STATISTICAL METHODS FOR THE SOCIAL AND BEHAVIORAL SCIENCES

A Series of Books in Psychology

Editors:

Richard C. Atkinson
Gardner Lindzey
Richard F. Thompson

STATISTICAL METHODS FOR THE SOCIAL AND BEHAVIORAL SCIENCES

LEONARD A. MARASCUILO
University of California, Berkeley

RONALD C. SERLIN
University of Wisconsin at Madison

W. H. FREEMAN AND COMPANY
NEW YORK

With Tom

Library of Congress Cataloging-in-Publication Data

Marascuilo, Leonard A.
  Statistical methods for the social and behavioral sciences.

  Bibliography: p.
  Includes index.
  1. Social sciences—Statistical methods.   I. Serlin,
Ronald C.   II. Title.
HA29.M2482   1988   519.5   87-398
ISBN 0-7167-1824-3

Printed in the United States of America
1 2 3 4 5 6 7 8 9 0 H 6 5 4 3 2 1 0 8 9 8

CONTENTS

This text grew out of our teaching the introductory course in statistics for behavioral scientists. Using explanations and material similar to those we use in our own classrooms, we take advantage here of the extra richness of detail and explanation that only a text can provide.

We were not completely satisfied with any of the books available for our course. We knew that students with only a knowledge of algebra can comprehend and use correctly the concepts and methods covered in a thorough introductory applied statistics course because we had seen our own students do so. But the available texts either covered topics superficially or immediately plunged into advanced topics at an intimidating pace.

While we provide extensive coverage of the most commonly needed statistical models, introductory or novice students should feel comfortable with this text. We include a solid introduction to statistics, beginning with a thorough discussion of descriptive statistics and of the philosophy underlying inferential statistics.

We help the student to understand that statistical strategies are rational and accessible. That is, they form a coherent approach to answering questions in both the scientific and nonscientific arenas and they are not restricted to people with superhuman mathematical capabilities. We emphasize throughout the overriding importance of the theoretical and practical interpretation of results, and we show students that they must think about their research questions before they can choose intelligently among the many statistical strategies available to them.

Whereas many texts begin with a study of probability theory, we introduce the topic after descriptive statistics. This allows us to explain that there is a clear need to discriminate between chance and nonchance sample outcomes in making inferences. Our approach to teaching probability theory underscores the notion that probability is a tool for making statistical decisions, not a separate body of knowledge unrelated to any sensible human endeavor. The relative lack of abstraction in our presentation allows a much better comprehension of the methods and purpose of probability theory. In addition, the highly verbal and conceptual beginning of the text, in which formulas are added gradually, alleviates the fear most students bring to the course. In this way the fear is not as likely to be exacerbated by the study of probability theory. Finally, nonparametric procedures are not relegated to a tacked-on chapter at the end of the text but are included as equally represented statistical strategies in the appropriate chapters.

The entire book can be covered in a two-semester sequence, but much of it is suited to a one-semester course. A one-semester course will most likely go through Chapter 32, probably skipping the material on alternative measures of association (Chapter 10), large-sample nonparametric procedures (Chapter 23), and tests of correlated proportions (Chapter 30). For a two-quarter course, we suggest leaving out the chapters beyond analysis of covariance.

The first half of the text provides a solid one-semester introduction to statistics that allows students to understand multiple-sample tests without requiring them to learn one-way analysis of variance. We present an extensive analysis of two-factor designs, but only a few sections on higher-order designs, because the two-factor presentation is so complete that students should be able to go on themselves to understand higher-order designs and to test contrasts in those designs. Wherever possible, the few heavily algebraic developments that we felt compelled to include are presented in chapter appendixes.

We highlight summaries of procedures in separate boxes. Although these summaries emphasize hand calculations for the most part, they lead to increasing emphasis on computers for complex analyses and higher-order ANOVA designs. We provide end-of-chapter exercises that allow the students to practice techniques already learned and to compare and contrast a variety of analysis options available to them. We also provide answers to exercises requiring calculations and an Instructor's Manual.

We take a spiral approach, continually linking new material to concepts that the student already knows or has learned. For example, Part I, covering statistics and descriptive statistics, opens with concepts that most students know from daily experience. We feel strongly that a subject as abstract as statistics is more easily learned when put into purposeful context. Thus we begin each Part with an overview of what is to come, and (with the exception of Part I) indicate why the upcoming material follows from what has been covered so far. New concepts and methods are introduced only after a need for them has been established. They are then revisited and extended as needed, often to motivate study of other, similar concepts and methods.

As an example of our emphasis on the motivation of concepts, let us briefly describe our treatment of probability theory. Once we have established a need for probability theory, we introduce the binomial formula in a coin-flipping example. We then use this discussion to present the concepts of hypothesis testing. We next discuss the sign test, since it is based on the binomial probability model. Upon encountering the problem of testing proportions for equality — showing that we need rules for sampling without replacement to solve the problems presented by the Fisher-Irwin exact test — we revisit probability theory to derive the required procedures. The two-sample and signed-rank Wilcoxon tests follow, since they are based on hypergeometric and binomial probability calculations. These procedures lead to the concept of the sampling distribution, and we show explicitly how critical regions based on sampling distributions are defined and used.

Our treatment of the phi coefficient affords another example of our approach. After the Pearson correlation coefficient is defined as a descriptive measure of association between two quantitative variables, phi is defined as a Pearson correlation coefficient calculated for two dichotomous variables. Because we stress even as early as the first chapter that measures of differences and measures of association form two sides of the same statistical coin, we can reintroduce phi as a measure of association in the two-sample binomial problem and show how it is tested for significance via the Fisher-Irwin exact test or the two-sample binomial test. After the Pearson chi-square test for 2×2 contingency tables is presented as the equivalent to the two-sample binomial test and as the large-sample approximation to the Fisher-Irwin test, and after the chi-square test is extended beyond the 2×2 case, the phi coefficient can be readily extended to Cramer's V.

The relationship between tests of association and the corresponding tests of differences is a recurring theme in the text. It is presented in terms of phi and the binomial test, the point biserial correlation coefficient and the t test, and eta-squared and ANOVA. The concepts of explained, unexplained, and total variability provide the basis for establishing these relationships. This approach allows us to unify seemingly different procedures and provides a strong lead-in to regression analysis.

ACKNOWLEDGMENTS

We are grateful to the following instructors, whose advice helped shape the form and content of this book: Alexa Beiser, Boston University; Patricia

Busk, University of San Francisco; Paul A. Games, Pennsylvania State University; Robert E. Hill, Jr., Ball State University; Dennis W. Leitner, Southern Illinois University; Joel R. Levin, University of Wisconsin at Madison; Keith R. Nelson, Beloit College; Dennis M. Roberts, Pennsylvania State University.

We want to acknowledge the many students who helped us with this text, chief among them Steve Paul and Kim Huff. Tom Little was magnificent and magnanimous in typing the manuscript at least seven times. Finally, the many contributions of Pat Busk in improving the text cannot be adequately acknowledged; we hope our heartfelt thanks will suffice.

Leonard A. Marascuilo

Ronald C. Serlin

STATISTICAL METHODS FOR THE SOCIAL AND BEHAVIORAL SCIENCES

PART I

VARIATION
AND
VARIANCE

One basic property of our physical, social, and psychological world is its variety. To understand the nature of our world in the face of this wide variability, we must start by defining very carefully what we observe, and we must be able to communicate our observations to others. Though we try to gain an understanding that is valid in as many different contexts as possible, we can only observe a very limited number of situations, because we are, unfortunately, restricted by time, expense, and circumstance. In the next six chapters we present and define methods that help to describe the similarities and differences among the observations that we make.

CHAPTER 1

The Variables
of Statistics

1-1. THE NATURE OF STATISTICS

From Gallup poll reports in newspapers to white-coated lab technicians advertising aspirin on television, you are often required to absorb and interpret the results of statistical analyses. In some cases, the results of experiments are said to be "highly significant," and, although this phrase is intended to indicate some sense of importance, there is no indication given of what "highly significant" actually means as used. This book is intended to provide you with a working knowledge of the terminology and methodology of statistics, so that you can understand statistical statements made by others and perform analyses of your own when needed.

Perhaps the major contributing factor in the recent increase in statistical information available to you is the emphasis on science and the methods of science in modern culture. Although the goals of science often involve the description and explanation of natural phenomena in terms of highly abstract theories, the beginnings of these theories and their ultimate support lie in observations, and observations are the raw materials of statistics.

As an example of this relationship between science and statistics, consider the scores of third-grade children on a standardized test of reading. In looking over these scores, suppose that a teacher notices that girls appear to obtain higher scores than boys. As a first step to formulating some theoretical explanation for such a phenomenon, the teacher might state as a hypothesis to be tested that girls obtain better scores than boys on this test, meaning, of course, that girls obtain higher scores than boys. Here, the observations are the children's scores, and the hypothesis serves as a low-level theory to be explored. The teacher, if knowledgeable, could use the methods of statistics to examine this hypothesis and to determine whether there was, indeed, a *statistical* difference between boys' and girls' scores on the test.

In addition to testing whether a hypothesis seems to be supported or disproved by the observations at hand, statistical models can be used to generate hypotheses. For example, the teacher above could pursue the study of the effects of sex differences in students' performance by examining available test scores, and statistical methods could be called upon to help determine other areas in which there seem to be sex-related differences among scores. In this way, it might be noticed that males with high reading scores also seem to have high math scores. These and other possible relationships could be examined in a preliminary way using statistical models.

In the preceding paragraphs, statistical methods were suggested as a means for examining both differences and similarities appearing in nature. The discovery and testing of hypotheses concerning similarities and differences in observations form two sides of the same statistical coin. As an example of the two-sided nature of statistical questions, consider the relationship between studying and grades. This relationship could be examined by comparing the amount of time A students study with the amount of study time of D students, to see if studying time seems to differ according to letter grade. On the other hand, the same question could be explored by seeing if there were a relatively consistent *association* between studying time and letter grades that is reflected by higher grades being achieved by students who study longer and lower grades being obtained by students who study less. The notion of exploring similarities and differences in data will form the conceptual basis of the organization of this book.

1-2. VARIETY, VARIATION, AND VARIANCE

According to the cliché, variety is the spice of life. It is also the subject matter of modern statistics. Because no two objects in nature are identical, they will not respond exactly the same way in all respects to a given force. The same is true of people. There may be general similarities in the way people respond to the threat of danger on a deserted city street late at night; a few will push ahead regardless of the danger, many will avoid the area, others will attempt to walk only in well-lit areas. With a little reflection, you could undoubtedly think of other actions that people might take, given such a threatening situation. But even within these individual gross responses, there are bound to exist considerable variations in their execution. Also, large variations will exist across people with respect to changes in involuntary sweating, increased blood pressure, shortness of breath, accelerated respiration, and secretions of cortical hormones. The characteristics that portray a complete picture of response to the situation for an individual are endless, and the ways that people respond to each of these characteristics are boundless. This is true for just about any stimulus people are exposed to during their daily lives.

Modern statistics is concerned with the study of variation and its relationship to causative factors, or what are believed to be causative factors, in the environment. This rather natural variation among all objects in the universe may help to make more explicit the interplay between science and statistics. Generating a description of the relationships among factors which comprise a phenomenon or a situation is a primary concern in science. Statistics can be used to select certain of the factors in a situation as possibly being causally related to others, with the hope being that those factors thus selected are the most important ones to include in the scientific description. Then, once we have decided upon a description (theory, law, hypothesis, etc.) that appears to be consistent with our observations and that seems to include all of the important factors, statistics can be used to test the adequacy of the description.

It is here, in the areas of factor selection and hypothesis testing, that the wide variations in nature become important. Our description must, in some way, depict the phenomenon in general terms, showing how, in spite of certain natural variations, the factors in the situation are related. Statisticians have invented a number of concepts that are used to describe the general properties of observations. Examples of such concepts include the mean (average) and the median (midvalue). At the same time, other statistical concepts are used to describe the amount of the variation in the observations. An example of these is known as the standard deviation. Using all these notions, statistics can be used to determine the adequacy of a scientific description by deciding whether the general descriptors seem to obey a law or conform to a hypothesis, when the variations in nature are taken into account.

Consider the following simple study in which a new method for the teaching of third-grade reading is to be contrasted with an old method that has been used for years in a certain school district. Once the pupils are assigned to the two programs, teaching begins, with the old method used in one group and the new method in the other. Following the training, a reading test is given to all the students. Here, each group's average score could be used to measure the general effects of the training. If the new program is successful, the difference in the group averages will be large; otherwise, it will be small. The resulting mean difference is compared to a second measure, the standard deviation, which describes the amount of variation that one expects to exist among the subjects within each of the two groups of the study. If the difference in the means is larger than what could be expected on the basis of chance variation, we can conclude that the effects of the two programs on the teaching of reading are different. On the other hand, if the difference is explainable strictly in terms of chance or random effects, no such decision would be made.

1-3. INDEPENDENT AND DEPENDENT VARIABLES

The reading scores example of Section 1-2 was based upon two factors. All of the factors which are involved in a situation are called *variables*. One of the variables was the type of program tested on the subjects, that is, the old program or the new program. The second variable consisted of scores generated from a reading test. The first variable is thought to affect the second, in that the difference in scores is thought to be caused by the different programs. Here the first variable is artificially or purposely created by the researcher. In fact, the researcher completely decides what will constitute the old program and the new program; such variables, which *seem* to have a causative effect upon other variables, are called *independent variables*. In many cases, independent variables are deliberately manipulated by an investigator. In this study, for example, the researcher would like to create a new method so that it produces test scores that tend to be higher than those produced by the old method. The test scores, on the other hand, are not manipulable directly. They are an outcome produced by the teaching programs and the random variation that exists among the students. Conceptually, variables such as test scores are thought to depend in some way on the independent variables; such variables, which *seem* to be causally influenced by the independent variable, are commonly referred to as *dependent variables*. Ideally, a researcher would like to say that changes in the independent variable cause or produce changes in the dependent variable. Sometimes, this cause and effect relationship may be stated with confidence. Unfortunately, more often than not, it cannot.

For example, it is not possible to conclude with certainty that an independent variable, smoking, causes occurrence of a dependent variable, lung cancer. Nor can it be concluded that an independent variable, a diet high in fat, causes the appearance of a dependent variable, cardiovascular disease. In a like manner, it cannot be concluded that an independent variable, cultural deprivation, causes changes in a dependent variable, school grades and academic performance. In all three cases, other variables have been proposed to explain variations in the incidence of lung cancer, cardiovascular disease, and performance in school. It may well be that cause and effect relationships exist, but with the knowledge available today, the relationships cannot be definitely proven.

Not all independent variables are manipulated by a researcher. For example, the number of cigarettes individuals smoke over a given period of time is self-determined, as is their amount of consumed fat. The lack of magazines or books in a home is influenced by many factors, with perhaps the most outstanding one being family income. Still, it is customary to refer to these nonmanipulated variables as independent variables. In these cases, the manipulation is not performed by a researcher, but is performed by nature or society, so that subjects enter a study with the *treatment* having been previously applied. The fact that not all independent variables are manipulated by a researcher should cause no difficulty in distinguishing independent from dependent variables.

1-4. QUALITATIVE AND QUANTITATIVE VARIABLES

Determining which variables in a given situation are likely to be independent variables and which are likely to be dependent is a good first step in both a scientific and a statistical analysis of a phenomenon. It forms part of a careful and close look at the problem under study. The next step in a statistical analysis involves examining the nature of the variables in question. Not only does such an examination help one better understand the exact nature of the hypothesis, but it will also determine the particular method of analysis that is appropriate. Consider again the example of the new method of teaching reading. Conceptually, the kind of teaching method used is thought to affect the students' reading scores; hence, the program type is considered the independent variable, and the reading scores are considered the dependent variable. But notice that these two variables are different in kind. The reading scores are *measured,* by counting the number of correct responses on a test, while the type of program can only be *described,* verbally. These two classifications of statistical variables are called *quantitative* and *qualitative,* respectively.

Qualitative variables are almost always defined in verbal terms that comprise mutually exclusive and exhaustive subclasses. This means that the verbal definition of the states of the variable must allow one to group all objects into at least one of the subclasses, at the same time guaranteeing that each object does not fall into more than one subclass. Examples of qualitative variables are:

1. Race: {Asian, black, white, other}
2. Sex: {male, female}
3. Marital Status: {single, married, widowed, divorced}
4. Social Class: {low, medium, high}

5. Attitude toward school integration: {strongly opposed, moderately opposed, neutral, moderately supportive, strongly supportive}
6. Amount of completed education: {some elementary school, elementary school graduate, some high school, high school graduate, some college, college graduate, some graduate school, doctorate}

Quantitative variables are variables whose properties are determined by counting or measuring. Inherent in the definition of a quantitative variable is a number that is associated with an object and without which the variable would not make sense. Examples of quantitative variables are:

1. Number of days off the job because of illness during the month of January: {0, 1, 2, . . . , 31}
2. Score on a 25-item spelling test: {0, 1, 2, . . . , 25}
3. Intelligence quotient: { . . . , 98, 99, 100, 101, . . . }
4. Weight of adult males on 21st birthday: {80 lb $\leq Y \leq$ 400 lb}
5. Time to run a 100-m dash: {10 sec $\leq Y \leq$ 20 sec}
6. Age at death: {0 $\leq Y \leq$ 140 yr}

Notice that, in certain cases, the distinction between qualitative and quantitative variables becomes somewhat clouded. For example, in the case of the fifth qualitative variable, attitude toward integration, the usual method of data collection involves asking a person to respond to a question on a five-point scale. Such a scale would typically range from 1, indicating strong opposition, to 5, denoting strong support. The reason that this variable is still considered to be qualitative is that the scale makes no sense unless the categories, described in verbal terms, are presented, along with the numbers. In this case there is no standard against which a given score can be compared; this can be contrasted with the standard used to measure time based on clocks kept at the United States Naval Observatory. In the case of the sixth variable, amount of completed education, no single number is associated with each individual in the given scheme. Thus, people with some high school education can have completed 9, 10, or 11 years of education, but you don't know exactly how much. If, on the other hand the amount of completed education had been specified by counting the number of years in school, this variable would have been considered a quantitative variable.

As is seen in the preceding discussion, qualitative variables can be classified as either *ordered* or *unordered*. Race, sex, and marital status are examples of unordered qualitative variables, since the categories used to define each of these variables cannot be placed in any low to high order. The order in which they are listed is of no importance and, indeed, trying to place them in any rational order is impossible. This is not true, however, of social class, attitude toward school integration, and amount of completed education. These qualitative variables are defined in terms of ordered classes. For these, the order is important, and to scramble the order would destroy the nature of the variable.

Like qualitative variables, quantitative variables are of two types, *discrete* and *continuous*. Number of days off the job, score on a test, and IQ are examples of discrete variables. A discrete variable is one that takes on a countable and, in practice, a finite set of values. It is possible to count the number of days a person has stayed off the job. In a like manner, one can count the number of correct answers on a test. Even though intelligence is thought to represent a continuum from low to high, IQ scores are reported to the nearest integer, and thus the corresponding set of IQ scores is countable. This is not true, however, of weights on 21st birthday, number of seconds to run the 100-m dash, and age at death. For these variables, all numbers between their respective minimum and maximum values are possible. A man on his 21st birthday could weigh 146.3454 . . . lb, run the 100-m dash in 13.6893 . . . seconds, and later die when he is 48.5699 . . . years of age. Even though there are no weight scales, no stop watches, or age counters that could give such accurate measures of weight, time, or age, it is clear that all decimal values in a finite range are possible measurements for these and other continuous variables. In practice, however, every measuring instrument, no matter how finely scaled, measures only to the nearest " . . . th" of a unit. In the final analysis, all continuous variables are measured discretely.

1-5. CONTINUOUS AND DISCRETE SCALES

All quantitative measurement is made on a discrete scale of values, since no measuring instrument is perfect. Most scales used in measuring adult weights are calibrated in pounds, and weights are reported to the nearest pound. Thus, a person who weighs 146 lb on such a scale is known to have a true weight that extends from a low of 145 lb 8 oz to a high of 146 lb 8 oz, since any weight in this range would be rounded to 146 lb. This means that his true weight is known to within an 8 oz (or ½ lb) error.

Many stop watches that are used to time runners in a 100-m dash read to hundredth of a second (0.01 sec). Thus, a person who runs the 100-m dash in 12.65 sec is known to have a true running time that extends from a low of 12.645 sec to a high of 12.655 sec. This means that the observed time of 12.65 seconds is within 0.005 sec of the true time.

The measurement of age is a little more complicated. In general, people report their age as that attained at their last birthday. Thus, a man who dies at age 48 is known to have a true age that extends from a low of exactly 48 years to a high of 48.9999 . . . years. Finally, it should be noted that age could be, and sometimes is, reported as age at nearest birthday. This makes the measurement of age similar to that used for weight and time. For this measurement, a man who dies at age 48 is known to have a true age that might be as low as 47.5 years or as high as 48.5 years.

1-6. EXERCISES

1-1. Define and illustrate the notions of an independent and dependent variable for the following situations. Do not use any variable repeatedly. Base all of your examples on research questions related to investigations on human behavior.

Type of independent variable	Type of dependent variable
a. Quantitative (continuous)	Quantitative (continuous)
b. Qualitative (unordered)	Quantitative (discrete)
c. Quantitative (continuous)	Qualitative (ordered)
d. Qualitative (unordered)	Qualitative (ordered)
e. Quantitative (discrete)	Quantitative (discrete)
f. Qualitative (ordered)	Qualitative (unordered)
g. Quantitative (discrete)	Qualitative (ordered)
h. Quantitative (continuous)	Qualitative (unordered)

1-2. Give an example of an endogenous (naturally occurring or nonmanipulated) independent variable for a study in which a researcher wishes to assess the impact of TV viewing upon reading comprehension of high school seniors. Answer the question for an exogenous (a deliberately manipulated) independent variable.

1-3. Give an example of a *true* cause and effect relationship. Also provide an example of what is, *seemingly*, a cause and effect relationship. Finally, provide an example of a relationship that is *not* a cause and effect relationship.

1-4. Explain why variables thought to be continuous are actually measured on a discrete number scale.

1-5. Consider a ruler which is calibrated in units of ⅛ in. What is the range of a person's true height if the observed (reported) height was 68⅝ in, if measurement was made to the:
a. nearest unit
b. last unit
c. next unit

CHAPTER 2

From a Sample of
Data to a Population

2-1. POPULATIONS AND SAMPLES

In statistics, as in science, one wishes to be able to make statements that are likely to be true in general. In this way, the third-grade teacher in Chapter 1, noticing certain trends in the scores of the students, is interested in making decisions that would apply to many third-grade classes taught, not just the one presently being taught. Similarly, any findings concerning the efficacy of the new reading program will be much more useful if they can be applied to many other students who might use it, not just the ones who took part in the experiment. This means that the basic unit of interest in statistics is not the sample observed, but a much larger group of possible individuals. The basic unit is called the *population* or *universe* and includes all people, objects, and concepts for which the subpopulation in the experiment, called a *sample,* can be considered representative. In certain cases, such as experiments in chemistry, the sample studied is considered essentially identical to all members of a like population. Because of the high purity and cleanliness available in such instances, there is no reason to think that the chemicals, test tubes, and other equipment used are significantly unlike all other examples of like materials. Unfortunately, such is not the case in the behavioral sciences. In fact, in many instances, the population corresponding to the sample in question is dynamic enough that it could only be considered hypothetical.

For example, consider the population of third-grade children, for which the class of Chapter 1 might be a representative sample. The dependent variable, scores on a reading test, was not measured on an entire population of third-grade children, but only upon a sample. But what constitutes a population of third-grade children? Certainly, other children who are now enrolled in third-grade classes belong to that population. Indeed, at one time or another, everyone who reads this book was also enrolled in third-grade classes. Next year's third-grade classes will contain students who are now enrolled in second-grade classes and should also be included. As can be seen, even a population of third-graders must be considered hypothetical.

The psychologist who studies how people respond to aggression may sample college sophomores enrolled in beginning psychology classes for her experiments, but her interest in psychology students may be minimal. She would like to make an inference about how *humans* respond to aggression.

The sociologist who studies gang fighting among teenaged youths with no father at home and with the sample taken from the caseloads of the local probation office is not interested in the specific youths that he studies in detail. Instead, he wishes to make statements about how groups of youths, in general, are expected to behave under similar situations. While there exists a population of teenaged youths without a father at home at any one time, it is a population that is dynamic and in constant flux. It changes with time and can never be localized and identified. Basically, all of the populations of the behavioral sciences have this abstract quality about them.

2-2. DESCRIPTIVE AND INFERENTIAL STATISTICS

All statistical analyses can be assigned to one of two broad research models. These two models are commonly referred to as *descriptive* and *inferential* statistics. The subject matter of the previous chapter, which consists of the methods that are used to describe typical sample values, variation about typical sample values, and relationships that exist between variables, is generally assigned to problems in descriptive statistics. Descriptive statistics are used whenever a researcher wishes to describe to someone else the findings and relationships that exist within a sample of observations. As a body of knowledge, descriptive statistics corresponds to the tip of the iceberg. It is a small, but important, part of statistical methodology.

Although researchers do need to describe their findings to others, as indicated in Section 2-1, they also want to use the sample findings to make corresponding statements about the population from which the sample came. This is the subject matter of inferential statistics. It consists of methods that allow a generalization of sample results to populations. The procedures that permit this leap from a small set of observable facts to a larger, nonobservable, set of similar facts are based upon simple probability concepts. We say that the concepts are simple because it seems that most people have an intuitive feeling about probability and how it works. We will consider some of these probability ideas. In particular, we will focus on the use of probability to develop rules that permit generalizations from a small, observable, sample to a larger, nonobservable, universe or population.

2-3. INTERNAL AND EXTERNAL VALIDITY

Before you can even begin thinking about detecting relationships in a sample or extending sample results to a population, you must ensure that any statement you make is scientifically sound. In particular, you want to be able to say, with confidence, that relationships or differences you detect in data are due to the variables you are investigating and not to other variables for which you neglected to account.

Since the populations of the behavioral sciences do not truly exist, researchers rely on samples to make their inferences about the abstractions we call populations. In a certain sense, a sample is just a chunk of a population. We hope that it is a good chunk. If it is, it will give rise to a study from which sample conclusions can be extended to the population. Such a study is said to have *external validity*. Not many studies in the behavioral sciences possess external validity, mainly because the part of the population used as the sample is not representative of the population to which the inference is to be made.

Even though external validity is not generally attainable, *internal validity* can be achieved in many situations. A study is said to have internal validity if the results can be attributed exclusively to the independent variables in the study and not to some other extraneous *confounding variables*. In the sciences, such internal validity is achieved through the use of *controlled* experiments, in which only one variable is allowed to vary at a time. The variables other than the one in question are those said to be controlled. By constructing such an experiment, the investigator can show more clearly that the changes in the independent variable do or do not correspond to changes in the dependent variable. On the other hand, if two or more independent variables are allowed to change at the same time without controls, it is impossible to say which of them, individually or in concert, are responsible for changes in the dependent variable. As will be seen later, two or more variables can be varied under very restrictive conditions, so as to evaluate their impact on the outcome variables. For now, however, we ignore these special cases and consider variations in only one independent variable and the effects that such variations have upon one dependent variable.

Suppose, for example, that the third-grade reading study had been performed on two classes with different initial reading abilities, and suppose that the new method had been applied only to the more able group of readers. If, at the end of the study, it is seen that the students trained with the new method have higher average scores, one would be hard pressed to conclude that the higher scores were a result of the new method. It is quite possible that the new method is no better than the old method and that the high scores only reflect the fact that the students were initially better readers. To make matters more complicated, the new program might help only already good readers and not poorer readers. Still another possibility is that different maturation rates could explain the differences, whereby the good readers would have improved even without the new program. It is obvious that such a study is poorly designed, since many possible explanations of the results are possible. In such instances, the factors involved in the study are said to be *confounded*. Whenever there is a confounding of factors, internal validity is destroyed. Fortunately, it is possible to eliminate the confounding of factors in most experimental studies.

2-4. RANDOM SAMPLES AND RANDOMIZATION

The methods for setting up samples with internal and/or external validity are based on the probabilities associated with the flipping of a coin, the rolling of a die, or the use of a table of random numbers. To set up a study with external validity, statisticians use a method based on a model called *simple random sampling*, which is defined as follows.

Definition of simple random sampling

A sampling procedure is said to generate a simple random sample if:

1. Each member of the population has an equal chance of being included in the sample.
2. Each member is selected independently of all other members, i.e., the selection (or nonselection) of any member has no effect on the selection (or nonselection) of any other member.

Condition 1 is referred to as the *equal probability* assumption, while Condition 2 is referred to as the *independence* assumption. Notice that, in order to create a study with external validity, you must start with the population and

---

Box 2-1   How to establish K randomized groups

Step 1. Consider a set of N members of some universe that are to be divided at random into K groups. Let the members be listed on a roster and given the numbers 1, 2, 3, . . . , N.

Step 2. Let the proposed sample sizes be denoted by $N_1, N_2, . . . , N_K$, so that $N_1 + N_2 + \cdots + N_K = N$.

Step 3. Enter a table of random numbers and record the first N different numbers that appear in the table that are also included in the roster.

Step 4. Define sample number one to consist of the first N_1 members identified by the corresponding random numbers. Define sample number two to consist of the next N_2 members identified by these random numbers. Continue the process until all samples are filled.

---

select sample members at random. This is a difficult procedure to apply because of the dynamic characteristics of human populations and the rather hypothetical nature of behavioral science populations. Therefore, we need another model.

This other model, called *randomization,* helps establish internal validity, in that it generates comparison groups that are likely to be similar, and any dissimilarity is due only to chance. In general, the samples produced by randomization can be very different from those generated by simple random sampling. Randomization's similarity to random sampling is quite apparent, except that we begin here with a sample, rather than the entire population. In either case, a random numbers table is recommended in selecting random and randomization samples. A table of random numbers is provided in Appendix A (Table A-1). The use of this table is explained in Section 2-5. Randomization of N objects into K groups is described in Box 2-1.

Definition of randomization

Randomization is the application of the principles of random sampling to a chunk from a population in which a number of equivalent groups are to be established whose differences from one another can only be attributed to chance.

As stated earlier, randomization almost always ensures internal, but not necessarily external validity. For example, suppose one applies randomization to a group of blind children in a state school for the blind. Because these children represent a unique group of blind students, results cannot be extended to all blind students. Most likely, these students come from middle-class environments and have parents with a strong commitment to education. Other, different kinds of families with blind children are excluded.

As indicated, randomization is simple random sampling applied to the chunk of the population that is available for study. If the chunk is a random sample from the universe, then randomization serves to ensure near uniformity across K samples, so that each sample is similar in form to the parent population. In this case, both internal and external validity are easier to defend. If a controlled experiment were performed on these samples, a researcher could conclude that, in the sample groups, differences were produced by the independent variable and by it alone. Furthermore, the researcher could extend the inference to the population of interest.

If, on the other hand, the chunk is a *convenience* sample, which is used because it is available, then randomization ensures uniformity across the samples so that internal validity is supported. In this case, a researcher can justify decisions about the effects of the independent variable upon the dependent variable if competing explanations can be ruled out as producing the difference. Even so, extending the inference to the population cannot, in general, be made. In this case, the inference must be made to a larger hypothetical group of people or objects that is similar in all respects to the convenience sample on which the randomization was performed. Remember that most chunks or convenience samples do not reflect the population characteristics as would a true random sample. Whereas internal validity is often attainable through randomization, external validity is only attainable through random sampling.

2-5. AN EXAMPLE

To explain better the nature of simple random sampling and randomization, consider the data in Table A-16. This table summarizes information collected on 238 students enrolled in a beginning biology class at a hypothetical university. On the basis of a coin toss, each student was assigned at random to one of two experimental programs. The programs, denoted by 1 and 2 in the table, were as follows:

1. Practical Condition: In addition to attendance at regular lectures, students worked for no pay at a local biological research laboratory for 4 hours per week. Further, they had to complete a five-page report on their experiences at the laboratory.
2. Discussion Condition: In addition to attendance at regular lectures, students attended two 2-hour discussion sections designed around the lectures and extra readings. They also had to complete a five-page report on a topic of interest that related to the content of the course.

These two programs of study constitute the major independent variable of the study. The dependent variable of the study is the student's score on the 100-point final exam. Other independent variables which could have an effect on the dependent variables, but which are not of major interest are sometimes called *covariates*. The covariates for this study, along with their codes are:

1. Sex: 0. Male   1. Female
2. College Board test score.
3. Response to the question: When you were in high school, did you have a class or part of a class that was devoted to the study of biology or some other biological science?   1. Yes   0. No
4. Major: 1. Humanities   2. Natural Sciences   3. Social Sciences   4. Other   5. Not known at this time
5. Score on a 30-point pretest designed to measure knowledge in biology.   ·

Let us now consider the concepts of internal and external validity in terms of the 238 students. If these 238 students comprise the entire population, then the selection of a random sample from the population tends to generate a study with external validity. If we then place the students from the simple random sample into one of the two programs using randomization procedures, the chances of a study having internal validity are enhanced. The ultimate result of these methods is twofold: First, any effects of confounding variables tend to be balanced out, and, second, any results generated by this study should be generalizable to the population of 238 students.

If, on the other hand, the sample of 238 students is considered a convenience sample because they are immediately available for testing the two programs, external validity is questionable. By randomly placing students into one program or another, the classes taking each program can be considered essentially alike. The randomizing procedure places students into each program in such a way that the effects of any confounding variables tend to balance out, establishing internal validity.

For teaching purposes, we will assume that the 238 students constitute a population of students and that the study in which the two programs are to be compared will be based on a simple random sample of students selected from the population of 238. Directions for selecting a random sample, using a random number table such as Table A-1, are provided in Box 2-2.

Suppose we wish to choose a random sample of size 40 from the roster and the data of Table A-16. To achieve this specialized selection, we use Table A-1. We associate each student with a number from 001 through 238. We then select 40 different three-digit numbers that cover that range. These numbers identify our sample.

We began by placing a finger anywhere on the table. It fell below the number 16, which appears as the intersection of the 11th two-digit column with row 29. Since $N = 238$ is a three-digit number, we add the number 8, which appears in the column immediately to the right of 16, to give us a first number, 168. We go down one row to the next number, 689, which is too large, and is discarded. Continuing in this way, the next acceptable number is

Box 2-2   Procedure for choosing a random sample from a roster

Step 1. Determine the size of the population to be sampled. Denote this number by N.

Step 2. Count the number of digits in N. This number, D, will equal the number of digits required for the random numbers you choose.

Step 3. Number the elements in the population consecutively from 1 to N, using D digits in these numbers. For example, if N were equal to 238, the first element would be assigned 001, the second 002, etc., with the last element assigned 238.

Step 4. To select a first number, place your finger on any D digit number in the random numbers table.

Step 5. If D is larger than 2, include as many digits as needed by incorporating numbers in columns to the right.

Step 6. Record this number if it is less than or equal to N.

Step 7. Move to the row immediately below the chosen number and record the second D digit number.

Step 8. Repeat the process until the desired sample size is reached. This may require moving to different columns after the bottom of the page is reached. If so, move on to the top of the next set of columns to the right and begin again to move down the columns, recording D digit numbers.

Step 9. If a random number is duplicated, discard the duplications, retaining the original, and continue.

Step 10. When the desired sample size is reached, return to the roster of elements to identify the elements in the universe that will form your sample.

Step 11. Record the data associated with the chosen elements.

055. The third acceptable number is 159. Using this procedure, the entire set of 40 different, acceptable, random numbers is given by:

168	055	159	201	053
022	131	236	074	135
144	123	102	024	017
171	148	187	104	037
162	001	078	195	011
039	115	140	190	071
021	047	094	016	127
040	034	061	136	088

The resulting sample is reported in Table 2-1.

2-6. VALIDITY IN PRACTICE

The students taking this course in biology represent a chunk of some population which almost defies description. For the most part, they are young people just out of high school, living not too far from the university in question. Some of them are in their last year of schooling and are trying to pick up credits to get a degree. Some come from states that are as far away as New York, Florida, and California. There are even students from foreign countries. They cover broad social classes. Some are taking this beginning course because they think they would like to major in biology. Some are there because their advisor told them to take the course. Others are taking it because it can be used as a prerequisite to medical school. Most of the students are white. There is a sprinkling of blacks, but very few Asians and no Native Americans are taking the course for credit. Compared to other classes, these students have very high College Board test scores and almost all of them are from the upper quartile of their graduating senior high school class. The students are not representative of all college students because other schools will have different demographic characteristics in their student bodies. It cannot be concluded that they represent college students who enroll for a beginning course in biology, because they don't. The population from which they came cannot be identified.

This, however, is not important for internal validity. As we recall, each student was given a code number and then a random process, such as the flipping of a coin, determined the program into which a student would be assigned. The random assignment, if successful, created two groups of students that are similar to one another in their distributions of all the characteristics named, as well as those we forgot about or ignored. The randomization was used to distribute all characteristics uniformly among the students in the two programs. This means that this study does have internal validity, provided that adequate controls are instituted. Under this condition, the researcher can say at the end of the study that employment in biological laboratories in the community had a specific type of impact upon the scores obtained by students on the final. If scores indicate greater knowledge about biology, the researcher can say that the program increased student knowledge or decreased it depending upon what is observed in the sample. Extraneous, or confounding, variables have been reduced as possible explanations for the final results because of the randomization.

In most situations, randomization and random sampling ensure internal and external validity. In cases in which human subjects are used, however, the assurance is doubtful. For example, one treatment may affect subjects in a negative way, so that they drop out of the study or else refuse to participate in a positive manner. Sometimes, competition may arise between the two groups and a heightened esprit de corps in one group may generate results that are not generalizable. A careful researcher will watch for these and other unexpected outcomes, even if randomization and random sampling have

Table 2-1. Random sample of 40 subjects selected from the population of Table A-16.

Code number	Sex	College Board score	High school biology	Major	Pretest score	Final	Experimental program
168	—	580	0	3	10	30	2
055	1	410	0	4	24	52	2
159	0	590	1	3	28	59	1
201	1	390	0	4	23	43	2
053	1	700	1	1	28	69	1
022	1	410	0	1	17	43	2
131	1	410	0	2	13	19	2
236	1	600	0	—	16	47	1
074	1	210	1	5	26	35	2
135	1	790	1	4	29	80	1
144	1	610	0	3	25	64	2
123	0	510	1	1	25	68	1
102	1	400	0	3	10	19	2
024	0	490	0	2	18	20	2
017	1	470	1	—	05	45	1
171	0	470	0	2	13	39	2
148	1	430	0	1	13	24	2
187	1	390	0	2	20	50	1
104	1	610	0	2	28	57	1
037	1	630	1	—	08	71	1
162	1	800	1	2	28	54	1
001	1	560	0	4	10	42	2
078	0	400	0	—	—	46	1
195	0	460	1	1	30	48	2
011	1	510	0	4	22	47	1
039	1	610	1	1	16	59	1
115	1	490	0	2	09	31	2
140	1	610	1	1	13	48	2

Table 2-1. *(Continued)*

Code number	Sex	College Board score	High school biology	Major	Pretest score	Final	Experimental program
190	1	500	1	2	30	68	1
071	1	490	0	4	17	47	2
021	0	610	0	4	14	42	1
047	0	600	0	1	03	38	1
094	0	610	0	1	16	59	1
016	1	430	1	1	17	43	1
127	—	470	1	5	15	35	1
040	1	610	0	3	13	45	1
034	—	500	1	1	15	21	1
061	0	460	0	5	16	37	1
136	0	610	1	3	30	67	1
088	1	540	0	1	17	31	2

been used. Humans are unpredictable and both males and females may be, to paraphrase the Duke in Verdi's *Rigoletto,* "as fickle as the wind."

It is not always clear to which populations the results can be generalized. In our example the two populations are hypothetical. The randomization procedure artificially created them. About the best that can be done is to describe the two samples in detail and claim that the populations are like the samples. This is done frequently in behavioral research, and it is a point to which the reader of scientific research articles should be attuned. Whenever you read a research article in the social sciences, careful attention should be given to the description of the sample on which the study is based. Usually, the researcher supplies this information to serve as a description of the universe that he or she believes serves as the population of interest.

Sometimes, preexisting records or files are used to obtain random samples. An example of this might be as follows. In a study of the effects of smoking upon the incidence of mortality from lung cancer, a researcher may solicit the assistance of a set of large hospitals or health plans for the purposes of conducting a *longitudinal* study which will follow a group of men of ages 50 to 59, for 10 or 15 years. From the case files of the cooperating hospitals or health groups, random samples can be selected using a table of random numbers.

Men selected into the sample may be asked to cooperate with the study by agreeing to undergo yearly medical check-ups and to contribute an hour's time, either to complete a questionnaire, or to undergo a person-to-person interview in which they are asked about their smoking habits. On the basis of this information, the men may be divided into groups consisting of nonsmokers, light smokers, moderate smokers, and heavy smokers. Of course, the definitions of the categories that define this independent variable would have been carefully worked out prior to the beginning of the study.

Note that, even though random samples were selected from the available files, the nature of the independent variable is such that assignment to the four groups violates both the principles of random sampling and randomization. The four groups of men are self-determined. Each man has decided for himself whether or not to smoke and, if he does smoke, on the number of cigarettes to smoke. The study does not have internal validity, and as such, it cannot possibly have external validity. Without internal validity there is no external validity, since invalid results cannot be generalized validly.

Because of the self-selection problem, researchers try to approach a study of this nature with an attempt to achieve as close an approximation to internal validity as is possible. To do this, they will gather other information, such as frequency of sexual intercourse, protein and carbohydrate intake, type of job usually engaged in, information on how leisure time is spent, X-ray and drug histories, use of alcohol, medical histories of parents, brothers, uncles, and even cousins. The list is long. If, at the end of the study period, the researcher can establish a relationship between smoking and lung cancer and also show that none of these other characteristics show any correlation with the incidence of mortality from lung cancer, the inference that smoking is the culprit has some credence.

This attempt to approximate internal validity is expensive and is not without errors. It is always possible that the wrong questions were asked and that the one key question concerning the cause of lung cancer was overlooked. This is part of the problem that exists for all such studies. Although random samples can be obtained from a roster such as hospital records, the records represent a chunk from some other population. Frequently the chunk is difficult to define in any meaningful fashion, so that the question of external validity immediately exists. The assignment of individuals to the categories of the independent variable is invariably based on self-selection; hence, the conditions for internal validity are violated from the start. Attempts to correct for this can always be in error in that the right information is not obtained.

There is a major conflict in educational research. The argument centers on why minority students as a group tend to obtain lower scores on intelligence and achievement tests. One school claims the low scores are produced more by heredity than by environmental forces. Such a conclusion may be illusory because of sampling difficulties. In most cases, the samples have been convenience samples that were available to researchers. The black school population of a northern urban school district is not like the black school population of a rural southern school district. Teaching programs for whites and blacks are not the same, even in a single school district. Home environments are not the same across races, even in a single school. Median family incomes are not equal across the races, even for families living in the same neighborhoods. The percentages of families with both mother and father at home are not the same across the races. The number of children per completed family is not the same across social classes. Vitamin, mineral, carbohydrate, and protein consumption across various ethnic groups is not the same. The list of differences is endless. To achieve internal validity is next to impossible, but the battle still rages.

The point of all this discussion is that without randomization, internal validity is not possible. This means that many studies in the social sciences are made without external validity, since without internal validity, there is no external validity. This is less true of internal validity, though this, too, is a problem for the social scientist. Because of these problems, researchers and critics tend to overevaluate and nitpick the research of others. In some cases, such criticisms are justified; but if data speak for themselves, as they sometimes do, then fault-finding in the research of others wastes time. As a reader of others' research, you must be critical, but you should not waste time looking for minor infractions of methodology and analysis. There probably has never been a perfect study in the social sciences, and there probably never will be. With enough diligence, you can criticize most studies on one point or another. Unless the criticism changes the implications of a study, you should consider the results as a first approximation to reality.

In the remaining chapters of this book, we shall return to the questions of internal and external validity, but we will not stress them. Statistical theory has little to say about these important research questions. For expository purposes, we will generally assume that either random samples or samples created by randomization are available for analysis. We will make these assumptions only to illustrate the use of standard statistical inference procedures. It is suggested that the reader evaluate each example for internal and external validity. As will be seen, many examples will not satisfy these conditions.

2-7. EXERCISES

2-1. Explain what is meant by external and internal validity. Use an example involving the study of human behavior.

2-2. While the samples of behavioral research are real, the populations are, in general, unreal.

Explain what this means in terms of the example you used to answer Exercise 2-1.

2-3. Compare and contrast:
   a. Simple random sampling with randomization.

b. A chunk, or convenience, sample with a random sample.

2-4. Describe how a chunk or convenience sample can be used to achieve internal validity in a study designed to compare two different teaching methods. Under what conditions would the method achieve external validity?

2-5. Select a random sample of 40 students from the roster of Table A-16. If possible, transfer the data to IBM cards or to a floppy disk to be used in future exercises. Have the computer print a list of your sample. Your sample will be used to teach you statistical theory and methods. If you use IBM cards, code your data as follows:

Column	Variable
1,2	Blank
3,4,5	Code number
6	Blank
7	Sex
8	Blank
9,10,11	College Board Score
12	Blank
13	High school biology
14	Blank
15	Major
16	Blank
17,18	Pretest score
19	Blank
20,21	Final score
22	Blank
23	Experimental program

2-6. Studies which do not involve random sampling or randomization are generally referred to as *observational studies*. Compare and contrast them to *experimental studies*, which are based on randomization or random sampling. In your discussion, consider the problems associated with internal and external validity.

2-7. One type of an observational study is a *retrospective* study. In a retrospective study on the effects of X-ray treatment upon birth defects, one might search hospital or doctor records until a group of 100 women who were X-rayed during pregnancy were found, and then *matched* with a group of 100 women who were not X-rayed, but were pregnant over the same period of time. Such a study might show the following results:

	X-rayed	Not X-rayed	Total
Abnormal Birth	30	2	32
Normal Birth	70	98	168
Total	100	100	200

The data seem to indicate that women who are pregnant should not be exposed to X-rays. Evaluate such a study with respect to internal and external validity. What confounding variables could be used to explain the outcome other than the one of X-raying during pregnancy?

2-8. Another example of an observational study is called a *prospective* study. As an example of a prospective study, consider a study on the effects of smoking upon the occurrence of lung cancer. In this typical prospective study, one identifies 100 men, aged 50 to 59, who have been smoking one or more full packages of cigarettes every day for 10 or more years. In addition, 100 men of the same age and other matching characteristics who have never smoked are identified. Both groups of men are followed for 10 years. The results of such a follow-up might produce the following results:

	Smokers	Nonsmokers	Total
Cancer	30	2	32
No cancer	70	98	168
Total	100	100	200

The data seem to indicate that smokers develop cancer in greater percentages than do nonsmokers. Evaluate such a study with respect to internal and external validity. What confounding variables could be used to explain the outcome, other than that of smoking excessive numbers of cigarettes?

2-9. Another example of an observational study is the *cross-sectional* study. In a cross-sectional study, one selects different aged groups of subjects and then tries to explain what happens as age increases. As an example, consider a study in which the use of standard English is tested on third-, fourth-, fifth-, and sixth-grade central city students who were evaluated in terms of a test with a perfect score of 100. Suppose the results were as follows:

Grade	Third	Fourth	Fifth	Sixth
Mean score	70	79	83	85
Number	100	91	80	72

These data suggest that, as students progress through elementary school, their knowledge and usage of standard English increases. Evaluate such a study with respect to internal and external validity. What confounding variables could be used to explain the outcome other than that of increasing years of exposure to standard English in school and the community?

2-10. Another form of an observational study is *cohort analysis*. In this kind of study, a single group of people is followed and their performance on a dependent variable is evaluated over time. An example is provided in a study of the dependent variable of Exercise 2-9, in which a single group of children entering the third grade is followed through their elementary school career. The results of such a study might be as follows:

Grade	Third	Fourth	Fifth	Sixth
Mean score	70	79	83	85
Number	100	91	80	72

Evaluate such a study with respect to internal and external validity. What confounding variables could be used to explain the outcome, other than that of increasing years of exposure to standard English in school and the community?

2-11. Most news reports released by the Gallup poll are based on a sampling of about 1300 to 1400 people. Do you believe this sample is large enough for predicting whether candidate A or B is more popular in the population from which the sample was actually collected? Why?

2-12. If you were conducting a survey of who was the more popular, candidate A or B, would you use:
   a. Voter registration rolls
   b. Telephone books
   c. Door to door canvassers
   to obtain your data? Comment about the internal and external validity of each choice.

2-13. Provide an example where descriptive statistics is all that is needed to answer a research question. Provide an example where inferential statistics are required.

2-14. A large university has 15,000 students, who are assigned individual code numbers. Today the code numbers range from 119062 to 147091. The administration wants a sample of 150 students to answer a questionnaire. Someone suggested that the administration go to a table of random numbers and select at random a number between 001 and 150. Suppose the number selected is 85. The administration has been told to have its computer select every 150th student on the roster, starting with the 85th student. This type of sampling is called *systematic* sampling. Under what conditions will it produce a random sample? Under what conditions would it be a sampling scheme to avoid?

CHAPTER 3

Graphic Methods and Pictorial Representations of Relationships

3-1. GRAPHS

As can be seen by examining Table 2-1, it appears that the numbers are without order and almost defy description. Yet, one wants to convey to other people any information that can be inferred from the sample about the population from which the sample came. One way to convey this information is to present it in a pictorial manner. Indeed, such is the nature of much research; findings can best be comprehended at once through the use of pictorial aids.

From a scientific point of view, experiments and surveys are performed in order to gain information about a given phenomenon. An experiment or survey gives one first-hand experience with a specific phenomenon in a variety of situations, and the measurements one makes during the investigation give a more precise numerical description of the relationships between the variables one measures. Unfortunately, numerical relationships such as these are also difficult to visualize. A pictorial representation, such as a graph, allows one to see differences and relationships that exist in the data.

Finally, graphs help others to understand the effects of various treatments, both in magnitude and in kind, on dependent variables in a controlled study or in a survey in which controls are frequently ignored. For expository purposes, we will consider controlled experiments only. Much of what will be said can be extended to survey studies. The controlled experiment tells how two variables are related; the hypothesis is that one variable affects the other in some way. A graph helps one see how values of the independent variable tend to be associated with different values of the dependent variable.

The data collected in a controlled experiment will often be in the form of two sets of numbers, each set consisting of the information gathered about the independent or dependent variable. Each set of numbers is then plotted along one or the other of the axes of the graph. By plotting one set of numbers along the vertical axis and the other along the horizontal axis, you will be able to tell at a glance if the two sets of numbers seem to vary with each other in a consistent fashion. When transferring data onto a graph, plan to plot the *dependent variable on the vertical axis* and the *independent variable on the horizontal axis*. These axes are often referred to as the Y axis and the X axis, respectively.

Occasionally, one may encounter some conceptual problems in deciding which variable in a study should be labeled the independent variable and which the dependent variable. For example, if one were planning to graph the time of day with fluctuations in the temperature at a location, it makes little sense to state that the time of day causes the temperature to change, and

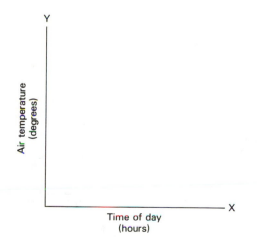

Figure 3-1.
The temperature and time of day labeled as dependent and independent variables.

Table 3-1.	Air temperature in degrees Fahrenheit as a function of time of day in a western city on July 1.

X, *time*	Y, *temperature (°F)*
6 A.M.	52
10 A.M.	58
2 P.M.	66
6 P.M.	61
10 P.M.	55
2 A.M.	54

certainly the reverse statement makes no sense at all. In such cases, it merely makes more sense to say that the temperature varies *as a function of the time* and to plot the temperature as the dependent variable along the Y axis.

Labeling. To help interpret a graph, label the axes clearly. Print the name of the dependent variable along the Y axis, and indicate the units used to measure this variable. Do the same when labeling the independent variable along the X axis. For the weather example, the results would be as shown in Figure 3-1.

Scaling. It is important that a graph be scaled effectively. A proper choice of scale fulfills three requirements. All the values assumed by the variable must fit onto the graph, these values should occupy about two thirds of the available graph space, and the scale should allow one to read values off the graph

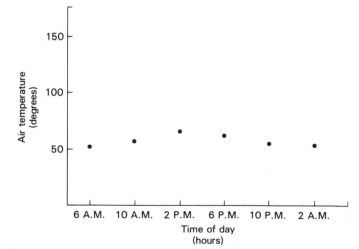

Figure 3-2.
Air temperature plotted against time of day on too fine a vertical scale.

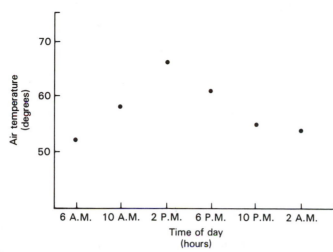

Figure 3-3.
Air temperature plotted against time of day on an appropriate vertical scale.

easily. For example, assume that temperatures have been measured at six different times as reported in Table 3-1. A possible choice of scale is shown in Figure 3-2. This choice is unfortunate, because all the Y values are squeezed into a small space on the graph. A much better choice is shown in Figure 3-3. All the Y values fit, but they are spread over a reasonable space on the graph. In order to improve the readability of a graph, choose a scale for the main graph paper divisions that are easily subdivided. Most graph paper has 10 subdivisions per main division, so scaling the main divisions with multiples of 1, 2, 5, or 10 yields the best results. Use 3, 7, and 9 only rarely. Write your scale numbers neatly along the main divisions.

Table 3-2.	Annual salary in thousands of dollars as a function of completed years of education.
X, years of schooling	**Y, annual salary**
3	2.5
6	5.1
7	7.0
9	8.4
11	10.5
12	11.0
15	12.5
16	16.7

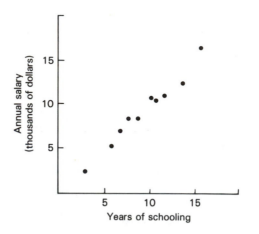

Figure 3-4.
Annual salary in thousands of dollars according to completed years of education.

The procedure used for scaling is the same for both the X and Y axes. The particular choice depends on the values assumed by each variable. Thus, the axes must be scaled separately, often resulting in an X axis scale that contains numbers entirely different from those used to scale the Y axis.

As an example, consider the paired sets of values of X and Y reported in Table 3-2. These paired points are shown plotted in Figure 3-4. This choice of axis scaling seems appropriate.

If it seems that a straight line best fits the data, the following procedure will prove useful. Assume you have plotted the points in Figure 3-5. First cover the upper half of the points and put an x at the center of the lower points, as shown. Then cover the lower points and put an x at the center of the upper points, as shown. Draw a straight line through the x's. The result is a line that fits your data well. The result is illustrated in Figure 3-6.

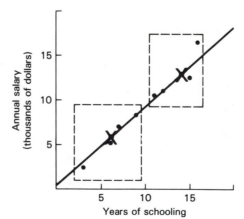

Figure 3-5.
An easy procedure for fitting a straight line.

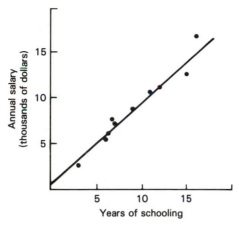

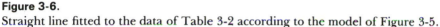

Figure 3-6.
Straight line fitted to the data of Table 3-2 according to the model of Figure 3-5.

3-2. STATISTICAL GRAPHS

Statisticians have developed a number of graphing methods that succinctly illustrate the basic information in a sample. These graphs are referred to as *bar graphs, line graphs, histograms,* and *percentage polygons.* Each is used to display the percentage of the sample or samples falling at or around a given value of an observed variable. In the case of a qualitative variable, such as stated college major, this would correspond to the percentage of science or humanities majors in the sample; in the case of a quantitative variable, such as score on the pretest, this would correspond to the percentage of students in the sample whose scores fell in the neighborhood of 17 points.

All four of these graph types are easy to make and to interpret. In each, the percentage is graphed as the dependent variable, since its value is a function of the category or score of the variable in question. Bar graphs are used for both ordered and unordered qualitative variables. Line graphs are used exclusively for discrete variables, while histograms and percentage polygons are used for both continuous and discrete variables. The construction of these graphs is illustrated for data taken from Table 2-1.

In the construction of any of these graphs, a word of caution is called for. While a researcher would like to convey information that is valid, it is possible to distort a graph so that it gives a false picture. This can be done by squeezing or lengthening the vertical or horizontal axes. To avoid such distortions, it is suggested that the vertical axis be about two thirds the length of the horizontal axis. This will help keep the distortion at a minimum.

Missing data cause problems in the construction of any statistical graph. We suggest that subjects that have missing information should not be considered part of the sample for the time being. Of course, they will be included in any other graph for which they have the requisite information. For example, when graphing the variable Major for the sample of Table 2-1, because there are four missing observations, we could act as though we have a sample of size 36.

3-3. STATISTICAL BAR GRAPHS

To illustrate the method for constructing a bar graph, consider the unordered qualitative variable Major and take the following steps. First, make a listing of all possible majors. In this case, the majors are: {humanities, natural sciences, social sciences, other, not known at this time}. Count the number of subjects that are members of these majors. The tallies and frequencies for the data of Table 2-1 are given in Table 3-3. Divide each frequency by the total number of observations in the sample and convert to a percentage by multiplying by 100. In this case, the percentages are as shown in Table 3-3. On a sheet of graph paper construct bars for each major, equal in height to the corresponding percentage. Put labels under each bar, label the vertical axis, and give the graph a title such as shown in Figure 3-7. In the case of a bar graph, one could add an extra category, No Response, as we have to represent subjects who did not respond to the particular question being graphed. For completeness, we provide directions for making a bar graph in Box 3-1.

The graph in Figure 3-7 represents a visual description of the composition of the sample with respect to stated major. Since the sample was chosen at random from the entire population, we expect that this composition also is fairly representative of the population from which the sample was drawn. As the graph in Figure 3-7 now stands, it provides little more information than if the relative percentage of students in each major grouping had been listed on a piece of paper. Such graphs are more informative when more than one sample is presented. For example, random samples drawn from the popula-

Table 3-3. Tally count for making a bar diagram for the variable major.

Category	Tally	Frequency	Percent
Humanities	ⅢⅢⅡ	12	30.0
Natural science	ⅢⅢ	8	20.0
Social science	ⅢⅠ	6	15.0
Other	ⅢⅡ	7	17.5
Unknown at this time	Ⅲ	3	7.5
No response	ⅢⅠ	4	10.0
Total		40	100.0

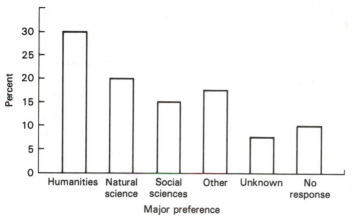

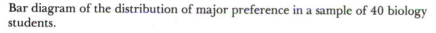

Figure 3-7.
Bar diagram of the distribution of major preference in a sample of 40 biology students.

tion in three successive years could be depicted on the same bar graph, with different colors or stripes to differentiate the samples. Then statements could be made from the graph as to the consistency of the population from year to year.

3-4. STATISTICAL LINE GRAPHS

The creation of a line graph is similar to the making of a bar graph. The steps to follow are the same, except that counting is performed on the numerical values of the variable and not categories. To illustrate the method of construction of a line graph, consider the discrete variable Score on the pretest.

Box 3-1   Procedure for making a bar graph

Step 1. List the categories. Make sure they cover all possible outcomes. In most cases, an "Other" and an "Unknown" category will be required.

Step 2. Count the number of subjects who fall into each category. Summarize the tallies in a column called frequency.

Step 3. Divide the frequency in each category by the total number of observations in the sample. Multiply the resulting proportion by 100 to place the frequencies on a percentage scale.

Step 4. On a sheet of graph paper, rule vertical and horizontal axes. Scale the vertical axis into equal width percentage intervals with the height of the axis being slightly larger than the largest category percentage.

Step 5. Across the horizontal axis, construct bars for each category equal in height to the category percentage.

Step 6. Put labels under each bar, label the vertical axis, and give the graph a title.

Begin by counting the number of subjects that obtain the possible numerical scores on the test. The tallies are summarized in Table 3-4 in the column headed frequency. Divide the frequency for each score of the variable by the total number of observations in the sample. Multiply the resulting proportion by 100 so as to place the frequencies on a percentage scale. On a sheet of graph paper, rule and scale the vertical and horizontal axes as shown in Figure 3-8. Divide the vertical axis into equal width percentage intervals with the height of the axis being slightly larger than the largest tabled percentage. Construct lines perpendicular to the horizontal axis above each value of the

Table 3-4.   Tally count for making a line graph for score on the biology pretest.

Pretest score	Tally	Frequency	Percent
0		0	0.0
1		0	0.0
2		0	0.0
3	|	1	2.6
4		0	0.0
5	|	1	2.6
6		0	0.0
7		0	0.0
8	|	1	2.6
9	|	1	2.6
10	‖|	3	7.7
11		0	0.0
12		0	0.0
13	⅀	5	12.8
14	|	1	2.6
15	‖	2	5.1
16	‖‖	4	10.3
17	‖‖	4	10.3
18	|	1	2.6
19		0	0.0
20	|	1	2.6
21		0	0.0

Table 3-4. *(Continued)*

Pretest score	Tally	Frequency	Percent
22	|	1	2.6
23	|	1	2.6
24	|	1	2.6
25	||	2	5.1
26	|	1	2.6
27		0	0.0
28	||||	4	10.3
29	|	1	2.6
30	|||	3	7.7
Total		39[a]	100.5[b]

[a] Total is based on known scores only.
[b] Total percentage is not 100.0, because of rounding errors.

variable, equal in height to the corresponding percentage. Put labels on the horizontal and vertical axes and give the graph a title, as shown in Figure 3-8. For completeness, we summarize the procedure for making a line graph in Box 3-2.

The information provided by the line graph, like that for the bar graph, can be used to make inferences about the population. The graph shows that the scores range from a low of 3 to a high of 30, with a major clustering of

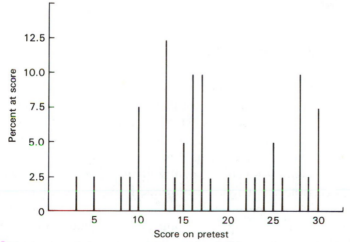

Figure 3-8.
Line graph of the distribution of pretest scores in a sample of 39 biology students.

Box 3-2   Procedure for making a line graph

Step 1. Count the number of subjects that obtain each of the possible values. Summarize the tallies in a column called frequency.

Step 2. Divide the frequency for each value by the total number of observations in the sample and multiply the resulting proportion by 100 to convert to a percentage scale.

Step 3. On a sheet of graph paper, rule vertical and horizontal axes. Scale the vertical axis using equal width percentage intervals, with the height of the axis being slightly larger than the highest tabled percentage. Also, scale the horizontal axis according to the rules given in Section 3-1.

Step 4. Construct lines perpendicular to the horizontal axis above each value of the variable, equal in height to the corresponding percentage.

Step 5. Label the axes and give the graph a title.

---

scores from 10 to 17 points and a secondary clustering occurring from 25 to 30 points. These clusterings allow a better description of the sample by revealing that it consists mainly of very good and average students, with relatively few poor or only slightly above average students.

It should be noted that not many researchers construct or report line graphs, not because they are invalid, but because they are not too informative if the range in values of the variable is large, such as in the example. When the range is large, researchers are more apt to use a histogram or percentage polygon to provide a graphic description of the sample. Unknown scores create a problem in the construction of line graphs and, as will be seen, for histograms and percentage polygons. Unfortunately, no satisfactory guidelines can be given to the solution of this problem. For now, it is suggested that unknown values be dropped from the analysis and that sample sizes be reduced accordingly.

3-5. STATISTICAL HISTOGRAMS

The making of a histogram is similar to the making of a combined bar and line graph, except that one must do a little planning. Technically, histograms are designed for continuous variables. Thus, if a discrete variable is going to be graphed using a histogram, the detailed discussion of the nature of such variables, presented in Section 1-5, must be called upon.

In that discussion, it was noted that the true score of an individual on a continuous variable is not actually known. This is due to the fact that such scores, measured on imperfect instruments, are rounded to the nearest unit of measurement. For example, the unit of measurement on the variable Score on the pretest, is 1 point. Thus, a discrete score of 2 corresponds, on a continuous scale, to a true score falling in the range between 1.5 and 2.5. This correction of discrete scores is called a *correction for continuity,* since we are relating the discrete scores to a continuous scale. The correction factor is set equal to one-half the difference between adjacent scores on the test.

For the scores on the pretest, the differences between adjacent test scores are equal to 1 test point. The correction for continuity is set equal to one-half this difference. Thus, a discrete score of 0 corresponds to the continuous range $-0.5 \leq Y \leq +0.5$; a discrete score of 1 correponds to the range $+0.5 \leq Y \leq +1.5$; etc.

Statistical histograms make use of the correction for continuity in setting up intervals of equal width. Sometimes, the lowest interval will extend below zero. It may seem inconceivable that scores on a test, for example, could possibly be negative. The test, however, measures a range whose limits are quite arbitrary. When a student gets a score of 0, it means that the test contained only questions that were too difficult. The student's true ability, however, is not zero in an absolute sense. Rather, with respect to this particular test, it is somewhat below the lower end point measured. If items were included on the test that were answered correctly by *all* students, none would get a zero and the problem would not appear. When you make a graph, and the lower end point is negative, use it in the same fashion you would any other lower end point.

Let us continue to set up a histogram. Determine the observed range of the variable in the sample using the continuity correction. The smallest observed score in the sample is equal to 3. In terms of the continuity correction, the lower limit to the interval containing 3 is 2.5. The largest observed value in the sample is equal to 30. In terms of the continuity correction, the upper limit of the interval containing 30 is 30.5. Thus, the observed range of scores in the sample on the continuous scale is given by:

$$\text{Range} = (\text{Largest upper limit}) - (\text{Smallest lower limit})$$
$$= 30.5 - 2.5 = 28$$

Divide the range into a set of equal width intervals. The number of intervals is generally taken to be no smaller than 8 and no larger than 12. If, for this example, the widths of each interval were to be set equal to 4, the number of intervals would be equal to $28/4 = 7$. This number of intervals is too small. If the width of each interval were to be set equal to 3, the number of intervals would be equal to $28/3 = 9.33$ or 10. Since this number is in the range of 8 to 12, we will use an interval width of 3.

In setting up the scale for the horizontal axis, we must recall that our completed graph of sample values is intended to reflect the nature of the population. For small samples, however, it is unlikely that the observed range is as large as the range of values in the population. To emphasize this in the graph, we make the lowest and highest interval end points smaller and larger, respectively, than the lowest and highest observed true scores.

Create the intervals by setting the lower end of the first interval slightly below the smallest lower true limit. A good procedure is to place the lower end of the first interval about one unit of measurement below the smallest lower true limit. In this case, the lower end of the first interval is $2.5 - 1 = 1.5$. Thus, the first interval is defined as $1.5 \leq Y \leq 4.5$. Note that this makes the midpoint of the first interval equal to the integer value of 3. The second interval is defined as $4.5 \leq Y \leq 7.5$. The remaining intervals are reported in Table 3-5. Note that in the sample, no values of the variable can ever equal endpoint values of the intervals.

Count the number of subjects that obtain scores in the various intervals. The tallies are summarized in Table 3-5 in the frequency column. Divide the frequency for each interval by the total number of observations in the sample for which numerical scores are available. Multiply the resulting proportions by 100 to place the frequencies on a percentage basis. On a sheet of graph paper, rule vertical and horizontal axes, as shown in Figure 3-9. Scale the vertical axis using equal width percentage intervals, with the height of the axis being slightly larger than the largest tabled percentage. On the horizontal axis, mark off the limits of the intervals reported in Table 3-5 and construct a bar over the interval equal in height to the tabled percentage. Put labels on the horizontal and vertical axes and give the graph a title, as in Figure 3-9.

The labeling of graphs is important, because they are used to convey information to oneself and to others. The axes should be clearly labeled so that the nature of the graph is self-evident. The advantage to the graphical

Table 3-5.   Tally count for making a histogram for score on the biology pretest.

Interval	Tally	Frequency	Percent
$1.5 \leq Y < 4.5$	|	1	2.6
$4.5 \leq Y < 7.5$	|	1	2.6
$7.5 \leq Y < 10.5$	卌	5	12.8
$10.5 \leq Y < 13.5$	卌	5	12.8
$13.5 \leq Y < 16.5$	卌 ||	7	17.9
$16.5 \leq Y < 19.5$	卌	5	12.8
$19.5 \leq Y < 22.5$	||	2	5.1
$22.5 \leq Y < 25.5$	||||	4	10.2
$25.5 \leq Y < 28.5$	卌	5	12.8
$28.5 \leq Y < 31.5$	||||	4	10.2
Total		39	99.8

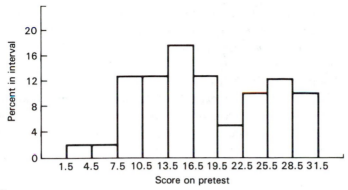

Figure 3-9.
Histogram of the distribution of pretest scores in a sample of 39 biology students.

picture of the data is lost if one must look in several places to put the pieces together.

Although the histogram of the pretest scores resembles the line graph of these scores, the histogram helps one to see trends in the data more clearly by smoothing out the individual bumps present in the line graph. Hence, al-

---

Box 3-3   Procedure for making a histogram

Step 1. Determine the magnitude of the difference between adjacent values of the variable and divide this magnitude by 2, to determine the correction for continuity.

Step 2. Determine the *range,* corrected for continuity, as:

$$\text{Range} = (\text{largest value} + \text{continuity correction}) - (\text{smallest value} - \text{continuity correction})$$

Step 3. Determine the proper interval width for the horizontal axis so as to create 8 to 12 intervals.

Step 4. Create the intervals by setting the lower end of the first interval one unit of measurement below the smallest *corrected* lower limit.

Step 5. Count the number of observations that fall in each interval.

Step 6. Divide the frequency for each interval by the total number of observations in the sample for which numerical scores are available. Multiply the resulting proportions by 100 to create a percentage scale.

Step 7. On a sheet of graph paper rule vertical and horizontal axes. Scale the vertical axis into equal width percentage intervals, with the height of the axis being slightly larger than the largest tabled percentage. Also, it is customary to scale the horizontal axis by marking off the limits of the intervals. This may be an instance where the scaling is not in multiples of 1, 2, 5, or 10. Construct a bar over each interval equal in height to the corresponding percentage.

Step 8. Label the axes and give the graph a title.

---

though the histogram still shows two high regions, one occurring between 8 and 19 points, the other between 23 and 30 points, the overall distribution of scores tends to show more regular features than in the line graph. Graphs with two such high regions are called *bimodal*. For completeness, we give directions for constructing a histogram in Box 3-3.

It should be noted that the vertical axis for a histogram actually indicates the percentage of test scores contained in the interval. Therefore, one should not label the axis simply "Percent." In general, histograms are used to describe the variation in a single sample, since it's somewhat difficult to differentiate two or more samples on a single histogram. When more than one sample is to be compared, percentage polygons are used.

3-6. STATISTICAL PERCENTAGE POLYGONS

The creation of a percentage polygon follows the same steps that are used to make a histogram, except that bars are not drawn over the respective intervals. Instead, above the midpoint of each interval, a point is placed at the height equal in value to the interval's percentage. The points are then joined by straight line segments to complete a closed polygon. The *relative frequency polygon* for the data of Table 3-5 is shown in Figure 3-10. We provide instructions for making a relative frequency polygon in Box 3-4.

When making a histogram, it is customary to indicate interval end points along the horizontal axis; when making a relative frequency polygon, midpoints are used. However, if one wanted to, one could also plot midpoints for a histogram.

As mentioned in Section 3-5, percentage polygons are often used to compare the distribution of scores for two or more groups of people. As an example, consider a comparison of the scores on the pretest of the males and females in our sample. Since we are interested in displaying these scores on the same graph, the same choice of intervals should be used for both groups.

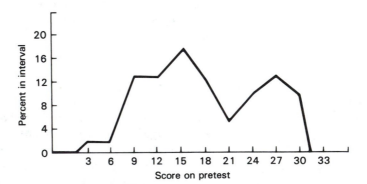

Figure 3-10.
Relative frequency polygon of the distribution of pretest scores in a sample of 39 biology students.

Box 3-4   Procedure for making a relative frequency polygon

Step 1. Complete the first six steps in the making of a histogram.

Step 2. Complete Step 7, but do not construct a bar over each interval. Instead, locate the midpoint of the interval, and mark a point above the midpoint equal in height to the relative frequency.

Step 3. Join the adjacent midpoints by straight lines. For the two extreme intervals, mark a point at the lower and upper interval limits on the horizontal axis. Extend the broken line segments to these lower and upper limits to complete the closed polygon.

The intervals used in the construction of the histogram in Section 3-5 are still appropriate in this particular case.

Further, since we are interested in comparing the graphs of the two groups, we should graph the percentages for each group in a given interval on the same scale. The percentage of scores in a given interval for each group is found by dividing the number of scores in the interval for that group by the number of people in the group. If we did not do this, the graph for the larger of the two groups would, in general, be higher than for the smaller group. The tallies and calculations for this graph are shown in Table 3-6, and the resulting graph is shown in Figure 3-11.

Table 3-6.   Tally count for making relative percentage polygons comparing pretest scores of males and females.

Interval	Males			Females		
	Tally	Frequency	Percent	Tally	Frequency	Percent
$1.5 \le Y < 4.5$	|	1	10.0		0	0.0
$4.5 \le Y < 7.5$		0	0.0	|	1	3.8
$7.5 \le Y < 10.5$		0	0.0	||||	4	15.4
$10.5 \le Y < 13.5$	|	1	10.0	||||	4	15.4
$13.5 \le Y < 16.5$	|||	3	30.0	||	2	7.7
$16.5 \le Y < 19.5$	|	1	10.0	||||	4	15.4
$19.5 \le Y < 22.5$		0	0.0	||	2	7.7
$22.5 \le Y < 25.5$	|	1	10.0	|||	3	11.5
$25.5 \le Y < 28.5$	|	1	10.0	||||	4	15.4
$28.5 \le Y < 31.5$	||	2	20.0	||	2	7.7
Total		10	100.0		26	100.0

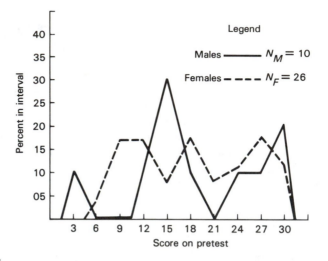

Figure 3-11.
Relative frequency polygons comparing pretest scores of a sample of 10 males and a sample of 26 females in a class of biology students.

Such a graph provides a good deal of information about the scores of the two groups. The scores for the females are much more uniformly distributed than for the males; that is, the females' scores are more evenly spread out across all values, while the males' scores are clustered around 15 and 27. It would seem that the females were somewhat more heterogeneous to start with than the males. It can thus be seen that the bimodal nature of the overall relative percentage polygon, Figure 3-10, is mainly due to the bimodal male distribution.

3-7. STATISTICAL CUMULATIVE RELATIVE FREQUENCY POLYGONS

Sometimes researchers construct a graph that is not normally used for descriptive purposes, but which can be used for analytical reasons. This graph is called the *cumulative relative frequency polygon.* Its construction follows the first steps involved in the making of a histogram or percentage polygon, except that some simple modifications follow. Complete the first six steps in the making of a histogram. Add an extra column to the tabulations of Table 3-5. Label this column *upper end points of the intervals,* as shown in Table 3-7. Add up the percentages, interval by interval, and record the resulting percentages. The percentage of scores less than, or equal to, 4.5 is given by 2.6 percent. The percentage of scores less than, or equal to, 7.5 is given by 2.6 percent + 2.6 percent = 5.2 percent. The percentage of scores less than, or equal to, 10.5 is given by 2.6 percent + 2.6 percent + 12.8 percent = 18.0 percent, etc. The remaining cumulative percentages are shown in Table 3-7. On a sheet of graph paper rule vertical and horizontal axes, as shown in Figure 3-12. Scale the vertical axis into equal-width percentage intervals so

Table 3-7. Cumulative percentages for score on the biology pretest.

Upper end points of the intervals	Cumulative percentages
4.5	2.6
7.5	5.2
10.5	18.0
13.5	30.8
16.5	48.7
19.5	61.5
22.5	66.6
25.5	76.8
28.5	89.6
31.5	99.8

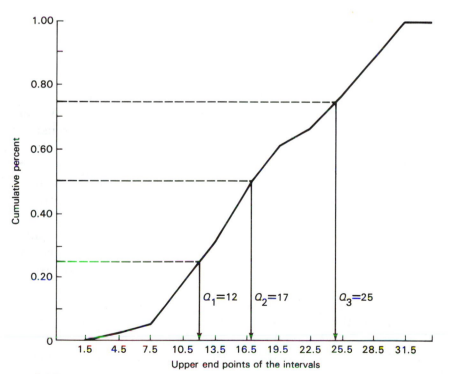

Figure 3-12.
Cumulative relative frequency polygon for the pretest scores in a sample of 39 biology students.

Box 3-5   Procedure for making a cumulative relative frequency polygon

Step 1. Complete the first six steps in the making of a histogram.
Step 2. Add an extra column labeled Upper End Points of the Intervals.
Step 3. Add up the percentages, interval by interval, and record the resulting percentages.
Step 4. On a sheet of graph paper, scale the vertical axis into equal width percentage intervals so that the last interval ends at 100 percent.
Step 5. On the horizontal axis, mark off the upper end points of the intervals, and place above each end point a mark whose Y value equals the cumulative percentage. Join the marks by straight line segments.
Step 6. Label the axes and give the graph a title.

---

that the last interval ends at 100 percent. On the horizontal axis, mark off the upper end points of the intervals, and place above each end point a mark at a height equal to the cumulative percentages. Join the marks by straight line segments. Put labels on the horizontal and vertical axes and give the graph a title. Note that the vertical axis is titled "Cumulative Percent." Directions for making a cumulative relative frequency polygon are shown in Box 3-5.

3-8. QUARTILES, DECILES, AND PERCENTILES

Cumulative percentage graphs are useful for determining test or variable *percentile* values. For example, the 90th percentile is the value of a variable that has the property that 90 percent of the observations are less than or equal to it. Only 10 percent of the observations exceed the 90th percentile value. The 25th percentile, sometimes called the *first quartile,* has the property that 25 percent of the observations are less than or equal to it. In a like manner, the 75th percentile, or third quartile, has the property that 75 percent of the observations are less than or equal to it. The 90th percentile is sometimes called the ninth *decile,* while the 10th percentile is frequently referred to as the first decile.

The 50th percentile (or the fifth decile or the second quartile) is generally called the *median.* It is the central value of the variable in that it divides the distribution in half. Exactly 50 percent of the observations exceed this central value and 50 percent of the observations are less than it. In the literature, the median is denoted as $\hat{M}$, $\hat{Q}_2$, $\hat{D}_5$, or $\hat{P}_{50}$. The first quartile is denoted as $\hat{Q}_1$ or $\hat{P}_{25}$, while the third quartile is denoted as $\hat{Q}_3$ or $\hat{P}_{75}$. The 10th percentile is denoted as $\hat{D}_1$ or $\hat{P}_{10}$ and the 90th percentile is denoted as $\hat{D}_9$ or $\hat{P}_{90}$. The caret over the letters $D, Q,$ and P is generally used to denote a value computed for a sample.

For the data of Table 3-7, it is seen that the approximate 5th percentile is equal to 7.5, the approximate 18th percentile is equal to 10.5, and the approximate 67th percentile is equal to 22.5. Other percentile values can be read from Figure 3-12 by laying a ruler across the vertical axis, parallel to the horizontal axis at the percentile value of interest, and then rotating the ruler through a 90° angle at the point the ruler cuts the graph. The corresponding percentile can be read at the point where the ruler cuts the horizontal axis. Following this procedure, one can verify that the 75th percentile is a number fairly close to 25, that the 25th percentile value is a number fairly close to 12 and that the median value is a number fairly close to 17. These three numbers give a researcher a good deal of information about the scores on the pretest. In this case, it is known that about 25 percent of the students obtain scores of 12 or less, about 50 percent obtain scores of 17 or less, and about 75 percent obtain scores of 25 or less. Note that the population percentile values are still unknown. However, a researcher would not hesitate to state that, in the population, the percentile values are numbers close to those reported in the sample. If the sample size is large, the deviations of the sample values from the population values will be small and the *confidence* in the statement will be strong; but, if the sample size is small, the confidence in the statement may not be strong, because, with small samples, the deviations may be large.

Percentile values can be approximated directly from Table 3-7 by using a process called *interpolation*. For example, let us compute the 40th percentile. We know that 30.8 percent of the scores are below 13.5 and 48.7 percent are below 16.5. Thus, the 40th percentile is between 13.5 and 16.5. The 40th percentile is $40 - 30.8 = 9.2$ percentage units above the 30.8th percentile and is part of the way into the interval bounded by the percentiles of 30.8 and 48.7. This interval contains $48.7 - 30.8 = 17.9$ percentage points. The 40th percentile is $9.2/17.9 = 0.5140$ of the way into the interval. The interval on the score scale is $16.5 - 13.5 = 3$ units wide. We estimate the 40th percentile as being $0.5140 \times 3 = 1.54$ units into the interval. Thus, $\hat{P}_{40} = 13.5 + 1.54 = 15.04$. Other values can be found in a similar fashion.

3-9. EXERCISES

3-1. Use a bar diagram to compare your sample of 40 students to the sample represented in Table 3-3 and Figure 3-7. What does the comparison suggest to you about random sampling?

3-2. What kind of graph should one construct for the responses to the following question? Why? How useful will your experience in this biology class be in your future life? 1. A great deal. 2. More than average. 3. Average. 4. Less than average. 5. Of no value at all.

3-3. Make a line graph for scores on the pretest for your sample of 40 students. Compare your results to Figure 3-8.

3-4. Make a histogram for the scores on the pretest for your sample of 40 students. Compare your results to those of Table 3-5 and Figure 3-9. What does the comparison suggest to you about random sampling?

3-5. Make a relative frequency polygon for the

scores on the pretest for your sample of 40 students. Place, on the same graph, the relative frequency polygon of Figure 3-10, but use a dotted or broken line to differentiate it from your sample. Compare the 2 graphs. Note: Use the same intervals as those in the text.

3-6. Make a cumulative percentage polygon for the scores on the pretest for your sample of 40 students. Use the graph to estimate $\hat{Q}_1$, $\hat{Q}_2$, and $\hat{Q}_3$. Compare your results to those reported for Figure 3-12. What does the comparison suggest to you about random sampling? Are you surprised?

3-7. Among the 238 students in Table A-16:
   a. 37 percent are male
   b. 25 percent have College Board scores below 445
   c. 54 percent did not have a previous course in high school biology
   d. 26 percent were natural science majors
   e. 51 percent were assigned to program 1

Determine a, b, c, d, and e for your sample, and give the information to your instructor, who will determine the average values for your class. Compare your results to these population values and to the class averages which will be supplied to you by your instructor. Are the results expected on the basis of random sampling? Why?

3-8. A sample of 40 represents $p = (^{40}\!/_{238}) \times 100 = 17$ percent of the population. Do you think this is large enough to make valid inferences about the 238 students in the full population? Answer this question when the data from your class are made available to you.

3-9. The distribution by major for the 238 students is as follows:

Major	Relative frequency
Humanities	29.0
Natural science	24.8
Social science	11.8
Other	11.3
Unknown	18.1
Missing data	5.0

Make a bar diagram for these data and for your sample on a single sheet of graph paper. How well does your sample agree with the population? Why does your sample differ from the population?

3-10. Bar diagrams are frequently represented by *pie charts*. A pie chart is a circle divided into wedges for which the central angle is proportional to the relative frequency of the graph categories. For the data of Exercise 3-9 the central angle for Humanities is equal to 0.290 $(360°) = 104.4°$. Report the results of Exercise 3-9 in terms of two pie charts for which the radii are set equal to 1 in. Which method do you prefer for representing such data; that of Exercise 3-9 or that of Exercise 3-10? Why?

CHAPTER 4

Measures of Central Tendency

4-1. MEASURES OF CENTRAL TENDENCY IN THE POPULATION

As was indicated in Chapters 1 and 2, statistics can be used to investigate differences and relationships in data, whether in the course of suggesting hypotheses for further testing or in examining whether a given hypothesis seemed to be supported by the data. It was indicated then that one could determine whether or not the sample information represented a real relationship in the population or merely a vagary due to sampling. One could do so by comparing the magnitude of a relationship present in sample data to the sizes of such relationships that one could expect solely due to the variability in nature. For example, if one found that a reading program improved student reading scores by six points and that one expected a chance gain of six points or more only 1 percent of the time, one would be likely to conclude that the students' reading ability was, indeed, improved by the program.

Clearly, in order to make such determinations, one must have an idea of the magnitude of the effect or relationship and the size of the variability present in nature. In this chapter, we will consider several of the more common measures used to summarize data, with the purpose of specifying where the center of a population is located. As was seen in the preceding chapter, graphs of information vary quite a bit. It seemed, for example, that the distribution of scores on the pretest differed for males and females; thus, the problem becomes one of summarizing the data in a way that reflects such differences.

Examination of the graphs considered in Chapter 3 might suggest three kinds of summary measures that have proved useful: the average, the median, and the mode. The average and median both attempt to define the center of the score distribution. The average, or sample mean, can be conceptualized in the following way. If we draw a relative frequency polygon for a set of data and then construct a metal replica of our polygon, the average is that score at which we would place our finger to balance the metal polygon; it represents the "center of gravity" of the score distribution. If, on the other hand, the scores are ordered from smallest to largest, the median is the middle score in the string. Finally, the mode is the score most frequently attained in the sample. It is for this reason that graphs in the previous chapter, having two most commonly attained scores, were called *bimodal.*

In the construction of the line graph, the histogram, and the percentage polygon for the scores on the pretest for the 40 biology students reported in Table 2-1, it was noted that the distribution of scores appeared to be bimodal. When this occurs, a researcher is inclined to believe that, perhaps, two different samples have been inadvertently mixed together. In this case, there is good reason to believe that the sample does consist of a mixing of two different unrelated samples, those who had or did not have a previous exposure to biology. At the time of the pretest, students in the class were asked: When you were in high school, did you have a class or part of a class that was devoted to the study of biology or some other biological science?

According to the figures in Table 4-1, 16 students responded Yes and 24 students responded No to this question. Certainly, pretest scores should depend to some extent upon how well the high school classes were taught and how concerned the students were about learning the subject matter. One would expect higher test scores from students who had these kinds of courses previously.

4-2. THE SAMPLE MEAN

One common example of a summary score is the *sample mean.* By definition, the sample mean of a group of observations is simply the sum of the observa-

Table 4-1. Scores on the biology pretest according to whether or not students had a high school course in one of the biological sciences.[a]

	Had a course	Did not have a course	
	28	10	
	28	24	
	26	23	
	29	17	
	25	13	
	5	16	
	8	25	
	28	10	
	30	18	
	16	13	
	13	13	
	30	20	
	17	28	
	15	10	
	15	22	
	30	9	
		17	
		14	
		3	
		16	
		13	
		16	
		17	
Sum of the scores	343	367	710
Number in group	16	23	39
Sample mean	21.4	16.0	18.2

[a] One student who did not have a high school course in the biological sciences did not take the pretest.

tions divided by the number of observations that constitute the group. In mathematical terms, the sample mean is defined as follows:

Definition of the sample mean

Let the observations in a sample be denoted by:

$$Y_1, Y_2, Y_3, \ldots, Y_N$$

where Y_1 = numerical value for the first observation
Y_2 = numerical value for the second observation
Y_3 = numerical value for the third observation
$\vdots$
Y_N = numerical value for the last, or Nth, observation

The sample mean, represented by $\bar{Y}$, is defined as:

$$\bar{Y} = \frac{1}{N}(Y_1 + Y_2 + Y_3 + \cdots + Y_N)$$

For the sample of 16 students who had a high school course in one of the biological sciences, the sample mean is equal to:

$$\bar{Y}_{Yes} = (28 + 28 + 26 + \cdots + 30)/16$$
$$= (343)/16 = 21.4375 = 21.4$$

For the sample of 24 students who did not have a high school course in one of the biological sciences, the sample mean, based on the 23 students who took the pretest, is equal to:

$$\bar{Y}_{No} = (10 + 24 + 23 + \cdots + 17)/23$$
$$= (367)/23 = 15.9565 = 16.0$$

For the entire sample of 39 students who took the pretest, the sample mean is equal to:

$$\bar{Y} = (343 + 367)/39 = (710)/39 = 18.2051 = 18.2$$

As can be seen, students who had a previous biological science course tended to have a mean score that was:

$$\bar{Y}_{Yes} - \bar{Y} = 21.4 - 18.2 = 3.2$$

points above the mean score of the entire group. Students who did not have such a course tended to have a mean score that was:

$$\bar{Y}_{\text{No}} - \bar{Y} = 16.0 - 18.2 = -2.2$$

or 2.2 points below the mean score of the entire group. The difference in the means between the groups is equal to:

$$\bar{Y}_{\text{Yes}} - \bar{Y}_{\text{No}} = 21.4 - 16.0 = 5.4 \text{ test points}$$

The hypothesis, or conjecture, that two samples had been mixed together appears to have been well founded in fact. Students who had a course in the biological sciences tended to outscore their classmates who did not have such classes by about five test points. On the other hand, if $\bar{Y}_{\text{Yes}} - \bar{Y}_{\text{No}}$ had been a number closer to zero, we might suspect that a previous course in biology was just as effective as no course in biology, at least in how students performed on the pretest.

4-3. THE SAMPLE MEDIAN

Another common measure of central tendency is the sample median, which was introduced in Section 3-8 as the 50th percentile value. In terms of the original observations, the sample median is defined as follows:

Definition of the sample median

Let the observations in a sample be ordered from the smallest to largest. Let the ordered observations be denoted by:

$$Y_1^o, Y_2^o, Y_3^o, \ldots, Y_N^o$$

where Y_1^o = the smallest, or first, ordered numerical value
Y_2^o = the second ordered numerical value
Y_3^o = the third ordered numerical value

.
.
.

Y_N^o = the largest, or Nth, ordered numerical value

The sample median is defined as:

$$\hat{M} = \begin{cases} \text{The middle ordered value, if } N \text{ is odd.} \\ \text{The mean value of the two mid-ordered values, if } N \text{ is even.} \end{cases}$$

For the data of Table 4-1, the ordered sample for the students who had a previous course in biology is given by:

$$5, 8, 13, 15, 15, 16, 17, 25, 26, 28, 28, 28, 29, 30, 30, 30$$

Since $N = 16$ is an even number, the median is the mean value of the two mid-observations $Y_8^o = 25$ and $Y_9^o = 26$, so that:

$$\hat{M}_{\text{Yes}} = (Y_8^o + Y_9^o)/2 = (25 + 26)/2 = 25.5$$

For the students who did not have a high school course in biology, the ordered sample is given by:

$$3, 9, 10, 10, 10, 13, 13, 13, 13, 14, 16, 16, 16, 17, 17,$$
$$17, 18, 20, 22, 23, 24, 25, 28$$

Since $N = 23$ is odd, the sample median value is the mid-value:

$$\hat{M}_{\text{No}} = Y_{12}^o = 16$$

For the total sample of 39 students who took the pretest, the sample median corresponds to the mid-value:

$$\hat{M} = Y_{20}^o = 17$$

As can be seen, students who had a biology course tended to have a median score that was:

$$\hat{M}_{\text{Yes}} - \hat{M} = 25.5 - 17 = 8.5$$

points above the median score of the entire group. Students who did not have such a course tended to have a median score that differed from the median of the entire group by:

$$\hat{M}_{\text{No}} - \hat{M} = 16 - 17 = -1$$

point. Their median was one point below the median of the entire group. The difference in medians between the two groups is equal to:

$$\hat{M}_{\text{Yes}} - \hat{M}_{\text{No}} = 25.5 - 16 = 9.5 \text{ test points}$$

This evidence also suggests that the two groups might be quite different in terms of this variable.

4-4. THE SAMPLE MODE

In Section 3-5, it was suggested that the combined sample of students possessed a bimodal distribution. This meant that the distribution had two modes. The sample mode is defined as follows:

Definition of the sample mode

The sample mode, $\hat{M}_0$, is the value of the variable that appears with the greatest frequency.

The sample of students who had high school biological science has two modes. The values of the modes are 28 and 30. The sample of students who did not have such a course has a single mode which appears at 13. In the combined sample, the mode is equal to 13. Thus, the mode also seems to distinguish students with previous biology experience from those without it.

4-5. SELECTING A SUMMARY MEASURE

In this chapter, three measures of central tendency were presented. Other measures of central tendency exist, but are used rarely. Since a sample may consist entirely of numbers that occur only once and thus may not possess a mode, the mode is almost never used in practice. In describing the distribution of a variable in a sample, both the mean and the median are useful, each supplying additional information. Which of these two better describes the sample depends on the exact nature of the distribution in question.

One characteristic of a distribution is its degree of symmetry. A *symmetric* distribution is one that possesses two halves that are identical. If a distribution is symmetric, the sample mean is generally preferred. If a distribution is *skewed*, that is, does not possess symmetry, the median is preferred since it would lie closer than would the mean to the part of the distribution where most of the scores fall. Examples of skewed and symmetric distributions appear in Figure 4-1. If the tail of a distribution extends to the right, the distribution is said to be *positively skewed;* if the tail extends to the left, the distribution is said to be *negatively skewed.* If the sample is large, skewness can be detected by examining the resulting histogram.

As will be seen later, the mean is quite often the preferred measure of central tendency because it is easily used in hypothesis testing. It will be shown in Chapter 20 that the distribution of sample means selected from many samples approaches a symmetric, known distribution when the size of the sample is large enough. This is true even for highly skewed distributions;

Negative skewness

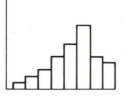

Symmetrical

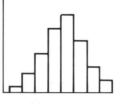

Positive skewness

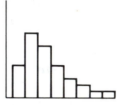

Figure 4-1.
Example of symmetric, positively skewed, and negatively skewed distributions.

thus, for samples of moderate size, skewness is of no great importance, and the mean is preferred even to the median.

4-6. THE WEIGHTED MEAN FOR K SAMPLES

Another reason that the mean is preferred over the median as a measure of central tendency is that sample means can be combined algebraically, whereas medians and modes cannot. For the data of Table 4-1 $\bar{Y}_{No} = 15.9565$, $\bar{Y}_{Yes} = 21.4375$, and $\bar{Y} = 18.2051$. As one might suspect, $\bar{Y}$ can be determined from $\bar{Y}_{No}$ and $\bar{Y}_{Yes}$. The sum of the pretest scores in the No group is 367 and in the Yes group is 343, so that the total across the two samples is 710. Since $\bar{Y}_{No} = (367)/23 = 15.9565$, we see that:

$$367 = 23(15.9565) = 23\bar{Y}_{No}$$

Similarly:

$$343 = 16(21.4375) = 16\bar{Y}_{Yes}$$

Box 4-1   Procedure for determining the weighted average of K sample means

Step 1. Determine the mean of each sample. Let the means be $\bar{Y}_1, \bar{Y}_2, \ldots, \bar{Y}_K$. Let the sample sizes be $N_1, N_2, \ldots, N_K$.

Step 2. Compute the weighted average as:

$$\bar{Y} = \frac{N_1\bar{Y}_1 + N_2\bar{Y}_2 + \cdots + N_K\bar{Y}_K}{N}$$

If we let $W_1 = N_1/N$, $W_2 = N_2/N$, $\ldots$, $W_K = N_K/N$ denote the weights, then:

$$\bar{Y} = W_1\bar{Y}_1 + W_2\bar{Y}_2 + \cdots + W_K\bar{Y}_K$$

Thus:

$$\bar{Y} = \frac{23\bar{Y}_{\text{No}} + 16\bar{Y}_{\text{Yes}}}{39} = (^{23}\!/_{39})\bar{Y}_{\text{No}} + (^{16}\!/_{39})\bar{Y}_{\text{Yes}}$$

In general, given $\bar{Y}_1$ based on N_1 observations and $\bar{Y}_2$ based on N_2 observations, the mean value of the combined group is given as the weighted average of the two means and is computed as:

$$\bar{Y} = \frac{N_1}{N}\bar{Y}_1 + \frac{N_2}{N}\bar{Y}_2$$

where $N = N_1 + N_2$. Directions for computing a *weighted average* are shown in Box 4-1.

4-7. STATISTICS AND PARAMETERS

The quantities that researchers compute from known sample values are called *statistics*. They are used as estimates of corresponding quantities in the population called *parameters*. Some statistics that we encountered in this chapter were the sample mean, $\bar{Y}$; the sample median, $\hat{M}$; and the sample mode, $\hat{M}_0$. Many other statistics will appear in later chapters. For example, we will consider the sample standard deviation in Chapter 5 and the sample correlation coefficient in Chapter 7. While sample values are computed from observed data, parameters remain unknown. If one knew the values of the parameters for a variable or sets of variables, research would not be required. For example, if we knew that the population mean score for certain students on a particular spelling test was equal to 24 points and that if we taught these students with a new program, the mean score would increase to 32 points, we would not have to research the method. For completeness, we provide definitions of the concepts of a population parameter and a sample statistic.

Definitions of a population parameter and a sample statistic

A population parameter is a quantity that serves to describe a specific characteristic of a population, such as its center or variation about its center.

A sample statistic is an estimate of a population parameter that is entirely based upon observed sample values.

4-8. EXERCISES

4-1. Determine for your sample of forty the mean, median, and mode for the scores on the pretest and compare your estimates with those of the entire group of 238 students. For the total group, the mean, median, and mode are 17.4, 16.0, and 16, respectively.

4-2. Report the results of Exercise 4-1 to your instructor, who will compute the average values for the class and return the information to you at a later time for class discussion.

4-3. What is the mean difference in pretest scores for the students in your sample who had, or did not have, a previous course in high school biology? How does it compare to the total group for which the mean values are 18.4 and 16.5?

4-4. Find the sample medians for the data of Exercise 4-3.

4-5. Find the mean, median, and mode for the College Board scores for your sample of 40 students. The values of these measures of central tendency for the 238 students are given by 528, 510, and 410, respectively. Compare your results to these values.

4-6. Find the mean values for the College Board scores for the students in your sample who were in study conditions 1 and 2. The corre-

sponding population values are 539 and 517. Do you think the groups are equivalent to one another on the characteristics measured by the College Board test scores? What is measured by the College Board test scores? Do you think it is an important variable to measure in this study? Why?

4-7. Reduce your majors to Humanities, Natural sciences, Social sciences, and Others and not known at this time. Find the mean values on the College Board test. Compare your results to those of the entire group. In this case the mean values are 523, 521, 586, and 521. Verify for your sample that:

$$\bar{Y} = W_1\bar{Y}_1 + W_2\bar{Y}_2 + W_3\bar{Y}_3 + W_4\bar{Y}_4$$

where

$$W_k = \frac{N_k}{N} \qquad \text{for } k = 1, 2, 3, \text{ and } 4$$

4-8. In a study of the effects of television viewing upon student learning, a school district was divided on the basis of 1980 census data into three social strata. A sample of third-grade children was chosen on each stratum and a record was kept of the number of hours each child spent viewing TV during the first Monday through Sunday in November. Results are as shown:

Stratum	Mean	Sample size
Low	15.6	27
Medium	6.3	36
High	8.4	47

Find the mean value for the school district.

4-9. For the data of Exercise 4-8, find the values of:

$$\hat{\alpha}_1 = \bar{Y}_1 - \bar{Y}, \ \hat{\alpha}_2 = \bar{Y}_2 - \bar{Y}, \ \text{and} \ \hat{\alpha}_3 = \bar{Y}_3 - \bar{Y}$$

and show that:

$$N_1\hat{\alpha}_1 + N_2\hat{\alpha}_2 + N_3\hat{\alpha}_3 = 0$$

Can you explain why that latter sum equals zero? What is measured by $\hat{\alpha}_1$, $\hat{\alpha}_2$, and $\hat{\alpha}_3$? These measures are called *treatment* or *group effects*.

4-10. Repeat the analysis of Exercise 4-9 for the data of Exercise 4-7.

4-11. Examine the histogram of Exercise 3-4. Describe the distribution in terms of the symmetry or skewness.

4-12. For the data of Exercise 4-7, what values are parameters and what values are statistics?

CHAPTER 5

Measures of Variation

5-1. MEASURES OF VARIATION IN THE POPULATION

In Chapter 4, we used two methods to measure group differences, each involving an examination of the difference in a summary statistic between two groups. One involved the difference in two sample means, the other the difference in two sample medians. It was said then that if the difference in the sample statistics that measure centers was a number close to zero, it would be concluded that the corresponding difference in the populations from which the samples came would also be close to zero.

Unfortunately, two problems still remain before such conclusions can be drawn about the population parameters. First, there is always a possibility that the samples, in spite of random sampling, are unlike their respective populations because of some vagary of sampling; and second, there is the related problem of determining what the term "close to zero" is likely to mean, given that there is always natural variation in the system being observed. Statisticians have developed techniques that minimize the risks involved in making inferences from sample data, and these methods are based on an examination of the variation within the sample that one could expect on the basis of chance alone. This within-group measure of variation is called the *standard deviation*. It is a measure of variation about the sample mean.

As we saw in Chapter 4, the sample mean is used as a summary measure that tends to describe a typical or central value in the sample. For example, consider the 16 students who had a prior course in high school biology. As we calculated in Section 4-2, the mean score on the pretest was 21.4. If we examine the scores of individual students, we note that not one student obtained exactly this test score, but still 21.4 does represent a mid-value score for a typical student. If we accept the sample mean as a reference point, we could compare each observation in the sample to it. In particular, we could compute the deviation of each observation from the sample mean by taking the difference between each observation and the sample mean. For the first observation listed in Table 5-1, the value of the deviation from the sample mean is given by:

$$d_1 = Y_1 - \bar{Y} = 28 - 21.4 = 6.6$$

While a typical student in the sample has a score of 21.4 points, student number one has a score that is 6.6 points above this hypothetical student. For student number six, the corresponding deviation is given by:

$$d_6 = Y_6 - \bar{Y} = 5 - 21.4 = -16.4$$

indicating that, relative to the typical student, student number six has a very low grade that is 16.4 points below the mean score. It is quite apparent that we could compute the deviation of each student score from the mean score. This has been done, and all of the deviations are listed in Table 5-1 in the column headed deviation scores. As a first thought, it might seem reasonable to sum the deviations and divide by the sample size to obtain an average deviation to use as a measure of within-sample variation. While this idea makes intuitive sense, it fails to create the desired end, since the sum of the deviations is zero. In our example, the sum of the deviations totals 0.6, not zero, because of rounding errors.

The same argument can be made about deviations of population scores about the population mean. If we could observe them, they would also add to zero. This idea of averaging deviations does have merit, however, for, although the sum of the deviations is zero, the sum of their squares is not. It is this fact that is used in defining the *standard deviation of the population*. This quantity is calculated by squaring the deviations, taking their sum, dividing

Table 5-1. Computation of the Sample Standard Deviations for the Two Samples of Table 4-1.

Students Who Had a Prior Course in High School Biology			Students Who Did Not Have a Prior Course in High School Biology.		
Score	Deviation score	d_i^2	Score	Deviation score	d_i^2
28	6.6	43.56	10	−6.0	36.00
28	6.6	43.56	24	8.0	64.00
26	4.6	21.16	23	7.0	49.00
29	7.6	57.76	17	1.0	1.00
25	3.6	12.96	13	−3.0	9.00
5	−16.4	268.96	16	0.0	0.00
8	−13.4	179.56	25	9.0	81.00
28	6.6	43.56	10	−6.0	36.00
30	8.6	73.96	18	2.0	4.00
16	−5.4	29.16	13	−3.0	9.00
13	−8.4	70.56	13	−3.0	9.00
30	8.6	73.96	20	4.0	16.00
17	−4.4	19.36	28	12.0	144.00
15	−6.4	40.96	10	−6.0	36.00
15	−6.4	40.96	22	6.0	36.00
30	8.6	73.96	9	−7.0	49.00
			17	1.0	1.00
			14	−2.0	4.00
			3	−13.0	169.00
			16	0.0	0.00
			13	−3.0	9.00
			16	0.0	0.00
			17	1.0	1.00
Total	0.6	1093.96		−1.0	763.00

by the number of observations, and then taking the square root. Note that squaring the deviations takes us away from the scale on which the measurements were made. By taking the square root, we return to the original scale of measurement. When one thinks about it, the solution is quite simple; the only difficulty is that, in practice, scores on the entire population are not observed. Rather, we deal with samples.

5-2. THE SAMPLE STANDARD DEVIATION

Of course, the same procedure can be performed on the sample observations. The mean can be calculated, each observation's deviation from this mean could be squared and added to all the others, the sum divided by the number of scores, and the square root taken of the result. The goal in this procedure is to approximate the population standard deviation. Unfortunately, the resultant statistic, based on the sample data, is a slight underestimate of the population standard deviation. This estimate can be improved, however, by dividing the sum of the squared deviations by a factor of $N - 1$, rather than N, before taking the square root. This definition of the sample standard deviation is as follows:

Definition of the sample standard deviation

Let the observations in a sample be denoted by:

$$Y_1, Y_2, Y_3, \ldots, Y_N$$

Let $d_1, d_2, d_3, \ldots, d_N$ represent the corresponding deviations from the sample mean, $\bar{Y}$, with:

$d_1 = Y_1 - \bar{Y}$ = the value of the deviation of the first observation from the sample mean

$d_2 = Y_2 - \bar{Y}$ = the value of the deviation of the second observation from the sample mean

$d_3 = Y_3 - \bar{Y}$ = the value of the deviation of the third observation from the sample mean

.
.
.

$d_N = Y_N - \bar{Y}$ = the value of the deviation of the last, or Nth, observation from the sample mean

The sample standard deviation is defined as:

$$S_Y = \sqrt{\frac{d_1^2 + d_2^2 + d_3^2 + \cdots + d_N^2}{N - 1}}$$

$$= \sqrt{\frac{(Y_1 - \bar{Y})^2 + (Y_2 - \bar{Y})^2 + (Y_3 - \bar{Y})^2 + \cdots + (Y_N - \bar{Y})^2}{N - 1}}$$

This definition is used to determine the standard deviations of the two samples of Table 5-1. For the students who answered Yes:

$$S_{Yes} = \sqrt{\frac{(6.6)^2 + (6.6)^2 + (4.6)^2 + \cdots + (8.6)^2}{16 - 1}}$$
$$= \sqrt{72.9307} = 8.5400 = 8.5$$

while for the students who answered No:

$$S_{No} = \sqrt{\frac{(-6.0)^2 + (8.0)^2 + (7.0)^2 + \cdots + (1.0)^2}{23 - 1}}$$
$$= \sqrt{34.6816} = 5.8891 = 5.9$$

As measures of *within-sample variation,* we see that the standard deviation for the group of students who had a course in high school biology exceeds that of the group who did not. The students who reported Yes show greater score variation.

5-3. THE SAMPLE VARIANCE

As we have already seen, sample averages can be compared by simply examining the difference in their numerical values. This is not true for standard deviations. While sample means tell us about the *location* of the center of a distribution, the standard deviation tells us about the extent or the *scale* of a distribution. A distribution with a large standard deviation is one that covers a wide range of values, while a distribution with a small standard deviation covers a narrow range of values. When comparing differences in location of two distributions, the difference in their central value has meaning, but when comparing the scales of two distributions it is their ratio that has greater meaning and usefulness. Even though it makes sense to compare the ratio of two standard deviations, it is not done in practice because the resulting ratio has undesirable statistical properties. Instead, statisticians recommend that the ratio of the square of the standard deviations be compared, since the properties of this ratio are easier to study. For the values of Section 5-2, the appropriate comparison is measured by the ratio:

$$\frac{S_{Yes}^2}{S_{No}^2} = \frac{72.9307}{34.6816} = 2.1029 = 2.1$$

Under this mode of comparison, it would be said that the variation among the scores for the students who had a course in high school biology is 2.1 times that observed among their counterparts who did not have such a course.

As will be seen, the squared standard deviation plays an important role in statistical theory and applications. Because of its unique importance, statisticians have given the squared standard deviation a name, referring to it as a *variance.* The definition of a sample variance is as follows:

Definition of the sample variance

The variance of a sample is equal to the square of the sample standard deviation. In particular, the sample variance is defined as:

$$S_Y^2 = \frac{d_1^2 + d_2^2 + d_3^2 + \cdots + d_N^2}{N-1}$$

$$= \frac{(Y_1 - \bar{Y})^2 + (Y_2 - \bar{Y})^2 + (Y_3 - \bar{Y})^2 + \cdots + (Y_N - \bar{Y})^2}{N-1}$$

The quantity used as the divisor in the definition of S_Y and S_Y^2 is called the *number of degrees of freedom* associated with the sample standard deviation or variance. It refers to the number of deviations that provide unique or nonredundant information about the variability in the sample. As we saw earlier:

$$d_1 + d_2 + d_3 + \cdots + d_N = 0$$

This means that the d values are not free to vary. They are restricted by the fact that their sum must be zero. Thus, if one knew the exact numerical values of all but one of the d values, the value of the remaining d value would also be known. For example, suppose one had a sample of size $N = 5$, and suppose one knew the values $d_1 = 2, d_2 = -6, d_4 = 7$, and $d_5 = 12$. With this information, it follows that the value of d_3 is known, since: $(+2) + (-6) + d_3 + (+7) + (+12) = 0$. Solving this equation for d_3, it is seen that: $d_3 = -2 + 6 - 7 - 12 = -15$.

5-4. EXERCISES

5-1. Determine the sample means, variances, and sample standard deviations on the pretest for the students who responded Yes and No to having had a previous course in high school biology in your own random sample. Compare your results to those of the entire group of students, for which the mean values are 18.4 and 16.5 and for which the standard deviations are 7.95 and 7.43.

5-2. How many degrees of freedom are associated

with your sample of students who:
  a. Responded Yes
  b. Responded No
  c. Make up the complete sample

5-3. Find the standard deviation for your sample on the pretest. For the entire group the standard deviation is 7.65.

5-4. How many standard deviations are there between the lowest score and the mean score on the pretest in your sample? Repeat this analysis for the top scoring student.

5-5. Determine S^2_{Yes}/S^2_{No} for your sample on the pretest. What does this tell you of the relative variance in the two samples? Compare your result to the parametric value of Exercise 5-1.

5-6. For the 238 students, the standard deviations of College Board scores for the five coded categories of major, in the order in which they are coded, is 110, 97, 106, 110, and 104, respectively. Do you think these values are close enough to one another to justify behaving as though they were equal to a common value?

CHAPTER 6

Transformations

6-1. DEFINITION OF THE SUMMATION SYMBOL, Σ

Up to this point, we have been able to avoid complex mathematical notation and formulas, but we have now reached the point where certain mathematical space-saving devices will prove useful. If you have not used mathematics to a great extent, note that, in many cases, mathematics serves chiefly as a shorthand notation that allows easy manipulation of concepts and relationships which might be long and complex when expressed in words. As an example of this, most algebra word problems are of a type that tend to be confusing and complex until expressed as equations. This is true of the shorthand symbol that indicates summation. As we will see, it saves writing, printing space, and makes relationships easier to manipulate. This symbol, Σ (the Greek letter sigma), is defined, discussed, and its use illustrated below.

Definition of the summation symbol, Σ (sigma)

Let $Y_1, Y_2, Y_3, \ldots, Y_N$ represent a set of numerical observations. We define, as a shorthand notation for their sum, the following algebraic expression:

$$\sum_{i=1}^{N} Y_i = Y_1 + Y_2 + Y_3 + \cdots + Y_N$$

where Σ is the symbol meaning *add*, and where i assumes the ordered set of numbers $1, 2, 3, \ldots, N$.

Any expression written using the summation notation consists of two parts: the summation symbol (sigma) and the set of numbers being summed. The summation symbol always indicates the first and last number in the sum. In the definition, for example, "$i = 1$" means that the first term in the sum is Y_1, and the N above the sigma means that the last term is Y_N. Thus, if we wanted to indicate that the sum only included the second through the ninth terms, we would write

$$\sum_{i=2}^{9} Y_i = Y_2 + Y_3 + \cdots + Y_9$$

The other part of the summation notation indicates the set of numbers being summed. If we had wanted to add the squares of the numbers instead of the numbers themselves, we could have written:

$$\sum_{i=1}^{N} Y_i^2 = Y_1^2 + Y_2^2 + \cdots + Y_N^2$$

In terms of this symbol, the sample mean is defined as:

$$\bar{Y} = \frac{1}{N} \sum_{i=1}^{N} Y_i$$

and the sample variance is defined as:

$$S_Y^2 = \frac{1}{N-1} \sum_{i=1}^{N} (Y_i - \bar{Y})^2$$

While we have used this definition to compute S_Y^2, few researchers compute it in this fashion. There are easier ways to compute S_Y^2 and S_Y that are well suited to the use of hand calculators.

6-2. COMPUTING FORMULAS FOR S_Y^2 and S_Y

In terms of the summation symbol, the computing formula for a sample variance is as follows:

Definition of the computing formula for S_Y^2

Let the observations in a sample be denoted by:

$$Y_1, Y_2, Y_3, \ldots, Y_N$$

Let:

$$\sum_{i=1}^{N} Y_i = Y_1 + Y_2 + Y_3 + \ldots + Y_N$$

and let:

$$\sum_{i=1}^{N} Y_i^2 = Y_1^2 + Y_2^2 + Y_3^2 + \cdots + Y_N^2$$

The computing formula for S_Y^2 is given by:

$$S_Y^2 = \frac{N \sum_{i=1}^{N} Y_i^2 - \left(\sum_{i=1}^{N} Y_i \right)^2}{N(N-1)}$$

The standard deviation can be found by taking the square root of S_Y^2.

For the $N = 16$ students of Table 4-1 who had a prior class in biology:

$$\sum_{i=1}^{16} Y_i = 28 + 28 + 26 + \cdots + 30 = 343$$

and

$$\sum_{i=1}^{16} Y_i^2 = 28^2 + 28^2 + 26^2 + \cdots + 30^2 = 8447$$

Substituting these numbers into the computing formula, we find that:

$$S_Y^2 = \frac{16(8447) - (343)^2}{16(16-1)} = \frac{17{,}503}{240} = 72.9292$$

This value agrees with the value computed in Section 5-2, based upon the definition of S_Y^2. The difference in values is a result of rounding errors. Of the two computed values, the one based on the computing formula just given has the greater accuracy. For this value:

$$S_Y = \sqrt{72.9292} = 8.5$$

6-3. TRANSFORMATION OF VARIABLES

As we saw in Section 6-1, the summation symbol, Σ, permits an expression of sums in a simple compact notation. Other useful properties of the Σ symbol are as follows.

　　Property 1. If A is a constant that is added to each value of Y, so that $y_i = Y_i + A$, then:

$$\sum_{i=1}^{N} y_i = \sum_{i=1}^{N} (Y_i + A) = \sum_{i=1}^{N} Y_i + NA$$

If the two outermost expressions of this equation are divided by N, we have:

$$\frac{1}{N} \sum_{i=1}^{N} y_i = \frac{1}{N} \sum_{i=1}^{N} (Y_i + A) = \frac{1}{N} \sum_{i=1}^{N} Y_i + \frac{1}{N}(NA)$$

from which it follows that:

$$\bar{y} = \bar{Y} + A$$

What was just illustrated is an algebraic relationship that is often referred to as the *translation* theorem. It is defined as follows:

The translation theorem for sample means

If a single constant, A, is added to every observation in a sample, then the mean value, $\bar{y}$, of the translated observations and the mean of the original observations, $\bar{Y}$, are related to one another by the following equations:

$$\bar{y} = \bar{Y} + A \qquad \text{and} \qquad \bar{Y} = \bar{y} - A$$

This theorem states that the mean of any distribution is increased by A units by adding A to each observation or is decreased by A units by subtracting A from each observation.

As an example, the United States Army has reported that the mean height of recruits during the past few years has been equal to 68.5 in. If one were to subtract 10 in from the height of every recruit measured, the mean height for the recruits would be reduced to $68.5 - 10 = 58.5$ in. On the other hand, if one were to add 8 in to the height of every recruit, the mean height would be shifted to a mean value of $68.5 + 8 = 76.5$ in.

Related to the translation theorem is another theorem, often referred to as the *scale* theorem. It operates as follows. If one were to multiply each observation in a sample by a constant and then compute a new sample mean, one would discover that the resulting mean would be identical to the original sample mean multiplied by the number that was used for the multiplication.

Property 2. If B is a quantity that is used as a constant multiplier to each value of Y, so that $y_i = BY_i$, then:

$$\sum_{i=1}^{N} y_i = \sum_{i=1}^{N} BY_i = B \sum_{i=1}^{N} Y_i$$

If the two outermost expressions of this equation are divided by N, we have:

$$\frac{1}{N} \sum_{i=1}^{N} y_i = B \left(\frac{1}{N} \sum_{i=1}^{N} Y_i \right)$$

from which it follows that:

$$\bar{y} = B\bar{Y}$$

Just illustrated is the scale theorem, which is defined as follows:

The scale theorem for sample means

If a single constant, B, serves as a common multiplier to every observation in a sample, then the mean value of the transformed observations, $\bar{y}$, and the mean of the original observations, $\bar{Y}$, are related to one another by the following equations:

$$\bar{y} = B\bar{Y} \quad \text{and} \quad \bar{Y} = (1/B)\bar{y}$$

If, for example, one were to multiply the height of every measured Army recruit by the common multiplier of $\frac{1}{12}$, transforming inches to feet, the mean height for the recruits would be changed to $\frac{1}{12}(68.5) = 5.7083 =$

5.7 ft. As indicated, this theorem is used when one converts inches to feet, feet to yards, inches to centimeters, pounds to ounces, etc.

If a researcher were to add or subtract the same constant from every observation in a sample and then compute the sample variance or standard deviation, the resulting measures would be equal in numerical value to the sample variance and standard deviation of the original sample. This identity of value is observed because the relative difference between any two observations remains the same, so that variation within the sample remains preserved. For example, consider subjects one and six of the sample of 16 students of Table 4-1. If eight points are added to each of their scores, we would find that the difference in the new scores is identical to their difference in the original sample. In this example, $Y_1 = 28$ and $Y_6 = 5$. The difference in these scores is given by $d = Y_1 - Y_6 = 28 - 5 = 23$. If we now add eight points to each score, we would have $y_1 = Y_1 + 8 = 28 + 8 = 36$, $y_6 = Y_6 + 8 = 5 + 8 = 13$ and $d = y_1 - y_6 = 36 - 13 = 23$.

In terms of standard deviations, $S_y = S_Y$, as we now show. Let each Y_i be changed to produce a new value, $y_i = Y_i + A$. By definition:

$$S_y^2 = \frac{1}{N-1} \sum_{i=1}^{N} (y_i - \bar{y})^2$$

If $y_i = Y_i + A$, we know that $\bar{y} = \bar{Y} + A$. Making these substitutions, it follows that:

$$S_y^2 = \frac{1}{N-1} \sum_{i=1}^{N} [(Y_i + A) - (\bar{Y} + A)]^2$$

$$= \frac{1}{N-1} \sum_{i=1}^{N} (Y_i - \bar{Y})^2 = S_Y^2$$

This proves the translation theorem for sample variances.

The translation theorem for sample variances

If a single constant, A, is added to every observation in a sample, then the variances of the new translated observations and the original observations are equal to one another. Thus:

$$S_y^2 = S_Y^2$$

If one were to multiply each observation in a sample by the same constant and then were to compute the sample variance or standard deviation, the resulting variance would equal the original variance multiplied by the square of the constant, and the resulting standard deviation would be equal to the original standard deviation multiplied by the constant. If the constant is larger than 1, the scale of the new variable will be expanded, but if the constant is less than 1, the scale will be compressed. For example, if the scores for subjects one and six were multiplied by 5, we would find that $y_1 = 5Y_1 = 5(28) = 140$ and $y_6 = 5(5) = 25$, so that their transformed difference would be given by $140 - 25 = 115 = 5(23)$, or five times their original difference. In terms of standard deviations, $S_y = 5S_Y$, and in terms of variance, $S_y^2 = 25S_Y^2$. This will now be shown.

Let each value of Y_i be changed to produce a new variable, $y_i = BY_i$. By definition:

$$S_y^2 = \frac{1}{N-1} \sum_{i=1}^{N} (y_i - \bar{y})^2$$

If $y_i = BY_i$, we know that $\bar{y} = B\bar{Y}$. Making these substitutions, it follows that:

$$S_y^2 = \frac{1}{N-1} \sum_{i=1}^{N} (BY_i - B\bar{Y})^2 = \frac{1}{N-1} \sum_{i=1}^{N} B^2(Y_i - \bar{Y})^2$$

$$= B^2 \left(\frac{1}{N-1} \sum_{i=1}^{N} (Y_i - \bar{Y})^2 \right) = B^2 S_Y^2$$

This proves the scale theorem for sample variances.

The scale theorem for sample variances

If a single constant, B, serves as a common multiplier to every observation in a sample, then the variance of the new transformed observations and the original observations are related to one another by means of the following equations:

$$S_y^2 = B^2 S_Y^2 \qquad \text{and} \qquad S_Y^2 = \frac{1}{B^2} S_y^2$$

The corresponding equations for the standard deviations are given by:

$$S_y = BS_Y \qquad \text{and} \qquad S_Y = \frac{1}{B} S_y$$

6-4. SAMPLE STANDARD SCORES

One of the problems inherent in the reporting of test scores, or any other measured variable, is that an individual number is without meaning. To know that Sue Riley got a score of 25 on a spelling test is to know nothing, unless one knows that 25 is a high score, a low score, or an average score. Unless a standard is available, interpretation is not possible.

For example, consider the reporting of the daily temperature. If we hear on the radio or TV that the expected noon temperature for tomorrow is to be near 80 °F, we know the appropriate kind of clothing to wear; similarly, if we hear a few weeks later that the expected noon temperature for the next day is going to be near 20 °F, we know that we should bundle up. We know this from experience and from the fact that we have available for comparison a reference point to which we can compare any reported temperature. In addition to a reference, we also have a scale that helps us to evaluate the temperature readings. Between 32 °F, water's freezing point, and 212 °F, water's boiling point, we have a gradient which permits us to interpret a reported temperature.

Test scores and other variables studied by behavioral researchers do not possess such anchor points that facilitate data interpretation. Because of this, artificial standards have been developed that provide a position from which to attack the problem. The solution is not ideal. On the other hand, it is useful and has been universally adopted by scientists in the social sciences.

The method is based upon the use of the sample mean as a reference point and the standard deviation as the unit of measure or comparison. As we saw in Section 5-1, subject number one in the group of students who had a prior course in biology deviated from the mean score of the group by +6.6 test points. If we use the standard deviation of the group as a scale unit, subject number one is $(6.6/8.5) = 0.7765 = 0.78$ standard deviations above the mean score. On the other hand, subject number six is $(-16.4/8.5) = -1.9294 = -1.93$ standard deviations away from the mean. The negative sign indicates that subject number six is below the mean of the group by 1.93 standard deviations. In these examples, we deviated from our rule of one significant decimal point when reporting standard scores. Standard scores are always reported to the nearest hundredth. In standard deviation units, the difference between these two students is given by $0.78 - (-1.93) = 2.71$ standard deviation units, a large statistical difference. Statisticians have been able to show that if one selected two people at random from a given population and measured some variable of interest on them, the expected value of the difference in their scores would be a number very close to 1.25 standard deviations. In this example, one has reason to believe that subjects one and six are very different in what they gained from their high school class in biology.

As indicated, standard scores are very easy to compute, mainly because the definition of a standard score is simple. The definition is as follows:

Definition of a sample standard score

Let Y represent an observation from a given sample. Let $\bar{Y}$ represent the mean of the sample. Let S_Y represent the standard deviation of the sample. The standard score associated with Y is defined as:

$$z = \frac{Y - \bar{Y}}{S_Y}$$

The standard score is often referred to as a z score.

The standard scores for the two samples of Table 5-1 are presented in Table 6-1.

As we saw in Section 6-3, variables could be translated to a new center with a different scale. Such transformed variables are used to a large extent by researchers in education. One example of transformed scores are *T scores*, which have a mean of 50 and a standard deviation of 10. They are computed by multiplying each z score by 10, adding 50 to the resulting product, and rounding to the nearest whole number. Thus, the T score for subject one of the group that did have a prior course in biology is given by $T = 10(0.78) + 50 = 7.8 + 50 = 57.8 = 58$. The corresponding T scores for the remaining students are reported in Table 6-1 under the column headed T scores.

College Board scores are also reported in standard score form. Educational Testing Service, which directs the use of this test, prefers to translate its scores so that the mean score equals 500 and the standard deviation equals 100. The transforming equation for their measurement scale is given by $(CBS) = 500 + 100z$. The college board scores reported in Table A-16 are based upon this transformation. Furthermore, it is worth noting that admission to the hypothetical university of Table A-16 is dependent upon having College Board scores that exceed 400, or that are greater than one standard deviation below the mean. If one examines the scores of Table A-16, it will be noted that a few students were admitted with scores below 400.

While random sampling is the preferred sampling procedure for research methodology, it sometimes generates unusual sample results. For example, it is possible to obtain, on a chance basis, one or two observations that seem out of line with respect to the other observations in a sample. When this occurs, there is a natural tendency to discard them from the sample. Such procedures are definitely frowned upon, unless it can be established that the unusual values are *outliers* and not members of the sampled population. One rule that researchers use in deciding whether or not a value is an outlier is to determine the standard score of a suspected outlier. If it exceeds ± 3 standard deviations, it is examined in greater detail to determine whether or not it is a true outlier.

For the 16 observations of Table 5-1, the standard score associated with $Y_6 = 5$ is equal to:

$$Z_1^{\circ} = \frac{Y_6 - \bar{Y}}{S_Y} = \frac{5 - 21.4}{8.54} = -1.92$$

Since $Z_1^{\circ} > -3$, it is concluded that the suspected observation is not an outlier and, as such, it must be retained in the sample.

Table 6-1. Standard z and T scores for the samples of Table 5-1.

Students Who Had a Prior Course in High School Biology			Students Who Did Not Have a Prior Course in High School Biology		
Score	z score	T score	Score	z score	T score
28	0.78	58	10	−1.02	40
28	0.78	58	24	1.36	64
26	0.54	55	23	1.19	62
29	0.89	59	17	0.17	52
25	0.42	54	13	−.51	45
5	−1.92	31	16	0.00	50
8	−1.58	34	25	1.53	65
28	0.78	58	10	−1.02	40
30	1.01	60	18	0.34	53
16	−0.64	44	13	−0.51	45
13	−0.99	40	13	−0.51	45
30	1.01	60	20	0.68	57
17	−0.52	45	28	2.03	70
15	−0.75	42	10	−1.02	40
15	−0.75	42	22	1.02	60
30	1.01	60	9	−1.19	38
			17	0.17	52
			14	−0.34	47
			3	−2.20	28
			16	0.00	50
			13	−0.51	45
			16	0.00	50
			17	0.17	52

6-5. EXERCISES

6-1. Find the standard deviation on the College Board scores for your sample.

6-2. Determine the standard deviations for the data of Exercise 4-6.

6-3. If $X_1 = 4, X_2 = 7, X_3 = 9$, and $X_4 = 16$, find the values of the following:

a. $\sum\limits_{i=1}^{4} X_i$

b. $\sum\limits_{i=1}^{4} (X_i + 3)$

c. $\sum\limits_{i=1}^{4} (X_i - 3)$

d. $\sum\limits_{i=1}^{4} 3X_i$

e. $\sum\limits_{i=1}^{4} (\frac{1}{3})X_i$

f. $\sum\limits_{i=1}^{4} X_i^2$

g. $\sum\limits_{i=1}^{4} (X_i + 3)^2$

h. $\sum\limits_{i=1}^{4} (X_i - 3)^2$

i. $\sum\limits_{i=1}^{4} (3X_i)^2$

j. $\sum\limits_{i=1}^{4} (\frac{1}{3}X_i)^2$

6-4. The average height of a sample of college basketball players is 6 ft, 2 in.

a. If 2 ft were to be subtracted from the height of each player, what would be the value of the average transformed height, in inches.

b. If 3 in were to be added to each player's height, what would be the value of the resulting mean?

c. What number should be subtracted from each height to give a mean transformed height of zero?

d. If each person's height were to be multiplied by 2.54, what would be the value of the resulting mean? Since 1 in = 2.54 cm, the resulting figure would represent the mean height of the players in the metric system.

6-5. The standard deviation of the sample of college basketball players mentioned in Exercise 6-4 is 4 in.

a. If 2 ft were to be subtracted from the height of each player, what would be the value of the standard deviation of the transformed heights?

b. If each person's height were to be multiplied by 2.54, what would be the value of the resulting sample variance?

6-6. A variable Y has a distribution with $\bar{Y} = 80$ and $S_Y = 36$. Find the values of A and B for transforming $y = A + BY$ so that $\bar{y} = 0$ and $S_y = 1$.

6-7. a. Find the z scores for each subject in your total sample on the pretest.

b. Show that within rounding error the sum of the z scores equals zero and that the sum of the squares of the z scores equals the degrees of freedom of the sample.

c. Show that $\bar{z} = 0$ and $S_z = 1$.

d. Find the T score for each student. How many standard deviations are there between the two students with lowest and highest scores? Compare this result with your answers to Exercise 5-4.

6-8. Is there reason to believe that the lowest and highest scores on the pretest for your sample are outliers?

6-9. For the entire group of 238 students, the lowest and highest scores on the college board test are $Y_1^o = 210$ and $Y_{238}^o = 820$. With a population mean of 528 and standard deviation of 105, is there reason to believe that Y_1^o and Y_{238}^o are outliers?

6-10. Suppose that a distribution of Y values is positively skewed. What can you say about the distribution of z or T scores?

PART **II**

CORRELATION AND ASSOCIATION

In the preceding chapters, we have introduced procedures for characterizing the typical values in samples and populations and how much the observations vary from the measures of central tendency. We have also presented methods for summarizing our observations graphically. So far, the techniques we have examined are useful for describing location and variability for a single variable at a time. Another important aspect of understanding the complexity in our surroundings involves describing the relationships among variables. In the next four chapters, we present methods for measuring the strength of various types of relationships between pairs of variables, including linear relationships between quantitative variables, ordered relationships between qualitative variables, and relationships between qualitative and quantitative variables.

CHAPTER 7

Measures of Covariation for Quantitative Variables

7-1. CORRELATION, COVARIATION, AND CAUSATION

In Chapter 4, it was suggested that pretest scores for the 238 students enrolled in the beginning biology course might be influenced by prior courses in high school biology. In particular, one might expect high pretest scores from students who had a prior course in biology and low scores from students who didn't have prior biology courses. This statement has the external appearance of a cause and effect relationship. It could be interpreted to mean that high scores on the test are caused by previous biology classes. This cause and effect connection is illusory. Other things could cause high or low grades. Time spent in study is one of them. Others could be suggested. The statement under investigation is really one of *correlation*. It says that high pretest scores are associated with a prior course in biology and low pretest scores are associated with no prior course in biology.

In this form, it is seen that a statement of correlation is simply a statement that connects a dependent variable with an independent variable in a specified manner. In this case, the dependent variable is score on the pretest and the independent variable is having or not having had a prior course in biology. Stating that two variables are correlated implies that as the scores on one variable change, the scores on the other variable tend to change in a systematic fashion. Another term that is often used in this context is *covariation*, perhaps a more descriptive term. As might be expected, there are many ways to identify and measure the correlation between two variables. We will examine some of them.

One of the major activities of researchers in the social sciences involves conducting investigations that attempt to identify cause and effect relationships between two variables. While these activities absorb a large amount of research money and time, the outcomes are, more often than not, ambiguous and conflicting. For example, we have all read that excessive smoking *causes* lung cancer and yet the cigarette manufacturers continue to insist that the observed relationship between smoking and lung cancer is only *correlational*. There are researchers in the biomedical sciences who agree with the cigarette manufacturers. Whether or not the relationship between smoking and lung cancer is one of cause and effect is still at issue; that it is correlational is without question. The existence of a correlation between two variables does not establish causality.

The relationship between cholesterol in the diet and cardiovascular disease is also only a correlational relationship. One can search the biomedical literature and find studies that assert a cause and effect relationship between these two variables; on the other hand, one can find studies that indicates that this is not so. While it is a fact that people with cardiovascular disease are found to have high levels of cholesterol in their blood, it still has not been decided whether or not the high cholesterol content causes the cardiovascular problem or whether the cardiovascular problem causes the high cholesterol level, or whether both have a common third source.

It is this reasoning that indicates why correlation does not imply causation. A correlation only indicates that two variables vary together. For example, if you put a pot of water on the stove to boil, you can see that the longer the pot sits on the heat, the hotter the water gets. The time and the water temperature vary together; they are correlated. But this correlation does not prove that time makes the water hotter, nor does the water's heat make the time change.

In the social sciences, the distinction between cause and effect and correlation is more difficult to untangle, since there are many more variables involved. Is poor school academic performance caused by cultural deprivation? Is male homosexual behavior caused by having an ineffectual father and a domineering mother? Is a high score on an intelligence test caused by inheriting particular genes from one's parents? Is the mid-century move to the suburbs caused by the movement of minority groups into the central cities? The list is endless, and yet the search for cause and effect continues. The establishment of a cause and effect relationship is difficult and, according to some, impossible. The establishment of a correlation is easy and, according to many, is the first step in proving a cause and effect relationship. Certainly, the establishment of correlation will lead us to investigate the relationship further.

7-2. THE SAMPLE SCATTER DIAGRAM

One way to illustrate, graphically, the relationship between two quantitative variables is to construct a *scatter diagram*. A scatter diagram is a two-dimensional graph of the paired observations of a dependent and independent variable measured on a sample of objects. As indicated in Section 3-1, the independent variable is generally denoted by X and is associated with the horizontal axis of the graph. The dependent variable is generally denoted by Y and is associated with the vertical axis of a graph. We will illustrate the drawing of a scatter diagram for the sample of students listed in Table 2-1 for which information is available. Since one might expect the scores on the final to be dependent in some fashion on the scores on the pretest, we shall take the pretest to be the independent variable and the scores on the final to be the dependent variable. Since a pretest score is missing for one student, we are forced to use information for only 39 students. We follow the directions in Box 7-1.

For the data in Table 2-1, the first person had a score on the final of 30 and a pretest score of 10. This led us to mark a point on the graph whose Y coordinate was 30 and whose X coordinate was 10. The entire scatter diagram is shown in Figure 7-1.

For these data, it appears that scores on the final have a tendency to increase as scores on the pretest increase. This statement seems to hold across

---

Box 7-1   Procedure for constructing a scatter diagram

Step 1. Prepare a reference system for the graph by drawing in the horizontal and vertical axes. The lengths of the two axes should be drawn to reduce possible distortion in the final graph. In general, this means that different scales will be required for each variable.

Step 2. Plot the paired observations.

Step 3. Label the axes and give the graph a title.

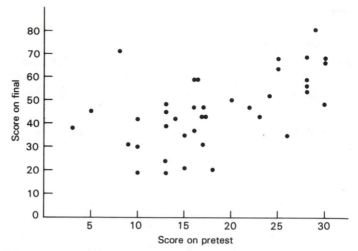

Figure 7-1.
Scatter diagram for scores on the biology pretest and the final examination for 39 biology students.

all students except the three who obtained the lowest scores on the pretest. When the values of the dependent variable increase with increases in values of the independent variable, it is said that the two variables are *positively correlated.* When the values of the dependent variable decrease with increases in values of the independent variable, it is said that the variables are *negatively correlated.*

The point (0, 0) is not always included in a scatter diagram. This is especially true if the smallest value for either X or Y is large. For example, if the smallest value of X were to equal 130, and the smallest value of Y were to equal 55, one might draw the axes through the point (120, 50).

7-3. THE SAMPLE CORRELATION COEFFICIENT

Like line graphs or histograms, scatter diagrams cannot be used for analytical investigations. Instead a summary measure similar to a mean or standard deviation is required. The summary measure that is used by researchers in the social sciences is called the *correlation coefficient.* Let us consider the kinds of properties such a summary measure should have.

First, we are interested in the covariation of the two variables, that is, whether they change together in a systematic way. We would want our summary measure to reflect these changes no matter how big or small are the numbers themselves. If our dependent variable increased by 10 points every time the independent variable increased 1 point, the summary measure should reflect this. It should not matter whether the dependent variable was increasing from 1 to 11 or from 1001 to 1011. Thus, we want a summary measure that does not depend on location of the actual scores; rather, it should be sensitive only to changes. Such a measure would be *location-free*.

Second, we would like our measure to reflect comparable relationships between pairs of variables even when the pairs may be measured on different scales. For example, assume we are interested in detecting a possible relationship between height and body weights. We want the measure of association to come out the same, whether we measure height in inches, feet, or meters and whether we measure weight in pounds, kilograms, or tons. Such a measure would be *scale-free*.

In Section 6-4, we learned how to compute standard scores. These measures are both scale-free and location-free of the original values. Because of this, we use standard scores to define the correlation coefficient. As implied by the term covariation, we want to compute a measure that is similar in form to the variances, but which indicates how the two variables change together. Such a measure, the sample correlation coefficient, is defined in the following manner. It is also referred to as the *Pearson product-moment correlation coefficient*.

Definition of the sample correlation coefficient

Let the standard scores for an independent variable, X, be denoted by:

$$\frac{X_1 - \overline{X}}{S_X}, \frac{X_2 - \overline{X}}{S_X}, \frac{X_3 - \overline{X}}{S_X}, \ldots, \frac{X_N - \overline{X}}{S_X}$$

with the standard score for the ith observation denoted by:

$$\frac{X_i - \overline{X}}{S_X}$$

Let the standard scores for a dependent variable, Y, be denoted by:

$$\frac{Y_1 - \overline{Y}}{S_Y}, \frac{Y_2 - \overline{Y}}{S_Y}, \frac{Y_3 - \overline{Y}}{S_Y}, \ldots, \frac{Y_N - \overline{Y}}{S_Y}$$

with the standard score for the ith observation denoted by:

$$\frac{Y_i - \overline{Y}}{S_Y}$$

The sample correlation coefficient is defined as:

$$r = \frac{1}{N-1} \sum_{i=1}^{N} \left(\frac{X_i - \overline{X}}{S_X} \right) \left(\frac{Y_i - \overline{Y}}{S_Y} \right)$$

Table 7-1. Computations to obtain the sample correlation coefficient for pretest scores and final scores for the 39 students of Table 2-1 with complete data

X	Y	$\dfrac{X-\bar{X}}{S_X}$	$\dfrac{Y-\bar{Y}}{S_Y}$	$\left(\dfrac{X-\bar{X}}{S_X}\right)\left(\dfrac{Y-\bar{Y}}{S_Y}\right)$
10	30	−1.09	−1.03	1.1227
24	52	0.77	0.38	0.2926
28	59	1.30	0.83	1.0790
23	43	0.64	−0.20	−0.1280
28	69	1.30	1.47	1.9110
17	43	−0.16	−0.20	0.0320
13	19	−0.69	−1.73	1.1937
16	47	−0.29	0.06	−0.0174
26	35	1.04	−0.71	−0.7384
29	80	1.43	2.18	3.1174
25	64	0.90	1.15	1.0350
25	68	0.90	1.41	1.2690
10	19	−1.09	−1.73	1.8857
18	20	−0.03	−1.67	0.0501
5	45	−1.76	−0.07	0.1232
13	39	−0.69	−0.45	0.3105
13	24	−0.69	−1.41	0.9729
20	50	0.24	0.25	0.0600
28	57	1.30	0.70	0.9100
8	71	−1.36	1.60	−2.1760
28	54	1.30	0.51	0.6630
10	42	−1.09	−0.26	0.2834
30	48	1.57	0.13	0.2041
22	47	0.50	0.06	0.0300
16	59	−0.29	0.83	−0.2407
9	31	−1.23	−0.96	1.1808
13	48	−0.69	0.13	−0.0897
30	68	1.57	1.41	2.2137
17	47	−0.16	0.06	−0.0096
14	42	−0.56	−0.26	0.1456
3	38	−2.03	−0.52	1.0556
16	59	−0.29	0.83	−0.2407
17	43	−0.16	−0.20	0.0320
15	35	−0.43	−0.71	0.3053
13	45	−0.69	−0.07	0.0483
15	21	−0.43	−1.61	0.6923
16	37	−0.29	−0.58	0.1682
30	67	1.57	1.34	2.1038
17	31	−0.16	−0.96	0.1536
710	1796	−0.02	0.00	21.0040

We illustrate the computation of this measure for the data of Table 7-1. These data represent pretest scores and final test scores for the 39 students of Table 2-1 for whom information was available. We begin by computing the means and standard deviations for the two variables. We summarize the computations as follows, and we carry two decimal places in the standard scores.

$$\sum_{i=1}^{39} X_i = 710 \qquad\qquad \sum_{i=1}^{39} Y_i = 1796$$

$$\sum_{i=1}^{39} X_i^2 = 15{,}066 \qquad\qquad \sum_{i=1}^{39} Y_i^2 = 91{,}952$$

$$\overline{X} = {710}/{39} = 18.21 \qquad\qquad \overline{Y} = {1796}/{39} = 46.05$$

$$S_X^2 = \frac{39(15{,}066) - (710)^2}{39(39 - 1)} \qquad\qquad S_Y^2 = \frac{39(91{,}952) - (1796)^2}{39(39 - 1)}$$

$$= 56.3252 \qquad\qquad\qquad = 243.2605$$

$$S_X = 7.51 \qquad\qquad\qquad S_Y = 15.60$$

Next, compute the standard scores as shown in Table 7-1. The correlation coefficient is now computed as:

$$r = [(-1.09)(-1.03) + (0.77)(0.38) + \cdots + (-0.16)(-0.96)]/(39 - 1)$$
$$= (21.0040)/38$$
$$= 0.5527$$
$$= 0.55$$

For these data, the value of the sample correlation coefficient is given by $r = 0.55$. We see that the correlation is positive. The scores on the final increase as the scores on the pretest increase. The meaning we can give to the number, 0.55, is a little more problematic and will be examined in Chapter 9.

7-4. THE SAMPLE COVARIANCE

We have introduced the correlation coefficient as a scale-free measure of association between two variables. Closely allied with the measures of correlation and variance is a scale-dependent measure of association called the *covariance*. Although the covariance is rarely used for descriptive purposes, it will be seen to play an important role in inferential statistics.

We can rewrite the formula for the correlation coefficient as:

$$r = \frac{\sum_{i=1}^{N} (X_i - \overline{X})(Y_i - \overline{Y})/(N - 1)}{S_X S_Y}$$

The covariance, denoted S_{XY}, is the numerator in this formula, so that r can be written as:

$$r = \frac{S_{XY}}{S_X S_Y}$$

The covariance is defined as follows.

Definition of the sample covariance

Let $d_{X_i} = X_i - \bar{X}$ and $d_{Y_i} = Y_i - \bar{Y}$. Then the sample covariance is given by:

$$S_{XY} = \text{Cov}(X, Y) = \frac{1}{N-1} \sum_{i=1}^{N} d_{X_i} d_{Y_i}$$

The calculating formula for the covariance is given by:

$$S_{XY} = \frac{N \sum_{i=1}^{N} X_i Y_i - \sum_{i=1}^{N} X_i \sum_{i=1}^{N} Y_i}{N(N-1)}$$

Notice the similarity in the definition and calculating formulas for the variance and covariance. If we calculate the covariance of a variable with itself, we actually are computing the variance of the variable. To see this, replace each X_i by Y_i in the formula for the covariance.

At this point in our development we will have little use for the covariance but when we get into some advanced inference procedures, the covariance will take on added importance.

7-5. COMPUTING FORMULA FOR THE SAMPLE CORRELATION COEFFICIENT

As might be expected, no one computes a correlation coefficient in terms of its definitional equation. The arithmetic computation can be significantly reduced by using a computing formula. The computing formula for the sample correlation coefficient is in Box 7-2.

For the data of Table 7-1:

$$\sum_{i=1}^{N} X_i = 10 + 24 + 28 + \cdots + 17 = 710$$

$$\sum_{i=1}^{N} Y_i = 30 + 52 + 59 + \cdots + 31 = 1796$$

Box 7-2   Procedure for computing r, in terms of a computing formula

Let the paired observations be denoted as:

$$(X_1, Y_1), (X_2, Y_2), \ldots , (X_i, Y_i), \ldots , (X_N, Y_N)$$

Step 1. Determine the values of

$$\sum_{i=1}^{N} X_i, \ \sum_{i=1}^{N} Y_i, \ \sum_{i=1}^{N} X_i^2, \ \sum_{i=1}^{N} Y_i^2, \text{ and } \sum_{i=1}^{N} X_i Y_i.$$

Step 2. Substitute these numbers into the formula below and perform the arithmetic:

$$r = \frac{N\left(\sum_{i=1}^{N} X_i Y_i\right) - \left(\sum_{i=1}^{N} X_i\right)\left(\sum_{i=1}^{N} Y_i\right)}{\sqrt{N\left(\sum_{i=1}^{N} X_i^2\right) - \left(\sum_{i=1}^{N} X_i\right)^2}\sqrt{N\left(\sum_{i=1}^{N} Y_i^2\right) - \left(\sum_{i=1}^{N} Y_i\right)^2}}$$

$$\sum_{i=1}^{N} X_i^2 = 10^2 + 24^2 + 28^2 + \cdots + 17^2 = 15{,}066$$

$$\sum_{i=1}^{N} Y_i^2 = 30^2 + 52^2 + 59^2 + \cdots + 31^2 = 91{,}952$$

$$\sum_{i=1}^{N} X_i Y_i = 10(30) + 24(52) + 28(59) + \cdots + 17(31)$$
$$= 35{,}162$$

$$r = \frac{39(35{,}162) - (710)(1796)}{\sqrt{39(15{,}066) - (710)^2}\sqrt{39(91{,}952) - (1796)^2}}$$

$$= \frac{96{,}158}{\sqrt{83{,}474}\sqrt{360{,}512}}$$

$$= \frac{96{,}158}{173{,}474} = 0.5543 = .55$$

7-6. ASSUMPTIONS FOR PROPER USE OF A SAMPLE CORRELATION COEFFICIENT

Of all the statistical measures that social scientists use for their research, the one that is the most difficult to interpret is the sample correlation coefficient. The problem of interpretation is no accident. It exists because the value of a sample correlation coefficient can be influenced by many factors. Some of these confounding influences can be controlled by a researcher, and some cannot. We shall describe four factors that could be troublesome.

1. The sample correlation coefficient is associated with a *linear* relationship between the independent and dependent variables. A relationship between two variables is said to be linear if, as the independent variable increases in equal unit changes, the dependent variable tends to increase or decrease in equal units. Examples of linear and nonlinear relationships are shown in Figure 7-2. Examples 1 and 2 illustrate relationships that are mainly linear. Example 1 illustrates a positive linear relationship between the independent and dependent variable. Example 2 illustrates a negative relationship. The sample correlation coefficient is a valid measure of association for these, and only these,

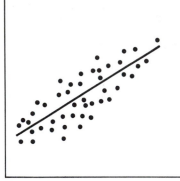

Example 1

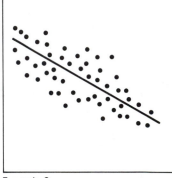

Example 2

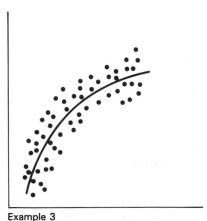

Example 3

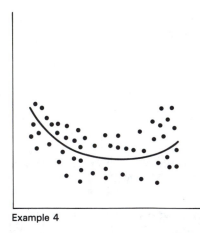

Example 4

Figure 7-2.
Examples of relationships between an independent variable, X, and a dependent variable, Y, that are primarily linear or nonlinear.

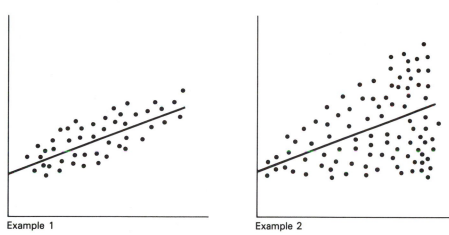

Figure 7-3.
Examples of homoscedastic and nonhomoscedastic variations about the straight line of a scatter diagram.

kinds of relationships. Examples 3 and 4 illustrate nonlinear relationships. For these kinds of relationships, the sample correlation coefficient is invalid and should not be used, because it tends to underestimate the strength of the association. For example, the sample correlation coefficient for Example 4 is given by $r = 0$, and yet the relationship between the X and Y variables is very strong. To avoid this possibly erroneous interpretation of a sample correlation coefficient, one should always examine the scatter diagram. If the association between the two variables does not seem to trace out a straight line, then one should not use the correlation coefficient as a measure of association. Other measures are available for nonlinear relationships.

2. The variability about the straight-line relationship between an independent and dependent variable must be *homoscedastic*. This means that the variance about the straight line must be equal for every value of the independent variable. For Example 1 of Figure 7-3, the variation about the trend line is constant, or nearly constant, for every value of X. This is not true for Example 2 in which it is seen that the variation increases as X increases. At low values of X, the variation about the line is small, but at large values of X, it is large. This tendency for the variance to increase with increases in the independent variable is common in growth studies. As an example, consider growth in height. If, at age 6, John Jones is 48 in tall and Robert Brown is 40 in tall, one would expect the difference between their heights at age 10 to exceed 8 in, since the taller boy is expected to grow at a faster rate than the shorter boy. With increases in age, the variance between their heights is expected to increase. For these and similar situations, the sample correlation coefficient is an invalid measure of association and should not be used. When the variance about the line remains constant with increases

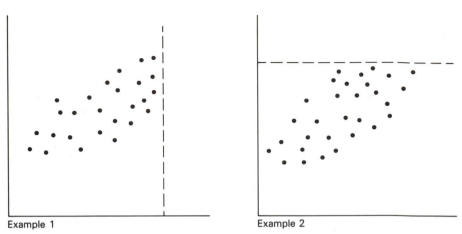

Figure 7-4.
Examples of truncated samples.

in the independent variable, the sample correlation coefficient is a valid measure. For heteroscedastic situations, statisticians have not provided appropriate measures of association.

3.   The range of the independent or dependent variable should not be *truncated.* A sample is said to be truncated if no observations are made either above or below a specified value on the independent or dependent variable. Examples of truncated samples are shown in Figure 7-4. Example 1 illustrates what the scatter diagram would look like if a truncation had taken place on the independent variable. This kind of truncation could be encountered in a study in which a researcher examines annual income and its relationship to age. If no measures are made on people over the age of 30, the distribution is truncated and the sample correlation coefficient will probably be too small, since we already know that income continues to increase with age. Example 2 illustrates a truncation on the dependent variable. This kind of truncation is often encountered in pretest-posttest studies performed by psychologists and researchers in education. In some learning studies, the posttest is too easy, so that many subjects achieve the maximum score. In such cases, the correlation coefficient will be too small.

4.   The appearance of *outliers,* observations that lie far from most values in a sample, can have an excessive effect upon the sample correlation coefficient. Because a sample correlation coefficient is, for the most part, an average of multiplied standard scores, outliers have a tendency to raise or lower the value of a sample correlation coefficient, depending upon the location of the outliers. Examples of outlier effects are shown in Figure 7-5. If an outlier with a low negative standard score on the independent variable is observed with a positive standard score on the dependent variable, the value of the sample correlation coefficient

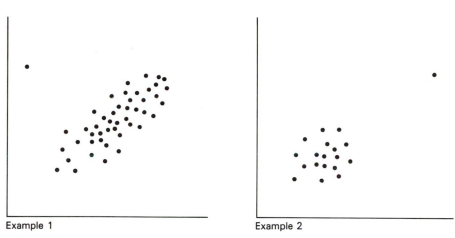

Example 1   Example 2

Figure 7-5.
Examples of outliers in a sample.

will be decreased as illustrated in Example 1. On the other hand, if both standard scores are large positive numbers, the sample correlation coefficient will be inflated as shown in Example 2.

Other sample characteristics can influence the value of a sample correlation coefficient. The four listed are the most important. Whenever one interprets a sample correlation coefficient, one should check to see that the general nature of the relationship between X and Y is linear, that the variance of the observations about the line is constant, that the distribution of the variables is not truncated, and that the sample contains no outliers.

7-7. THE POPULATION CORRELATION COEFFICIENT

Throughout this chapter, we have referred to r as the sample correlation coefficient. Of course, our goal is to describe the relationship that exists between two variables in the population from which the sample came. In this sense, we say that r is the sample estimate of the population correlation coefficient. The population correlation coefficient is denoted by the Greek letter ρ (rho). Its range is from -1 to $+1$.

7-8. EXERCISES

7-1. Draw the scatter diagram for the pretest scores and final test scores for your sample of students. Does your sample satisfy the four conditions for a valid correlation coefficient?

7-2. Determine the correlation coefficient between pretest scores and final test scores for your sample of students. Compare the results to that of the entire group of 238 students for which the value is 0.42.

7-3. Report the value of your correlation coefficient of Exercise 7-2 to your instructor. Your instructor will make a relative frequency polygon of the data for your class and discuss the results with you at a later time.

7-4. Suppose you transformed your pretest and final test scores to T scores and then computed the correlation coefficient between the two sets of paired T scores. What relationship would this correlation coefficient have to the value you found in Exercise 7-2?

CHAPTER 8

Measuring Linear Relationships

8-1. LINEAR RELATIONSHIPS AND EQUATIONS

As indicated in Section 7-6, the sample correlation coefficient is used to measure the strength of a linear relationship between an independent and a dependent variable. Measuring the strength of the association is only part of the research task. Another part is to determine more exactly the nature of the relationship. This is found by determining the equation of the straight line that best describes the data. Once the exact nature of the equation is known, it can be used to predict unknown values of a dependent variable, given specified values of the independent variable. Because so many relationships of the social sciences can be approximated by a linear equation, researchers use straight-line relationships to describe the association between two variables.

For that reason, we shall need to examine, in some detail, linear equations and how they are used to make predictions.

We begin by recalling that it takes two points to determine a straight line. Once the line is determined, it can then be described in terms of two constants, the *intercept* and the *slope* of the line. In terms of the notation of Figure 8-1, we see that as soon as the points (X_1, Y_1) and (X_2, Y_2) are placed on a sheet of graph paper, a straight line can be drawn by placing a ruler between the two points and simply tracing the line that passes through the two points. We also see that the line will cut the Y axis at the point where $X = 0$. The vertical distance between the point where the line cuts the Y axis and the horizontal axis is called the intercept of the line. The intercept is denoted by B_0. The slope of the line is defined as the amount of increase in the line for each unit increase in X. The slope is denoted by B_1. Given any two points on the line, the values of B_0 and B_1 can be found. Thus, the equation of a straight line can be determined by simply knowing the values of B_0 and B_1.

Definition of the equation of a straight line

Let B_0 be the intercept of a straight line and let B_1 be the slope. With these two constants the equation of a straight line is given by:

$$Y = B_0 + B_1 X$$

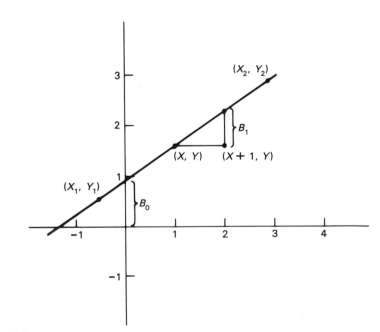

Figure 8-1.
The graph of a straight line.

Box 8-1   Procedure for graphing a straight line

Step 1. Rule vertical and horizontal axes on the graph paper.

Step 2. Determine the intercept of the equation, B_0. Plot the point $(0, B_0)$.

Step 3. Choose any value of X that is near the end of the positive X axis of the graph. Call this value X_E. Substitute this value into the equation to determine the corresponding value of Y. This gives $Y_E = B_0 + B_1 X_E$.

Step 4. Plot the point (X_E, Y_E).

Step 5. Place a ruler between the two points and trace out the resulting line.

Step 6. Label the axes and give the graph a title.

Notice that if $X = 0$, $Y = B_0 + B_1(0) = B_0$, the value of the intercept. In addition, the change in the line from X to $X + 1$ is given by:

$$[B_0 + B_1(X + 1)] - [B_0 + B_1 X] = B_1$$

the value of the slope. These values are shown in Figure 8-1. We will use the definition to graph the equation of a straight line following the directions in Box 8-1.

As an example, let us plot the line $Y = 3 + 1.5X$. By comparing this equation to

$$Y = B_0 + B_1 X$$

we see that the intercept, B_0, is 3, and the slope, B_1, is 1.5. We then put a dot on the Y axis 3 units above the X axis. Next, we can choose any value for the X coordinate. Choose a point near the positive end of the X axis. With the scale shown in Figure 8-2, a good choice might be $X_E = 10$. Next, the Y value for a point on the line, with $X_E = 10$, is given by:

$$Y_E = 3 + 1.5 X_E = 3 + 1.5(10) = 18$$

The point (10,18) is then plotted on the graph. Finally, a line is drawn that goes through the two plotted points, and the graph is labelled and given a title, as shown in Figure 8-2.

If B_0 is negative, the intercept will cut the Y axis at a point below the horizontal X axis. If B_0 is positive, the intercept will cut the Y axis at a point above the X axis. If B_1 is negative, the line will have values that decrease with increases in the X variable. If B_1 is positive, the line will have values that increase with increases in the X variable. For most of the variables encountered in the social sciences, B_0 and B_1 are positive. Further, negative values of X and Y are rarely encountered, so that most linear equations are defined only if X and Y are positive.

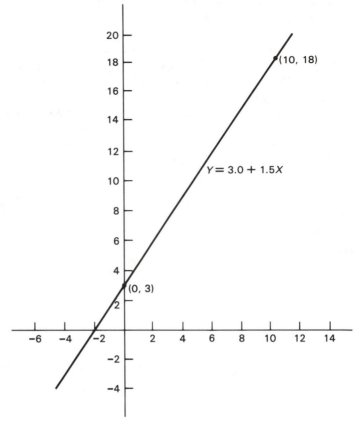

Figure 8-2.
The graph of the equation $Y = 3.0 + 1.5X$.

8-2. ESTIMATING THE LINEAR EQUATION FOR A SAMPLE

One of the problems in determining the equation of a sample is that one could determine as many straight lines as there are pairs of points in the scatter diagram. For the scatter diagram of Figure 7-1, you could determine 741 different straight lines by drawing lines through every possible pair of points. The result would be chaotic. To avoid this, statisticians have derived methods to obtain an average line that can be used to describe the general linear trend in a set of sampled data. The resulting best fitting straight line is determined from a knowledge of the means, the standard deviations, and the correlation coefficient between the two variables of interest. The equations for determining the best average value of B_0 and B_1 are presented in Box 8-2. The little "hat," or caret, on top of the Y is used to indicate that this equation is estimated from the sample.

Box 8-2   Procedure for determining and graphing the linear equation for a sample

Step 1. Determine the values of $\overline{X}$, $\overline{Y}$, S_X, S_Y, and r.

Step 2. Determine the values of B_0 and B_1, using the equations:

$$B_0 = \overline{Y} - r \frac{S_Y}{S_X} \overline{X}$$

and:

$$B_1 = r \frac{S_Y}{S_X}$$

Step 3. In terms of the above expressions, the best equation is given by:

$$\hat{Y} = B_0 + B_1 X$$

or by:

$$\hat{Y} = \left(\overline{Y} - r \frac{S_Y}{S_X} \overline{X}\right) + \left(r \frac{S_Y}{S_X}\right) X$$

Step 4. Plot this equation according to the procedures indicated in Box 8-1.

As an example, for the data of Table 7-1, we find that:

$$\overline{X} = 18.2051 \qquad \overline{Y} = 46.0513$$
$$S_X = 7.5050 \qquad S_Y = 15.5968$$
$$r = 0.5543$$

Thus, according to the equations given in Box 8-2,

$$B_0 = \overline{Y} - r \frac{S_Y}{S_X} \overline{X}$$

$$= 46.0513 - (0.5543) \frac{15.5968}{7.5050} (18.2051) = 25.0801 = 25.08$$

and:

$$B_1 = r \frac{S_Y}{S_X} = (0.5543) \frac{15.5968}{7.5050} = 1.1519 = 1.15$$

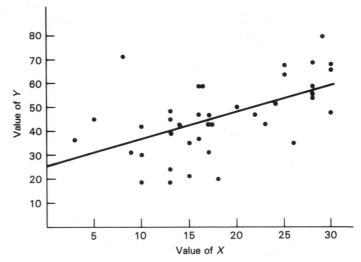

Figure 8-3.
The graph of the equation $\hat{Y} = 25.08 + 1.15X$ superimposed on the scatter diagram of Figure 7-1.

In terms of these numbers, the best straight-line equation for the data is given by:

$$\hat{Y} = 25.08 + 1.15X$$

For this equation, the intercept is 25.08 and the slope equals 1.15. With these two values, the equation is plotted as shown in Figure 8-3.

8-3. USING A LINEAR EQUATION TO PREDICT UNKNOWN VALUES

Once the values of B_0 and B_1 are known, they can be used to predict the value of a dependent variable from knowledge of the independent variable. For example, suppose a student not included in the sample of Table 7-1 had a pretest score of $X = 20$. We could use the sample equation to predict that the score on the final for such a student would be a number close to:

$$\hat{Y} = 25.08 + 1.15(20) = 48.08 = 48$$

If, indeed, the score turned out to be exactly equal to 48, we would feel very pleased. Unfortunately, such accuracy in prediction is not always possible. However, the number 48 has a very simple interpretation. It is actually the average score on the final that we would expect to observe for all students who obtained a score of 20 on the pretest. Some students will score above 48 and some will score below, but the average for all the students would be a number close to 48. In the total population of 238 students, ten had a score of

20 on the pretest. Their scores on the final were given by 57, 50, 50, 50, 18, 50, 77, 50, 35, and 60, with a mean equal to $\overline{Y}_{20} = 49.7$, a number fairly close to the predicted value of 48.

It should be noted that prediction is never perfect. It is always made with error, and this is because sample correlation coefficients between an independent and dependent variable are almost always less than one in value. If a sample correlation coefficient were to equal plus or minus one, the prediction would be perfect. No error would be encountered. On the other hand, if the sample correlation coefficient were to equal zero, no accurate prediction would be possible. As the sample r changes from zero to plus or minus one, the accuracy of prediction increases. Since most correlation coefficients observed in the social sciences range in value of 0.4 to 0.6, the accuracy of prediction is not very high. This means that prediction in these sciences is really a prediction of trend and not one of accuracy. Thus, if one reads that aggression in teenagers is related to family income, it does not mean that one can predict with accuracy the amount of aggression that a specific teenager will exhibit, given his family income. Instead, the statement must be interpreted in a looser fashion to say that, in general, aggression is expressed more forcibly among teenagers who come from families with low yearly incomes and that it tends to be expressed in a more mild form among teenagers who come from wealthy families.

We have examined the prediction of scores using only one predictor variable. Often there are situations in which the accuracy of prediction can be improved by using more than one independent variable. We will describe such methodology in detail in later chapters.

8-4. REGRESSION TO THE MEAN

Before continuing with our discussion, let us embark on an important digression that will provide a basis for understanding much of the material which will follow. Consider a sample in which there is a perfect linear relationship between X and Y. That is, the two are functionally related. As an example, suppose that students' heights were recorded in inches, X, and then in centimeters, Y; or that number of correct answers on a test were computed, X, followed by number of errors on the same test, Y. In such cases, once a person's X value is given, the Y value can be given exactly. It is similarly true, though not proved here, that whenever a perfect linear relationship exists between two variables within a sample, each individual's Z score on Y will correspond exactly to the Z score on X. Thus, an individual who is two standard deviations above the mean on X will also be two standard deviations above the mean on Y; one who is half a standard deviation below the mean of X will be half a standard deviation below the mean of Y, etc.

Because of this property of perfect linear relationships within a sample, it is easy to devise a prediction rule in cases where an individual's Y performance is unknown. The rule is simply predict the same Z score on Y as was obtained on X. Thus:

$$\hat{Z}_{Y_i} = Z_{X_i}$$

where $\hat{Z}_{Y_i}$ represents the predicted standard score for the ith individual on variable Y. It should be mentioned that this rule applies to all variables for which $r_{XY} = +1.00$, such as height in inches and height in centimeters. In cases where there is a perfect negative relationship for which $r_{XY} = -1.00$, such as number correct and number of errors on the same test, the rule becomes simply:

$$\hat{Z}_{Y_i} = -Z_{X_i}$$

Thus, knowing that a perfect linear relationship exists between two variables and, given information about a Z score on X, one need only predict the same Z score on Y. In the case of a negative relationship, the sign of the predicted scores would be reflected, or changed.

The prediction rules, as outlined above, apply only to variables which are perfect linear functions of each other. A very similar prediction rule can be applied, even for less-than-perfect relationships. It forms the basis of the phenomenon called *regression toward the mean*. In particular, when two variables are not perfectly correlated, a person's score on the predicted variable is, on the average, not as extreme as it is on the predictor variable. In other words, a value on Y is generally closer to the group mean than would be expected solely from the knowledge of the score on X. The prediction equation, therefore, regresses the predicted score on Y to a point somewhere between the initial Z score on X and zero, the standardized mean. The amount of this regression is inversely related to the magnitude of r_{XY}. In particular, the prediction equation is given by:

$$\hat{Z}_{Y_i} = r_{XY}Z_{X_i}$$

Note that only one equation is needed here, since r_{XY} carries the plus and minus signs that were used previously. From this it may be seen that if two variables are perfectly correlated, that is, if $r_{XY} = \pm1.00$, one would be a perfect linear function of the other. In this case, a predicted Z score on Y would be exactly the same as it was on X, and no regression would have occurred. On the other hand, if two variables are completely uncorrelated, $r_{XY} = 0$, regression would be total so that $\hat{Z}_{Y_i} = 0$. For other values of r_{XY}, the amount of regression to the mean would range from slight for values close to ±1.00 to a great deal for values close to zero. This is easy to demonstrate.

Consider the first student of Table 7-1, who has an X score of 10. The standard X score for this person is equal to:

$$Z_{X_1} = \frac{X_1 - \overline{X}}{S_X} = \frac{10 - 18.2051}{7.5050} = -1.0933$$

As we have shown, the predicted score for this person is calculated as:

$$\hat{Y}_1 = 25.0801 + 1.1519(10) = 36.5991$$

so that the predicted standard score is given by:

$$\hat{Z}_{Y_1} = \frac{\hat{Y}_1 - \overline{Y}}{S_Y} = \frac{36.5991 - 46.0513}{15.5968} = -0.6060$$

which, relatively speaking, is closer to the mean Y value than is the observed X value to its mean. If we consider the ratio of the two standard scores, we obtain:

$$\frac{\hat{Z}_{Y_1}}{Z_{X_1}} = \frac{-0.6060}{-1.0933} = 0.5543$$

the value of the correlation coefficient. This means that a predicted standard score for the Y variable is $(100)r$ percent of the standard score on the X value.

The regression to the mean phenomenon was discovered by Sir Francis Galton at the turn of the century. He noted that short parents tended to have taller children while tall parents tend to have shorter children. He assumed that this regression to the mean effect was biological in nature and helped to produce stable populations. Today we know that such regression could be explained by the fact that variables are imperfectly related, with correlation coefficients less than one.

Another expression of regression to the mean can be seen in the empirical fact that dull parents have children brighter than themselves, while bright parents have children duller than themselves. This does not mean that *all* dull parents have brighter children. Instead, it means that *on the average,* they tend to have brighter children. At the same time, it is not true that *all* bright parents have duller children. *On the average,* they do. Thus, bright parents can have children brighter than themselves but typically the reverse is true. The same is true for dull parents. Generally their children are brighter, but not always.

The effects of regression to the mean are quite subtle and often appear in unexpected ways in research in the social sciences. Many examples can be provided from the evaluation of many mental health programs. In its most typical form, a standardized personality inventory such as the Minnesota Multiphasic Personality Inventory (MMPI), is given to a group of patients upon admission to a mental health clinic. At the time of this initial testing, most clients are distraught and are undergoing significant psychological stress. Because of this, their personality profile demonstrates high degrees of abnormalities. Being under stress, these individuals tend to score on the extreme end of the personality scales set up for the MMPI. Once admitted to the clinic, clients are treated and then retested with the MMPI at a later date, such as one or two weeks after admission. Most retest scores are closer to the mean of the normal population, and almost always the director of the clinic, as well as the staff, conclude that the treatment and the clinic program are highly successful. This is a conclusion which is most likely invalid.

Since test and retest scores for the MMPI are positively correlated, it is no wonder that upon a second testing, clients' scores *move* toward the mean of the normal population. The movement toward the mean may be related to the treatment offered to the clients; yet, at the same time it must be noted that a large part of the movement could be attributed to the regression to the mean. The effect of the treatment, if any, is confounded with the regression toward the mean. When extreme groups are used and when the test – retest correlation is in the neighborhood of 0.3 to 0.6, the regression effect will be large.

Another example is provided in the controversy related to the stability of IQ test scores. There are studies in the literature in which groups of children with very low IQ scores are given a second test following some educational program. Without exception, the IQ scores increase, often dramatically. The authors of such studies claim that the increase is due to the training. Like the mental health improvement studies, the proposed explanation for the increased IQ is invalid. In all probability, the increase is a regression to the mean, resulting from the selection of subjects from the extreme low end of the distribution and the correlation between test and retest scores on the IQ test.

Regression effects are common. The prudent researcher will always be cognizant of their possible occurrence and watch out for them so that they do not become competing explanations for treatment effects. One way to avoid drawing incorrect inferences in an analysis of the effects of treatment on extreme groups is to include a control group, generated by the method of randomization. Because both groups represent extreme populations, both will experience regression. If the treatment is effective, the change in the treatment group will differ from that in the control group.

8-5. EXERCISES

8-1. Determine B_0 and B_1 for your sample of students for the pretest scores and final test scores. Compare this to the population values of 35.11 and 0.75.

8-2. Find your equation of the "best fitting line" and graph it onto your scatter diagram from Exercise 7-1. Also, plot the population values with red ink on a dotted line. Compare the two lines.

8-3. For your data, what is the predicted value of Y for $X = 15$? For $X = 20$? Report these results to your instructor. The results will be summarized and presented for discussion at a later time.

8-4. A psychologist argued that the Stanford-Benet IQ test was biased against children with low cognitive skills. To prove his point, he took 50 children who scored 85 or less on the test and gave them a second test. On the first test the mean score was given by $\bar{Y}_1 = 81$. On the second test the mean score had risen to $\bar{Y}_2 = 88$. Did he prove his point? Why?

8-5. Suppose the same psychologist of Exercise 8-4 had given a second test to children with IQ scores above 115. Can you make an intelligent guess about the mean value of Y on the second testing? On what basis are you making this guess?

Measuring Explained and Unexplained Variation

9-1. VARIATION ABOUT A STRAIGHT-LINE

It was stated in Section 8-3 that the size of the correlation coefficient is related to the accuracy of predictions based on an estimated straight line. In this chapter, we will examine the nature of the relationship between accuracy and the correlation coefficient. In order to do so, let's consider how we might choose our line so that it represents the data in a scatter diagram in the "best" possible fashion.

If we were to "eyeball" a line for our scatter diagram, we would try to draw it so that it comes close to the greatest number of points. That is, we would try to draw the "best" line in such a way that most of the points in the scatter plot are not very far from this line. This is precisely how the coefficients, B_0 and

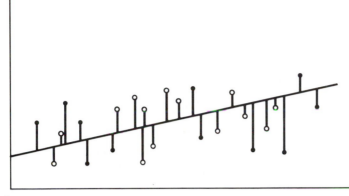

Figure 9-1.
Deviations of the observations from the best-fitting straight line.

B_1, given in Section 8-2, are chosen. For these values of B_0 and B_1, the line $\hat{Y} = B_0 + B_1 X$ is just that line from which the points in the scatter plot deviate least. Typical deviations are represented in Figure 9-1.

The amount of deviation of the points on the scatter diagram from the "best" line plays an important role in the interpretation of the correlation coefficient. Indeed, it was mentioned in Section 7-6 that the *nature* of these deviations determines in large part whether or not a correlation coefficient is a valid summary measure, since it is assumed in the calculation of the correlation coefficient that the deviations about the line are random and homoscedastic for all values of X. We can examine these deviations in a more precise fashion by referring to Figure 9-2. Our goal in this examination is to develop a measure which reflects how close the points are to the line.

9-2. EXPLAINED AND UNEXPLAINED DEVIATIONS ABOUT THE BEST-FITTING STRAIGHT LINE

Consider the geometry illustrated in Figure 9-2. For this discussion, let (X_i, Y_i) be the values of X and Y observed in the ith sample element. Let $\bar{Y}$ be the sample mean of the N values of the dependent variable Y, and let $\hat{Y} = B_0 + B_1 X$ be the equation of the best-fitting straight line.

Recall that the variance of the Y variable is calculated by summing the square of each deviation from the mean, $\bar{Y}$. In Figure 9-2, the deviation of the point (X_i, Y_i) from $\bar{Y}$ is represented by the distance d_{T_i}, called the *total deviation*. Since we have chosen our "best" line so that the points in the sample lie close to it, we expect our line to be closer, in most cases, to the observations than is $\bar{Y}$.

The distance d_{E_i} represents the deviation of our line from the mean $\bar{Y}$. Since we have hypothesized a relationship between Y and X, we are not surprised

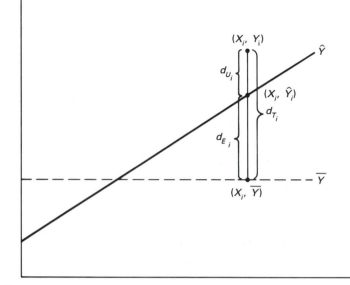

Figure 9-2.
Explained and unexplained deviations for an observed sample value.

that our line varies from $\bar{Y}$. In fact, we could easily feel that the proposed relationship *explains* the line's variation, since postulating the existence of a relationship demands some systematic change in the dependent variable whenever the independent variable changes. It is for this reason that we label this deviation as d_{E_i}, the *explained deviation*.

The distance of points from the prediction line, on the other hand, is *unexplained* by the relationship between Y and X. It is therefore labeled d_{U_i}, the *unexplained deviation*. Finally, these two deviations are seen in Figure 9-2 to sum to d_{T_i}. With this notation:

$d_{T_i} = Y_i - \bar{Y}$ = total deviation of the ith observation from the sample mean on the dependent variable Y.

$d_{U_i} = Y_i - \hat{Y}_i$ = unexplained deviation between the ith observation and the value predicted from the equation $\hat{Y}_i = B_0 + B_1 X_i$.

$d_{E_i} = \hat{Y}_i - \bar{Y}$ = explained deviation between the predicted value for the ith observation and the mean of the sample on the dependent variable Y.

Further, with this notation, we see from Figure 9-2 that:

$$d_{T_i} = d_{U_i} + d_{E_i}$$

or

(Total deviation) = (Unexplained deviation) + (Explained deviation)

Note that if B_1 were equal to zero (and thus, that r were equal to zero), the best-fitting equation would be given simply as $\hat{Y} = \bar{Y}$, and the value of $\hat{Y}_i - \bar{Y}$ would be equal to zero for every observation. In all other cases, $\hat{Y}_i - \bar{Y}$ would be different from zero. This means that $\hat{Y}_i - \bar{Y}$ is related to the correlation between Y and X. We will examine this further.

We illustrate the determination of these deviations for the first pair of observations in Table 7-1. For $Y_1 = 30$ and $X_1 = 10$, the predicted value of Y is given by $\hat{Y}_1 = 25.0801 + 1.1519(10) = 36.60$. For the entire sample of 39 students, $\bar{Y} = 46.05$. Thus:

$$d_{T_1} = Y_1 - \bar{Y} = 30 - 46.05 = -16.05$$

$$d_{U_1} = Y_1 - \hat{Y}_1 = 30 - 36.60 = -6.60$$

$$d_{E_1} = \hat{Y}_1 - \bar{Y} = 36.60 - 46.05 = -9.45$$

We see that:

$$d_{T_1} = d_{U_1} + d_{E_1} = (-6.60) + -9.45 = -16.05$$

The remaining values of d_{T_i}, d_{U_i}, and d_{E_i} are summarized in Table 9-1. Note that, except for rounding errors:

$$\sum_{i=1}^{N} d_{T_i} = \sum_{i=1}^{N} d_{U_i} = \sum_{i=1}^{N} d_{E_i} = 0$$

Since these sums are all equal to zero, we cannot use them to generate measures of how close the points are to the line. To generate measures of *goodness of fit*, we can proceed just as we did for defining the sample variance and square the deviations before adding.

In terms of these squared deviations:

1. Sum of squares of the total deviations equals:

$$SS_T = \sum_{i=1}^{N} (Y_i - \bar{Y})^2$$
$$= (-16.05)^2 + (5.95)^2 + (12.95)^2 + \cdots + (-15.05)^2$$
$$= 9243.8975 = 9243.90$$

2. Sum of squares of the unexplained deviations equals:

$$SS_U = \sum_{i=1}^{N} (Y_i - \hat{Y}_i)^2$$
$$= (-6.60)^2 + (-0.73)^2 + (1.67)^2 + \cdots + (-13.66)^2$$
$$= 6402.5072 = 6402.51$$

Table 9-1. Total deviations, unexplained deviations, and explained deviations for each of the $N = 39$ observations of Table 7-1 for $\hat{Y} = 25.0801 + 1.1519X$

Y	$\hat{Y}$	$d_T = Y - \bar{Y}$	$d_U = Y - \hat{Y}$	$d_E = \hat{Y} - \bar{Y}$
30	36.60	−16.05	−6.60	−9.45
52	52.73	5.95	−0.73	6.68
59	57.33	12.95	1.67	11.28
43	51.57	−3.05	−8.57	5.52
69	57.33	22.95	11.67	11.28
43	44.66	−3.05	−1.66	−1.39
19	40.05	−27.05	−21.05	−6.00
47	43.51	0.95	3.49	−2.54
35	55.03	−11.05	−20.03	8.98
80	58.49	33.95	21.51	12.44
64	53.88	17.95	10.12	7.83
68	53.88	21.95	14.12	7.83
19	36.60	−27.05	−17.60	−9.45
20	45.81	−26.05	−25.81	−0.24
45	30.84	−1.05	14.16	−15.21
39	40.05	−7.05	−1.05	−6.00
24	40.05	−22.05	−16.05	−6.00
50	48.12	3.95	1.88	2.07
57	57.33	10.95	−0.33	11.28
71	34.30	24.95	36.70	−11.75
54	57.33	7.95	−3.33	11.28
42	36.60	−4.05	5.40	−9.45
48	59.64	1.95	−11.64	13.59
47	50.42	0.95	−3.42	4.37
59	43.51	12.95	15.49	−2.54
31	35.45	−15.05	−4.45	−10.60
48	40.05	1.95	7.95	−6.00
68	59.64	21.95	8.36	13.59
47	44.66	0.95	2.34	−1.39
42	41.21	−4.05	0.79	−4.84
38	28.54	−8.05	9.46	−17.51
59	43.51	12.95	15.49	−2.54
43	44.66	−3.05	−1.66	−1.39
35	42.36	−11.05	−7.36	−3.69
45	40.05	−1.05	4.95	−6.00
21	42.36	−25.05	−21.36	−3.69
37	43.51	−9.05	−6.51	−2.54
67	59.64	20.95	7.36	13.59
31	44.66	−15.05	−13.66	−1.39
Total 1796	1795.96	0.05	0.04	0.01

3. Sum of squares of the explained deviations equals:

$$SS_E = \sum_{i=1}^{N} (\hat{Y}_i - \bar{Y})^2$$
$$= (-9.45)^2 + (6.68)^2 + (11.28)^2 + \cdots + (-1.39)^2$$
$$= 2840.0287 = 2840.03$$

Except for rounding errors it should be noted that:

$$SS_T = SS_U + SS_E$$

We say that the goodness of fit of the regression line to the data is good if SS_E is large and SS_U is small; otherwise, it is said to be poor. Because SS_E and SS_U add to SS_T, the goodness of fit can be measured by the ratio of SS_E to SS_T.

For this ratio, if $SS_E = 0$, then $SS_E/SS_T = 0$, whereas, if $SS_E = SS_T$, then $SS_E/SS_T = 1$. This suggests that SS_E/SS_T could be used as a measure of association in much the same way as the correlation coefficient, except that it can never be negative in value.

Let's examine this ratio for the data of Table 9-1. For these data, we see that:

$$\frac{SS_E}{SS_T} = \frac{2840.0287}{9243.8975} = 0.3072$$

Thus, the explained sum of squares is 30.7 percent of the total sum of squares. This suggests that a substantial part of the variation in the final exam scores can be explained by the variation in the pretest scores. This is not too surprising, since we have already seen that the correlation coefficient between the two sets of scores is given by $r = 0.5543$. What is remarkable, however, is that r is related in a direct numerical fashion to the ratio of SS_E to SS_T. In point of fact, it can be shown that $r^2 = SS_E/SS_T$. For this example, $r^2 = 0.5543^2 = 0.3072$. This means that r^2 has a simple interpretation. In particular, r^2 is a measure of how much of the dispersion in the dependent variable is explainable in terms of the independent variable.

In this case, it would be said that about 31 percent of the variation in the final exam scores can be explained by the variation of the scores on the pretest given to the students at the beginning of the biology class. While r is difficult to interpret, r^2 is not. The importance of this statement cannot be over-emphasized. Research is performed to determine the amount of variation in a dependent variable that is explainable by its correlation with an independent variable. The determination of the amount of explained variation is given simply as r^2. This means that one need not perform the lengthy calculations shown in Table 9-1 to determine this value. All one need do is compute the value of r and then square it.

9-3. QUALITATIVE INDEPENDENT VARIABLES

Up to now, our discussion of correlation has focused on the case in which both the independent and dependent variables are of a quantitative nature. This is very restricting, since much of the research in the social sciences utilizes qualitative independent variables and quantitative dependent variables. This creates a problem in measuring association in terms of a correlation coefficient, because one variable is not quantitative. However, the model of explained and unexplained deviations can be extended to cover the case in which the independent variable is qualitative and the dependent variable is quantitative. We illustrate the model in terms of the data of Table 2-1.

Consider the qualitative variable, College major. Possible *levels* for this variable are (1) Humanities; (2) Natural sciences; (3) Social sciences; (4) Other; and (5) Not known at this time. As a dependent measure, consider the scores on the final examination. For these two variables, one might like to

Table 9-2.   Scores on the final exam in terms of College major

	(1) Humanities	(2) Natural sciences	(3) Social sciences	(4) Other	(5) Not known	
	69	19	30	52	47	
	43	20	59	43	35	
	68	39	64	80	45	
	24	50	19	42	71	
	48	57	45	47	46	
	59	54	67	47	35	
	48	31		42	37	
	38	68				
	59					
	43					
	21					
	31					
Total	551	338	284	353	316	1842
Mean score	45.92	42.25	47.33	50.43	45.14	46.05
Sample size	12	8	6	7	7	40

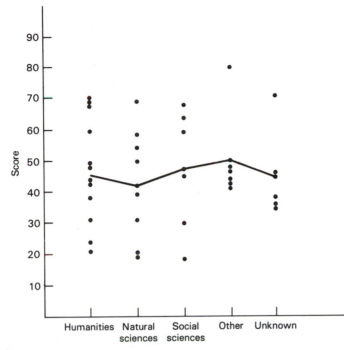

Figure 9-3.
The scatter diagram for the data of Table 9-2.

determine whether final examination scores are associated with College major. The paired data, College major and final examination score, are summarized in Table 9-2. If one desired, one could construct a scatter diagram to illustrate the variation within and between the groups. This has been done in Figure 9-3 with College major presented in the same order as it appeared on the questionnaire distributed to the students. It should be noted that the order of the groups is of no importance, and they can be switched around without influencing the analyses and interpretation of the data. This is different from the model in which both variables were quantitative. In that case, numerical order cannot be disturbed without influencing analysis and interpretation.

When the independent variable is qualitative, no best-fitting line can be determined. In the regression model of Chapter 8, the best-fitting straight line represented an average straight line. Since no single average line can be fit to the scatter diagram, we need a different method for determining an *average line*. A little reflection suggests that a reasonable substitute could be found by computing the average of each group and using the average values in place of the predicted linear equation values. With these values, a prediction line, based upon the individual mean values of each sample, can be drawn on the scatter diagram. This line is referred to as the *empirical* prediction line. It is shown in Figure 9-3 for the data of Table 9-2. For the most part, the empirical prediction line appears to be horizontal to the X axis. If there is a correlation between College major and scores on the final, it appears that it is weak. As indicated, the empirical prediction line is assuming the role of the best-fitting line used for relating two quantitative variables to one another. This substitution of group means for a straight-line prediction value is the key to measuring association for the model in which the independent variable is qualitative and the dependent variable is quantitative.

9-4. EXPLAINED AND UNEXPLAINED VARIATION ABOUT AN EMPIRICAL LINE

Paralleling the model of Section 9-2, let Y_i be the observed value of Y for the ith element. Let $\bar{Y}$ be the sample mean of all the observations and let $\hat{Y}_i$ be the predicted sample mean value. With this notation:

$d_{T_i} = Y_i - \bar{Y} =$ total deviation for the ith observation from the total sample mean.

$d_{U_i} = Y_i - \hat{Y}_i =$ unexplained deviation between the ith observation and the value predicted by the sample mean of the group of which Y_i is a member.

$d_{E_i} = \hat{Y}_i - \bar{Y} =$ explained deviation between the mean predicted and the total sample mean.

With this notation:

$$(Y_i - \bar{Y}) = (Y_i - \hat{Y}_i) + (\hat{Y}_i - \bar{Y})$$

Note that if each sample mean were to equal the mean of the total sample, then each $\hat{Y}_i - \bar{Y}$ would equal zero, so that every total deviation would equal an unexplained deviation. Because the sample means are not equal to the same value, we know that the explained deviations are different from zero and, therefore, College major will probably explain some of the variation in the test scores.

For the first subject, $Y_1 = 69$. The predicted value for each Humanities major is given by the mean value of 45.92. Across all subjects, $\bar{Y} = 46.05$. Thus:

$$d_{T_1} = Y_1 - \bar{Y} = 69 - 46.05 = 22.95$$
$$d_{U_1} = Y_1 - \hat{Y}_1 = 69 - 45.92 = 23.08$$

and

$$d_{E_1} = \hat{Y}_1 - \bar{Y} = 45.92 - 46.05 = -0.13$$

As can be seen:

$$d_{T_1} = d_{U_1} + d_{E_1} = 23.08 + (-0.13) = 22.95$$

The remaining values of d_{T_i}, d_{U_i}, and d_{E_i} are summarized in Table 9-3.

If we examine the column headed $d_U = Y - \hat{Y}$, we note that the first 12 d_U values sum to zero. This is also true for the next eight values that are associated with the sample of Natural Science majors. This sum to zero exists for each of the five samples. This means that the deviations are restricted in each sample, so that across the complete sample, the number of degrees of freedom for the d_U values is given by:

$$(N_1 - 1) + (N_2 - 1) + \cdots + (N_K - 1) = N - K$$

As a result, the number of degrees of freedom for SS_U is given by $N - K$, where K equals the number of groups. In this case, $K = 5$, so that $N - K = 40 - 5 = 35$. In addition, we see that the explained deviations are equal to a common value for each of the subjects within a given sample. Thus, for the 12 Humanities major subjects, each has an explained deviation of -0.13 points.

In terms of these deviation components:

$$SS_T = \sum_{i=1}^{N} (Y_i - \bar{Y})^2$$
$$= 22.95^2 + (-3.05)^2 + 21.95^2 + \cdots + (-9.05)^2$$
$$= 9243.90$$

$$SS_U = \sum_{i=1}^{N} (Y_i - \hat{Y}_i)^2$$
$$= 23.08^2 + (-2.92)^2 + (22.08)^2 + \cdots + (-8.14)^2$$
$$= 8978.32$$

and

$$SS_E = \sum_{i=1}^{N} (\hat{Y}_i - \bar{Y})^2$$
$$= (-0.13)^2 + (-0.13)^2 + (-0.13)^2 + \cdots + (-0.91)^2$$
$$= 265.64$$

Again, we note that, except for rounding errors:

$$SS_T = SS_U + SS_E = 8978.32 + 265.64 = 9243.96$$

so that the association measure corresponding to r^2 is given by:

$$\frac{SS_E}{SS_T} = 265.64/9243.96 = 0.0287 = 0.03$$

Table 9-3. Total deviations, unexplained deviations, and explained deviations for each of the $N = 40$ observations of Table 9-2.

Y	$\hat{Y}$	$d_T = Y - \bar{Y}$	$d_U = Y - \hat{Y}$	$d_E = \hat{Y} - \bar{Y}$
69	45.92	22.95	23.08	−0.13
43	45.92	−3.05	−2.92	−0.13
68	45.92	21.95	22.08	−0.13
24	45.92	−22.05	−21.92	−0.13
48	45.92	1.95	2.08	−0.13
59	45.92	12.95	13.08	−0.13
48	45.92	1.95	2.08	−0.13
38	45.92	−8.05	−7.92	−0.13
59	45.92	12.95	13.08	−0.13
43	45.92	−3.05	−2.92	−0.13
21	45.92	−25.05	−24.92	−0.13
31	45.92	−15.05	−14.92	−0.13
19	42.25	−27.05	−23.25	−3.80
20	42.25	−26.05	−22.25	−3.80
39	42.25	−7.05	−3.25	−3.80
50	42.25	3.95	7.75	−3.80
57	42.25	10.95	14.75	−3.80
54	42.25	7.95	11.75	−3.80
31	42.25	−15.05	−11.25	−3.80
68	42.25	21.95	25.75	−3.80
30	47.33	−16.05	−17.33	1.28
59	47.33	12.95	11.67	1.28
64	47.33	17.95	16.67	1.28
19	47.33	−27.05	−28.33	1.28
45	47.33	−1.05	−2.33	1.28
67	47.33	20.95	19.67	1.28
52	50.43	5.95	1.57	4.38
43	50.43	−3.05	−7.43	4.38
80	50.43	33.95	29.57	4.38
42	50.43	−4.05	−8.43	4.38
47	50.43	0.95	−3.43	4.38
47	50.43	0.95	−3.43	4.38
42	50.43	−4.05	−8.43	4.38
47	45.14	0.95	1.86	−0.91
35	45.14	−11.05	−10.14	−0.91
45	45.14	−1.05	−0.14	−0.91
71	45.14	24.95	25.86	−0.91
46	45.14	−0.05	0.86	−0.91
35	45.14	−11.05	−10.14	−0.91
37	45.14	−9.05	−8.14	−0.91
Total 1842	1842.01	0.00	−0.01	0.01

To distinguish this measure from r^2, the symbol $\hat{\eta}^2$ is used. It is called the *correlation ratio*. As we see, $\hat{\eta}^2$ is the ratio of the explained sum of squares to the total sum of squares and has the same interpretation as r^2. In this case, it is very small. Final test scores are not related to College major. We define the correlation ratio here.

Definition of the correlation ratio

The correlation ratio is defined as the ratio of the sum of squares of explained deviations to the sum of squares of total deviations. Thus

$$\hat{\eta}^2 = \frac{SS_E}{SS_T}$$

As might be expected, no researcher would compute $\hat{\eta}^2$ in the manner illustrated in Table 9-3. If one thinks about the way the deviations of Table 9-3 are computed, it becomes apparent that explained components are defined in terms of sample means and unexplained components are defined in terms of sample variances as indicated in Box 9-1.

For the data of Table 9-2, begin by first computing the mean value of each sample and the mean of the total group. The results are summarized in Table 9-4. With these values:

$$SS_E = 12(0.0169) + 8(14.4400) + \cdots + 7(0.8281)$$
$$= 265.64$$

Next, we determine the value of SS_U by first computing the variance for each sample. The results are summarized in Table 9-5. With these values:

$$SS_U = 11(252.2651) + 7(321.6429) + \cdots + 6(157.4762)$$
$$= 8978.32$$

Finally:

$$\hat{\eta}^2 = \frac{SS_E}{SS_E + SS_U} = \frac{265.64}{265.64 + 8978.32} = \frac{265.64}{9243.96}$$
$$= 0.0287$$

In this case, the goodness of fit of the empirical regression line to the data is poor.

If each sample mean were to equal the total sample mean, SS_E would equal zero, so that all the variation is unexplained. As the variation between the means increases, the value of SS_E increases and so does the value of $\hat{\eta}^2$. Thus, large values of $\hat{\eta}^2$ correspond to large differences in the sample means across the groups.

Box 9-1   Directions for computing the sample correlation ratio

Step 1. Compute the means of the K samples and denote them as:

$$\bar{Y}_1, \bar{Y}_2, \ldots, \bar{Y}_K$$

Let the corresponding sample sizes be denoted as:

$$N_1, N_2, \ldots, N_K$$

Let the mean of all the observations be denoted as $\bar{Y}$.

Step 2. Compute:

$$SS_E = N_1(\bar{Y}_1 - \bar{Y})^2 + N_2(\bar{Y}_2 - \bar{Y})^2 + \cdots + N_K(\bar{Y}_K - \bar{Y})^2$$

Step 3. Compute the variances of the K samples and denote them as:

$$S_1^2, S_2^2, \ldots, S_K^2$$

Step 4. Compute:

$$SS_U = (N_1 - 1)S_1^2 + (N_2 - 1)S_2^2 + \cdots + (N_K - 1)S_K^2$$

Step 5. Compute:

$$SS_T = SS_E + SS_U$$

and:

$$\hat{\eta}^2 = \frac{SS_E}{SS_T}$$

Table 9-4. Computation table for finding SS_E

Sample k	N_k	Total	$\bar{Y}_k$	$\bar{Y}_k - \bar{Y}$	$(\bar{Y}_k - \bar{Y})^2$
1	12	551	45.92	−0.13	0.0169
2	8	338	42.25	−3.80	14.4400
3	6	284	47.33	1.28	1.6384
4	7	353	50.43	4.38	19.1844
5	7	316	45.14	−0.91	0.8281
Total	40	1842	46.05		

Table 9-5. Computation table for finding SS_U

Sample	N_k	Sum of squares	Sample variance
1	12	28,075	$\dfrac{12(28,075) - (551)^2}{12(12-1)} = 252.2651$
2	8	16,532	$\dfrac{8(16,532) - (338)^2}{8(8-1)} = 321.6429$
3	6	15,352	$\dfrac{6(15,352) - (284)^2}{6(6-1)} = 381.8667$
4	7	18,899	$\dfrac{7(18,899) - (353)^2}{7(7-1)} = 182.9524$
5	7	15,210	$\dfrac{7(15,210) - (316)^2}{7(7-1)} = 157.4762$

9-5. EXERCISES

9-1. Determine the value of SS_E, SS_U, SS_T, and r^2 for the pretest and final for your data and compare them to the values reported in the text.

9-2. Explain in your own words the meaning of explained and unexplained variation.

9-3. Find the total, explained, and unexplained deviations for the two subjects of your sample with the most extreme X scores.

9-4. Describe what happens to the d_E values when $r = 0$ and when $r = 1$.

9-5. Examine your sample for differences in mean final test scores as they relate to major, i.e., compute $\hat{\eta}^2$ for your sample. For the 238 students, $\eta^2 = 0.0418$. Compare the two values.

9-6. Draw the scatter diagram for the data of Exercise 9-5.

9-7. Review Exercises 4-8 and 4-9. Interpret the results of those exercises in light of the discussion in this chapter.

CHAPTER**10**

Measures of Association for Other Models

10-1. OTHER MEASURES OF ASSOCIATION

As we have seen, the correlation coefficient, r, is used to measure the association between an independent and dependent quantitative variable, while the correlation ratio, $\hat{\eta}^2$, is used to measure the association between a qualitative independent variable and a quantitative dependent variable. It is worth noting that the correlation ratio also finds use for quantitative dependent variables with ordered qualitative independent variables. Whereas r is restricted to linear relationships, $\hat{\eta}^2$ is not. Other measures of association exist that are used when the relationship between the variables is not linear. The most commonly used measure of association for nonlinear relationships is *Spearman's rank correlation coefficient*, r_S. This measure is an ordinary correlation coefficient based on the substitution of the integers, 1, 2, . . . , N, for the originally observed values of the independent and dependent variables. The *point-biserial correlation coefficient, r_{pb}*, is used when the independent variable is dichotomous and the dependent variable is quantitative. For this special model, the square of the sample point-biserial correlation coefficient and the sample correlation ratio are identical. Thus, r_{pb} serves as a conceptual link between r and $\hat{\eta}^2$. The *phi coefficient, $\hat{\phi}$,* is a measure of association that is used when both the independent and dependent variables are dichotomous. As will be seen, it is calculated in the same way as the correlation coefficient.

10-2. SPEARMAN'S RANK CORRELATION COEFFICIENT, r_s

If a scatter diagram involving two quantitative variables suggests to a researcher that the relationship between the two variables is not linear, the ordinary sample correlation coefficient is known to be an invalid measure of association. If the relationship appears to be increasing or decreasing in a *monotonic* way, Spearman's rank correlation coefficient can be used to estimate the strength of the association. In particular, a relationship is said to be *monotonic increasing* if increases in X tend to correspond to increases in Y. The relationship is said to be *monotonic decreasing* if increases in X tend to be accompanied by decreases in Y. Examples of monotonic relationships are shown in Figure 10-1. If the relationship is always decreasing or always increasing, it is said to be *strictly monotonic.*

The Spearman rank correlation coefficient is found by ranking the observations for each variable, substituting the integers 1, 2, 3, . . . , N, and then computing the sample correlation coefficient on the ranks. We illustrate the use of this measure for the data of Table 10-1. These data represent two variables for which a linear association is not apparent in the scatter diagram,

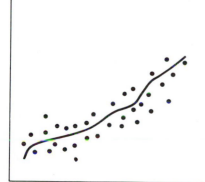
Monotonic increasing

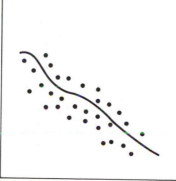
Monotonic decreasing

Figure 10-1.
Examples of monotonic relationships.

Table 10-1.   Relationship between months on the job and
hourly salary for 22 different union members
doing the same or related job, but located in 11
different factories

Months on job	Hourly salary	Rank on months	Rank on salary
1	4.10	1	4
2	4.15	2	7.5
4	6.30	3	21
5	4.15	4	7.5
7	4.12	5	5
10	3.75	6.5	1
10	3.82	6.5	2
14	4.02	9.5	3
14	4.18	9.5	9.5
14	5.83	9.5	15
14	5.83	9.5	15
23	4.14	12	6
39	4.25	13	11
40	4.18	14	9.5
55	6.19	15	18.5
69	4.30	17.5	12
69	5.61	17.5	13
69	5.83	17.5	15
69	6.25	17.5	20
72	6.58	20	22
110	6.05	21.5	17
110	6.19	21.5	18.5
Total		253	253

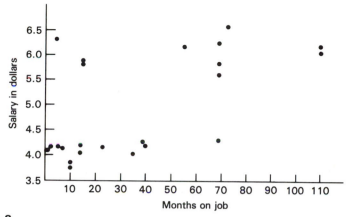

Figure 10-2.
The scatter diagram for the data of Table 10-1.

shown in Figure 10-2. For this study, a sample of 22 union members doing the same or related jobs in 11 different factories in the same community were polled on:

$$X: \quad \text{Months on the job}$$

and:

$$Y: \quad \text{Salary earned per hour}$$

Certain union members claimed that the relationship between months on the job and hourly salary was not equitable across factories, and they petitioned their union to resolve the grievance. The data and the computations for computing r_s are summarized in Table 10-1. We begin by ranking the data from 1 to N for each variable. We break ties by assigning mean ranks to the tied values. For the two workers tied at 10 months on the job, the ranks of 6 and 7 are averaged to give 6.5 to each worker. Letting r_{1i} stand for the rank of X_i and r_{2i} stand for the rank of Y_i, we now compute r_s on the ranks:

$$\sum_{i=1}^{22} r_{1i} = 1 + 2 + 3 + \cdots + 21.5 = 253$$

$$\sum_{i=1}^{22} r_{1i}^2 = 1^2 + 2^2 + 3^2 + \cdots + 21.5^2 = 3784$$

$$\sum_{i=1}^{22} r_{2i} = 4 + 7.5 + 21 + \cdots + 18.5 = 253$$

$$\sum_{i=1}^{22} r_{2i}^2 = 4^2 + 7.5^2 + 21^2 + \cdots + 18.5^2 = 3791.5$$

$$\sum_{i=1}^{22} r_{1i} r_{2i} = 1(4) + 2(7.5) + 3(21) + \cdots + 21.5(18.5) = 3439$$

Box 10-1   How to compute a Spearman rank correlation coefficient

Step 1. Rank the data from 1 to N for each variable. Check to see that the sum of the ranks in each column adds to $\frac{1}{2}N(N + 1)$.

Step 2. Follow the steps of section 7-4, where X_i is replaced by r_{1i} and Y_i is replaced by r_{2i}.

$$r_S = \frac{22(3439) - 253(253)}{\sqrt{22(3784) - (253)^2}\sqrt{22(3791.5) - (253)^2}}$$

$$= \frac{11649}{19321} = 0.6029 \approx 0.60$$

We provide directions for computing r_S in Box 10-1.

10-3. THE POINT-BISERIAL CORRELATION COEFFICIENT, r_{pb}

The point-biserial correlation coefficient is used to measure the association between a dichotomous variable and a quantitative variable. In most cases, the dichotomous variable is one that indicates group membership. As an example, consider the data of Table 10-2 which is taken from the data of Table 2-1. In this table, scores on the final examination are reported in terms of the program to which each student was assigned. With the final as the dependent variable, an indicator independent variable is created by letting $X = 0$ for every student who is assigned to Program 1 and by letting $X = 1$ for every student who is assigned to Program 2. With this artificially created independent variable, sometimes called a *dummy variable,* one can ask if performance on the final is associated with the program to which a student is assigned. The answer is found by computing the corresponding sample correlation coefficient. For completeness, we define the point-biserial correlation coefficient as follows.

Definition of the point-biserial correlation coefficient

The point-biserial correlation coefficient is an ordinary sample correlation coefficient, for which the independent variable is dichotomous. If the independent variable is a dummy variable that indicates class or group membership, one should set $X = 0$ for all observations in one of the groups, and $X = 1$ for all of the observations in the remaining group.

Table 10-2. Scores on the final examination for students assigned to the two experimental programs

Program 1		Program 2	
X	Y	X	Y
0	59	1	30
0	69	1	52
0	47	1	43
0	80	1	43
0	68	1	19
0	45	1	35
0	50	1	64
0	57	1	19
0	71	1	20
0	54	1	39
0	46	1	24
0	47	1	42
0	59	1	48
0	68	1	31
0	42	1	48
0	38	1	47
0	59	1	31
0	43		
0	35		
0	45		
0	21		
0	37		
0	67		

We illustrate the computation of the point-biserial correlation coefficient for the data of Table 10-2, using the directions of Box 10-2. As the scatter diagram of Figure 10-3 suggests, students in Program 1 tend to obtain higher scores than students in Program 2. For the data of Table 10-2:

$$\sum_{i=1}^{40} X_i = 0 + 0 + 0 + \cdots + 1 = 17$$

$$\sum_{i=1}^{40} X_i^2 = 0^2 + 0^2 + 0^2 + \cdots + 1^2 = 17$$

$$\sum_{i=1}^{40} Y_i = 59 + 69 + 47 + \cdots + 31 = 1842$$

$$\sum_{i=1}^{40} Y_i^2 = 59^2 + 69^2 + 47^2 + \cdots + 31^2 = 94068$$

and:

$$\sum_{i=1}^{40} X_i Y_i = 0(59) + 0(69) + 0(47) + \cdots + 1(31) = 635$$

With these values:

$$r_{pb} = \frac{40(635) - (17)(1842)}{\sqrt{40(17) - (17)^2}\sqrt{40(94068) - (1842)^2}}$$

$$= \frac{-5914}{12024} = -0.4918 = -0.49$$

The negative correlation indicates that higher mean scores are obtained for students who worked at a local biological research laboratory for 4 hours per week. For these students, the group dummy code was set at $X = 0$. Thus,

---

Box 10-2   How to compute the point-biserial correlation coefficient

Step 1. Introduce a dummy variable by letting $X = 0$ for all of the observations in one of the samples. Let $X = 1$ for all of the observations in the remaining sample.
Step 2. Compute:

$$\sum_{i=1}^{N} X_i, \ \sum_{i=1}^{N} X_i^2, \ \sum_{i=1}^{N} Y_i, \ \sum_{i=1}^{N} Y_i^2, \text{ and } \sum_{i=1}^{N} X_i Y_i$$

Step 3. Substitute the numbers found in Step 2 into the computing formula for r.

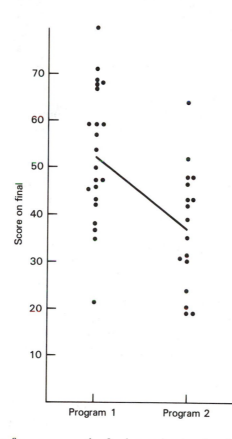

Figure 10-3.
The scatter diagram for scores on the final examination for the students in the two experimental programs.

as the dummy scores increase from $X = 0$ to $X = 1$, the mean scores decrease from $\bar{Y}_1 = 52.48$ to $\bar{Y}_2 = 37.35$. Of the total variation, $r_{pb}^2 = (-0.49)^2 = 0.24$, or 24 percent is explainable in the difference between the two programs. As we see from Figure 10-3, the empirical regression line goes through the separate group means. Since we have set X equal to zero for the subjects in Program One, the line intersects the Y axis at a height equal to the mean of the group coded zero. Thus, for dummy coding, the intercept, B_0, equals the mean of the group coded zero. In this case, $B_0 = \bar{Y}_1$. Further, since the height of the line changes from $\bar{Y}_1$ to $\bar{Y}_2$ as X increases from 0 to 1, the slope can be calculated as:

$$B_1 = \frac{\bar{Y}_2 - \bar{Y}_1}{1 - 0} = \bar{Y}_2 - \bar{Y}_1$$

Hence, with dummy coding, the slope equals the difference between the means of the groups coded 1 and 0, respectively. The linear equation for this coding scheme reduces to:

$$\hat{Y} = B_0 + B_1 X = \bar{Y}_1 + (\bar{Y}_2 - \bar{Y}_1)X$$

We will extend this result in Chapter 47.

Finally, it should be noted that r_{pb} could be computed as a correlation ratio. If it had been computed as a correlation ratio, it would be seen that the results would be identical. Because $\hat{\eta}^2 = 0$ when the group means are equal to one another, we see that $r_{pb} = 0$ whenever $\bar{Y}_1 = \bar{Y}_2$. Also, there are shortcut computing formulas for the determination of r_{pb}. One of these short-cut methods is described in Section 32-6.

10-4. THE PHI COEFFICIENT, $\hat{\phi}$

The phi coefficient is used to measure the relationship between two dichotomous variables. It is computed as an ordinary sample correlation coefficient after the classes of each variable are indicated by dummy variables. As an example, consider the data of Table 10-3 which is taken from the data of Table 2-1. It was the subjective decision of the instructor teaching the class in biology that a passing grade on the final was any score greater than or equal to 40 and that all scores below 40 were indicative of a failing grade. The distribution of students according to program and final grade status is as shown in Table 10-3. As can be seen, 19, or 82.6 percent, of the students assigned to Program 1 passed the final, while only 8, or 47.1, percent of the students assigned to Program 2 passed the final. There appears to be a correlation between success on the final and the particular assigned program of instruction. We can measure this correlation in terms of the phi coefficient. For completeness, we define the phi coefficient as follows.

Table 10-3. Distribution of passing and failing students on the final exam according to the program assigned to the student

Y \ X	Program 1 X = 0	Program 2 X = 1	Total
Passed final Y = 0	19	8	27
Failed final Y = 1	4	9	13
Total	23	17	40

Definition of the phi coefficient

The phi coefficient is an ordinary sample correlation coefficient, where the two classes of both the independent and dependent variables are identified with dummy variables that take on the values 0 and 1.

The assignment of the numbers 0 and 1 to the two classes of each of the variables is arbitrary. All possible assignments generate the same absolute value for $\hat{\phi}$. Directions for computing $\hat{\phi}$ are given in Box 10-3.

For the data of Table 10-3:

$$\sum_{i=1}^{40} X_i = 0(23) + 1(17) = 17$$

$$\sum_{i=1}^{40} X_i^2 = 0^2(23) + 1^2(17) = 17$$

$$\sum_{i=1}^{40} Y_i = 0(27) + 1(13) = 13$$

$$\sum_{i=1}^{40} Y_i^2 = 0^2(27) + 1^2(13) = 13$$

and:

$$\sum_{i=1}^{40} X_i Y_i = 0(0)(19) + 1(0)(8) + 0(1)(4) + 1(1)(9) = 9$$

Box 10-3   How to compute a ϕ (phi) coefficient

Step 1. Set up the 2 × 2 table of interest.

Step 2. Assign the dummy values $X = 0$ and $X = 1$ to the two classes of the independent variable and then assign the dummy values $Y = 0$ and $Y = 1$ to the two classes of the dependent variable.

Step 3. Compute:

$$\sum_{i=1}^{N} X_i, \ \sum_{i=1}^{N} X_i^2, \ \sum_{i=1}^{N} Y_i, \ \sum_{i=1}^{N} Y_i^2, \text{ and } \sum_{i=1}^{N} X_i Y_i$$

Step 4. Substitute the numbers found in Step 3 into the computing formula for r.

so that:

$$\hat{\phi} = \frac{40(9) - 17(13)}{\sqrt{40(17) - 17^2}\sqrt{40(13) - 13^2}} = \frac{139}{370.46} = 0.3752 = 0.38$$

Computational formulas exist for the simple determination of $\hat{\phi}$. If the totals of Step 3 of Box 10-3 are compared to the figures of Table 10-3, it is seen that all of the totals appear in the table. This means that the computations of Step 3 can be completely ignored. The numbers required to compute $\hat{\phi}$ are shown in Table 10-4. As we see, these frequencies are associated with $X = 1$ and $Y = 1$. The same result can be obtained by using the frequencies associated with $X = 0$ and $Y = 0$. Another computational formula is presented in Section 16-4.

In this example, we have computed $\hat{\phi}$ for a case in which there are clearly defined independent and dependent variables. The independent variable is program membership and the dependent variable is success in passing the final examination. It makes no sense to think of program membership as depending on score on the final examination. The phi coefficient is not restricted to cases in which there is a definite independent variable. In fact, it is most commonly encountered in a *one*-sample situation where the two variables are *interdependent,* with neither serving as an independent nor a dependent variable. For example, consider the 40 subjects of Table 2-1 and the variables Y_1: Sex and Y_2: High-school biology. This is clearly a *one*-sample problem, and the best we can do is to determine whether sex and taking biology are interrelated.

We summarize the data in Table 10-5, including students on which both pieces of information are available. For these data, $\hat{\phi} = -0.02$. This distinction between cases in which an independent variable exists and those in which neither variable is clearly independent is important.

Table 10-4. Figures needed to determine $\hat{\phi}$ for the data of Table 10-3

X / Y	Program 1 X = 0	Program 2 X = 1	Total
Passed final Y = 0			
Failed final Y = 1		9	13
Total		17	40

Table 10-5. Sex and taking high-school biology for the 40 students of Table 2-1.

Taking high-school biology	Sex		Total
	Males	Females	
Yes	4	10	14
No	7	16	23
Total	11	26	37

10-6. EXERCISES

10-1. Thirteen sixth-grade students were given a spelling test and a reading vocabulary test. Both tests contained 25 items. The data are shown below.

Student	Spelling test	Vocabulary test
1	25	24
2	23	25
3	19	23
4	22	18
5	12	17
6	18	20
7	19	16
8	6	14
9	11	13
10	4	10
11	7	8
12	10	12
13	6	15

Compute the Spearman rank correlation coefficient on these data. Interpret what you find.

Compare it to the Pearson product moment correlation coefficient.

10-2. What is the association between type of program and final test scores for your sample of biology students? In addition to $\hat{\eta}^2$ what measure of association would be appropriate to answer this question? Why? Compute this measure and interpret your results.

10-3. In a study in which the effects of reinforcement upon learning was being examined, 38 four-year old children were randomly divided into two groups. Children in Group 1 were rewarded with candy every time they made a correct response to a problem designed to teach conservation of matter. Children in Group 2 were given a verbal reward for correct responses. Results are as shown. Determine $\hat{\phi}$ for these data. Is learning the task related to the method of reinforcement?

Number of trials to learn task	Group 1 (candy)	Group 2 (verbal)	Total
Less than 5	12	9	21
Six or more	4	13	17
Total	16	22	38

PART III

STATISTICAL METHODS BASED ON EXACT DISTRIBUTIONS

Until now, we have emphasized the description of samples and populations. If the sample is representative of the population, we have a vague feeling that we can use the sample information to talk intelligently about the population. In the preceding chapters, we have seen repeatedly that sample descriptors will differ from the population characteristics that we are trying to measure. Even under similar conditions, we know that sample statistics will differ from trial to trial due to chance factors. In the next chapters, we examine the laws of chance, or probability theory, and show how they are used in inferential statistics to generalize from the sample to the population. The methods of inferential statistics which we describe allow us to answer questions and specify limits on the population characteristics that we estimate in the sample.

CHAPTER 11

Probability and Statistical Errors of the First Kind

11-1. THE ROLE OF PROBABILITY IN STATISTICS—DESCRIPTIVE AND INFERENTIAL STATISTICS

The procedures we presented in the preceding chapters have dealt with the problem of describing sample information. In so doing, we have emphasized that the sample descriptors (the mean, median, variance, and correlation coefficient) have been used in an attempt to extend our information by inference to a description of the population from which the sample came. Such procedures comprise *descriptive statistics*.

We now turn to a different problem, one that comprises a much larger body of statistical theory. In Chapter 1, it was noted that statistics can be used in the testing and generation of hypotheses. Such was the case, for example, when the third-grade teacher wished to decide whether the difference between boys' and girls' scores on the reading test could be explained by chance variations alone. Hypothesis testing and other such decisions about population parameters are in the province of *inferential statistics.*

Unfortunately, because of the variability always present in nature, exact decisions cannot be made. Rather, a decision is based on the relative likelihood of the data arising because of chance. For example, if one flipped a coin 20 times and it always came up tails, some uncertainty as to the fairness of the coin would naturally arise. This suspicion is not generated because 20 tails in a row is an impossible result, but rather that it is an extremely unlikely result. Similarly, if a teacher could establish that an observed difference in boys' and girls' sample mean test scores was a quite unlikely occurrence, the assumption or hypothesis that the population mean scores for boys and girls were equal would be questioned.

Probability theory is used to supply the information concerning how likely it is that the data could have resulted from chance alone. Thus, probability forms the basis of statistical decisions and, as a result, must be studied and understood.

11-2. THE RULES OF PROBABILITY THEORY

As indicated earlier, most people seem to have an intuitive idea about probability. If you were to ask someone on the street, "What is the probability of a head coming up in the tossing of a coin?" the almost universal answer would be, "It's one-half." If you were to ask why, the typical response might be, "The coin has two sides and chance determines which side will come up." The answer is correct and the explanation is sound, provided that the coin isn't loaded. Similarly, suppose one asked, "What is the probability of throwing a four if one were to roll a six-sided die?" The most likely answer is, "It's one-sixth because the die has six sides and chance determines which side will show up." This answer is also correct and the explanation sound for a fair die. These answers, which people seem to know intuitively, are based upon the formal definition of probability, which we now state.

Definition of probability for equally likely events

Consider an event, E, which could be the outcome of a random or chance process. The probability of the event, E, occurring is defined as the ratio of the number of ways E could occur to the total number of different ways that outcomes could be generated by the process, provided that all outcomes have an equal chance of occurring. We denote the probability of the event, E, as:

$$P(E) = \frac{\text{Number of ways the event } E \text{ can occur}}{\text{Number of ways any event can occur}}$$

For the coin tossing example, the random process is the tossing of the coin. The possible outcomes are *heads* and *tails*. Of these two possible outcomes, only one is heads. Thus, the probability of heads is defined as the ratio ½, provided that the coin is not loaded to favor heads or tails. For the rolling of the die example, the random process is the shaking and the rolling of the die. The possible outcomes are one, two, three, four, five, and six spots. Of these six possible outcomes, only one is the appearance of the four. Thus, the probability of a four appearing is defined as the ratio ⅙ provided that the die is not loaded to favor any one, or group, of the six possible outcomes.

The problem becomes a bit more involved if you ask, "What is the probability of two heads appearing if the coin is tossed two times in succession?" Here you might obtain an answer of ⅓, ¼, or any other fraction. Intuition begins to break down at this point. Even so, if we add another idea to the model, the solution of this problem becomes simpler. Note that the outcome on the first toss can in no way influence the outcome on the second toss if the person doing the tossing gives the coin a thorough shaking before the tossing takes place. This means that the outcome on the second tossing is left to chance in such a way that it is completely independent of the outcome on the first tossing. This idea of *independence* is one of the basic building blocks of the statistical inference model to be developed in later chapters. We now provide a definition of this important statistical concept.

Definition of statistical independence

Consider two events, E_1 and E_2. The two events are said to be independent if the probability of either event occurring is not influenced in any way by the particular outcome of the other event. This means that:

$$P(E_1) \text{ is not influenced by } E_2 \text{ occurring}$$

and

$$P(E_2) \text{ is not influenced by } E_1 \text{ occurring}$$

A direct consequence of this definition is expressed as the multiplication theorem of probability theory, which we now define.

Definition of the multiplication theorem of probability theory

Two events are said to be statistically independent if the probability of their joint occurrence can be represented by the product of their individual probabilities. We denote the probability of two independent events as:

$$P(E_1 \text{ and } E_2) = P(E_1)P(E_2)$$

For more than two independent events, the probability of their joint occurrence equals the product of the probabilities of their separate occurrences.

In terms of this definition, we see that the probability of two heads in two consecutive tosses of a fair coin is given by $\frac{1}{2} \times \frac{1}{2}$, or $\frac{1}{4}$, because the events are independent. A head or a tail occurring on the first toss does not influence the outcome of the second toss. In a like manner, the probability of two tails is also given by $\frac{1}{2} \times \frac{1}{2}$, or $\frac{1}{4}$.

Another question that might be even more difficult to answer is, "What is the probability of obtaining one head and one tail if a coin is tossed two times?" Again, the answers might vary from $\frac{1}{3}$ to $\frac{1}{4}$, or to any other fraction. If we add another idea to the model, the solution of this problem also becomes simpler. Note that the first toss could produce a head and the second toss could produce a tail. On the other hand, the first toss could produce a tail and the second toss could produce a head. Thus, there are two different ways to produce one head and one tail in two consecutive tosses of a coin. If the two events can not both occur at the same time, it follows that the total probability of interest is the simple sum of the two separate probabilities. Since the probability of a head followed by a tail is given by $\frac{1}{2} \times \frac{1}{2}$, or $\frac{1}{4}$, and since the probability of a tail followed by a head is given by $\frac{1}{2} \times \frac{1}{2}$, or $\frac{1}{4}$, the probability of one head and one tail is given by $\frac{1}{4} + \frac{1}{4} = \frac{1}{2}$. This example illustrates the calculation of the probability of the joint occurrence of two events which are known to be mutually exclusive. For completeness, we now provide a definition of mutually exclusive events.

Definition of mutually exclusive events

Consider two events, E_1 and E_2. The two events are said to be mutually exclusive if the appearance of either event precludes the appearance of the other.

As a consequence of this definition, since two mutually exclusive events can not both occur simultaneously, we have, for such events, that

$$P(E_1 \text{ and } E_2) = 0$$

A further consequence of this definition is given by the addition theorem of probability theory.

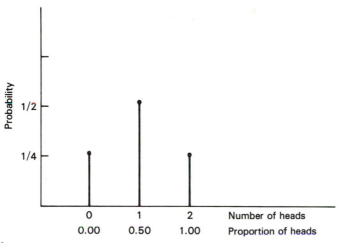

Figure 11-1.
Graphic representation of the probability distribution of the number of heads appearing when an unloaded coin is tossed twice.

Definition of the addition theorem of probability theory

Consider two events, E_1 and E_2. The probability that either E_1 or E_2 occurs is given by:

$$P(E_1 \text{ or } E_2) = P(E_1) + P(E_2)$$

provided that the events are mutually exclusive. For more than two mutually exclusive events, the probability of any one occurring equals the sum of the probabilities of their separate occurrence.

If we let the outcomes of the coin tossing be denoted by X: {number of heads} and the probabilities by $P(X = x)$ where $x = 0, 1, 2$, we can illustrate the probabilities for two coin tosses by the line graph of Figure 11-1. Note that this line graph is similar to the line graph model of Section 3-4, except that the vertical scale is *probability* and not *percentage*. Also notice that $\frac{1}{4} + \frac{1}{2} + \frac{1}{4} = 1$. Such a graph depicts a *probability distribution*, which is a relationship that associates or connects a set of values of a variable, X, with its corresponding probabilities, $P(X = x)$.

11-3. TREE DIAGRAMS

One way to generate the probability distribution for the number of heads in three, four, five, or more independent tosses of a coin is to draw a *tree diagram*

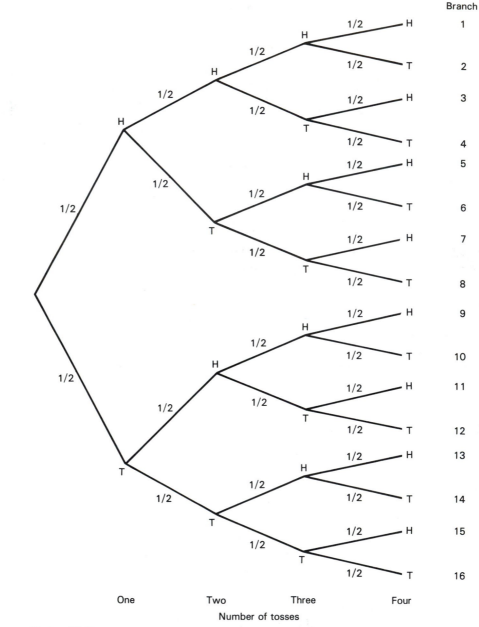

Figure 11-2.
The tree diagram for the tossing of a coin four times.

and then compute the probabilities of each *branch* by multiplying the probabilities associated with each *segment* of the total branch. This is illustrated in Figure 11-2 for four tosses of a coin. As can be seen, there are 16 complete branches to the tree. The top branch is defined by the segments H,H,H,H. The probability of this branch is given by:

$$P(H \text{ and } H \text{ and } H \text{ and } H) = P(H)P(H)P(H)P(H)$$
$$= (\tfrac{1}{2})(\tfrac{1}{2})(\tfrac{1}{2})(\tfrac{1}{2}) = \tfrac{1}{16}$$

The branch below the upper branch is defined by the segments H,H,H,T. The probability of this branch is given by:

$$P(H \text{ and } H \text{ and } H \text{ and } T) = P(H)P(H)P(H)P(T)$$
$$= (\tfrac{1}{2})(\tfrac{1}{2})(\tfrac{1}{2})(\tfrac{1}{2}) = \tfrac{1}{16}$$

The remaining branches and their probabilities are summarized in Table 11-1. As can be seen, the probabilities of each branch are equal to $\tfrac{1}{16}$. Because there are 16 branches, the total probability for the entire tree is equal to $16 \times \tfrac{1}{16} = 1$.

We can now use this table to find the probabilities of zero, one, two, three, or four heads. As we see in Table 11-1, branch 1 is the only branch that has four heads. Thus, the probability that X equals 4 is given by $\tfrac{1}{16}$. We denote this probability by

$$P(X = 4) = \tfrac{1}{16}$$

Branches 2, 3, 5, and 9 have three heads. Thus, the probability that X equals 3

Table 11-1.   The 16 complete branches, or set of outcomes, for the four independent tossings of an unloaded coin

| | Outcome on toss | | | | | Number of heads |
Branch	One	Two	Three	Four	Probability	in the four tosses
1	H	H	H	H	$\tfrac{1}{16}$	4
2	H	H	H	T	$\tfrac{1}{16}$	3
3	H	H	T	H	$\tfrac{1}{16}$	3
4	H	H	T	T	$\tfrac{1}{16}$	2
5	H	T	H	H	$\tfrac{1}{16}$	3
6	H	T	H	T	$\tfrac{1}{16}$	2
7	H	T	T	H	$\tfrac{1}{16}$	2
8	H	T	T	T	$\tfrac{1}{16}$	1
9	T	H	H	H	$\tfrac{1}{16}$	3
10	T	H	H	T	$\tfrac{1}{16}$	2
11	T	H	T	H	$\tfrac{1}{16}$	2
12	T	H	T	T	$\tfrac{1}{16}$	1
13	T	T	H	H	$\tfrac{1}{16}$	2
14	T	T	H	T	$\tfrac{1}{16}$	1
15	T	T	T	H	$\tfrac{1}{16}$	1
16	T	T	T	T	$\tfrac{1}{16}$	0

is given by 4 × ¹⁄₁₆ or ⁴⁄₁₆. We denote this probability by

$$P(X = 3) = \tfrac{4}{16}$$

Branches 4, 6, 7, 10, 11, and 13 have two heads. Thus, the probability that X equals 2 is given by 6 × ¹⁄₁₆ or ⁶⁄₁₆. We denote this probability by

$$P(X = 2) = \tfrac{6}{16}$$

Branches 8, 12, 14, and 15 have one head. Thus, the probability that X equals 1 is given by 4 × ¹⁄₁₆ or ⁴⁄₁₆. We denote this probability by

$$P(X = 1) = \tfrac{4}{16}$$

Finally, only branch 16 has zero heads. Thus, the probability that X equals 0 is given by ¹⁄₁₆. We denote this probability by

$$P(X = 0) = \tfrac{1}{16}$$

The entire probability distribution is shown in Figure 11-3. As with outcomes for two tosses:

$$\tfrac{1}{16} + \tfrac{4}{16} + \tfrac{6}{16} + \tfrac{4}{16} + \tfrac{1}{16} = 1$$

The tree diagram that represents the outcomes for a single toss has two complete branches. The tree diagram for two tosses has $4 = 2^2$ branches. The tree diagram for four tosses has $16 = 2^4$ branches. It should be clear that the tree diagram with N tosses has 2^N branches, a number that becomes very large

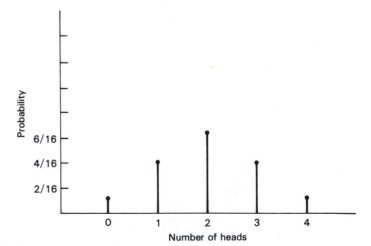

Figure 11-3.
Probability distribution of the number of heads appearing when an unloaded coin is tossed four times.

Table 11-2. Probability distribution of heads in 20 independent tosses of an unloaded coin

Number of heads X	P(X = x)
0	0.0000
1	0.0000
2	0.0002
3	0.0011
4	0.0046
5	0.0148
6	0.0370
7	0.0739
8	0.1201
9	0.1602
10	0.1762
11	0.1602
12	0.1201
13	0.0739
14	0.0370
15	0.0148
16	0.0046
17	0.0011
18	0.0002
19	0.0000
20	0.0000
Total	1.0000

as soon as N gets large. For ten tosses, $2^{10} = 1024$ and for 20 tosses $2^{20} = 1,048,576$. Fortunately, we will not have to draw such a gigantic tree, since tables have been prepared by statisticians that we can use whenever we have a research question that requires the computations for the corresponding tree.

As another example, consider the probabilities for a tree based on 20 tosses. The probabilities are reported in Table 11-2 and graphically shown in

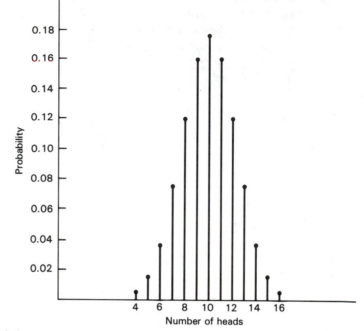

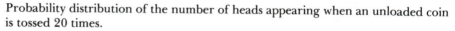

Figure 11-4.
Probability distribution of the number of heads appearing when an unloaded coin is tossed 20 times.

Figure 11-4. The graph is quite striking. We see that the probabilities are essentially zero for zero, one, two, three, and four heads. The probabilities start to increase in an orderly fashion from 0.015 for five heads to 0.176 for ten heads. Then the probabilities begin to decrease in the same orderly fashion in which they increase, until at 15 heads the probability has reduced to 0.015. Again, the probabilities for 16, 17, 18, 19, and 20 heads are very close to zero. In fact, if one were to toss a coin 20 times and observe 0, 1, 2, 3, 4, 16, 17, 18, 19 or 20 heads, one would be very surprised. Any one of these outcomes is very unlikely. On the other hand, the appearance of close to ten heads is expected, since about half of the tosses should be heads and half should be tails. But note that the probability of exactly ten heads is only equal to 0.176. Even so, one might not be surprised to find that in 20 tosses, 7, 8, 9, 10, 11, 12 or even 13 heads appeared. Chance could be used to explain a deviation of plus or minus three heads from expectation, without much difficulty. However, one might begin to be suspicious if 6 or 14 heads were to appear because their probability of occurrence is given by only 0.037. In other words, in every 1000 experiments in which a coin is tossed 20 times, one would expect only 37 of them to generate 6 heads and 37 of them to yield 14 heads. These are pretty low odds, and such an outcome would certainly cause one to wonder. Note the implications of what is being stated. We are essentially suggesting that we partition the set of outcomes into three mutually exclusive sets that relate to our belief in the fairness of a coin that is to be tossed 20 times. We would definitely question the fairness of the coin if {0, 1, 2, 3, or 4} or {16, 17, 18, 19, or 20} heads were to occur. We would not question the fairness of the coin if {7, 8, 9, 10, 11, 12, or 13} heads were to be observed. We might be left in doubt if {5 or 6} or {14 or 15} heads were to appear.

11-4. DECISION RULES AND TYPE I ERRORS

In Section 11-3, we took the possible set of outcomes and divided them into three sets that reflected our belief about the fairness of a coin, given the evidence of 20 independent tosses. One set was associated with a denial of fairness. Another set was associated with affirmation of fairness. Finally, one set left us in doubt. We could eliminate our doubt by splitting the outcomes into two sets by including the outcomes 5 and 15 in the set of outcomes that would lead us to question the fairness of the coin, and by including the outcomes 6 and 14 in the set of outcomes that would not lead us to question the fairness of the coin. If we were to do this, we would have a simple rule of behavior for testing any coin. The rule would read as follows.

Decision rule for testing the fairness of a coin based on 20 independent tosses

If {0, 1, 2, 3, 4, 5, 15, 16, 17, 18, 19 or 20} heads were to appear when a coin is tossed 20 times, question the belief that the probability of a head is ½ and that the coin is unloaded. If {6, 7, 8, 9, 10, 11, 12, 13, or 14} heads were to appear when a coin is tossed 20 times, do not question the belief that the probability of a head is ½ and that the coin is unloaded.

Note that there is a small risk of being wrong and making a false decision by concluding that the coin is loaded when it really is not. The probability of this error is given by the addition theorem for mutually exclusive events as:

$$P(X = 0) + P(X = 1) + P(X = 2) + P(X = 3) + P(X = 4)$$
$$+ P(X = 5) + P(X = 15) + P(X = 16) + P(X = 17) + P(X = 18)$$
$$+ P(X = 19) + P(X = 20)$$
$$= 0.0000 + 0.0000 + 0.0002 + 0.0011$$
$$+ 0.0046 + 0.0148 + 0.0148 + 0.0046 + 0.0011$$
$$+ 0.0002 + 0.0000 + 0.0000$$
$$= 0.0414$$

This is a small risk of declaring that a specific coin is loaded when really it is not. If we were to test 1000 coins that were known to be unloaded, tossing each 20 times, and if we used the stated rule, we would make errors about 41 times out of 1000. Those are pretty good odds, but we could do better by including 5 and 15 heads in the set of outcomes that would lead us not to question the fairness of the coin. If we were to do this, the risk of error would be reduced to 0.0118, or 12 out of 1000.

In any case, a decision is in order. We must choose between a risk of 0.0118 and 0.0414. We must come to a compromise and the compromise that is made seems to vary from situation to situation and from researcher to researcher. Among social science researchers, most will settle for a false rejection risk that does not exceed 0.05. Whereas this solution is not ideal, it is a solution that is workable and this workability may serve as its main justification. It has worked well in the past and we suspect that it will work well in the future.

In essence, we have presented the solution adopted by many researchers in the social sciences concerning the extension of the findings in a sample to corresponding statements in the relevant population. According to the model adopted, there exists a *hypothesis to be tested*. In the example, the hypothesis is that the coin is unloaded. If p = probability of heads, the hypothesis says that $p = \frac{1}{2}$. There exists a risk of saying the coin is loaded, when in fact, it is not. If this error were to occur, it would be said that a *type I error* had been made. To reduce the risk of making this error, a *level of significance* is selected. This states how large a risk of a type I error will be tolerated. In this example, the risk of a type I error would be set equal to 0.0414. Once this risk is specified, a *decision rule* is created. For this example, the decision rule reads: "Reject the hypothesis that the coin is not loaded if the number of heads in the sample were to equal {0, 1, 2, 3, 4, 5, 15, 16, 17, 18, 19, or 20}." The researcher would now toss the coin 20 times, count the number of heads generated by the tossing, and then use the decision rule to decide whether or not the hypothesis should be retained. We close this chapter with the definitions of these terms.

Definition of the hypothesis under test

The hypothesis to be tested by a statistical test is a statement that specifies the numerical values or relationships of the parameters of a probability distribution.

Sometimes, the hypothesis under test is called the *null* hypothesis, and is labeled H_0. For the experiment in which a coin is tossed 20 times, H_0 is given as $H_0: p = \frac{1}{2}$.

Definition of a type I error

A type I error is said to have been made if a researcher rejects a tested hypothesis that is in fact true.

A type I error occurs whenever the sample results lead one to reject the hypothesis being tested, although the observations actually result from the unlikely chance fluctuations allowable under the hypothesis being tested. For the coin tossing experiment, a type I error will be committed if we conclude that the coin is unfair, $P \neq \frac{1}{2}$, when it is in fact fair, $P = \frac{1}{2}$.

Probability of a type I error

The probability of a type I error is the probability of rejecting the hypothesis under test when it should be retained. It is generally denoted by the symbol, α, called alpha.

A type I error is sometimes called an *alpha error*. For tossing a coin 20 times, α was set at 0.0414. With this risk of a type I error, the *critical region* consists of the outcomes yielding 0, 1, 2, 3, 4, and 5 heads and 15, 16, 17, 18, 19, or 20 heads.

Definition of the critical or rejection region

The critical region of a statistical test consists of the set of outcomes that are least compatible with the hypothesis under test.

Definition of a decision rule

A decision rule is a statement that tells a researcher when to reject a tested hypothesis. If the sample statistics are in the critical or rejection region of the test, the hypothesis is rejected.

The decision rule is stated as soon as the alpha level has been decided upon and before the data is collected by a researcher. For the above experiment, the decision rule can be stated as:

Decision Rule: Reject H_0 if $X \leq 5$ or if $X \geq 15$, where
X = number of heads in 20 tosses.

11-5. EXERCISES

11-1. Set up the tree diagram for four independent tosses of a coin for which $P(H) = \frac{2}{3}$ and $P(T) = \frac{1}{3}$. To obtain the probability of a single branch must you use the multiplication or addition theorem of probability theory?

11-2. From the tree diagram of Exercise 11-1, find $P(X = 0)$, $P(X = 1)$, $P(X = 2)$, $P(X = 3)$, and $P(X = 4)$. To obtain these probabilities must you use the multiplication or addition theorem of probability theory?

11-3. The model of Section 11-4 holds for the trial by jury model used in American courts of law. For that test, define the following terms:
a. Hypothesis under test
b. Type I error
c. Probability of a type I error
d. Rejection rule
e. Rejection region

11-4. Consider a deck of cards consisting of four suits: (clubs, diamonds, hearts, and spades), with values: (2, 3, 4, 5, 6, 7, 8, 9, 10, jack, queen, king, and ace). If a single card is drawn from the deck, what is the probability that it is a:
a. King?
b. Queen?
c. King or queen?
d. Heart?
e. King or heart?
f. King and a heart?

11-5. If two cards are selected from the deck of Exercise 11-4, what is the probability that the first card is a king and the second card is a queen, if the first card is returned to the deck before drawing the second card?

11-6. For the data of Table 11-2, what is the probability of:
a. $X = 5$
b. $X = 5$ or 7
c. $X_1 = 5$ and $X_2 = 7$, if X_1 refers to a result found by Alice Adams and X_2 refers to a result found by Bob Brown.
d. $X_1 = 10$ and $X_2 = 10$, where X_1 and X_2 are as defined in (c).
e. $X = 0, 1, 2, 3, 4, 16, 17, 18, 19,$ or 20.

11-7. Why would the decision rule for $N = 20$:

Reject H_0 if X is 9, 10, or 11

not be acceptable for testing $H_0: p = \frac{1}{2}$?

11-8. A test contains ten items that can be scored as correct or wrong. How many branches has the tree diagram for representing this test?

11-9. Answer Exercise 11-8 if the responses are scored as correct, wrong, or no answer.

11-10. A classroom contains 12 boys and 15 girls. If a student is selected at random, what is the probability that a boy will be selected?

11-11. If two students are selected with replacement from the classroom of Exercise 11-10, what is the probability that:
a. Both students are boys?
b. One student is a boy?
c. Neither of the students is a boy?

11-12. If A and B are mutually exclusive with $P(A) = 0.3$ and $P(B) = 0.6$, find:
a. $P(A$ and $B)$
b. $P(A$ and not $B)$

c. P(not A and B)
d. P(not A and not B)
To help you, complete the following table:

	A	Not A	Total
B			0.6
Not B			
Total	0.3		

11-13. If A and B of Exercise 11-12 are independent rather than mutually exclusive, find:
a. P(A and not B)
b. P(not A and B)
c. P(not A and not B)

11-14. A roulette wheel has 18 black numbers, 18 red numbers, and 2 green numbers (0 and 00). If a roulette wheel is spun twice, what is
a. The probability of 2 black numbers?
b. The probability of 1 black number?
c. The probability of 0 black numbers?

11-15. If a person plays roulette on a wheel like that of Exercise 11-14, and bets on black:
a. Find the probability of winning on one trial.
b. How many times should a person expect to win in 100 trials?

11-16. Two six-sided dice are tossed together. Let $X_1 =$ number of spots on 1 die and $X_2 =$ number of spots on the other die. Find
a. Probability that $Y = X_1 + X_2 = 2$
b. Probability that $Y = X_1 + X_2 = 3$
c. Probability that $Y = X_1 + X_2 = 7$
d. Probability of getting $Y = 7$ on two consecutive rolls of the dice

CHAPTER 12

Probability and Statistical Errors of the Second Kind

12-1. TYPE II ERRORS

In Section 11-4, we defined a type I error as the rejection of a tested hypothesis that should have been retained. Since no way exists to eliminate completely the possibility of this kind of error in any experimental or observational study, short of studying the entire population of interest, we control the risk of making this error by pooling the extreme outcomes to define the critical region. In this formulation, we paid no attention to the fact that data could lead to a nonrejection of the hypothesis when it should be rejected. This other side of the coin is referred to as a type II error. As a definition, we have the following.

Definition of a type II error

A type II error is said to have been made if a researcher does not reject a tested hypothesis that should have been rejected.

A type II error is sometimes called a *beta* (β) *error*.

As we will see in later chapters, more attention is placed upon the avoidance of a type I error than on the avoidance of a type II error. Only the type I error rate can be strictly controlled, so that type I errors are considered to be serious errors, in that the consequences of having made a type I error could be devastating. As an example, consider a court trial in which a man is accused of having committed a premeditated murder. The jury must make a decision concerning the guilt or innocence of the accused murderer. If the jury decides that the person is guilty when he really is guilty, the principle of justice has been satisfied. This is also true if the jury decides upon innocence when the accused actually is innocent. However, errors occur if the jury declares the accused to be innocent when the decision should be guilt, or if the jury declares the accused to be guilty when innocence would be the correct decision. The consequences of making these errors are not equal. The sending of an innocent person to jail, and possibly to death, is the error which is most frightful to us. We would be most unhappy if an innocent person were to be convicted of a murder he or she had not committed. For this reason, we associate our type I error with this invalid decision. As a result, we ask the jury to test:

$$H_0: \quad \text{The accused is innocent}$$

against the alternative:

$$H_1: \quad \text{The accused is guilty}$$

H_1 is called the *alternative hypothesis* and is the logical complement to the null hypothesis. We provide a definition of this important concept.

Definition of the alternative hypothesis

The alternative hypothesis is a statement that specifies the conclusion drawn upon rejection of the null hypothesis.

The alternative hypothesis is sometimes called the *research hypothesis*.

Under this model, a type I error occurs if an innocent person is sent to jail, while a type II error occurs if a guilty person is set free, never again to be tried for the murder actually committed. While it is true that the release of a guilty person into society where he or she can murder again is horrifying to think about, our system of justice maintains that it is worse to send an innocent person to jail for a crime not committed.

The distinction between type I and type II errors is easy to demonstrate for studies in the biological sciences. For example, consider a doctor who decides to test a patient for diabetes. With respect to a single test, one possible error involves diagnosing a *false positive*. This occurs when the patient is said to have diabetes when the patient does not. A *false negative* occurs when the patient is diagnosed as free from diabetes when this diagnosis is wrong. This latter error is, of course, the more serious. If the patient is incorrectly diagnosed as being free of diabetes, there continues to be a health menace to the patient. Except for the immediate concern and treatment, the identification of a false positive is not very serious, because the suspected patient could be given further tests, at which time the identification of a false positive would be confirmed. The most extreme case would involve the small costs of making extra tests. In any case, it is clear that the hypotheses tested on the patient are:

$$H_0: \quad \text{Patient has diabetes}$$

against the alternative:

$$H_1: \quad \text{Patient does not have diabetes}$$

Another example from public health can help clarify the distinction between the two types of errors. Every day, public health officials are involved in testing public drinking water for purity and safety. A declaration that the water is safe to drink when it is *not* safe to drink is a very serious error. People who drink the water may become ill and, in some cases, die. On the other hand, the declaration that the water is unsafe, when really safe, may cause inconvenience to people in that the water supply may be closed until further investigation shows it to be safe, or, if it is not turned off, greater quantities of chemical purifiers may be added to the water. The cost here is only time and money. Thus, the public health worker tests:

$$H_0: \quad \text{Water is not safe to drink}$$

against the alternative:

$$H_1: \quad \text{Water is safe to drink}$$

In the social sciences, the consequences of making a type I or type II error are not so great and, in many cases, the costs in money, time, pain, or agony are not so clear and often are debatable. As an example, consider the following situation, in which a school district wishes to test a new reading program for the teaching of reading to children who are labelled *poor readers.* If, as a result of an experiment, it is concluded that the new program is better than the old program when, in fact, it is not, one type of error has occurred. On the other hand, if it is concluded that the new program is no better than the old program when, in fact, it *is* better, another type of error has occurred. Which of these two errors is the more serious?

Consider the consequences of making these two errors. If the new program is adopted when, in reality, the old program is just as or more effective, money would have been wasted in establishing the new program and the students may suffer by not being brought up to their full potential. On the other hand, if the old program is retained when, in reality, the new program is better, the students again will suffer. With both kinds of error, students will suffer, but since we do not want school boards to waste taxpayers' money, we consider the type I error to be the more serious error. Therefore, we ask the school board to test:

H_0:   There is no difference between the old and new programs

against the alternative:

H_1:   The new program is superior to the old program

The reason that we will emphasize discussion of the type I error and will have little to say about the type II error is that the control for a type I error is relatively easy, while the control for a type II error is more difficult. To control the risk of a type I error, we simply decide upon the size of the critical region we desire. In the court trial, the jury is told to choose innocence if there is the slightest shadow of doubt about guilt. The testing program for diabetes would probably be considered successful if the proportion of false positives is kept below 1 percent. Because the consequences of making a type I error in testing drinking water are extremely grave, the probability of a type I error most certainly would be controlled at some figure such as $\alpha = 0.00000001$. On the other hand, in the education study, one could, perhaps, tolerate a type I error of size $\alpha = 0.05$ or $\alpha = 0.01$. Unfortunately, the control for the type II error is not so easy. The difficulty will be apparent in the example of the following section where it will be seen that control is possible only if an alternative hypothesis can be stated exactly. In most behavioral research, this level of specificity is not attainable.

12-2. CONTROLLING THE TYPE II ERROR: AN EXAMPLE

Consider the tree diagram of Figure 11-2, which was used to determine the probability distribution of the number of heads appearing in four tosses of a fair coin. The probabilities for each branch are reported in Table 11-1 for the condition that $P(H) = P(T) = \frac{1}{2}$. Suppose we knew that, if the coin were unfair, its probability distribution would be defined by $P(H) = \frac{2}{3}$ and $P(T) = \frac{1}{3}$. If this were the case, we could test:

$$H_0: \quad P(H) = \frac{1}{2}$$

against the alternative:

$$H_1: \quad P(H) = \frac{2}{3}$$

with the decision rule:

Decision Rule: Reject H_0 if the number of heads is 3 or 4

With this decision rule, the probability of a type I error is given by:

$$\alpha = P(X = 3 \text{ or } X = 4)$$
$$= P(X = 3) + P(X = 4)$$

As shown in Section 11-3, $P(X = 3) = \frac{4}{16}$ and $P(X = 4) = \frac{1}{16}$, so that:

$$\alpha = \frac{4}{16} + \frac{1}{16} = \frac{5}{16} = 0.3125$$

which is a rather large probability of a type I error.

Note that the decision rule determines the probability of a type I error. Alpha is simply the probability of observing an outcome in the critical region, assuming that H_0 is true. In a similar manner, the decision rule determines the probability of a type II error. Note that a type II error occurs if the observed outcome is not in the critical region, assuming that H_1 is true. For the example, this occurs if the number of heads is 0, 1, or 2. These three outcomes constitute the nonrejection region of the test. We can determine their probability of occurrence by repeating the computations of Table 11-1, but with $P(H) = \frac{2}{3}$ and $P(T) = \frac{1}{3}$. These computations are summarized in Table 12-1. As we see, branch 1 has four heads so that:

$$P(X = 4) = \frac{16}{81}$$

Branches 2, 3, 5, and 9 have three heads, so that:

$$P(X = 3) = \frac{32}{81}$$

Branches 4, 6, 7, 10, 11, and 13 have two heads, so that:

$$P(X = 2) = \frac{24}{81}$$

Table 12-1.   Probabilities of the 16 branches of Table 11-1 for $P(H) = \frac{2}{3}$

Branch	Probability for $P(H) = \frac{2}{3}$
1	$(\frac{2}{3})(\frac{2}{3})(\frac{2}{3})(\frac{2}{3}) = \frac{16}{81}$
2	$(\frac{2}{3})(\frac{2}{3})(\frac{2}{3})(\frac{1}{3}) = \frac{8}{81}$
3	$(\frac{2}{3})(\frac{2}{3})(\frac{1}{3})(\frac{2}{3}) = \frac{8}{81}$
4	$(\frac{2}{3})(\frac{2}{3})(\frac{1}{3})(\frac{1}{3}) = \frac{4}{81}$
5	$(\frac{2}{3})(\frac{1}{3})(\frac{2}{3})(\frac{2}{3}) = \frac{8}{81}$
6	$(\frac{2}{3})(\frac{1}{3})(\frac{2}{3})(\frac{1}{3}) = \frac{4}{81}$
7	$(\frac{2}{3})(\frac{1}{3})(\frac{1}{3})(\frac{2}{3}) = \frac{4}{81}$
8	$(\frac{2}{3})(\frac{1}{3})(\frac{1}{3})(\frac{1}{3}) = \frac{2}{81}$
9	$(\frac{1}{3})(\frac{2}{3})(\frac{2}{3})(\frac{2}{3}) = \frac{8}{81}$
10	$(\frac{1}{3})(\frac{2}{3})(\frac{2}{3})(\frac{1}{3}) = \frac{4}{81}$
11	$(\frac{1}{3})(\frac{2}{3})(\frac{1}{3})(\frac{2}{3}) = \frac{4}{81}$
12	$(\frac{1}{3})(\frac{2}{3})(\frac{1}{3})(\frac{1}{3}) = \frac{2}{81}$
13	$(\frac{1}{3})(\frac{1}{3})(\frac{2}{3})(\frac{2}{3}) = \frac{4}{81}$
14	$(\frac{1}{3})(\frac{1}{3})(\frac{2}{3})(\frac{1}{3}) = \frac{2}{81}$
15	$(\frac{1}{3})(\frac{1}{3})(\frac{1}{3})(\frac{2}{3}) = \frac{2}{81}$
16	$(\frac{1}{3})(\frac{1}{3})(\frac{1}{3})(\frac{1}{3}) = \frac{1}{81}$

Branches 8, 12, 14, and 15 have one head, so that:

$$P(X = 1) = \frac{8}{81}$$

Finally, only Branch 16 has zero heads, so that:

$$P(X = 0) = \frac{1}{81}$$

Thus, the probability of a type II error is given by:

$$\beta = P(X = 0 \text{ or } X = 1 \text{ or } X = 2)$$
$$= P(X = 0) + P(X = 1) + P(X = 2)$$
$$= \frac{1}{81} + \frac{8}{81} + \frac{24}{81}$$
$$= 0.4074$$

which is a rather large probability of a type II error.

As this example shows, the probability of a type II error is dependent upon:

1. The decision rule that is used to reject H_0.
2. The risk of a type I error, because the size of alpha is actually determined by the critical region.

3. The value of the population parameter as defined under the alternative hypothesis.
4. The number of trials.

The problem in specifying the risk of a type II error is now clear. Rarely does a researcher have an idea as to the values of the population parameters, given that the alternative is true. If he did, the determination of the probability of a type II error would be simple; otherwise, it is impossible to achieve. If, in the example, we had not known that $P(H) = \frac{2}{3}$, there would have been no way to determine the probability of a type II error.

As will be demonstrated in Exercise 12-2, the risk of a type II error can be reduced by increasing the number of trials. In practice, this is achieved by increasing the number of subjects in an experiment. But even here problems exist. To determine the size of the sample for a study that will make the risk of a type II error as small as desired, a researcher must know the values of the parameters specified by the alternative hypothesis. In general, this is not known. Thus, to minimize the risk of a type II error, researchers choose the largest sample size available.

12-3. EXERCISES

12-1. Find the probability of a type II error if a coin is tossed four times, where the decision rule says to reject H_0: coin is fair if $X = 3$ or 4, and where $P(H) = \frac{3}{4}$ and $P(T) = \frac{1}{4}$ under H_1.

12-2. Find the probability of a type II error if a coin is tossed six times, where the decision rule says to reject H_0 if $X = 5$ or 6, and where $P(H) = \frac{2}{3}$ and $P(T) = \frac{1}{3}$.

12-3. There is an item on a standardized reading test that is very difficult. The probability of a correct response is given by $p = \frac{1}{3}$. Miss Jones has 6 students in her class that will take this test. What is the probability that

a. All six get the item correct?
b. Five get the item correct?

12-4. Miss Jones of Exercise 12-3 decides to give special training to her students. If she is successful, she expects $p = \frac{1}{3}$ to change to $p = \frac{3}{4}$. If it does change to $p = \frac{3}{4}$, find the probability that
a. All six get the item correct.
b. Five get the item correct.

12-5. For the example of Exercises 12-3 and 12-4, what is
a. H_0?
b. H_1?
c. The probability of a type II error if the critical region consists of $X = 5$ or 6 correct answers?

CHAPTER 13

Permutations and Binomial Probability Theory

13-1. PROBABILITIES AND POPULATIONS

As we saw in Chapter 11, simple rules allowed us to specify all of the possible outcomes and the associated probabilities of the specific events we examined. In these cases, we had direct knowledge of the population parameters; we knew, in a sense, what the sample values should be. For example, if one were to flip a coin 1000 times, approximately 500 heads and 500 tails would be expected. If the results deviate greatly from these values, we do not necessarily assume that the population values for a fair coin are different from half heads and half tails. Instead we examine the coin and the flipping process for possible unfairness. The theoretical probabilities represent population values that are to be expected if the theory is correct.

This expectation of ours has direct implications for hypothesis testing. If our *sample* values differ from those in the *population*, we suspect that the sample is unlike the population in some way. Indeed, if we assume that the theory is correct, we can specify in advance of sampling a decision rule and rejection region based on exact probability values that can lead us to decide whether or not the theory should be maintained. Unfortunately, in many cases, such as in experiments examining test scores, we cannot specify all possible outcomes because of their great number and because the theory may not be exact. In these cases, we shall have to rely on approximations. Even exact probability problems become difficult in practice when the number of possible outcomes becomes large, for then the specification of the rejection region involves adding up a great number of extremely small probabilities. Fortunately, we shall see that approximation techniques can also be used in these instances to provide a workable solution and format.

Finally, a great many problems of behavioral research can be solved by direct application of probability theory. This, in practice, involves a great savings in time and energy, because there is no need to perform an experiment to compute sample values that serve as estimates of population parameters that are already known. Indeed, such is the nature of some problems in probability theory that, should one perform an empirical probability experiment, the outcomes might not be believed until the theoretical answer had been mathematically worked out to support the empirical findings.

The definition of the probability of an event, E, was expressed in Chapter 11 as:

$$P(E) = \frac{\text{Number of ways } E \text{ can occur}}{\text{Number of ways any event can occur}}$$

As implied in this definition, the calculation of probabilities involves the counting of events. Although the counting of heads and tails in coin flipping may have seemed simple and, perhaps, obvious, the counting rules that can be illustrated using basic examples have widespread use. The more important rules will be discussed in the next section.

Throughout, we will be trying to analyze problems, such as the coin-flipping problem, with hypothesis testing in mind. As we saw in the example of Section 11-3, we needed to determine how likely it was to observe less than 4 or greater than 16 heads in 20 independent coin tosses. In doing so, we found the probabilities associated with *exactly* 4, 3, 2, 1, and 0 heads arising, and then added these together. We did the same for 16, 17, 18, 19, or 20 heads. Thus, our problem was reduced to finding a rule that specified the probability of a certain number of heads appearing in 20 tosses. In the four-coin example, we first found the number of different outcomes possible and then found the number of these that contained the desired number of heads. We did not do this for the 20-coin example, but we now present methods that can be used for this purpose. These considerations lead us to the development of a set of counting rules that can be used to compute theoretical probabilities.

13-2. PERMUTATIONS

Let us consider three six-sided dice, and let us count the number of outcomes these dice could produce upon tossing. The first die could have any of its six sides facing up. For each of these possibilities, the second die could have any of its six sides facing up, so that the two dice can yield $6(6) = 6^2 = 36$ different outcomes. The third die can also land in six ways; therefore, the three dice can yield $6(36) = 216$ or:

$$6(6)(6) = 6^3$$

different outcomes. Similarly, four dice could result in:

$$6(6)(6)(6) = 6^4$$

outcomes, and so on, for any number of dice. In general, if we have N dice, they could produce 6^N outcomes. Even more generally, if each of N trials could occur in a ways, the total number of outcomes, T, that could happen is given by:

$$T = a^N$$

In the above example, each die could turn up any one of six faces, so $a = 6$. For four dice, there are $T = 6^4$ different outcomes. As another example, we saw in Chapter 11 all of the outcomes that four coins could produce. Because each coin has two sides, $a = 2$. With four coins, $N = 4$ and, thus, the four coins can yield:

$$T = 2^4 = 16$$

outcomes.

We have just seen how to count the total number of events that can occur when each of N trials can produce a outcomes. This number is used as the denominator for computing probabilities of events of this kind.

Now consider a slightly different problem. Assume we have five books: {Algebra, Biology, Chemistry, Drama, and English} which, for brevity, we will refer to as books {A, B, C, D, and E}. Let us say we want to choose the books at random and place them next to one another on a shelf. In how many different possible orders or arrangements could this be done? There are five possibilities for the first book placed on the shelf. For each one of these five possibilities, four other books could be placed next to it, because the placement of one of the five books on the shelf leaves only four books from which to choose the second. Thus, there are $5(4) = 20$ possible orders for placing two books on the shelf. These are:

$$\{AB, AC, AD, AE, BA, BC, BD, BE, CA, CB, CD, CE,$$
$$DA, DB, DC, DE, EA, EB, EC, ED\}$$

Similarly, after the second book is placed, there are only three books left to be chosen. Each of these remaining three books could be placed to the right of any one of the 20 orders of two books listed above, giving rise to $3(20) = 60$ possible orders in which three of the five books could be shelved. Continuing in this way, we see that the entire set of five books can be shelved in

$$5(4)(3)(2)(1) = 120 \text{ orders}$$

In general, if we have N elements to be selected, we can select them in:

$$P = N(N - 1)(N - 2) \; . \; . \; . \; (3)(2)(1)$$

orders. The number of orders that results is usually written in shorthand notation as $N! = N(N - 1)(N - 2) \; . \; . \; . \; (3)(2)(1)$. This symbol, $N!$, is read as "N factorial."

Now let's consider placing only two of these books on the shelf. Again, as we saw above, we can choose the first book from all five and the second book from the remaining four, so that the two books can thus be placed in $5(4) = 20$ orders. Note that this result can also be written, in terms of factorials, as:

$$P = \frac{5(4)(3)(2)(1)}{3(2)(1)} = \frac{5!}{3!} = \frac{5!}{(5 - 2)!}$$

This expression suggests a general formula for the number of different orders in which X objects can be selected from a total of N objects and then ordered. The number of orders is referred to as the number of *permutations*, which we specify as a definition.

Definition of permutations

A permutation is a distinct arrangement of objects in which order is important. The number of permutations of X objects chosen from N objects can be written as:

$$P_X^N = \frac{N!}{(N - X)!}.$$

PERMUTATIONS AND BINOMIAL PROBABILITY THEORY

To make this definition of P_X^N consistent with our example for the ordering of five books we need to define 0!. As we have shown, the number of orders for placing all books on the shelf is given by:

$$P_5^5 = 5(4)(3)(2)(1) = 5!$$

From the formula we also see that:

$$P_5^5 = \frac{5!}{(5-5)!} = \frac{5!}{0!}$$

So as to have consistency in this symbolism, it is customary to define 0! as equal to 1.

As an example, consider a raffle in which 100 tickets are sold to 100 different individuals. If five tickets are then drawn out of a barrel in order, the number of possible orderings is given by:

$$P_5^{100} = \frac{100!}{(100-5)!} = \frac{100!}{95!} = \frac{100(99)(98)(97)(96)(95!)}{95!}$$
$$= 100(99)(98)(97)(96) = 9,034,502,400$$

Notice that, in this simple case, we could have reasoned out the answer in the same fashion as we figured the number of orders possible in shelving two of our five books.

Let us again consider the book-shelving problem, but this time let us assume that two of the books are identical. That is, let us say that in the five books we have two Algebra and one each of Biology, Chemistry, and Drama. In how many orders can the five books be shelved? In calculating this, let us write down two particular orders of the original five books:

ABCDE   and   EBCDA

Now, in our new sample, we have replaced E by another A. When we do this for the above two orders, we have:

ABCDA   and   ABCDA

which are identical. A little reflection shows that the 120 different orders for the original set of books can be reduced to 60 identical pairs of orders when the extra A replaces the E. Thus, the number of distinct orders is given by $\frac{120}{2} = 60$. In terms of factorials, this reduces to $\frac{5!}{2!}$.

What if we have three identical books, so that the five books consist of AAABC? Consider, for example, these orders from the original set:

ABCDE, ABCED, DBCAE, DBCEA, EBCAD, and EBCDA

When the D and E are replaced by A, all six of these orders become identical. We see that the number of distinct permutations is reduced from 120 to $5!/3! = 20$. Similar reasoning shows that, in general, if I of the objects are identical out of N, the number of *distinct* permutations of these objects is given by $N!/I!$.

This rule can be extended to more than one set of identical objects. For instance, let us suppose the five books were A, A, B, B, C. Then, by the above reasoning, of the $5! = 120$ possible orders of the distinct books A, B, C, D, E, we have only $5!/2!2!1! = 30$ orders of the books A, A, B, B, and C.

Definition of permutations in its most general form

In general, given N objects, of which I_1 are identical, I_2 are different from I_1 but are themselves identical, and so on, up to the last I_K identical objects, then the number of distinct permutations is given by:

$$P = \frac{N!}{I_1!I_2! \cdots I_K!}$$

where $N = I_1 + I_2 + \cdots + I_K$.

Thus, we can use this formula to write down the number of permutations of the books A, A, B, B, B to be $P = 5!/2!3! = 5(4)/2 = 10$. Note that, in this case, we have only two groups of distinct objects which comprise the original five. This is the same case as having only heads and tails as outcomes in coin tosses. If we tossed a coin five times, we can find out in how many orders two heads and three tails could have occurred; it is given by the same formula as above:

$$P = \frac{5!}{2!(5-2)!} = \frac{5!}{2!3!} = 10$$

In this context, the formula $[N!/x!(N-x)!]$ for the number of distinct orders of N objects in which x and $(N-x)$ are identical is called the *binomial coefficient*. Because this coefficient plays an important role in statistical models, we give it a special definition.

Definition of the binomial coefficient

Consider N trials that can result in one of two outcomes, A and B. The number of permutations giving rise to x outcomes of Type A and $(N-x)$ outcomes of Type B is given by:

$$P = \frac{N!}{x!(N-x)!}$$

and is denoted $\binom{N}{x}$. Since:

$$\frac{N!}{x!(N-x)!} = \frac{N!}{(N-x)!x!}$$

it follows that:

$$\binom{N}{x} = \binom{N}{N-x}$$

13-3. BINOMIAL PROBABILITIES

We saw in Chapter 11 that probability computations can be made easy with the use of a tree diagram. As an example, consider Figure 13-1 which diagrams the tree for flipping three fair dice, and consider the outcomes to be: T: {a 2 comes up}; and $\overline{T}$: {a 2 does not come up}. Let X be the number of twos that appear on the three dice. It is clear that, on each toss, T has a probability of $P(T) = \frac{1}{6}$ of occurring, and $\overline{T}$ has a probability of $P(\overline{T}) = \frac{5}{6}$ of occurring, as there are five numbers other than 2. Now let us use this diagram to write the probabilities of 0, 1, 2, and 3 twos arising in three die tosses. For either 0 or 3 twos, there is only one path possible. For 0 twos, we have:

$$P(X = 0) = \frac{5}{6}(\frac{5}{6})(\frac{5}{6}) = \frac{125}{216}$$

and for three twos we have:

$$P(X = 3) = \frac{1}{6}(\frac{1}{6})(\frac{1}{6}) = \frac{1}{216}$$

Now, let us examine $P(X = 1)$. First, we notice that there are three paths which lead to this outcome, and these are starred in the diagram. The probability $P(X = 1)$ is given by the sum:

$$P(X = 1) = \frac{1}{6}(\frac{5}{6})(\frac{5}{6}) + \frac{5}{6}(\frac{1}{6})(\frac{5}{6}) + \frac{5}{6}(\frac{5}{6})(\frac{1}{6})$$
$$= 3(\frac{1}{6})(\frac{5}{6})^2 = \frac{75}{216}$$

Similarly, there are three paths associated with 2 twos, and the sum is given by:

$$P(X = 2) = \frac{1}{6}(\frac{1}{6})(\frac{5}{6}) + \frac{1}{6}(\frac{5}{6})(\frac{1}{6}) + \frac{5}{6}(\frac{1}{6})(\frac{1}{6})$$
$$= 3(\frac{1}{6})^2(\frac{5}{6}) = \frac{15}{216}$$

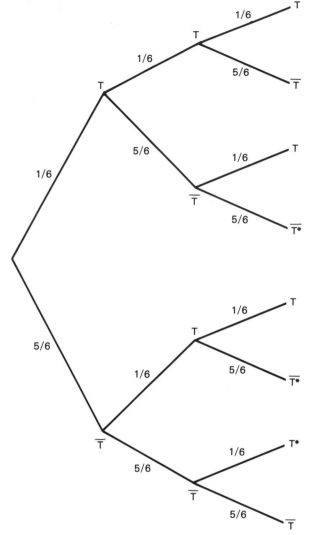

Figure 13-1.
The tree diagram for the tosses of three dice.

Notice two things about these results. First, we already know how many paths generate a specific number of twos. This can be calculated from the binomial coefficient with $N = 3$ and $X = x$. Second, and more important, the probability of each of the paths leading to the same outcome is the same. We should have expected this. For example, to calculate the probability of a branch containing a single two, we would need to multiply together one $P(T)$ and two $P(\bar{T})$'s. This is true no matter in which order the T and the two $\bar{T}$'s occur. Hence, they should all be the same. The following definition of binomial probabilities pools together the results of this discussion.

Definition of binomial probabilities

The probabilities associated with x outcomes of one kind and $N - x$ outcomes of another kind resulting from N independent identical trials is given by:

$$P(X = x) = \binom{N}{x} p^x q^{N-x}$$

where X is the discrete variable associated with the number of outcomes of a certain kind, x is the number of these outcomes that actually occur, p is the probability that one of these outcomes occurs, and $q = 1 - p$ is the probability that one of these outcomes does not occur on a given trial.

For example, let X represent the number of twos appearing in throwing three dice. Let p represent the probability that a two appears on one of the dice, and let q be the probability that a two does not appear on this die. Then:

$$p = \tfrac{1}{6} \quad \text{and} \quad q = \tfrac{5}{6}$$

and:

$$P(X = 0) = \binom{3}{0} p^0 q^{(3-0)} = \frac{3!}{3!0!} (\tfrac{1}{6})^0 (\tfrac{5}{6})^3 = (\tfrac{5}{6})^3$$

$$P(X = 1) = \binom{3}{1} p^1 q^{(3-1)} = \frac{3!}{2!1!} (\tfrac{1}{6})^1 (\tfrac{5}{6})^2 = 3(\tfrac{1}{6})(\tfrac{5}{6})^2$$

$$P(X = 2) = \binom{3}{2} p^2 q^{(3-2)} = \frac{3!}{2!1!} (\tfrac{1}{6})^2 (\tfrac{5}{6})^1 = 3(\tfrac{1}{6})^2(\tfrac{5}{6})$$

$$P(X = 3) = \binom{3}{3} p^3 q^{(3-3)} = \frac{3!}{0!3!} (\tfrac{1}{6})^3 (\tfrac{5}{6})^0 = (\tfrac{1}{6})^3$$

In the above calculations, we used the fact that any number raised to the zero power is 1. Notice that these are the same probabilities that were generated from the tree diagram.

13-4. USING BINOMIAL PROBABILITY THEORY TO TEST A SIMPLE STATISTICAL HYPOTHESIS

One of the reasons for presenting binomial probability theory in some detail is that this model provides a simple introduction to statistical inference. As an example, consider an evaluation of an educational program designed to reduce recidivism among teenage boys who have been apprehended for the use of drugs on a high school campus. During the 4 years before the initiation of the new education program designed to reduce drug usage, 70 percent of the students arrested for drug abuse were apprehended a second time within 1 month of their initial arrest. After 1 year of the program, it was decided to test the program for effectiveness. As part of the evaluation, it was decided to use the month of October as a test period to determine whether the recidivism rate had *decreased*. If it had not decreased, the recidivism rate should be equal to 70 percent, whereas if it had decreased, the rate should be reduced. Thus, we wish to test:

$$H_0: \quad \text{Recidivism rate has not changed}$$

against:

$$H_1: \quad \text{Recidivism rate has reduced}$$

Transforming these into statistical hypotheses, we have:

$$H_0: \quad p = 0.7$$

and

$$H_1: \quad p < 0.7$$

We now need to construct a decision rule that tells us when to reject H_0. To do this we need to know how many trials were made during October, since we already know that with no change, $p = 0.7$. Because $N = 14$ arrests were made in October, we know that we are dealing with a binomial variable for which $p = 0.7$ and $N = 14$. If we now assume that apprehensions are distributed independently among the boys, we know that X has a binomial distribution so that:

$$P(X = x) = \binom{14}{x}(0.7)^x(0.3)^{N-x}$$

We can now construct an $\alpha = 0.05$ decision rule by building up the distribution of X, the number of boys arrested for a second time during the month of November. The probability values are shown in Table 13-1. Since the alternative hypothesis specifies that $p < 0.7$, we build up the critical region to include outcomes that are consistent with this alternative. We would never conclude that $p < 0.7$ if all 14 students were recidivists. The outcome that is most in agreement with the alternative is the one for which $X = 0$. The next is $X = 1$, etc. For the values in Table 13-1, we see that the $\alpha = 0.05$ critical

Table 13-1. Binomial probabilities for $N = 14$ and $p = 0.7$

Value of X	P(X = x)
14	$\binom{14}{14}(0.7)^{14}(0.3)^{0} = 0.0067822$
13	$\binom{14}{13}(0.7)^{13}(0.3)^{1} = 0.0406932$
12	$\binom{14}{12}(0.7)^{12}(0.3)^{2} = 0.1133596$
11	$\binom{14}{11}(0.7)^{11}(0.3)^{3} = 0.1943307$
10	$\binom{14}{10}(0.7)^{10}(0.3)^{4} = 0.2290326$
9	$\binom{14}{9}(0.7)^{9}(0.3)^{5} = 0.1963136$
8	$\binom{14}{8}(0.7)^{8}(0.3)^{6} = 0.1262016$
7	$\binom{14}{7}(0.7)^{7}(0.3)^{7} = 0.0618130$
6	$\binom{14}{6}(0.7)^{6}(0.3)^{8} = 0.0231798$
5	$\binom{14}{5}(0.7)^{5}(0.3)^{9} = 0.0066228$
4	$\binom{14}{4}(0.7)^{4}(0.3)^{10} = 0.0014192$
3	$\binom{14}{3}(0.7)^{3}(0.3)^{11} = 0.0002212$
2	$\binom{14}{2}(0.7)^{2}(0.3)^{12} = 0.0000237$
1	$\binom{14}{1}(0.7)^{1}(0.3)^{13} = 0.0000016$
0	$\binom{14}{0}(0.7)^{0}(0.3)^{14} = 0.0000000$
Total	0.9999948

region is defined by $X = 0, 1, 2, 3, 4, 5,$ and 6, since:

$$P(X \leq 6) = 0.0000000 + 0.0000016 + \cdots + 0.0231798$$
$$= 0.0314680$$

is less than $\alpha = 0.05$, whereas:

$$P(X \leq 7) = 0.0314680 + 0.0618130 = 0.0932810$$

exceeds $\alpha = 0.05$. Thus, our decision rule is given by:

Decision Rule: Reject H_0 if X is 0, 1, 2, 3, 4, 5, or 6

This example shows that it is not always possible to generate a decision rule where the probability is exactly equal to 0.05, 0.01, or any preassigned value. When this happens, it is customary to define the decision rule so that it is

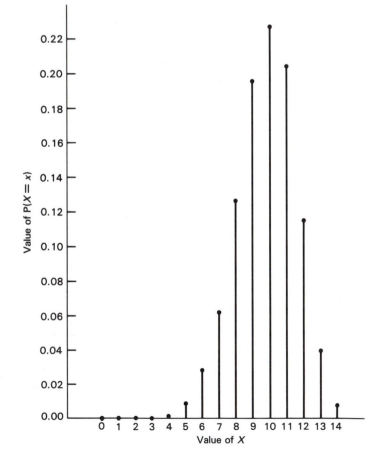

Figure 13-2.
The binomial distribution for $N = 14$ and $p = 0.7$.

smaller than the *nominal* value desired. In point of fact, three boys were arrested for a second time in November. Since X = 3 is in the critical region, the hypothesis is rejected and it is concluded that the recidivism rate has been reduced. The new education program appears to be effective.

For completeness, we provide the probabilities for the complete set of possible outcomes in graphic form in Figure 13-2.

13-5. EXERCISES

13-1. Given an unfair coin, whose probability of coming up heads on a given toss is P(H) = ¾, find the probability of getting four heads in five tosses.

13-2. A bag of sweets contains 20 pieces of candy, 15 of which a child likes and five of which he hates. He samples from the bag, at random, five times. Find the probability of his choosing four pieces he likes if he replaces the chosen piece each time.

13-3. A test contains four multiple choice items, each with four alternatives, one of which is correct. If you guess the answers to each question, purely at random, what is the probability that you get three or more correct answers on the test?

13-4. A "friend" possesses a coin reputed to be so fair that it always alternates heads and tails. Do you believe that the coin is fair? Why, or why not?

13-5. You want to determine if a die is fair, so you perform the following experiment: You roll the die ten times and note on how many rolls the number showing was either 1, 2, or 3. Before you roll the die, you make a decision rule that, if the numbers "3 or less" turn up on the die either 0, 1, 2, 8, 9, or 10 times, you will conclude the die is unfair. What is the probability that your decision will be wrong?

13-6. Using the formulas of this chapter, find the following. Show which formula you used in each calculation.

a. The number of ways three heads and 17 tails can occur in a toss of 20 coins.
b. The number of permutations of six distinct books.
c. The number of permutations of six books if three are identical.
d. The number of orders in which three out of six distinct books can be chosen.

13-7. Thirty percent of maze-bright rats can run a complicated maze correctly on the first trial. One hundred rats, of which 80 were maze-bright, were caged in an area that caught fire one evening. In saving the rats the cage labels of 14 rats were lost. It was thought that the 14 rats were maze-bright rats. Set up an $\alpha = 0.05$ decision rule for testing the rats to determine whether or not they were maze-bright. Specify H_0 and H_1. What is the decision if three of the rats ran the maze correctly on the first trial?

13-8. Ten percent of the customers going into an ice cream store order chocolate ice cream. One night, nine out of the first 16 customers ordered chocolate ice cream. Is this an unusual event? Why?

13-9. The median score on a standardized reading test is 500. In a class of 20 students, 16 had scores above 500. Does this suggest that the teacher is doing an outstanding job?

13-10. In a classroom of 27 students, 13 caught measles during the month of March. Can binomial theory be used to evaluate this event? Why?

13-11. Roulette tables in Nevada contain 18 red numbers, 18 black numbers, and two green numbers. A particular roulette wheel was spun 10 times and produced nine red outcomes and one green outcome. Should bettors be wary of this wheel?

13-12. In Nevada, a player needs to cover his "color" bet with $1, when playing roulette. If he bets on red, and red comes up, he gets his dollar bet back with one extra dollar. If a black or green comes up, he loses his dollar. Should a rational person play this game? Why?

13-13. If one bets $1 on red on each spin of a roulette wheel, as described in Exercise 13-11, how much money should one be expected to have after 100 spins of the wheel?

13-14. The state of California began issuing license plates with 7 characters as follows:

number, letter, letter, letter, number, number, number

How many license plates can be generated if all 26 letters, A, B, . . . Z and all 10 digits, 0, 1, . . . 9 are allowed repetition.

CHAPTER 14

The Sign Test

14-1. STATISTICAL HYPOTHESIS TESTING

In Chapters 11, 12, and 13, we presented a general description of statistical hypothesis testing using coin-tossing as an illustration. We now wish to move in the direction of the social scientist and show how the coin-tossing model can be used for testing behavioral hypotheses. This will entail a discussion of the sign test and an introduction to *confidence interval estimation theory*. At first, our presentation of confidence intervals will be descriptive and more in the form of *how to do it* and less in its theoretical aspects. The theory will come later and should be understandable, provided a few examples of its use have been mastered. Of all the statistical tests in use today, it is interesting to note that the oldest test is based on the coin-tossing model described earlier. We now describe it in detail.

14-2. THE SIGN TEST

The oldest known use of a statistical test procedure took place in 1710. At that time, Dr. John Arbuthnott, the personal physician to Queen Anne, used the birth registration statistics of the City of London to test the hypothesis that Divine Providence ensured that the proportion of males born in the city exceeded the proportion of females born during the same time period. His test procedure was based upon the coin-tossing model that was presented in the previous chapters. The sex of a child could be associated with the tossing of a coin in that the appearance of a head was analogous to the birth of a boy, while the appearance of a tail was analogous to the birth of a girl. If the probability of a male birth were equal to ½, then over a 20-year period one would expect males to outnumber females about half the time, while females would outnumber males the remaining half of the time. This means that the decision rule of Section 11-4 could be used to test the hypothesis that over a 20-year period the probability of a male birth equalled the probability of a female birth. The decision rule would be to reject the hypothesis of equal probabilities if males outnumbered females for 0, 1, 2, 3, 4, 5, 15, 16, 17, 18, 19, or 20 years. Actually, Arbuthnott obtained records for more than 20 years and found that males were born in consistently greater numbers than were females, a finding which is true, even today. While Arbuthnott thought that males were born in greater numbers so as to fight wars and contribute to economic and social progress, modern day geneticists have different, often biochemical, hypotheses to explain the greater number of male births.

As a more contemporary use of this test, consider a study in which an educational psychologist wishes to determine whether or not verbal or candy reinforcement after correct responses would help preschool children learn the distinctions between *greater than, equal to,* and *less than.* Because individual differences in intelligence could influence the outcome of the study, teachers were asked to rank order a sample of students according to perceived intelligence and ability to solve problems involving spatial relationships. Once the children were rank ordered, they were paired, with the two highest ranking students constituting the first pair, the next two ranking students constituting the second pair, and the two lowest ranking students constituting the last pair. The members of each pair were then assigned, on the basis of a coin toss, to either a candy reinforcement schedule or a verbal reinforcement schedule. This randomization process was performed to ensure that all uncontrollable variables are approximately equally distributed between the children in the candy and verbal reinforcement conditions of the study. Once the assignment was completed, each child was instructed and tested individually by the researcher. During the instruction and testing period, 15 problems were given to each child. Five involved the concept of *greater than,* five involved the concept of *equal to,* and five involved the concept of *less than.*

We can think of the 14 pairs of students as representing some large universe of paired children. The independent variable of the study consists of the two reinforcement conditions: candy and verbal. These conditions define two hypothetical universes of children with each universe identified with the reinforcement conditions. The dependent measure is the number of correct responses. This variable has a distribution that may differ across the two conditions. We hypothesize that the two distributions are identical.

Suppose this hypothesis were true and suppose we treated each matched pair of subjects as a single unit. We can do this by computing a difference score for each pair and checking to see whether or not the candy reinforcement subject obtained a higher score than his or her verbal reinforcement control subject. If the distributions were identical, about half of the differences would be positive and half would be negative. Thus, the hypothesis could be stated as H_0: $P(+) = P(-) = 0.5$. In this form, we see that we are testing a hypothesis about the parameter of a binomial variable. With this in mind, let us examine the data reported in Table 14-1.

Table 14-1. Number of correct solutions made by 14 pairs of preschool children that were randomly assigned to a candy or a verbal reinforcement schedule in the learning of the concepts *Greater Than, Equal To,* or *Less Than*

Pair	Type of Reinforcement		Difference score	Sign
	Candy	Verbal		
1	12	13	−1	−
2	13	12	+1	+
3	10	15	−5	−
4	14	8	+6	+
5	12	13	−1	−
6	9	12	−3	−
7	13	10	+3	+
8	8	9	−1	−
9	6	8	−2	−
10	9	13	−4	−
11	5	8	−3	−
12	7	9	−2	−
13	8	4	+4	+
14	1	8	−7	−

The first thing to note is that the scores decrease as the pair number increases. This is expected since the children were rank ordered on the subjective perceptions of teacher ratings of intelligence and aptitude. It is also seen that in four of the pairs, the difference in the candy and verbal scores is positive (+). In these pairs, children given the candy reinforcement outperformed their matched pair assigned to the verbal reinforcement group. On the other hand, 10 children in the verbal reinforcement condition outperformed their matched pair assigned to the candy reinforcement condition, so that differences in candy and verbal scores for these pairs is negative (−). If one had a decision rule related to the number of positive or negative deviations, one could make a judgment as to which of the two methods aided the learning of the three related concepts.

Because the criterion variable for the test is based upon the number of positive and negative differences, this test is called the sign test. Under this model, the generation of the decision rule is very simple. If we let X equal the number of positive differences, we can find the probability that 0, 1, 2, . . . , 13, 14 of the pairs have a higher score in the candy reinforcement condition. If chance is the sole explanation of what occurs, then

P(Candy reinforcement score > Verbal reinforcement score)
$$= P(\text{plus deviation}) = P(\text{negative deviation}) = \tfrac{1}{2}$$

so that, under binomial theory

$$P(X = 0) = \binom{14}{0}(\tfrac{1}{2})^0(\tfrac{1}{2})^{14}$$

$$P(X = 1) = \binom{14}{1}(\tfrac{1}{2})^1(\tfrac{1}{2})^{13}$$
etc.

Fortunately, we do not have to compute these probabilities to set up the decision rule for this investigation or for any other investigation based on a coin-tossing model, since tables of decision rules have been prepared by others. One such table is given in the Appendix as Table A-2. This table is titled "Critical Values for the Sign Test." It is entered by specifying the value of N, the number of matched pairs, and α, the probability of a type I error. If we set α equal to 0.05, we can read the decision rule for $N = 14$ by entering Table A-2 in the percentile columns headed 0.025 and 0.975. These percentile values are selected since we wish $\alpha/2$ to be in the lower and upper tails of the distribution. We split the α equally between the two tails because there is no way to know before the experiment begins which method of training will be superior. For the two tabled percentile values, we read in Table A-2 the two numbers 2 and 12. These critical values define the $\alpha = 0.05$ two-tailed decision rule for testing the identity of the two population distributions. In particular, the decision rule is:

Decision Rule: Reject the hypothesis of the identity of distributions if the number of positive differences among the matched pairs is given by 0, 1, 2, 12, 13, or 14.

In this case, the number of positive deviations equals 4. Therefore, we do not reject the hypothesis. We conclude that no statistically significant difference exists between the candy and verbal reinforcement conditions. Thus, the independent variable, type of reinforcement, has no influence on the dependent variable, number of correct responses. Remember that this decision may not be valid. There is the chance that a type II error has been made. Just because a tested hypothesis has not been rejected, one does not have proof that H_0 is true. One only has data that is not incompatible with H_0. So, when it is said that type of reinforcement has no influence on the dependent variable, an understanding of what is meant must be supplied. Technically, one should only say that H_0 has not been rejected or that no evidence has been found that H_0 is false. Until more, or better, data are collected, one is advised to act as though H_0 is true. Whether or not it *is* true can never be known with certainty. It is an unfortunate state of affairs, but it is the one that exists with the statistical hypothesis testing model.

As this example illustrates, the sign test is a very simple test to perform. Perhaps that is why it is the first recorded statistical test. The steps for the performance of the sign test are given in Box 14-1.

Box 14-1   How to perform the sign test

Step 1. State the hypothesis to be tested. In particular, the hypothesis states that the median of the difference values is zero. In statistical form, H_0 is given by:

$$H_0: \quad P(+) = P(-) = 0.5$$

Step 2. Select the risk of a type I error that one is willing to accept. Most social scientists are satisfied if $\alpha = 0.05$.

Step 3. Let X = number of positive differences in the sample. Use Table A-2 to obtain the appropriate decision rule.

Step 4. Collect the data and determine the number of positive differences, X.

Step 5. Make a decision. If X is in the critical region, reject H_0. If X is not in the critical region, don't reject H_0.

14-3. ASSUMPTIONS TO JUSTIFY THE SIGN TEST

The justification of the sign test is easy to achieve. In fact, of all statistical tests that have been developed by statisticians, this is the easiest one to justify. It is based on one major assumption and that is that the observations between matched pairs are statistically independent. This means that measurements made on any one pair can in no way influence the measurements made on any other pair. In the example, independence was attained by the individual testing of each child. This could have been destroyed if the children had been permitted to talk to one another about their individual experiences with the tester. It is hoped that the tester told the children not to discuss the instruction and testing period with children who had not been previously tested and that the children followed this advice, if it was given. If the observations between the pairs are correlated, the test is invalid. Correlation within the pairs is of no danger. In fact, it is expected and desired. If there is no correlation within the pairs, it turns out that the sign test is not a very effective test. Other tests exist that are better. This suggests that an implicit assumption of the sign test is that paired observations are correlated. If they are not, the test should not be performed.

Because the sign test is actually a test of H_0: $P(+) = P(-) = \frac{1}{2}$, and since our dependent measures are quantitative difference scores, we need to be more exact in our statement of H_0. As we know, the median divides the distribution of a quantitative variable into two equal segments, so that $P(+) = P(-) = \frac{1}{2}$. The mean does not, unless the distribution is symmetrical. Thus, the sign test must be related to the median of a distribution and not to the mean, unless the distribution is symmetrical. In most research studies there is no way to determine whether or not this condition has been satisfied because of the small number of observations. Because the test is based on difference scores, a correct statement of H_0 is that the median value of the difference scores is zero, that is, H_0: $M_d = 0$. Note that with this notation we are making a distinction between a sample statistic and a population parameter. The sample median difference is denoted by $\hat{M}_d$, whereas the population median difference is denoted by M_d. The distinction between sample statistics and population parameters is maintained throughout this book.

The distinction between a mean difference and a median difference may be confusing the first time around. For the data of Table 14-1, $\bar{Y}_C = 9.07$, $\bar{Y}_V = 10.14$, and $\bar{Y}_d = -1.07$. In addition, we see that $\bar{Y}_C - \bar{Y}_V = -1.07$, so that $\bar{Y}_d$ is, indeed, equal to $\bar{Y}_C - \bar{Y}_V$. However, this relationship does not hold for the medians. For the data of Table 14-1, $\hat{M}_C = 9.5$, $\hat{M}_V = 9.5$, and $\hat{M}_d = -1.5$. Thus, we see that $\hat{M}_C - \hat{M}_V \neq \hat{M}_d$.

Thus, the sign test cannot be used to test:

$$H_0: \quad M_C - M_V = 0$$

Instead, it is used to test:

$$H_0: \quad M_d = 0$$

If we rank order the differences for the data of Table 14-1, we obtain the following ordered values:

$$-7, -5, -4, -3, -3, -2, -2, -1, -1, -1, +1, +3, +4, +6$$

For this ranking, the median difference is equal to:

$$\hat{M}_d = \frac{d_7^0 + d_8^0}{2} = \frac{-2 - 1}{2} = -1.5$$

a number not too distant from $M_d = 0$. Note that, even though the observed sample median difference is equal to -1.5, we still make the strong conclusion that the unknown population median difference is equal to zero.

14-4. THE CONFIDENCE INTERVAL FOR THE MEDIAN DIFFERENCE OF THE SIGN TEST

Every research study entails the risk of making a type I error. This occurs whenever the tested hypothesis is rejected, when in point of fact, it should be retained as true or as perhaps true until better and stronger evidence against its truth has been obtained. In the example, we have concluded that the differences between candy and verbal reinforcements are not *statistically significant*. By this it is meant that H_0 was not rejected by the sign test. The decision could be wrong.

Scientists in the hard sciences have known of the existance of errors in measurement almost from the birth of their sciences. Even their best measurements are made with error, and, as a consequence, they report their measurements with an estimate of the magnitude of the error. In reporting the temperature at which an unknown solid melts, a metallurgist would not hesitate to state that the melting point of this material is $936° \pm 5°$. The best estimate of the temperature at which the material melts is $936°$, but it could be any temperature between $936° - 5° = 931°$ and $936° + 5° = 941°$. In terms of a continuous interval, one might say that the melting point of this unknown solid is given by $931° \leq X° \leq 941°$.

This method of summarizing statistical findings has been widely adopted by statisticians. The method is based upon a specification of a type I error that one is willing to tolerate in testing the hypothesis of no difference or no effect of the independent variable upon the dependent variable. The method can be illustrated with the data of Table 14-1.

As indicated by the interval for the example using the melting point of an unknown solid, our goal is to specify a set of populations from which we think our sample could have come. In doing so, we begin by postulating a single value for the median difference of the population and then determining whether or not our sample values seem to fit with the postulated median difference. If the sample value seems to be like the kind we would expect when sampling from the population, we feel that the postulated value *could be* the median difference of the *actual* population from which the sample was drawn. We then postulate a different value for the population median and evaluate its likelihood when compared to the sample. We repeat the process until we have the entire set of values that we think the population median difference is likely to be.

Our decision concerning whether or not the sample could reasonably have come from a population with a certain postulated median is based on the same statistical logic as we used for the sign test. Let's review that logic. We postulate as a null hypothesis that the median difference in the population is zero. If this is so, then we think that the differences in the sample should reflect this by half being positive and half being negative. Of course, we know the sample values will only rarely be precisely half negative. Even though we can examine only the outcome of one experiment, we conceptualize the observed experiment to be one of a large number of similar experiments that could hypothetically be conducted. Using probability laws, we calculate that in 95 percent of the hypothetical experiments, the number of values less than the postulated population median *should* range from 3 to 11. With the number of differences less than the median denoted X, then if H_0 is true we would expect $X \leq 2$ or $X \geq 12$ to occur in less than 5 percent of the large number of hypothetical experiments.

Whereas the value of the postulated median difference, $M_d = 0$, is of primary interest in the testing situation, the logic just outlined could be applied to any hypothesized population median. For example, let's suppose the population median difference was given by $M_d = 1$. Then the number of differences in the sample less than $+1$ should be close to one-half. Only 5 percent of the time would we expect the sample to contain $X \leq 2$ or $X \geq 12$ differences less than $+1$. In our sample, 10 differences were less than $+1$, 3 were larger, and one equaled $+1$. Since 10 is not an unreasonable number of differences less than $+1$ to be found in the sample, we would not reject the hypothesis that the population median difference was $+1$. Similarly, if we postulate a population median difference of $M_d = +3$, we would have 11 sample differences smaller than the hypothetical value. This is still within the expected range.

But as soon as we postulate a population median difference greater than $+3$, for example, $M_d = 3.001$, we find 12 differences in our sample less than this value. Thus, we feel that the largest value the population median could be, while not being too incompatible with our sample values, would be $+3$. In a similar fashion, we would postulate smaller values than zero as possible population medians. We would find that, as soon as we hypothesize a value less than -4, for example, $M_d = -4.003$, we would have only two sample values which were smaller. Thus, -4 would be the lowest reasonable population median difference. We would state that it is reasonable to conclude that the population median difference was between -4 and $+3$, or:

$$-4 \leq M_d \leq +3$$

In terms of this interval, it would be said that the population median difference is unknown, but it is probably no less than -4 and no greater than $+3$.

One does not have to test many values to determine these limits. The procedure we have just examined can be simplified greatly. We have ordered the data from smallest to largest in Section 14-3. This ordered listing is:

$$-7, -5, -4, -3, -3, -2, -2, -1, -1, -1, +1, +3, +4, +6$$

We have seen that a plausible set of hypothesized population median values was given by:

$$-4 \leq M_d \leq +3$$

Let us now examine the connection between the critical value of 2, our ordered sample data, and this interval of plausible values for the population median. The lower limit for this interval, $M_{\text{Lower}} = -4$, is the third ordered data point from the bottom, whereas the upper limit for the interval, $M_{\text{Upper}} = +3$, is the third ordered sample value from the top. The reason that the limits on the interval are the third from the bottom and top is that the critical value for the test equals two. It is the third ordered sample value from the bottom that has two numbers less than it, and it is the third ordered sample value from the top that has two numbers greater than it. The decision rule is related to the limits on the interval through the lower critical value for the test. If we let the lower critical value be specified as L, then the lower limit for the interval is the sample value d^o_{L+1}. In a similar fashion, the upper limit would be $L + 1$ places from the top. If we denote the upper critical value for the test as U, then the sample value that is $(L + 1)$ places from the top is equal to d^o_U. Hence, the interval of plausible population values is given by:

$$d^o_{L+1} \leq M_d \leq d^o_U$$

In terms of our present example, $L = 2$ and $U = 12$, so the interval is:

$$d^o_3 \leq M_d \leq d^o_{12}$$

which is

$$-4 \leq M_d \leq +3$$

The interpretation of this interval is important and must be understood. Many research findings are based upon this model. In our example, we do not know the true value of M_d in the universe of matched pair difference values. According to the sample results, it could be as low as -4 with the scores on the verbal reinforcement condition exceeding those on the candy condition by 4 points. On the other hand, it could be as high as $+3$ points with the candy condition being more effective than the verbal condition. We just don't know the truth on the basis of these data. Since $M_d = 0$ is in the interval, we will risk saying that no difference exists. This is exactly the same decision that was made with the sign test. This is always the case. If the interval includes zero, the sign test will lead to nonrejection of H_0. If the interval does not include zero, the sign test will lead to the rejection of H_0. This means that a test of the hypothesis can be performed by using the interval that is believed to contain the value of the unknown population parameter. If zero is in the interval, the hypothesis is not rejected. If zero is not in the interval, the hypothesis is rejected.

The interval computed by this procedure is called a *confidence interval*. A confidence interval defines a range of values for the unknown parameter that are compatible with the sample statistics. Thus, the sample median of $\hat{M}_d = -1.5$ could be generated from a population in which the median difference is between a low value of -4 and a high value of $+3$. Since this interval was based upon a risk of a probability of a type I error controlled at $\alpha = 0.05$, the interval is called a 95-percent confidence interval. Because confidence intervals play a major role in empirical research, we provide a general definition that will find repeated applications in the rest of this book.

Definition of a confidence interval

Consider a population and any parameter that defines some characteristic of the population. Let us denote this parameter of interest with the Greek letter θ (theta). With the risk of a type I error set at α, determine from the sample the $\alpha/2$ and $1 - \alpha/2$ estimate of the lower and upper limit for θ. Let these limits be θ_{Lower} and θ_{Upper}. The $(1 - \alpha)$ percent confidence interval for θ is defined as the range of values of the unknown parameter that is compatible with the sample statistic. Algebraically, it is denoted as:

$$\theta_{\text{Lower}} \le \theta \le \theta_{\text{Upper}}$$

If we wanted, we could have defined a 99-percent confidence interval by using the decision rule based on the 0.005 and 0.995 critical values. According to the figures of Table A-2, the critical values are given by $L = 1$ and $U = 13$. Therefore, the limits for the 99-percent confidence interval would be defined by $d_{L+1}^o = d_2^o$ and $d_U^o = d_{13}^o$. For these values, $d_2^o = -5$ and $d_{13}^o = +4$, so that the 99-percent confidence interval for the median difference is given by:

$$-5 \leq M_d \leq +4$$

As can be seen, this interval is considerably wider than that obtained for the 95-percent confidence interval. This is to be expected because a 99-percent confidence interval has a smaller probability of a type I error. Thus one can reduce the probability of a type I error to a very small value, if desired, but the problem in doing so is that the confidence interval expands in size so that the reduced risk of a type I error produces an interval that has less utilitarian value. For that reason, most researchers in the social sciences let $\alpha = 0.05$, and this is what we will do in the remaining chapters. The procedure for setting up a confidence interval is described in Box 14-2.

As a final note to this section, we note that the theory used to obtain a confidence interval for the median difference can be used to obtain a confidence interval for the *median* of a population. As an example, consider the ordered observations for the candy reinforcement group. The ordered values are given by:

$$1, 5, 6, 7, 8, 8, 9, 9, 10, 12, 12, 13, 13, 14$$

The third ordered values from either end of the above series are $Y_3^o = 6$ and

---

Box 14-2   How to determine the confidence interval for M_d of the sign test

Step 1. Select the value of α. Most social scientists let $\alpha = 0.05$.

Step 2. Determine the decision rule from Table A-2. Let the rule be:

$$\text{Reject } H_0 \text{ if } X \leq L, \text{ or if } X \geq U$$

Step 3. Rank order the differences as:

$$d_1^o, d_2^o, \ldots, d_{N-1}^o, d_N^o$$

Step 4. Find the two limiting values defined by:

$$d_{L+1}^o \quad \text{and} \quad d_U^o$$

Step 5. Report the confidence interval as:

$$d_{L+1}^o \leq M_d \leq d_U^o$$

$Y_{13}^0 = 13$. Thus, the 95-percent confidence interval for M_C is given by:

$$6 \le M_C \le 13$$

In like manner, the 95-percent confidence interval for the verbal reinforcement group is given by:

$$8 \le M_V \le 13$$

14-5. THE PROBLEM OF DEVIATIONS EQUAL TO ZERO

In most matched-pair studies of the social sciences, deviations whose values are equal to zero are encountered. Such deviations cannot be counted as positive deviations or as negative deviations. The counting solution used most frequently for this situation is to count each zero deviation as half of a plus sign. For example, suppose a study with 22 pairs has eight positive deviations, nine negative deviations, and five zero deviations. The five zero deviations are reassigned equally to the positive and negative deviations, to give $8 + \frac{1}{2}(5) = 10.5$ plus deviations and $9 + \frac{1}{2}(5) = 11.5$ negative deviations. These figures are then used to conduct the sign test and to obtain the confidence interval.

14-6. ONE- AND TWO-TAILED TESTS

The example of Section 14-4 has been based upon an alternative hypothesis that stated that the unknown median difference was not equal to zero. Another alternative could be that the median difference was greater than zero. These two alternatives illustrate what are called two- and one-tailed tests. Most research performed in the social sciences is based upon two-tailed alternatives, although one-tailed alternatives can be justified in many cases. In the previous example, one could justify a one-tailed alternative if the theory suggested, for example, that verbal reinforcement was more effective.

In testing two-tailed hypotheses, the risk of a type I error is split equally between the two tails of the distribution of the test statistic. We do so because we are willing to reject the two-tailed null hypothesis, $H_0: M_d = 0$, if the median difference of the population from which our sample came is either larger or smaller than zero. In the one-tailed case, however, we are only interested in rejecting the null hypothesis if the median difference of the population from which our sample came is different from zero in the specified direction. If the theory were true, and verbal reinforcement is more effective, we would be wasting the type I error probability assigned to the inappropriate tail. If the goal of the study is to increase the median score as much as possible, the researcher is truly interested in testing a one-tailed alternative. Hence, in testing this alternative, we do not split our alpha into two parts.

The null hypothesis of interest states that the candy reinforcement produces scores that are higher than, or equivalent to, those produced by the verbal reinforcement. The alternative hypothesis is that the candy reinforcement yields lower scores than the verbal reinforcement. Recall that our difference scores were calculated by subtracting the values in the verbal condition from those in the candy condition. That is:

$$d = \text{Candy score} - \text{Verbal score}$$

Under the null hypothesis, since the candy reinforcement scores are higher than, or equal to, the verbal scores, we should tend to get positive or zero differences. Hence, we write:

$$H_0: \quad M_d \geq 0$$

Similarly, under the alternative hypothesis the candy scores should be lower than the verbal, and we write:

$$H_1: \quad M_d < 0$$

The test criterion, X, is the number of positive differences in the sample. Under H_0, we would expect many such differences. The only way we would be convinced that H_0 was false would be to find very few positive differences in the sample. Therefore, we put all of our α into the lower end of the distribution of the number of positive differences, X, creating a rejection region that contains α percent of the smallest possible X values. For our example, the one-sided critical value for the test of the alternative $M_d < 0$ is found in Table A-2, for $N = 14$ and $\alpha = 0.05$, to be equal to 3. Our decision rule would be:

Decision Rule: Reject H_0 if $X \leq 3$.

In this case, since there were $X = 4$ positive signs, we would again not reject H_0. If the alternative had been $M_d > 0$, we would have used the critical value at the upper end of the distribution. For this alternative, the decision rule would be:

Decision Rule: Reject H_0 if $X \geq 11$.

Following the discussion of confidence intervals in Section 14-4, we can also build one-tailed confidence intervals. We again seek values of the population median difference that are consistent with our data.

At this point, we could repeat the argument presented earlier for two-

---

Box 14-3 **Procedure for setting up one-tailed confidence intervals using the sign test**

Step 1. Find the critical value, L, in Table A-2 for N and α.

Step 2. If the alternative hypothesis states that $M_d > 0$, the confidence interval is given by:

$$M_d \geq d^o_{L+1}$$

Step 3. If the alternative hypothesis states that $M_d < 0$, the confidence interval is given by:

$$M_d \leq d^o_{N-L}$$

---

tailed confidence intervals, but because of redundancy, we simply provide directions for finding the appropriate critical values in the sign test table and for setting up the one-sided confidence interval. As a first step, find the critical value, L, associated with N and α. If the alternative states that $M_d < 0$, the appropriate limit for the one-sided confidence interval is d^o_{N-L}. For our example, $N = 14$ and $\alpha = 0.05$, $L = 3$, so that the limit $d^o_{N-L} = d^o_{14-3} = d^o_{11} = +1$. Our confidence interval is given by:

$$M_d \leq +1$$

Note that $M_d = 0$ is in this interval. This agrees with the corresponding test of H_0. On the other hand, if the alternative states that $M_d > 0$, the appropriate limit is d^o_{L+1}, and the confidence interval is given by:

$$M_d \geq d^o_{L+1}$$

We provide directions for one-tailed confidence intervals for the median difference based on sign test theory in Box 14-3.

14-7. CONFIDENCE INTERVALS FOR PERCENTILES

In the previous sections we described procedures for estimating the median difference in terms of a point or an interval estimate. As indicated in Section 14-4, the same model can be used to estimate the median of a population. To do this one follows the steps of Boxes 14-2 and 14-3 using the ordered values $Y^o_1, Y^o_2, \ldots, Y^o_N$ in place of the ordered $d^o_1, d^o_2, \ldots, d^o_N$.

Also we now see how to obtain the confidence interval for any percentile value of any population. For example, to find the confidence interval for the third quartile, one determines $X = L$ and $X = U$ using the binomial formula with $p = 0.75$ and $q = 0.25$. Thus, the lower limit is found by determining the largest L that makes:

$$\sum_{x=0}^{L} \binom{N}{x}(0.75)^x(0.25)^{N-x} \leq 0.025$$

and the smallest U that makes:

$$\sum_{x=U}^{N} \binom{N}{x}(0.75)^x(0.25)^{N-x} \leq 0.025$$

These values of L and U are used to give the 95-percent confidence interval for Q_3 as:

$$Y_{L+1}^{\circ} \leq Q_3 \leq Y_U^{\circ}$$

14-8. EXERCISES

14-1. Comment about the internal and external validity of the study reported in Table 14-1.

14-2. Use the sign test to analyze the data of a study in which the effectiveness of a drug to induce relaxed sleep was being made. Sixteen patients were identified who reported that their sleep for the previous three nights was very disturbed and not at all relaxing. These 16 patients were given the drug and upon waking the next morning were asked how their sleep was, when compared to the three previous nights. Their responses were as follows:

1. Better	9. Better
2. Better	10. The same
3. Better	11. Better
4. Worse	12. The same
5. The same	13. Worse
6. Better	14. Better
7. Better	15. Better
8. Worse	16. The same

a. Analyze the data by discarding responses of *The same*.

b. Analyze the data by assigning *The same* responses to *Better* and *Worse* so as to make rejection of the hypothesis more difficult.

c. Use a coin to assign *The same* responses to the choices *Better* and *Worse* and then analyze the data.

d. Of the three methods which do you prefer? What are the advantages and disadvantages in the use of these three methods to break tied observations?

14-3. As part of a reading study, 26 children were rank ordered on the basis of a reading readiness test. They were then paired. By means of a coin toss, one member of each pair was assigned to either a traditional reading program or to a new innovative program. Following five weeks of training, the students were tested on a 25-item test. The results were as shown in the following table.

Pair	Score under traditional program	Score under new program
1	25	24
2	23	25
3	19	23
4	22	18
5	12	17
6	18	20
7	19	16
8	6	14
9	11	13
10	4	10
11	7	8
12	10	12
13	6	15

Note that the test is top heavy; that is, many students passed most of the items suggesting that the test was perhaps too easy. However, is there any reason to believe that the new program is any better than the old program in its effect upon the scores on the particular reading test given to the students to assess the effectiveness of the new program? Which is a better statement of the hypothesis under test?

$$H_0: \quad \mu_1 - \mu_2 = 0$$

or

$$H_0: \quad M_d = 0$$

Defend your answer.

14-4. Find the mean and median on the final for the two experimental conditions in your sample of size 40. Find the difference in the means and the difference in the medians for the two groups. Find the mean and median of the difference scores. Does $\hat{M}_d = \hat{M}_1 - \hat{M}_2$,

and does $\bar{Y}_d = \bar{Y}_1 - \bar{Y}_2$? Explain what is going on. What bearing does this have on the interpretation of a sign test decision?

14-5. Why is the lower limit to the confidence interval for M_d defined by X_{L+1}°, and not by X_L°?

14-6. If one thinks about our introduction to the sign test in terms of the hypothesis tested by Dr. John Arbuthnott, it becomes clear that he was only interested in alternatives where $p > \frac{1}{2}$. What would be the decision rule for the test if $N = 20$?

14-7. In a study of reading, an investigator obtained measurements on the number of eye fixations per line of print for 20 normal first-grade children. The results are as shown. Find a 95-percent confidence interval for the median number of fixations.

Adina	9.2
Bill	23.8
Carolyn	13.8
Denise	22.6
Elvira	13.8
Francine	30.8
Georgetta	14.0
Harold	10.3
Ira	19.4
Joyce	13.7
Kevin	22.9
Leonard	12.6
Mary	18.6
Nellie	More than 40
Peter	13.6
Quincy	14.7
Ruthie	More than 40
Sadie	More than 40
Terence	38.2
Ollie	More than 40

14-8. In a study in which visually handicapped children were tested, the median number of fixations per line was found to be 37.9. Are the data of Exercise 14-7 compatible with this median value?

14-9. In a study in which two methods for teaching children how to read were being tested, two different teacher-made tests were used to evaluate the teaching methods. Results are as shown for four different classrooms of children for pre-assigned matched pairs. Is there reason to believe that one method is superior to the other? Use the results shown here.

School 1 (Test 1)				School 2 (Test 2)			
Class A		Class B		Class C		Class D	
M_1	M_2	M_1	M_2	M_1	M_2	M_1	M_2
8	13	10	15	28	31	28	36
9	10	12	9	26	22	29	25
15	20	13	16	27	21	28	28
14	18	14	18	40	50	26	31
13	12	5	7	42	49	40	41
		8	6	47	50		
		12	20	36	39		

14-10. Why can the sign test be justified for the data of Exercise 14-9? Is one sign test based on all four classes treated as one group better than four separate sign tests applied to each separate group? Why?

14-11. The binomial distribution with $p = \frac{1}{2}$ and any N can be used to test H_0: $p = \frac{1}{2}$. As an example, consider a study in which $N = 20$ mice are given two trials to run a T maze in which food is placed in the right turn runway. Would you say that the mice have learned the maze if 16 turn to the right on the third trial?

14-12. In a study in which a new reading program was compared to an old program, the following statistics were generated. Analyze each program with $\alpha_{OLD} = \alpha_{NEW} = 0.05$.

Number of students who	Old program	New program	Total
Improved	3	12	15
Did not improve	17	8	25
Total	20	20	40

14-13. In Exercise 14-12 you were asked to perform each statistical test with $\alpha = 0.05$. What is the total risk of a type I error under these directions?

14-14. Compute the ϕ coefficient for the data of Exercise 14-12. Relate it to the conclusions you made in Exercise 14-12. There is a problem. Explain what is happening.

14-15. Use Exercise 14-12 and 14-14 as models and examine the following data to determine whether boys and girls in a 3rd-grade class are guessing when choosing between True and False to a test question that is appropriate for a 6th-grade class.

Response	Boys	Girls	Total
Correct	18	16	34
Wrong	4	3	7
Total	22	19	41

CHAPTER 15

Combinations and Hypergeometric Probability Theory

15-1. SAMPLING WITHOUT REPLACEMENT

In Chapter 13, we derived formulas for calculating probabilities associated with binomial trials. Using a tree diagram, we were able to see that all orders of outcomes leading to a particular coin-flipping result had the same probability. For example, a head followed by a tail in two flips of a fair coin has the same probability as a tail followed by a head. To derive the binomial probability formula, we simply found the probability of any particular order and then multiplied this probability by the number of orders possible. Because the sign test could be formulated in terms of a sequence of independent binomial trials, we could use binomial theory to set up acceptance and rejection regions for this test. Unfortunately, the binomial probability model does not allow us to calculate the probabilities required for testing two population proportions for equality or for certain other tests. In order to do so, we will need to examine a model for which the trials are not independent and for which the probabilities of particular outcomes can change as the trials proceed. In this chapter, we will examine these probability calculations by considering the model of sampling without replacement.

As an example of changing probabilities across trials, consider the selection of two playing cards from a 52-card bridge deck. If one draws a heart on the first draw, the probability of drawing a heart on the second draw is given by $P = {}^{12}\!/\!{}_{51}$, but if a card other than a heart is drawn on the first draw, the probability of drawing a heart on the second draw is given by $P = {}^{13}\!/\!{}_{51}$. In this case, the probabilities change after the first trial, because the deck contains 52 cards on the first drawing and 51 on the second. We say that the deck of cards represents a universe with a *finite* number of elements. If we were to replace the first card in the deck before we drew the second card, the distinction would be unnecessary because at both trials the probability of a heart would be given by $P = {}^{13}\!/\!{}_{52} = {}^{1}\!/\!{}_{4}$, so that binomial theory could be applied. However, in research we rarely, if ever, return subjects to the universe so that they may be selected a second, third, fourth, etc., time. In research, we sample without replacement. Thus, there is another good reason for examining sampling without replacement. In order to examine probabilities associated with sampling without replacement, we will present the concept of conditional probabilities and the hypergeometric probability formula.

15-2. CONDITIONAL PROBABILITY

Consider again the five books, A through E, from Chapter 13. The probability of selecting book A first is $\frac{1}{5}$, as we have seen. What is the probability of selecting book A *second*? If we replace the book on the shelf after we select it, then the probability remains $\frac{1}{5}$. There is still one A out of five books when we select the second book. This is true regardless of which book we selected first. Thus, when sampling with replacement, the probabilities on a particular trial do not depend on what has gone before: the trials are *independent.*

On the other hand, if we do not replace the books after we select them, then the probability of selecting A second *depends* on which book was selected first. If the first book was A, then there is no A to be selected second and the probability of A would be zero. If any other book than A has been selected first, then out of the four books remaining, one is an A, and the probability would be $\frac{1}{4}$. We say that the process of sampling without replacement involves *dependent* trials, since the probabilities for a given trial depend on the particular configuration present at that time.

We see, then, that when trials are not independent, there is no unambiguous answer to the question, "What is the probability of selecting A second?" Without further information one must respond, "It depends." To aid our discussion, we will introduce the term *conditional probability* so that the above question has a definite answer. We can then respond, "If A was selected first, then the probability of selecting A second is zero." We use the symbol $P(E_2|E_1)$ to represent "the probability that E_2 occurs, given E_1 also occurs." Thus:

$$P(\text{A second}|\text{no A first}) = \frac{1}{4}$$

indicates that the probability of selecting A second is ¼ if any book other than A is selected first.

To calculate conditional probabilities, we limit ourselves only to those outcomes that satisfy the given condition. For the situation above, there are 16 cases that have a non-A selected first. They are:

BA, BC, BD, BE, CA, CB, CD, CE, DA, DB, DC, DE, EA, EB, EC, ED

These 16 outcomes are the only cases that satisfy the given condition. Of these, only four contain an A second. Hence:

$$P(\text{A second}|\text{no A first}) = \frac{4}{16} = \frac{1}{4}$$

as before. Notice that the denominator is the number of events in which a book other than A can be selected first, and the numerator represents the number of events in which a non-A was selected first and then an A was selected second. We can generalize this result to form a definition of conditional probability.

Definition of conditional probability

Let E_1 occur in $n(E_1)$ ways, and let E_1 and E_2 occur together in $n(E_1 \text{ and } E_2)$ ways. Then the conditional probability of E_2, given that E_1 also occurs, is defined as:

$$P(E_2|E_1) = \frac{n(E_1 \text{ and } E_2)}{n(E_1)}$$

15-3. MULTIPLICATION RULE FOR JOINT OCCURRENCE OF EVENTS

In Section 15-2, we saw that a conceptual way to define independent events would be that *independence* refers to two outcomes whose individual occurrences do not affect the probabilities of one another. We shall now see how the concept of conditional probability can allow us to calculate the probability of two events occurring together. From the definition of probability presented in Chapter 11, we have for the probability of E_1 and E_2 occurring together:

$$P(E_1 \text{ and } E_2) = \frac{n(E_1 \text{ and } E_2)}{n(A)}$$

where $n(A)$ is the number of ways that any event can happen. If we now multiply and divide the right side by $n(E_1)$, we have:

$$P(E_1 \text{ and } E_2) = \frac{n(E_1 \text{ and } E_2)}{n(A)} \left(\frac{n(E_1)}{n(E_1)} \right)$$

This does not change the equality, because we are multiplying by a quantity equal to 1. But since the multiplication and division on the right side can be done in any order without affecting the result, we can rearrange the factors to yield:

$$P(E_1 \text{ and } E_2) = \frac{n(E_1)}{n(A)} \left(\frac{n(E_1 \text{ and } E_2)}{n(E_1)} \right)$$

The first ratio on the right is just the definition of $P(E_1)$. The second ratio we see to be the conditional probability $P(E_2|E_1)$. Hence, we have the result:

$$P(E_1 \text{ and } E_2) = P(E_1)P(E_2|E_1)$$

This is the multiplication rule for the probability of the joint occurrence of E_1 and E_2, and the result does not depend on whether or not E_1 and E_2 are independent events.

Definition of multiplication theorem

Whether or not E_1 and E_2 are independent, the probability of their joint occurrence is given by:

$$P(E_1 \text{ and } E_2) = P(E_1)P(E_2|E_1)$$

We found in Chapter 11 that, for independent events, the probability of the joint occurrence of E_1 and E_2 was given by:

$$P(E_1 \text{ and } E_2) = P(E_1)P(E_2)$$

By comparing formulas, we see that, if E_1 and E_2 are independent, we must have:

$$P(E_2) = P(E_2|E_1)$$

This result makes sense. The notion of independence implies that the probability of E_2 occurring does not depend on whether or not the event E_1 occurs. This means two things: first, if two events are independent, there is an unequivocal meaning to the probability of either one, say E_2 occurring, and this is given by $P(E_2)$; and, second, if E_1 and E_2 are independent, then all probabilities of E_2 conditioned on E_1 are the same and are equal to $P(E_2)$.

As an example, consider the data of Table 15-1, which represents the frequencies of students of Table 2-1 who are above or below the median on the College Board test and the final examination. For these data, the median College Board score was 505, and the median on the final exam was 45.5. Let us represent students who were above or below the median on the College Board test as CA and CB, respectively. Similarly, FA and FB will denote students who were above or below the median on the final exam. Notice that the marginal totals in Table 15-1 give us what we already know, that 50 percent of the scores on each test fall above the median. The probability of above median College Board scores is given by:

$$P(CA) = {}^{20}\!/_{40} = \tfrac{1}{2}$$

as is:

$$P(CB) = \tfrac{1}{2}$$

$$P(FA) = \tfrac{1}{2}$$

and:

$$P(FB) = \tfrac{1}{2}$$

By using the formula:

$$P(E_1 \text{ and } E_2) = P(E_1)P(E_2|E_1)$$

Table 15-1. Distribution of College Board and final exam scores for the 40 students of Table 2-1, (classification is based on sample medians)

| | Classification | College Board | | |
		Below (CB)	Above (CA)	Total
Final {	Below (FB)	14	6	20
Exam {	Above (FA)	6	14	20
	Total	20	20	40

we see that:

$$P(CA \text{ and } FA) = P(CA)P(FA|CA)$$
$$= {}^{20}\!/_{40}({}^{14}\!/_{20}) = {}^{14}\!/_{40}$$

Recall that independence implies that:

$$P(E_2) = P(E_2|E_1)$$

which says that two events are independent if the probability of the second event does not depend on the particular outcome of the first event. For the example above, we have:

$$P(FA) = {}^{20}\!/_{40} \quad \text{and} \quad P(FA|CA) = {}^{14}\!/_{20}$$

Hence, being above or below the median on the final is not independent of being above or below the median on the College Board test.

As we saw in Chapter 11, if E_1 and E_2 are mutually exclusive, then

$$P(E_1 \text{ or } E_2) = P(E_1) + P(E_2)$$

Let us examine the case when E_1 and E_2 are not mutually exclusive. Consider tossing a coin two times in succession. Let HH represent the outcome of a head on both tosses. Let HT represent the outcome of a head on the first toss and a tail on the second toss. These events are mutually exclusive because on any one tossing of the coin two times in succession both of these events cannot occur at the same time. The complete set of possible outcomes for tossing a coin twice is given by: {HH, HT, TH, and TT}. These four events are mutually exclusive. Define E_1 to be the event "head on the first toss" and E_2 to be "head on the second toss". Clearly, E_1 does not preclude E_2, since a head is a possible outcome on each toss. What is the probability, $P(E_1 \text{ or } E_2)$, of getting a head either on the first or the second toss? Merely by counting the outcomes, we see that E_1 or E_2 can occur in three out of the four cases. Hence, $P(E_1 \text{ or } E_2) = {}^3\!/_4$. We can also calculate this result by adding the events which satisfy E_1: {HH and HT} to the events which satisfy E_2: {TH and HH} and then subtracting the events in which they both occur simultaneously. The subtraction is required, since we have counted HH twice, once for E_1 and once for E_2. Algebraically, we have:

$$\begin{aligned} P(E_1 \text{ or } E_2) &= P(E_1) + P(E_2) - P(E_1 \text{ and } E_2) \\ &= [P(HH) + P(HT)] + [P(HH) + P(TH)] - [P(HH)] \\ &= P(HH) + P(HT) + P(TH) \\ &= P(E_1 \text{ or } E_2) \end{aligned}$$

as we desired. Notice that our rule for $P(E_1 \text{ or } E_2)$, when E_1 and E_2 are mutually exclusive is a special case of this formula. If the events are mutually exclusive, it is impossible for them to occur together, that is, $P(E_1 \text{ and } E_2)$ = 0. Hence, for mutually exclusive events:

$$P(E_1 \text{ or } E_2) = P(E_1) + P(E_2) - P(E_1 \text{ and } E_2)$$
$$= P(E_1) + P(E_2) - 0$$
$$= P(E_1) + P(E_2)$$

as we had before.

Addition rule for the probability of two events

Whether or not E_1 and E_2 are mutually exclusive

$$P(E_1 \text{ or } E_2) = P(E_1) + P(E_2) - P(E_1 \text{ and } E_2)$$

15-4. COMBINATIONS

For completeness, we now derive a formula for the number of unique groups of objects called *combinations*. Unlike permutations, which are distinguished as a collection of objects whose order is important, a combination is described solely in terms of the objects comprising the group. Thus, ABCDE and ABDCE are two different permutations of our books, but they comprise the same combination, since the groups each contain the books A, B, C, D, and E. In a combination, order is unimportant.

Let us calculate the number of distinct combinations that could be formed by choosing only two of the five books. We already know how many permutations are possible. The number is:

$$P_2^5 = \frac{5!}{(5-2)!} = \frac{5!}{3!} = 20$$

They are:

AB AC AD AE BC BD BE CD CE DE
BA CA DA EA CB DB EB DC EC ED

If we examine these permutations, we find pairs of them, such as AB and BA, that represent the same combination. Thus, of the 20 permutations, there are 10 such pairs, and therefore there are only 10 distinct combinations of size two that can be formed from the five books.

If we now consider how many combinations of size three can be formed, we will be able to derive a general formula for combinations. Again, we know how many permutations are possible:

$$P_3^5 = \frac{5!}{(5-3)!} = \frac{5!}{2!} = 60$$

But this time, the six permutations ABC, ACB, BAC, BCA, CAB, and CBA all represent a single combination. From the previous example of size two combinations and from the present example of size three combinations, we see that among the total number of permutations, there are sets of them that represent a single combination, and these sets contain as many permutations as there are orders of two or three objects. That is, two objects can be ordered in 2! or two ways. Three objects can be ordered in 3!, or 6 ways. For the present example, then, there are $^{60}/_6$, or 10, combinations possible.

In general, if we have N objects from which we wish to select x objects, then the number of combinations possible, C_x^N, is given by:

$$C_x^N = \frac{P_x^N}{x!} = \frac{\dfrac{N!}{(N-x)!}}{x!} = \frac{N!}{x!(N-x)!} = \binom{N}{x}$$

Notice that the formula for the number of combinations is identical to that for finding the number of permutations of N objects which are members of two classes, such as heads and tails. The shorthand notation, $\binom{N}{x}$, is used interchangeably for either case: $\binom{N}{x}$ refers to both the number of combinations of x objects chosen from N objects and to the number of permutations of two types of N objects, where x are identical and where $(N-x)$ are identical. Without a context, what the formula refers to, that is, either permutations or combinations, is ambiguous. We now define C_x^N formally.

Definition of combinations

Consider a set of N objects which are to be grouped in sets of size x. The number of such groups is given by:

$$C_x^N = \frac{N!}{x!(N-x)!} = \binom{N}{x}$$

The x objects that constitute the members of each group are called a combination.

As an example, consider the number of five-card hands that can be dealt from a 52-card bridge deck. This can be calculated by finding the number of distinct five-card combinations that can be drawn from 52 objects. It is given by:

$$C_5^{52} = \binom{52}{5} = 2{,}598{,}960$$

As another example, now let us compute the number of two-ace hands possible. Of the aces, there are $C_2^4 = \binom{4}{2} = 6$ ways to select two that appear in the hand. For each of these combinations, there are $C_3^{48} = \binom{48}{3} = 17{,}296$ combinations possible for the 3 non-aces chosen for the hand. Hence, the total number of hands containing two aces and three non-aces is the product of these, and the probability of getting a hand with two aces is then:

$$P(2 \text{ aces}) = \frac{\binom{4}{2}\binom{48}{3}}{\binom{52}{5}} = \frac{6(17{,}296)}{2{,}598{,}960} = 0.0399$$

This example illustrates a result referred to as the hypergeometric formula. We derive it in the following section.

15-5. HYPERGEOMETRIC PROBABILITIES

We can use the formula for the number of distinct permutations of N objects, I_1 and I_2 of which are identical, to solve an often encountered problem. Assume one has a bag containing 100 marbles, 75 of which are yellow, Y, and 25 of which are green, G. Assume further that we select a sample of five marbles at random. What is the probability of getting $3Y$ and $2G$ in the sample, if the selection is made without replacement?

In order to solve this problem, we must first write down the total number of distinct permutations of the 100 marbles. This is given by:

$$n(T) = \frac{100!}{75!25!} = \binom{100}{25} = \binom{100}{75}$$

Now, we can divide the 100 marbles into two groups with five in the sample, S, and 95 not in the sample, $\bar{S}$. Of the five in our sample, three are yellow and two are green. Hence, there are

$$n(S) = \frac{5!}{3!2!} = \binom{5}{3} = \binom{5}{2}$$

possible distinct orders. For each of these orders, the remaining 95 marbles can be ordered in

$$n(\bar{S}) = \frac{95!}{72!23!} = \binom{95}{72} = \binom{95}{23}$$

ways, since there are $72Y$ and $23G$ identical marbles remaining. Hence, the desired probability is given by:

$$P = \frac{\dfrac{5!}{3!2!}\left(\dfrac{95!}{72!23!}\right)}{\dfrac{100!}{75!25!}} = \frac{5!95!75!25!}{3!2!72!23!100!} = 0.2691$$

Let us rearrange the factorial products in the probability as follows:

$$P = \frac{\dfrac{75!}{3!72!}\left(\dfrac{25!}{2!23!}\right)}{\dfrac{100!}{5!95!}}$$

Let us also note that we can represent the three factorial fractions in terms of the binomial coefficients:

$$\frac{100!}{5!95!} = \binom{100}{5}$$

$$\frac{75!}{3!72!} = \binom{75}{3}$$

and:

$$\frac{25!}{2!23!} = \binom{25}{2}$$

It can be seen, then, that our result can be written as:

$$P = \frac{\binom{75}{3}\binom{25}{2}}{\binom{100}{5}}$$

In this form, P is referred to as a hypergeometric probability. The frequencies used to define a hypergeometric probability can be represented by the numbers in Table 15-2. We now provide a definition for this important probability formula.

Definition of hypergeometric probabilities

Let us consider a sample of N objects in which A are alike and $B = (N - A)$ are alike. Let a sample of size n be selected from the N objects. The probability, P, that the sample has a objects of type A and b objects of type B is given by:

$$P = \frac{\binom{A}{a}\binom{B}{b}}{\binom{N}{n}} = \frac{\binom{A}{a}\binom{N-A}{n-a}}{\binom{N}{n}}$$

See Table 15-3 for the general layout of a, b, A, B, n, and N.

As an example, consider a deck of 52 playing cards. Four of these cards are aces, and 48 are not. If a poker hand is dealt with five cards selected at random, the probability of a pair of aces can be found from constructing a

Table 15-2. Example illustrating the use of the hypergeometric formula

	Color of Marbles		
Number	Yellow	Green	Total
In bag	75	25	100
In sample	3	2	5

Table 15-3. The general model for the hypergeometric formula

	Quality A	Quality B	Total
Population	A	B	N
Sample	a	b	n

Table 15-4. Table for determining the probability of two aces in a five-card poker hand

	Aces	Nonaces	Total
Deck	4	48	52
Hand	2	3	5

table such as Table 15-4. The probability of a pair of aces and three other cards in the poker hand is given by:

$$P(2 \text{ aces}) = \frac{\binom{4}{2}\binom{48}{3}}{\binom{52}{5}} = 0.0399$$

which is the same result seen earlier.

15-6. EXERCISES

15-1. A classroom consists of 20 students. How many different samples of size
   a. 5 can be generated from the group?
   b. 10 can be generated from the group?
   c. 15 can be generated from the group?

15-2. The class of Exercise 15-1 consists of 8 boys and 12 girls. How many samples of five students contain
   a. zero boys
   b. one boy
   c. two boys
   d. three boys
   e. four boys
   f. five boys

15-3. What are the probabilities of *a* through *f* of Exercise 15-2?

15-4. One of the boys in the classroom of Exercise 15-1 is an A+ student. What is the probability that this student is in the samples *a* through *f* of Exercise 15-3?

15-5. Bridge is a card game in which two partners named East and West play against two other players called North and South. The players are seated at the table as shown here:

North

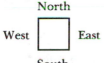

West [ ] East

South

The players make bids against the opposing team until a decision is made, at which time bidding stops. After the first card is played by West, North places his cards on the table for everyone to see. Upon seeing North's cards South can plan her strategy. Suppose that South has 5 spades in her hand and that North has 3. This means that five spades are divided between East and West. What is the probability that
   a. East has all five spades
   b. East has four spades
   c. East has three spades
   d. East has two spades
   e. East has one spade
   f. East has zero spades

15-6. Mr. Jones has nine umbrellas. Two are green. If he selects an umbrella at random each morning when he leaves for work, what is the probability that
   a. on Monday he selects a green one?
   b. he selects a green one on Monday and Tuesday?
   c. he selects a green one two times during the week?
   Are you using sampling with or without replacement? Why?

15-7. A shelf contains 10 red, 18 black, 17 blue, and 20 green covered books. If you select six books at random from the shelf, what is the probability that one is red, two are black, one is blue, and two are green? Are you using sampling with or without replacement?

15-8. A club consists of 100 men who are either lawyers or liars. If 70 are liars, and 60 are lawyers, how many are lying lawyers?

15-9. If you select one card from a deck of 52 cards, what is the probability that the card is either a heart or a jack?

15-10. A card is selected from a deck of 52 cards and is seen to be the two of hearts. If it is not returned to the deck, what is the probability that the next card selected is
a. a two
b. the two of diamonds
c. a heart
d. a heart or a two

15-11. The employees of a small bank can be divided as follows:

Years of service	Males	Females	Total
Less than or equal to 5	5	10	15
More than 5	15	5	20
Total	20	15	35

How many committees of size 4 can be generated from this bank consisting of one representative from each of the four groups?

15-12. How many committees of size 4 can be formulated for the bank of Exercise 15-11? What is the probability that the committee consists of one member from each group if the selection is at random?

15-13. Suppose that the males with more than 5 years of service and the females with less than 5 years form a committee of size four. How many committees of size four can you create from these ten people with:
a. 1 male with less than 5 years experience
b. 3 males with more than 5 years experience
c. 2 females with less than 5 years experience

d. 1 female with more than 5 years experience

15-14. If an employee of Exercise 15-11 is selected in a raffle to represent the bank at its yearly convention, what is the probability that the employee is
a. male
b. has more than 5 years of experience
c. is male with more than 5 years experience
d. is male or has more than 5 years experience

15-15. Keno is a game that is played in Nevada. Eighty ping-pong balls are numbered from 1 to 80 and placed in an air chamber where 20 are forced out to be played. A witless victim can play the game by betting a dollar that some or all of the numbers he selects will also be selected by the casino. If our witless victim selects 8 numbers, what is the probability that
a. 8 of his numbers are selected
b. 7 of his numbers are selected
c. 6 of his numbers are selected
d. 5 of his numbers are selected
e. 4 of his numbers are selected
f. 3 of his numbers are selected
g. 2 of his numbers are selected
h. 1 of his numbers is selected
i. 0 of his numbers is selected

15-16. Assume the payoffs are as follows:

Number Selected	Payoff for $1 Bet
8	$25,000
7	1,100
6	90
5	5
4	0
3	0
2	0
1	0
0	0

Would you play this game? Why?

15-17. Consider the set of seven consecutive integers: {1, 2, 3, 4, 5, 6, 7}:

a. In how many ways can one permute the integers?

b. In how many ways can one select three of the integers?

c. For the combinations of (b), let $T = r_1 + r_2 + r_3$, so that T represents the sum of the three integers. Find the distribution of T and graph it.

The distribution of T is called the Wilcoxon distribution. It will be seen again in Chapter 18.

15-18. When 34 public colleges in Michigan are classified by 1966 enrollment, under 12,000; 12,000 or more, and type, two-year; four-year, the following table results:

Enrollment	Four-Year B	Two-Year $\bar{B}$	Total
Under 12,000 A	7	22	29
12,000 or more $\bar{A}$	5	0	5
Total	12	22	34

Consider selecting one college at random from the 34. Represent, symbolically, and compute the probability of selection of:

a. A college with enrollment under 12,000

b. A four-year college

c. A four-year college with enrollment under 12,000

d. A two-year college with enrollment of 12,000 or more

e. A college that is either a school with enrollment under 12,000 or a four-year college

f. A college with enrollment under 12,000, given that the college is a four-year college

15-19. The following data are reported for the performance of 100 students on two items of a test:

Item 1 \ Item 2	Pass (B)	Fail ($\bar{B}$)	Total
Pass (A)	40	20	60
Fail ($\bar{A}$)	10	30	40
Total	50	50	100

If a single student is selected at random, what is the probability that the student will:

a. Pass Item 1 and Item 2?

b. Pass Item 1, but fail Item 2?

c. Pass Item 1 or Item 2 (A or B)?

d. Pass Item 2, if the student has passed Item 1?

e. Is performance on the two items independent?

f. If five students are chosen at random without replacement, what is the probability that each of them will fail at least one item?

15-20. You are playing *Let's Make a Deal*, and you are faced with five curtains. Behind four of the curtains are prizes of unbelievable wealth. Behind the other curtain is a sign reading, "ZONK, You Lose All." Find the probability of choosing, at random, only the four winning curtains in four different guesses.

15-21. A classroom contains 12 boys and 6 girls. In how many orders of 18 students can the teacher prepare a roster which is labelled only according to sex?

15-22. The state of California began issuing license plates with 7 characters as follows:

number, letter, letter, letter, number, number, number

How many license plates can be generated if all 26 letters, A, B, . . . , Z and all 10 digits, 0, 1, . . . , 9 are allowed, and no letter or number can be repeated.

CHAPTER 16

The Fisher – Irwin Test

16-1. A PROBLEM OF PROPORTIONS

In Chapter 15, we derived formulas for calculating probabilities when sampling without replacement. We mentioned at that time that we could use these probabilities to set up acceptance and rejection regions in much the same way that we used binomial probabilities to do so for the sign test. Under the sign test model, the dependent variable was quantitative. Often, however, we need to examine hypotheses involving qualitative variables. Hypergeometric probabilities allow us to test such hypotheses.

Consider a mock trial to be held in a law school. The judge, jury, defendant, and prosecuting and defense attorneys are all law students. The case hinges on a philosophical point about which all of the law students are quite opinionated in one direction, A, or another, $\overline{A}$. After listening to the prosecutor for some time, and eyeing the jurors, the defense attorney realizes that no legal argument can save the defendant. Rather, the jurors' minds are already made up. So the defense attorney decides to show that the trial is unfair because the jury does not represent the defendant's peers.

The defense attorney's reasoning is as follows. The jury may be considered to be a sample from a particular population, J. If the jury's population seems to correspond to that of all law students, then there is no reason to question the jury's fairness. To examine this question, the prosecutor samples, at random, 38 law students. This sample also represents a population, L, perhaps different from the jury's population. We want to determine whether or not the jury and the random sample of law students seem to come from the same population.

As an indication of the similarity of the two populations, we can compare the proportion of people in each population that are on the A side of the philosophical issue. If the two proportions are equal, then the J population and the L population feel equally about the issue. In such a case, the population difference, $\Delta = P_J - P_L$, would equal zero, and, under random sampling, we would expect the sample difference, $\hat{\Delta} = \hat{P}_J - \hat{P}_L$, to be near zero also. Values of $\hat{\Delta}$ that were far from zero would call into question the equality of P_J and P_L. The Fisher–Irwin test examines the hypothesis of the equality of proportions in two populations, based on the proportions in two independent samples. In the next section, we present the test of H_0: $\Delta = 0$ versus H_1: $\Delta \neq 0$.

16-2. HYPERGEOMETRIC PROBABILITIES USED IN HYPOTHESIS TESTING

We can use the hypergeometric formula to determine the probability of particular values of $\hat{\Delta}$ arising by chance, when sampling at random from populations in which $\Delta = 0$. Table 16-1 shows the numbers of A and $\overline{A}$ people in the jury and law student samples. Of the 50 people, 30 are type A and 20 are type $\overline{A}$. The hypergeometric formula allows us to calculate the probability

Table 16-1. Observed jury and law student samples

Sample	A	$\overline{A}$	Total
Jury	3	9	12
Law student	27	11	38
Total	30	20	50

that the jury group will contain a particular number, f_{AJ}, of type A people when the 50 people are separated into two groups at random, so that the jury group has 12 people and the student group has 38. If the two populations represented by the jury and student samples, indeed, have equal proportions of A people, then $\hat{\Delta}$ should not be far from zero. If the proportions are unequal, then $\hat{\Delta}$ should deviate significantly from zero. In terms of the hypergeometric probabilities, we are able to set up a rejection region containing no more than the least likely α percent of $\hat{\Delta}$ values. If the $\hat{\Delta}$ value actually observed is among these, we would reject the hypothesis of equal population proportions.

Our immediate problem is to determine the complete set of $\hat{\Delta}$ values that could be generated by chance for 12 jurors and 38 students. The way we do this is to hold the margins of Table 16-1 fixed and place in the upper left cell the value $f_{AJ} = 0$. The table is then completed and the probability is computed. With $f_{AJ} = 0$, the remaining frequencies are found to be $f_{\bar{A}J} = 12$, $f_{AL} = 30$ and $f_{\bar{A}L} = 8$, so that:

$$\hat{\Delta} = \hat{P}_J - \hat{P}_L = \frac{f_{AJ}}{N_J} - \frac{f_{AL}}{N_L} = \frac{0}{12} - \frac{30}{38} = -0.7895$$

Table 16-2. Values of f_{AJ}, $\hat{P}_J$, $\hat{P}_L$, $\hat{\Delta}$, and their probabilities

f_{AJ}	$\hat{P}_J$	$\hat{P}_L$	$\hat{\Delta}$	Probability
0	0.0000	0.7895	−0.7895	0.00000
1	0.0833	0.7632	−0.6799	0.00004
2	0.1667	0.7368	−0.5701	0.00066
3	0.2500	0.7105	−0.4605	0.00562
4	0.3333	0.6842	−0.3509	0.02844
5	0.4167	0.6579	−0.2412	0.09100
6	0.5000	0.6316	−0.1316	0.18958
7	0.5833	0.6053	−0.0220	0.26000
8	0.6667	0.5789	0.0878	0.23359
9	0.7500	0.5526	0.1974	0.13435
10	0.8333	0.5263	0.3070	0.04702
11	0.9167	0.5000	0.4167	0.00900
12	1.0000	0.4737	0.5263	0.00071

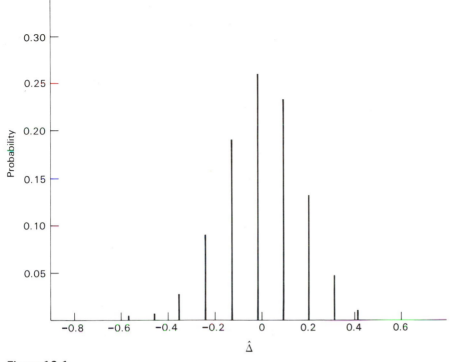

Figure 16-1.
Hypergeometric probabilities for $\hat{\Delta} = \hat{p}_1 - \hat{p}_2$ based on Table 16-2.

and:

$$P = \frac{\binom{N_J}{f_{AJ}}\binom{N_L}{f_{AL}}}{\binom{N_J + N_L}{f_{AJ} + f_{AL}}} = \frac{\binom{12}{0}\binom{38}{30}}{\binom{50}{30}} = 0.00000$$

We next replace $f_{AJ} = 0$ by $f_{AJ} = 1$, complete the table, compute $\hat{\Delta}$, and its corresponding P. This process is repeated for $f_{AJ} = 2, 3, \ldots, 12$. Results are as shown in Table 16-2. Figure 16-1 is a graph of the probabilities.

Table 16-3 contains those values of $\hat{\Delta}$ that are furthest from zero and the probabilities of their arising by chance from the combined group of 50 people. If we wish to specify the least likely $\hat{\Delta}$ values, we would start with the $\hat{\Delta}$ furthest from zero. Notice that these least likely values are the $\hat{\Delta}$ having the smallest probability. If we wish to amass a rejection region containing no more than 5 percent of the outcomes, we would begin with $\hat{\Delta} = -0.7895$, since its value is furthest from 0.

We would then include $\hat{\Delta} = -0.6798$, continuing in this fashion until we included $\hat{\Delta} = -0.3509$ in the rejection region. At this point, the cumulative

Table 16-3.   Unlikely values of $\hat{\Delta}$ and their probabilities

$\hat{\Delta}$	Probability	Cumulative probability
−0.7895	0.00000	0.00000
−0.6798	0.00004	0.00004
−0.5701	0.00066	0.00070
0.5263	0.00071	0.00141
−0.4605	0.00562	0.00703
0.4167	0.00900	0.01603
−0.3509	0.02844	0.04447
0.3070	0.04702	0.09149

probability of selecting by chance an outcome in the rejection region equals 4.4 percent, as shown in Table 16-3. If we try to include $\hat{\Delta} = 0.3070$, the type I error rate would increase beyond 5 percent, to 9.1 percent. Hence, we decide to include only the first seven $\hat{\Delta}$ values shown in Table 16-3. We would reject the hypothesis that the two populations have equal proportions of A-type people, H_0: $P_J = P_L$, if the observed $\hat{\Delta}$ value is among those in the rejection region. In the example, the observed $\hat{\Delta} = -0.4605$ is in the rejection region. Thus, we conclude, with a type I error rate of 4.4 percent, that the population represented on the jury is not the same as that represented by the sample of law students. The defense attorney has made her case.

16-3. THE FISHER–IRWIN EXACT TEST

As we have seen, the hypergeometric formula allows us to calculate the exact probabilities of outcomes in the rejection region of the Fisher–Irwin exact test. Just as we did in the sign test, we include in the rejection region those outcomes that are least likely under the null hypotheses of equal population proportions. If the observed $\hat{\Delta}$ is one of the α percent least likely, we reject the null hypotheses. We provide steps for performing the Fisher–Irwin exact test in Box 16-1.

16-4. TESTING THE $\hat{\phi}$ COEFFICIENT FOR SIGNIFICANCE

We saw in Chapter 10 that one could calculate a correlation coefficient using the data in a 2 × 2 table, provided the categories were dummy coded. As we

---

Box 16-1   **How to perform the Fisher–Irwin exact test of the hypothesis H_0:**
$P_1 = P_2$

Step 1. Display the data in a 2 × 2 table, as shown in Table 16-4. Let F_{11} represent the
set of possible numbers of sample 1, type A individuals.

Table 16-4.   A typical contingency table for testing the
hypothesis $H_0: P_1 = P_2$.

	Group 1	Group 2	Total
A	f_{11}	f_{12}	$f_{1.}$
$\overline{A}$	f_{21}	f_{22}	$f_{2.}$
Total	N_1	N_2	N

Step 2. Determine those values of F_{11} and $\hat{\Delta}$ that are least likely under H_0. The
smallest value of F_{11} is usually near zero, and the largest is near N_1. Depending on the table, values of F_{11} equal to zero or N_1 may not be possible. An
example of such a table is shown in Table 16.5.

Step 3. Calculate the probabilities of the least likely outcomes using the hypergeometric formula. The probability of getting f_{11} type A individuals is given by:

$$P(F_{11} = f_{11}) = \frac{\binom{N_1}{f_{11}}\binom{N_2}{f_{12}}}{\binom{N}{f_{1.}}}$$

Step 4. Using these probabilities, include in the rejection region extreme values of $\hat{\Delta}$
until the cumulative probability is close to, but does not exceed, the desired α
percent type I error rate. If the test is one-tailed, cumulative probabilities are
taken from the tail that is most compatible with H_1. If the test is two-tailed,
build up the critical region from both tails, using the extreme values of $\hat{\Delta}$
selected from both positive and negative values.

Step 5. If the observed value of $\hat{\Delta}$ is included in the rejection region, conclude that H_0
is false, and that the two population proportions, P_1 and P_2, are not equal.

---

recall, this coefficient was called phi (ϕ). There are two major reasons for
examining $\hat{\phi}$. First, as we stated in Chapter 2, questions concerning differences are often conceptually the same as questions involving association. The
possibility of different proportions of A people existing in two populations
was addressed in Section 16-2. The defense attorney could instead have
asked whether or not there was some association between being an A-type
person and being simultaneously on the jury.

Table 16-5. Example of limitations on the value of f_{11}

	Group 1	Group 2	Total
A	F_{11}		2
$\overline{A}$			8
Total	7	3	10

This question is one of association, and $\hat{\phi}$ measures this association in the sample. Second, we noted in Chapter 10 that the square of a correlation coefficient represented the proportion of variation in the dependent variable that is explained by the independent variable. Since the $\hat{\phi}$ coefficient is a correlation coefficient for dichotomous data, $\hat{\phi}$ will perform the same role as r when both the independent and dependent variables are dichotomous. For both of these reasons, it would be advantageous to be able to test $\hat{\phi}$ for significance. In what follows we will use ϕ (without the caret) to represent the population correlation coefficient. In addition, we will now show that $\hat{\phi}$ can be found in terms of $\hat{\Delta}$, so that a test of:

$$H_0: \quad \phi = 0$$

is the same as a test of:

$$H_0: \quad \Delta = 0$$

Hence, we can use the Fisher–Irwin test for either hypothesis.

As can be seen in Table 16-2, once the margins of the table are known, the entire distribution of $\hat{\Delta}$ is determined by f_{11}, the proportion of A-type people in the first sample. The same thing is true of $\hat{\phi}$. If we code the variables of Table 16-4 (in Box 16-1) so that $X = 1$ represents Group 1, $X = 0$ represents Group 2, $Y = 1$ represents the A category, and $Y = 0$ represents the $\overline{A}$ category, we can show that

$$\hat{\phi} = \frac{Nf_{11} - N_1 f_{1.}}{\sqrt{N_1 N_2 f_{1.} f_{2.}}}$$

Once $N_1, N_2, f_{1.}$, and $f_{2.}$ are fixed, $\hat{\phi}$ depends only on f_{11}. Thus, the distribution of $\hat{\phi}$ is identical to the distribution of $\hat{\Delta}$ we have already displayed in Table 16-2. If the hypothesis of equal population proportions is rejected, then we can, at the same time, conclude that the population ϕ is not equal to zero.

To make this fact even more explicit, consider the previous formula for $\hat{\phi}$. Because

$$f_{11} + f_{12} = f_{1.}$$

and

$$N = N_1 + N_2$$

we can substitute for N and $f_{1.}$ and algebraically simplify to obtain:

$$\hat{\phi} = \frac{\hat{p}_1 - \hat{p}_2}{\sqrt{\dfrac{f_{1.}f_{2.}}{N_1 N_2}}} = \sqrt{\frac{N_1.N_2.}{f_{1.}f_{2.}}}\,\hat{\Delta}$$

For the data of Table 16-1:

$$\hat{\phi} = \sqrt{\frac{12(38)}{30(20)}}\left(\frac{3}{12} - \frac{27}{38}\right) = \sqrt{\frac{12(38)}{30(20)}}\,(-0.4605) = -0.4015$$

Since $\hat{\Delta} = -0.4605$ is in the critical region, the hypothesis $H_0\!: \phi = 0$ is rejected. We provide directions for testing $H_0\!: \phi = 0$ in Box 16-2.

In this example, we have continued to emphasize the connection between questions regarding differences and questions dealing with association. In this case, the two types of questions are interchangeable. Because there is a clearly defined independent variable, jury membership, and a clearly defined dependent variable, attitude toward A, the problem can certainly be phrased in terms of differences. On the other hand, examining the association between these two variables, attitude is associated with group membership, and this still implies that attitude depends on the group to which one belongs. The interchangeability of the two views cannot alter the fact that two samples are involved and that sample membership is an independent variable. However, as pointed out in Section 10-6, the ϕ coefficient is encountered more frequently in social science research in the one-sample case in which there is neither an independent nor dependent variable.

Box 16-2   Procedure for testing $H_0\!: \phi = 0$

Step 1. Perform the Fisher–Irwin test and reject H_0 if $\hat{\Delta}$ is in the critical region.
Step 2. Estimate ϕ as

$$\hat{\phi} = \sqrt{\frac{N_1 N_2}{f_{1.}f_{2.}}}\,\hat{\Delta}$$

16-5. THE TWO-SAMPLE MEDIAN TEST

The Fisher–Irwin two-sample test is quite flexible. Of course, it is most directly used when the dependent variable is dichotomous. Variables such as {Pass, Fail}, {Lived, Died}, {Male, Female}, etc., are defined in such a way that they fit naturally into a Fisher–Irwin framework. Other variables may be used as dependent variables, even though they are quantitative, if the hypothesis of interest involves the proportion of such scores falling into dichotomous categories.

For example, consider two new mathematics units designed to improve algebraic ability, and let us assume that a test has been created to assess these units' effectiveness. A teacher wishes to determine if one unit is better than the other. To do so, the teacher examines the scores obtained by two random samples of students, one sample using the first treatment, G_1, and the other using the second, G_2, to see if either group has a higher median score then the other. The scores are listed in Table 16-6.

To distinguish sample medians from population medians, we denote sample medians, as we have been doing, by $\hat{M}$ and the population median by M. With this notation, the null hypothesis being examined here is that the two population medians, M_1 and M_2, are equal. It is given by:

$$H_0: \quad M_1 = M_2 = M_0$$

where M_0 is the common median value. If this is so, then each sample can be considered to be drawn from the same population, and our best estimate of the common population median is derived by combining the two samples into a single group. For the data of Table 16-6, this would result in a combined group of 20 observations, whose median would be the average of the 10th and 11th ordered observation:

$$\hat{M}_0 = \frac{37 + 38}{2} = 37.5$$

Table 16-6. Algebra test scores for two treatment groups.

G_1		G_2		
17	27	30	43	55
22	28	32	47	58
22	37	35	54	59
24	42	38	55	60

Table 16-7. Data for the Fisher–Irwin median test

	G_1	G_2	Total
Below median	7	3	10
Above median	1	9	10
Total	8	12	20

At the same time, each of the two samples provides its own estimate of $\hat{M}_0$. If the two samples come from populations with the same median, we would expect half of the observations in each population to be below M_0 and half above. Then, an equivalent statement of the above null hypothesis would be:

$$H_0: \quad P_1 = P_2 = \tfrac{1}{2}$$

where P is the proportion above the median M_0. Further, if this is the case, we would expect half of the observations in each sample to be above $\hat{M}_0$. With this in mind, we see that we are examining the hypothesis of the equality of two population proportions, and this can be done by using the Fisher–Irwin test.

To continue our example, we note that only one subject of sample one is above $\hat{M}_0 = 37.5$, while nine of the second sample observations are above this value. These data are condensed into the 2×2 table shown in Table 16-7. We then proceed to calculate the probabilities of extreme values of $\hat{\Delta} = \hat{P}_1 - \hat{P}_2$ using the hypergeometric distribution. The results are shown in Table 16-8. Since we have not specified a directional alternative, the rejection region would consist of $\hat{\Delta}$ values taken from both tails of the distribution

Table 16-8. Extreme values of $\hat{\Delta}$ and their probabilities for the median test

f_{11}	$\hat{\Delta}$	Probability	Cumulative probability
8	0.8333	0.00036	0.00036
0	−0.8333	0.00036	0.00072
7	0.6250	0.00953	0.01025
1	−0.6250	0.00953	0.01978
6	0.4167	0.07502	0.09480
2	−0.4167	0.07502	0.16982

Box 16-3   Procedure for the two-sample median test

Step 1. Rank order the observations in each sample.
Step 2. Treat the two samples as one sample and find the median value of the total sample. Denote this median value as $\hat{M}_0$.
Step 3. Count the number of cases above and below $\hat{M}_0$ in each sample and set up a 2 × 2 contingency table similar to Table 16-4. If there are values in either sample equal to $\hat{M}_0$, place them in the contingency table so as to make the value of $\hat{\Delta}$ closer to zero.
Step 4. Perform the Fisher–Irwin test.

---

of $\hat{\Delta}$. In this case, the $\hat{\Delta}$ values are $\{-0.8333, -0.625, 0.625, 0.8333\}$. The type I error rate is given by $\alpha = 0.0198$, the cumulative probability of these four outcomes. Because the observed $\hat{\Delta} = 0.625$ lies in the rejection region, we would conclude that the two populations seem to have different median values. Therefore, the treatments are not equally effective. We provide directions for performing the two-sample median test in Box 16-3.

16-6. COMPUTING BINOMIAL AND HYPERGEOMETRIC PROBABILITIES

The determination of binomial and hypergeometric probabilities requires the direct computation of $\binom{N}{x}$, which refers to: (1) the number of permutations of N objects divided into two sets in which x are identical and in which the remaining objects are different, but also identical, or (2) the number of combinations of x objects selected from N objects. While the contexts are different, the arithmetic computations are the same. To facilitate these computations, tables of $\binom{N}{x}$ have been prepared. One such table appears as Table A-3 in the appendix. This table can be used to compute hypergeometric probabilities such as:

$$P(X = 3 \text{ and } Y = 7) = \frac{\binom{10}{3}\binom{9}{7}}{\binom{19}{10}}$$

with ease. Entering Table A-3, we see that $\binom{10}{3} = 120$, $\binom{9}{7} = 36$, and $\binom{19}{10} = 92{,}378$, so that:

$$P(X = 3 \text{ and } Y = 7) = \frac{120(36)}{92{,}378} = 0.0468$$

Inspection of Table A-3 shows that the figures possess a symmetry. This symmetry is used when $X + Y$ exceeds 10. Since $\binom{N}{x} = \binom{N}{N-x}$, we see, for example, that $\binom{19}{5} = \binom{19}{14}$. This property is used to compute probabilities such as:

$$P(X = 8 \text{ and } Y = 7) = \frac{\binom{10}{8}\binom{9}{6}}{\binom{19}{14}}$$

In this case $\binom{10}{8} = 45$, $\binom{9}{6} = 84$, and $\binom{19}{14} = \binom{19}{5} = 11{,}628$, so that:

$$P(X = 8 \text{ and } Y = 7) = \frac{45(84)}{11{,}628} = 0.3251$$

16-7. EXERCISES

16-1. Divide the male students of your sample of 40 into two classes:

c_1: Above a score of 15 on the pretest
c_2: Below or equal to a score of 14 on the pretest

and complete the following contingency table:

Group	Program one	Program two	Total
c_1			
c_2			
Total			

a. Test H_0: $P(c_1|\text{One}) = P(c_1|\text{Two})$
   against
   H_1: H_0 is false
b. What is the $\alpha = 0.05$ decision rule?

16-2. A group of 18 school children were classified as to whether they were inner- or outer-directed and whether or not they were a wanted child at birth. Results are as shown.

Y \ X	Wanted at birth	Not wanted	Total
Inner	8	1	9
Outer	2	9	11
Total	10	10	20

a. What is the $\hat{\phi}$ coefficient for these data?
b. Is there reason to believe that $\phi = 0$ at $\alpha = 0.05$?

16-3. Two wines were tested by two sets of independent judges. Each set of judges tested only one wine, which was compared to a standard. The judges were told to rate the wine as superior or inferior to the standard. Results are as shown.

Rating	Wine A	Wine B	Total
Superior	6	4	10
Inferior	2	4	6
Total	8	8	16

Are there any differences in the ratings of the wines?

16-4. Another group of judges was asked to rate both wines against each other. The judges were told to select the best of the two wines. Because taste sequence can bias the results, half of the judges tasted Wine A first. The second half tested Wine B first. Results are as shown.

	Order of tasting		
Preferred wine	A first	B first	Total
A	6	2	8
B	2	6	8
Total	8	8	16

Does order of presentation make a difference in the ratings?

16-5. In a study in which a group of 3-year old children were temporarily abandoned by their mother in a nursery room setting, an attempt was made to see if the child would turn to a male or female attendant upon the discovery that mother was not in the room. To control the sex difference of the attendant they were dressed in similar outfits: tennis shoes, blue denim trousers, and a sweatshirt with the logo of the college. They were also similar in height, weight, hair color, and general features. Results are as shown.

Person	Sex of child		
sought	Male	Female	Total
Male	6	9	15
Female	9	2	11
Neither	5	9	14
Total	20	20	40

These data can be investigated in terms of three Fisher–Irwin tests. Do the analysis using

a. $\alpha_1 = \alpha_2 = \alpha_3 = 0.05$
b. $\alpha_1 = \alpha_2 = \alpha_3 = \frac{1}{3}(0.05) = 0.0167$

Which analysis would you recommend, a or b? Why?

CHAPTER 17

The Matched-Pair Wilcoxon Test

17-1. INFORMATION IN SAMPLE DATA

Researchers collect samples because sample data contain information about the parameters of a population. As a result, a researcher would like to extract the maximum information the sample possesses about the parameters. In a certain sense, the matched-pair sign test is wasteful of the information the sample contains about the median or mean difference in the populations under study. It pays no attention to the magnitude of the sample differences. It considers only the positive or negative quality of the differences. This means that when a researcher uses the sign test for testing no difference in population centers, each difference is treated with equal value and weight, regardless of its size. For example, a difference of $+7$ is given the same

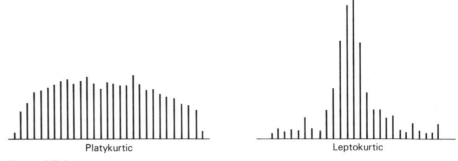

Figure 17-1.
Examples of platykurtic and leptokurtic distributions.

importance as a difference of $+1, -13, -4, +18$, or any other number. All differences are treated as providing the same amount of information about the mean or median difference in the population. Large sample differences suggest large population differences, while small differences do not. One statistical test that treats the sample differences with weights correlated with magnitude is the matched-pair Wilcoxon test. This test is very similar to the sign test. It differs from the sign test in that the differences are ranked from 1 to N, and then the sum of the ranks associated with positive differences is used to test the hypothesis of no difference in population centers. It is based upon the same assumption of independence between differences as the sign test, but the distribution of population differences must be symmetrical. Fortunately, if the hypothesis is true in the matched-pair design, the distribution of population differences is always symmetrical. If the hypothesis is false, it is known that under most conditions this test has a higher probability of rejecting the hypothesis of identical centers than does the sign test applied to the same data. It is known to be a better test if the distribution of the differences is platykurtic. A distribution is said to be *platykurtic* if it has a wide, broad peak and a large variance. If the distribution has a sharp peak with most of the distribution concentrated around the center of the distribution, the distribution is said to be *leptokurtic*. Examples of platykurtic and leptokurtic distributions are shown in Figure 17-1. If a distribution is known to be leptokurtic, then the sign test is the preferred test.

17-2. THE MATCHED-PAIR WILCOXON TEST

Decision rules for the matched-pair Wilcoxon test can be derived from the tree diagrams that are used to obtain decision rules for the sign test. The only difference is that the branches are treated differently. By now, it should be apparent that one does not actually have to construct an appropriate tree diagram, since a complete listing of the branches can be made in the manner illustrated in Table 11-1 for the tree of Figure 11-2. Such a listing is provided in Table 17-1 for a study in which $N = 5$ trials are considered. In this diagram, a $(+)$ sign is recorded for a positive difference, and a $(-)$ sign recorded for a negative difference, just as they were for the sign test. We now part company with the sign test and, instead of simply counting the number of $(+)$ deviations, we rank them according to their *absolute* magnitude. This means that we assign ranks to the differences, completely ignoring the sign of the difference. The ranking is represented by the first row of Table 17-1, where we represent the sign in terms of a dummy code. These ranks are used to calculate the matched-pair Wilcoxon statistic which is defined as follows.

Definition of the matched-pair Wilcoxon statistic

Let x_i represent a dummy code where:

$$x_i = 1, \text{ if the } i\text{th ordered difference is } (+)$$

and:

$$x_i = 0, \text{ if the } i\text{th ordered difference is } (-)$$

Let:

$$r_i = 1, 2, 3, \ldots, N$$

We define the Wilcoxon matched-pair statistic in terms of the dummy code, x_i, and the ranks, r_i, as:

$$T = \sum_{i=1}^{N} x_i r_i$$

In terms of this definition, the value of T for branch 1 is given by:

$$T_1 = 1(1) + 1(2) + 1(3) + 1(4) + 1(5) = 15$$

while for branch 7, T is given by:

$$T_7 = 1(1) + 1(2) + 0(3) + 0(4) + 1(5) = 8$$

Values of T for the remaining branches are shown in Table 17-1.

   We can now see the difference that exists between the sign test and the Wilcoxon matched-pair test. Consider branches 2, 3, 5, 9, and 17. For the sign test, all five branches are equivalent since each contains four plus signs. They are given equal emphasis in the sign test. But that is not true for the Wilcoxon matched-pair test, where it is seen that the T values are given,

Table 17-1. The $2^5 = 32$ branches of the complete set of outcomes for $N = 5$ independent trials

Branch \ Rank	1	2	3	4	5	$T = \sum\limits_{i=1}^{5} x_i r_i$
1	+	+	+	+	+	15
2	+	+	+	+	−	10
3	+	+	+	−	+	11
4	+	+	+	−	−	6
5	+	+	−	+	+	12
6	+	+	−	+	−	7
7	+	+	−	−	+	8
8	+	+	−	−	−	3
9	+	−	+	+	+	13
10	+	−	+	+	−	8
11	+	−	+	−	+	9
12	+	−	+	−	−	4
13	+	−	−	+	+	10
14	+	−	−	+	−	5
15	+	−	−	−	+	6
16	+	−	−	−	−	1
17	−	+	+	+	+	14
18	−	+	+	+	−	9
19	−	+	+	−	+	10
20	−	+	+	−	−	5
21	−	+	−	+	+	11
22	−	+	−	+	−	6
23	−	+	−	−	+	7
24	−	+	−	−	−	2
25	−	−	+	+	+	12
26	−	−	+	+	−	7
27	−	−	+	−	+	8

Table 17-1. *(Continued)*

Branch \ Rank	1	2	3	4	5	$T = \sum_{i=1}^{5} x_i r_i$
28	−	−	+	−	−	3
29	−	−	−	+	+	9
30	−	−	−	+	−	4
31	−	−	−	−	+	5
32	−	−	−	−	−	0

Table 17-2. Probability distribution of the Wilcoxon matched-pair statistic for $N = 5$ independent trials

t		f	$P(T = t)$	$P(T \le t + \frac{1}{2})$
0	ǀ	1	0.03125	0.03125
1	ǀ	1	0.03125	0.06250
2	ǀ	1	0.03125	0.09375
3	ǁ	2	0.06250	0.15625
4	ǁ	2	0.06250	0.21875
5	ǁǀ	3	0.09375	0.31250
6	ǁǀ	3	0.09375	0.40625
7	ǁǀ	3	0.09375	0.50000
8	ǁǀ	3	0.09375	0.59375
9	ǁǀ	3	0.09375	0.68750
10	ǁǀ	3	0.09375	0.78125
11	ǁ	2	0.06250	0.84375
12	ǁ	2	0.06250	0.90625
13	ǀ	1	0.03125	0.93750
14	ǀ	1	0.03125	0.96875
15	ǀ	1	0.03125	1.00000

respectively, by 10, 11, 12, 13, and 14. If the largest difference is negative, $T = 10$, while if the smallest difference is negative, $T = 14$. As we see, T takes into account the *magnitude* of the differences. This is not true of the sign test statistic. It thoroughly ignores the magnitude and is, thus, wasteful of the information that the differences have about the population median difference, M_d.

Table 17-2 and Figures 17-2 and 17-3 provide tabular and graphic illustrations of the probability distribution of T. We see that T is a discrete random variable with a distribution that is symmetric about $T = 7.5$ and that T assumes all the discrete integer values from $T = 0$ to $T = 1 + 2 + 3 + 4 + 5 = 15$. In the general case, based on N pairs, T is symmetric about:

$$\mu_T = M_T = \frac{N(N+1)}{4}$$

and it covers the range from $T = 0$ to $T = 1 + 2 + 3 + \cdots + N = N(N+1)/2$. Since the space between each discrete value for T is unity, the correction for continuity equals $\pm \frac{1}{2}$. This correction is shown in the last column of Table 17-2 and is used for drawing the *cumulative probability polygon* of Figure 17-3.

As an example of the use of the test, consider a study in which $N = 5$ emotionally disturbed children were observed for 1 hour on each of two consecutive days. Suppose that a record was kept of the number of times each participated in antisocial behavior. The results are as shown in the Before column of Table 17-3. Suppose that on day 3, a behavior modification schedule was imposed upon the children, a schedule designed to stop the undesirable behavior. On days 4 and 5, a record was again kept of the number of times each child exhibited antisocial behavior over the two 1-hour observa-

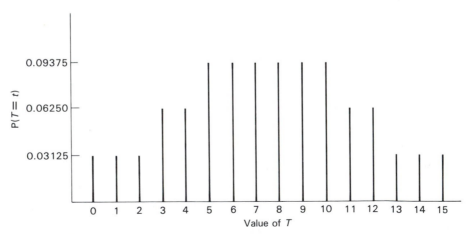

Figure 17-2.
Distribution of the matched-pair Wilcoxon statistic for $N = 5$.

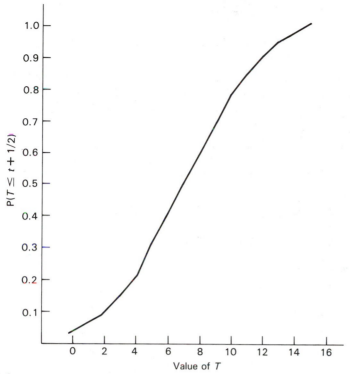

Figure 17-3.
Cumulative probabilities for the matched-pair Wilcoxon statistic for $N = 5$.

tion periods. The results are as shown in the After column of Table 17-3. On the basis of these data, we want to know if the behavior-modification intervention was successful. We do this by hypothesizing that it was not. If it had no effect, then the median of the difference values in the population from which these five children were selected should be equal to zero. If it was successful, then the After scores should be smaller than the Before scores, so that the

Table 17-3.   Number of antisocial behavior incidents shown by $N = 5$ children before and after a behavior-modification intervention

Child	Before	After	Difference	Sign	Rank
Arlene	6	2	4	+	3
Bob	12	4	8	+	5
Connie	8	9	−1	−	1
David	3	0	3	+	2
Elmer	11	6	5	+	4

median of the difference scores:

$$d = Y_{\text{Before}} - Y_{\text{After}}$$

should be positive. If we rank the difference scores, taking into account the magnitude of the difference, T should be an outcome of the distribution shown in Table 17-2. If the alternative were true, T should be large and so we would suspect the truth of:

$$H_0: \quad M_d = 0$$

To test H_0 against:

$$H_1: \quad M_d > 0$$

we need a decision rule that indicates when H_0 should be rejected. As a first choice, we can set up the rule:

Decision Rule 1:   Reject H_0 if $T = 15$.

With this rule, the risk of a type I error is equal to $\alpha_1 = P(T = 15) = 0.03125$. Since this is less than 0.05, we might consider the rule:

Decision Rule 2:   Reject H_0 if $T = 14$ or 15.

With this rule, the risk of a type I error is equal to:

$$\alpha_2 = P(T = 14 \text{ or } 15) = P(T = 14) + P(T = 15)$$
$$= 0.03125 + 0.03125 = 0.0625$$

This is larger than 0.05, so we choose Decision Rule 1. For the data of Table 17-3:

$$T = 0(1) + 1(2) + 1(3) + 1(4) + 1(5) = 14$$

With Decision Rule 1, we cannot reject H_0. If we had used Decision Rule 2, we would have rejected H_0.

As an aside, this example points out the problem of using small samples. With a small sample, the chances for rejecting a false hypothesis are reduced, since the critical region contains a small set of potential values. If we could have increased the sample size to $N = 10$, an α of 0.05 decision rule could be stated that contains the outcomes $T = 45, 46, 47, \ldots, 54, 55$. With this larger set of values, the chances for rejecting H_0 are greatly enhanced.

In practice, one does not need to generate the distribution of T each time this test is used. Fortunately, it has been done by others and decision rules have been tabled. These rules are summarized in Table A-4 for various probabilities of making a type I error. This table is titled "Critical Values for the Matched-Pair Wilcoxon Test." It is entered by specifying the value of N, the number of matched pairs, and α, the probability of a type I error. We illustrate the use of this test for the data of Table 17-4, which are taken from Table 14-1. This example has the added problem that some of the difference scores are tied at a common value. Strictly speaking, the matched-pair Wilcoxon test is not valid when there are tied values; however, one can approximate the probabilities of T if there are a few tied values and if one assigns midrank values to the tied values. This is the procedure adopted in this example, and this is the procedure that is recommended when using this test.

If there should be differences whose values are zero, they should be divided equally between the (+) and (−) deviations, and half the rank total should be assigned to each. For example, if there were five differences whose value is zero, 2.5 should be assigned (+) ranks and 2.5 should be assigned (−) ranks. Normally, the zero values would be ranked 1, 2, 3, 4, 5 for a total rank assignment of $1 + 2 + 3 + 4 + 5 = 15$. This total is now divided by five, so

Table 17-4. Computations for the matched-pair Wilcoxon test for the data of Table 14-1

Pair	Difference score	Value of x_i	Value of r_i	$x_i r_i$
1	−1	0	2.5	0
2	+1	1	2.5	2.5
3	−5	0	12	0
4	+6	1	13	13
5	−1	0	2.5	0
6	−3	0	8	0
7	+3	1	8	8
8	−1	0	2.5	0
9	−2	0	5.5	0
10	−4	0	10.5	0
11	−3	0	8	0
12	−2	0	5.5	0
13	+4	1	10.5	10.5
14	−7	0	14	0
Total			105	34

Box 17-1   How to do the matched-pair Wilcoxon test

Step 1. Complete the first two steps for the sign test.

Step 2. Use Table A-4 to obtain the appropriate decision rule. Let T_L and T_U denote the lower $\%_2$ value of T and the upper $1 - \%_2$ value of T. Let the decision rule be:

     Decision Rule: Reject H_0 if $T \le T_L$ or if $T \ge T_U$.

Step 3. Compute the differences. Assign ranks to the differences, ignoring the sign associated with each difference. If there are differences whose value is zero, divide their rank total equally between the plus and minus values. If there are tied values, assign midranks.

Step 4. Compute:

$$T = \sum_{i=1}^{N} x_i r_i$$

and make a decision.

---

that midranks of 3 are assigned to the zero differences. 2.5 are considered $(+)$ and 2.5 are considered $(-)$, so that 7.5 is assigned to the negative rank sum and 7.5 is assigned to the positive rank sum. In Table 17-4 there are no zero differences, and so the problem does not exist.

Ignoring the sign of the differences, it is seen that four of the differences are equal to plus or minus one. These four differences are assigned the mean rank value of $\frac{1}{4}(1 + 2 + 3 + 4) = 2.5$. The remaining ranks are as shown in Table 17-4. For this example, the sum of the ranks assigned to the positive differences is given by:

$$T = 2.5 + 13 + 8 + 10.5 = 34$$

To decide whether or not this value of T represents a significant difference in population centers at $\alpha = 0.05$, we read from Table A-4 that the 0.025 and 0.975 percentile values are given by 21 and 84. In terms of these numbers, the $\alpha = 0.05$, two-tailed decision rule reads is:

     Decision Rule: Reject the hypothesis of no difference in scores if the value of T is given by $T \le 21$ or $T \ge 84$.

Since $T = 34$ is not in the rejection region, the hypothesis that the median difference in the population is zero is not rejected. We provide directions for the matched-pair Wilcoxon test in Box 17-1.

Note that the box provides directions for a two-sided alternative. Step 2 can be modified to provide a one-tailed test. For example, if H_1 states that $M_d > 0$, you would select the upper $(1 - \alpha)$ point for the decision rule, while if $M_d < 0$, the lower α point would be used to select the correct decision rule.

17-3. THE CONFIDENCE INTERVAL FOR THE MEDIAN DIFFERENCE OF THE MATCHED-PAIR WILCOXON TEST

Just as the decision rule of the sign test can be used to obtain a confidence interval for the median difference, so can the decision rule of the matched-pair Wilcoxon test be used in the same way. The only difference in the procedure is that it is time-consuming. One begins by computing all possible two-sample estimates of the population median difference, that is, all

$$\hat{M}_{ii'} = \tfrac{1}{2}(d_i^0 + d_{i'}^0)$$

These are rank ordered and their median is taken as an estimate of the population median difference. An easy way to find this estimate is to create a

Table 17-5. Computations required to obtain the confidence interval for the median difference of the matched-pair Wilcoxon test

Value of d_i	−7.0	−5.0	−4.0	−3.0	−3.0	−2.0	−2.0	−1.0	−1.0	−1.0	+1.0	+3.0	+4.0	+6.0
−7.0	−7.0	−6.0	−5.5	−5.0	−5.0	−4.5	−4.5	−4.0	−4.0	−4.0	−3.0	−2.0	−1.5	−0.5
−5.0		−5.0	−4.5	−4.0	−4.0	−3.5	−3.5	−3.0	−3.0	−3.0	−2.0	−1.0	−0.5	0.5
−4.0			−4.0	−3.5	−3.5	−3.0	−3.0	−2.5	−2.5	−2.5	−1.5	−0.5	0.0	1.0
−3.0				−3.0	−3.0	−2.5	−2.5	−2.0	−2.0	−2.0	−1.0	0.0	0.5	1.5
−3.0					−3.0	−2.5	−2.5	−2.0	−2.0	−2.0	−1.0	0.0	0.5	1.5
−2.0						−2.0	−2.0	−1.5	−1.5	−1.5	−0.5	0.5	1.0	2.0
−2.0							−2.0	−1.5	−1.5	−1.5	−0.5	0.5	1.0	2.0
−1.0								−1.0	−1.0	−1.0	0.0	1.0	1.5	2.5
−1.0									−1.0	−1.0	0.0	1.0	1.5	2.5
−1.0										−1.0	0.0	1.0	1.5	2.5
+1.0											1.0	2.0	2.5	3.5
+3.0												3.0	3.5	4.5
+4.0													4.0	5.0
+6.0														6.0

triangular table of average differences and to locate the median of the mean differences. The triangular matrix for the data of Table 17-4 is shown in Table 17-5. The numbers in the matrix are found by averaging the differences in the margins of the table that are associated with the intersecting row and column for each tabled entry. In this case $\hat{M}_d = -1.5$.

In addition, this table can be used to determine a confidence interval for the population median difference, since a relationship exists between the Wilcoxon signed rank test and values in the table. First, provided that one counts half of the mean differences whose value is zero as positive, the number of positive values in the table equals the Wilcoxon signed rank statistic, T. A check of the positive and zero differences of Table 17-5 shows that:

$$T = 31 + \tfrac{1}{2}(6) = 34$$

Second, the minimum number of positive mean differences that could be obtained for any set of data is zero, and the maximum is $N(N+1)/2$, the same range possible for the Wilcoxon signed rank statistic. Therefore, the tabled critical values for the Wilcoxon test can be used to construct a two-tailed confidence interval in the same manner as that used for the sign test in Chapter 14. In particular, the interval is bounded by the average values in the $T_L + 1$ position and in the T_U position from the bottom. In this example, the lower limit to the confidence interval is defined as the average difference associated with the $T_L + 1 = 21 + 1 = 22$d smallest average. The upper limit is associated with the 22d largest average, or the $T_U = 84$th value from the bottom. For the data of Table 17-4, the lower limit equals -3 and the upper limit equals $+1$, so that $-3 \leq M_d \leq +1$. Since $M_d = 0$ is in the interval, we can conclude that the median difference in the populations is not significantly different from zero. This interval is considerably smaller than that

---

Box 17-2 **How to determine the $(1 - \alpha)$ percent confidence interval for M_d of the matched-pair Wilcoxon test**

Step 1. Rank order the differences and record them in the first row and column of the data matrix.

Step 2. Fill in the upper triangle of the matrix of average differences corresponding to intersecting rows and columns.

Step 3. Order the $\hat{M}_{ii'}$ from smallest to largest. Denote these ordered values as $\hat{M}_{ii'}^0$.

Step 4. Find the lower $\alpha/2$ critical value in Table A-4. The lower limit to the confidence interval corresponds to the $T_L + 1$ smallest average in the triangular matrix. Find the upper $(1 - \alpha/2)$ critical value in Table A-4. The upper limit to the confidence interval corresponds to the T_U ordered average in the triangular matrix. For one-tailed intervals, the limits are obtained using the α critical value or the $1 - \alpha$ critical value.

reported for the sign test. For the sign test, the interval extended from -4 to $+3$ for a range of seven test points. For the Wilcoxon test, the range is only four test points. Clearly, the Wilcoxon model is more precise than the sign test model. We provide directions for computing the $(1 - \alpha)$ percent confidence interval for M_d in Box 17-2.

Like the sign test model, the matched-pair Wilcoxon model can be used to estimate the median of a population, obtain a confidence interval for M, and test $M = 0$. One merely replaces paired differences with the one-sample ordered observations, $Y_1^0, Y_2^0, \ldots, Y_N^0$.

17-4. EXERCISES

17-1. Two methods for the treatment of skin cancer were applied over a 10-year period in a large university research hospital. Patients were provided information about the two treatments; they then volunteered to accept either treatment, and then treatments were applied at random to members of each pair. Pairs were established by sex and age and by proximity of date on which treatment began. The dependent variable is the number of years that treatment was judged successful by a panel of doctors who did not know which treatment had been applied to each patient.

Pair	Chemotherapy	Radiology
1	9.2	8.7
2	8.7	9.3
3	6.2	7.2
4	1.4	6.8
5	8.3	7.7
6	7.6	6.2
7	5.5	5.9
8	6.2	6.2
9	1.3	5.4
10	2.1	3.2
11	1.6	3.1

Pair	Chemotherapy	Radiology
12	4.2	4.7
13	1.3	2.6
14	1.9	3.9
15	2.7	2.9
16	1.6	1.6
17	0.8	0.8

a. Apply the matched-pair Wilcoxon test to these data.

b. Find the 95-percent confidence interval for the median difference.

17-2. Apply the sign test to the data of Exercise 17-1 and determine the 95-percent confidence interval for the median difference.

17-3. The median number of correct responses on a 30-item recall task was 15 items when high school students were tested. The words used in the recall task bore no apparent relationship to each other. An investigator interested in the effect of categorization of words on the students' recall used a similar list containing related words scattered at random throughout the list. The scores reported are the number of words recalled on the 30-item list of related words by a random sample of 10 high school students. The hypothesis to be tested is that median number recalled for the list of partially related words is 15. Do the test and find the 95-percent confidence interval for the median improvement.

Number correct	Number correct minus median
13	−2
14	−1
20	5
28	13
21	6
24	9
23	8
11	−4
29	14
22	7

17-4. Analyze the data of Exercise 17-3 in terms of the sign test model.

17-5. In a study in which the effects of diet upon maze-running were being evaluated, the following statistics were generated.

Litter	Diet one	Diet two
1	7	8
2	8	9
3	12	10
4	20	12
5	15	14
6	9	10
7	20	15
8	13	10

Litter	Diet one	Diet two
9	20	15
10	9	9
11	14	13
12	20	20
13	16	14
14	20	18
15	14	6
16	13	12
17	20	14
18	20	13

The dependent variable is the number of trials it takes a rat to make five consecutive successful runs. No rat was given more than 20 trials. Previous studies had suggested that Diet two produced greater learning than Diet one.

a. Do these data support the latter observation?

b. Determine the 95-percent confidence interval for the median difference.

17-6. In a study in which a new reading program was being compared to an old, or traditional, reading program, 32 poor readers were given a pretest designed to measure their reading skills. On the basis of the pretest, the students were rank ordered and randomly assigned in pairs to the two treatments. Results are as shown.

	Old program		New program	
Pair	Pretest	Posttest	Pretest	Posttest
1	17	28	16	30
2	18	20	18	38
3	20	29	19	28

	Old program		New program	
Pair	Pretest	Posttest	Pretest	Posttest
4	20	35	20	35
5	23	35	22	39
6	23	38	25	43
7	26	37	27	40
8	27	37	27	50
9	27	38	27	44
10	29	29	28	47
11	31	40	30	46
12	31	41	32	38
13	32	40	35	50
14	35	44	35	51
15	35	47	37	49
16	40	47	43	49

a. Perform the sign test and the matched-pair Wilcoxon test for each program.
b. Obtain the 95-percent confidence interval for the median difference under the sign test and Wilcoxon models for each program.

CHAPTER 18

The Two-Sample Wilcoxon Test and the Mann–Whitney U Test

18-1. USING RANKS TO COMPARE TWO DISTRIBUTIONS

In Chapter 17, we saw how ranks could be used to test the hypothesis that the median difference of a set of matched-pair data is equal to zero. We now wish to consider the same problem, but for the case in which the data are not matched. In particular, we are going to see how you compare two samples selected at random from completely separate populations.

The test is normally referred to as the Wilcoxon two-sample test. A second form of this test is frequently encountered. It is called the Mann–Whitney U test. While these tests seem to test different hypotheses, they actually provide tests of the same hypothesis. This identity of function is illustrated in this chapter.

18-2. THE TWO-SAMPLE WILCOXON TEST

As an example of the use of this test, consider the data of Table 18-1, which represents the number of times seven patients returned to a mental health therapy clinic following two different types of initial treatments. In treatment one, three subjects were given a 30-minute person-to-person interview with a public health social worker, in which the nature of the therapy was discussed. In treatment two, the same information was presented to four subjects via a prerecorded 30-minute television tape. The program staff wanted to know if attendance would be hindered by the use of the video tape for, if it was not, the interviewers could be released for other staff activities.

To test the hypothesis of no treatment effects, the Wilcoxon test requires that the original data be replaced by ranks. To achieve this ranking, the data are ordered and then ranks are assigned, independent of sample membership. The ranks are then used to generate the criterion variable for the two-sample Wilcoxon test. In particular, this test uses the ranks $\{1, 2, \ldots, (N_1 + N_2)\}$ as a population of values. If attendance is unaffected by the type of treatment given to the subjects, then all possible assignments of the ranks to the data are equally likely. For the data of Table 18-1, ranks 1, 2, and 5 are assigned to the interviewed subjects, while ranks 3, 4, 6, and 7 are assigned to the TV subjects. If we knew the probabilities associated with the distribution of ranks, we could define a decision rule that would enable us to test the hypothesis that the median difference in the number of visits for the two groups of subjects is zero. Why the hypothesis is one about the value of M_d will become apparent from the discussion in Section 18-5. In any case, the Wilcoxon two-sample test is used to test the hypothesis H_0: $M_d = 0$ against H_1: $M_d \neq 0$. As might be expected, this test can be modified to generate directional, or one-tailed, tests. In addition, as was the case for the sign test, the null hypothesis specifies identity of the two population distributions.

Table 18-1. Number of visits to a mental health therapy clinic for a group of seven patients for six months

Original data		Rank data	
Interview	Film	Interview	Film
1	8	1	3
7	10	2	4
11	12	5	6
	15		7
Total		8	20

In a manner similar to that used for computing the probabilities for the sign test and the matched-pair Wilcoxon test, we could generate a tree diagram, define a variable on each branch, count the branches with common values, find the probabilities for the various outcomes, and define a decision rule. The only problem with this approach is that the tree diagram requires a large amount of drawing space because of the great number of branches. For this reason, we only provide a tabulation of the complete set of branches by indicating the ranks that would be assigned.

To simplify the presentation, note that:

$$(1 + 2 + 5) + (3 + 4 + 6 + 7) = 28$$

and that this constant sum of 28 holds for all assignments of the ranks. Thus, if one knew that the ranks 2, 4, and 7 were assigned to the smaller sample, ranks 1, 3, 5, and 6 must of necessity be assigned to the larger sample, so that:

$$(2 + 4 + 7) + (1 + 3 + 5 + 6) = 28$$

This means that we can simplify the tabulation if we decide to work with only one of the samples. If, in addition, we focus on the smaller sample, we can further simplify the arithmetic and, at the same time, be on our way to a definition of the two-sample Wilcoxon test, as follows:

Definition of the two-sample Wilcoxon statistics

If we let $r_1, r_2, \ldots, r_{N_1}$ be the ranks assigned to the smaller sample, the Wilcoxon statistic is defined as:

$$T_W = r_1 + r_2 + \cdots r_{N_1} = \sum_{i=1}^{N_1} r_i$$

For our example:

$$T_W = r_1 + r_2 + r_3$$

where r_1 is the rank assigned to the smallest value in the smaller sample and r_3 is the rank assigned to the largest value. The complete set of assignments and corresponding values of T_W are shown in Table 18-2. For the moment, let us ignore the column labelled U. We will return to it in Section 18-3.

As we see, the smallest value of T_W occurs for the ranks 1, 2, and 3. For this assignment, $T_W = 6$. The largest value occurs for the ranks 5, 6, and 7. For

Table 18-2. The complete set of assignments of three ranks from the set of integers 1, 2, 3, 4, 5, 6, and 7 to the smaller of two samples where $N_1 = 3$ and $N_2 = 4$

r_1	r_2	r_3	$T_W = \Sigma\, r_i$	U
1	2	3	6	12
1	2	4	7	11
1	2	5	8	10
1	2	6	9	9
1	2	7	10	8
1	3	4	8	10
1	3	5	9	9
1	3	6	10	8
1	3	7	11	7
1	4	5	10	8
1	4	6	11	7
1	4	7	12	6
1	5	6	12	6
1	5	7	13	5
1	6	7	14	4
2	3	4	9	9
2	3	5	10	8
2	3	6	11	7
2	3	7	12	6
2	4	5	11	7
2	4	6	12	6
2	4	7	13	5
2	5	6	13	5
2	5	7	14	4
2	6	7	15	3
3	4	5	12	6

(continued)

Table 18-2. The complete set of assignments of three ranks from the set of integers 1, 2, 3, 4, 5, 6, and 7 to the smaller of two samples where $N_1 = 3$ and $N_2 = 4$ *(Continued)*

r_1	r_2	r_3	$T_W = \Sigma\, r_i$	U
3	4	6	13	5
3	4	7	14	4
3	5	6	14	4
3	5	7	15	3
3	6	7	16	2
4	5	6	15	3
4	5	7	16	2
4	6	7	17	1
5	6	7	18	0

Table 18-3. Distribution of T_W and U for $N_1 = 3$ and $N_2 = 4$

T_W	U	f	$P(T_W = t)$	$P(T_W \le t + \tfrac{1}{2})$
6	12 |	1	0.02857	0.02857
7	11 |	1	0.02857	0.05714
8	10 ||	2	0.05714	0.11428
9	9 |||	3	0.08571	0.20000
10	8 ||||	4	0.11429	0.31428
11	7 ||||	4	0.11429	0.42857
12	6 |||||	5	0.14286	0.57143
13	5 ||||	4	0.11429	0.68572
14	4 ||||	4	0.11429	0.80000
15	3 |||	3	0.08571	0.88572
16	2 ||	2	0.05714	0.94282
17	1 |	1	0.02857	0.97139
18	0 |	1	0.02857	1.00000
		35		

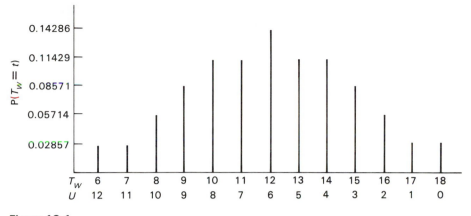

Figure 18-1.
Distribution of the two-sample Wilcoxon statistic for $N_1 = 3$ and $N_2 = 4$.

this assignment, $T_W = 18$. Also note that some values of T_W repeat. We have tallied them, and have summarized the distribution in Table 18-3. The complete tree diagram is defined by $C_3^7 = \binom{7}{3} = 35$ branches. We now calculate the probability of each value of T_W, assuming that each branch is equally likely. For example, $P(T_W = 12) = 5/35 = 0.14286$. The distribution is shown graphically in Figures 18-1 and 18-2. As can be seen, the distribution is symmetrical about $T_W = 12$. This value is clearly the median of the distribution, as well as the mode and mean.

We can now generate a decision rule for our example. Since we are testing a

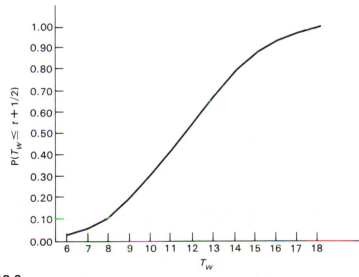

Figure 18-2.
Cumulative probabilities for the two-sample Wilcoxon statistic for $N_1 = 3$ and $N_2 = 4$.

nondirectional alternative, we will need to construct the decision rule from both tails of the distribution. As a first trial, let us consider the following:

Decision Rule: Reject H_0 if $T_W = 6$ or if $T_W = 18$.

With this rule, the risk of a type I error is given by:

$$\alpha = P(T_W = 6) + P(T_W = 12)$$
$$= 0.02857 + 0.02857 = 0.05714$$

For most situations, this rule would not be acceptable because α exceeds 0.05. With such small sample sizes, it is not possible to produce a rule that satisfies the condition that $\alpha \le 0.05$, and so we are forced to compromise and adopt this as a usable decision rule. In this case, $T_W = 1 + 2 + 5 = 8$. Because $T_W = 8$ is not in the critical region defined by $T_W = 6$ or $T_W = 12$, the hypothesis is not rejected. Thus, it is concluded that the TV film is as effective as the interview and is therefore recommended.

In practice, one does not need to generate a decision rule each time this test is performed, for others have done it and prepared tables that are easy to use. One such table appears in the appendix as Table A-5. This table is entered by specifying the values of N_1 and N_2 and α, the risk of a type I error that one is willing to tolerate. For example, if $N_1 = 5$ and $N_2 = 8$, the two-tailed decision rule with $\alpha = 0.05$ is given by:

Decision Rule: Reject H_0 if $T_W \le 21$ or if $T_W \ge 49$.

The table can also be used for directional tests. For example, the decision rule for testing:

$$H_0: \quad M_d = 0$$

against:

$$H_1: \quad M_d > 0$$

with $N_1 = 3$, $N_2 = 7$, and $\alpha = 0.05$ is given by:

Decision rule: Reject H_0 if $T_W \ge 25$.

We provide directions for performing the two-sample Wilcoxon test in Box 18-1.

As an example, consider the data of Table 18-4 which lists the original ordered data and the corresponding ranks for 18 subjects who were either exposed to the interview schedule or video film. Tied values are broken by

---

Box 18-1   How to perform the two-sample Wilcoxon test

Step 1. Rank order the data in each sample. Let N_1 refer to the size of the smaller sample, if one exists.

Step 2. Assign ranks 1, 2, 3, . . . , $(N_1 + N_2)$ to the ranked observations, paying no attention to sample membership. Assign rank 1 to the smallest value and rank $(N_1 + N_2)$ to the largest value. If there are tied ranks, break the ties by assigning midrank values to the corresponding ties.

Step 3. Compute the value of the Wilcoxon statistic, which is defined as the sum of the ranks associated with the smaller sample, $T_W = \sum\limits_{i=1}^{N_1} r_i$

Step 4. Determine the appropriate decision rule from the critical values of Table A-5.

Step 5. Make a decision.

Table 18-4.   Number of visits to a mental health therapy clinic for a group of 18 patients observed over six months of treatment

Original data		Rank data	
Interview	Film	Interview	Film
1	1	2.5	2.5
1	1	2.5	2.5
3	2	6.0	5.0
7	9	7.0	8.5
9	13	8.5	10.0
15	18	11.0	13.0
16	26	12.0	15.0
20	29	14.0	16.0
	31		17.0
	42		18.0
Total		63.5	107.5

assigning midranks. Thus, the four values tied at 1 visit are ranked $\frac{1}{4}(1 + 2 + 3 + 4) = 2.5$ and the two values tied at 9 visits are ranked $\frac{1}{2}(8 + 9) = 8.5$. As we see:

$$T_W = 2.5 + 2.5 + \cdots + 14 = 63.5$$

With $N_1 = 8$, $N_2 = 10$, and $\alpha = 0.05$, the two-tailed decision rule read from Table A-5 is given by:

Decision Rule: Reject H_0 if $T_W \leq 53$ or if $T_W \geq 99$.

Since $T = 63.5$ is not in the critical region, we do not reject H_0, and we conclude that, in the universe from which the patients came, $M_d = 0$. Since attendance is not affected by the type of initial visit, it is reasonable to recommend the use of the video film so that the public health social workers can be used for other duties.

Strictly speaking, the rules of Table A-5 are valid only if the number of tied values is small, such as in our example. If there are many ties, then one is advised to generate the decision rule via a tree diagram. The probabilities for T_W are determined under the assumption that attendance figures for all subjects are independent from one another. This is equivalent to saying that observations between and within samples are independent.

18-3. CONCORDANT AND DISCORDANT PAIRED OBSERVATIONS

Mann and Whitney examined the same null hypothesis as Wilcoxon, but from a different perspective. They felt that if one compared each Sample 1 observation to each Sample 2 observation, and if H_0 were true, about half of the comparisons would show a larger value in Sample 2 than in Sample 1, and in about half of the comparisons the reverse would be true. Thus, they realized that the *number of comparisons* in which an observation from Sample 1 was less than an observation from Sample 2 would provide a test statistic for examining H_0. This led them to formulate the concept of concordant and discordant pairs of observations.

Concordant and discordant pairs are defined as follows.

Definition of concordant and discordant pairs

Two pairs of ordered numbers (X_1, Y_1) and (X_2, Y_2) are said to be:

> *a.* Concordant if $X_1 < X_2$ and $Y_1 < Y_2$
> *b.* Discordant if $X_1 < X_2$ and $Y_1 > Y_2$

and

> *c.* Tied if either $X_1 = X_2$ or $Y_1 = Y_2$

For example:

$(X_1, Y_1) = (3, 7)$ and $(X_2, Y_2) = (6, 12)$
are concordant, since $3 < 6$ and $7 < 12$.
$(X_1, Y_1) = (3, 7)$ and $(X_2, Y_2) = (8, 4)$
are discordant, since $3 < 8$ and $7 > 4$.
$(X_1, Y_1) = (3, 7)$ and $(X_2, Y_2) = (6, 7)$
are tied, since $3 < 6$ and $7 = 7$.

and

$(X_1, Y_1) = (3, 5)$ and $(X_2, Y_2) = (3, 13)$
are tied, since $3 = 3$ and $5 < 13$.

To see how concordant and discordant pairs are associated with the test of $H_0: M_d = 0$, consider the rank data of Table 18-1 in terms of sample membership. Let us introduce a dummy variable, X, to represent sample membership. If we let $X = 0$ represent membership in Sample 1, and $X = 1$ represent membership in Sample 2, we can summarize the rank data of Table 18-1 as:

	Sample 1			Sample 2			
X	0	0	0	1	1	1	1
Y	1	2	5	3	4	6	7

From this representation, let's make a complete list of all possible between-group pairs (X_1, Y_1) and (X_2, Y_2) (Table 18-5), and examine them for concordance. There are ten concordant pairs and two discordant pairs. The total number of possible group pairs between sample comparisons is given by $N = N_1 N_2 = 3(4) = 12$. For the data of Table 18-5, the number of concordant and discordant pairs between samples is given by 10 and 2, respectively. As indicated above, the number of concordances provides information about the value of M_d in the population. If the median difference, $M_d = 0$, one would expect to find that about half of the comparisons would be concordant and half discordant. If the $M_d < 0$, one would expect to find many discordant pairs whereas, if $M_d > 0$, most pairs would be concordant. Thus, the number of concordances can be used to test H_0. Historically, C was proposed as a measure for testing $H_0: M_d = 0$ at about the same time that Wilcoxon proposed the use of T_W. Mann and Whitney suggested that the smaller-sized sample be identified with the value $X = 0$, and they labeled the number of concordances U. In this form, the test is called the Mann–Whitney U test.

As an example of how the distribution of U is generated, consider the 35 branches of Table 18-2. For the first branch with ranks 1, 2, and 3, $U = 12$. Remaining values of U for the other branches are reported in the last column

Table 18-5. Table of concordant and discordant pairs of ranks for the data of Table 18-1.

Pairs			
(X_1, Y_1)	(X_2, Y_2)	Concordant	Discordant
(0, 1)	(1, 3)	✓	
(0, 1)	(1, 4)	✓	
(0, 1)	(1, 6)	✓	
(0, 1)	(1, 7)	✓	
(0, 2)	(1, 3)	✓	
(0, 2)	(1, 4)	✓	
(0, 2)	(1, 6)	✓	
(0, 2)	(1, 7)	✓	
(0, 5)	(1, 3)		✓
(0, 5)	(1, 4)		✓
(0, 5)	(1, 6)	✓	
(0, 5)	(1, 7)	✓	
Total		10	2

of Table 18-2. Clearly, there is a direct connection between T_W and U. The relationship is as follows:

$$U = N_1 N_2 + \frac{N_1(N_1 + 1)}{2} - T_W$$

For $N_1 = 3$ and $N_2 = 4$:

$$U = 3(4) + \frac{3(4)}{2} - T_W = 18 - T_W$$

When $T_W = 6$, $U = 18 - 6 = 12$, and when $T_W = 18$, $U = 18 - 18 = 0$. For the data of Table 18-1, $T_W = 8$ and $U = 18 - 8 = 10$. Thus, if one knows the value of T_W, the value of U can be computed directly, without having to count concordances, discordances, and ties.

18-4. THE MANN—WHITNEY U TEST

The Mann—Whitney U test can always be substituted for the two-sample Wilcoxon test, since both are based upon the same probability distributions.

Thus, one can generalize decision rules for U directly from the decision rules for T_W. In practice, this is not necessary since Mann and Whitney provided tables of critical values for common values of α. A shortened table appears in the appendix as Table A-6. As an example of how this table is used, consider the data of Table 18-4. For these data, $N_1 = 8$ and $N_2 = 10$. With $\alpha = 0.05$ divided equally between the two tails of the distribution of U, the decision rule for testing:

$$H_0: M_d = 0 \quad \text{against} \quad H_1: M_d \neq 0$$

is seen to be:

Decision Rule: Reject H_0 if $U \leq 17$ or if $U \geq 63$.

Rank order the data in each sample separately and count the number of concordances, discordances, and ties for each observation. For example, consider the first ordered subject of sample 1 in Table 18-4. This subject is tied with the first two subjects in Sample 2, since they have $Y = 1$, and then is concordant with the eight other subjects in Sample 2. The same is true for the second ordered subject in Sample 1. For the third ordered subject in Sample 1, whose $Y = 3$, there are discordances with the three subjects in Sample 2 with scores less than 3, and there are seven concordances with subjects in Sample 2 whose scores are greater than three. Results for the first ordered subject are shown in Column 1 of Table 18-6, as are the results for the remaining values. Since $N_2 = 10$, the total number of pairs to be examined is

Table 18-6. Short-cut procedures for determining U for the data of Table 18-4.

				Value of Y in smaller sample					
	1	1	3	7	9	15	16	20	Total
C	8	8	7	7	6	5	5	4	50
D	0	0	3	3	3	5	5	6	25
T	2	2	0	0	1	0	0	0	5
Total	10	10	10	10	10	10	10	10	80

given by $N = N_1 N_2 = 8(10) = 80$. For these data, the proportion of concordant pairs is given by:

$$\hat{P} = \frac{U}{N_1 N_2} = {}^{50}\!/\!80 = 0.625$$

Furthermore, if $M_d = 0$, then U would be expected to be near a value of 40. In that case:

$$P = {}^{40}\!/\!80 = 0.50$$

so that the test of $H_0: M_d = 0$ is identical to the test of $H_0: P = 0.50$.

As we see, five between-sample pairs are tied. Like the two-sample Wilcoxon test, ties provide a problem in that the critical values for U are determined under the condition that ties do not occur. To overcome this problem, ties are divided equally among the concordant and discordant pairs. If the number of ties is small, the error made in using the tabled decision rules is negligible. For the data of Table 18-5 the corrected value for ties U is

$$U_C = U + \tfrac{1}{2}T = 50 + \tfrac{1}{2}(5) = 52.5$$

Since $U_C = 52.5$ is not in the critical region defined by $U \leq 17$ and $U \geq 63$, H_0 is not rejected. This agrees with the decision made when the Wilcoxon test was used. If we had wanted, we could have determined U from T_W. For the data of Table 18-4, we have seen that $T_W = 63.5$, so that:

$$U = N_1 N_2 + \frac{N_1(N_1 + 1)}{2} - T_W$$

$$= 8(10) + \frac{8(8 + 1)}{2} - 63.5 = 52.5$$

We provide directions for performing the Mann–Whitney U test in Box 18-2.

18-5. CONFIDENCE INTERVAL FOR THE MEDIAN DIFFERENCE

One of the major advantages of the Mann–Whitney U test over the Wilcoxon version is that the Mann–Whitney test leads to a confidence interval for the median difference. Denote the ordered observations in the smaller sample by $Y^o_{11}, Y^o_{12}, \ldots, Y^o_{1N_1}$, and those in the larger sample by $Y^o_{21}, Y^o_{22}, \ldots, Y^o_{2N_2}$. Note that if $Y^o_{1i} < Y^o_{2i'}$, it follows that $d_{ii'} = Y^o_{2i} - Y^o_{1i'} > 0$, whereas if $Y^o_{1i} > Y^o_{2i'}$, it follows that $d_{ii'} = Y^o_{2i} - Y^o_{1i'} < 0$. Thus, U represents the number of pairs for which $d_{ii'}$, is positive. If, in addition, H_0 is true, then the sample median

---

Box 18-2   How to perform the Mann–Whitney U test

Step 1. Rank order the data in each sample.

Step 2. Associate a dummy variable with each sample. Let the dummy value of 0 be associated with the smaller sample and the dummy value of 1 be associated with the larger sample.

Step 3. Count the number of pairs that are concordant or tied between samples. The Mann–Whitney U statistic is the number of concordant pairs. If there are ties:

$$U = C + \tfrac{1}{2}T$$

Step 4. Determine the decision rule for U from Table A-6.

Step 5. Make a decision.

---

difference, $\hat{M}_d$, provides an estimate of the population M_d. Furthermore, one can find a $(1 - \alpha)$ percent range for the population M_d in terms of the decision rules of Table A-6 and values of $d_{ii'}$. As we saw, the $\alpha = 0.05$ decision rule for rejecting H_0 with $N_1 = 8$ and $N_2 = 10$ is given by:

Decision Rule: Reject H_0 if $U \le 17$ or if $U \ge 63$.

We can use this rule to find the confidence interval for M_d by computing each of the $N = N_1 N_2 = 80$ ordered differences, $d_{ii'} = Y^o_{1i} - Y^o_{2i'}$. In particular, it can be shown that the lower and upper limits to the confidence interval are given by the ordered differences:

$$d^o_{(\text{Lower})} = d^o_{U_{\alpha/2}+1} \quad \text{and} \quad d^o_{(\text{Upper})} = d^o_{U_{1-(\alpha/2)}}$$

In this case, $d^o_{(\text{Lower})} = d^o_{18}$ and $d^o_{(\text{Upper})} = d^o_{63}$. An easy way to find d^o_{18} and d^o_{63} is shown in Table 18-7. This simplification is based on the directions given in Box 18-3. For the data of Table 18-7:

$$d^o_{18} = -6 \quad \text{and} \quad d^o_{63} = 22$$

so that:

$$-6 \le M_d \le 22$$

Since $M_d = 0$ is contained in the interval, we again do not reject H_0. In addition, we see that the sample median difference is given by:

$$\hat{M}_d = \frac{d^o_{40} + d^o_{41}}{2} = \frac{8 + 8}{2} = 8$$

Table 18-7. Procedure for finding the confidence interval for the M_d of the data of Table 18-4.

				Value of the larger sample						
	1	1	2	9	13	18	26	29	31	42
Value of smaller sample										
1	0	0	1	8	12	17	25	28	30	41
1	0	0	1	8	12	17	25	28	30	41
3	−2	−2	−1	6	10	15	23	26	28	39
7	−6	−6	−5	2	6	11	19	22	24	35
9	−8	−8	−7	0	4	9	17	20	22	33
15	−14	−14	−13	−6	−2	3	11	14	16	27
16	−15	−15	−14	−7	−3	2	10	13	15	26
20	−19	−19	−18	−11	−7	−2	6	9	11	22

Note that the number of positive differences in Table 18-6 is given by $C = 50$ and that the number of zero differences is given by $T = 5$, so that $U = C + \frac{1}{2}T = 50 + \frac{1}{2}(5) = 52.5$. Thus, a very simple way to compute U is to follow the directions for setting up the $(1 - \alpha)$ percent confidence interval for M_d and determine U by counting the number of positive and zero differences. This is the procedure we recommend, since it gives rise to the value of

---

Box 18-3   How to compute a confidence interval for the median difference

Step 1. Rank order the values of each sample.

Step 2. List the two sets of ordered samples in a two-dimensional table with the smaller sample listed in the vertical margin.

Step 3. Complete the matrix of differences by calculating all the algebraic differences between the vertical and horizontal margins.

Step 4. Determine the ordered values for the confidence interval by selecting the appropriate critical region from Table A-6. The limits for the confidence interval are found by rank ordering the differences and using as the lower limit the ordered difference defined by $U_{\alpha/2} + 1$ and the upper limit the ordered difference defined by $U_{1-(\alpha/2)}$. For one-tailed intervals, the limits are obtained using $U_\alpha + 1$ or $U_{1-\alpha}$.

U and provides a point and interval estimate of M_d. If $N_1 N_2$ is odd, the point estimate of M_d is given by

$$d^o_{\left(\frac{N_1 N_2 + 1}{2}\right)}$$

and if $N_1 N_2$ is even by

$$\frac{d^o_{\left(\frac{N_1 N_2}{2}\right)} + d^o_{\left(\frac{N_1 N_2}{2} + 1\right)}}{2}$$

In addition, the $(1 - \alpha)$ percent confidence interval for M_d is given by:

$$d^o_{U_{\alpha/2} + 1} \leq M_d \leq d^o_{U_{1 - (\alpha/2)}}$$

18-6. SYMMETRIC DISTRIBUTIONS AND A TEST OF THE MEAN DIFFERENCE IN PAIRED OBSERVATIONS

In many situations, a researcher can make a stronger statement about the difference in two distributions other than that available in declaring that $M_d = 0$ or $M_d \neq 0$. If the distribution of $d_{ii'}$, is symmetrical, it follows that the median of the differences is identical to the mean of the differences, which in turn is equal to the difference in the means. In general, one cannot state with certainty that a distribution is symmetrical, but an examination of the distri-

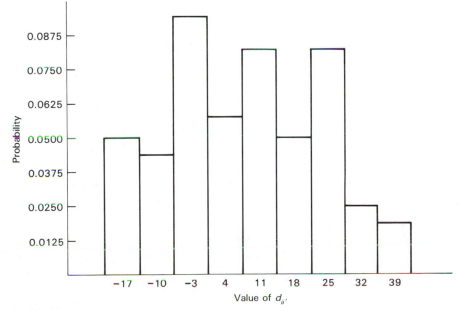

Figure 18-3.
Distribution of the $d_{ii'}$ values of Table 18-7.

bution of the differences allows a ballpark characterization of the symmetry property of the sample differences. Figure 18-3 provides a visual impression of the distribution of the differences generated in Table 18-7. While there is a slight skewness to the distribution, it may appear symmetrical enough to conclude that the distribution in the population is symmetrical. With this decision, we can conclude with some degree of assurance that the mean difference is not statistically different from zero. The point estimate of $\bar{d} = \bar{Y}_2 - \bar{Y}_1$ is given by $\bar{d} = 8.175 \simeq 8.2$. This is very close to $\hat{M}_d = 8$, supporting the belief that the distribution is symmetrical.

18-7. EXERCISES

18-1. Apply the Wilcoxon test to the smaller gender group in your sample of 40 subjects who are classified into Programs 1 and 2 and for which the dependent variable is score on the final.
  a. What are H_0 and H_1?
  b. What is the decision rule for $\alpha = 0.05$?
  c. What is the decision?

18-2. Find the 95-percent confidence interval for M_d. Under what condition can the statement about M_d be translated into a statement about μ_d?

18-3. Write a short paragraph on the findings generated from Exercises 18-1 and 18-2.

18-4. In a study of consumer buyer habits a researcher was stationed at a checkout stand in a large supermarket and targeted for research every tenth male and female that passed through the checkout stand and paid the cashier for the merchandise. As the merchandise was rung up on the cash register, the researcher kept a second record on foods that had brand name labels and which could have been purchased using the store's own label. The amount spent on the brand labels was determined and compared to the cost for the store's brand. For example, Buyer 1 purchased $8.32 of brand label food that could have been purchased using the store's label at $7.83, for a saving of 49¢. Results for the first ten men and ten women in the study are as follows:

Men	Women
+0.49	+1.33
+0.63	−0.17
+0.18	−0.22
−0.03	+0.61
+0.17	+0.31
+1.26	+0.99
+0.33	+1.42
+0.41	+0.88
+0.91	+2.61
+0.84	+1.02

Is there a sex difference in the buying habits?

18-5. Find the 95-percent confidence interval for the median difference for the data of Exercise 18-4.

18-6. What assumptions must you make to justify the test of Exercise 18-4? Are they reasonable in this case?

18-7. Find the variances for the two groups of Exercise 18-4. Is there reason to believe that they differ? If they do, what impact does this have upon the conclusions of Exercise 18-4?

18-8. Comment about the internal and external validity of the conclusions of Exercise 18-4.

PART IV

PROCEDURES BASED ON THE NORMAL DISTRIBUTION

We have used exact probability distributions to produce tests and confidence intervals for small samples. These methods become unwieldly for even moderate sample sizes, and most investigators would not wish to perform the required calculations. Fortunately, there are excellent approximations to the required probabilities. These approximations are based on a theoretical distribution known as the normal distribution. We describe the properties of the normal distribution, and we show how it is used to test hypotheses and set up confidence intervals for population parameters in one- and two-sample situations.

CHAPTER 19

The Normal Distribution

19-1. STATISTICAL INFERENCE MODELS

In Chapter 11, we examined the basic principles of statistical inference, the process by which a researcher is able to stretch sample findings into corresponding statements about the population from which the sample came. We saw that probability theory served as the starting point for this model, in that statistical inference procedures are based on the probabilities of the possible outcomes of a chance process. Furthermore, we saw that inferences were made according to a decision rule generated from a division of the outcomes into two sets. One set consisted of outcomes compatible with the hypothesis being tested, while the other set, called the critical region, consisted of outcomes that were incompatible with the hypothesis.

An example of this inference model was given in Chapter 11 in terms of hypotheses about the flipping of a coin 20 times. In that example, we were able to list the probabilities associated with each of the values of the variable, the number of heads appearing. This was done in advance to data collection, provided we could specify the proper value of p, the probability of heads appearing on a given toss. In testing fair coins, we assumed a value, $p = \frac{1}{2}$, and determined the probabilities associated with all possible outcomes. Separating the outcomes into two sets based on cumulating probabilities, we were able to specify in advance of the data collection a decision rule for rejecting the hypothesis under test.

We assumed throughout the example that the results of coin-flipping could be approximated closely by the rules of probability theory. As intuition suggests, the approximation will be good if the flipping of the coin results in a truly random process. Thus, the key element in defining critical regions and decision rules is the proper choice of a probability distribution to approximate the distribution of the variable in question. If the approximation is good, and if the approximate distribution we choose is well-known and has easily determined percentile values, then the definition of critical regions and decision rules is at once accurate and simple to apply.

We were able to succeed in the examples of Chapters 11 to 18 because the set of outcomes was not large. We now wish to develop the theory for a number of statistical tests that can be applied in cases where the set of outcomes is large. It is surprising that many, if not most, of the statistical tests that are used by researchers can be derived from a single theory, based upon a very specific probability distribution with a long history. This distribution is called the *normal distribution*.

19-2. THE NORMAL DISTRIBUTION

Making use of first principles, one can derive the normal distribution. However, since the derivation requires the knowledge of calculus and advanced mathematics, we will introduce the normal distribution as a definition or mathematical model. As will be seen, the definition is phrased in terms of probabilities. By studying, in detail, its probability properties, the nature of the normal distribution can be understood. We define the normal distribution as follows.

Definition of the normal distribution

A continuous variable is said to have a normal probability distribution if its probabilities correspond to the probability values reported in Table A-7.

Some of the properties of a variable that has a normal distribution are that:

1. The underlying variable, Y, is continuous
2. The range of values of the continuous variable is unbounded
3. The distribution is symmetric about its center
4. The distribution is unimodal
5. The distribution is defined entirely in terms of two parameters, the mean, μ_Y (mu), and the standard deviation, σ_Y (sigma)

Each time a different μ_Y or σ_Y is specified, a different normal distribution is defined. Thus, there are actually many normal distributions, comprising a *family*. Other properties of the normal distribution, to two decimal places, that should be committed to memory are shown in Figures 19-1 and 19-2.

19-3. AN EXAMPLE OF A NORMAL DISTRIBUTION

Many biological variables appear to have distributions that can be adequately described by the normal distribution. One of these is the distribution of adult heights. There are good reasons why variables such as human heights have a normal distribution, and we will examine them in Section 20-4. Suppose, as an example, it is known that the heights of entering male collegiate freshmen at a midwestern university are normally distributed with a mean height of 69 in and a standard deviation of 2 in. If this is true, then we know from the percentages reported in Figures 19-1 and 19-2, that:

1. About 68 percent of the entering male freshmen have heights between $\mu_Y - \sigma_Y = 69 - 2 = 67$ in and $\mu_Y + \sigma_Y = 69 + 2 = 71$ in
2. About 95 percent of the entering male freshmen have heights between $\mu_Y - 2\sigma_Y = 69 - 2(2) = 65$ in and $\mu_Y + 2\sigma_Y = 69 + 2(2) = 73$ in
3. Almost 100 percent of the entering male freshmen have heights between $\mu_Y - 3\sigma_Y = 69 - 3(2) = 63$ in and $\mu_Y + 3\sigma_Y = 69 + 3(2) = 75$ in

In addition, we know that approximately:

4. The 2nd percentile height value is $P_{0.02} = \mu_Y - 2\sigma_Y = 69 - 2(2) = 65$ in
5. The 16th percentile height value is $P_{0.16} = \mu_Y - 1\sigma_Y = 69 - 1(2) = 67$ in
6. The 50th percentile height value is $P_{0.50} = \mu_Y - 0\sigma_Y = 69 - 0(2) = 69$ in

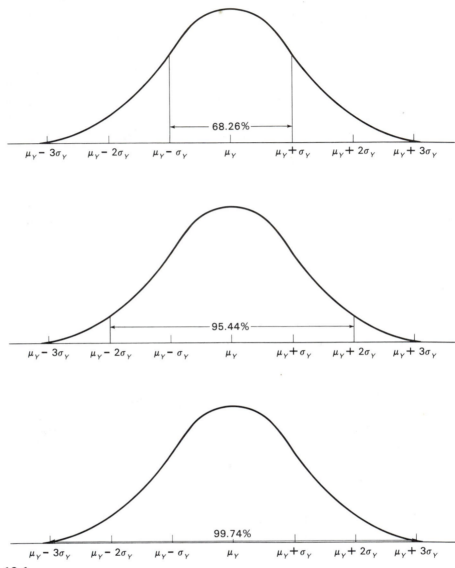

Figure 19-1.
Central probabilities of the normal distribution with mean of μ_Y and standard deviation σ_Y.

7. The 84th percentile height value is $P_{0.84} = \mu_Y + 1\sigma_Y = 69 + 1(2) = 71$ in

8. The 98th percentile height value is $P_{0.98} = \mu_Y + 2\sigma_Y = 69 + 2(2) = 73$ in

These eight separate pieces of information were derived strictly from the knowledge that entering freshmen heights can be adequately described by a normal distribution with a mean of 69 and a standard deviation of 2. This is not all the information that can be gleaned from these initial conditions. For example, we can determine the fifth percentile, the first quartile, the third

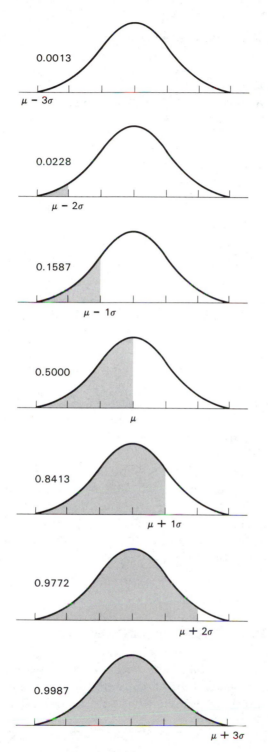

Figure 19-2.
Cumulative probabilities of the normal distribution with mean μ_Y and standard deviation σ_Y.

Box 19-1   Procedure for determining a percentile value for a normal variable

Step 1. Determine the value of μ_Y and σ_Y.

Step 2. Select the percentile value of interest, P_p.

Step 3. Find the value of Z_p in Table A-7 for the corresponding value of p. The percentile value is given by:

$$P_p = \mu_Y + Z_p \sigma_Y$$

Step 4. Substitute the values of μ_Y and σ_Y into the equation. The result is the p percentile.

---

quartile, or any other percentile value of interest by referring to the information summarized about the normal distribution in Table A-7. For example, by finding the Y value associated with the cumulative probability of Table A-7, we see that:

9. The 5th percentile value is defined by $P_{0.05} = \mu_Y - 1.645\sigma_Y = 69 - 1.645(2) = 69 - 3.29 = 65.71$ in

10. The 1st quartile value is defined by $P_{0.25} = \mu_Y - 0.674\sigma_Y = 69 - 0.674(2) = 69 - 1.35 = 67.65$ in

11. The 3rd quartile value is defined by $P_{0.75} = \mu_Y + 0.674\sigma_Y = 69 + 0.674(2) = 69 + 1.35 = 70.35$ in

12. The 95th percentile value is defined by $P_{0.95} = \mu_Y + 1.645\sigma_Y = 69 + 1.645(2) = 69 + 3.29 = 72.29$ in

As these examples show, percentile values for a normally distributed variable can be determined from the figures of Table A-7. Directions for determining the percentile value for any normally distributed variable are shown in Box 19-1.

19-4. THE STANDARD NORMAL DISTRIBUTION

In Section 6-4, we introduced the notion of a sample standard score. In particular, it was stated that if $\bar{Y}$ and S_Y were the sample mean and standard deviation of N observations, then the sample standard score associated with the value of Y is defined as:

$$Z = \frac{Y - \bar{Y}}{S_Y}$$

From these transformed values, one could compute T scores as:

$$T = 10Z + 50$$

As might be expected, one can do exactly the same thing in the population, provided that μ_Y and σ_Y are known. The definition of a population standard value is as follows.

Definition of a population standard value

Let Y represent an observation from a given population, let μ_Y represent the mean of the population, and let σ_Y represent the standard deviation of the population. The standard value associated with Y is defined as:

$$Z = \frac{Y - \mu_Y}{\sigma_Y}$$

As in the sample, Z actually measures the number of standard deviations that exist between Y and μ_Y. For the example of Section 19-3, the number of standard deviations between an average student's height of 69 in and one whose height is 62 in is given by:

$$Z = \frac{Y - \mu_Y}{\sigma_Y} = \frac{62 - 69}{2} = -3.5$$

standard deviations.

An interesting property of a standard value, Z, determined for a variable, Y, which has a normal distribution is that the distribution of Z is also normal, and its mean and standard deviation are equal to zero and one, respectively. A variable that has this property is said to be a *standard normal* variable, defined as follows.

Definition of a standard normal variable

Let

$$Z = \frac{Y - \mu_Y}{\sigma_Y}$$

where Y is normal with mean μ_Y and standard deviation σ_Y. The transformed variable, Z, is also normal, but with mean value of $\mu_Z = 0$ and standard deviation $\sigma_Z = 1$. It is called a standard normal variable.

An important implication of this definition is that any normally distributed variable, whatever its mean and standard deviation, can be transformed into a standard normal variable by a simple subtraction of the population mean and a division of the resulting difference by the population standard deviation. The resulting distribution will be normal with a mean of zero and a standard deviation of one. The importance of this fact is that a researcher needs only a single table of the standard normal distribution, for all other normal distributions can be related to it. As a matter of fact, Table A-7 is the table of the normal distribution with mean of zero and standard deviation of one.

Table A-7 can be used to determine the percentage of male heights that is less than a certain height. For example, what percentage of the males are less than 70 in tall? To answer this question, we determine the standard score corresponding to $Y = 70$. In this case:

$$Z = \frac{Y - \mu_Y}{\sigma_Y} = \frac{70 - 69}{2} = 0.5$$

We now wish to determine the probability that a standard normal value is less than 0.5. We enter Table A-7 with $Z = 0.5$ and read that the area below 0.5 is given by 0.6915. Thus, we conclude that about 69 percent of the males are less than 70 in in height.

19-5. CORRECTING FOR CONTINUITY

Even though the normal distribution is defined for a continuous variable, many of the variables observed by researchers in the social sciences are discrete, and so the correction for continuity described in Section 3-5 is called for. We illustrate the use of the correction by example. IQ scores, as determined from the Stanford-Binet test of mental abilities, have a discrete distribution. Scores are always reported as whole integers and never as fractions or decimals. Furthermore, the test has been constructed so that, in the standardizing population, $\mu_Y = 100$ and $\sigma_Y = 16$. If we agree that a discrete score, Y, represents a true score in an interval of $Y \pm \frac{1}{2}$, we can determine the proportion of the population that has an IQ score of 100, greater than 110, or in the interval 95 to 105, or any other interval of interest. We'll illustrate the procedure for $Y = 100$, and we'll see how to determine percentile values not listed in the table.

The discrete score of $Y = 100$ corresponds to the continuous interval 99.5 to 100.5. Since Table A-7 reports cumulative probabilities, we can determine the proportion of interest by first determining the $P(Y < 100.5)$ and then subtracting from it the $P(Y < 99.5)$. The remainder will be the proportion of people having an IQ equal to 100. Under this model:

$$P(Y = 100) = P(Y < 100.5) - P(Y < 99.5)$$

In terms of the transformation equation, we have, for $Y = 100.5$, that:

$$Z = \frac{100.5 - 100}{16} = \frac{0.5}{16} = 0.0313$$

Since this number is not in Table A-7, we will find an approximation to the correct value using interpolation. Corresponding to $Z = 0.00$, the cumulative probability is 0.50, while a Z value of 0.05 corresponds to a cumulative probability of 0.5199. Because the desired Z value lies between a Z of 0.00 and a Z of 0.05, we know that the corresponding cumulative probability lies between 0.5000 and 0.5199.

The assumption underlying interpolation is that as Z moves a certain fraction of the way through the interval between 0.00 and 0.05, the corresponding cumulative probability moves the same fraction of the way between 0.5000 and 0.5199. Thus, if we find the fraction that Z has moved into the interval, we can calculate the cumulative probability that is this same fraction of the width of the probability interval. This is the desired cumulative probability.

For the desired $Z = 0.0313$, the fraction that Z has moved into the interval is:

$$\frac{0.0313 - 0.00}{0.05 - 0.00} = 0.626$$

The desired cumulative probability is the same fraction through the interval between 0.50 and 0.5199. That is:

$$\Delta_{100.5} = 0.626(0.5199 - 0.50) = 0.626(0.0199) = 0.0125$$

So the desired cumulative probability corresponding to $Z = 0.0313$ is equal to:

$$P(Y < 100.5) = 0.5000 + 0.0125 = 0.5125$$

For $Y = 99.5$:

$$Z = \frac{99.5 - 100}{16} = \frac{-0.5}{16} = -0.0313$$

From Table A-7, we see that this value lies between -0.05 and 0.00, so we set up the following fraction:

$$\frac{-0.0313 - (-0.05)}{-0.05 - 0.00} = 0.374$$

The desired cumulative probability is the same fraction of distance from 0.4801 to 0.50. The desired distance is thus:

$$\Delta_{99.5} = 0.374(0.50 - 0.4801)$$
$$= 0.374(0.0199)$$
$$= 0.0074$$

and the corresponding cumulative probability is:

$$P(Y < 99.5) = 0.4801 + 0.0074 = 0.4875$$

Finally, $P(Y = 100) = 0.5125 - 0.4875 = 0.0250$. This means that 2.5 percent of the population has an IQ score that is exactly equal to the mean value of 100.

19-6. NORMAL PROBABILITY PAPER

Since the normal distribution is a mathematical abstraction, no distribution of the real world possesses an exactly normal distribution. Yet, the distribution of many variables can be described adequately by the normal distribution. This means that criteria are needed to determine when the normal distribution description is acceptable. Statisticians have developed many exact and approximate tests that can be used to determine whether or not the normal distribution model is useful for descriptive and analytical purposes. One of the simpler approximate tests is to graph the cumulative relative frequencies on graph paper, called *normal probability paper,* which is similar to regular graph paper except that one axis is scaled to the standard normal distribution. An exact normal distribution generates a straight line on normal probability paper. If the resulting graph is not linear, we conclude that the distribution is not normal. We illustrate the test in terms of the biology pretest data of Table 3-7. While the example is based on a grouped frequency table, the method also works for individual scores, provided that a correction for continuity is applied. For this example, the cumulative relative frequencies and upper end points are as shown in Table 19-1.

For the example, we use $^{39}\!/_{39.5} = 0.987$ as the last cumulative relative frequency. When these data are graphed, as in Figure 19-3, we see that the line connecting the points is relatively straight. Hence, we conclude that the distribution is near normal. Directions for this visual test are provided in Box 19-2.

Table 19-1. Values for testing normality of distribution for grouped biology pretest data

Upper end point	Cumulative relative frequency
4.5	0.026
7.5	0.052
10.5	0.180
13.5	0.334
16.5	0.513
19.5	0.641
22.5	0.692
25.5	0.794
28.5	0.896
31.5	0.987

Box 19-2   Procedure for testing graphically for normality of distributions

Step 1. If the data are not grouped, rank order them. Make the correction for continuity by adding one-half the unit of measurement to each value of the observed variable. These corrected values are the ones used because we graph cumulative relative frequencies.

Step 2. Obtain the cumulative relative frequencies. Since the normal distribution is unlimited in range, the 100th percentile cannot be determined. For graphing purposes, determine the last cumulative relative frequency as $[N/(N + \frac{1}{2})]$.

Step 3. Mark the upper end points of the interval along the horizontal axis if the data are grouped. For ungrouped data, use a convenient working scale. Note that no label is needed for the vertical axis, as it is already marked.

Step 4. For ungrouped data, plot on the normal probability paper the cumulative relative frequencies against the corrected values. For grouped data, plot the cumulative relative frequencies against the upper end points of the intervals.

Step 5. Join the plotted points by straight line segments. If the resulting broken line graph is almost linear, conclude that the distribution of the variable can be described as a normal distribution.

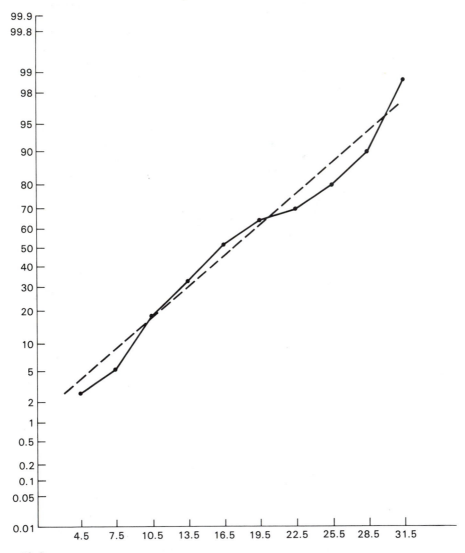

Figure 19-3.
Cumulative relative frequencies for the data of Table 3-7 plotted on normal probability graph paper.

19-7. EXERCISES

19-1. Over many years of data collection it has been learned that the height of varsity basketball players at a midwestern university is nearly normally distributed with a mean of 77 in and with a standard deviation of 1.5 in:

  a. Find the 68-percent central range of heights.
  b. Find the 95-percent central range of heights.
  c. Find the 99-percent central range of heights.
  d. Find the 25th percentile.
  e. Find the 40th percentile.
  f. Find the 85th percentile.
  g. Find $P(Y \leq 78)$.
  h. Find $P(75 \leq Y \leq 78)$.

19-2. If two members are selected from the population of Exercise 19-1:

  a. What is the probability that both are taller than 77 in?
  b. What is the probability that both are taller than 78 in? (See Exercise 19-1g.)
  c. What is the probability that one is taller than 77 in and the other is taller than 78 in?
  d. What is the probability that either is taller than 78 in?

19-3. Stanford-Binet IQ test scores can be described adequately in terms of a normal distribution with $\mu_Y = 100$ and $\sigma_Y = 16$. If a subject is drawn at random and given the test, what is the probability that his IQ:

  a. Exceeds 105?
  b. Is exactly equal to 105?

19-4. For your sample of 40 students, plot on one sheet of normal probability paper the final test scores of:

  a. Students in Program 1.
  b. Students in Program 2.
  c. Describe what is shown by the graph.

CHAPTER 20

The Central Limit Theorem

20-1. THE ROLE OF THE NORMAL DISTRIBUTION IN STATISTICAL INFERENCE

The sudden appearance of the normal distribution in Chapter 19 may have seemed somewhat arbitrary. There are reasons, however, why this distribution is the one on which the major part of statistical inference theory is based and why it has been the necessary choice over all other distributions for approximating distributions in nature.

In the nineteenth century, many scientists assumed that the normal distribution represented a natural law, because it was apparent that many biological variables, such as height of adults, length of full-grown arms, birth weight of rodents, and scores of other biological characteristics could be adequately described by the probabilities dictated by the normal distribution. Even earlier, astronomers knew that their errors of measurement in making observations could be described by deviations whose distributions were similar to the normal distribution.

While scientists were seeing the normal distribution appearing in large collections of data, mathematicians were finding that the normal distribution could be used to solve statistical problems with greater ease than could other possible distributions when applied to the same problems. Since it was easy for statisticians to study and work with the normal distribution mathematically, it gained immediate acceptance over other contenders. That it could be used as a good first approximation to other distributions also facilitated its acceptance as a working model. However, it was one other property that placed it in the center of statistical theory: in classical probability theory it kept appearing in a natural way whenever mathematical statisticians began to study the distributions that arose as sample sizes were allowed to become extremely large. It is mainly for this latter reason that the normal distribution serves as the center of statistical inference. Researchers generally use large samples to test hypotheses and to estimate parameter values. Their decision process is generally based on statistics that almost invariably generate normal distributions, even though the original variables of study will not necessarily follow a normal distribution.

This convergence to the normal distribution comes about because of a remarkable property of statistical variables which is summarized in a unique mathematical theorem called the *central limit theorem*. As might be expected, the proof of the central limit theorem requires considerable knowledge of theoretical mathematics and statistics. As a result, we cannot prove the theorem in this book; however, we can illustrate how it operates, even for a small sample size. The demonstration will not be perfect, but by studying the method of generation, we can appreciate and understand the reasons for the appearance of the normal distribution, even without a knowledge of advanced mathematics. Because our demonstration and the central limit theorem itself involve the mean and variance of a population, we will need to define these concepts first.

20-2. THE MEAN AND VARIANCE OF FINITE AND INFINITE POPULATIONS

As we proceed, we must distinguish sample sizes from population sizes. We will continue to use $N, N_1, N_2, \ldots$ to represent sample sizes and we will use $\mathcal{N}, \mathcal{N}_1, \mathcal{N}_2, \ldots$ to represent population sizes. In most cases, these latter values will remain unknown. We begin our discussion for finite populations where $\mathcal{N}$ is known.

Because we are dealing with population values, we must use the formulas appropriate to population parameters. For the population mean, the formula is identical to that used for calculating sample means. In particular:

$$\mu_Y = \frac{1}{\mathcal{N}} \sum_{i=1}^{\mathcal{N}} Y_i$$

Identity of formulas for the population and sample variance does not hold true as it does for $\overline{Y}$ and μ_Y. Because, in the population of Y values, μ_Y is known, no degrees of freedom are required to estimate μ_Y. Thus, the population variance is defined as:

$$\sigma_Y^2 = \frac{1}{\mathcal{N}} \sum_{i=1}^{\mathcal{N}} (Y_i - \mu_Y)^2$$

We now provide formal definitions of μ_Y and σ_Y^2.

Definition of μ_Y and σ_Y^2 for finite populations with known size

The mean value of a population of $\mathcal{N}$ elements is defined as

$$\mu_Y = \frac{1}{\mathcal{N}} \sum_{i=1}^{\mathcal{N}} Y_i$$

The variance of a population of $\mathcal{N}$ elements is defined as

$$\sigma_Y^2 = \frac{1}{\mathcal{N}} \sum_{i=1}^{\mathcal{N}} (Y_i - \mu_Y)^2$$

The standard deviation is simply the square root of σ_Y^2.

If we had an entire population for which the mean and variance were to be calculated, we would use these formulas in just the same way as we used the formulas for the sample mean and variance. That is, to calculate μ_Y, we would add all of the values in the population and divide by $\mathcal{N}$. Because populations are usually enormous in size, we would take advantage of any shortcuts that we had available. For example, if there were 1250 Y values equal to 2, we wouldn't add these numbers; rather, we would find this contribution to the sum by multiplying 2 by 1250, so that after adding the 1250 values of 2 we would get 2500. This procedure would be followed for any values that appeared a sizable number of times.

To codify this result, let us say that in the population the value y_1 appears f_1 times, y_2 appears f_2 times, and so on. The f_j stand for the frequency of occurrence of y_j. In addition, let us say that there are J distinct values of Y in the population. Notice this notation. Y_i is the value of the ith observation. This value could be any one of the numbers $y_1, y_2, \ldots, y_j, \ldots, y_J$. For example, on the biology pretest there were $J = 31$ distinct values possible, the scores 0, 1, 2, . . . , 29, 30. The score of the ith person, Y_i, could be any of these 31 values. Then, to find μ_Y, we would calculate:

$$\mu_Y = \frac{1}{N}\sum_{i=1}^{N} Y_i = \frac{1}{N}\sum_{j=1}^{J} f_j y_j$$

By rearranging terms, this formula can be rewritten as

$$\mu_Y = \frac{1}{N}\sum_{j=1}^{J} f_j y_j = \sum_{j=1}^{J} \frac{f_j}{N} y_j = \sum_{j=1}^{J} p_j y_j = \sum_{j=1}^{J} y_j p_j$$

where p_j is the proportion of the total N individuals who have the score y_j. By similar reasoning, the variance, σ_Y^2, can be written thus:

$$\sigma_Y^2 = \frac{1}{N}\sum_{i=1}^{N} (Y_i - \mu_Y)^2 = \sum_{j=1}^{J} (y_j - \mu_Y)^2 p_j$$

With some simple algebra, a computing formula for σ_Y^2 can be derived and shown to be given by

$$\sigma_Y^2 = \sum_{j=1}^{J} y_j^2 p_j - \mu_Y^2$$

We now provide definitions of μ_Y and σ_Y^2 for infinite universes or for theoretical statistical variables.

Definition of μ_Y and σ_Y^2 for infinite populations

The mean value of a theoretical or infinite population is defined as

$$\mu_Y = \sum_{j=1}^{J} y_j p_j$$

The variance of a theoretical or infinite population is defined as

$$\sigma_Y^2 = \sum_{j=1}^{J} (y_j - \mu_Y)^2 p_j$$

The standard deviation is the square root of σ_Y^2. Implicit in this definition is that $p_1 + p_2 + \cdots + p_J = 1$.

Sometimes the mean value of Y is called the *expected value* of Y and is denoted by the symbol $E(Y)$. Thus:

$$E(Y) = \sum_{j=1}^{J} y_j p_j = \mu_Y$$

In addition, the variance of Y is sometimes denoted as $\text{Var}(Y)$. In terms of expected values:

$$\sigma_Y^2 = \text{Var}(Y) = E(Y - \mu_Y)^2$$

The latter term can be expanded algebraically and shown to provide the previous computing formula for σ_Y^2:

$$\text{Var}(Y) = E(Y^2) - [E(Y)]^2$$
$$= \sum_{j=1}^{J} y_j^2 p_j - \mu_Y^2$$

This latter formula is the preferred one for determining the value of σ_Y^2.

As an example of the use of these formulas, let us find the mean and variance of a binomial variable for $N = 5$ tosses of a coin and $p = \frac{1}{2}$. In this case, $J = 6$, since Y, the number of heads, can take on the values 0, 1, . . . , 5. In this case, knowledge of $\mathcal{N}$ is not required, since we know that the relative frequencies of occurrence are given by the probabilities $p_0 = 0.03125$, $p_1 = 0.15625$, $p_2 = 0.31250$, $p_3 = 0.31250$, $p_4 = 0.15625$, and $p_5 = 0.03125$. Thus, we have

$$\mu_Y = E(Y) = \sum_{j=1}^{6} y_j p_j$$
$$= 0(0.03125) + 1(0.15625) + \cdots + 5(0.03125)$$
$$= 2.5$$

and

$$\sigma_Y^2 = E(Y^2) - \mu_Y^2 = \sum_{j=1}^{6} y_j^2 p_j - \mu_Y^2$$
$$= [0^2(0.03125) + 1^2(0.15625) + \cdots + 5^2(0.03125)] - 2.5^2$$
$$= 1.25$$

In Section 22-3, we will see that for any binomial variable, $\mu_Y = Np$ and $\sigma_Y^2 = Np(1 - p)$.

The expected value $E(Y)$ and variance $\text{Var}(Y)$ play the same role for populations as $\bar{Y}$ and S_Y^2 do for samples. As we saw in Section 6-3, one could find sample means and variances for transformed variables using the scale and translation theorems. We now wish to provide the corresponding theorems for population parameters.

Scale and translation theorems for population parameters

If a single constant A is added to every observation in a population so that $y = Y + A$, then the expected value $E(y)$ of the translated observations and the expected value $E(Y)$ of the original observations are related to one another by the formula

$$E(y) = E(Y) + A$$

and the variances are related to one another by

$$\mathrm{Var}(y) = \mathrm{Var}(Y)$$

If a single constant B serves as a common multiplier to every observation in a population so that $y = BY$, then the expected value of the transformed observations, $E(y)$, and the expected value of the original observations, $E(Y)$, are related to one another by

$$E(y) = BE(Y)$$

and the variances are related to one another by

$$\mathrm{Var}(y) = B^2\mathrm{Var}(Y)$$

20-3. LINEAR COMBINATIONS OF VARIABLES

As we will see, the central limit theorem is a statement about the probability distribution of a certain kind of variable called a *linear combination*. We have actually seen linear combinations in previous chapters even though we did not identify them explicitly. A linear combination is simply the weighted sum of other variables. A linear combination is defined as follows.

Definition of a linear combination

Let $Y_1, Y_2, \ldots, Y_L$ be a set of variables and let $W_1, W_2, \ldots, W_L$ be a set of arbitrary constants, called *weights*. The new variable,

$$T = W_1Y_1 + W_2Y_2 + \cdots + W_LY_L$$

is called a linear combination of the Y variables

While the definition of T states that the weights are arbitrary, it should be noted that in all applications the weights are selected with foresight to produce useful weighted sums. The sample mean is an example of such a linear form in which all of the weights are set equal to $1/N$. In particular:

$$\bar{Y} = \frac{1}{N} Y_1 + \frac{1}{N} Y_2 + \frac{1}{N} Y_3 + \cdots + \frac{1}{N} Y_N.$$

Linear combinations are variables with probability distributions. Because of this, they possess an expected value, $E(T)$; a variance, $\text{Var}(T)$; and a standard deviation, σ_T. Let us illustrate how the expected value and variance would be determined in terms of first principles and definitions. The results of this demonstration will show that the mean and variance of a linear combination are given by the following:

Mean value and variance of a linear combination

Let

$$T = W_1 Y_1 + W_2 Y_2 + \cdots + W_L Y_L$$

If $\mu_1, \mu_2, \ldots, \mu_L$ are the mean values of the Y variables, then the mean value of T is given by

$$\mu_T = W_1 \mu_1 + W_2 \mu_2 + \cdots + W_L \mu_L$$

If $\sigma_1, \sigma_2, \ldots, \sigma_L$ are the standard deviations of the Y variables, then the variance of T is given by

$$\sigma_T^2 = W_1^2 \sigma_1^2 + W_2^2 \sigma_2^2 + \cdots + W_L^2 \sigma_L^2$$

provided that the Y variables are uncorrelated.

Consider two brown bags, each containing balls bearing numbers. Let the balls of bag 1 be numbered 1 and 3, and let the other bag contain balls numbered 0, 3, and 6. For the first bag,

$$\mu_1 = \sum_{j=1}^{2} y_j p_j = 1(\tfrac{1}{2}) + 3(\tfrac{1}{2}) = 2$$

and

$$\sigma_1^2 = \sum_{j=1}^{2} y_j^2 p_j - \mu_1^2 = 1^2(\tfrac{1}{2}) + 3^2(\tfrac{1}{2}) - 2^2 = 1$$

Similarly, for the second bag,

$$\mu_2 = \sum_{j=1}^{3} y_j p_j = 0(\frac{1}{3}) + 3(\frac{1}{3}) + 6(\frac{1}{3}) = 3$$

and

$$\sigma_2^2 = \sum_{j=1}^{3} y_j^2 p_j - \mu_2^2 = 0^2(\frac{1}{3}) + 3^2(\frac{1}{3}) + 6^2(\frac{1}{3}) - 3^2 = 6$$

Let us draw one observation from each bag and compute for all possible draws the values of

$$T_2 = W_1 Y_1 + W_2 Y_2$$

As a specific example, let us suppose that W_1 and W_2 are both equal to unity, so that

$$T_2 = (1)Y_1 + (1)Y_2 = Y_1 + Y_2$$

which is simply the sum of the two numbers. The results are summarized in Table 20-1. For the six values shown, we find:

$$\mu_T = \sum_{j=1}^{6} t_j p_j = 1(\frac{1}{6}) + 4(\frac{1}{6}) + \cdots + 9(\frac{1}{6}) = 5$$

Table 20-1. All possible values of $T_2 = Y_1 + Y_2$ and $T_2^* = 2Y_1 + Y_2$ for two populations consisting of values Y_1: (1, 3) and Y_2: (0, 3, 6).

Value of Y_1	Value of Y_2	T_2	T_2^*
1	0	1	2
1	3	4	5
1	6	7	8
3	0	3	6
3	3	6	9
3	6	9	12

We see that this result is identical to

$$\mu_T = W_1\mu_1 + W_2\mu_2 = (1)2 + (1)3 = 5$$

In addition, we see that

$$\sigma_T^2 = \sum_{j=1}^{6} t_j^2 p_j - \mu_T^2 = 1^2(\tfrac{1}{6}) + 4^2(\tfrac{1}{6}) + \cdots + 9^2(\tfrac{1}{6}) - 5^2$$
$$= 7$$

Again, we see that this result is identical to

$$\sigma_T^2 = W_1^2\sigma_1^2 + W_2^2\sigma_2^2 = (1^2)1 + (1^2)6 = 7$$

To continue with this example, suppose we now let $W_1 = 2$ and $W_2 = 1$ and then calculate all possible values of $T_2^* = 2Y_1 + Y_2$. These values are also shown in Table 20-1. Now, we find:

$$\mu_{T_2^*} = \sum_{j=1}^{6} t_j^* p_j = 2(\tfrac{1}{6}) + 5(\tfrac{1}{6}) + \cdots + 12(\tfrac{1}{6}) = 7$$

which agrees with

$$\mu_{T_2^*} = W_1\mu_1 + W_2\mu_2 = (2)2 + (1)3 = 7$$

Further,

$$\sigma_{T_2^*}^2 = \sum_{j=1}^{6} t_j^{*2} p_j - \mu_{T_2^*}^2 = 2^2(\tfrac{1}{6}) + 5^2(\tfrac{1}{6})$$
$$+ \cdots + 12^2(\tfrac{1}{6}) - 7^2 = 10$$

which also agrees with:

$$\sigma_{T_2^*}^2 = W_1^2\sigma_1^2 + W_2^2\sigma_2^2 = (2^2)1 + (1^2)6 = 10$$

We have provided these examples for a purpose. The lession is that μ_T and σ_T^2 do not have to be computed in terms of definitional or calculating formulas, provided that $\mu_1, \mu_2, \ldots, \mu_L$ and $\sigma_1^2, \sigma_2^2, \ldots, \sigma_L^2$ are known. When these values are available, we know that

$$\mu_T = W_1\mu_1 + W_2\mu_2 + \cdots + W_L\mu_L$$

and

$$\sigma_T^2 = W_1^2\sigma_1^2 + W_2^2\sigma_2^2 + \cdots + W_L^2\sigma_L^2$$

We now state the central limit theorem:

The central limit theorem

Let

$$T = W_1 Y_1 + W_2 Y_2 + \cdots + W_L Y_L$$

be a linear combination with

$$\mu_T = W_1 \mu_1 + W_2 \mu_2 + \cdots + W_L \mu_L$$

and

$$\sigma_T^2 = W_1^2 \sigma_1^2 + W_2^2 \sigma_2^2 + \cdots + W_L^2 \sigma_L^2$$

If L is *large* or, more precisely, is allowed to increase without limit, then the distribution of T approaches a *normal* distribution with mean μ_T and standard deviation σ_T.

20-4. AN EMPIRICAL DEMONSTRATION OF THE CENTRAL LIMIT THEOREM

We will illustrate the operation of the central limit theorem by means of an example. It should be noted that the final result is not dependent upon the example that is used. Because we must work with a finite set of numbers, we cannot expect the demonstration to be ideal. Instead, we must be satisfied to show general tendencies. For our example, we begin with the following simple model.

Consider two populations of balls contained in two separate brown paper bags. Let bag 1 consist of three red balls with the labels 1, 2, and 3. Let bag 2 consist of four green balls with the labels 2, 4, 6, and 10. Let us select one ball from each bag, read the values on the balls, and then compute

$$T_2 = 3Y_1 + \tfrac{1}{2}Y_2$$

where

$$Y_1 = \text{value of the red ball selected}$$

and

$$Y_2 = \text{value of the green ball selected}$$

As we saw in Chapter 11, any random process can be described by means of a tree diagram. For this example, the tree would contain $3(4) = 12$ branches. This tree is shown in Figure 20-1. As can be seen, the first branch is defined for $Y_1 = 1$ and $Y_2 = 2$, the value of T_2 being given by $T_2 = 3(1) + \frac{1}{2}(2) = 4$. For the twelfth branch, $Y_1 = 3$, $Y_2 = 10$, and $T_2 = 3(3) + \frac{1}{2}(10) = 14$. The resulting line graph for T_2 is shown in Figure 20-2. Note, in the distribution of T_2, that two values are tied at $T_2 = 8$ and at $T_2 = 11$. This suggests that the probability of T_2 is concentrating somewhere toward the middle of the distribution.

We now repeat that the central limit theorem involves summing a large number of variables and we have so far only considered a sum of two variables. We now go to a sum of three variables. To the two populations of balls contained in the two separate brown bags, we add a third population of blue balls contained in a third brown bag. Let these balls be labeled with the

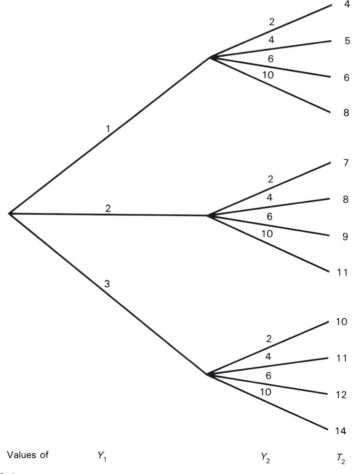

Values of Y_1 Y_2 T_2

Figure 20-1.
Tree diagram for two trials for $T_2 = 3Y_1 + 0.5Y_2$.

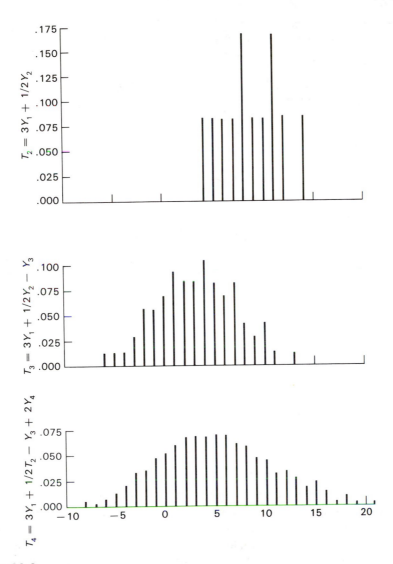

Figure 20-2.
Example illustrating convergence upon the normal distribution because of the operation of the central limit theorem.

numbers 1, 4, 5, 6, 7, and 10. Our new procedure is to select one ball from each bag and then compute

$$T_3 = 3Y_1 + \tfrac{1}{2}Y_2 - Y_3$$

where

$$Y_1 = \text{value of the red ball selected}$$

$$Y_2 = \text{value of the green ball selected}$$

$$Y_3 = \text{value of the blue ball selected}$$

Table 20-2. Tree diagram of the example of Section 20-2, illustrated as a three-dimensional table for $T_3 = 3Y_1 + \frac{1}{2}Y_2 - Y_3$.

Value of Y_1	Value of Y_2	Value of Y_3					
		1	4	5	6	7	10
1	2	③	0	−1	−2	−3	−6
	4	4	1	0	−1	−2	−5
	6	5	2	1	0	−1	−4
	10	7	4	3	2	1	−2
2	2	6	3	2	1	0	−3
	4	7	4	3	2	1	−2
	6	8	5	④	3	2	−1
	10	10	7	6	5	4	1
3	2	9	6	5	4	3	0
	4	10	7	6	5	4	1
	6	11	8	7	6	5	2
	10	13	10	9	8	7	4

This is repeated for all possible values of Y_1, Y_2, and Y_3. The tree diagram for T_3 has $3(4)(6) = 72$ branches. Because of space limitations, we illustrate these possible outcomes of T_3 only in table form (Table 20-2). For example, when $Y_1 = 1$, $Y_2 = 2$, and $Y_3 = 1$, we get $T_3 = 3(1) + \frac{1}{2}(2) - 1(1) = 3$. This branch and its T_3 value are represented in Table 20-2 as the single-circled value. The branch $Y_1 = 2$, $Y_2 = 6$, and $Y_3 = 5$, with $T_3 = 3(2) + \frac{1}{2}(6) - 1(5) = 4$, is shown as the double-circled value. All 72 branches are as indicated. As can be seen, the range in values extends from a low of -6 to a high of 13. The frequencies are as shown in Table 20-3. Finally, the line graph for the distribution is shown in Figure 20-2. Because of the discreteness of the variable, exact identity to the continuous normal distribution cannot be attained. However, the closeness to normality is striking. There are two clearly defined long tails and a concentration of the probability around the center of the distribution.

We now add another brown bag to the group of three. Let this new bag contain four yellow balls with the labels -1, 0, 1, and 4. We now draw one ball from each bag and compute T_4 for all possible choices of Y_1, Y_2, Y_3, and Y_4:

$$T_4 = 3Y_1 + \frac{1}{2}Y_2 - Y_3 + 2Y_4$$

Table 20-3. Tally count for the T values and probabilities of Table 20-2, where $T_3 = 3Y_1 + \frac{1}{2}Y_2 - Y_3$.

Value of T	Tally	Frequency	Probability
−6	|	1	0.0139
−5	|	1	0.0139
−4	|	1	0.0139
−3	||	2	0.0278
−2	||||	4	0.0556
−1	||||	4	0.0556
0	ЖЖ	5	0.0694
1	ЖЖ||	7	0.0972
2	ЖЖ|	6	0.0833
3	ЖЖ|	6	0.0833
4	ЖЖ|||	8	0.1111
5	ЖЖ|	6	0.0833
6	ЖЖ	5	0.0694
7	ЖЖ|	6	0.0833
8	|||	3	0.0417
9	||	2	0.0278
10	|||	3	0.0417
11	|	1	0.0139
12		0	0.0000
13	|	1	0.0139
Total		72	1.0000

The tree diagram for this new variable has $3(4)(6)(4) = 288$ branches. Because of its immense size, we do not draw it. The tallies for this new variable are as shown in Table 20-4, and the corresponding line graph is shown in Figure 20-2. As before, the similarity to the normal distribution is impressive. The truly remarkable point is that a convergence to the normal distribution has appeared, even though the distributions in the four bags are each nonnormal. Two of the distributions are symmetrical, and two are skewed in a positive direction; yet, the distribution of T_4 is very close to normal in form.

Table 20-4. Tally count for the T values where $T = 3Y_1 + \frac{1}{2}Y_2 - Y_3 + 2Y_4$.

Value of T	Tally	Frequency	Probability
−8	|	1	0.0035
−7	|	1	0.0035
−6	||	2	0.0069
−5	|||	3	0.0104
−4	卌|	6	0.0208
−3	卌||	7	0.0243
−2	卌||||	10	0.0347
−1	卌卌|||	13	0.0451
0	卌卌卌	15	0.0521
1	卌卌卌||	17	0.0590
2	卌卌卌卌	20	0.0694
3	卌卌卌卌	20	0.0694
4	卌卌卌卌	20	0.0694
5	卌卌卌卌	20	0.0694
6	卌卌卌卌	20	0.0694
7	卌卌卌|||	18	0.0625
8	卌卌卌|	16	0.0556
9	卌卌卌|	16	0.0556
10	卌卌||	12	0.0417
11	卌卌	10	0.0347
12	卌卌|	11	0.0382
13	卌|||	8	0.0278
14	卌	5	0.0174
15	卌||	7	0.0243
16	|||	3	0.0104
17	||	2	0.0069
18	|||	3	0.0104
19	|	1	0.0035
20		0	0.0000
21	|	1	0.0035
Total		288	1.0000

This is also apparent in the graphing of the cumulative relative frequencies on normal probability paper, illustrated in Figure 20-3. It is worth pointing out that if the original distributions are already normal, then the distribution of T will also be normal.

The great power contained in the central limit theorem should not be overlooked. It is a remarkable property about numbers. Many decisions by researchers are based upon the existence of this theorem, and this research affects all of us in our everyday lives. It is for this reason that knowledge of modern statistics is nearly a requirement for participation in a modern society.

In this section we have shown how the normal distribution appears as a consequence of the summing together of several variables. As we have seen, the distribution of T_3 resembles a normal distribution more than does the

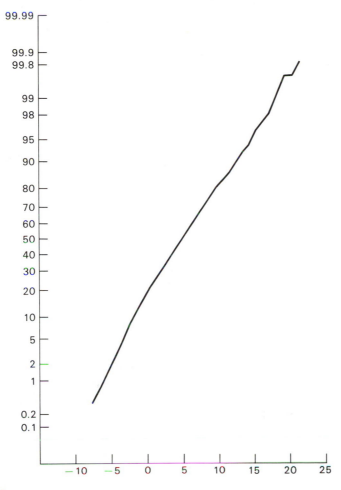

Figure 20-3.
Cumulative relative frequencies for T_4 of Figure 20-2 plotted on normal probability graph paper.

distribution of T_2, and we have also noted that the similarity to a normal distribution for T_4 is even greater than that for T_3. If we were to add a fifth brown bag containing a population of six numbered purple balls, the resulting distribution of T_5 would be even closer in appearance to the normal distribution. If we were to continue the process and allow the number of populations to increase indefinitely, we would find that the limiting distribution would be exactly normal. That, in essence, is what the central limit theorem states. Now we can see why errors of measurement and many other variables seem to follow a normal distribution.

According to the central limit theorem, any variable that is defined as the sum of other, random variables will have a probability distribution that converges to the normal distribution. Yet there are exceptions. Not all variables have normal distributions. One such exception is adult body weight. Another exception is family income, which is positively skewed. A third example is the time required to react to a visual stimulus. In this case, there exists a minimum reaction time below which it is humanly impossible to respond. Thus, the reaction time of a large number of people will be truncated in a small interval near the minimum, and the distribution will be positively skewed.

20-5. EXERCISES

20-1. Suppose Y_1 has a distribution with $\mu_{Y_1} = 10$, $\sigma_{Y_1}^2 = 10$; Y_2 has a distribution with $\mu_{Y_2} = 12$, $\sigma_{Y_2}^2 = 20$; and Y_3 has a distribution with $\mu_{Y_3} = 14$, $\sigma_{Y_3}^2 = 30$. Find the mean and variance of:

 a. $T_a = Y_1 + Y_2 + Y_3$
 b. $T_b = \frac{1}{3}(Y_1 + Y_2 + Y_3)$
 c. $T_c = 2Y_1 - 3Y_2 + 7Y_3$
 d. $T_d = 2Y_1 + 3Y_2 + 5Y_3$

20-2. Suppose Y_1, Y_2, and Y_3 are normal. Find:

 a. $P(T_a \leq 40)$
 b. $P(T_b \leq 14)$
 c. $P(70 \leq T_c \leq 90)$
 d. $P(T_d \leq 95)$

20-3. A fair die has six faces for which the probability of any face is equal to $\frac{1}{6}$. Find the expected value of Y, the outcome on a single toss. Find Var(Y).

20-4. Suppose two dice are tossed. Find $E(T)$ and Var(T) for $T = Y_1 + Y_2$ where Y_1 is the outcome on the first die and Y_2 is the outcome on the second die.

20-5. Repeat Exercise 20-4 for 10 dice and find $P(T \geq 40)$.

20-6. Find $P_{.025}$ and $P_{.975}$ for the T of Exercise 20-4. How can the numbers $P_{.025}$ and $P_{.975}$ be used to test the fairness of a die that is tossed 10 times in succession?

CHAPTER 21

The Sampling Distribution of $\overline{Y}$

21-1. AN EXAMPLE USING THE CENTRAL LIMIT THEOREM

As an example of the use of the central limit theorem, consider the following. Suppose that four entering freshmen are selected at random from the population of Section 19-3, where $\mu = 69$ and $\sigma = 2$. If the heights of the four students are given by $Y_1 = 70$, $Y_2 = 68$, $Y_3 = 74$, and $Y_4 = 71$, should one be surprised? The mean height of these four students is given by:

$$\overline{Y} = \tfrac{1}{4}(70 + 68 + 74 + 71) = 70.75 \text{ in}$$

This is 1.75 in above the average value of 69.

The selection of a student at random is analogous to choosing a ball at random from a brown bag. Selecting student 1 is similar to choosing a ball from a bag in which $\mu_1 = 69$ and $\sigma_1 = 2$. The same brown-bag model holds for students 2, 3, and 4. In this example, the populations are identical, not different as they were in Section 20-4. Thus, we know that $\mu_1 = \mu_2 = \mu_3 = \mu_4 = 69$ and $\sigma_1 = \sigma_2 = \sigma_3 = \sigma_4 = 2$. Since we would like our linear combination to represent the mean, we let $W_1 = W_2 = W_3 = W_4 = \frac{1}{4}$, so that we now have

$$T = \tfrac{1}{4}Y_1 + \tfrac{1}{4}Y_2 + \tfrac{1}{4}Y_3 + \tfrac{1}{4}Y_4$$

which is exactly identical to $\overline{Y}$. Since $\overline{Y}$ is a linear combination, we also know that

$$\begin{aligned}
\mu_T = \mu_{\overline{Y}} &= \tfrac{1}{4}\mu_1 + \tfrac{1}{4}\mu_2 + \tfrac{1}{4}\mu_3 + \tfrac{1}{4}\mu_4 \\
&= \tfrac{1}{4}(69) + \tfrac{1}{4}(69) + \tfrac{1}{4}(69) + \tfrac{1}{4}(69) = 4(\tfrac{1}{4})(69) \\
&= 69 = \mu_Y
\end{aligned}$$

and

$$\begin{aligned}
\sigma_T^2 = \sigma_{\overline{Y}}^2 &= (\tfrac{1}{4})^2\sigma_1^2 + (\tfrac{1}{4})^2\sigma_2^2 + (\tfrac{1}{4})^2\sigma_3^2 + (\tfrac{1}{4})^2\sigma_4^2 \\
&= (\tfrac{1}{16})2^2 + (\tfrac{1}{16})2^2 + (\tfrac{1}{16})2^2 + (\tfrac{1}{16})2^2 \\
&= (4)(\tfrac{1}{16})2^2 \\
&= \frac{2^2}{4} = 1 = \frac{\sigma_Y^2}{4}
\end{aligned}$$

Surprisingly, the effects of the central limit theorem can be seen, even for sample sizes as small as 4, so long as the populations from which the samples come do not differ too greatly from normal. Since heights tend to be close to normal, it follows by the central limit theorem that the distribution of $\overline{Y}$ is approximately normal; therefore, we can determine the percentile value of $\overline{Y} = 70.75$ in by computing the associated standard score for this value and consulting Table A-7 for the corresponding percentile value. Thus:

$$P(T < 70.75) = P\left(Z < \frac{T - \mu_T}{\sigma_T}\right) = P\left(Z < \frac{70.75 - 69}{1}\right)$$
$$= P(Z < 1.75) = 0.9599$$

Thus, the mean value of $\overline{Y} = 70.75$ in corresponds to the 96th percentile value. It seems that the four selected students are not typical of the students at the school. They seem to be taller than expected.

21-2. THE DISTRIBUTION OF $\overline{Y}$ WHEN SAMPLING WITH REPLACEMENT

In Section 21-1, we saw that the population mean and variance of

$$T = \tfrac{1}{4}Y_1 + \tfrac{1}{4}Y_2 + \tfrac{1}{4}Y_3 + \tfrac{1}{4}Y_4$$

were given by

$$\mu_{\bar{Y}} = \mu_Y \qquad \text{and} \qquad \sigma_{\bar{Y}}^2 = \frac{\sigma_Y^2}{4}$$

These parameter values actually represent a general result for any $T = \bar{Y}$, based on N independent observations. The general results are as follows.

The sampling distribution of $\bar{Y}$

Consider the universe of mean values generated by the complete set of

$$\bar{Y} = \frac{1}{N} \sum_{i=1}^{N} Y_i$$

that can be generated from a universe of Y_i values. If N is large, this distribution is approximately normal because of the central limit theorem. Its mean, variance, and standard deviation are

$$\mu_{\bar{Y}} = \mu_Y$$

$$\sigma_{\bar{Y}}^2 = \frac{\sigma_Y^2}{N}$$

and

$$\sigma_{\bar{Y}} = \frac{\sigma_Y}{\sqrt{N}}$$

size, not only for large samples.

These formulas are among the most frequently used formulas of empirical research. We will encounter them repeatedly in the pages that follow.

As an illustration of one property of the sampling distribution of the sample mean, suppose that scores on a test are distributed with $\mu_Y = 200$ and $\sigma_Y = 50$, as illustrated in Figure 21-1 as P_{one}. If we now sample an exceptionally large number of samples of size $N = 4$ from this population, and if we compute the sample mean for each sample, we would generate the sampling distribution shown in Figure 21-1 as P_{four}. As we know, for samples of size four we have

$$\mu_{\bar{Y}} = \mu_Y = 200$$

and

$$\sigma_{\bar{Y}} = \frac{\sigma_Y}{\sqrt{N}} = {}^{50}\!/_2 = 25$$

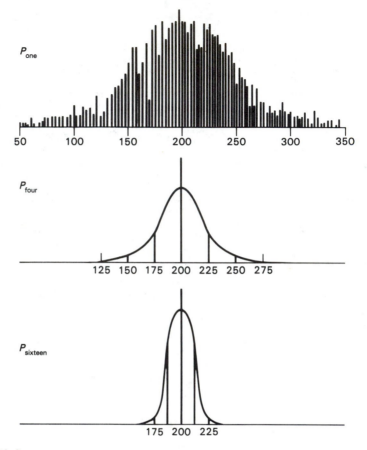

Figure 21-1.
The sampling distribution of the mean, $\bar{Y}$, for samples of size $N = 1, 4,$ and 16, where Y is normal with mean, $\mu_Y = 200$ and standard deviation $\sigma_Y = 50$.

Because $\sigma_{\bar{Y}} < \sigma_Y$, the values of $\bar{Y}$ spread less about the mean than the values of Y.

If we now select samples of size $N = 16$ from the original population, the distribution of the sample means would have

$$\mu_{\bar{Y}} = \mu_Y = 200$$

and

$$\sigma_{\bar{Y}} = \frac{\sigma_Y}{\sqrt{16}} = 12.5$$

This distribution is shown in Figure 21-1 as P_{sixteen}. As we can see, increasing the sample size produces sampling distributions that are more and more compact.

21-3. ONE-SAMPLE TEST ABOUT A POPULATION MEAN WHEN THE VALUE OF THE POPULATION VARIANCE IS KNOWN

In the examples in Sections 21-1 and 21-2, we have provided an indication of the use of the central limit theorem. We have also illustrated how the normal distribution is used to test hypotheses about the population mean values. We now wish to expand on those examples.

   We will now describe a statistical test for which we assume that the value of σ_Y is known. Suppose that, in a certain large urban school district, it has been noted that the mean score on the College Board test has been deteriorating over time. Suppose that the reasons for the changes are unknown, but that it has been suggested that teachers are no longer teaching adequately in the classroom, that the students have failed to learn how to read in elementary school, that the students are spending more time watching television than they spend on homework, and so on. Since there is no way to prove or disprove any of these charges, the school board has decided to try an experimental program in which 15 students are selected at random from the population of 4539 seniors. The program is to consist of a 10-week course in which the students are given training in answering questions that have appeared on previous College Board tests. To prepare the course, teachers from the mathematics department have studied the previous tests and then prepared 10 lesson plans on how to solve problems similar to those used there. Teachers in the English, science, and social science departments have done the same. Altogether, 40 lesson plans have been prepared for use in the special class, which then meets for 40 minutes a day for 10 weeks. The test is administered two weeks after the completion of the special training.

   The independent variable of the study consists of the 40 lesson plans and the instructional periods. The dependent variable of the study consists of the 15 scores obtained by the students at the time of testing. Suppose the 15 scores, reported in rank order, are as follows:

$$380, \quad 440, \quad 440, \quad 450, \quad 490, \quad 490, \quad 500, \quad 530,$$
$$540, \quad 570, \quad 610, \quad 640, \quad 680, \quad 740, \quad 780$$

As can be seen, the median score is equal to $\hat{M} = Y_8^o = 530$, and the mean score is determined thus:

$$\bar{Y} = \frac{1}{15}(380 + 440 + 440 + \cdots + 780)$$
$$= \frac{1}{15}(8280) = 552$$

   As we know, College Board test scores tend to approximate a normal distribution with a mean value of 500 and a standard deviation of 100. If we now adopt this model as a valid description of what the test scores would be like if no program were instituted, we can develop the appropriate statistical tests with ease. For the test we are illustrating, the hypothesis H_0 to be examined states that the lesson plans and the class instruction have no influence upon the distribution of test scores and, thus, that the mean score in the population of 4539 students is 500. At the same time, if the program is successful, the mean score will exceed 500 in value. Unfortunately, it is also conceivable that the program will not be beneficial, especially if it has not been pretested. This means that the new program could actually produce a lowering of the mean value to some number less than 500. This indicates that for our alternative hypothesis we cannot afford to ignore the possibility of either occurrence. Transferring these statements to statistical hypothesis statements, we have the following two propositions to evaluate:

H_0:   The lesson plans and teaching program
have no impact on student test scores

and

H_1:   The lesson plans and teaching program do
have an impact on student test scores

In symbolic terms, these two propositions are equivalent to:

$$H_0: \quad \mu_Y = \mu_0 = 500$$

and

$$H_1: \quad \mu_Y = \mu_1 \neq 500$$

where μ_0 is the hypothetical value of μ_Y if H_0 is true and μ_1 is the value of μ_Y if H_0 is false.

We know that the sampling distribution of $\bar{Y}$ is normal and that $\mu_{\bar{Y}} = \mu_Y$ and $\sigma_{\bar{Y}} = \sigma_Y / \sqrt{N}$. Thus, given these two values, we can specify the entire probability distribution of sample means. We know, for example, that 68 percent of the sample means fall within one standard deviation of the population mean. Further, 95 percent of the sample means fall within 1.96 standard deviations of the population mean. If we were to construct a critical region, we would include in this region the most unlikely 5 percent of the values of $\bar{Y}$. Equivalently, we could determine the Z value of our given sample mean according to the equation

$$Z_{\bar{Y}} = \frac{\bar{Y} - \mu_{\bar{Y}}}{\sigma_{\bar{Y}}}$$

Since the alternative hypothesis states that μ_Y may either exceed 500 or be less than 500, we must split the probability of a type I error and place .025 in each tail of the normal distribution. With this split of the type I error probability,

---

Box 21-1   Procedure for testing $H_0: \mu_Y = \mu_0$ versus $H_1: \mu_Y \neq \mu_0$, if σ_Y is known

Step 1. State the value of μ_0.
Step 2. Determine the value of $\bar{Y}$.
Step 3. Determine the value of $\sigma_{\bar{Y}} = \sigma_Y/\sqrt{N}$.
Step 4. Compute:

$$Z_{\bar{Y}} = \frac{\bar{Y} - \mu_{\bar{Y}}}{\sigma_{\bar{Y}}}$$

Step 5. Determine the decision rule. With $\alpha = .05$, the decision rule is:

Decision Rule: Reject H_0 if $Z_{\bar{Y}} < -1.96$ or if $Z_{\bar{Y}} > 1.96$

Step 6. Make a decision.

---

the $\alpha = .05$ decision rule is as follows:

Decision Rule: Reject H_0 if $Z_{\bar{Y}} \leq -1.96$ or if $Z_{\bar{Y}} \geq 1.96$

For the observed data and the a priori assumptions, we have $\mu_{\bar{Y}} = \mu_Y = 500$ and $\sigma_{\bar{Y}} = \sigma_Y/\sqrt{N} = 100/\sqrt{15} = 25.82$, so that

$$Z_{\bar{Y}} = \frac{552 - 500}{25.82} = \frac{52}{25.82} = 2.01$$

Since the observed $Z = 2.01$ is in the critical region, the hypothesis that $\mu_Y = 500$ is rejected. We have reason to believe that the program has influenced the mean score of the test. Inspection of the data suggests that the mean score has been increased.

Directions for testing the hypothesis that a population mean is equal to some predetermined numerical value, provided that the sample is large or else selected at random from a normal population, are given in Box 21-1.

21-4. THE CONFIDENCE INTERVAL FOR μ_Y WHEN σ_Y IS KNOWN

Consider the example of Section 21-3. Suppose the population mean is actually equal to $\mu_Y = 500$ and that $\sigma_Y = 100$. For $N = 15$, we find that 95 percent of all sample means will be between the quantities

$$\bar{Y}_L = \mu_Y - 1.96 \frac{\sigma_Y}{\sqrt{N}} = 500 - 1.96 \frac{100}{\sqrt{15}} = 449.39$$

and

$$\bar{Y}_U = \mu_Y + 1.96 \frac{\sigma_Y}{\sqrt{N}} = 500 + 1.96 \frac{100}{\sqrt{15}} = 550.61$$

so that the 95 percent central range for $\bar{Y}$ is given thus:

$$449.39 < \bar{Y} < 550.61$$

provided that it is known that $\mu_Y = 500$. In terms of the population parameters μ_Y and σ_Y^2 (which, we must recall, are unknown in most cases), the same logic would indicate that 95 percent of the sample means satisfy the inequality

$$\mu_Y - 1.96 \frac{\sigma_Y}{\sqrt{N}} < \bar{Y} < \mu_Y + 1.96 \frac{\sigma_Y}{\sqrt{N}}$$

This is an inequality about $\bar{Y}$, and it is equivalent to the two inequalities

$$\mu_Y - 1.96 \frac{\sigma_Y}{\sqrt{N}} < \bar{Y} \quad \text{and} \quad \bar{Y} < \mu_Y + 1.96 \frac{\sigma_Y}{\sqrt{N}}$$

Inequalities are algebraically like equations in that the same number can be added to or subtracted from both sides of the inequality without changing the correctness of the inequality. This means that each inequality can be algebraically solved for μ_Y. Thus, in 95 percent of the cases,

$$\mu_Y < \bar{Y} + 1.96 \frac{\sigma_Y}{\sqrt{N}} \quad \text{and} \quad \bar{Y} - 1.96 \frac{\sigma_Y}{\sqrt{N}} < \mu_Y$$

Putting the two inequalities together, we have that, 95 percent of the time,

$$\bar{Y} - 1.96 \frac{\sigma_Y}{\sqrt{N}} < \mu_Y < \bar{Y} + 1.96 \frac{\sigma_Y}{\sqrt{N}}$$

If we reconsider the example of Section 14-4, where we were interested in the melting point of a metal, we see that this interval is similar to the interval the metallurgist used:

$$931° \leq X \leq 941°$$

which was thought to contain the true melting point. Another way this interval appeared was as follows:

$$X = 936° \pm 5°$$

This indicates that the estimate of the melting point is $936°$, with an error of $\pm 5°$. Similarly, the estimate of μ_Y is $\bar{Y}$, with an error of $\pm 1.96 \sigma_Y/\sqrt{N}$, and we can write:

$$\mu_Y = \bar{Y} \pm 1.96 \frac{\sigma_Y}{\sqrt{N}}$$

These inequalities about μ_Y state that μ_Y is trapped between two numbers a large proportion of the time. This is quite a remarkable statement when it is recalled that in almost all research investigations μ_Y is unknown. As a matter of fact, if μ_Y were known, research about it would be unnecessary. Research studies are performed to estimate the values of μ_Y, σ_Y^2, and other population parameters, and for this reason, the trapping of an unknown parameter value like μ_Y between two numbers is of extreme practical importance.

Because confidence intervals can be calculated by examining the acceptance regions, and because the acceptance region contains $1 - \alpha$ percent of the distribution, we typically refer to these intervals as $1 - \alpha$ percent confidence intervals. Box 21-2 provides directions for determining the confidence interval of the mean of a normally distributed variable.

For the College Board data of Section 21-3, we concluded that the mean score is different from 500. Our best guess is that it has increased by 52 points, the increase seen for the 15 test subjects. However, the estimate may not be valid for the 4539 students. That value might be too small, or it might be too large. If we compute the confidence interval, however, we then have

---

Box 21-2 Procedure for determining the $1 - \alpha$ percent confidence interval for μ_Y if σ_Y is known

Step 1. Select a large enough random sample from the population of interest to allow the central limit theorem to apply.

Step 2. Compute the sample mean $\bar{Y}$.

Step 3. For an α risk of a type I error, choose

$$Z_{\alpha/2} = \alpha/2 \text{ percentile value of the standard normal distribution}$$

and

$$Z_{1-\alpha/2} = 1 - \alpha/2 \text{ percentile value of the standard normal distribution}$$

Step 4. Compute the $1 - \alpha$ percent confidence interval for μ_Y as follows:

$$\bar{Y} + Z_{\alpha/2} \frac{\sigma_Y}{\sqrt{N}} < \mu_Y < \bar{Y} + Z_{1-\alpha/2} \frac{\sigma_Y}{\sqrt{N}}$$

an idea of the minimum and maximum change. In this case, the 95 percent confidence interval is given by

$$\mu_Y = \bar{Y} \pm 1.96\sigma_{\bar{Y}} = 552 \pm 1.96(25.82) = 552 \pm 51$$

Thus, we see that the new mean is most likely larger than 501, but smaller than 603. As indicated, the interval is very wide.

Note that N, the sample size, appears in the denominator of the quantity that is added to and subtracted from $\bar{Y}$. This means that the confidence interval for μ_Y can be made as small as desired by choosing a large enough sample size. One other condition that affects the width of the confidence interval is the number used as the multiplier of $\sigma_Y/\sqrt{N}$. In the last equation given, the multipliers are -1.96 and $+1.96$, the 2.5 and 97.5 percentile values of the standard normal distribution. One could use other values, such as -1.00 and $+1.00$, the 16th and 84th percentile values of the standard normal distribution. With $Z = \pm 1.00$, narrow intervals can be obtained with small sample sizes.

On the other hand, we could have used as a multiplier the values -2.58 and $+2.58$, the 0.5 and 99.5 percentile points of the standard normal distribution. Using these values, we would obtain very wide intervals. Unless the sample size is large, the interval may be too wide to be useful. Naturally, scientists would prefer narrow intervals; however, narrow intervals may involve a large probability of being wrong. This is where we face the problems indicated in Section 11-4. For $Z = \pm 1.00$, we know that 32 percent of the means are excluded from the interval determination. For $Z = \pm 1.96$, 5 percent of the means are excluded, while for $Z = \pm 2.58$, only 1 percent are excluded. These percentages are precisely the long-run risks of error in declaring that μ_Y is in the computed interval when, in fact, it is not. In testing hypotheses in Chapter 11, we did not want to entail a large risk of rejecting H_0 when it was true; here, we do not want to entail a large risk of declaring that μ_Y is in the computed interval when, in fact, it is not. This suggests that a compromise is in order. Most researchers will risk a type I error rate of $\alpha = .05$ and will use $Z = \pm 1.96$ to determine their confidence interval, feeling that the risk is not overly high and the intervals are not too broad at this risk level.

We would like to explore in depth the notion of risk in decision making. We have often mentioned error rates associated with type I and type II errors. This is a good place in the development of statistical theory to indicate how these error rates relate to specific investigations. For example, we have just tested the hypothesis that $\mu_Y = 500$. What does $\alpha = .05$ truly signify about our conclusions for this test? Note that only one study has been performed, and the data have led us to only one conclusion, which is either correct or incorect. What is the probability that our decision is correct?

To help in understanding the answer to this question, consider a simple experiment which you should actually perform. Take a coin and flip it. While the coin is in the air, what is the probability that it will land with heads up? Of course, with a fair coin, the answer is one-half. After the coin lands, look at it. Now what is the probability that the coin has landed with heads up? The answer depends on which side *is* up. Suppose the coin has tails up. Then the probability that heads is up is zero. On the other hand, if heads *is* up, the probability is one. Once the coin has landed, the results are historical fact, and heads is either up or not.

The same is true of our decision concerning $H_0: \mu_Y = 500$. Once we have made a decision rule, collected the data, and made a decision, the data are historical facts and our decision is either correct or incorrect. Unfortunately, we never know whether or not we have made a correct decision, but the probability of our being correct is either one or zero, depending on the unknown true nature of μ_Y.

We can now answer the question regarding the meaning of $\alpha = .05$. Suppose a researcher performs 1000 studies during a lifetime, and suppose each is conducted with $\alpha = .05$. Suppose further that in each of the 1000 studies, H_0 is true. Then the type I error rate means that close to 5 percent of the studies should generate data that cause the researcher to reject H_0. In these 50 studies, a type I error has been committed. In this sense, we say that $\alpha = .05$ is a *long-run* risk of making a type I error over a large number of studies.

Performance of the statistical test required that we know the value of μ_0 if H_0 is true. This is highly restrictive, because in most investigations, this information is lacking. But what is of significance is that knowledge of μ_0 is not needed to determine the limits of the confidence interval. For the confidence interval, we need only the value of the sample mean. Since the sample mean is always known, the confidence interval can always be determined if $\sigma_{\bar{Y}}$ is known.

We should emphasize another interpretation for a confidence interval. A confidence interval defines the set of values of μ_Y that, for the given value of $\bar{Y}$, would not lead us to reject the hypothesis being examined. Thus, the sample mean of $\bar{Y} = 552$ could be drawn at random from a population whose mean value could be as low as 501 or as high as 603. As we see, $\mu_Y = 500$ is excluded, and we can use the confidence interval to conclude that $H_0: \mu_Y = 500$ is to be rejected. In fact, $\mu_Y = 499$ is also excluded, as are all numbers not in the range extending from a low of 501 to a high of 603.

This confidence interval model assumes that the value of σ_Y is known. In practice, this is almost never true, and so the model is mainly of academic interest. Further, it is assumed that N is large enough that the distribution of the sample mean approaches normality according to the central limit theorem. For most behavioral studies, where population distributions tend to be not too far from normal, this condition is satisfied if N is larger than 30. If N is less than 30, or if the distributions do not seem to be normal, then the reliance upon the central limit theorem is questionable. The smaller the sample size, the less one can rely on the theorem. It is under this condition that a researcher should adopt the sign test or the matched-pair Wilcoxon test to compare the population median with a specific value. If, in addition, the distribution is symmetrical, the hypotheses can be stated directly in terms of means and the sign and the matched-pair Wilcoxon tests become the *nonparametric* analogs to the procedures presented here.

If the parent population is normal, the dependency upon the central limit theorem can be completely ignored. In practice, it is next to impossible to determine whether or not a sample has been selected from a distribution that is normal in form. We have seen that we could use normal probability paper to help decide whether or not the assumed normality of the distribution is reasonable, and we recommend that this procedure be used.

21-5. THE DISTRIBUTION OF $\overline{Y}$ WHEN SAMPLING WITHOUT REPLACEMENT

The discussion in Section 21-2 examined results derived for sampling with replacement. Let us continue this discussion by sampling from a population composed of the numbers 1, 7, 10, 11, and 14. The mean value of this population is given by

$$\mu_Y = \tfrac{1}{5}(1 + 7 + 10 + 11 + 14) = 8.6$$

and its variance is given by

$$\sigma_Y^2 = \tfrac{1}{5}[(1 - 8.6)^2 + (7 - 8.6)^2 + \cdots + (14 - 8.6)^2]$$
$$= 19.44$$

If we draw samples of size 3 with replacement from the population, we know that

$$\mu_{\overline{Y}} = \mu_Y = 8.6$$

and

$$\sigma_{\overline{Y}}^2 = \frac{\sigma_Y^2}{N} = \frac{19.44}{3} = 6.48$$

Let us now list all of the samples of size $N = 3$ that can be produced under sampling *without* replacement. There are only $\binom{N}{r} = \binom{5}{3} = 10$ possible samples instead of the $N^3 = 5^3 = 125$ different samples that can be produced under sampling with replacement. With such a smaller number of samples we should not be surprised to find that the variability between the samples is significantly reduced. As we will see, that is indeed the case.

Table 21-1. All possible samples of size 3 that can be generated from the population 1, 7, 10, 11, and 14.

Sample			$\bar{Y}$
1	7	10	6.00
1	7	11	6.33
1	7	14	7.33
1	10	11	7.33
1	10	14	8.33
1	11	14	8.67
7	10	11	9.33
7	10	14	10.33
7	11	14	10.67
10	11	14	11.67

We list the 10 samples in Table 21-1. The 10 sample means are given by

6.00   6.33   7.33   7.33   8.33   8.67   9.33   10.33   10.67   11.67

and their mean is given by

$$\mu_{\bar{Y}} = \tfrac{1}{10}(6.00 + 6.33 + \cdots + 11.67) = 8.6$$

Here we see that even when we sample without replacement, the expected value of the sample mean is still equal to the population mean.

Let us now calculate the variance of the means, $\sigma_{\bar{Y}}^2$. As before, we treat these 10 values as a population, so that:

$$\sigma_{\bar{Y}}^2 = \tfrac{1}{10}[(6.00 - 8.60)^2 + (6.33 - 8.60)^2 + \cdots + (11.67 - 8.60)^2]$$
$$= 3.24$$

Clearly, $\sigma_{\bar{Y}}^2$ is much smaller than the value obtained by sampling with replacement. Even though the two variances in this illustration are in a ratio of 1 to 2, the exact relationship for the general case is not obvious. While we could generate the correct connection in terms of simple algebra, we prefer to state it simply as follows.

The mean and variance of $\bar{Y}$ for sampling without replacement

The sampling distribution of $\bar{Y}$ has as its parameters $\mu_{\bar{Y}}$ and $\sigma_{\bar{Y}}^2$. If the sampling is without replacement, the mean, variance, and standard deviation are as follows:

$$\mu_{\bar{Y}} = \mu_Y$$

$$\sigma_{\bar{Y}}^2 = \frac{\sigma_Y^2}{N}\left(\frac{\mathcal{N} - N}{\mathcal{N} - 1}\right)$$

$$\sigma_{\bar{Y}} = \frac{\sigma_Y}{\sqrt{N}}\sqrt{\frac{\mathcal{N} - N}{\mathcal{N} - 1}}$$

where $\mathcal{N}$ is the population size and N is the sample size. If $N/\mathcal{N} < 0.05$, then $(\mathcal{N} - N)/(\mathcal{N} - 1)$ may be dropped from $\sigma_{\bar{Y}}$ without serious statistical effects.

For our example, we had $\mathcal{N} = 5$, $N = 3$, and $\sigma_Y^2 = 19.44$, so that

$$\sigma_{\bar{Y}}^2 = \frac{19.44}{3}\left(\frac{5 - 3}{5 - 1}\right) = 3.24$$

Three important features of sampling without replacement can be examined. First, if $N = 1$, we are selecting individual observations from the population, and the mean of each sample of size 1 is equal to the observation. Thus, the population of sample means is identical to the original population of observations. In this case, we would have

$$\sigma_{\bar{Y}}^2 = \frac{\sigma_Y^2}{N}\left(\frac{\mathcal{N} - N}{\mathcal{N} - 1}\right) = \frac{\sigma_Y^2}{1}\left(\frac{\mathcal{N} - 1}{\mathcal{N} - 1}\right) = \sigma_Y^2$$

Because each sample mean is an observation from the original population, the variance of the means must equal the population variance, and our result agrees with this fact. Second, if the sample size equals the size of the population, then only one sample and one sample mean are possible. The variance of this single mean is zero, since when $N = \mathcal{N}$,

$$\sigma_{\bar{Y}}^2 = \frac{\sigma_Y^2}{\mathcal{N}}\left(\frac{\mathcal{N} - N}{\mathcal{N} - 1}\right) = \frac{\sigma_Y^2}{\mathcal{N}}\left(\frac{\mathcal{N} - \mathcal{N}}{\mathcal{N} - 1}\right) = 0$$

Finally, for a particular sample size N, if the size of the population becomes large, the ratio $(\mathcal{N} - N)/(\mathcal{N} - 1)$ approaches unity and the effects of sampling without replacement become minor. That is, if we sample without replacement from a large population, we effectively approximate samples with replacement.

21-6. THE DISTRIBUTION OF A SAMPLE TOTAL

In Sections 21-2 and 21-5, we specified the parameters of the distribution of $\overline{Y}$ for sampling with and without replacement from a finite universe. Sometimes we are not interested in $\overline{Y}$ as a criterion variable, but rather in $T = N\overline{Y}$. Examples have been encountered in the Fisher-Irwin test, the sign test, and the two forms of the Wilcoxon test. As we will see, knowing the distribution of the sample total will enable us to extend these models to large samples. If we make use of the scale theorem of Section 20-2, we see that

$$\mu_T = N\mu_Y$$

for sampling both with and without replacement; that

$$\sigma_T^2 = N^2\sigma_{\overline{Y}}^2 = N^2\frac{\sigma_Y^2}{N} = N\sigma_Y^2$$

for sampling with replacement; and that

$$\sigma_T^2 = N^2\frac{\sigma_Y^2}{N}\left(\frac{\mathcal{N}-N}{\mathcal{N}-1}\right) = N\sigma_Y^2\left(\frac{\mathcal{N}-N}{\mathcal{N}-1}\right)$$

for sampling without replacement.

21-7. EXERCISES

21-1. Define the following terms in your own words. Do not use the definitions in the text.
   a. Central limit theorem
   b. Repeated random sampling
   c. Linear combination
   d. Sampling without replacement
   e. Population of sample means
   f. The mean of the population of sample means
   g. The variance of the population of sample means

21-2. Suppose that six basketball players are selected from the population of Exercise 19-1. If their mean height is $\bar{Y} = 75$ in, should we be surprised?

21-3. What are H_0 and H_1 in Exercise 21-2?

21-4. Suppose that nine students are selected at random from a school population of 50,000 students and given the Stanford-Binet test of mental abilities. Should we be surprised if the mean value is $\bar{Y} = 106$?

21-5. What are H_0 and H_1 for Exercise 21-4?

21-6. Suppose Y is normally distributed with $\mu_Y = 80$ and $\sigma_Y^2 = 40$. Find the mean and variance of $\bar{Y} = \frac{1}{5}(Y_1 + Y_2 + Y_3 + Y_4 + Y_5)$. Suppose that $\bar{Y} = 84$. Should we be surprised? Why?

21-7. Find the 95 percent central range for the means of:

   a. Exercise 21-2
   b. Exercise 21-4

21-8. Consider a population of $N = 25$ schools. If schools are
   a. Sampled with replacement
   b. Sampled without replacement
   how many samples of size $N = 4$ can be generated from this population?

21-9. If the mean salary of teachers in the schools of Exercise 21-8 is given by $\mu_Y = \$22,000$ and if $\sigma_Y = \$1500$, find the mean and variance of the sampling distribution of $\bar{Y} = \frac{1}{4}(Y_1 + Y_2 + Y_3 + Y_4)$.

21-10. In a survey of spending habits in the purchase of food, $N = 80$ families with two school-age children were randomly identified in a large urban community and asked to keep a record for 10 weeks of all money spent on food. The mean amount was given by $\bar{Y} = \$82.26$. In a study made 5 years earlier, $\mu_Y = \$72.18$ and $\sigma_Y = \$10.62$. Has the amount spent on food changed over the past 5 years if the earlier study is used as a reference?
   a. What are H_0 and H_1?
   b. What is the test statistic?
   c. What is the $\alpha = .05$ decision rule?
   d. What is the decision?
   e. What is the 95-percent confidence interval for the population mean?
   f. What assumptions have you made?

CHAPTER 22

The Mean and Variance of Discrete Distributions

22-1. PARAMETRIC AND NONPARAMETRIC TESTS

In Chapter 11, we began a presentation of statistical tests and confidence interval procedures for methods based on replacing originally observed data by ranks. As was shown, the matched-pair Wilcoxon test and the two-sample Wilcoxon or Mann-Whitney U test could be used for testing differences between distributions. While it is not obvious, the sign test and the Fisher-Irwin test can also be expressed as tests based on ranks.

Tests based on replacing originally observed data by ranks or other values are commonly referred to as *nonparametric tests*. The assumptions required to justify such tests are minimal. The assumption common to all of these tests is that the observations within a sample must be independent and, if two samples are involved, the observations between samples must also be independent.

This simplicity does not hold for what are known as *parametric tests*. Consider the example of Section 21-1. There we examined whether four people could have been sampled from a population whose mean height was given by $\mu_Y = 69$. That test used the original height data of the four subjects measured and it also made use of the known fact that the distribution of heights could be approximated by the normal distribution. Tests that are based upon this latter assumption of normality are generally referred to as parametric tests. While this comparison of parametric and nonparametric tests is overly simplified, it is sufficient for most cases.

Whereas researchers in the social sciences have tended to prefer parametric over nonparametric tests, it is our contention that nonparametric tests should be preferred because of their minimal assumption requirements and because they possess good statistical power. Our recommendation is especially valid for small-sample situations because, in those cases, a researcher does not have sufficient data to make meaningful decisions about the probability distributions of pertinent data. A histogram based on 10 to 15 subjects will provide very little information about the form and extent of a distribution. In addition, plots on normal probability paper will not be too informative, because of the small sample sizes. So what should one do? We recommend the use of the nonparametric tests. They can almost always be justified. Unfortunately, there is a catch. The calculation of exact probability levels is difficult when sample sizes are large. As might be expected, however, the situation really is not as much of a loss as it might appear, since all of these tests are based on measures that can be written as linear combinations and can, therefore, be treated as approximately normally distributed, provided the number of terms in the sum is large. To treat them in this way, however, we need to know the values of the mean and standard deviation of the normal distribution to which the criterion used for the decision processes converges.

22-2. PROBABILITIES AS POPULATION PARAMETERS

In Section 11-1, we saw that the probability that heads will come up in the toss of a fair coin is ½. We went on to note that, should the results of a coin-flipping experiment differ greatly from the theoretical probabilities, we would suspect the coin of being unfair. We would not assume that the population values for a fair coin were different from half heads and half tails. In this sense, the theoretical probabilities represent population values that are expected if the theory is correct.

22-3. THE MEAN AND VARIANCE OF THE NUMBER OF SUCCESSES IN N BINOMIAL TRIALS

In describing population parameters, one must be very careful in defining the variable whose mean one is seeking. If we are dealing with a binomial variable, such as the flipping of a coin, we are usually interested in a fixed number of tosses, which we will denote as N. For example, we may be interested in counting the number of times heads appears in $N = 20$ flips of a coin. Our variable of interest, which we can call T, is the total number of times heads appears in our experiment. We wish now to calculate the *average* number of occurrences of heads we would expect to appear in a large number of 20-coin experiments. We will call this value μ_T. We show that the mean number of successes in N binomial trials is given by $\mu_T = Np$ and that the variance is given by $\sigma_T^2 = Npq$.

To find the mean and variance of the number of successes in N independent binomial trials, we define the total number of heads in N trials as

$$T = \sum_{i=1}^{N} X_i = X_1 + X_2 + \cdots + X_N,$$

where each X_i is called a dummy, or indicator, variable, defined:

$$X_i = \begin{cases} 0 \text{ if the outcome is tails (with probability } p_0) \\ 1 \text{ if the outcome is heads (with probability } p_1). \end{cases}$$

Since trials are identical, we know that the expected values for all trials must equal one another. Let us denote the mean of each trial by μ_X. Thus, it follows that

$$\mu_T = E(T) = N\mu_X$$

We now determine the value of μ_X. From Section 20-2, we know that

$$\mu_X = 0p_0 + 1p_1 = p_1$$

In terms of binomial theory notation, $p_0 = q$ and $p_1 = p$. Thus:

$$\mu_X = p$$

and we see that $E(T) = Np$, as we set out to show.

We now find σ_T^2. Using the results of Section 20-3, we know that for such a sum of the independent random variables X_i,

$$\sigma_T^2 = \sigma_{X_1}^2 + \sigma_{X_2}^2 + \cdots + \sigma_{X_N}^2 = \sum_{i=1}^{N} \sigma_{X_i}^2 = N\sigma_X^2$$

Since all of the trials are identical, we have only to find the variance of one of them.

Again, each of the trials has only two outcomes, $\{0, 1\}$, with probabilities $p_0 = q$ and $p_1 = p$. As we have just shown, $\mu_X = p$. Thus:

$$\sigma_X^2 = (0^2 p_0 + 1^2 p_1) - p^2 = p_1 - p^2 = p - p^2 = p(1 - p) = pq$$

We have then, for N identical trials, that $\sigma_T^2 = Npq$. We summarize the results as follows:

The mean and variance of a binomial variable

The mean number of successes in N trials of a binomial variable with probability of success p on any one trial is given by

$$\mu_T = E(T) = Np$$

and the variance is given by

$$\sigma_T^2 = \text{Var}(T) = Npq$$

where

$$q = 1 - p$$

Thus, for 20 flips of a fair coin with $p = q = \frac{1}{2}$, we have

$$\mu_T = 20(\tfrac{1}{2}) = 10 \quad \text{and} \quad \sigma_T^2 = 20(\tfrac{1}{2})(\tfrac{1}{2}) = 5$$

22-4. MEAN AND VARIANCE OF A PROPORTION FOR *N* TRIALS

In the preceding sections, we have derived the mean and variance of the number of successes, T, achieved in N binomial trials. Often, however, results are reported as proportions. Such is the procedure, for example, for the results of a Gallup poll. For this reason, we will also calculate the mean and variance of the proportion of successes in N binomial trials.

If we again let T represent the number of successes in N trials and if we let $\hat{p}$ represent the proportion of success in these trials, we have:

$$\hat{p} = \frac{T}{N}$$

since the proportion of successes is their number divided by the total number of trials.

Since $\hat{p}$ is related to T in this way, we can use the results of Section 20-2, the scale theorem for means and for variances, to derive the desired results. In particular, if a new variable $\hat{p}$ is equal to an old variable T divided by a constant N, then the mean of the new variable equals the old mean divided by N:

$$E(\hat{p}) = \mu_{\hat{p}} = \frac{\mu_T}{N} = \frac{Np}{N} = p$$

Further, the variance of the new variable equals the variance of the old variable divided by N^2. Thus,

$$\sigma_{\hat{p}}^2 = \frac{\sigma_T^2}{N^2} = \frac{Npq}{N^2} = \frac{pq}{N}$$

For our 20-flip example, $\mu_{\hat{p}} = p = \frac{1}{2}$. Hence, on the average, we would expect half of the results to be heads. Similarly:

$$\sigma_{\hat{p}}^2 = \frac{pq}{N} = \frac{(\frac{1}{2})(\frac{1}{2})}{20} = \frac{1}{80}$$

That is, if we wrote down the proportions from an extremely large number of 20-flip experiments, the variance of these tallied proportions should be close to $\frac{1}{80}$. We summarize the results as follows.

The mean and variance of the sampling distribution of a proportion based on N trials

The mean and variance of $\hat{p} = T/N$ are given by

$$\mu_{\hat{p}} = E(\hat{p}) = p$$

and

$$\sigma_{\hat{p}}^2 = \text{Var}(\hat{p}) = \frac{pq}{N}$$

Like the formulas for $\mu_{\bar{Y}}$ and $\sigma_{\bar{Y}}^2$, these formulas are among the most frequently called upon of empirical research. We shall see many applications of them in later pages.

22-5. LARGE-SAMPLE MEANS FOR NONPARAMETRIC TESTS

As we implied in Section 22-1, in large-sample situations the central limit theorem allows us to approximate exact probabilities with the normal distribution. To do so, we need to know the mean and variance of the appropriate normally distributed variable. In the cases of the sign, matched-pair Wilcoxon, two-sample Wilcoxon, and Fisher-Irwin tests and the Spearman rank correlation test, the dependent variable can be written as a linear combination, so that the central limit theorem can be used. We present the values of the means of the dependent measure for these tests.

Means for common nonparametric statistics

Test	Criterion	Mean
Sign	$T_{(+)}$	$\frac{1}{2}N$
Matched-pair Wilcoxon	T	$\dfrac{N(N+1)}{4}$
Two-sample Wilcoxon	T_W	$N_1\left(\dfrac{N_1 + N_2 + 1}{2}\right)$
Mann-Whitney	U	$\dfrac{N_1 N_2}{2}$
Fisher-Irwin	f_{11}	$N_1 p_0$
Spearman's rho	r_S	0

We now derive these results.

The sign test   The dependent variable can be written as

$$T = \sum_{i=1}^{N} x_i$$

where x_i represents variables that take on the value $x_i = 1$ if the sign of the ith difference is positive and 0 otherwise. Under the null hypothesis examined by the sign test, the probability $p = \frac{1}{2}$ that a particular difference is positive. Hence, each x_i is a dichotomous variable with underlying binomial parameter $p = \frac{1}{2}$. Since x_i represents independent random variables, we know that the mean of T is given by

$$\mu_T = Np = N(\tfrac{1}{2}) = \frac{N}{2}$$

The matched-pair Wilcoxon test   We defined the dependent variable as

$$T = \sum_{i=1}^{N} x_i r_i$$

where each x_i is also a binomial variable that takes on the value $x_i = 0$ or 1, depending on the sign of the difference; r_i stands for the ranks of the differences themselves. Since T is again written as a linear combination, we know that

$$\mu_T = \sum_{i=1}^{N} r_i \mu_{x_i}$$

Here, too, under the null hypothesis examined, each x_i has a probability of $\frac{1}{2}$ of equalling 1, so $\mu_{x_i} = p = \frac{1}{2}$. Hence

$$\mu_T = \sum_{i=1}^{N} r_i(\tfrac{1}{2}) = \tfrac{1}{2} \sum_{i=1}^{N} r_i$$

If there are no ties in the raw scores, the summation involves the addition of the first N integers. We know the result of this summation to be

$$\sum_{i=1}^{N} r_i = \frac{N(N+1)}{2}$$

If midranks are assigned to tied scores, the sum is unchanged, so that

$$\mu_T = \tfrac{1}{2} \left(\frac{N(N+1)}{2} \right) = \frac{N(N+1)}{4}$$

Two-sample Wilcoxon test   Under the null hypothesis examined in the two-sample Wilcoxon procedure, the dependent variable is the sum of the ranks in the smaller group

$$T = \sum_{i=1}^{N_1} r_i$$

We can again apply the rules for the mean of a linear combination. As we saw in Section 21-6

$$\mu_T = N_1 \mu_{r_i}$$

Each rank represents an observation sampled at random from a population consisting of the integers from 1 to N. Over an enormous number of trials, the expected value of these ranks is the mean of the population. We know the sum of the first N integers to be $N(N+1)/2$, so that

$$\mu_{r_i} = \frac{N(N+1)/2}{N} = \frac{N+1}{2}$$

Hence

$$\mu_T = N_1 \left(\frac{N+1}{2} \right)$$

Since $N = N_1 + N_2$, it follows that

$$\mu_T = N_1 \left(\frac{N_1 + N_2 + 1}{2} \right)$$

For the Mann-Whitney U statistic

$$\mu_U = \frac{N_1 N_2}{2}$$

The Irwin-Fisher test   Under the null hypothesis, we have $p_1 = p_2 = p_0$. If the null hypothesis is true, our best estimate of p_0 is obtained from combining the two samples into one large sample of $N = N_1 + N_2$ subjects. If we use the notation that $T = f_1$. of the subjects in the combined sample are of type A, then our best estimate of p_0 is given by

$$\hat{p}_0 = \frac{f_1.}{N} = \frac{f_{11} + f_{12}}{N_1 + N_2}$$

Further, under the null hypothesis, we can consider the N subjects to be assigned to the two groups entirely at random. We can thus depict our dependent variable, $T = f_{11}$, the number of type A subjects in the first group, as

$$T = f_{11} = \sum_{i=1}^{N_1} x_i$$

where each $x_i = 1$ if the ith subject is of type A, and 0 otherwise. Although there is a marked similarity here to previous linear combinations, we emphasize that the probability of any x_i equalling 1 changes as we select subjects, due to the sampling being performed without replacement.

Nevertheless, we have seen in Section 21-5 that the mean remains unchanged when sampling without replacement. Hence, we still have

$$\mu_{f_{11}} = E(f_{11}) = \mu_{x_1} + \mu_{x_2} + \cdots + \mu_{x_{N_1}}$$
$$= p_0 + p_0 + \cdots + p_0 = N_1 p_0$$

just as in the binomial case.

Spearman's rho   Because the algebra involved with determining the mean value of Spearman's rho is complex, we simply report the results. For Spearman's rho

$$\mu_{r_S} = E(r_S) = 0$$

22-6. LARGE-SAMPLE VARIANCES FOR NONPARAMETRIC TESTS

We now present the variances of the dependent variables for the same test procedures. It should be noted that two of these variables (for the sign and matched-pair Wilcoxon tests) are defined in terms of sampling with replacement while the others involve sampling without replacement. For the latter cases, we use the relationship defined in Section 21-6 for correcting the variance to conform to the model of sampling without replacement. The variances are presented in the following list.

Variances for common nonparametric statistics

Test	Variance
Sign	$\dfrac{N}{4}$
Matched-pair Wilcoxon	$\frac{1}{4} \sum_{i=1}^{N} r_i^2$
Two-sample Wilcoxon	$\dfrac{N_1 N_2}{(N_1 + N_2 - 1)} \sigma_{r_i}^2$
Mann-Whitney	$\dfrac{N_1 N_2}{(N_1 + N_2 - 1)} \sigma_{r_i}^2$
Fisher-Irwin	$\dfrac{N_1 N_2 p_0 q_0}{N_1 + N_2 - 1}$
Spearman's rho	$\dfrac{1}{N - 1}$

We now derive these results.

The sign test   We defined

$$T = \sum_{i=1}^{N} x_i$$

Therefore, we know the variance of T to be

$$\sigma_T^2 = \sum_{i=1}^{N} \sigma_{x_i}^2$$

Because each x_i is a binomial variable, its variance is equal to

$$\sigma_{x_i}^2 = pq = (\tfrac{1}{2})(\tfrac{1}{2}) = \tfrac{1}{4}$$

since each $p = \tfrac{1}{2}$. Hence

$$\sigma_T^2 = \tfrac{1}{4} + \tfrac{1}{4} + \cdots + \tfrac{1}{4} = \frac{N}{4}$$

The match-pair Wilcoxon procedure   We have

$$T = \sum_{i=1}^{N} x_i r_i$$

Hence

$$\sigma_T^2 = \sum_{i=1}^{N} r_i^2 \sigma_{x_i}^2$$

Since the x_i are binomial variables, each of their variances is given by

$$\sigma_{x_i}^2 = pq = (\tfrac{1}{2})(\tfrac{1}{2}) = \tfrac{1}{4}$$

Therefore

$$\sigma_T^2 = \sum_{i=1}^{N} r_i^2 / 4 = \tfrac{1}{4} \sum_{i=1}^{N} r_i^2$$

where the summation indicates the addition of the square of the assigned ranks and midranks. If there are no ties, these are the first N integers. With no ties, this is known to be

$$\sum_{i=1}^{N} r_i^2 = \frac{N(N+1)(2N+1)}{6}$$

so that without ties,

$$\sigma_T^2 = \tfrac{1}{4}\left(\frac{N(N+1)(2N+1)}{6}\right) = \frac{N(N+1)(2N+1)}{24}$$

The two-sample Wilcoxon test   The case here is similar, although we must remember to correct for sampling without replacement. We again have

$$T = \sum_{i=1}^{N_1} r_i$$

Because we are sampling without replacement, we have

$$\sigma_T^2 = N_1 \sigma_{r_i}^2 \left(\frac{\mathcal{N}-N}{\mathcal{N}-1}\right)$$

where $\sigma_{r_i}^2$ represents the variance of the ranks and midranks involved. Because we consider the ranks to constitute our population, we have

$$\sigma_{r_i}^2 = \frac{\displaystyle\sum_{i=1}^{\mathcal{N}} (r_i - \mu_{r_i})^2}{\mathcal{N}}$$

We can expand the numerator to yield

$$\sum_{i=1}^{\mathcal{N}} (r_i - \mu_{r_i})^2 = \sum_{i=1}^{\mathcal{N}} r_i^2 - \mathcal{N}\mu_{r_i}^2$$

for which we know that

$$\mu_{r_i} = \frac{N_1 + N_2 + 1}{2} = \frac{\mathcal{N}+1}{2}$$

Therefore

$$\sigma_{r_i}^2 = \frac{\displaystyle\sum_{i=1}^{\mathcal{N}} r_i^2}{\mathcal{N}} - \frac{(\mathcal{N}+1)^2}{4}$$

Because $N_1 + N_2 = \mathcal{N}$, we can see that $\mathcal{N} - N_1 = N_2$, so that:

$$\sigma_T^2 = \frac{N_1 N_2}{\mathcal{N}-1}\,\sigma_{r_i}^2 = \frac{N_1 N_2}{N_1 + N_2 - 1}\,\sigma_{r_i}^2$$

If there are no ties, then

$$\sum_{i=1}^{N} r_i^2 = \frac{N(N+1)(2N+1)}{6} \qquad \text{and} \qquad \sigma_T^2 = \frac{N_1 N_2}{12}(N+1)$$

The Irwin-Fisher test   For this test, we wrote

$$T = f_{11} = \sum_{i=1}^{N_1} x_i$$

If we were sampling with replacement, we already know that we would have:

$$\sigma_{f_{11}}^2 = N_1 p_0 q_0$$

since each x_i would be a binomial variable. Hence, to correct for sampling without replacement, we would have

$$\sigma_{f_{11}}^2 = N_1 p_0 q_0 \left(\frac{N - N_1}{N - 1} \right)$$

Again, $N - N_1 = N_2$, so that

$$\sigma_{f_{11}}^2 = \frac{N_1 N_2}{N_1 + N_2 - 1}(p_0 q_0)$$

Spearman's rho   Because the algebra involved in determining the variance of Spearman's rho is complex, we just report the results. For Spearman's rank correlation coefficient

$$\sigma_{r_S}^2 = \frac{1}{N - 1}$$

The mean and variances calculated in these last two sections can now be used to calculate rejection regions, based on a normal approximation to the exact probabilities. We shall show how this is done in the next chapter.

22-7. EXERCISES

22-1. A coin is to be tossed 75 times. Find the expected number of times heads occurs and the variance of the number of heads if:
a. $p = \frac{1}{2}$
b. $p = \frac{2}{3}$
c. $p = \frac{3}{4}$

22-2. From past experience it is known that 32 percent of all drivers convicted of drunk driving are under the age of 21. If a judge sees 83 drivers in a four-week period who are accused of driving while drunk and if 38 are under the age of 21, should he be surprised?

22-3. Find the mean and variance of $\hat{p}$ for the three conditions of Exercise 22-1.

22-4. Find the mean and variance for the matched-pair Wilcoxon statistic if $N = 20$ and there are no ties.

22-5. Determine the 68th percentile for the variable of Exercise 22-4.

22-6. Find the mean and variance for the two-sample Wilcoxon statistic if $N_1 = 8, N_2 = 12$, and there are no ties.

22-7. Determine the 32d percentile of the variable of Exercise 22-6.

22-8. Find the mean and variance for the Fisher-Irwin statistic if $N_1 = 10$, $N_2 = 15$, and $p_0 = .8$.

22-9. Determine the 5th and 95th percentile of the variable of Exercise 22-8.

22-10. Repeat exercise 22-9 for $p_0 = .5$ and compare the results.

CHAPTER 23

Large-Sample Nonparametric Tests

23-1. INTRODUCTION

In Chapter 22, we were able to find the means and variances of the six test criteria we used earlier in exact probability tests. Using these means and variances in conjunction with the central limit theorem, we will be able to calculate approximate critical values to use in the testing of hypotheses. In a sense, we will be able to use the approximation to extend our tables to any sample sizes desired. Once the normal approximation yields the critical values, they will be used as if they were tabled values, in precisely the same manner as we used the exact tabled values in previous chapters.

23-2. CORRECTING FOR CONTINUITY

Whenever the probabilities of a discrete variable are approximated by a continuous variable, one must make a correction for continuity. As an example, consider the 20 tosses of a coin reported in Table 11-2 and discussed in Section 11-3. Suppose we wish to use the normal distribution to approximate the probabilities found in Table 11-2. To determine the probability of getting $X = 5$ or fewer heads in 20 tosses, we must add the probabilities of getting 0, 1, 2, 3, 4, and 5 heads. As a continuous variable, $X \leq 5$ covers the continuous range less than or equal to 5.5. Since the underlying variable has a binomial distribution, we know that

$$E(X) = Np = 20(\tfrac{1}{2}) = 10$$

and

$$\mathrm{Var}(X) = Npq = 20(\tfrac{1}{2})(\tfrac{1}{2}) = 5$$

We need to find $P(X \leq 5.5)$. In this case:

$$P(X \leq 5.5) = P\left(Z \leq \frac{5.5 - 10}{\sqrt{5}}\right) = P(Z \leq -2.01) = 0.022$$

This is in agreement with the cumulative probability $P(X \leq 5)$, which can be obtained from the figures of Table 11-2. In like manner, had we desired to find the probability that $X \geq 15$, we would have needed to consider the continuous range greater than or equal to 14.5. Notice that each of these corrections for continuity yields a range beginning one-half unit closer to the expected value of $E(X) = 10$. For the upper tail:

$$P(X \geq 14.5) = P\left(Z \geq \frac{14.5 - 10}{\sqrt{5}}\right) = P(Z \geq 2.01) = 0.022$$

In practice, we rarely calculate probabilities. Rather, we use the Z values themselves to make decisions about hypotheses under test. We have noticed that the correction for continuity involves subtracting $\tfrac{1}{2}$ if $X > E(X)$ or adding $\tfrac{1}{2}$ if $X < E(X)$. Directions for correcting for continuity are provided in Box 23-1.

23-3. CRITICAL VALUES FOR LARGE-SAMPLE NONPARAMETRIC TESTS

In Sections 22-5 and 22-6, we provided the expected values and variances for five discrete test criteria. We will now indicate how these values can be used to

---

Box 23-1   Procedure for correcting for continuity

Step 1. Determine X, $E(X)$, and $\text{Var}(X)$.
Step 2. If $X > E(X)$, calculate Z as follows:

$$Z = \frac{X - \frac{1}{2} - E(X)}{\sqrt{\text{Var}(X)}}$$

If $X < E(X)$, calculate Z thus:

$$Z = \frac{X + \frac{1}{2} - E(X)}{\sqrt{\text{Var}(X)}}$$

---

derive critical values for the associated test procedures. Let us denote any of the five criteria as X. As in the previous section, we know that the cumulative distribution of X can be approximated by the normal distribution. Specifying the $\alpha/2$ percentile of the distribution of X as $P_{\alpha/2}$, we then have, using the correction for continuity,

$$Z_{\alpha/2} = \frac{P_{\alpha/2} + \frac{1}{2} - E(X)}{\sqrt{\text{Var}(X)}}$$

Solving for $P_{\alpha/2}$ yields:

$$P_{\alpha/2} = [E(X) - \frac{1}{2}] + Z_{\alpha/2}\sqrt{\text{Var}(X)}$$

Since $P_{\alpha/2}$ will not be an integer, we use as the lower critical value L the integer below $P_{\alpha/2}$. Similarly, the upper critical value U will be the integer above $P_{1-\alpha/2}$, where

$$P_{1-\alpha/2} = [E(X) + \frac{1}{2}] + Z_{1-\alpha/2}\sqrt{\text{Var}(X)}$$

Directions for finding the lower and upper critical values using the normal approximation are provided in Box 23-2.

23-4. THE LARGE-SAMPLE SIGN TEST

The expected value and variance of T_+, the sign test criterion, are:

$$E(T_+) = \frac{N}{2} \quad \text{and} \quad \text{Var}(T_+) = \frac{N}{4}$$

Box 23-2   Procedure for finding the lower and upper critical values using the normal approximation

Step 1. For the particular test criterion of interest, X, find the mean $E(X)$ and the variance $\text{Var}(X)$ from the tables in Sections 22-5 and 22-6.

Step 2. The lower critical value L is the integer below:

$$P_{\alpha/2} = [E(X) - \tfrac{1}{2}] + Z_{\alpha/2} \sqrt{\text{Var}(X)}$$

The upper critical value U is the integer above:

$$P_{1-\alpha/2} = [E(X) + \tfrac{1}{2}] + Z_{1-\alpha/2} \sqrt{\text{Var}(X)}$$

Step 3. For one-tailed tests
(a) if the alternative hypothesis indicates a large value of X, then the critical value is the integer above:

$$P_{1-\alpha} = [E(X) + \tfrac{1}{2}] + Z_{1-\alpha} \sqrt{\text{Var}(X)}$$

(b) If the alternative hypothesis indicates a small value of X, then the critical value is the integer below:

$$P_{\alpha} = [E(X) - \tfrac{1}{2}] + Z_{\alpha} \sqrt{\text{Var}(X)}$$

In practice, for the sign test, "large" means that N is greater than 25.

As an example of the use of this test, consider a study in which 36 small shop owners in a major metropolitan center were asked the question:

During the past calendar year, by what percentage did you increase your employees' wages? ____ percent

The reason for asking this question is that the investigator wants to determine whether or not the pay increases met the cost-of-living increases resulting from inflation. Results are shown in Table 23-1. For the time period shown, the cost of living had increased by 12.8 percent. If the store owner kept pay raises in line with the inflation rate, the median difference between practice and theory should be zero. Therefore, consider the hypothesis

$$H_0: \quad M_d = 0$$

against

$$H_1: \quad M_d \neq 0$$

Table 23-1. Responses to the question concerning wage increases to employees in 1980.

Employer	Percent increase	Amount above 12.8	Rank of (+) deviations	Rank of (−) deviations
1	8.0	−4.8		27
2	2.1	−10.7		36
3	17.3	+4.5	24.5	
4	6.4	−6.4		31
5	12.2	−0.6		3
6	10.8	−2.0		12
7	2.3	−10.5		35
8	7.9	−4.9		28
9	14.6	+1.8	9.5	
10	18.2	+5.4	30	
11	13.2	+0.4	1	
12	9.1	−3.7		21.5
13	9.8	−3.0		18
14	10.2	−2.6		15
15	10.0	−2.8		17
16	13.6	+0.8	5.5	
17	9.1	−3.7		21.5
18	3.7	−9.1		34
19	10.2	−2.6		15
20	11.4	−1.4		8
21	11.9	−0.9		7
22	13.6	+0.8	5.5	
23	8.6	−4.2		23
24	14.7	+1.9	11	
25	8.3	−4.5		24.5
26	9.2	−3.6		20
27	12.2	−0.6		3
28	14.6	+1.8	9.5	
29	15.3	+2.5	13	

Table 23-1 *(Continued).*

Employer	Percent increase	Amount above 12.8	Rank of (+) deviations	Rank of (−) deviations
30	10.2	−2.6		15
31	8.1	−4.7		26
32	9.3	−3.5		19
33	6.2	−6.6		32
34	17.9	+5.1	29	
35	3.8	−9.0		33
36	12.2	−0.6		3
Total			138.5	527.5

where

$$d = \text{percent increase} - \text{inflation rate}$$

Note that this is a slightly different use of the sign test from the examples described in Chapter 14. In this case, 12.8 percent serves as a standard against which each shop is being compared. Such comparisons are frequently encountered in program evaluation investigations and in research using economic or socioeconomic variables.

For our example, $N = 36$, and $\alpha = .05$, so we have

$$P_{\alpha/2} = (^{36}\!/_2 - \tfrac{1}{2}) - 1.96\sqrt{^{36}\!/_4} = 11.62$$

so that $L = 11$, and

$$P_{1-\alpha/2} = (^{36}\!/_2 + \tfrac{1}{2}) + 1.96\sqrt{^{36}\!/_4} = 24.38$$

so that $U = 25$. In our example, $T_+ = 10$, and so we reject the null hypothesis. In addition, the 95 percent confidence interval for M_d is given by:

$$d_{12}^{\circ} \leqq M_d \leqq d_{25}^{\circ}$$

Ordering the data from smallest to largest yields $-10.7, -10.5, -9.1, \ldots$, $+4.5, +5.1, +5.4$. For these data,

$$d_{12}^{\circ} = -3.7 \quad \text{and} \quad d_{25}^{\circ} = -0.6$$

so that the 95 percent confidence interval for M_d is given by

$$-3.7 \leqq M_d \leqq -0.6$$

Note that $M_d = 0$ is not included in the interval. This is not surprising, since H_0 was rejected.

23-5. THE LARGE-SAMPLE MATCHED-PAIR WILCOXON TEST

The expected value and variance of the matched-pair Wilcoxon statistic T are defined by

$$E(T) = \frac{N(N+1)}{4} \quad \text{and} \quad \text{Var}(T) = \frac{1}{4} \sum_{i=1}^{N} r_i^2$$

where T is the sum of the ranks associated with the positive deviations. For the data of Table 23-1,

$$E(T) = \frac{36(37)}{4} = 333$$

If there are ties in the data, midranks are assigned to the tied values. Recall that in calculating T, the ranks assigned to differences of zero are considered to be half positive and half negative. A general form for the variance, which is *always* correct, is given in Section 22-6 as:

$$\text{Var}(T) = \frac{1}{4} \sum_{i=1}^{N} r_i^2$$

where r_i is the actual rank or midrank assigned to the ith difference.
For the present example, we have:

$$\text{Var}(T) = \frac{1}{4}(27^2 + 36^2 + 24.5^2 + \cdots + 3^2)$$
$$= \frac{1}{4}(16,200) = 4050$$

and

$$\sigma_T = \sqrt{4050} = 63.64$$

Thus, the critical values are given by

$$P_{.025} = (333 - 0.5) - 1.96(63.64) = 207.77$$

so that $L = 207$, and

$$P_{.975} = (333 + 0.5) + 1.96(63.64) = 458.23$$

so that $U = 459$. Because, for these data, $T = 138.5$, we reject the null hypothesis. In the matrix of $\hat{M}_{ii'} = (d_i^0 + d_{i'}^0)/2$, one would have to identify $\hat{M}_{208}^0$ and $\hat{M}_{459}^0$. Because of the gargantuan nature of the task, we do not present a table of the average differences, but merely state the result. We find that $\hat{M}_{208}^0 = -3.65$ and that $\hat{M}_{459}^0 = -0.90$, giving us the confidence interval

$$-3.65 \leqq M_d \leqq -0.90$$

Notice that this interval is narrower than the sign-test confidence interval.

In general, the Wilcoxon procedure will be preferred over the sign test if the distribution of differences is flat. If the distribution is peaked, the sign test will usually be more powerful.

23-6. THE TWO-SAMPLE WILCOXON TEST/MANN-WHITNEY U TEST FOR LARGE SAMPLES

As shown in Sections 22-5 and 22-6, the expected value and variance of the two-sample Wilcoxon test statistic are given by

$$E(T_W) = N_1\left(\frac{N_1 + N_2 + 1}{2}\right) \quad \text{and} \quad \text{Var}(T_W) = \frac{N_1 N_2}{(N_1 + N_2 - 1)}\,\sigma_{r_i}^2$$

where T_W is the sum of the ranks of the smaller sample. For the Mann-Whitney U test:

$$E(U) = \frac{N_1 N_2}{2} \quad \text{and} \quad \text{Var}(U) = \frac{N_1 N_2}{(N_1 + N_2 - 1)}\,\sigma_{r_i}^2$$

where U is the number of concordant pairs. In general, the large-sample form of these tests can be justified if N_1 and N_2 are greater than 10 or if $N_1 + N_2 > 20$.

As an example of the large-sample form of this test, consider the data of Table 23-2, which appear in rank order. We wish to test the hypothesis that the median difference in the pretest scores between the two groups is zero.

Since there are ties in the data, the general formula for $\text{Var}(T_W)$ must be used. For this example:

$$\sigma_{r_i}^2 = \frac{\sum_{i=1}^{N} r_i^2 - N\left(\frac{N+1}{2}\right)^2}{N}$$

$$= \frac{20{,}510 - 15{,}600}{39} = 125.8974$$

so that

$$\text{Var}(T_W) = \frac{16(23)}{38}(125.90) = 1219.22$$

Table 23-2. Ranked data taken from Table 4-1.

Previous course in one of the biological sciences		No previous course in one of the biological sciences	
Original data	Rank	Original data	Rank
5	2	3	1
8	3	9	4
13	10	10	6
15	14.5	10	6
15	14.5	10	6
16	17.5	13	10
17	21.5	13	10
25	29.5	13	10
26	31	13	10
28	33.5	14	13
28	33.5	16	17.5
28	33.5	16	17.5
29	36	16	17.5
30	38	17	21.5
30	38	17	21.5
30	38	17	21.5
		18	24
		20	25
		22	26
		23	27
		24	28
		25	29.5
		28	33.5
Sum of ranks	394		386

and

$$\sigma_{T_W} = \sqrt{1219.22} = 34.92$$

For the Wilcoxon test:

$$P_{\alpha/2} = \left[16\left(\frac{16 + 23 + 1}{2} \right) - \frac{1}{2} \right] - 1.96\sqrt{\frac{16(23)}{38}} (125.8974) = 251.06$$

so that $L = 251$, and

$$P_{1-\alpha/2} = \left[16\left(\frac{16 + 23 + 1}{12} \right) + \frac{1}{2} \right]$$

$$+ 1.96\sqrt{\frac{16(23)}{38}} (125.8974) = 388.94$$

so that $U = 389$. Since $T_W = 394$, we reject the null hypothesis.

For the Mann-Whitney U test:

$$P_{\alpha/2} = (184 - 0.5) - 1.96(34.92) = 115.06$$

so that $L = 115$, and

$$P_{1-\alpha/2} = (184 + 0.5) + 1.96(34.92) = 252.94$$

so that $U = 253$. The matrix of differences is shown in Table 23-3. For this table:

$$d^o_{116} = -12 \qquad \text{and} \qquad d^o_{253} = 0$$

so that

$$-12 \leqq M_d \leqq 0$$

In this case, the test and the interval procedure do not agree, since there are a great number of zero values in Table 23-3. We offer the following explanation for the apparent discrepancy. An examination of Table 23-3 shows that there are 103 positive differences and 14 zero values, so that $U = 103 + \frac{1}{2}(14) = 110$. This value of U is less than the critical value 115, and so we would reject H_0 on the basis of both the Wilcoxon and the Mann-Whitney tests, as expected. Because there are 14 zeros, we treat half as positive deviations and half as negative deviations. This means that the 253d ordered difference is treated as if it were negative, and hence both limits of the confidence interval are negative. The interval, therefore, theoretically excludes zero and would also indicate rejection.

Table 23-3. Determination of the 95 percent two-sided confidence interval for the median difference for the data of Table 23-2.

Large Sample								Small Sample								
	5	8	13	15	15	16	17	25	26	28	28	28	29	30	30	30
3	-2	-5	-10	-12	-12	-13	-14	-22	-23	-25	-25	-25	-26	-27	-27	-27
9	4	1	-4	-6	-6	-7	-8	-16	-17	-19	-19	-19	-20	-21	-21	-21
10	5	2	-3	-5	-5	-6	-7	-15	-16	-18	-18	-18	-19	-20	-20	-20
10	5	2	-3	-5	-5	-6	-7	-15	-16	-18	-18	-18	-19	-20	-20	-20
10	5	2	-3	-5	-5	-6	-7	-15	-16	-18	-18	-18	-19	-20	-20	-20
13	8	5	0	-2	-2	-3	-4	-12	-13	-15	-15	-15	-16	-17	-17	-17
13	8	5	0	-2	-2	-3	-4	-12	-13	-15	-15	-15	-16	-17	-17	-17
13	8	5	0	-2	-2	-3	-4	-12	-13	-15	-15	-15	-16	-17	-17	-17
13	8	5	0	-2	-2	-3	-4	-12	-13	-15	-15	-15	-16	-17	-17	-17
14	9	6	1	-1	-1	-2	-3	-11	-12	-14	-14	-14	-15	-16	-16	-16

−14	−14	−14	−13	−13	−13	−12	−10	−8	−7	−6	−5	−2
−14	−14	−14	−13	−13	−13	−12	−10	−8	−7	−6	−5	−2
−14	−14	−14	−13	−13	−13	−12	−10	−8	−7	−6	−5	−2
−13	−13	−13	−12	−12	−12	−11	−9	−7	−6	−5	−4	−1
−12	−12	−12	−11	−11	−11	−10	−8	−6	−5	−4	−3	0
−12	−12	−12	−11	−11	−11	−10	−8	−6	−5	−4	−3	0
−12	−12	−12	−11	−11	−11	−10	−8	−6	−5	−4	−3	0
−10	−10	−10	−9	−9	−9	−8	−6	−4	−3	−2	−1	2
−9	−9	−9	−8	−8	−8	−7	−5	−3	−2	−1	0	3
−1	−1	−1	0	0	0	1	3	5	6	7	8	11
0	0	0	1	1	1	2	4	6	7	8	9	12
1	1	1	2	2	2	3	5	7	8	9	10	13
1	1	1	2	2	2	3	5	7	8	9	10	13
3	3	3	4	4	4	5	7	9	10	11	12	15
8	8	8	9	9	9	10	12	14	15	16	17	20
11	11	11	12	12	12	13	15	17	18	19	20	23
16	16	16	17	17	17	18	20	22	23	24	25	28

23-7. LARGE-SAMPLE FORM OF THE FISHER-IRWIN TEST

As we saw in Sections 22-5 and 22-6, the expected value and variance of the Fisher-Irwin statistic f_{11}, the number of successes in sample 1, are given by

$$E(f_{11}) = N_1 p_0 \quad \text{and} \quad \text{Var}(f_{11}) = \frac{N_1 N_2}{N_1 + N_2 - 1}(p_0 q_0)$$

The distribution of this statistic can be approximated by the normal distribution if $N_1 p_0 > 5$, $N_2 p_0 > 5$, $N_1 q_0 > 5$, and $N_2 q_0 > 5$. Even though large-sample conditions may be satisfied, the Z statistic, as reported, cannot be used, because p_0 and q_0 are unknown.

Fortunately, there is a way around this problem, and that is to replace p_0 by a value estimated from the data. Consider asking $N_1 = 49$ males and $N_2 = 49$ females the question:

Should the U.S. government continue to provide financial subsidies to farmers who grow tobacco? Yes ____ No ____

Suppose the results are as shown in Table 23-4. Let us examine the data and try to determine whether or not the two samples could have come from populations with equal binomial parameters. To do so, we consider the hypothesis

$$H_0: \quad p_1 = p_2 = p_0$$

While neither of the two population values is specified by the null hypothesis, the two are assumed to be equal to one another and to the common unknown value p_0. In sample 1, $\hat{p}_1$ is an estimate of p_1, just as $\hat{p}_2$ is an estimate of p_2 in sample 2. Since both are estimates of the common value p_0, we can pool the information in the two samples to obtain a single estimate of p_0. In sample 1, $\hat{p}_1 = f_{11}/N_1$, and in sample 2, $\hat{p}_2 = f_{12}/N_2$, where f_{11} equals the number of

Table 23-4. Responses to the question concerning tobacco subsidies for two samples of size 49.

	Males	Females	Total
Agree	35	21	56
Disagree	14	28	42
Total	49	49	98

agreements in sample 1 and f_{12} equals the number of agreements in sample 2. Because the two samples come from populations with equal binomial parameters, we can conceive of them as one sample consisting of $N = N_1 + N_2$ binomial trials, each trial with the true parameter p_0. We therefore add the number of agreements in both samples and divide by the total sample size to estimate p_0. If we call this pooled estimate $\bar{p}$, then

$$\bar{p} = \frac{f_{11} + f_{12}}{N_1 + N_2} = \frac{f_{1.}}{N}$$

This result can also be written in terms of the individual sample proportions. Since $\hat{p}_1 = f_{11}/N_1$, it follows that $f_{11} = N_1 \hat{p}_1$. In like manner, $f_{12} = N_2 \hat{p}_2$, so that

$$\bar{p} = \frac{f_{11} + f_{12}}{N_1 + N_2} = \frac{N_1 \hat{p}_1 + N_2 \hat{p}_2}{N_1 + N_2} = \frac{N_1}{N_1 + N_2} \hat{p}_1 + \frac{N_2}{N_1 + N_2} \hat{p}_2$$

Thus, $\bar{p}$ is a weighted average of the separate proportions in the two samples. For our example, $\hat{p}_1 = {}^{35}\!/_{49} = 0.7143$ and $\hat{p}_2 = {}^{21}\!/_{49} = 0.4286$. We now estimate $\bar{p}$. Pooling the samples, we see that $f_{1.} = 35 + 21 = 56$ of the 98 subjects are in agreement with the statement. Therefore, $\bar{p} = {}^{56}\!/_{98} = 0.5714$. We could also find $\bar{p}$ from the equation

$$\bar{p} = \frac{N_1 \hat{p}_1 + N_2 \hat{p}_2}{N_1 + N_2} = \frac{49(0.7143) + 49(0.4286)}{49 + 49} = \frac{35 + 21}{98}$$

$$= 0.5714$$

Substituting this estimate of p_0 into the formulas for mean and variance, we find:

$$P_{\alpha/2} = [49(0.5714) - 0.5] - 1.96\sqrt{\frac{49(49)}{(49 + 49 - 1)}(0.5714)(0.4286)}$$

$$= 22.67$$

so that $L = 22$. Similarly:

$$P_{1-\alpha/2} = [49(0.5714) + 0.5] + 1.96\sqrt{\frac{49(49)}{(49 + 49 - 1)}(0.5714)(0.4286)}$$

$$= 33.32$$

so that $U = 34$. Since $f_{11} = 35$, we reject the null hypothesis. Note that we can also conclude that the phi coefficient based on the data of Table 23-4 is significantly different from zero.

Although we have rejected the null hypothesis, it does not make much sense to find a confidence interval for f_{11}. Rather than statements about f_{11}, we are interested in confidence intervals for the population proportions. Because of this, we introduce tests based on the proportions directly.

23-8. TEST FOR A SINGLE PROPORTION

In Section 22-4 we showed that the expected value and variance of a sample proportion are given by

$$E(\hat{p}) = p \quad \text{and} \quad \text{Var}(\hat{p}) = \frac{pq}{N}$$

We now examine the theory for testing a single proportion for statistical significance. As will be seen, the sign test is a special case of this test. As an example, consider a study in which a researcher wishes to test the hypothesis that whites in a small town tend to send their children to private schools. At the time of the 1980 census, 27 percent of the children in small cities who were between the ages of 5 and 18 were classified as nonwhite. In September, 1216 of the total public school enrollment of 4015 in this small town were nonwhite, so that the proportion of nonwhite students was $\hat{p} = {}^{1216}\!/_{4015} = 0.3029$. The researcher wants to know whether the school data are compatible with the census data, or whether they support the hypothesis that whites tend to use private schools. We test

$$H_0: \quad p \le 0.27$$

against

$$H_1: \quad p > 0.27$$

using critical values from the normal distribution. The large-sample form of this test requires that $Np > 5$ and $Nq > 5$.

In this case, $\hat{p}$ has a sampling distribution with

$$E(\hat{p}) = p = 0.27$$

and

$$\text{Var}(\hat{p}) = \frac{pq}{N} = \frac{(0.27)(0.73)}{4015} = 0.000049$$

With

$$\hat{p} = {}^{1216}\!/_{4015} = 0.3029$$

we have

$$Z = \frac{\hat{p} - p}{\sqrt{pq/N}} = \frac{0.3029 - 0.2700}{0.0070} = \frac{0.0329}{0.0070} = 4.70$$

With $\alpha = .05$, H_0 is rejected because $Z = 4.70 > Z_{.95} = 1.645$. There are 3 percent more nonwhites than expected. In this case, we have not made a correction for continuity, because of the large sample size. More explicitly, for proportions, the correction for continuity is given by $\pm 1/2N$. When $1/2N \leq 0.01$, the correction is usually ignored. Notice, also, the way H_0 is stated. The research question is a one-tailed hypothesis. In order to conclude that the proportion of nonwhites is greater than $p = 0.27$, the null hypothesis must cover the opposite possibility. We provide procedures in Box 23-3 for testing $H_0: p = p_0$.

In our example, we saw that $p = 0.27$ is not a valid statement. Since p is unknown, we estimate it from the data as $\hat{p} = 0.3029$. We use this value to find a confidence interval for p.

As we saw, $\mathrm{Var}(\hat{p}) = pq/N$. Unfortunately, we cannot compute this number, because p is unknown. Of course, we could estimate p using $\hat{p}$. If we did

---

Box 23-3   **Procedure for using a large-sample test statistic to examine the null hypothesis $H_0: p = p_0$ ($Np > 5$ and $Nq > 5$)**

Step 1. Determine the percentage $\hat{p}$ of successes, or agreements, in the sample by taking the number of successes T and dividing by the number of trials:

$$\hat{p} = \frac{T}{N}$$

Step 2. With $\mu_{\hat{p}} = p_0$, determine the value of

$$\sigma_{\hat{p}} = \sqrt{\frac{p_0 q_0}{N}}$$

Step 3. Determine the value of the test statistic:

$$Z_{\hat{p}} = \frac{\hat{p} - p_0}{\sigma_{\hat{p}}} = \frac{\hat{p} - p_0}{\sqrt{\dfrac{p_0 q_0}{N}}}$$

Step 4. Find the critical values $Z_{\alpha/2}$ and $Z_{1-\alpha/2}$ in the table of the standard normal curve. Reject H_0 if $Z_{\hat{p}} < Z_{\alpha/2}$ or if $Z_{\hat{p}} > Z_{1-\alpha/2}$. For a one-tailed test, put all of the α in one tail.

---

this, we would have an estimate of $\text{Var}(\hat{p})$ given by

$$\hat{\sigma}_{\hat{p}}^2 = \frac{\hat{p}\hat{q}}{N}$$

If we took the square root, we would have an estimate of the standard deviation of the distribution of $\hat{p}$. This estimate is called a *standard error* and is used to differentiate the *estimated value* from the population value, $\sigma_{\hat{p}}$. We will denote it as

$$SE_{\hat{p}} = \sqrt{\frac{\hat{p}\hat{q}}{N}}$$

Because this measure plays such an important role in statistical applications, we give it a prominent place in our list of definitions.

Definition of the standard error of a proportion

The standard error of a sample proportion is defined:

$$SE_{\hat{p}} = \sqrt{\frac{\hat{p}\hat{q}}{N}}$$

It serves as an estimate of

$$\sigma_{\hat{p}} = \sqrt{\frac{pq}{N}}$$

We provide directions in Box 23-4 for obtaining a confidence interval for a proportion or binomial probability.

In this particular situation we have tested a one-tailed hypothesis. Therefore the corresponding confidence interval must be one-tailed. Let us say that the true proportion is p. The confidence interval contains all values of p that are compatible with the data. In this case, if we perform a sequence of one-tailed hypothesis tests in order to amass all values of p leading to nonrejection, we would expect that, 95 percent of the time,

$$\hat{p} < p + 1.645 \; SE_{\hat{p}}$$

Solving for p to form the confidence interval, we have

$$\hat{p} - 1.645 \; SE_{\hat{p}} < p$$

Box 23-4 **Procedure for obtaining a large-sample confidence interval for p**

Step 1. Estimate p from the data as follows:

$$\hat{p} = \frac{T}{N} = \frac{\text{number of successes}}{\text{number of trials}}$$

Step 2. Determine the value of the standard error:

$$SE_{\hat{p}} = \sqrt{\frac{\hat{p}\hat{q}}{N}}$$

Step 3. Report the interval as follows:

$$\hat{p} + Z_{\alpha/2}SE_{\hat{p}} < p < \hat{p} + Z_{1-\alpha/2}SE_{\hat{p}}$$

For a one-tailed interval, place all of the α in one tail.

For our example, this yields

$$0.3029 - 1.645\sqrt{\frac{0.3029(0.6971)}{4015}} < p$$

or

$$0.2910 < p$$

This indicates that the nonwhite proportion of students in the public schools of small cities exceeds 0.2910. Therefore, it is larger than the 27 percent expected from the census data.

23-9. THE TWO-SAMPLE BINOMIAL TEST OF EQUAL PROPORTIONS

The large sample form of the Fisher test discussed in Section 23-7 is rarely encountered in the literature. More commonly, the form described here is used. For this test, consider the following linear combination:

$$T = \hat{p}_1 - \hat{p}_2 = W_1\hat{p}_1 + W_2\hat{p}_2$$

for which $W_1 = +1$ and $W_2 = -1$. Thus, as we know from Section 20-3,

$$E(T) = W_1 E(\hat{p}_1) + W_2 E(\hat{p}_2) = (+1)(p_1) + (-1)(p_2) = p_1 - p_2$$

If H_0 is true, $E(T) = p_0 - p_0 = 0$. Also, we know that

$$\text{Var}(T) = W_1^2 \text{Var}(\hat{p}_1) + W_2^2 \text{Var}(\hat{p}_2)$$

$$= (+1)^2 \frac{p_1 q_1}{N_1} + (-1)^2 \frac{p_2 q_2}{N_2} = \frac{p_1 q_1}{N_1} + \frac{p_2 q_2}{N_2}$$

If H_0 is true, then

$$\text{Var}(T) = \frac{p_0 q_0}{N_1} + \frac{p_0 q_0}{N_2}$$

so that

$$Z = \frac{T - E(T)}{\sqrt{\text{Var}(T)}} = \frac{\hat{p}_1 - \hat{p}_2}{\sqrt{\dfrac{p_0 q_0}{N_1} + \dfrac{p_0 q_0}{N_2}}}$$

has a normal distribution with mean of zero and standard deviation of one. However, it cannot be computed, since p_0 is unknown.

If we replace p_0 by $\bar{p}$, we have the more widely used approximation for the large-sample Fisher-Irwin test, the *two-sample binomial* test. We provide directions for testing $H_0: p_1 = p_2$ in Box 23-5.

With $\bar{p} = 0.5714$, $\bar{q} = 0.4286$, and

$$\hat{\sigma}_{\hat{p}_1 - \hat{p}_2} = \sqrt{0.5714(0.4286)(\frac{1}{49} + \frac{1}{49})} = \sqrt{0.01} = 0.1$$

our test statistic becomes:

$$Z = \frac{\hat{p}_1 - \hat{p}_2}{\hat{\sigma}_{\hat{p}_1 - \hat{p}_2}} = \frac{0.7143 - 0.4286}{0.1} = \frac{0.2857}{0.1} = 2.86$$

Since this value is larger than 1.96, we reject H_0, concluding that these two samples do not come from populations with equal binomial parameters.

As usual, once we reject the null hypothesis, we are interested in making a statement about the kinds of populations from which our samples may have come. To do this, we set up a confidence interval. As we saw in the one-sample procedure of Section 23-8 when we set up confidence intervals, we can no longer assume we know anything about the values of the population parameters in question. Because of this, we use the formula

$$\sigma_{\hat{p}_1 - \hat{p}_2}^2 = \sigma_{\hat{p}_1}^2 + \sigma_{\hat{p}_2}^2 = \frac{p_1 q_1}{N_1} + \frac{p_2 q_2}{N_2}$$

to determine the standard deviation of $\hat{p}_1 - \hat{p}_2$. Unfortunately, this model fails for the same reason that it did for the one-sample case. The values p_1 and

Box 23-5   **Large-sample procedure for testing** H_0: $p_1 = p_2 = p_0$ $(N_1 p_0 > 5,$ $N_2 p_0 > 5$, $N_1 q_0 > 5$, and $N_2 q_0 > 5)$

Step 1. Estimate $\hat{p}_1$ and $\hat{p}_2$ in each sample.
Step 2. Estimate p_0 by finding

$$\bar{p} = \frac{N_1 \hat{p}_1 + N_2 \hat{p}_2}{N_1 + N_2} = \frac{f_{11} + f_{12}}{N_1 + N_2}$$

and compute

$$SE_{\hat{p}_1 - \hat{p}_2} = \sqrt{\frac{\bar{p}\bar{q}}{N_1} + \frac{\bar{p}\bar{q}}{N_2}}$$

Step 3. Compute:

$$Z = \frac{\hat{p}_1 - \hat{p}_2}{\sqrt{\bar{p}\bar{q}(1/N_1 + 1/N_2)}}$$

Step 4. Enter the table of the standard normal curve to select the critical values $Z_{\alpha/2}$ and $Z_{1-\alpha/2}$ for the specified value of α. If the test is one-tailed, place the risk in one tail of the distribution.
Step 5. Reject H_0 if $Z < Z_{\alpha/2}$ or if $Z > Z_{1-\alpha/2}$ for a two-tailed test. For a one-tailed test compare Z to the single critical value.

p_2 are unknown, and so the estimates of $\hat{p}_1$ and $\hat{p}_2$ must be called upon. Whenever sample values are used to estimate a population standard deviation of a statistic, the resulting estimate is called a standard error. Since this standard error is so important for studies using binomial variables, we provide the following definition.

The standard error of the difference in two proportions

The standard error of $\hat{p}_1 - \hat{p}_2$ is defined:

$$SE_{\hat{p}_1 - \hat{p}_2} = \sqrt{\frac{\hat{p}_1 \hat{q}_1}{N_1} + \frac{\hat{p}_2 \hat{q}_2}{N_2}} = \sqrt{SE_{\hat{p}_1}^2 + SE_{\hat{p}_2}^2}$$

It serves as an estimate of:

$$\sigma_{\hat{p}_1 - \hat{p}_2} = \sqrt{\frac{p_1 q_1}{N_1} + \frac{p_1 q_2}{N_2}} = \sqrt{\sigma_{\hat{p}_1}^2 + \sigma_{\hat{p}_2}^2}$$

The $1 - \alpha$ percent confidence interval for $\hat{p}_1 - \hat{p}_2$ is given by

$$(\hat{p}_1 - \hat{p}_2) + Z_{\alpha/2} SE_{\hat{p}_1 - \hat{p}_2} < p_1 - p_2 < (\hat{p}_1 - \hat{p}_2) + Z_{1-\alpha/2} SE_{\hat{p}_1 - \hat{p}_2}$$

In our example, we have $\hat{p}_1 = 0.7143$, so that:

$$SE_{\hat{p}_1}^2 = \frac{\hat{p}_1 \hat{q}_1}{N_1} = \frac{0.7143(0.2857)}{49} = 0.0042$$

Similarly, we have $\hat{p}_2 = 0.4286$, so that:

$$SE_{\hat{p}_2}^2 = \frac{\hat{p}_2 \hat{q}_2}{N_2} = \frac{0.4286(0.5714)}{49} = 0.0050$$

Therefore:

$$SE_{\hat{p}_1 - \hat{p}_2}^2 = 0.0042 + 0.0050 = 0.0092$$

and

$$SE_{\hat{p}_1 - \hat{p}_2} = \sqrt{0.0092} = 0.0957$$

Our confidence interval then becomes:

$$(0.7143 - 0.4286) - 1.96(0.0957)$$
$$< p_1 - p_2 < (0.7143 - 0.4286)$$
$$+ 1.96(0.0957)$$
$$0.2857 - 0.1876 < p_1 - p_2 < 0.02857 + 0.1876$$
$$0.0981 < p_1 - p_2 < 0.4733$$

Box 23-6   Large-sample procedure for determining a confidence interval for $p_1 - p_2$

Step 1. Estimate $\hat{p}_1$ and $\hat{p}_2$, as in Step 1 of the test procedure.
Step 2. Determine

$$SE_{\hat{p}_1 - \hat{p}_2} = \sqrt{\frac{\hat{p}_1 \hat{q}_1}{N_1} + \frac{\hat{p}_2 \hat{q}_2}{N_2}}$$

Step 3. Find the appropriate critical values for the specified value of α, as in Step 4 of the test procedure.
Step 4. Form the confidence interval

$$(\hat{p}_1 - \hat{p}_2) + Z_{\alpha/2} SE_{\hat{p}_1 - \hat{p}_2} < p_1 - p_2 < (\hat{p}_1 - \hat{p}_2) + Z_{1-\alpha/2} SE_{\hat{p}_1 - \hat{p}_2}$$

For a one-tailed confidence interval, place α in one tail.

We thus conclude that our samples could have come from populations whose binomial parameters differ by as little as 10 percent but by no more than 47 percent. In Box 23-6 we present procedures for setting up a confidence interval for the difference in two binomial parameters. Note that this method is valid only for large samples.

23-10. EXERCISES

23-1. For the matched-pair Wilcoxon test, find the upper 95 percent critical value for $N = 10$ in Table A-4. Use the normal approximation corrected for continuity and determine how close the approximate value is to the exact value.

23.2. For the two-sample Wilcoxon test, find the 97.5 percent upper critical value for $N_1 = 8$ and $N_2 = 9$. Use the normal approximation corrected for continuity and determine how close the approximate value is to the exact value.

23-3. Find the 95 percent confidence interval for the median score on the final examination for students in program 1 and program 2 for your sample of 40 subjects. Use:
a. The sign-test model
b. The matched-pair Wilcoxon model

23-4. Compare students in program 1 with those in program 2 on the final examination for your sample of 40 subjects. Use:
a. The two-sample Wilcoxon test
b. The two-sample Mann-Whitney U test

23-5. Describe how you would find a confidence interval for the median difference of Exercise 23-4.

23-6. What is the difference between the analysis in Exercise 23-3 and that in Exercise 23-4? Which would you recommend for comparing program 1 to program 2? Why?

23-7. In a large Southern city a group tried to pass an ordinance that allowed landlords to practice rent discrimination on the basis of sexual orientation of potential renters. At the time of the voting the referendum was defeated with $p = 0.69$ and $q = 0.31$. Following the voting, a sample of heterosexuals, bisexuals, and homosexuals were polled on how they voted. Results are as shown.

Group	Heterosexual	Bisexual	Homosexual
For	29	5	8
Against	24	27	34
Total	53	32	42

Are there differences in how these groups voted?

23-8. Find the 95 percent confidence intervals for the proportions in the three populations represented in Exercise 23-7.

23-9. Find the 25th and 75th percentiles of $\hat{p}$ for the three groups of Exercise 23-7.

23-10. For the sign test, find the 2.5 percent and 97.5 percent critical values for $N = 24$ in Table A-2. Use the normal approximation corrected for continuity and determine how close the approximate values are to the exact values.

CHAPTER 24

Tests on Correlation Coefficients

24-1. THE SMALL-SAMPLE TEST OF SPEARMAN'S RHO

We have so far provided directions for small-sample tests based on ranks and proportions, but we have not yet provided directions for testing Spearman's rho for small samples. We do so now. Tables of critical values are available for testing Spearman's rank measure of correlation for statistical significance. A shortened version of such a table appears in the Appendix as Table A-8. This table is entered with N, the sample size, and α, the desired risk of a type I error. In this case, the values of r_s are read directly. For example, consider the data in Table 24-1. The decision rule for testing

$$H_0: \quad \rho_s = 0 \quad \text{against} \quad H_1: \quad \rho_s \neq 0$$

Table 24-1. Scores on a pre- and posttest given to 12 students reading under grade level.

Subjects ranked according to pretest score	X: Score on pretest	Y: Score on posttest
1	18	23
2	21	22
3	23	28
4	36	35
5	39	50
6	40	46
7	40	50
8	50	47
9	55	58
10	57	52
11	58	60
12	60	58

Box 24-1   Procedure for testing Spearman's rank correlation coefficient for significance

Step 1. Compute r_S.

Step 2. Find a decision rule in Table A-8 for N equal to the number of paired observations and α equal to the desired risk of a type I error.

Step 3. Reject H_0 if $r_S \leq r_{S:\alpha/2}$, or if $r_S \geq r_{S:1-\alpha/2}$, if the test is two-tailed. If the test is one-tailed, place the risk of a type I error in the appropriate tail of the distribution of r_S.

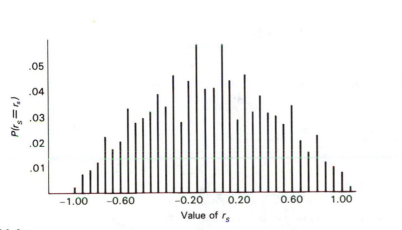

Figure 24-1.
The distribution of Spearman's rho for $N = 6$.

for $N = 12$ and $\alpha = .05$ is given as follows:

Decision Rule: Reject H_0 if $r_S \leq -0.59$ or if $r_S \geq 0.59$

For the data of Table 24-1, $r_S = 0.92$, and H_0 is rejected. In Box 24-1 we provide directions for testing ρ_S for statistical significance. Figure 24-1 provides a visual impression of the distribution of r_S for $N = 6$. As we see, it is symmetrical and bimodal, but with mean and median equal to zero.

24-2. THE LARGE-SAMPLE TEST OF SPEARMAN'S RHO

As reported in Sections 22-5 and 22-6,

$$E(r_S) = 0 \quad \text{and} \quad \text{Var}(r_S) = \frac{1}{N-1}$$

so that

$$Z = \frac{r_S - 0}{1/\sqrt{N-1}} = r_S \sqrt{N-1}$$

can be used to test

$$H_0: \quad \rho_S = 0 \quad \text{against} \quad H_1: \quad \rho_S \neq 0$$

For example, if $r_S = 0.32$ and $N = 60$, $Z = 0.32\sqrt{60-1} = 2.46$, so that one would reject the hypothesis that $\rho_S = 0$, with $\alpha = .05$. In Box 24-2, we provide directions for the large-sample test of $\rho_S = 0$. For this approximation, N is considered large if $N \geq 30$.

24-3. TESTING A SINGLE CORRELATION COEFFICIENT FOR SIGNIFICANCE

In Chapter 7, we introduced the correlation coefficient as a measure of association between two variables. We now wish to provide methods for

---

Box 24-2   Procedure for testing $\rho_S = 0$ in large samples

Step 1. Compute r_S and $Z = r_S \sqrt{N-1}$.
Step 2. Reject H_0 if $Z < Z_{\alpha/2}$ or if $Z > Z_{1-\alpha/2}$. For a one-tailed alternative, place the entire risk of a type I error in one tail of the distribution of Z.

testing correlation coefficients for statistical significance. In Sections 24-1 and 24-2, we provided directions for testing Spearman's rho for statistical significance. For large samples, the method of Section 24-2 can be used to test any correlation for statistical significance. In fact, it is the preferred method of many researchers. We will present an alternative model in Section 32-7.

Whereas we test whether or not an association exists between two variables by determining whether or not the population correlation coefficient equals zero, there are times when we wish to test whether ρ is equal to a specified value ρ_0. A case in point occurs in the following example. According to genetic theory many family traits are correlated among siblings. For example, genetic theory states that IQ test scores should show a correlation of $\rho = 0.5$ for brothers born of the same mother and father, provided that the union of parents throughout the population is random. As a test of the theory, the records of a large school district were searched to identify brothers whose birthdays were not more than two years apart and for whom Kuhlman-Anderson IQ test scores were available. The number of brother pairs that satisfied the two criteria was given by $N = 49$. The sample correlation for these 49 pairs was given by $r = 0.58$, seeming to support the theoretical value of $\rho = 0.5$. However, one still must perform a statistical test to determine whether or not the theory is supported by the empirical data.

The test that is used was developed by Fisher and is based upon a transformation of the correlation coefficients to a new scale referred to as the *Fisher z* scale. Tables of the transformed values have been prepared, and a condensed version of these tables is presented in Table A-9. Using advanced techniques, Fisher was able to show that the standard deviation of the distribution of z is given approximately by

$$\sigma_z = \frac{1}{\sqrt{N-3}}$$

and that

$$Z_r = \frac{z_r - z_\rho}{\sigma_z}$$

could be approximated by a standard normal variable with mean of zero and standard deviation of 1. We illustrate the use of the table and the corresponding test for the example with $N = 49$ and $r = 0.58$. One begins by finding the value of the Fisher z transformation for the observed sample correlation coefficient of $r = 0.58$ and for the theoretical population correlation coefficient of $\rho = 0.50$. From Table A-9 the corresponding Fisher z values for $r = 0.58$ and $\rho = 0.50$ are given respectively by $z_r = 0.663$ and $z_\rho = 0.549$. For $\alpha = .05$, the corresponding decision rule is given thus:

Decision Rule: Reject H_0 if $Z_r < -1.96$ or if $Z_r > 1.96$

Box 24-3   Procedure for testing $H_0: \rho = \rho_0$ against $H_1: \rho \neq \rho_0$

Step 1. Determine the sample value of r.

Step 2. In Table A-9, determine the values of z_r and z_ρ associated with r and ρ_0, respectively.

Step 3. Compute:

$$Z_r = \frac{z_r - z_\rho}{1/\sqrt{N-3}}$$

Step 4. Refer Z_r to the standard normal distribution. Reject H_0 if Z_r is in the critical region defined by

$$Z_r < Z_{\alpha/2}$$

or if

$$Z_r > Z_{1-\alpha/2}$$

For the data:

$$Z_r = \frac{0.663 - 0.549}{1/\sqrt{46}} = \frac{0.663 - 0.549}{0.147} = 0.77$$

Since $Z_r = 0.77$ is not in the rejection region, H_0 is not rejected. The data do not disagree with the theory that $\rho = 0.5$.

For completeness, in Box 24-3 we list the steps required to test $H_0: \rho = \rho_0$ against the alternative $H_1: \rho \neq \rho_0$.

The confidence interval for ρ can be found by finding a confidence interval for z_ρ and then reading backward in Table A-9 for the upper and lower values of the confidence interval. For the example, we have

$$z_r + Z_{\alpha/2}\frac{1}{\sqrt{N-3}} < z_\rho < z_r + Z_{1-\alpha/2}\frac{1}{\sqrt{N-3}}$$

and

$$0.663 - 1.96(1/\sqrt{46}) < z_\rho < 0.663 + 1.96(1/\sqrt{46})$$

so that

$$0.663 - 0.289 < z_\rho < 0.663 + 0.289$$

$$0.374 < z_\rho < 0.952$$

Box 24-4   Procedure for determining the $1 - \alpha$ percent confidence interval for ρ

Step 1. Determine the values of

$$z_L = z_r + Z_{\alpha/2}\,\frac{1}{\sqrt{N - 3}}$$

and

$$z_U = z_r + Z_{1-\alpha/2}\,\frac{1}{\sqrt{N - 3}}$$

Step 2. Find the ρ_L and ρ_U values in Table A-9 that correspond to z_L and z_U.

Step 3. The $1 - \alpha$ percent confidence interval for ρ is given by

$$\rho_L < \rho < \rho_U$$

We now enter Table A-9 with $z_L = 0.374$ and $z_U = 0.952$ and find the values $\rho_L = 0.36$ and $\rho_U = 0.74$, so that the 95 percent confidence interval for ρ is given by:

$$0.36 < \rho < 0.74$$

In Box 24-4 we provide directions for obtaining a confidence interval for ρ.

24-4. TESTING TWO CORRELATION COEFFICIENTS FOR EQUALITY

Often, a researcher has estimated correlation coefficients from two independent populations and wishes to test them for equality. This is true for the following example. In the search of student records described in Section 24-3, 38 sister pairs were identified for which $r = 0.44$. On the surface, this value appears to be considerably smaller than the value obtained for the brother pairs. According to genetic theory, the two population correlation coefficients should be equal. Fisher showed that two correlation coefficients could also be tested for equality using the same z transformation. If we let r_1 and r_2 refer to the two sample correlation coefficients and N_1 and N_2 refer to the number of pairs in each sample, then the appropriate test statistic is given by

$$Z_{r_1 - r_2} = \frac{z_1 - z_2}{\sqrt{\dfrac{1}{N_1 - 3} + \dfrac{1}{N_2 - 3}}}$$

where z_1 and z_2 are the Fisher z transformations corresponding to r_1 and r_2.

This statistic is derived as follows. Note that

$$T = z_1 - z_2$$

is a linear combination of z_1 and z_2 where $W_1 = +1$ and $W_2 = -1$. Therefore:

$$\mu_T = (+1)\mu_{z_1} + (-1)\mu_{z_2} = \mu_{z_1} - \mu_{z_2}$$

If H_0 is true, then $\mu_{z_1} = \mu_{z_2}$, so that $\mu_T = 0$. In addition:

$$\sigma_T^2 = (+1)^2\sigma_{z_1}^2 + (-1)^2\sigma_{z_2}^2 = \sigma_{z_1}^2 + \sigma_{z_2}^2$$

Since $\sigma_{z_1}^2 = 1/(N_1 - 3)$ and $\sigma_{z_2}^2 = 1/(N_2 - 3)$, it follows that

$$\sigma_T^2 = \frac{1}{N_1 - 3} + \frac{1}{N_2 - 3}$$

Thus:

$$Z_{r_1 - r_2} = \frac{T - \mu_T}{\sigma_T} = \frac{z_1 - z_2}{\sqrt{\dfrac{1}{N_1 - 3} + \dfrac{1}{N_2 - 3}}}$$

Just as in the one-sample case, $Z_{r_1 - r_2}$ has a standard normal distribution with mean of zero and a standard deviation of 1 when the tested hypothesis is true. Thus, the α percent decision rule for testing $H_0: \rho_1 = \rho_2$ against $H_1:$ $\rho_1 \neq \rho_2$ is:

Decision Rule: Reject H_0 if $Z_{r_1 - r_2} < Z_{\alpha/2}$ or if $Z_{r_1 - r_2} > Z_{1-\alpha/2}$

For the observed data, $z_1 = 0.663$ and $z_2 = 0.472$, so that:

$$Z_{r_1 - r_2} = \frac{0.663 - 0.472}{\sqrt{\dfrac{1}{49 - 3} + \dfrac{1}{38 - 3}}} = \frac{0.191}{0.224} = 0.85$$

For $\alpha = .05$, the decision rule is:

Decision Rule: Reject H_0 if $Z_{r_1 - r_2} < -1.96$ or if $Z_{r_1 - r_2} > 1.96$

Since $Z_{r_1 - r_2} = 0.85$ is not in the rejection region, the hypothesis is not rejected. The data do not disagree with the theory that $\rho_1 = \rho_2$. In Box 24-5 we show the steps required to test $H_0: \rho_1 = \rho_2$.

Unfortunately, no one knows how to set up a confidence interval for

---

Box 24-5   Procedure for testing $H_0: \rho_1 = \rho_2$ against $H_1: \rho_1 \neq \rho_2$

Step 1. Compute r_1 and r_2.
Step 2. Determine the values of z_1 and z_2 from Table A-9.
Step 3. Compute:

$$Z_{r_1-r_2} = \frac{z_1 - z_2}{\sqrt{\dfrac{1}{N_1 - 3} + \dfrac{1}{N_2 - 3}}}$$

Step 4. Reject H_0 if $Z_{r_1-r_2} < Z_{\alpha/2}$ or if $Z_{r_1-r_2} > Z_{1-\alpha/2}$.

$\rho_1 - \rho_2$. The mathematics has proved intractable. On the other hand, correlation coefficients can be pooled, provided it is known that they come from populations with identical values. The pooling is based on the Fisher z. For two correlations, the pooled Fisher $\bar{z}$ is given as follows:

$$\bar{z} = W_1 z_1 + W_2 z_2$$

where

$$W_1 = \frac{N_1 - 3}{(N_1 - 3) + (N_2 - 3)} \quad \text{and} \quad W_2 = \frac{N_2 - 3}{(N_1 - 3) + (N_2 - 3)}$$

For our example, $W_1 = (49 - 3)/[(49 - 3) + (38 - 3)] = 0.5679$. In like manner, $W_2 = 0.4321$. With these weights,

$$\bar{z} = (0.5679)(0.663) + (0.4321)(0.549) = 0.581$$

so that $\bar{r}$, read from Table A-9, is equal to 0.52. The variance of $\bar{z}$ is given by the definition in Section 20-3:

$$\sigma_{\bar{z}}^2 = W_1^2 \sigma_1^2 + W_2^2 \sigma_2^2$$

With substitution for W_1^2, W_2^2, σ_1^2, and σ_2^2 in terms of N_1 and N_2, this variance simplifies to:

$$\sigma_{\bar{z}}^2 = \frac{1}{(N_1 - 3) + (N_2 - 3)}$$

In this case:

$$\sigma_{\bar{z}}^2 = \frac{1}{46 + 35} = \frac{1}{81} = 0.0123$$

Thus, the 95 percent confidence interval for $\bar{z}$ is given by

$$0.581 - 1.96\sqrt{0.0123} < \bar{z} < 0.581 + 1.96\sqrt{0.0123}$$

$$0.364 < \bar{z} < 0.798$$

so that the 95 percent confidence interval for the average ρ is given by

$$0.35 < \bar{\rho} < 0.66$$

24-5. EXERCISES

24-1. Find the 95 percent confidence interval for ρ_{xy} for your sample of 40 students for:

    y: score on final

    x: score on pretest

24-2. Is there reason to believe that $\rho_{xy} = 0$ for the data of Exercise 24-1?

24-3. Does it make sense to test $\rho_{xy} = 0.5$ for the data of Exercise 24-1? Why?

24-4. For your sample of 40 subjects find r_{xy} for:

    y: score on final

    x: score on pretest

for students in program 1 and program 2.

24-5. Use the data of Exercise 24-4 and test

$$H_0: \quad \rho_{xy}^{(1)} = \rho_{xy}^{(2)}$$

using $\alpha = .05$.

24-6. Can one find a confidence interval for $\rho_{xy}^{(1)} - \rho_{xy}^{(2)}$ for Exercise 24-5?

24-7. If H_0 of Exercise 24-5 is not rejected, *pool* the data to obtain a single estimate of ρ_{xy}. Compare this estimate to that obtained in Exercise 24-1.

24-8. In a nutrition study, the following statistics were obtained on four groups of college students. In the study, calorie intake was correlated with initial weight.

Type of Student		r_{xy}	Number
G_1	College students with weights 20 lb or more below accepted standards	0.40	20
G_2	College students of normal weights	0.60	20
G_3	College students with weights 20 lb or more above accepted standards	0.55	20
G_4	College athletes in varsity sports	0.20	20

a. These data can be analyzed in terms of $C = \binom{4}{2} = 6$ pairwise comparisons. Perform the six tests.

b. For a decision rule, analyze each test with $\alpha = .05$.

c. For a decision rule, analyze each test with $\alpha = \frac{1}{6}(0.05) = 0.0083$.

d. What is the difference between parts b and c? Which would you recommend? Why?

24-9. Pool the nonsignificantly different r values in Exercise 24-8c and find a 95 percent confidence interval for their common value.

PART V

PROCEDURES BASED ON THE CHI-SQUARE DISTRIBUTION

Although the normal distribution has been seen to have great utility in solving one- and two-sample problems, it does not provide an adequate approximation to the probabilities required for a single test of the equality of more than two population parameters. Statisticians have been able to derive other continuous distributions that yield good approximations to the exact probabilities needed in these cases. One of these distributions, called the chi-square distribution, is introduced in Chapter 25. This distribution is used primarily in testing hypotheses and calculating confidence intervals in the multiple-sample extension of the Fisher-Irwin exact test for qualitative dependent variables. Other tests for qualitative dependent variables are also based on the chi-square distribution. Its use for these purposes is presented in the chapters that follow.

The Chi-Square Distribution

25-1. STATISTICAL DISTRIBUTIONS AND TEST STATISTICS

We have already seen in the preceding chapters an example of one kind of statistical distribution: the normal distribution. In addition, examples have been given of the use of this distribution for both exact and approximate probability computations. It is time now to state in detail how use is made of such distributions in general, and to introduce another commonly encountered statistical distribution.

As in the case of the normal distribution, statistical distributions in general tell us the kinds of values to expect when dealing with certain variables. Thus, in the case of a normally distributed variable, such as the sample mean for a large sample, we know that 95 percent of the time, the value of

$$Z = \frac{\bar{Y} - \mu_Y}{\sigma_Y / \sqrt{N}}$$

should fall between -1.96 and 1.96. This kind of statement is important, and it can be generalized to other distributions and situations. If we can refer the distribution of any variable in question to one of the standard tabled statistical distributions, such as Z, we immediately know all of the percentile values of the variable.

In Chapter 14 and Chapters 16 through 19, we saw how statistical decision rules are determined using exact probability calculations. The tests which we considered are only the most common ones out of hundreds available for use in these testing situations, and each would require its own calculation of exact probabilities. As we have seen in the examples we have considered, the calculations become tedious even for moderate sample sizes.

It is because the criterion variables in these tests can be written as linear combinations that the central limit theorem is of such great importance to us. Instead of requiring many probability calculations, we can set up decision rules merely by referring to a widely useful set of the tabled probabilities of the standard normal distribution.

Unfortunately, not all test statistics have distributions that can be approximated by the normal distribution. In cases lacking this advantage, one cannot refer to the standard normal distribution to determine decision rules. We thus need to find other distributions that can be used in this manner.

25-2. THE CHI-SQUARE DISTRIBUTION

As an example of a statistical distribution that will be very useful to us in future work, we introduce the chi-square distribution. As one might expect, statistical distributions are rarely examined as idle curiosities; rather, they are generated in order to describe the distribution of population and sample variables that are of interest. As we shall see, the chi-square distribution specifies probability values for sums of squared normal variables.

The symbol denoting the chi-square distribution is the Greek letter chi, χ, with an exponent of 2, denoting "squared"; thus, χ^2. This distribution is generated from the standard normal distribution and actually represents a family of distributions, each defined by its associated number of degrees of freedom.

Consider a variable that follows the standard normal distribution. From previous experience, we have become familiar with the percentiles of this distribution. For example, 68 percent of the observations chosen at random from this distribution fall between -1 and 1. Now each time we sample a value from the normal distribution, let us square it and plot the distribution of the square of values from the standard normal distribution. We see that any time the value of Z lies between -1 and 1, the square, Z^2, lies between 0 and 1. Similarly, any time the value of Z lies between -1.96 and 1.96, Z^2 lies between 0 and $1.96^2 = 3.84$. The chi-square distribution with one degree of freedom is defined as the distribution of the square of a standard normal distribution. Algebraically, we write

$$\chi_1^2 = Z^2$$

Definition of χ_1^2, chi-square with one degree of freedom

Consider a normally distributed variable, Z, with $\mu_Z = 0$ and $\sigma_Z = 1$. Draw repeated samples of size 1 from this distribution. Square each sample value. Over an infinite number of samplings, the squared Z values have a distribution which is named chi-square with degrees of freedom $\nu = 1$. The degrees of freedom characterize the distribution.

As we have already begun to indicate, the percentiles of χ_1^2 can be generated from those of Z. Since, for example, 95 percent of the values of Z lie between -1.96 and 1.96, then 95 percent of the values of χ_1^2 lie between 0 and 3.84. Similarly, 68 percent of the χ_1^2 values lie between 0 and 1. Figure 25-1 shows a graph of the distribution of χ_1^2. This graph is peaked near $\chi_1^2 = 0$, since the Z distribution is peaked near $Z = 0$. Conceptually, the χ_1^2 distribution represents the Z distribution flipped over the y axis by the act of squaring.

We can easily find the mean of χ_1^2 from our knowledge of the mean and variance of Z. For χ_1^2, the mean value over an enormous number of trials is

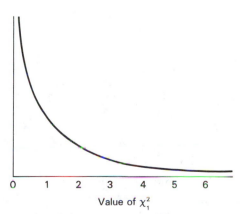

Figure 25-1.
The chi-square distribution with $\nu = 1$.

given by

$$\mu_{\chi_1^2} = \frac{\sum\limits_{i=1}^{N} Z_i^2}{N}$$

But from the formula for the variance of Z, we have

$$\sigma_Z^2 = \frac{\sum\limits_{i=1}^{N} (Z_i - \mu_Z)^2}{N} = \frac{\sum\limits_{i=1}^{N} Z_i^2}{N}$$

since $\mu_Z = 0$. Because $\sigma_Z^2 = 1$, we see that $\mu_{\chi_1^2} = 1$. Unfortunately, the case is not so simple for the variance of χ_1^2, so we merely state the result that $\sigma_{\chi_1^2}^2 = 2$.

More generally, we define the chi-square distribution with K degrees of freedom as the sum of the squares of K independent standard normal variables:

$$\chi_K^2 = Z_1^2 + Z_2^2 + \cdots + Z_K^2$$

Since each squared Z variable represents a positive quantity, the peak of the χ_K^2 distribution moves out farther from the vertical axis as K increases. We can derive the mean and variance of χ_K^2, because χ_K^2 is written as the sum of independent random variables. Thus, by the rule for linear combinations:

$$\mu_{\chi_K^2} = \mu_{Z_1^2} + \mu_{Z_2^2} + \cdots + \mu_{Z_K^2}$$

We have seen that the mean of a χ_1^2 variable equals 1. Since each term in the sum just given represents the mean of a χ_1^2 variable, we have:

$$\mu_{\chi_K^2} = 1 + 1 + \cdots + 1 = K$$

Similarly, we have:

$$\sigma_{\chi_K^2}^2 = \sigma_{Z_1^2}^2 + \sigma_{Z_2^2}^2 + \cdots + \sigma_{Z_K^2}^2$$

Here, each term represents the variance of a χ_1^2 variable, which we have already said equals 2. Hence:

$$\sigma_{\chi_K^2}^2 = 2 + 2 + \cdots + 2 = 2K$$

Finally, as K increases, the central limit theorem states that the χ_K^2 distributions approach normality. This is true in spite of the obvious extreme skewness of the χ_1^2 distribution. A graph of the typical χ_K^2 distribution is shown in Figure 25-2.

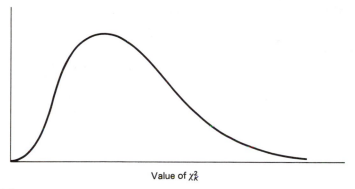

Value of χ_k^2

Figure 25-2.
A typical chi-square distribution.

Definition of χ_K^2, chi-square with K degrees of freedom

Consider K independent standard normal variables $Z_1, Z_2, \ldots, Z_K$. The sum of the squares of these variables has a chi-square distribution with K degrees of freedom. The parameter that characterizes the family of chi-square distributions is generally denoted by the Greek letter v (nu). Thus, we know that

$$\mu_{\chi_v^2} = v$$

and

$$\sigma_{\chi_v^2}^2 = 2v$$

Let us now consider two independent chi-square variables, one having two degrees of freedom and the other three degrees of freedom. Then, by our definition:

$$\chi_2^2 = Z_1^2 + Z_2^2$$

and

$$\chi_3^2 = Z_3^2 + Z_4^2 + Z_5^2$$

We have written χ_2^2 as the sum of different squared Z variables from those we used for χ_3^2, because we specified that they were independent. We can see, then, that the sum of the two χ^2 variables is also a χ^2 variable, since

$$\chi_2^2 + \chi_3^2 = Z_1^2 + Z_2^2 + Z_3^2 + Z_4^2 + Z_5^2 = \chi_5^2$$

which is a χ^2 variable with five degrees of freedom. This relationship holds for the distribution of the sum of any two independent χ^2 variables. In general, $\chi_{v_1}^2 + \chi_{v_2}^2 = \chi_{v_1+v_2}^2$. This relationship is of considerable importance to the advanced statistical models presented in Part VII. Because of its importance, we present it as a definition.

The additive or decomposition property of chi-square variables

Consider Q chi-square variables, χ_1^2, χ_2^2, . . . , χ_Q^2, with degrees of freedom v_1, v_2, . . . , v_Q. If these variables are independent, their sum $\chi_1^2 + \chi_2^2 + \cdots + \chi_Q^2$ is a χ^2 variable with degrees of freedom $v = v_1 + v_2 + \cdots + v_Q$.

Percentile values of the chi-square distribution have been determined. A shortened version of this family is presented in Table A-10. This table is entered with the percentile of interest and the value of v. For example, the 95th percentile of the chi-square distribution with $v = 30$ is given by $\chi_{30:0.95}^2 = 43.77$.

For degrees of freedom exceeding 30, percentiles of the χ^2 distribution can be determined from the following approximation:

$$\chi_{v:P}^2 \approx v\left(1 - \frac{2}{9v} + Z_P \sqrt{\frac{2}{9v}}\right)^3$$

For example, to find $\chi_{30:0.95}^2$, by the approximation, we have $v = 30$ and $P = 0.95$, so that:

$$\chi_{30:0.95}^2 \approx 30\left[1 - \frac{2}{9(30)} + 1.645 \sqrt{\frac{2}{9(30)}}\right]^3$$
$$\approx 43.77$$

25-3. EXERCISES

25-1. Use the percentiles of the normal distribution to determine the proportion of values from a chi-square distribution with one degree of freedom that would lie between 0 and 4.

25-2. What are the mean and variance of a chi-square distribution with 3 degrees of freedom? With 11 degrees of freedom? With 100 degrees of freedom?

25-3. If values are drawn at random from independent chi-square distributions with 3, 8, and 14 degrees of freedom, respectively, and then summed, the distribution of the sums thus obtained in repeated sampling is chi-square with how many degrees of freedom?

25-4. According to the central limit theorem, percentiles of the chi-square distribution with 200 degrees of freedom can be approximated using those of a normal distribution with a mean of 200 and a variance of 400. Find the 95th percentile of such a chi-square distribution using this approximation.

25-5. A more accurate approximation is given in Section 25-2. Use this approximation to find the 95th percentile of a chi-square distribution with 200 degrees of freedom. Compare your answer from Exercise 25-4 with this more accurate approximation.

CHAPTER 26

Tests of Association for Qualitative Variables

26-1. THE PHI COEFFICIENT AND THE FISHER-IRWIN TEST

In Section 10-4, the phi coefficient was introduced as a measure of association for two dichotomous variables, and in Sections 16-4 and 23-7 it was shown how the exact form and the large-sample form of the Fisher-Irwin test could be used to test

$$H_0: \quad \phi = 0$$

against

$$H_1: \quad \phi \neq 0$$

We wish to reexamine the test for the phi coefficient in terms of yet another approximation. We take this second look to enable ourselves to generalize to contingency tables with more than two rows or columns.

26-2. THE KARL PEARSON STATISTIC AND THE PHI COEFFICIENT

Even though the sample phi coefficient is calculated as an ordinary sample correlation coefficient between two variables whose values must be either 0 or 1, the tests for correlation coefficients presented in Chapter 24 cannot be used to determine whether or not a population phi coefficient is significantly different from zero. Different tests are required in the case of the phi coefficient because the variables used to calculate phi do not satisfy the conditions of normality and homoscedasticity mentioned in Sections 7-6 and 24-3. One model that has gained wide acceptance was proposed near the turn of the century by Karl Pearson in the form of a statistic he named *chi-square*. The computation of the statistic is quite straightforward.

The Karl Pearson statistic is based upon a comparison of the observed and expected frequencies which would be encountered in each cell of a two-dimensional contingency table, given that it is known that no association exists between the two variables of interest. As an illustration of the model used to estimate these expected frequencies, consider the data of Table 10-3, which yield a phi coefficient of $\hat{\phi} = 0.38$. In particular, consider the students assigned to the two programs of the study. If there were no differences in the two programs, one would expect an equal proportion of students to pass the final examination in each group. In the combined group of 40 students, 27, or 0.675, passed the examination. Under the hypothesis of no association, one would expect 0.675 of the 23 students assigned to program 1 to pass. Thus, the number of students in this program expected to pass is given by $23(0.675) = 15.525$. This expected frequency is slightly less than the observed frequency of 19. For the 17 subjects assigned to program 2, the

Table 26-1. Estimated expected frequencies for the data of Table 10-3, assuming that there is no association between type of program and passing or failing the final.

	Program 1	Program 2	Total
Passed final	15.525	11.475	27
Failed final	7.475	5.525	13
Total	23	17	40

number expected to pass, given that program effects are identical, is $17(0.675) = 11.475$. This is slightly larger than the observed frequency of 8. Now consider the students who failed the final. For the combined group, 13, or 0.325, of the students failed. If this proportion is applied to the 23 and 17 students in the experimental programs, it is seen that the expected frequencies are given by $23(0.325) = 7.475$ and $17(0.325) = 5.525$, respectively. The results are summarized in Table 26-1.

Now that we know the frequencies to expect under the hypothesis of no association between the variables, we can compare the observed and expected frequencies. What Karl Pearson suggested is that the comparison should be based upon a statistic whose value will be close to zero when there is no association and whose value will be large if the hypothesis of no association is false. A statistic having these desired properties is defined as follows.

Definition of the Karl Pearson statistic

Let the two rows of a 2×2 contingency table be denoted by $i = 1$ and $i = 2$. Let the columns be denoted by $j = 1$ and $j = 2$. Let the observed frequencies f_{ij} of the corresponding cells be denoted by f_{11}, f_{12}, f_{21}, and f_{22}. Let the corresponding estimated expected frequencies be denoted by F_{11}, F_{12}, F_{21}, and F_{22}. In terms of these numbers, the Karl Pearson statistic is defined by

$$X^2 = \sum_{i=1}^{2} \sum_{j=1}^{2} \frac{(f_{ij} - F_{ij})^2}{F_{ij}}$$

As can be seen, X^2 equals zero when all of the observed frequencies f_{ij} equal the expected frequencies F_{ij}. Otherwise, X^2 will be greater than zero, the magnitude being dependent upon the deviations between the f_{ij} and the F_{ij}. We illustrate the application of this definition to the data of Tables 10-3 and 26-1. From these tables we see that

$$f_{11} = 19, \quad f_{12} = 8, \quad f_{21} = 4, \quad \text{and} \quad f_{22} = 9$$

and

$$F_{11} = 15.525, \quad F_{12} = 11.475, \quad F_{21} = 7.475, \quad \text{and} \quad F_{22} = 5.525$$

In terms of these figures, the value of the Karl Pearson statistic is

$$X^2 = \frac{(19 - 15.525)^2}{15.525} + \frac{(8 - 11.475)^2}{11.475} + \frac{(4 - 7.475)^2}{7.475} + \frac{(9 - 5.525)^2}{5.525}$$
$$= 0.7778 + 1.0523 + 1.6155 + 2.1856 = 5.63$$

Examination of the figures in Tables 10-3 and 26-1 shows all corresponding marginal totals in the tables to be identical. Also, the total sample sizes are equal. This identity of marginal totals is not accidental. Because of the arithmetic process that is used to estimate the frequencies, certain restrictions are placed upon the numbers that go into the four cells in the body of the table. For example, as soon as the number 15.525 is placed in the upper left-hand cell, the frequency 11.475 in the upper right-hand cell is determined, since the two frequencies must sum to 27. In a like manner, the number 7.475 is determined as soon as 15.525 is placed in the table, since $15.525 + 7.475$ sums to 23. Finally, the lower right-hand cell frequency is also determined, since $7.475 + 5.525$ sums to the required 13 and since $11.475 + 5.525$ sums to the required 17. The estimated frequencies in Table 26-1 are said to have one degree of freedom.

We began this section with a discussion of the phi coefficient and have wound up with a discussion of the Karl Pearson statistic. It may not be obvious, but a simple relationship exists between the phi coefficient and the Karl Pearson statistic for a 2×2 table. The relationsip is as follows.

Relationship between X^2 and $\hat{\phi}$ for a 2×2 table

If X^2 is the Karl Pearson statistic for a 2×2 table, the corresponding $\hat{\phi}$ coefficient is given by

$$\hat{\phi} = \sqrt{\frac{X^2}{N}}$$

where N is the size of the sample.

For the data of Tables 10-3 and 26-1, $X^2 = 5.63$, so that

$$\hat{\phi} = \sqrt{5.63/40} = \sqrt{0.1408} = 0.3752 \approx 0.38$$

which is the value reported earlier.

26-3. THE TEST OF $\phi = 0$ FOR LARGE SAMPLES

It is quite clear that the Karl Pearson statistic makes intuitive sense; the value is small when there is no association, and it is large when there is association. Pearson made a careful study of the distribution of X^2 under repeated random sampling and was able to show that it was approximated by the distribution of χ_1^2 given in Section 25-2, provided all the F_{ij} exceed 5. This means that the Karl Pearson statistic for a 2×2 table has, upon repeated sampling, a theoretical distribution that is close to the chi-square distribution with one

---

Box 26-1   Large-sample procedure for testing $H_0: \phi = 0$ against the alternative $H_1: \phi \neq 0$, for $F_{ij} > 5$

Step 1. Set up the 2×2 table of observed frequencies f_{11}, f_{12}, f_{21}, and f_{22}.

Step 2. Estimate the corresponding expected frequencies F_{11}, F_{12}, F_{21}, and F_{22}, and check that all F_{ij} exceed 5.

Step 3. Compute:

$$X^2 = \sum_{i=1}^{2} \sum_{j=1}^{2} \frac{(f_{ij} - F_{ij})^2}{F_{ij}}$$

where $i = 1$ refers to the first row, $i = 2$ refers to the second row, $j = 1$ refers to the first column, and $j = 2$ refers to the second column.

Step 4. Reject the hypothesis of no association between the variables if X^2 exceeds the $1 - \alpha$ percentile of the chi-square distribution with one degree of freedom.

Step 5. If H_0 is rejected, estimate the population phi coefficient as follows:

$$\hat{\phi} = \sqrt{\frac{X^2}{N}}$$

where N is the size of the sample.

---

degree of freedom, provided H_0 is true. When H_0 is false, X^2 will be large. For this reason we place all of the α into the upper tail of the χ^2 distribution. Since this table has $\nu = 1$ degree of freedom and all $F_{ij} > 5$, the decision rule for testing $H_0: \phi = 0$ against $H_1: \phi \neq 0$ is as follows:

Decision Rule: Reject H_0 if $X^2 > 3.84$

Since $X^2 = 5.63$ is greater than 3.84, we reject H_0 and conclude that there is an association between the kind of laboratory experience described and passing the final examination. In terms of the proportions passing, we would conclude that students in program 1 have a better chance of passing the final than do students in program 2. Directions for testing $H_0: \phi = 0$ using the X^2 statistic of Karl Pearson are provided in Box 26-1.

There is reason to believe that X^2 is still approximated by the chi-square distribution, even if some of the F_{ij} are less than or equal to 5. The rule we have provided, although more stringent, is easily followed and provides great assurance that the approximation is adequate.

26-4. TESTING FOR ASSOCIATION IN AN $I \times J$ CONTINGENCY TABLE

The Karl Pearson test of Section 26-2 extends in a straightforward manner to the case in which the number of rows or columns in the resulting contingency

Table 26-2. Joint frequency distribution of eye and hair color of 212 students enrolled in a beginning biology class.

Y: Hair color	X: Eye color					
	Brown	Hazel	Green	Gray	Blue	Total
Black	45	8	7	2	7	69
Red	6	6	9	5	13	39
Blond	3	6	6	4	18	37
Dark-brown	50	8	2	2	5	67
Total	104	28	24	13	43	212

table exceeds 2. As an example, consider the data of Table 26-2, which were obtained from a survey of the students enrolled in the beginning biology class. The expected frequencies, under the hypothesis of no association, are estimated in the same manner as in Section 26-2 and are reported in Table 26-3. The estimated expected frequencies for brown-eyed black-haired students is given by $F_{11} = 104(69/212) = 33.85$. For brown-eyed redheads, $F_{21} = 104(39/212) = 19.13$. The corresponding figures for brown-eyed blond-haired students is given by $F_{31} = 104(37/212) = 18.15$. Since the number of brown-eyed students is equal to 104, it follows that $F_{41} = 104 - 33.85 - 19.13 - 18.15 = 32.87$. This last result could also be computed as $F_{41} = 104(67/212) = 32.87$. In any case, column 1 has three degrees of freedom. This is also true for the expected frequencies of columns 2, 3, and 4. There are no degrees of freedom available for filling the estimated expected frequencies of the last

Table 26-3. Estimated expected frequencies for Table 26-2.

Y: Hair color	X: Eye color					
	Brown	Hazel	Green	Gray	Blue	Total
Black	33.85	9.11	7.81	4.23	14.00	69
Red	19.13	5.15	4.42	2.39	7.91	39
Blond	18.15	4.89	4.19	2.27	7.50	37
Dark-brown	32.87	8.85	7.58	4.11	13.59	67
Total	104	28	24	13	43	212

column, since these frequencies are determined as soon as columns 1, 2, 3, and 4 are known. Thus, the number of degrees of freedom for the table is $v = 12$. An easy way to compute v is to note that $v = (I-1)(J-1)$, where $I =$ number of columns and $J =$ number of rows. In this example $I = 5$ and $J = 4$, and so $v = (5-1)(4-1) = 12$, as already noted. For completeness, we define the Karl Pearson statistic for an $I \times J$ table.

Definition of the Karl Pearson statistic for an $I \times J$ contingency table

For an $I \times J$ contingency table, the Karl Pearson statistic is computed as follows:

$$X^2 = \sum_{i=1}^{I} \sum_{j=1}^{J} \frac{(f_{ij} - F_{ij})^2}{F_{ij}}$$

Under the hypothesis of no association, X^2 is approximately χ_v^2, where $v = (I-1)(J-1)$.

For the observed data,

$$X^2 = \frac{(45 - 33.85)^2}{33.85} + \frac{(6 - 19.13)^2}{19.13} + \cdots + \frac{(5 - 13.59)^2}{13.59}$$
$$= 77.92$$

From Table A-10, the 95th percentile value for the χ^2 distribution with $v = 12$ degrees of freedom is given by $\chi^2 = 21.03$. Since $X^2 = 77.92 > 21.03$, the hypothesis of no association is rejected. We now know that there is an association between eye color and hair color and would, therefore, like to estimate the strength of the relationship. The measure that is commonly used for this situation is called *Cramer's measure of association*, or the mean square contingency coefficient. For a 2×2 contingency table this measure is identical to the phi coefficient. To distinguish it from ϕ, we can denote it by ϕ', but more frequently it is denoted as V.

If M equals the smaller of $I-1$ and $J-1$, one can estimate the strength of association between X and Y by means of the following relation:

$$\hat{V} = \sqrt{\frac{X^2}{MN}}$$

For the data, $I - 1 = 4 - 1 = 3$ and $J - 1 = 5 - 1 = 4$, so that

$$\hat{V} = \sqrt{\frac{77.92}{3(212)}} = \sqrt{0.1225} = 0.35$$

For all practical purposes, $\hat{V}$ can be interpreted as a simple correlation coefficient.

Definition of Cramer's measure of association

Let

$$X^2 = \sum_{i=1}^{I} \sum_{j=1}^{J} \frac{(f_{ij} - F_{ij})^2}{F_{ij}}$$

be the value of the Karl Pearson statistic for an $I \times J$ contingency table. Let M equal the smaller of $I - 1$ and $J - 1$. Cramer's $\hat{V}$ is defined as follows:

$$\hat{V} = \sqrt{\frac{X^2}{NM}}$$

Box 26-2   **Procedure for testing $H_0: V = 0$ against the alternative $H_1: V \neq 0$**

Step 1. For all cells, compute:

$$F_{ij} = \frac{f_{i.} f_{.j}}{N}$$

where

$$f_{i.} = \text{frequency in the } i\text{th row}$$

and

$$f_{.j} = \text{frequency in the } j\text{th column}$$

Step 2. Compute:

$$X^2 = \sum_{i=1}^{I} \sum_{j=1}^{J} \frac{(f_{ij} - F_{ij})^2}{F_{ij}}$$

Step 3. Reject the hypothesis of no association if X^2 exceeds the $1 - \alpha$ percentage point of the chi-square distribution with $v = (I - 1)(J - 1)$ degrees of freedom.

Step 4. If H_0 is rejected, estimate the population V coefficient as

$$\hat{V} = \sqrt{\frac{X^2}{MN}}$$

where N is the size of the sample and M is the smaller of $I - 1$ and $J - 1$.

The Karl Pearson statistic is based upon two assumptions. First, all observations in the table must be statistically independent, and second, the expected frequencies for all cells must be values greater than 5.

In our example, seven of the cells have expected frequencies that are smaller than 5, and so the second assumption appears not to be satisfied. The assumption of independence between subjects appears to be satisfied, since eye color and hair color are genetic traits that are assigned to individuals at the time of conception by strictly natural processes. Of course, the assumption of independence between subjects could be violated if sisters, brothers, cousins, or other relatives were included in the study.

Directions for the chi-square test are provided in Box 26-2.

26-5. CONTINGENCY TABLES WITH ORDERED CATEGORIES

The Karl Pearson test of independence is designed to examine association whenever the dependent variable is qualitative. This means it can be used for both unordered and ordered qualitative variables. However, if both variables are ordered it tends to underestimate the strength of the ordinal association. Fortunately, Spearman's rho can be used in this special case. We illustrate the method by using the data of Table 26-4, which were obtained from the biology students of Table 2-1 on the last day of class. At that time, students were asked to complete a questionnaire which contained the following item:

As a result of your experiences and new knowledge acquired in this class, would you consider a career in biology, medicine, or some other of the life sciences? Definitely Yes ____   Maybe ____   Definitely No ____

The responses to this question, along with the final class grades, are reported in Table 26-4 for students who completed the questionnaire item.

Table 26-4. Ordered contingency table of responses to a questionnaire item and final course grades for a group of students taking beginning biology.

Y	1: A	2: B	X 3: C	4: D or F	Total
1. Definitely yes	18	51	21	5	95
2. Maybe	3	23	8	5	39
3. Definitely no	0	13	16	17	46
Total	21	87	45	27	180

Table 26-5. Computational table for Spearman's rho for
ordered-category variables.

Y	X	f_{XY}	r^Y	r^X
1	1	18	48	11
1	2	51	48	65
1	3	21	48	131
1	4	5	48	167
2	1	3	115	11
2	2	23	115	65
2	3	8	115	131
2	4	5	115	167
3	1	0	157.5	11
3	2	13	157.5	65
3	3	16	157.5	131
3	4	17	157.5	167

One might want to know whether or not attitudes are correlated with grades
in the course. The measurement of this association is illustrated.

We begin by setting up a computational table, as illustrated in Table 26-5,
to determine the value of r_S. First let us rank the Y values. Consider the 95
respondents coded as $Y = 1$. If they differed in attitude, their rank values
would be given by $r^Y = 1, 2, \ldots, 95$; but, since we cannot make such a
differentiation in attitude, we assign an average rank of:

$$\overline{R}_1^Y = \frac{1}{95}(1 + 2 + \cdots + 95)$$
$$= \frac{1}{95}\left[\frac{95(1 + 95)}{2}\right] = \frac{1 + 95}{2} = 48$$

Note that the addition process can be avoided because the mean rank is
simply the average of the smallest and largest ranks assigned to the set. In like
manner, the mean ranks for the coded values of $Y = 2$ and $Y = 3$ are given by

$$\overline{R}_2^Y = \frac{96 + 134}{2} = 115 \quad \text{and} \quad \overline{R}_3^Y = \frac{135 + 180}{2} = 157.5$$

respectively. For the grade assignments, $\overline{R}_1^X = (1 + 21)/2 = 11$, $\overline{R}_2^X = (22 +
108)/2 = 65$, $\overline{R}_3^X = (109 + 153)/2 = 131$, and $\overline{R}_4^X = (154 + 180)/2 = 167$.

These values are reported in Table 26-5. In terms of these mean ranks,

$$\Sigma r^Y = 95(48) + 39(115) + 46(157.5) = 16{,}290$$
$$\Sigma (r^Y)^2 = 95(48)^2 + 39(115)^2 + 46(157.5)^2 = 1{,}875{,}742.50$$
$$\Sigma r^X = 21(11) + 87(65) + 45(131) + 27(167) = 16{,}290$$
$$\Sigma (r^X)^2 = 21(11)^2 + 87(65)^2 + 45(131)^2 + 27(167)^2 = 1{,}894{,}154$$
$$\Sigma (r^Y r^X) = 18(48)(11) + 51(48)(65) + \cdots + 17(157.5)(167) = 1{,}643{,}367$$

With these values,

$$
r_S = \frac{180(1{,}643{,}367) - (16{,}290)^2}{\sqrt{180(1{,}875{,}742.50) - 16{,}290^2}\ \sqrt{180(1{,}894{,}154) - 16{,}290^2}}
$$
$$
= \frac{295{,}779{,}530}{\sqrt{337{,}617{,}360}\ \sqrt{340{,}921{,}190}} = \frac{295{,}779{,}530}{337{,}322{,}450}
$$
$$
= 0.8768
$$

In terms of the large-sample test of $H_0: \rho_S = 0$, described in Section 24-2,

$$Z_r = r_S\sqrt{N-1} = (0.8768)\sqrt{180-1} = 11.73$$

Since Z_r is in the $\alpha = .05$ critical region defined by $Z_r < -1.96$ or $Z_r > 1.96$, we reject the hypothesis of no association. Thus, we have reason to believe that grades in the biology course are correlated with intentions to consider a career in the life sciences. Inspection of the data suggests that the association is positive, with high grades associated with the response category "definitely yes" and low grades associated with the response category "definitely no." This positive association is also reflected in the positive algebraic sign in the value of the test statistic.

Although this chapter focuses on the chi-square distribution, we have included the Spearman rho procedure here because it is one that can be used to analyze contingency tables for the special case of ordered values. Including it here should highlight the fact that different analyses are required for measures of association for ordered and unordered categorical data. The Karl Pearson test ignores order on the two variables. The Spearman rho test focuses on the order and is therefore more powerful and is to be preferred in the case of ordered variables.

26-6. EXERCISES

26-1. In a study on the relationship between age and women's attitudes toward abortion, 96 Catholic women were interviewed and asked:

Would you have an abortion for a child you did not want? Yes _____   No _____

Results are as follows:

Response	Age		Total
	Under 30	Over 30	
Yes	31	6	37
No	11	48	59
Total	42	54	96

Find $\hat{\phi}$ and test $H_0: \phi = 0$.

26-2. In the study of Exercise 26-1, the following data were generated for women who said that their family size was completed, i.e., those who said they did not have plans for more children. All respondents are Catholic. Find $\hat{V}$ for these data and test $H_0: V = 0$.

Yearly family income, $	Number of children in completed family				Total
	0	1	2	3 or more	
0–10,000	12	8	7	14	41
10,000–25,000	6	10	4	12	32
25,000–50,000	1	3	9	10	23
More than 50,000	0	1	5	8	14
Total	19	22	25	44	110

26-3. Can Spearman's rho be applied to the data of Exercise 26-2? Why? Which would you use: r_s or $\hat{V}$? Compute r_s and test ρ_s for significance.

26-4. In a study on who provides information to women who have abortions, 272 women who had had an abortion at a large central-city hospital were asked:

Whom did you consult about having an abortion?

a. Minister, rabbi, or other religious leader (only)
b. Doctor (only)
c. Family members (only)
d. Consultant (only)
e. Combination of a, b, c, d, e
f. No one

Results are as shown for the women by religion.

Source of information	Catholic	Protestant	Jewish	Other	Total
a	10	2	8	2	22
b	27	61	21	29	138
c	11	7	0	3	21
d	6	3	0	12	21
e	7	10	7	10	34
f	21	8	0	7	36
Total	82	91	36	63	272

Find $\hat{V}$ for these data and test $H_0: V = 0$.

26-5. In Exercise 26-3 many of the cells have F_{ij} values that are less than 5. What effect do they have on V? One way to reduce the effects of small sample sizes is to *pool* columns or rows that are qualitatively similar. Do this, compute $\hat{V}$, and test $H_0: V = 0$.

26-6. In a survey of adults' feelings about liberal versus conservative politics, a group of 100 adults were classified into liberal or conservative categories on the basis of a questionnaire. They were then given a short paragraph to read that was taken from the Preamble to the Constitution. Those who did not recognize the passage were asked if they agreed with the ideas expressed. Results are as shown.

	Category		
Response	Liberal	Conservative	Total
Agree	49	10	59
Disagree	12	14	26
Total	61	24	85

Is there a reason to believe, in the population of people who could have been polled, that $\phi = 0$? Use $\alpha = .05$ to answer this question.

26-7. In the survey of Exercise 26-6, people were classified according to religious persuasion and asked, "Should school boards fire teachers who are homosexual?" Results are as shown.

Response	Liberal Christian	Conservative Christian	Jewish	Other	Total
Yes	5	17	2	2	26
No	20	4	13	8	45
No opinion	5	4	5	15	29
Total	30	25	20	25	100

Determine Cramer's $\hat{V}$ and test $H_0: V = 0$.

26-8. Remove the "no opinion" row from Exercise 26-7 and reanalyze the data. What is your opinion about the practice of collapsing or removing categories?

CHAPTER **27**

Tests of Homogeneity
or Identity of
Distributions

27-1. HOMOGENEITY VERSUS INDEPENDENCE

The example of Section 26-4 was based upon a single sample of 212 students who were classified according to eye color and hair color. One could not readily conceive of the data reported in Table 26-4 as being generated from a preselected sample of redheads, a preselected sample of blond students, and so on, who were then classified according to eye color nor could one readily imagine the data to have been collected from a preselected sample of brown-eyed people, blue-eyed people, and so on, who were then classified according to hair color. In this study, eye color and hair color alike were noted only after the single sample of 212 subjects was selected.

Table 27-1. Frequency distribution of four groups of students and how they responded to the question about reducing crime in the streets.

| | Group | | | | |
Response	Males majoring in sociology	Males in other majors	Females majoring in sociology	Females in other majors	Total
1. Penalties	1	5	0	10	16
2. Police	6	16	2	12	36
3. Welfare	16	8	19	7	50
4. None	20	10	15	13	58
Total	43	39	36	42	160

For the data of Table 27-1, however, a researcher preselected 43 male students who were majoring in sociology. Three other groups of students were purposefully selected by the researcher to compare the effects of two categories of majors among male students and among female students, to compare male students with female students, and probably to compare the types of majors among all students. While in the study of eye and hair color only one sample was selected, for the data of Table 27-1 four samples were selected.

Consider the data shown in Table 27-1, which is based upon responses to the following question that was asked of a group of students in a first-year sociology class at the end of the term:

A number of suggestions have been proposed to reduce crime in the streets. Which suggestion do you think will do the most to reduce crime?

1. Increase penalties for convicted offenders.
2. Increase the number of city police.
3. Increase welfare payments and/or social services.
4. None of the above.

In this case, there are two clearly defined independent variables. They consist of the two categories of majors and the two sexes. The dependent variable consists of the responses to the question about reducing crime in the streets. The researcher wanted to know whether the responses that the subjects made to the question about reducing crime in the streets were related to gender, major, or some combination of gender and major. This question can be answered by testing the hypothesis that the resulting distributions of responses are identical for the four purposely created independent groups of students.

This hypothesis of the identity of distributions across several populations is refered to as one of *homogeneity*. The test of this hypothesis was proposed by Karl Pearson. Unfortunately, the Karl Pearson test of homogeneity of distribution is often confused with the Karl Pearson test of independence between two qualitative variables. This confusion is easy to understand. As we shall see, the test statistics for both are identical, and the probabilities for both can be approximated by chi-square distributions with $v = (I-1)(J-1)$ degrees of freedom. The two tests, however, are based on different assumptions. The test of independence is a *one*-sample test, in that N paired observations are made on two variables. The test of homogeneity is a *multiple*-sample test in which groups of subjects are sampled and observations are made on a single dependent variable.

27-2. THE MULTIPLE-SAMPLE TEST OF HOMOGENEITY

The Karl Pearson statistic can be used to test the hypothesis that multiple samples have been selected from independent populations in which the distribution of the dependent variable is the same across all populations. This can be tested by means of the Karl Pearson statistic:

$$X^2 = \sum_{i=1}^{I} \sum_{j=1}^{J} \frac{(f_{ij} - F_{ij})^2}{F_{ij}}$$

For the observed frequencies of Table 27-1 and the estimated expected

Table 27-2. Expected frequencies for the data of Table 27-1.

	Group				
Response	Males majoring in sociology	Males in other majors	Females majoring in sociology	Females in other majors	Total
1. Penalties	4.3000	3.9000	3.6000	4.2000	16
2. Police	9.6750	8.7750	8.1000	9.4500	36
3. Welfare	13.4375	12.1875	11.2500	13.1250	50
4. None	15.5875	14.1375	13.0500	15.2250	58
Total	43	39	36	42	160

frequencies of Table 27-2,

$$X^2 = \frac{(1-4.30)^2}{4.30} + \frac{(6-9.675)^2}{9.675} + \cdots + \frac{(13-15.225)^2}{15.225}$$
$$= 40.28$$

Since $v = (I-1)(J-1) = (4-1)(4-1) = 9$, the 95 percent decision rule for rejecting the hypothesis of homogeneity is as follows:

Decision Rule: Reject H_0 if $X^2 > \chi^2_{9:.95} = 16.92$

Since $X^2 = 40.28 > 16.92$, the hypothesis of homogeneity is rejected. The distribution of responses across the four groups of students differs.

Directions for testing the hypothesis of homogeneity of distributions are given in Box 27-1. Notice the complexity of the hypothesis of homogeneity. It

---

Box 27-1   The Karl Pearson test of homogeneity of distributions

Step 1. Consider the J populations categorized on a qualitative variable defined by I mutually exclusive categories. Let the population probability for the ith category in population j be denoted as p_{ij}. Consider the complex hypothesis

$$H_0:\quad \begin{bmatrix} p_{11} = p_{12} = \cdots = p_{1J} \\ p_{21} = p_{22} = \cdots = p_{2J} \\ \vdots \quad \vdots \quad \vdots \quad \vdots \\ p_{I1} = p_{I2} = \cdots = p_{IJ} \end{bmatrix}$$

and its alternative

$$H_1:\quad H_0 \text{ is false}$$

Step 2. Determine the value of each $F_{ij} = N_{.j}\hat{P}(f_i)$, where $N_{.j} =$ frequency in the jth sample and $\hat{P}(f_i) = f_i/N$, where $f_i =$ frequency in the ith row and $N = N_{.1} + N_{.2} + \cdots + N_J$.

Step 3. Compute the Karl Pearson statistic:

$$X^2 = \sum_{i=1}^{I} \sum_{j=1}^{J} \frac{(f_{ij} - F_{ij})^2}{F_{ij}}$$

Step 4. Reject H_0 if $X^2 > \chi^2_{v:1-\alpha}$ where $v = (I-1)(J-1)$.

Step 5. Measure the strength of the association in terms of Cramer's V.

states that the individual category probabilities are equal across the complete set of populations. In other words, within each row, probabilities are equal from column to column. If this hypothesis is rejected, one might seem to be faced with a nightmare, because the reasons for rejection are not obvious. Consider our example: Was H_0 rejected because males majoring in sociology differed from males majoring in other subjects in how they responded to the first category, dealing with penalties? Or was the rejection due to the fact that males and females differed in their responses to category 3 or category 4? If one thinks about it, the rejection might have resulted from a large number of such explanations. Which ones would be correct? The Karl Pearson test fails to provide the answer. Something else is needed, as we shall see in Chapter 28.

27-3. EXERCISES

27-1. What are the differences and similarities between the Karl Pearson tests of homogeneity and independence?

27-2. In a prospective study on the effects of smoking on lung disease, two groups of men over the age of 50 were followed for 20 years by way of a prepaid hospital plan. Subjects were classified at the beginning of the study as smokers or nonsmokers. At the end of the study the following statistics were generated:

Lung disease	Smoker	Nonsmoker	Total
Present	271	36	307
Absent	2461	1605	4066
Total	2732	1641	4373

Test the hypothesis $H_0: p_S = p_{NS}$ using the Karl Pearson statistic.

27-3. In the study of Exercise 27-2, a followup investigation was made of the men who suffered from lung disease. For one of the studies the following statistics were generated:

Use of coffee for an average day	Smoker	Nonsmoker	Total
0 cups	42	18	60
1 cup	83	10	93
2 or more cups	146	8	154
Total	271	36	307

Use the Karl Pearson test for the hypothesis of homogeneity.

27-4. In a study of the effects of social status upon attendance at cultural events, the employees of a large Western bank were classified as
a. Top management
b. Middle management
c. Regular clerical employees
d. Service employees

From each of the groups, 50 employees were sampled and asked,

During the months of October and November, how many times did you go to an opera, concert, play, or other cultural event?

Responses are as shown.

Attendance	a	b	c	d	Total
0	4	10	15	30	59
1	1	12	10	2	25
2	7	6	15	2	30
3 or more	38	22	10	16	86
Total	50	50	50	50	200

Column header: Status (spanning a, b, c, d)

Use the Karl Pearson test for the hypothesis of homogeneity.

27-5. Note that in Exercise 27-4 both variables are ordered. The Karl Pearson test ignores the order. One can assign the code numbers 1, 2, 3, and 4 to the ordered categories and compute Spearman's rho. Do this and test for significance.

CHAPTER **28**

Multiple Comparisons
for Tests of Homogeneity

28-1. MULTIPLE COMPARISONS FOR PROPORTIONS

In Chapters 26 and 27 we provided models for analyzing contingency tables under the hypothesis of independence or homogeneity. In some cases, we specified the exact nature of H_0 and H_1, and in others we did not. We now want to close the discussion concerning the exact nature of H_0 and H_1 for those models. In particular we will consider tests of H_0 for homogeneity in this chapter and tests of H_0 for independence in Chapter 49. To simplify our discussion of homogeneity, consider the data of Table 28-1. These data are taken from a study designed to measure the effects of teenage crime upon city life. In the study, the following question was asked of parent-teacher associa-

Table 28-1. Responses to the question "Do you think that teenage street crime in your city exceeds, on the average, that of the nation?" for the four cities cited in Section 28-1.

Response	New York	Detroit	Topeka	Seattle	Total
Yes	120	175	60	30	385
No	60	35	100	120	315
Total	180	210	160	150	700

tion officers in New York, Detroit, Topeka, and Seattle:

Do you think that teenage street crime in your city exceeds, on the average, that of the nation? Yes ——   No ——

As we see, the data of Table 28-1 involve four independent binomial samples. First we let 1 represent New York; 2, Detroit; 3, Topeka; and 4, Seattle. Then the apparent hypothesis of homogeneity is:

$$H_0: \quad p_1 = p_2 = p_3 = p_4$$

The simplest way to state the alternative is:

$$H_1: \quad H_0 \text{ is false}$$

Although H_0 is clear in meaning, H_1 is not. What does it mean to state "H_0 is false"? A large test statistic means only that H_0 should be rejected; it does not provide information as to why H_0 is thought to be false. The reasons for a rejection are definitely of value to a researcher, because they provide clues to the question "Why?"

Until a few years ago, there was no answer to this question, but a break-through was achieved, in a different context, in 1953, by Scheffé. Later, in 1961, Dunn improved upon Scheffé's answer. We will consider both solutions in the context of contingency-table analysis. Scheffé did not propose his method for these models, nor did Dunn propose hers. Their methods were proposed originally for quantitative variables, but in the mid-1960s, Good-man extended their work to cover contingency tables. It is his method that we will describe.

A hypothesis such as $H_0: p_1 = p_2 = p_3 = p_4$ is referred to as an *omnibus hypothesis* and can be contrasted to a simple *pairwise* hypothesis such as $H_0: p_1 = p_2$. When a simple hypothesis such as this is tested via the Fisher-Irwin test and when H_0 is rejected, the reason for the rejection is known immediately. Rejection of H_0 means that $p_1 \neq p_2$. With this in mind, we might think that the appropriate alternative to H_0 should be a statement about the following set of $C = \binom{4}{2} = 6$ Fisher-Irwin hypotheses, stated as *pairwise differences:* that $p_1 - p_2 \neq 0$, or $p_1 - p_3 \neq 0$, or $p_1 - p_4 \neq 0$, or $p_2 - p_3 \neq 0$, or $p_2 - p_4 \neq 0$, or $p_3 - p_4 \neq 0$. Unfortunately, such simplicity is incorrect.

Scheffé made a study of this problem for quantitative variables, and he saw that H_1 did involve pairwise comparisons, but it also involved complex comparisons. More explicitly, he learned that the number of such comparisons is unlimited. For example, consider p_1, p_2, and p_3. The comparisons involving these three parameters include the following, among others:

$$p_1 - \tfrac{1}{2}(p_2 + p_3) \neq 0$$

$$p_1 - (^{210}\!/_{370}\, p_2 + {}^{160}\!/_{370}\, p_3) \neq 0$$

$$\vdots$$

There is no limit to the number of such comparisons. Scheffé found that rejection of H_0 meant that at least one of these comparisons was statistically different from zero. Such comparisons are called *contrasts* and have the following structure and properties.

Definition of a contrast

Assume that a parameter of interest is measured on K populations. A contrast in the parameters $\theta_1, \theta_2, \ldots, \theta_K$ is a linear combination of the form

$$\psi = W_1\theta_1 + W_2\theta_2 + \cdots + W_K\theta_K$$

but one in which the weights are restricted to satisfy the condition

$$W_1 + W_2 + \cdots + W_K = 0$$

A sample estimate of ψ is given by

$$\hat{\psi} = W_1\hat{\theta}_1 + W_2\hat{\theta}_2 + \cdots + W_K\hat{\theta}_K$$

where $\hat{\theta}_1, \hat{\theta}_2, \ldots, \hat{\theta}_K$ are estimates of the parameters generated in the K samples.

We now show that our comparisons regarding p_1, p_2, p_3, and p_4 are contrasts. For $p_1 - p_2$, we have $W_1 = 1$, $W_2 = -1$, $W_3 = 0$, and $W_4 = 0$, and our condition is satisfied:

$$1 - 1 + 0 + 0 = 0$$

For $p_1 - p_3$, $W_1 = 1$, $W_2 = 0$, $W_3 = -1$, and $W_4 = 0$. Again, we find:

$$1 + 0 - 1 + 0 = 0$$

For $p_1 - \frac{1}{2}(p_2 + p_3)$, $W_1 = 1$, $W_2 = -\frac{1}{2}$, $W_3 = -\frac{1}{2}$, and $W_4 = 0$, and:

$$1 - \tfrac{1}{2} - \tfrac{1}{2} + 0 = 0$$

Finally, for $p_1 - (^{210}/_{370}\, p_2 + {^{160}/_{370}}\, p_3)$, $W_1 = 1$, $W_2 = -^{210}/_{370}$, $W_3 = -^{160}/_{370}$, and $W_4 = 0$, with:

$$1 - {^{210}/_{370}} - {^{160}/_{370}} + 0 = 0$$

The linear combination

$$3p_1 + 7p_2 - 15p_3 - 9p_4$$

is not a contrast, since $W_1 = 3$, $W_2 = 7$, $W_3 = -15$, and $W_4 = -9$ and when these are summed, the result is -14, not zero.

Since a contrast is a linear combination, we know from Section 20-3 that the sampling distribution of $\hat{\psi} = W_1 \hat{\theta}_1 + W_2 \hat{\theta}_2 + \cdots + W_K \hat{\theta}_K$ is known. Its properties are as follows.

Properties of contrasts

If the sample sizes are sufficiently large, then the sample estimate

$$\hat{\psi} = W_1 \hat{\theta}_1 + W_2 \hat{\theta}_2 + \cdots + W_K \hat{\theta}_K$$

tends to have a normal distribution with

$$E(\hat{\psi}) = \psi = W_1 \theta_1 + W_2 \theta_2 + \cdots + W_K \theta_K$$

and

$$\mathrm{Var}(\hat{\psi}) = W_1^2 \mathrm{Var}(\hat{\theta}_1) + W_2^2 \mathrm{Var}(\hat{\theta}_2) + \cdots + W_K^2 \mathrm{Var}(\hat{\theta}_K)$$

If $\mathrm{Var}(\hat{\theta}_1)$, $\mathrm{Var}(\hat{\theta}_2)$, . . . , $\mathrm{Var}(\hat{\theta}_K)$ are unknown, they can be estimated in the samples as $SE^2_{\hat{\theta}_1}$, $SE^2_{\hat{\theta}_2}$, . . . , $SE^2_{\hat{\theta}_K}$, so that an estimate of $\mathrm{Var}(\hat{\psi})$ is given by

$$SE^2_{\hat{\psi}} = W_1^2 SE^2_{\hat{\theta}_1} + W_2^2 SE^2_{\hat{\theta}_2} + \cdots + W_K^2 SE^2_{\hat{\theta}_K}$$

The correct H_0 and H_1 for all *omnibus* tests are

$$H_0: \quad \text{All } \psi = \sum_{k=1}^{K} W_k \theta_k = 0$$

and

$$H_1: \quad \text{At least one } \psi \neq 0$$

If H_0 is rejected, a researcher can search for at least one $\psi \neq 0$. Rejection of H_0 guarantees that at least one such contrast exists. Unfortunately, it may not be interpretable, and it may not be easy to find.

The question remains concerning how one finds the significant contrasts in a test of homogeneity of proportions. This problem was solved by Goodman. He found that each contrast should be tested as

$$H_0: \quad \psi = 0$$

against

$$H_1: \quad \psi \neq 0$$

by computing

$$Z = \frac{\hat{\psi} - 0}{SE_{\hat{\psi}}}$$

and rejecting H_0 if Z is in the critical region of the test.

The problem that Goodman had to solve involved determining the decision rule to apply to each of the Z values. Without doubt, using $Z = \pm 1.96$ would not do. To investigate why this is true, suppose we had two tests, based on Z_1 and Z_2. If the tests of Z_1 and Z_2 were mutually exclusive, the probability of making a type I error for the test of $H_0^{(1)}: \psi_1 = 0$ or $H_0^{(2)}: \psi_2 = 0$ would be given by:

$$
\begin{aligned}
P(\text{type I error for } H_0^{(1)} \text{ or } H_0^{(2)}) &= P(\text{type I error for } H_0^{(1)}) \\
&\quad + P(\text{type I error for } H_0^{(2)}) \\
&= \alpha_1 + \alpha_2 = .05 + .05 = .10
\end{aligned}
$$

Unfortunately, in the present context the tests are not mutually exclusive, since the two tests use common data; however, $\alpha_1 + \alpha_2 = .10$ certainly is an upper bound on the risk of at least one type I error in the two tests. Thus, when events are not mutually exclusive, we will have:

$$
\begin{aligned}
P(I_1 \text{ or } I_2) &\leq P(I_1) + P(I_2) \\
&= \alpha_1 + \alpha_2
\end{aligned}
$$

where I_1 refers to the event of a type I error on the first test and I_2 refers to the corresponding error on the second test. In any case, as the number of tests increases, the probability of making one or more type I errors among the set of tests also increases and eventually approaches unity.

Following the derivation made by Scheffé, Goodman found that the appropriate decision rule for testing an infinite set of contrasts for statistical significance, so that the risk of committing at least one type I error in the set of tests is equal to α, is:

Decision Rule: Reject H_0: $\psi = 0$ in favor of H_1: $\psi \neq 0$ if $Z = \hat{\psi}/SE_{\hat{\psi}}$ is less than $-S^*$ or greater than S^*, where $S^* = \sqrt{\chi^2_{\nu:1-\alpha}}$ and where ν = the number of degrees of freedom for the omnibus test of homogeneity.

Alternatively, one can test the hypothesis H_0: $\psi = 0$ by examining the confidence interval,

$$\hat{\psi} - \sqrt{\chi^2_{\nu:1-\alpha}}\, SE_{\hat{\psi}} < \psi < \hat{\psi} + \sqrt{\chi^2_{\nu:1-\alpha}}\, SE_{\hat{\psi}}$$

and then rejecting H_0 if $\psi = 0$ is not in the interval. The Goodman procedure for testing homogeneity of proportions is described in Box 28-1.

If we perform the Karl Pearson test on the data of Table 28-1, we see that $X^2 = 172.05$. With $\alpha = .05$, H_0 is rejected, since $\chi^2_{3:.95} = 7.81$. Thus, we know that some contrast in the p_k is different from zero. Let us apply Goodman's procedure to the data of Table 28-1. We begin by making all *pairwise comparisons* among the four cities. For the comparison of New York to Detroit:

$$\hat{\psi}_{1\,vs.\,2} = \hat{p}_1 - \hat{p}_2 = {}^{120}\!/_{180} - {}^{175}\!/_{210} = 0.6667 - 0.8333 = -0.1666$$

with

$$\begin{aligned} SE^2_{\hat{\psi}_{1\,vs.\,2}} &= (1)^2 SE^2_{\hat{p}_1} + (-1)^2 SE^2_{\hat{p}_2} \\ &= \frac{\hat{p}_1\hat{q}_1}{N_1} + \frac{\hat{p}_2\hat{q}_2}{N_2} \\ &= {}^{1}\!/_{180}\,({}^{120}\!/_{180})({}^{60}\!/_{180}) + {}^{1}\!/_{210}\,({}^{175}\!/_{210})({}^{35}\!/_{210}) = 0.001896 \end{aligned}$$

Thus

$$Z_{1\,vs.\,2} = \frac{\hat{\psi}_{1\,vs.\,2}}{SE_{\hat{\psi}_{1\,vs.\,2}}} = \frac{-0.1666}{0.0435} = -3.83$$

The remaining comparisons are summarized in Table 28-2. Each is compared with $S^* = \sqrt{\chi^2_{3:.95}} = \sqrt{7.81} = 2.79$. As can be seen, each city is statistically different from the others in how it responds to the question.

If one "*data-snoops*" and makes *eyeball inspections* of the data, it looks as

---

Box 28-1   **Goodman's post hoc procedure for identifying statistically significant contrasts for a dichotomous dependent variable measured across K independent groups**

Step 1. Perform the omnibus Karl Pearson test using the statistic X^2.

Step 2. If H_0 is not rejected, do not make an investigation for significant contrasts, for none will be found.

Step 3. If H_0 is rejected, assign meaningful weights to

$$\psi = \sum_{k=1}^{K} W_k \theta_k$$

and test $H_0 : \psi = 0$ versus $H_1 : \psi \neq 0$, using

$$Z = \frac{\hat{\psi} - 0}{SE_{\hat{\psi}}}$$

or

$$\hat{\psi} - S^* SE_{\hat{\psi}} < \psi < \hat{\psi} + S^* SE_{\hat{\psi}}$$

where

$$\nu = K - 1$$

and

$$S^* = \sqrt{\chi^2_{\nu:1-\alpha}}$$

Step 4. Reject H_0 if $Z < -S^*$ or if $Z > S^*$, or if the confidence interval does not contain zero.

---

though New York and Detroit are somewhat similar and that they differ, jointly, from Topeka and Seattle. This hypothesis can be tested. For these data,

$$\hat{\psi} = (^{180}\!/_{390}\, \hat{p}_1 + {}^{210}\!/_{390}\, \hat{p}_2) - (^{160}\!/_{310}\, \hat{p}_3 + {}^{150}\!/_{310}\, \hat{p}_4)$$
$$= {}^{295}\!/_{390} - {}^{90}\!/_{310} = 0.4661$$

$$SE^2_{\hat{\psi}} = \left[\left(\frac{180}{390}\right)^2 \frac{\hat{p}_1 \hat{q}_1}{N_1} + \left(\frac{210}{390}\right)^2 \frac{\hat{p}_2 \hat{q}_2}{N_2} \right]$$
$$+ \left[\left(\frac{-160}{310}\right)^2 \frac{\hat{p}_3 \hat{q}_3}{N_3} + \left(\frac{-150}{310}\right)^2 \frac{\hat{p}_4 \hat{q}_4}{N_4} \right]$$
$$= 0.001095$$

Table 28-2. The six post hoc comparisons among the response proportions of Table 28-1.

Comparison	Differences in proportions $\psi = p_k - p_{k'}$	Value of $SE_{\hat{\psi}} = \sqrt{\dfrac{\hat{p}_k \hat{q}_k}{N_k} + \dfrac{\hat{p}_{k'} \hat{q}_{k'}}{N_{k'}}}$	Value of $Z_{p_k - p_{k'}}$
1 vs. 2	−0.1666	0.0435	−3.83
1 vs. 3	0.2917	0.0520	5.61
1 vs. 4	0.4667	0.0480	9.72
2 vs. 3	0.4583	0.0469	9.77
2 vs. 4	0.6333	0.0424	14.94
3 vs. 4	0.1750	0.0510	3.43

and

$$Z = \frac{\hat{\psi}}{SE_{\hat{\psi}}} = \frac{0.4661}{0.0331} = 14.08$$

The suspicion has been supported. New York and Detroit, taken collectively, differ from Topeka and Seattle, taken collectively. A contrast like the one just examined is referred to as a *complex contrast.* Whereas the number of *pairwise* contrasts is limited to $C = \binom{K}{2}$, the number of complex contrasts is exceedingly large.

Other hypotheses could be generated. There are an infinity of them. Most don't make any sense. In fact, we can find no other meaningful questions to ask of these data.

28-2. POST HOC AND A PRIORI MULTIPLE COMPARISONS

The method described in Section 28-1 is referred to as a *post hoc method of multiple comparisons,* since it is embarked upon following the rejection of an omnibus hypothesis. It is not employed if H_0 is not rejected. While it is an important method, it has one drawback: it distributes the risk of a type I error over an infinite set of contrasts, for which only a small number are meaningful and interpretable. Thus, it is wasteful in how it uses α, the risk of a type I error.

This limitation prompted another look at the problem by Dunn. She reasoned that if one could *count* the number of comparisons and hypotheses to test before one collected data, one should be able to distribute the risk of a type I error among the contrasts of direct interest. For example, suppose one wished to test five contrasts and hold the risk of committing at least one type I error in the set equal to .05. Dunn suggested doing each test at $^{.05}\!/_5 = .01$ and using the following for the decision rule:

Decision Rule: Reject H_0 if $Z < Z_{.005} = -2.58$

or if $Z > Z_{.995} = +2.58$

The method makes sense, and it is statistically sound and easy to use. The critical values appear in Table A-11. For contingency-table data, the appropriate critical values are listed in the column headed ∞, which lists the appropriate values derived from the normal distribution. Thus, for $C = 5$ contrasts we read, for $\alpha = .05$, the value 2.58. Note that under this model a type I error is said to occur if 1, 2, 3, 4, or more type I errors are made. Thus, the method is said to control the probability of committing at least one type I error.

Because the method is based upon an a priori identification of interesting contrasts, no omnibus test is performed. In addition, the procedure is performed assuming the truth of the omnibus null hypothesis. As an example, assume we are interested only in the pairwise comparisons, and consider the data for New York and Detroit. A comparison of the proportions for these two cities would test the hypothesis

$$H_0:\quad p_1 = p_2$$

Because this study involves four samples and because we wish to compare the four cities, whether through pairwise contrasts or more complex ones, the estimation of $\bar{p}$ must be based on all four samples. For the four cities of the study:

$$\bar{p} = \frac{120 + 175 + 60 + 30}{180 + 210 + 160 + 150} = \frac{385}{700} = .55$$

This estimate, along with $\bar{q} = 1 - \bar{p} = 1 - .55 = .45$, is used in each of the $\binom{4}{2} = 6$ pairwise tests. Thus, for the New York–Detroit comparison:

$$Z_{p_1-p_2} = \frac{\dfrac{120}{180} - \dfrac{175}{210}}{\sqrt{\dfrac{(.55)(.45)}{180} + \dfrac{(.55)(.45)}{210}}}$$

$$= \frac{0.6667 - 0.8333}{\sqrt{0.0025536}} = \frac{-0.1666}{0.0505} = -3.30$$

The remaining five tests are summarized in Table 28-3. With $\alpha = .05, C = 6$.

Table 28-3. The six a priori pairwise comparisons among the response proportions of Table 28-1.

Comparison	Difference in proportions $p_k - p_{k'}$	Value of $\sqrt{\dfrac{\overline{pq}}{N_k} + \dfrac{\overline{pq}}{N_{k'}}}$	Value of $Z_{p_k - p_{k'}}$
1 vs. 2	−0.1666	0.0505	−3.30
1 vs. 3	0.2917	0.0541	5.39
1 vs. 4	0.4667	0.0550	8.49
2 vs. 3	0.4583	0.0522	8.78
2 vs. 4	0.6333	0.0532	11.90
3 vs. 4	0.1750	0.0565	3.10

and $v = \infty$, Table A-11 is entered to find the critical value of 2.64. The decision rule for each test is given as follows:

Decision Rule: Reject H_0 if $Z_{p_k - p_{k'}} < -2.64$ or if $Z_{p_k - p_{k'}} > 2.64$

Since -3.30 is less than -2.64, we reject the H_0 involving New York and Detroit. More PTA officers in Detroit agree with the question than do those of New York. In addition, we see that each of the cities seems to differ from all of the others in responses to the question. We provide directions for this procedure in Box 28-2.

Notice the similarity in the Z values between the *a priori* and *post hoc* methods. The important difference between the two methods is in the critical values. For the post hoc method the critical values are given by $S^* = \pm 2.79$, whereas for the a priori method the critical values are given by $Z = \pm 2.64$. Thus, the a priori method has a greater chance of rejecting the hypotheses associated with the individual C contrasts of specific interest.

28-3. MULTIPLE COMPARISONS FOR AN $I \times J$ TEST OF HOMOGENEITY

The procedure described in Section 28-2 is not restricted to a dichotomous response variable. Suppose the following question had been asked of the citizens:

A number of suggestions have been proposed to reduce crime in the streets. Which of the following suggestions do you think will do the most to reduce crime?

Box 28-2   Procedure for performing a priori pairwise comparisons among proportions

Step 1. List the comparisons of interest. Let the number of comparisons be denoted by C.

Step 2. Determine the proportion in each of the samples.

Step 3. Determine the value of $\bar{p}$ and $\bar{q}$, where

$$\bar{p} = \frac{f_{11} + f_{12} + \cdots + f_{1K}}{N_1 + N_2 + \cdots + N_K}$$

for each of the comparisons, and let $\bar{q} = 1 - \bar{p}$.

Step 4. Define each contrast as

$$\psi_c = W_1 p_1 + W_2 p_2 + \cdots + W_K p_K$$

and estimate ψ_c as follows:

$$\hat{\psi}_c = W_1 \hat{p}_1 + W_2 \hat{p}_2 + \cdots + W_K \hat{p}_K$$

with

$$SE^2_{\psi_c} = \bar{p}\bar{q} \left(\frac{W_1^2}{N_1} + \frac{W_2^2}{N_2} + \cdots + \frac{W_K^2}{N_K} \right)$$

Step 5. Test each $H_0 : \psi_c = 0$ with

$$Z_c = \frac{\hat{\psi}_c}{SE_{\hat{\psi}_c}}$$

Step 6. Obtain the decision rule from Table A-11, using:

$$\alpha = \text{probability of a type I error}$$

$$C = \text{number of contrasts}$$

and

$$\nu = \infty$$

Step 7. Make the decisions.

1. Increase police enforcement and criminal penalties.
2. Institute stronger handgun control laws.
3. Legalize heroin and other drugs.
4. Other.

In this example, the proportions of response in each of the response categories can be compared between cities by using the methods of Section 28-2. With the responses shown in Table 28-4, this would mean that we can compare the cities for the proportion of responses within each *row* of the table. Here, there would be 6 pairwise contrasts in each row for a total of 24 contrasts, so that the critical value for a planned analysis would be given by:

$$Z = \pm 3.08 \quad \text{for} \quad \alpha = .05$$

The comparison of New York with Detroit in row 1 is given as follows:

$$Z_{p_{11}-p_{12}} = \frac{100/180 - 80/210}{\sqrt{1/180 \, (280/700)(420/700) + 1/210 \, (280/700)(420/700)}}$$

$$= \frac{0.1746}{0.0498} = 3.51$$

New York and Detroit differ in their views concerning increased enforcement and penalties. Remaining comparisons are reported in Table 28-5. We provide directions for this procedure in Box 28-3.

In addition, we could have been interested in testing contrasts that cut across rows. If so, such contrasts must be included in the value of C. For example, the comparison of New York with Detroit with rows 1 and 2 combined is given by

$$\hat{\psi} = (\hat{p}_{11} + \hat{p}_{21}) - (\hat{p}_{12} + \hat{p}_{22})$$

Table 28-4. Response to the question "Which suggestions do you think will do the most to reduce crime in the street?"

Response	New York	Detroit	Topeka	Seattle	Total
1	100	80	30	70	280
2	50	90	70	20	230
3	10	30	20	20	80
4	20	10	40	40	110
Total	180	210	160	150	700

Table 28-5. All possible pairwise comparisons for the data of Table 28-4.

Row	Cities	Comparison	Standard error under H_0	$Z_{p_{ij}-p_{ij'}}$ under H_0	Standard error under H_1	$Z_{p_{ij}-p_{ij'}}$ under H_1
1	1–2	0.1746	0.0498	3.51[a]	0.0499	3.50
	1–3	0.3681	0.0532	6.92[a]	0.0482	7.64[b]
	1–4	0.0889	0.0542	1.64	0.0551	1.61
	2–3	0.1935	0.0514	3.76[a]	0.0456	4.25[b]
	2–4	−0.0857	0.0524	−1.64	0.0527	−1.63
	3–4	−0.2792	0.0557	−5.01[a]	0.0511	−5.46[b]
2	1–2	−0.1508	0.0477	−3.16[a]	0.0478	−3.16
	1–3	−0.1597	0.0510	−3.13[a]	0.0515	−3.10
	1–4	0.1445	0.0519	2.78	0.0434	3.33
	2–3	−0.0089	0.0493	−0.18	0.0520	−0.17
	2–4	0.2953	0.0502	5.88[a]	0.0440	6.71[b]
	3–4	0.3042	0.0533	5.71[a]	0.0480	6.33[b]
3	1–2	−0.0873	0.0323	−2.70	0.0296	−2.95
	1–3	−0.0694	0.0346	−2.01	0.0349	−1.99
	1–4	−0.0777	0.0352	−2.21	0.0326	−2.38
	2–3	0.0179	0.0334	0.54	0.0389	0.46
	2–4	0.0096	0.0340	0.28	0.0368	0.26
	3–4	−0.0083	0.0362	−0.23	0.0412	−0.20
4	1–2	0.0635	0.0370	1.72	0.0276	2.30
	1–3	−0.1389	0.0395	−3.52[a]	0.0415	−3.35
	1–4	−0.1556	0.0402	−3.87[a]	0.0430	−3.62
	2–3	−0.2024	0.0382	−5.30[a]	0.0373	−5.43[b]
	2–4	−0.2191	0.0389	−5.63[a]	0.0390	−5.62[b]
	3–4	−0.0167	0.0414	−0.40	0.0498	−0.34

[a] Significant at $\alpha \leq .05$, critical value equals ± 3.08.
[b] Significant post hoc at $\alpha \leq .05$, critical value equals ± 4.11.

Note that:

$$\hat{p}_{NY} = \hat{p}_{11} + \hat{p}_{21} = \text{proportion of people in New York who chose response categories 1 or 2}$$

In like manner,

$$\hat{p}_{D} = \hat{p}_{12} + \hat{p}_{22} = \text{corresponding proportion of people in Detroit who chose response categories 1 or 2}$$

For the data,

$$\hat{p}_{11} + \hat{p}_{21} = {}^{100}/_{180} + {}^{50}/_{180} = {}^{150}/_{180}$$

Box 28-3   Procedure for performing a row-by-row a priori multiple pairwise comparison investigation in an $I \times J$ test of homogeneity

Step 1. Count the total number of comparisons of interest for the complete $I \times J$ table. Denote this number by C.

Step 2. Consider the frequencies in row 1. Call them $f_{11}, f_{12}, \ldots, f_{1J}$. Convert them to proportions by defining $\hat{p}_{11} = f_{11}/N_1$, $\hat{p}_{12} = f_{12}/N_2$, $\ldots$, $\hat{p}_{1J} = f_{1J}/N_J$.

Step 3. Determine the value of $\bar{p}_1$ for row 1:

$$\bar{p}_1 = \frac{f_{11} + f_{12} + \cdots + f_{1J}}{N_1 + N_2 + \cdots + N_J} = \frac{f_{1.}}{N}$$

and $\bar{q}_1 = 1 - \bar{p}_1$.

Step 4. For the contrasts based on the first row, complete steps 4 and 5 of Box 28-2.

Step 5. Repeat steps 1 through 4 for the remaining rows in the table.

Step 6. Obtain the decision rule from Table A-11, using as parameters:

$$\alpha = \text{probability of a type I error}$$

$$C = \text{total number of contrasts of interest for the table}$$

and

$$\nu = \infty$$

Step 7. Make the decisions.

---

and

$$\hat{p}_{12} + \hat{p}_{22} = {}^{80}\!/\!{}_{210} + {}^{90}\!/\!{}_{210} = {}^{170}\!/\!{}_{210}$$

The squared standard error for $\hat{\psi}$ is given by

$$SE_{\hat{\psi}}^2 = \frac{1}{N_1} (\bar{p}_{1.} + \bar{p}_{2.})[1 - (\bar{p}_{1.} + \bar{p}_{2.})] + \frac{1}{N_2} (\bar{p}_{1.} + \bar{p}_{2.})[1 - (\bar{p}_{1.} + \bar{p}_{2.})]$$

where

$$\bar{p}_{1.} = \frac{f_{1.}}{N} \qquad \text{and} \qquad \bar{p}_{2.} = \frac{f_{2.}}{N}$$

For the data of Table 28-4, the contrast comparing New York with Detroit combining responses 1 and 2 is given by

$$\hat{\psi} = (^{100}/_{180} + {}^{50}/_{180}) - (^{80}/_{210} + {}^{90}/_{210}) = {}^{150}/_{180} - {}^{170}/_{210} = 0.0238$$

with

$$SE_{\hat{\psi}}^2 = {}^{1}/_{180}(^{510}/_{700})(^{190}/_{700}) + {}^{1}/_{210}(^{510}/_{700})(^{190}/_{700})$$
$$= 0.00204$$

so that

$$Z = \frac{\hat{\psi}}{SE_{\hat{\psi}}} = \frac{0.0238}{\sqrt{0.00204}} = \frac{0.0238}{0.0452} = 0.53$$

Truly, the homogeneity model is a very complicated model. To reject H_0 is generally not sufficient. The reasons for the rejection are of paramount interest. As indicated, finding the reason may not be simple. By examining contrasts, the reasons can be found.

Sometimes a researcher does not know which contrasts to examine and which to ignore. In this case, a post hoc analysis must be performed with the

---

Box 28-4   Procedure for performing post hoc multiple comparisons in an $I \times J$ contingency table for a test of homogeneity

Step 1. Perform the test of homogeneity using X^2.

Step 2. If H_0 is not rejected, do not perform an analysis on any contrast. If H_0 is rejected, define contrasts of interest in row i as

$$\hat{\psi} = W_1 \hat{p}_{i1} + W_2 \hat{p}_{i2} + \cdots + W_J \hat{p}_{iJ}$$

Determine:

$$SE_{\hat{\psi}}^2 = W_1^2 \frac{\hat{p}_{i1}\hat{q}_{i1}}{N_1} + W_2^2 \frac{\hat{p}_{i2}\hat{q}_{i2}}{N_2} + \cdots + W_J^2 \frac{\hat{p}_{iJ}\hat{q}_{iJ}}{N_J}$$

and reject H_0 if

$$Z = \frac{\hat{\psi}}{SE_{\hat{\psi}}}$$

is less than $-S^*$ or greater than $+S^*$, where $S^* = \sqrt{\chi_{\nu:1-\alpha}^2}$, and where $\nu = (I-1)(J-1)$.

Z values read from Table A-11 replaced by $S^* = \sqrt{\chi^2_{\nu:1-\alpha}}$, where $\nu =$ the number of degrees of freedom for the omnibus test. Directions for this model are given in Box 28-4, and post hoc results for the 24 pairwise contrasts are indicated in Table 28-5.

We repeat that contrasts can be defined for combined rows. For those that are, the described procedure is valid except that the formula for SE^2_{ψ} is slightly more complex and is not amenable to a simple representation. For the combined-rows comparison of New York and Detroit, we could write the squared standard error as follows for a post hoc contrast:

$$SE^2_{\psi} = \hat{p}_{NY}\hat{q}_{NY}/N_{NY} + \hat{p}_{D}\hat{q}_{D}/N_{D}$$

28-4. EXERCISES

28-1. Perform a planned analysis with $\alpha = .05$ on the data of Exercise 23-7. Let the contrasts of interest be the following:

$$\psi_1 = p_{hetero} - p_{bi}$$

$$\psi_2 = p_{hetero} - p_{homo}$$

$$\psi_3 = p_{bi} - p_{homo}$$

28-2. Use the contrasts of Exercise 28-1 and carry out a post hoc analysis. Compare the two studies.

28-3. How many pairwise comparisons can be generated for the data of Exercise 27-4? What are the critical values for $\alpha = .05$? What are the critical values for a post hoc analysis? How many contrasts could one do in a planned analysis before the Dunn critical value exceeded the Scheffé critical value?

28-4. Compare the four status groups of Exercise 27-4 on response (3 or more) using pairwise contrasts and:
   a. The planned critical value of Exercise 28-3
   b. The post hoc critical value of Exercise 28-3

CHAPTER 29

Statistical Methods for Correlated Proportions

29-1. CORRELATED QUALITATIVE MEASURES

Up to now our discussion of contingency tables has dealt with cases where each individual is included in the table only once. That is somewhat restricting, because many studies entail two measurements made at different times or at the same time. We've already seen examples where the sign test or the matched-pair Wilcoxon test was used in cases where measurements were taken before and after treatment or where matched pairs were established prior to data collection. As an example of where one could obtain correlated measures on a dichotomous dependent variable, consider a study in which $N = 200$ Asian students are asked in the ninth grade and again when they are in the twelfth grade to respond to the questionnaire item:

The most important qualities of a husband are determination and ambition. True (1) or False (0)

Results might appear as shown in Table 29-1. The observant reader immediately sees that something is wrong, because the total sample size appears to be 400 instead of 200. The problem is that each student is counted twice: once at time 1 and again at time 2.

The way the data are presented clouds the fact that the individual subject responses are correlated. For example, a student who says "true" at time 1 is

Table 29-1. Responses by 200 Asian students to the item "The most important qualities of a husband are determination and ambition." True (1) or False (0). Repeated at two time periods.

| | Time | | |
Response	1	2	Total
True (1)	110	82	192
False (0)	90	118	208
Total	200	200	400

Table 29-2. Responses by 200 Asian students to the item "The most important qualities of a husband are determination and ambition." True (1) or False (0). Repeated at two time periods.

Subject	Time 1	Time 2
1	True (1)	True (1)
2	False (0)	True (1)
3	True (1)	True (1)
⋮	⋮	⋮
200	True (1)	False (0)
Total (true)	110	82
Total (false)	90	118
Total	200	200

expected to say "true" at time 2, unless some attitude change has been introduced in three or more years of high school instruction. The responses are truly representative of matched-pair data and should be reported as shown in Table 29-2. Clearly, presentation of the data in this form is cumbersome. Fortunately, the data can be presented in a compact form that is easy to interpret and comprehend; such a form is shown in Table 29-3. The frequency of (1, 1) responses is tabulated, as are the remaining frequencies, those for the response sets (0, 1), (1, 0), and (0, 0). With this tabulation and the notation of Table 29-4, we now see that the marginal totals of 110 and 82 are the ones of interest, for $\hat{p}_{1.} = {}^{110}\!/_{200} = .55$ and $\hat{p}_{.1} = {}^{82}\!/_{200} = .41$ measure the proportion of students who report "true" at time 1 and time 2, respectively. If these students experienced no change in attitude over time, we would find that $\hat{\Delta} = \hat{p}_{1.} - \hat{p}_{.1} = 0$; however, in this case, $\hat{\Delta} = .55 - .41 = .14$, indicating that some of the students have made a shift in attitude to "false." Our immediate problem is to determine whether the shift is significantly

Table 29-3. The McNemar contingency table for a dichotomous variable measured at two points in time.

	Time 2		
Time 1	True (1)	False (0)	Total
True (1)	60	50	110
False (0)	22	68	90
Total	82	118	200

Table 29-4. The frequency distribution for a 2×2 McNemar table for testing $H_0: p_{.1} = p_{1.}$ or $H_0: p_{10} = p_{01}$, where $N = f_{01} + f_{10}$.

	Time 2		
Time 1	1	0	Total
1	f_{11}	f_{10}	$f_{1.}$
0	f_{01}	f_{00}	$f_{0.}$
Total	$f_{.1}$	$f_{.0}$	N

different from zero. This decision is made by performing the McNemar test for correlated proportions.

29-2. THE McNEMAR TEST FOR CORRELATED PROPORTIONS

The statistical theory for the McNemar test for correlated proportions is quite simple. Note that the proportion of subjects who choose 1 at time 1 is $\hat{p}_{1.} = f_{1.}/N$ and the proportion of subjects who choose 1 at time 2 is $\hat{p}_{.1} = f_{.1}/N$. If there has been no change in attitude, we would expect to find that $\hat{p}_{.1}$ is approximately equal to $\hat{p}_{1.}$. The McNemar hypothesis is therefore best stated thus:

$$H_0: \quad p_{.1} = p_{1.}$$

If H_0 is true, the proportion of "true" responses is the same at time 1 and time 2. That is, H_0 involves the marginal identity of distributions.

Again, consider the 2×2 frequency data and note that $f_{.1} = f_{11} + f_{01}$ and that $f_{1.} = f_{11} + f_{10}$. If, in the sample, we were to note that $\hat{p}_{.1} = \hat{p}_{1.}$, then it would follow that

$$\hat{p}_{.1} = \frac{f_{11}}{N} + \frac{f_{01}}{N} = \frac{f_{11}}{N} + \frac{f_{10}}{N} = \hat{p}_{1.}$$

so that

$$\frac{f_{01}}{N} = \frac{f_{10}}{N}$$

or so that

$$\hat{p}_{01} = \hat{p}_{10}$$

This indicates that the proportion who change from response 0 at time 1 to response 1 at time 2 is equal to the proportion who change from response 1 at time 1 to response 0 at time 2. Clearly, if these proportions are equal, then the distributions of 1 and 0 at time 1 and time 2 must be identical. In addition, we also see that $\hat{p}_{.1}$ and $\hat{p}_{1.}$ must be correlated proportions, since they both involve $f_{11}/N = \hat{p}_{11}$. If $\hat{p}_{11}$ is large, $\hat{p}_{.1}$ and $\hat{p}_{1.}$ must be large, whereas if $\hat{p}_{11}$ is small, $\hat{p}_{.1}$ and $\hat{p}_{1.}$ must be small. For this reason, the McNemar test is often called a test of correlated proportions.

If we write the null hypothesis as

$$H_0: \quad \Delta = p_{.1} - p_{1.} = 0$$

then we can form a test statistic based upon the sample estimator

$$\hat{\Delta} = \hat{p}_{.1} - \hat{p}_{1.}$$

if we know $E(\hat{\Delta})$ and $\text{Var}(\hat{\Delta})$. Under H_0, $E(\hat{\Delta}) = p_{.1} - p_{1.} = 0$. It can be shown that

$$\text{Var}(\hat{\Delta}) = \frac{1}{N}\left[(p_{01} + p_{10}) - (p_{01} - p_{10})^2\right]$$

Under H_0, this reduces to

$$\text{Var}(\hat{\Delta}) = \frac{1}{N}(p_{01} + p_{10})$$

so that we would have

$$Z = \frac{\hat{p}_{.1} - \hat{p}_{1.}}{\sqrt{\dfrac{1}{N}(p_{01} + p_{10})}} = \frac{\hat{p}_{01} - \hat{p}_{10}}{\sqrt{\dfrac{1}{N}(p_{01} + p_{10})}}$$

Since p_{01} and p_{10} are not known, $\hat{p}_{01}$ and $\hat{p}_{10}$ are substituted for them in the test statistic. When we make this substitution and simplify the formula, we have as a test statistic

$$Z = \frac{f_{01} - f_{10}}{\sqrt{f_{01} + f_{10}}}$$

For our example:

$$Z = \frac{50 - 22}{\sqrt{50 + 22}} = 3.30$$

Since this is in the rejection region defined by $Z < -1.96$ and $Z > 1.96$, H_0 is rejected.

We now provide directions for obtaining a $1 - \alpha$ percent confidence interval for $\Delta = p_{.1} - p_{1.}$. We estimate Δ by $\hat{\Delta} = .14$. In addition:

$$SE_{\hat{\Delta}}^2 = \frac{1}{N}\left[(\hat{p}_{01} + \hat{p}_{10}) - (\hat{p}_{01} - \hat{p}_{10})^2\right]$$

For our data,

$$SE_{\hat{\Delta}}^2 = \frac{1}{200}\left[\frac{50}{200} + \frac{22}{200} - \left(\frac{50}{200} - \frac{22}{200}\right)^2\right] = .001702$$

so that

$$SE_{\hat{\Delta}} = \sqrt{.001702} = .0413$$

Box 29-1   Directions for the McNemar test of correlated proportions

Step 1. Set up the contingency table shown in Table 29-4.
Step 2. Determine the values of

$$\hat{p}_{01} = \frac{f_{01}}{N} \quad \text{and} \quad \hat{p}_{10} = \frac{f_{10}}{N}$$

Step 3. Determine the value

$$Z = \frac{f_{01} - f_{10}}{\sqrt{f_{01} + f_{10}}}$$

Step 4. Reject H_0 if $Z < Z_{\alpha/2}$ or if $Z > Z_{1-\alpha/2}$.
Step 5. If H_0 is rejected, determine the $1 - \alpha$ percent confidence interval as:

$$\Delta = \hat{\Delta} \pm Z_{\alpha/2} SE_{\hat{\Delta}}$$

where

$$\hat{\Delta} = \hat{p}_{.1} - \hat{p}_{1.} = \hat{p}_{01} - \hat{p}_{10}$$

and

$$SE_{\hat{\Delta}}^2 = \frac{1}{N} [(\hat{p}_{01} + \hat{p}_{10} - (\hat{p}_{01} - \hat{p}_{10})^2]$$

where N is the total sample size.

Finally, the 95 percent confidence interval for Δ is given as follows:

$$\Delta = \hat{\Delta} \pm 1.96 \, SE$$
$$= .14 \pm 1.96(.0413)$$
$$= .14 \pm .08$$

Directions for performing the McNemar test of correlated proportions are provided in Box 29.1.

29-3. INTERNAL SYMMETRY AND MARGINAL HOMOGENEITY

The McNemar test can be extended in two different ways. One way is to increase the number of categories from two to three or more. For this extension, two different tests appear: the Bowker test of internal symmetry and the

Table 29-5.   A Bowker contingency table with identical margins and internal changes.

	Time 2			
Time 1	Category 1	Category 2	Category 3	Total
Category 1	10	5	5	20
Category 2	8	6	16	30
Category 3	2	19	29	50
Total	20	30	50	100

Stuart test of marginal homogeneity. A second way to extend the McNemar test is to increase the number of measurements from two to three or more. This extension is called the Cochran Q test. We describe the Bowker test in Section 29-4, Stuart's test in Section 29-5, and the Cochran Q test in Section 42-5.

For the McNemar test the hypotheses

$$H_{01}: \quad p_{01} = p_{10}$$

and

$$H_{02}: \quad p_{.1} = p_{1.}$$

are interchangeable. H_{01} is referred to as a test of deviation from symmetry, and H_{02} as a test of marginal homogeneity. If the probabilities for the *change cells* are equal (i.e., if $p_{01} = p_{10}$), then the *marginal* probabilities must be equal ($p_{.1}$ must be equal to $p_{1.}$). That is not true when the number of categories is three or more. When the categories increase to three or more, two different hypotheses may be tested, because the marginal probabilities can remain the same at time 1 and 2, even though people change their category membership by large degrees. An example is provided in Table 29-5, for which the Bowker test is used to test for internal change. The Stuart test, on the other hand, is a test of homogeneity of marginal probabilities at times 1 and 2.

29-4. THE BOWKER TEST OF INTERNAL CHANGE

For the Bowker extension, suppose the question of Section 29-2 had been:

The most important qualities of a husband are determination and ambition. True (1), I am not sure (2), or False (3) and suppose the results had been as presented in Table 29-6. Note that the subjects in the (1, 1), (2, 2), and (3, 3) cells provide no information about whether the students have made a shift over time. If we look into the 3×3 table, we see that we can generate three 2×2 McNemar tables and can test each for significance. These tables are summarized in Table 29-7. The three

Table 29-6. The Bowker contingency table for a trichotomous variable measured at two points in time.

| | Time 2 | | | |
Time 1	True (1)	Questionable (2)	False (3)	Total
True (1)	50	18	40	108
Questionable (2)	6	22	10	38
False (3)	9	5	40	54
Total	65	45	90	200

Table 29-7. Three McNemar tables that can be generated from Table 29-6 without collapsing categories.

Time 1	Time 2	
	Column 1	Column 2
Row 1	50	18
Row 2	6	22
	Column 1	Column 3
Row 1	50	40
Row 3	9	40
	Column 2	Column 3
Row 2	22	10
Row 3	5	40

large-sample forms of the McNemar statistics for these tables are:

$$Z_{12} = \frac{6 - 18}{\sqrt{6 + 18}} = -2.4495$$

$$Z_{13} = \frac{9 - 40}{\sqrt{9 + 40}} = -4.4286$$

and

$$Z_{23} = \frac{5 - 10}{\sqrt{5 + 10}} = -1.2910$$

The Bowker test examines the three McNemar hypotheses simultaneously. In this case, the hypothesis is

$$H_0: \quad p_{12} = p_{21}$$
$$p_{13} = p_{31}$$
$$p_{23} = p_{32}$$

Continuing with our example, the Bowker test statistic is defined simply as follows:

$$X_B^2 = Z_{12}^2 + Z_{13}^2 + Z_{23}^2$$
$$= \frac{12^2}{24} + \frac{31^2}{49} + \frac{5^2}{15}$$
$$= 6.00 + 19.61 + 1.67$$
$$= 27.28$$

It can be shown that the probability distribution of X_B^2 can be approximated by the chi-square distribution with $v = \binom{K}{2}$, where K is the number of categories. In this case, $v = \binom{3}{2} = 3$, so that the $\alpha = .05$ decision rule for rejecting the hypothesis of no internal change is given by the following:

Decision Rule: Reject H_0 if $X_B^2 \geq \chi_{3:.95}^2 = 7.81$

Thus, H_0 is rejected.

At this point, one would like to know why H_0 has been rejected. One way to make this decision is to examine *all* 2×2 McNemar tables. For this post hoc model, a McNemar table is said to be significant if its Z^2 is larger than $S^2 = \chi_{v:1-\alpha}^2$, or if its Z value is less than $-S$ or greater than $+S$. In this case, $S^2 = 7.81$, so that the table involving rows and columns 1 and 3 is one possible reason for the rejection of H_0.

Table 29-8. Three McNemar tables that can be generated from Table 29-6 by collapsing two rows and two columns together.

	Time 1	
Time 2	Columns 1 and 2	Column 3
Rows 1 and 2	96	50
Row 3	14	40
	Columns 1 and 3	Column 2
Rows 1 and 3	139	23
Row 2	16	22
	Columns 2 and 3	Column 1
Rows 2 and 3	77	15
Row 1	58	50

There are other tables that may be responsible for the rejection, because the Bowker test is an omnibus test of all possible McNemar tables. We have examined only three of them. Three more can be generated by collapsing rows and columns. These tables are shown in Table 29-8. The Z^2 values for these tables are given by:

$$Z^2_{(12)3} = \frac{(14-50)^2}{14+50} = 20.25$$

$$Z^2_{(13)2} = \frac{(16-23)^2}{16+23} = 1.26$$

and

$$Z^2_{(23)1} = \frac{(58-15)^2}{58+15} = 25.33$$

Thus, we conclude that the tables based on rows (1 and 2) with 3 and rows (2 and 3) with 1 also can be used to explain the statistically significant findings. As indicated, the three major changes are those associated with:

1. 40 subjects who said "true" at time 1 and "false" at time 2
2. 50 subjects who said "true" or "questionable" at time 1 and "false" at time 2
3. 58 subjects who said "true" at time 1 and "questionable" or "false" at time 2

In short, it seems that students changed from a general position of "true" at time 1 to a general position of "false" at time 2.

When N is large, the test statistic can be written as:

$$X_B^2 = \sum_{k=1} \sum_{k'=1} \frac{(f_{kk'} - f_{k'k})^2}{f_{kk'} + f_{k'k}} \qquad k < k'$$

The assumptions for the Bowker test are identical to those of the McNemar test. Each pair of observations at times 1 and 2 is independent of all other observations. Directions for performing the Bowker test are provided in Box 29-2.

Box 29-2   Procedure for the Bowker test

Step 1. To test the hypothesis

$$H_0: \quad p_{kk'} = p_{k'k}$$

set up all $v = \binom{K}{2}$ 2×2 McNemar tables.

Step 2. For each of the v tables compute

$$Z_{kk'} = \frac{f_{kk'} - f_{k'k}}{\sqrt{f_{kk'} + f_{k'k}}}$$

Step 3. Determine the value of the Bowker statistic

$$X_B^2 = \sum_k \sum_{k'} Z_{kk'}^2$$

Step 4. Reject the hypothesis of no internal change if

$$X_B^2 \geq \chi_{v:1-\alpha}^2$$

Step 5. If H_0 is rejected, examine all 2×2 McNemar tables that can be generated from the $K \times K$ contingency table by computing the Z^2 values. A significant difference is said to exist if

$$Z^2 \geq S^2 = \chi_{v:1-\alpha}^2$$

29-5. THE STUART TEST OF MARGINAL HOMOGENEITY

The test statistic of the Stuart test of marginal homogeneity has a complicated structure and requires knowledge of matrix algebra for its determination. Since a knowledge of matrix algebra is not a requirement for the use of this book, we do not provide a formula for the test statistic.

Since the marginal homogeneity hypothesis under test for a $K \times K$ contingency table is:

$$p_{1.} = p_{.1}$$

$$p_{2.} = p_{.2}$$

$$H_0: \qquad \vdots \qquad \vdots$$

$$p_{K.} = p_{.K}$$

the procedure we present is based upon a planned repeated use of the model associated with the McNemar test applied to each corresponding pair of marginal frequencies. For the kth category, the test statistic is given by

$$Z = \frac{\hat{p}_{k.} - \hat{p}_{.k}}{SE_{\hat{p}_{k.} - \hat{p}_{.k}}}$$

In Section 29-1, we presented the standard error for the McNemar sample statistic $\hat{\Delta}$. In the Stuart model, the standard error is given by

$$SE^2_{\hat{p}_{k.} - \hat{p}_{.k}} = \frac{1}{N}(\hat{p}_{k.} + \hat{p}_{.k} - 2\hat{p}_{kk})$$

To perform the test for the kth category, we compare

$$Z = \frac{\hat{p}_{k.} - \hat{p}_{.k}}{\sqrt{\frac{1}{N}(\hat{p}_{k.} + \hat{p}_{.k} - 2\hat{p}_{kk})}}$$

with the value read from Table A-11 for $C = K$ and $df = \infty$. For the data of Table 29-6, we have

$$Z_1 = \frac{108/200 - 65/200}{\sqrt{1/200\,[108/200 + 65/200 - 2(50/200)]}} = \frac{0.215}{0.0427} = 5.03$$

In like manner:

$$Z_2 = \frac{0.035}{0.0312} = 1.12 \qquad \text{and} \qquad Z_3 = \frac{-0.180}{0.040} = -4.50$$

Box 29-3   Procedure for Stuart's test of marginal homogeneity

Step 1. For each value of k, compute:

$$Z_k = \frac{\hat{p}_{k.} - \hat{p}_{.k}}{\sqrt{\frac{1}{N}(\hat{p}_{k.} + \hat{p}_{.k} - 2\hat{p}_{kk})}}$$

with the critical value Z read from Table A-11 for $C = K$ and df $= \infty$.

Step 2. Conclude that $p_{k.}$ does not equal $p_{.k}$ if Z_k exceeds the critical value in absolute magnitude.

With $K = 3$, we find in Table A-11 that the rejection region is given by $Z < -2.39$ or $Z > 2.39$. There is a significant change between "true" at time 1 and "true" at time 2. About 22 percent fewer subjects find the proposition true at time 2. There is also a significant change between "false" at time 1 and "false" at time 2. About 18 percent more of the subjects report "false" at time 2.

Directions for a planned investigation of Stuart's test of marginal homogeneity are presented in Box 29-3. The assumptions for the test are identical to those of the McNemar and Bowker tests. The pairs of observations between subjects are independent, whereas the paired observations for each subject are thought to be correlated.

29-6. INTERPRETING SIGNIFICANT FINDINGS IN THE BOWKER AND STUART TESTS

The variables of the Bowker and Stuart tests are assumed to be unordered. These tests are not optimum for detecting a shift in direction if the categories of the dependent variable are ordered, as are those encountered in attitude measures (strongly agree, agree, disagree, strongly disagree). For ordered categories, the matched-pair Wilcoxon test can be used to test for identity in marginal distributions.

The Bowker test can show statistically significant changes from one category to another category from time 1 to time 2 even when there is no change in the marginal distributions. This situation is illustrated in Table 29-5. The reverse case cannot occur. If there is no internal change, there can be no marginal change.

For the data of Table 29-6, the Stuart test results show that the proportion responding "false" has increased over time. It does not allow us to say where the initial "true" responses went, nor does it tell us from where the subsequent "false" responders came. The Bowker test results allow us to conclude that there are more people shifting from "true" to "questionable" than from "questionable" to "true" and from "true" to "false" than from "false" to "true." Hence, the greatest movement involves those who responded "true" initially. These people moved both to "questionable" and to "false," but only the "false" proportion has been significantly increased. From this example, we see that both tests should be performed in order to best understand the nature of the changes occurring.

29-7. EXERCISES

29-1. In addition to the Asian Students, the study of Table 29-3 also included a sample of blacks, whites, and others. The statistics for these three groups are as follows:

		Blacks		Whites		Others	
Time 2	Time 1	(1)	(0)	(1)	(0)	(1)	(0)
(1)		72	30	243	112	148	63
(0)		30	41	208	381	57	64

    a. Perform each of the McNemar tests at $\alpha = .05$.

    b. Examine each of the four sets of data at $\alpha = \frac{1}{4}(.05) = .0125$.

    c. Which model would you recommend: a or b? Why?

29-2. Compare the Asians with the blacks by examining the following confidence interval:

$$\psi = [(\hat{p}_{.1} - \hat{p}_{1.})_A - (\hat{p}_{.1} - \hat{p}_{1.})_B]$$

$$\pm \; Z_{\alpha/2} \sqrt{SE^2_{\hat{\Delta}_A} + SE^2_{\hat{\Delta}_B}}$$

29-3. Make all pairwise comparisons for the four ethnic groups, using the model of Exercise 29-2. Test each contrast at $\alpha = .05/C$, where C equals the number of contrasts.

29-4. Suppose that the study of Table 29-6 also includes a sample of whites and that the data for the whites are as follows:

		Time 2			
Time 1	(1)	(2)	(3)	Total
(1)	133	61	216	410
(2)	40	67	53	160
(3)	37	189	153	379
Total	210	317	422	949

    a. Apply the Bowker test to these data.

    b. Make a post hoc analysis of the data.

29-5. Use the model of Exercise 29-2 and compare internal change of the Asians with the whites. Use a total $\alpha = .05$.

29-6. Apply the Stuart test to the data of Exercise 29-4.

29-7. Apply the model of Exercise 29-2 to compare marginal change of the Asians with the whites for the data of Exercise 29-4. Use a total $\alpha = .05$.

CHAPTER 30

The Sampling Distribution of S_Y^2 and S_Y

30-1. THE SAMPLING DISTRIBUTION OF S_Y^2

In Chapter 25, we presented the chi-square distribution. The distribution itself serves a very important role in a great number of statistical procedures where the underlying variable has a normal distribution. We will examine chi-square-distributed variables in that context.

Suppose we have a random sample of size N from a normally distributed population with mean μ_Y and variance σ_Y^2. For each of the observations Y_i, we can compute a standard score

$$Z_{Y_i} = \frac{Y_i - \mu_Y}{\sigma_Y}$$

If we now square the Z scores and add them, we have a variable

$$\chi_N^2 = Z_1^2 + Z_2^2 + \cdots + Z_N^2$$

$$= \sum_{i=1}^{N} \frac{(Y_i - \mu_Y)^2}{\sigma_Y^2}$$

which has a χ^2 distribution with N degrees of freedom.

In the appendix to this chapter we show that the distribution of the sample variance is related to that of a chi-square variable. In particular it is shown that

$$\chi_{N-1}^2 = \frac{(N-1)S_Y^2}{\sigma_Y^2}$$

As an example of how the chi-square distribution is used, assume that a population variance is known to equal 100. What is the probability that a sample of size 11 drawn from this population at random will have a variance greater than 160? We know that $(N-1)S_Y^2/\sigma_Y^2$ has a chi-square distribution with $\nu = 11 - 1 = 10$. Substituting the values of N, S_Y^2, and σ_Y^2 into the formula, we find that

$$\chi_{N-1}^2 = \frac{(N-1)S_Y^2}{\sigma_Y^2} = \frac{(11-1)160}{100} = 16$$

By entering the chi-square table (Table A-10) with 10 degrees of freedom, we find that the probability of getting a value less than 16 is as follows:

$$P(\chi_{10}^2 < 16) = .90$$

so that only 10 percent of the time would we expect a sample variance of 160 or larger.

30-2. THE USE OF CHI-SQUARE AS A TEST STATISTIC

As mentioned in Section 25-1, if we know the distribution of a variable of interest, we can set up a test statistic whose observed values can be compared with tabled percentile values to determine whether or not any observed value is likely or unlikely. In the present case, the value of $(N-1)S_Y^2/\sigma_Y^2$ can be used as such a test statistic and compared with the chi-square distribution. When $(N-1)S_Y^2$ is much larger than a hypothesized σ_Y^2 value, the ratio of the two is large; when $(N-1)S_Y^2$ is much smaller than σ_Y^2, the ratio is small. Most of the time, we would expect $(N-1)S_Y^2/\sigma_Y^2$ to lie close to $(N-1)$, which is the mean of a χ_{N-1}^2 variable. These insights can be used to test whether a sample is likely to have come from a population with a particular hypothesized variance. For a two-tailed test, we set up the hypotheses of interest as

$$H_0: \quad \sigma_Y^2 = \sigma_0^2$$

and

$$H_1: \quad \sigma_Y^2 \neq \sigma_0^2$$

To examine this H_0 with a 5 percent risk of a type I error, we enter a chi-square table with $v = N - 1$ and find the .025 and .975 percentile values. Then, if our sample comes from the hypothesized population, we expect the test statistic to lie between $\chi_{.025}^2$ and $\chi_{.975}^2$ approximately 95 percent of the time. If, on the other hand, our sample variance is so large that $(N-1)S_Y^2/\sigma_0^2$ exceeds $\chi_{N-1:.975}^2$, or is so small that the test statistic is less than $\chi_{N-1:.025}^2$, we conclude that the sample comes from a population whose variance does not equal σ_0^2. Our decision rule is then given as follows:

$$\text{Decision Rule:} \quad \text{Reject } H_0 \text{ if } \frac{(N-1)S_Y^2}{\sigma_0^2} > \chi_{N-1:.975}^2$$

$$\text{or if } \frac{(N-1)S_Y^2}{\sigma_0^2} < \chi_{N-1:.025}^2$$

We see that this procedure is essentially the same as those we examined in Section 25-1, where we compared test statistics with the Z distribution. Once we know the appropriate statistical distribution to use, our test statistic and decision rule can be formulated immediately.

As an example, consider a sample of size $N = 19$, drawn from an unspecified population. We wish to test the hypothesis that the population from which the sample is drawn has a variance equal to 30. If the sample variance equals 20, what should be concluded? The hypotheses to be tested are

$$H_0: \quad \sigma_Y^2 = 30$$

and

$$H_1: \quad \sigma_Y^2 \neq 30$$

Here, the test statistic is given by

$$\chi^2 = \frac{(19-1)20}{30} = 12$$

From Table A-10, we find that

$$\chi_{18:.025}^2 = 8.23 \quad \text{and} \quad \chi_{18:.975}^2 = 31.53$$

Since χ^2 is not in either rejection region, we do not reject H_0.

Box 30-1   One-sample procedure for testing H_0: $\sigma_Y^2 = \sigma_0^2$

Step 1. Determine the value of S_Y^2.

Step 2. Compute

$$\chi^2 = \frac{(N-1)S_Y^2}{\sigma_0^2}$$

where σ_0^2 is specified by

$$H_0: \quad \sigma_Y^2 = \sigma_0^2$$

Step 3. For $H_1: \sigma_Y^2 \neq \sigma_0^2$, enter Table A-10 with $v = N - 1$ and $\alpha/2$ and $(1 - \alpha/2)$ to define the rejection rule:

Decision Rule: Reject H_0 if $\chi^2 < \chi^2_{v:\alpha/2}$

or if $\chi^2 > \chi^2_{v:1-\alpha/2}$

For $H_1: \sigma_Y^2 > \sigma_0^2$, enter Table A-10 with $v = N - 1$ and $(1 - \alpha)$ to define the following decision rule:

Decision Rule: Reject H_0 if $\chi^2 > \chi^2_{v:1-\alpha}$

For $H_1: \sigma_Y^2 < \sigma_0^2$, use the following decision rule:

Decision Rule: Reject H_0 if $\chi^2 < \chi^2_{v:\alpha}$

We provide directions for testing the variance of a sample for significance in Box 30-1.

30-3. CONFIDENCE INTERVAL FOR σ_Y^2

In a manner similar to that used in Section 21-4 for the population mean, confidence intervals can be derived for the population variance. From the previous section, we see that 95 percent of the time we expect the test statistic to lie above $\chi^2_{N-1:.025}$ and below $\chi^2_{N-1:.975}$. The two parts of this statement can be written as inequalities. That is, 95 percent of the time we expect

$$\frac{(N-1)S_Y^2}{\sigma_Y^2} < \chi^2_{N-1:.975}$$

and

$$\frac{(N-1)S_Y^2}{\sigma_Y^2} > \chi^2_{N-1:.025}$$

As before, we can turn these inequalities into statements about the unknown population variance σ_Y^2. This gives us

$$\frac{(N-1)S_Y^2}{\chi_{N-1:.975}^2} < \sigma_Y^2$$

and

$$\frac{(N-1)S_Y^2}{\chi_{N-1:.025}^2} > \sigma_Y^2$$

Finally, we combine these last two inequalities into a confidence interval for σ_Y^2. We expect that 95 percent of the time

$$\frac{(N-1)S_Y^2}{\chi_{N-1:.975}^2} < \sigma_Y^2 < \frac{(N-1)S_Y^2}{\chi_{N-1:.025}^2}$$

For the example of Section 30-2, we would have, with $N=19$ and $S_Y^2 = 20$,

$$\frac{(18)20}{31.53} < \sigma_Y^2 < \frac{(18)20}{8.23}$$

$$11.42 < \sigma_Y^2 < 43.74$$

Notice that the hypothesized variance equal to 30 is included in this region, so we would not reject the previous null hypothesis. In addition, however, the confidence interval tells us the entire range of values for the variance of the population from which we think our sample is likely to have been drawn.

We provide directions for obtaining a $1 - \alpha$ percent confidence interval for a population variance in Box 30-2.

Box 30-2   Procedure for obtaining a $1 - \alpha$ percent confidence interval for σ_Y^2

Step 1. Determine S_Y^2.

Step 2. In Table A-10, find the values of

$$\chi_{N-1:\alpha/2}^2 \qquad \text{and} \qquad \chi_{N-1:1-\alpha/2}^2$$

Step 3. Determine the limits of the interval:

$$\frac{(N-1)S_Y^2}{\chi_{N-1:1-\alpha/2}^2} < \sigma_Y^2 < \frac{(N-1)S_Y^2}{\chi_{N-1:\alpha/2}^2}$$

30-4. PROPERTIES OF THE SAMPLING DISTRIBUTIONS OF S_Y^2 AND S_Y

We will illustrate in this section two important properties of sample measures of variability. We will show that S_Y^2 is an unbiased estimate of σ_Y^2, meaning that, on the average, S_Y^2 provides an estimate of σ_Y^2 that is on target. At the

Table 30-1. All possible samples of size 2 that can be generated from the population 1, 3, 4, 6, 7, and 9 for sampling with replacement.

Sample		$\overline{Y}$	S_Y^2	S_Y
1	1	1.0	0.00	0.00
1	3	2.0	2.00	1.41
1	4	2.5	4.50	2.12
1	6	3.5	12.50	3.54
1	7	4.0	18.00	4.24
1	9	5.0	32.00	5.66
3	1	2.0	2.00	1.41
3	3	3.0	0.00	0.00
3	4	3.5	0.50	0.71
3	6	4.5	4.50	2.12
3	7	5.0	8.00	2.83
3	9	6.0	18.00	4.24
4	1	2.5	4.50	2.12
4	3	3.5	0.50	0.71
4	4	4.0	0.00	0.00
4	6	5.0	2.00	1.41
4	7	5.5	4.50	2.12
4	9	6.5	12.50	3.54
6	1	3.5	12.50	3.54
6	3	4.5	4.50	2.12
6	4	5.0	2.00	1.41
6	6	6.0	0.00	0.00
6	7	6.5	0.50	0.71
6	9	7.5	4.50	2.12
7	1	4.0	18.00	4.24
7	3	5.0	8.00	2.83
7	4	5.5	4.50	2.12
7	6	6.5	0.50	0.71
7	7	7.0	0.00	0.00
7	9	8.0	2.00	1.41
9	1	5.0	32.00	5.66
9	3	6.0	18.00	4.24
9	4	6.5	12.50	3.54
9	6	7.5	4.50	2.12
9	7	8.0	2.00	1.41
9	9	9.0	0.00	0.00

same time, we will see that S_Y is a biased estimate of σ_Y. In most cases, it is *too small*. Although we can prove these results mathematically, we will instead provide a heuristic demonstration of these properties. In Chapter 31, we will see how statisticians have adjusted for the underestimation of σ_Y by introducing a new statistical distribution, called the *t* distribution.

For this development consider the population of values 1, 3, 4, 6, 7, and 9. The 36 samples of size 2 that can be generated from that population are listed in Table 30-1, along with their corresponding means, variances, and standard deviations. For the population,

$$\mu_Y = \frac{1 + 3 + 4 + 6 + 7 + 9}{6} = 5.0$$

so that

$$\sigma_Y^2 = \frac{(1-5)^2 + (3-5)^2 + \cdots + (9-5)^2}{6} = 7.00$$

If we now compute the mean value of the 36 sample variances, we have that:

$$\mu_{S_Y^2} = \frac{0.00 + 2.00 + \cdots + 2.00 + 0.00}{36} = 7.00$$

Thus, we see that S_Y^2 is an unbiased estimate of σ_Y^2, since the mean value of all possible S_Y^2 values that can be generated from the parent population is equal to σ_Y^2.

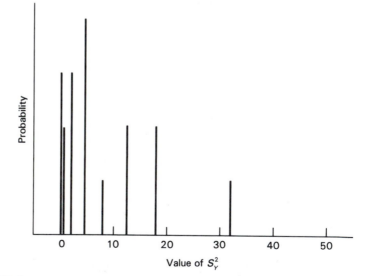

Figure 30-1.
The sampling distribution of S_Y^2 for the finite population consisting of the numbers 1, 3, 4, 6, 7, and 9.

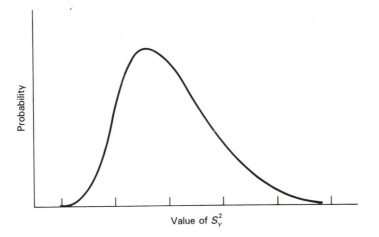

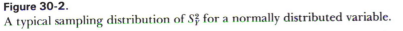

Figure 30-2.
A typical sampling distribution of S_Y^2 for a normally distributed variable.

The distribution of S_Y^2 is shown in Figure 30-1. As we see, the distribution is highly skewed. If we had used a normally distributed population, the distribution would resemble that of Figure 30-2.

Let us now consider the mean of the S_Y values. This mean is given as follows:

$$\mu_{S_Y} = \frac{0.00 + 1.41 + \cdots + 1.41 + 0.00}{36} = 2.12$$

On the other hand, $\sigma_Y = \sqrt{7} = 2.65$. Since μ_{S_Y} does not equal σ_Y, we know that S_Y is a biased estimator of σ_Y and, even more, that it is biased toward the negative side. On the average it is too small.

30-5. APPENDIX

The sampling distribution of S_Y^2 is associated with the chi-square distribution. This can be shown by adding $\bar{Y}$ to and subtracting it from the numerator in the expression

$$\chi_N^2 = \sum_{i=1}^{N} \frac{(Y_i - \mu_Y)^2}{\sigma^2}$$

as follows:

$$\sum_{i=1}^{N} (Y_i - \mu_Y)^2 = \sum_{i=1}^{N} [(Y_i - \bar{Y}) + (\bar{Y} - \mu_Y)]^2$$

We now expand the sum inside the brackets by squaring to get:

$$\sum_{i=1}^{N} (Y_i - \mu_Y)^2 = \sum_{i=1}^{N} (Y_i - \bar{Y})^2 + 2 \sum_{i=1}^{N} (Y_i - \bar{Y})(\bar{Y} - \mu_Y) + \sum_{i=1}^{N} (\bar{Y} - \mu_Y)^2$$

The second term on the right includes a factor of $(\bar{Y} - \mu_Y)$, which is constant over the summation. Hence, it can be moved to the left of the summation sign. Doing this and taking one further step, we get

$$2 \sum_{i=1}^{N} (Y_i - \bar{Y})(\bar{Y} - \mu_Y) = 2(\bar{Y} - \mu_Y) \sum_{i=1}^{N} (Y_i - \bar{Y}) = 0$$

since the sum of deviations about the mean equals zero. This leaves:

$$\sum_{i=1}^{N} (Y_i - \mu_Y)^2 = \sum_{i=1}^{N} (Y_i - \bar{Y})^2 + \sum_{i=1}^{N} (\bar{Y} - \mu_Y)^2$$

Because we can write the sample variance as

$$S_Y^2 = \frac{\sum_{i=1}^{N} (Y_i - \bar{Y})^2}{N - 1}$$

we can solve for the sum of squared deviations to find:

$$\sum_{i=1}^{N} (Y_i - \bar{Y})^2 = (N - 1)S_Y^2$$

Substituting this value into the preceding equation and dividing both sides by σ_Y^2 gives us, finally:

$$\frac{\sum_{i=1}^{N} (Y_i - \mu_Y)^2}{\sigma_Y^2} = \frac{(N - 1)S_Y^2}{\sigma_Y^2} + \frac{N(\bar{Y} - \mu_Y)^2}{\sigma_Y^2}$$

The term on the left, as we have seen, is the sum of N independent squared Z variables. Hence, its distribution is that of χ_N^2. The term on the far right can be manipulated as follows:

$$\frac{N(\bar{Y} - \mu_Y)^2}{\sigma_Y^2} = \frac{(\bar{Y} - \mu_Y)^2}{\sigma_Y^2/N} = \left(\frac{\bar{Y} - \mu_Y}{\sigma_Y/\sqrt{N}}\right)^2 = \left(\frac{\bar{Y} - \mu_Y}{\sigma_{\bar{Y}}}\right)^2 = Z^2$$

which we know to be distributed as a χ_1^2 variable. Hence, we have:

$$\chi_N^2 = \frac{(N - 1)S_Y^2}{\sigma_Y^2} + \chi_1^2$$

By the rule for the addition of chi-square variables, $(N-1)S_Y^2/\sigma_Y^2$ must be distributed as a χ_{N-1}^2 variable.

30-6. EXERCISES

30-1. A group of $N = 25$ low-achieving third-grade students was given a standardized test of reading ability. According to the publisher's manual, $\sigma_Y = 20$. For the sample of students, $S_Y = 12$. Is there reason to believe that the variance of low-ability students is different from that of the standardizing population?

30-2. For the data of Exercise 30-1, is there reason to believe that $\sigma_Y < 20$?

30-3. Find the 95 percent confidence interval for the data of Exercise 30-1.

30-4. Find the 95 percent confidence interval for Exercise 30-2.

30-5. Find the 95 percent confidence intervals for σ_Y^2 for your sample of 40 students on the final test for:
a. Students in program 1.
b. Students in program 2.

30-6. Split the risk of a type I error between the two groups in Exercise 30-5 and find the corresponding confidence intervals. Which method would you recommend, that of Exercise 30-5 or that of Exercise 30-6? Why?

PART VI

PROCEDURES BASED ON THE *t* DISTRIBUTION

Although we have presented a test for the population variance, it is rare that a researcher will have a preconceived notion of what value to use in the test. The tests we have thus far presented for the population mean, however, which are based on the normal distribution, require knowledge of the numerical value of the population standard deviation. To overcome this apparent drawback, another distribution, known as the *t* distribution, has been identified and found useful in place of the normal distribution. We introduce the *t* distribution in Chapter 31, and we show in the chapters that follow how to use it to test hypotheses and calculate confidence intervals for the population mean in one-, two-, and multiple-sample investigations.

The t Distribution

31-1. THE "STUDENT" DISTRIBUTION

In Chapter 21, we provided methods for testing $H_0: \mu_Y = \mu_0$, provided that the value of the variance was known. In general, most research involves situations where the value of this parameter is unknown. In this case, one is compelled to estimate the population standard deviation with a sample value and then use the estimated value for hypothesis testing or for defining a confidence interval. Estimating the value of a standard deviation when the population value is unknown is not a new problem to us. Earlier, we learned how to estimate the standard deviation from the sample values by computing the sample standard deviation. If the sample size is large, the sample estimate will be a good estimate of the population standard deviation. This, however, is not true when the sample size is small. In general, a sample standard deviation tends to be too small as an estimator of the population standard deviation.

This underestimate inherent in the sample standard deviation was discovered early in the development of modern statistics. Because of it, methods were sought that could adjust for the biased nature of sample standard deviations. In 1908, Gossett produced a solution that was published under the pen name *Student*. He suggested that the population standard deviation be replaced by the sample standard deviation and that the critical values taken from the normal distribution be replaced by values from a new set of distributions that he generated and that he named t.

We now make a few statements about the t distribution. First of all, like the chi-square distribution, there are multiple distributions that are often referred to as a family of t distributions. Each particular t distribution is defined by one parameter, called the number of degrees of freedom of the distribution. This number is usually denoted by the Greek letter ν (nu) and is generally equal to the number of degrees of freedom that are used to estimate the standard deviation of a population. As was discussed in Section 5-3, the number of degrees of freedom used to estimate σ_Y is given by $\nu = N - 1$. Like the standard normal distribution, each of the t distributions is symmetrical about zero; however, unlike the standard normal distribution, the standard deviations of the t distributions are greater than 1. This means that the tail percentile values of the t distribution are farther from zero than the corresponding values observed for the standard normal distribution. These more extreme values compensate for the overly small values assumed by the sample standard deviation. That these values are more extreme is shown in Table A-12, which lists the critical values for the t distribution. For example, if we look in the table at the bottom row for the 97.5 percentile value, $\nu = \infty$, we read the familiar 1.96 value. Moving up the table to 25 degrees of freedom, we read the larger value of 2.06. For 20 degrees of freedom, the corresponding 97.5 percentile value is 2.09. For 15 degrees of freedom, the tabled value is 2.13 and for 10 degrees of freedom, we read 2.23. For degrees of freedom of 9 or less, the increase in the tabled values is rapid, corresponding to the increase in the error of the sample standard deviation as an estimate of the population standard deviation. We shall denote the α percentile values of the t distribution as $t_{\nu:\alpha}$. Thus, $t_{23:.975} = 2.07$ corresponds to the 97.5 percentile value of the t distribution with $\nu = 23$ degrees of freedom.

The family of t_ν distributions is defined from the standard normal distribution and the family of χ^2_ν distributions. As an example, we know that

$$Z = \frac{\bar{Y} - \mu_0}{\sigma_Y / \sqrt{N}}$$

is distributed as a standard normal variable if the distribution of $\bar{Y}$ is normal.

In Chapter 30, we also saw that

$$\chi_v^2 = (N - 1) \frac{S_Y^2}{\sigma_Y^2}$$

is distributed as χ_v^2 with $v = N - 1$ if the distribution of Y is normal. The family of t distributions is defined:

$$t_v = \frac{Z}{\sqrt{\chi_v^2/v}}$$

If we substitute the appropriate terms into t_v, we have for the one sample model that

$$t_v = \frac{\dfrac{\bar{Y} - \mu_0}{\sigma_y/\sqrt{N}}}{\sqrt{\dfrac{(N - 1)\, S_Y^2/\sigma_Y^2}{N - 1}}} = \frac{\bar{Y} - \mu_0}{S_Y/\sqrt{N}}$$

In this form, we see that t_v has the structure of a Z variable, except that S_Y replaces σ_Y. Thus, even though σ_Y is unknown, so that Z cannot be computed, we see that t_v can always be determined from the sample statistics $\bar{Y}$ and S_Y, provided that μ_0 is specified. As we shall see in Chapters 32 through 34, this is of considerable value in practice. For completeness, we provide a definition of t_v.

Definition of t_v

Consider a variable Z which is normal with $\mu_Z = 0$ and $\sigma_Z^2 = 1$. Let χ_v^2 refer to a variable that is distributed as χ_v^2 with v degrees of freedom. Then, t_v is defined:

$$t_v = \frac{Z}{\sqrt{\chi_v^2/v}}$$

Using advanced methods, it can be shown that

$$E(t_v) = 0 \qquad \text{and} \qquad \text{Var}(t_v) = \frac{v}{v - 2}$$

Note that $\text{Var}(t_v) > 1$.

31-2. EXERCISES

31-1. Find the 95th percentile of a *t* distribution with
  a. 10 degrees of freedom
  b. 15 degrees of freedom
  c. 25 degrees of freedom

31-2. Find the 2.5 and 5.0 percentiles of a *t* distribution with

  a. 10 degrees of freedom
  b. 30 degrees of freedom

31-3. Assume we know that the 90th percentile of a *t*-distributed variable equals 1.333. How many degrees of freedom are associated with this *t* distribution?

CHAPTER 32

Tests Based on the t Distribution

32-1. ONE-SAMPLE TEST ABOUT A POPULATION MEAN IF THE POPULATION VARIANCE IS UNKNOWN

The procedure of Section 21-3 is based upon the assumption that the standard deviation of the population is known. In most investigations, the value of σ_Y is not known. With this in mind, let us take a second look at the data of Section 21-3, where we tested the hypothesis that $\mu_Y = 500$ in terms of the sample mean, $\overline{Y} = 552$, and the population standard deviation, $\sigma_Y = 100$.

Experience has shown that the substitution of a new teaching method has a tendency to change the variation among the students who are given the training. Some methods tend to increase the variance, while others decrease the variance. Although it is difficult to specify the kinds of methods that tend to increase or decrease the variance, the assumption of known variance is not necessary, since one can always estimate the variance from the sample and use it as a substitute for the unknown population value. Upon the substitution of S_Y for σ_Y, one transfers the model from that of the normal distribution to that of the t distribution discussed in Chapter 31. For the example of Section 21-3, our test statistic becomes:

$$t_{\bar{Y}} = \frac{\bar{Y} - \mu_{\bar{Y}}}{S_Y/\sqrt{N}}$$

As we see, $t_{\bar{Y}}$ specifies the number of standard deviations between $\bar{Y}$ and μ_Y, but here the sample standard deviation is used as the reference value. The decision rule is determined from the t distribution with $v = N - 1$ degrees of freedom. Let us repeat that the critical value specifies the maximum number of standard deviations that one could expect between $\bar{Y}$ and μ_Y for the preselected risk of a type I error. The denominator of $t_{\bar{Y}}$ is called the standard error of $\bar{Y}$. As we see, it serves as an estimate of $\sigma_{\bar{Y}} = \sigma_Y/\sqrt{N}$, the standard deviation of the sampling distribution of $\bar{Y}$. For completeness, we provide a definition of $SE_{\bar{Y}}$.

Definition of the standard error of a mean

The standard error of a mean is an estimate of $\sigma_{\bar{Y}} = \sigma_Y/\sqrt{N}$ determined from a sample and is defined:

$$SE_{\bar{Y}} = \frac{S_Y}{\sqrt{N}}$$

In Box 32-1 we summarize the steps for the one-sample t test.
For the example, $\mu_{\bar{Y}} = 500$. For the data,

$$\sum_{i=1}^{15} Y_i = 8280 \qquad \text{and} \qquad \sum_{i=1}^{15} Y_i^2 = 4{,}761{,}800$$

Hence:

$$\bar{Y} = \frac{1}{N} \sum_{i=1}^{15} Y_i = \frac{8280}{15} = 552$$

and

$$S_{\bar{Y}}^2 = \frac{N \sum_{i=1}^{N} Y_i^2 - \left(\sum_{i=1}^{N} Y_i\right)^2}{N(N-1)} = \frac{15(4{,}761{,}800) - 8280^2}{15(14)} = 31{,}660$$

Box 32-1   Procedure for testing $H_0: \mu_Y = \mu_0$ versus $H_1: \mu_Y \neq \mu_0$ if σ_Y is unknown

Step 1. State the value of μ_0.

Step 2. Determine the value of $\overline{Y}$ and S_Y^2.

Step 3. Determine the value of $SE_{\overline{Y}} = S_Y/\sqrt{N}$.

Step 4. Compute:

$$t_{\overline{Y}} = \frac{\overline{Y} - \mu_0}{SE_{\overline{Y}}}$$

Step 5. Determine the decision rule. With the α of interest and $\nu = N - 1$, the decision rule is as follows:

Decision Rule: Reject H_0 if $t_{\overline{Y}} < t_{\nu : \alpha/2}$ or if $t_{\overline{Y}} > t_{\nu : 1 - \alpha/2}$

Step 6. Make a decision.

Therefore

$$SE_{\overline{Y}} = \sqrt{\frac{S_Y^2}{N}} = \sqrt{\frac{13{,}660}{15}} = \sqrt{910.67} = 30.18$$

which yields

$$t_{\overline{Y}} = \frac{\overline{Y} - \mu_0}{SE_{\overline{Y}}} = \frac{552 - 500}{30.18} = 1.72$$

Our decision rule would then be stated as follows, with $\nu = N - 1 = 14$ and $\alpha = .05$:

Decision Rule: Reject H_0 if $t_{\overline{Y}} < t_{14 : .025} = -2.14$

or if $t_{\overline{Y}} > t_{14 : .975} = 2.14$

Since $1.72 < 2.14$, we do not reject H_0.

While the test in Section 21-3 leads to a rejection of H_0, the test in this section concludes with the nonrejection of H_0. The apparent inconsistency is easy to resolve: the assumed standard deviation of $\sigma_Y = 100$ for the normal curve test must be too small. The standard deviation of the sample of 15 students is given by $S_Y = \sqrt{13{,}660} = 117$, a number greater than 100. Either the students of the school district in question are less homogeneous than the students on whom the test was standardized, or else the training has made them more heterogeneous than the standardizing group. It is possible that both alternatives apply to these students. The important point is that knowledge of the population variance is not needed to perform the *t* test. It is for this reason that the *t* test is preferred over the normal curve test.

32-2. THE CONFIDENCE INTERVAL FOR μ_Y WHEN σ_Y IS UNKNOWN

If σ_Y is unknown, one estimates it from the data and substitutes S_Y into the confidence interval equation in place of σ_Y. In addition, each Z value is replaced by the corresponding t distribution value. In particular, the $1 - \alpha$ percent confidence interval for μ_Y is found as shown in Box 32-2.

For the College Board data analyzed in Section 32-1, the number of degrees of freedom associated with S_Y is given by $v = N - 1 = 15 - 1 = 14$, $t_{14:.025} = -2.14$ and $t_{14:.975} = 2.14$. Hence:

$$\mu_Y = \bar{Y} \pm 2.14 \, SE_{\bar{Y}} = 552 \pm 2.14(30.18) = 552 \pm 65$$

Thus, in the population of 4539 seniors, the new program could produce a mean value as low as 487 or as high as 617. Any value of μ_Y between these limits could have produced a sample mean value of 552. Since $\mu_Y = 500$ is in the interval, $H_0: \mu_Y = 500$ is not rejected. This means that a test of H_0 can be achieved by simply computing the confidence interval for μ_Y and checking to see whether the hypothesized value of μ_Y is in the interval. If μ_Y is in the interval, H_0 is not rejected; otherwise, it is rejected. As will be seen, this strategy will be used with increasing frequency in the later chapters of this book.

Finally, we call the resulting confidence interval a 95 percent confidence interval. It may or may not be a true statement about μ_Y, since the population mean may or may not be contained between 487 and 617. We can never know for sure. The best we can do is hope that the confidence interval is a true statement. The probability that it is a true statement, however, is 1 or 0. *It is not .95.*

Early in the book you were asked to obtain your own random sample to use for the exercises. You should now determine the confidence interval for your sample. You will discover that the confidence interval for every member of your class will differ from yours and that others' will also differ from one another. Some of them will be valid statements about μ_Y and some will not be valid statements. If your class contains 100 students, close to 95 of the computed intervals will be valid statements, while about 5 of them will be type I errors. In practice there is no way to determine which of the intervals represent type I errors, since one never knows μ_Y. Because we cannot identify the possible type I errors, we behave as though each of the intervals were correct.

32-3. THE MATCHED-PAIR *t* TEST

A special case of the test described in Section 32-2 is encountered frequently in behavioral research. The most common situation involves two measures

---

Box 32-2 The $1 - \alpha$ percent confidence interval for μ_Y if σ_Y is unknown

With the risk of a type I error chosen to equal α, the $1 - \alpha$ percent confidence interval for μ_Y is given by:

$$\bar{Y} + t_{\nu:\alpha/2}\frac{S_Y}{\sqrt{N}} < \mu_Y < \bar{Y} + t_{\nu:1-\alpha/2}\frac{S_Y}{\sqrt{N}}$$

where

$$t_{\nu:\alpha/2} = \alpha/2 \text{ percentile value of the } t \text{ distribution with with } \nu = N - 1$$

and

$$t_{\nu:1-\alpha/2} = 1 - \alpha/2 \text{ percentile value of the } t \text{ distribution with } \nu = N - 1$$

For directional confidence intervals, if the alternative is

$$H_1: \quad \mu > \mu_0$$

then the confidence interval is given by

$$\mu > \bar{Y} + t_{\nu:\alpha}\frac{S_Y}{\sqrt{N}}$$

If the alternative is

$$H_1: \quad \mu < \mu_0$$

then the confidence interval is given by

$$\mu < \bar{Y} + t_{\nu:1-\alpha}\frac{S_Y}{\sqrt{N}}$$

In another form, the nondirectional confidence interval can be written as

$$\mu_Y = \bar{Y} \pm t_{\nu:\alpha/2}\frac{S_Y}{\sqrt{N}}$$

---

taken at different times on each subject in the study. For example, blood pressure may be measured before and after the administration of a tranquilizer. In this case, the researcher wishes to know whether the tranquilizer lowers the blood pressure of the tested subjects.

Assume that a sample consists of 10 hyperactive children, and assume that blood pressures before and after the administration of a tranquilizer are as shown in Table 32-1. Since the observations are paired for each subject, we can take the difference between the "before" measure and the "after" measure to obtain a difference score. For the 10 subjects of Table 32-1, the ordered difference scores are as follows:

$$-5, \quad 10, \quad 20, \quad 20, \quad 25, \quad 30, \quad 35, \quad 40, \quad 45, \quad 45$$

We now see that we have reduced the original two-variable problem to a one-sample problem based on the 10 difference scores. The methods of Section 32-2 can be used to test the hypothesis

$$H_0: \quad \mu_B - \mu_A = 0$$

versus the alternative

$$H_1: \quad \mu_B - \mu_A > 0$$

which is a *directional alternative*.

For these data,

$$\sum_{i=1}^{10} d_i = 265 \qquad \text{and} \qquad \sum_{i=1}^{10} d_i^2 = 9325$$

Table 32-1. Blood pressure readings on 10 hyperactive children before and after administration of a tranquilizer.

Subject	Before	After	Difference
1	155	110	45
2	160	120	40
3	140	145	−5
4	145	125	20
5	155	145	10
6	160	115	45
7	150	120	30
8	175	155	20
9	170	145	35
10	165	140	25

so that

$$\bar{d} = 26.5$$

$$S_d = 15.9948$$

and

$$t_{\bar{d}} = \frac{\bar{d} - 0}{S_d / \sqrt{N}} = \frac{26.5 - 0}{15.9948 / \sqrt{10}} = \frac{26.5000}{5.0580} = 5.24$$

With $\alpha = .05$, the one-tailed decision rule for rejecting H_0 with $v_1 = N - 1 = 10 - 1 = 9$ degrees of freedom is as follows:

Decision Rule: Reject H_0 if $t_{\bar{d}} > 1.83$

We reject H_0. The 95 percent confidence interval for $\mu_B - \mu_A$ is given by

$$\mu_B - \mu_A > 26.5 - 1.83(5.0580) = 17.24$$

32-4. THE TWO-SAMPLE t TEST FOR EQUAL POPULATION MEAN VALUES

The two-sample t test is based on the assumption that the variances of the two populations from which the samples are drawn are equal and must be estimated by pooling the information in the two samples. If it *is* assumed that the two samples come from populations whose variances are equal, then each sample variance is an estimate of the population variance. We must find a way to use the information provided by the two sample estimates to obtain a single estimate of the population variance.

We recall that we began a discussion of this problem in Section 9-4. At that point, we tried to keep the notation simple, but now we need to be more explicit in the identification of sample values. For this, let the first sample be denoted by

$$Y_{11}, Y_{21}, \ldots, Y_{i1}, \ldots, Y_{N_1 1}$$

where Y_{i1} represents the value of Y for the ith element in group 1. With this notation, the mean for group 1 is denoted thus:

$$\bar{Y}_{.1} = \frac{1}{N_1} \sum_{i=1}^{N_1} Y_{i1}$$

The variance is defined as

$$S_{\bar{Y}_1}^2 = \frac{1}{N_1 - 1} \sum_{i=1}^{N_1} (Y_{i1} - \bar{Y}_{.1})^2$$

so that

$$(N_1 - 1)S_{\bar{Y}_1}^2 = \sum_{i=1}^{N_1} (Y_{i1} - \bar{Y}_{.1})^2 = SS_{U_1}$$

which is the sum of squares of the unexplained deviations in sample 1. In a like manner,

$$(N_2 - 1)S_{\bar{Y}_2}^2 = \sum_{i=1}^{N_2} (Y_{i2} - \bar{Y}_{.2})^2 = SS_{U_2}$$

measures the variability about the mean in sample 2 only. Thus, pooling these two measures of variability, we see that

$$SS_U = SS_{U_1} + SS_{U_2} = (N_1 - 1)S_{\bar{Y}_1}^2 + (N_2 - 1)S_{\bar{Y}_2}^2$$

measures the overall variability within the two samples. Since the first term is based on $v_1 = N_1 - 1$ degrees of freedom and the second term is based on $v_2 = N_2 - 1$ degrees of freedom, this measure of overall variability is based on

$$v = v_1 + v_2 = (N_1 - 1) + (N_2 - 1) = N_1 + N_2 - 2$$

degrees of freedom. Hence, we define the pooled estimate of the common population variance, called the *mean square within*, as follows:

$$MS_W = \frac{(N_1 - 1)S_{\bar{Y}_1}^2 + (N_2 - 1)S_{\bar{Y}_2}^2}{N_1 + N_2 - 2}$$

The hypothesis we wish to test is $H_0: \mu_{Y_1} - \mu_{Y_2} = 0$, against $H_1: \mu_{Y_1} - \mu_{Y_2} \neq 0$. To test this hypothesis, consider the mean difference

$$\bar{d} = \bar{Y}_1 - \bar{Y}_2$$

Since it is a linear combination, we know that, under H_0:

$$\mu_{\bar{d}} = \mu_{Y_1} - \mu_{Y_2} = 0$$

and

$$\text{Var}(\bar{d}) = (+1)^2 \text{Var}(\bar{Y}_1) + (-1)^2 \text{Var}(\bar{Y}_2) = \frac{\sigma_{Y_1}^2}{N_1} + \frac{\sigma_{Y_2}^2}{N_2}$$

Since $\sigma_{\bar{Y}_1}^2$ and $\sigma_{\bar{Y}_2}^2$ are unknown and assumed to be equal, we can replace them in this formula with their best estimate, MS_W. With this substitution, the test statistic for the two-sample t test becomes

$$t_{\bar{d}} = \frac{\bar{Y}_1 - \bar{Y}_2}{\sqrt{\dfrac{MS_W}{N_1} + \dfrac{MS_W}{N_2}}}$$

Let us apply this test to the data of Table 4-1. Summary statistics for these data are reported in Table 32-2. For these statistics:

$$MS_W = \frac{(16 - 1)8.54^2 + (23 - 1)5.89^2}{(16 - 1) + (23 - 1)} = 50.1946$$

with:

$$v = (16 - 1) + (23 - 1) = 16 + 23 - 2 = 37$$

With these values:

$$t_{\bar{d}} = \frac{21.44 - 15.96}{\sqrt{\dfrac{50.1946}{16} + \dfrac{50.1946}{23}}} = \frac{5.48}{\sqrt{5.3196}} = \frac{5.48}{2.31} = 2.37$$

With $\alpha = .05$ and $v = 37$, the two-tailed decision rule, read from Table A-12, is given as follows:

Decision Rule: Reject H_0 if $t_{\bar{d}} > 2.02$ or if $t_{\bar{d}} < -2.02$

H_0 is rejected, since $t_{\bar{d}} = 2.34$ is larger than 2.02. We summarize the steps for performing the two-sample t test in Box 32-3.

Table 32-2. Sample statistics for the data of Table 4-1.

Group	1	2
Mean	21.4	16.0
Standard deviation	8.54	5.89
Sample size	16	23

Box 32-3   Method for performing the two-sample t test of $\mu_{Y_1} - \mu_{Y_2} = 0$

Step 1. Compute the mean and standard deviation of each sample.

Step 2. Estimate the pooled variance:

$$MS_W = \frac{(N_1 - 1)S_1^2 + (N_2 - 1)S_2^2}{N_1 + N_2 - 2}$$

Step 3. Compute

$$t_{\bar{d}} = \frac{\bar{Y}_1 - \bar{Y}_2}{\sqrt{MS_W/N_1 + MS_W/N_2}}$$

Step 4. Compute

$$v = N_1 + N_2 - 2$$

Step 5. Determine the decision rule from Table A-12.

Step 6. Make a decision.

The denominator of the two-sample t test is called the standard error of the difference of two means for independent samples. We provide a definition of it at this point.

The standard error of the difference of two means

The standard error of the difference of two means is defined as follows:

$$SE_{\bar{d}} = \sqrt{\frac{S_1^2}{N_1} + \frac{S_2^2}{N_2}}$$

If the population variances are equal, then:

$$SE_{\bar{d}} = \sqrt{\frac{MS_W}{N_1} + \frac{MS_W}{N_2}}$$

where

$$MS_W = \frac{(N_1 - 1)S_1^2 + (N_2 - 1)S_2^2}{N_1 + N_2 - 2}$$

These standard errors are used as estimates of the population value

$$\sigma_{\bar{Y}_1 - \bar{Y}_2} = \sqrt{\frac{\sigma_{Y_1}^2}{N_1} + \frac{\sigma_{Y_2}^2}{N_2}}$$

Box 32-4 How to set up a $1 - \alpha$ percent confidence interval for $\mu_{\bar{d}} = \mu_{Y_1} - \mu_{Y_2}$

Step 1. Compute

$$\bar{d} = \bar{Y}_1 - \bar{Y}_2$$

and

$$SE_{\bar{d}} = \sqrt{\frac{MS_W}{N_1} + \frac{MS_W}{N_2}}$$

Step 2. With the risk of a type I error set equal to α, determine $t_{v:\alpha/2}$ and $t_{v:1-\alpha/2}$ from Table A-12.

Step 3. Determine the confidence interval:

$$\mu_{\bar{d}} = \bar{d} \pm t_{v:\alpha/2}SE_{\bar{d}}$$

For a one-tailed confidence interval, put all of the α into the appropriate tail.

Finally, we note that one can place a two-tailed confidence interval around $\mu_{\bar{d}} = \mu_{Y_1} - \mu_{Y_2}$ by using

$$\mu_{\bar{d}} = \mu_{Y_1} - \mu_{Y_2} = (\bar{Y}_1 - \bar{Y}_2) \pm t_{v:\alpha/2}SE_{\bar{d}}$$

For our example,

$$\mu_{\bar{d}} = 5.48 \pm 2.02(2.31) = 5.48 \pm 4.67$$

or

$$0.81 < \mu_{Y_1} - \mu_{Y_2} < 10.15$$

Directions for this model appear in Box 32-4.

32-5. THE WELCH-ASPIN TEST FOR EQUAL POPULATION MEAN VALUES

The two-sample t test described in the previous section is based on the following assumptions:

1. Independence of observations within each sample
2. Independence of observations between the two samples
3. Equal variance in both populations
4. Normality of observations

If only assumptions 1, 2, and 3 are satisfied, one can always justify the use of the two-sample Wilcoxon test or the Mann-Whitney U test. The disadvantages in the use of these tests are that they are cumbersome to carry out if the sample sizes are large and that the determination of a confidence interval is complicated. If the normality assumption is justified but the assumption of equal variance is not, the critical values taken from the t distribution are incorrect. Welch and Aspin showed, however, that the t distribution could be used to provide an approximation to the correct values. Their procedure involves using the individual sample variances and adjusting the degrees of freedom of the t test. We now describe this useful test.

We will illustrate the use of the Welch-Aspin test with the data of Table 32-2. If we replace each population standard deviation by the corresponding sample standard deviation, the test statistic for the Welch-Aspin test is defined:

$$t_d^* = \frac{\bar{Y}_1 - \bar{Y}_2}{\sqrt{S_{Y_1}^2/N_1 + S_{Y_2}^2/N_2}}$$

If we now substitute the sample values, we have that

$$t_d^* = \frac{21.4 - 16.0}{\sqrt{\dfrac{8.54^2}{16} + \dfrac{5.89^2}{23}}} = \frac{5.4}{\sqrt{6.0666}} = \frac{5.4}{2.46} = 2.19$$

Since we have substituted sample standard deviations for population standard deviations, we know we cannot use the normal distribution to define a decision rule that tells us when to reject H_0. Instead, we must use the t distribution with the appropriate number of degrees of freedom. As shown by Welch and Aspin, the degrees of freedom are given by v^*, where v^* is found from the equation

$$\frac{1}{v^*} = \frac{1}{v_1}\left(1 - \frac{W_1}{W}\right)^2 + \frac{1}{v_2}\left(1 - \frac{W_2}{W}\right)^2$$

For our example, v_1, v_2, W_1, W_2, and W are defined as follows:

$$v_1 = N_1 - 1 = 16 - 1 = 15$$

$$v_2 = N_2 - 1 = 23 - 1 = 22$$

$$W_1 = \frac{N_1}{S_{Y_1}^2} = \frac{16}{8.54^2} = 0.2194$$

$$W_2 = \frac{N_2}{S_{Y_2}^2} = \frac{23}{5.89^2} = 0.6630$$

$$W = W_1 + W_2 = 0.2194 + 0.6630 = 0.8824$$

With these values,

$$\frac{1}{\nu^*} = \frac{1}{15}\left(1 - \frac{0.2194}{0.8824}\right)^2 + \frac{1}{22}\left(1 - \frac{0.6630}{0.8824}\right)^2 = 0.0404$$

so that

$$\nu^* = \frac{1}{0.0404} = 24.75 \approx 24$$

Since the parameters of the t distribution must be integers, it is customary to define ν^* as the next lower integer. In this case, the next lower integer is 24. The $\alpha = .05$ decision rule, read from Table A-12, is as follows:

Decision Rule: Reject H_0 if $t^* < -2.06$ or if $t^* > 2.06$

Since $t_{\bar{d}}^* = 2.19$ is larger than 2.06, we reject H_0 and conclude that students who have had a prior course in biology, on the average, obtain higher scores than students who have not had such a course.

We summarize the steps for doing the Welch-Aspin test in Box 32-5.

Since a two-tailed test of hypothesis has been performed, a two-tailed confidence interval is in order. The confidence interval is given by:

$$(\bar{Y}_1 - \bar{Y}_2) + t^*_{\nu^*:\alpha/2}SE_{\bar{d}} < \mu_{\bar{d}} < (\bar{Y}_1 - \bar{Y}_2) + t^*_{\nu^*:1-\alpha/2}SE_{\bar{d}}$$

$$5.4 - 2.06(2.46) < \mu_{\bar{d}} < 5.4 + 2.06(2.46)$$

$$0.33 < \mu_{\bar{d}} < 10.48$$

Box 32-5   How to perform the Welch-Aspin test of $\mu_{Y_1} - \mu_{Y_2} = 0$

Step 1. Compute the mean and standard deviation of each sample.
Step 2. Compute

$$t_{\bar{d}}^* = \frac{\bar{Y}_1 - \bar{Y}_2}{\sqrt{S_{Y_1}^2/N_1 + S_{Y_2}^2/N_2}}$$

Step 3. Determine ν^* from

$$\frac{1}{\nu^*} = \frac{1}{\nu_1}\left(1 - \frac{W_1}{W}\right)^2 + \frac{1}{\nu_2}\left(1 - \frac{W_2}{W}\right)^2$$

where $W_1 = N_1/S_{Y_1}^2$, $W_2 = N_2/S_{Y_2}^2$, and $W = W_1 + W_2$.
Step 4. Determine the decision rule from Table A-12.
Step 5. Make a decision.

Note that $\mu_{Y_1} - \mu_{Y_2} = 0$ is not in the interval. This is expected, since the hypothesis that $\mu_{Y_1} - \mu_{Y_2} = 0$ has been rejected.

32-6. THE POINT BISERIAL CORRELATION COEFFICIENT AND THE TWO-SAMPLE t TEST

In Chapter 1, we indicated that the testing of hypotheses concerning differences in centers and the examination of hypotheses concerning associations between two variables form two sides of the same statistical coin. In Chapter 4, we saw how to measure differences in population centers, and in Section 32-4 we learned how to test these differences for statistical significance using the t test, provided the population variances are known to be equal. In Chapter 10, we learned how to measure the association between an independent and a dependent variable in terms of the correlation coefficient. Focusing on the independent-dependent nature of the two-sample procedure for comparing two means, we may begin to think that one could connect the two-sample model with a correlation problem.

When there are only two groups in a study, we saw, in Section 10-3, that the qualitative variable representing group membership can be quantified by introducing a dichotomous *indicator* or *dummy variable*. With this quantification, one can compute r_{pb}, the point biserial correlation coefficient. For the data of Table 4-1, let us define our indicator variable as

$$X = 0 \qquad \text{if the subject did not take high school biology}$$

and

$$X = 1 \qquad \text{if the subject took high school biology}$$

With this quantification,

$$\sum_{i=1}^{N} X_i = 1 + 1 + \cdots + 1 + 0 + 0 + \cdots + 0 = 16(1) + 23(0) = 16$$

$$\sum_{i=1}^{N} X_i^2 = 1^2 + 1^2 + \cdots + 1^2 + 0^2 + 0^2 + \cdots + 0^2 = 16(1) + 23(0) = 16$$

$$\sum_{i=1}^{N} Y_i = 28 + 28 + \cdots + 30 + 10 + 24 + \cdots + 17 = 710$$

$$\sum_{i=1}^{N} Y_i^2 = 28^2 + 28^2 + \cdots + 30^2 + 10^2 + 24^2 + \cdots + 17^2 = 15{,}066$$

$$\sum_{i=1}^{N} X_i Y_i = 1(28) + 1(28) + \cdots + 1(30) + 0(10) + 0(24) + \cdots$$
$$+ 0(17) = 343$$

Thus:

$$r_{pb} = \frac{39(343) - 16(710)}{\sqrt{39(16) - 16^2}\ \sqrt{39(15,066) - 710^2}} = \frac{2017}{5542.42} = 0.3639 = .36$$

The positive value reflects the fact that, as the indicator variable increases from 0 to 1, the sample means increase from 16.0 to 21.4. We would conclude that a moderate correlation exists between scores on the midterm and whether or not students have had high school biology. Higher mean scores are obtained for students who have had a high school biology course. Of the total variation, $r_{pb}^2 = 0.3639^2 = 0.13$, or 13 percent, is explained by the difference between the two programs.

The point biserial correlation coefficient equals zero when the two sample means are equal. It is different from zero whenever the sample means are different from one another. Thus, the two-sample t test, used to test equality of means, can also be used to test $H_0: \rho_{pb} = 0$ against $H_1: \rho_{pb} \neq 0$. However, researchers tend to use a different form of this test. It can be shown that the test statistic required to test $H_0: \rho_{pb} = 0$ is given as:

$$t_{r_{pb}} = \frac{r_{pb}\sqrt{N-2}}{\sqrt{1 - r_{pb}^2}}$$

As was true of the two-sample test, the degrees of freedom for the test are given by $\nu = N_1 + N_2 - 2$, or, if $N = N_1 + N_2$, by $\nu = N - 2$. Thus, to test the significance of a point biserial correlation coefficient, one proceeds as shown in Box 32-6.

We illustrate the test with the data of Table 4-1. As we saw, the value of the point biserial correlation coefficient is equal to $r_{pb} = 0.36$. Thus, to test $H_0: \rho_{pb} = 0$ against the alternative $H_1: \rho_{pb} \neq 0$, the appropriate $\alpha = .05$ decision rule is defined as follows:

Decision Rule: Reject H_0 if $t_{r_{pb}} < -2.02$ or if $t_{r_{pb}} > 2.02$

Box 32-6   Procedure for testing $H_0: \rho_{pb} = 0$ against $H_1: \rho_{pb} \neq 0$

Step 1. Compute the value of r_{pb}.

Step 2. Compute

$$t_{r_{pb}} = \frac{r_{pb}\sqrt{N-2}}{\sqrt{1 - r_{pb}^2}}$$

Step 3. Reject H_0 if $t_{r_{pb}} < t_{N-2:\alpha/2}$ or if $t_{r_{pb}} > t_{N-2:1-\alpha/2}$.

For these data,

$$t_{r_{pb}} = \frac{0.3639 \sqrt{39-2}}{\sqrt{1-(0.3639)^2}} = 2.37$$

which is the same value as calculated in Section 32-4 for the two-sample t test. Since $t_{r_{pb}} = 2.37$ is greater than 2.02, we reject H_0 and conclude that $\rho_{pb} \neq 0$. Not only are the two t statistics identical, but the degrees of freedom for the two tests are also identical.

As we have seen, the test of $H_0: \mu_{Y_1} = \mu_{Y_2}$ and the test of $H_0: \rho_{pb} = 0$ are equivalent. Thus, one can test both hypotheses at the same time. Typically, researchers test $H_0: \mu_{Y_1} = \mu_{Y_2}$. If H_0 is rejected, it follows that $\mu_{Y_1} \neq \mu_{Y_2}$ and that $\rho_{pb} \neq 0$. If H_0 is not rejected, one concludes that $\mu_{Y_1} = \mu_{Y_2}$ and that $\rho_{pb} = 0$.

Incidentally, the relationship between t and r_{pb} provides a simple way to compute r_{pb}. First, perform the t test as described in Section 32-4. Then determine r_{pb} as a solution to the equation involving t and r_{pb}. The solution is given by

$$r_{pb}^2 = \frac{t^2}{v + t^2}$$

For these data,

$$r_{pb}^2 = \frac{2.37^2}{37 + 2.37^2} = 0.1318$$

so that $r_{pb} = 0.3630$, the value, except for rounding errors, reported earlier. Since $X = 0$ is associated with no high school biology and $X = 1$ is associated with high school biology, we assign a positive sign to r_{pb} because the mean associated with $X = 1$ is larger than the mean associated with $X = 0$.

32-7. TESTING A SINGLE CORRELATION COEFFICIENT FOR SIGNIFICANCE

In the previous section, we saw how to test the point biserial correlation coefficient for statistical significance. In particular, we saw that the test statistic used to decide between $H_0: \rho_{pb} = 0$ and $H_1: \rho_{pb} \neq 0$ had a t distribution with $v = N - 2$ degrees of freedom. As we know from Section 32-6, a sample point biserial correlation coefficient is merely a special case of an ordinary correlation coefficient for which the independent variable is scored as 0 and 1. One can test an ordinary correlation coefficient for statistical significance by following the steps described in Section 32-6 for the point biserial correlation coefficient. For the ordinary correlation coefficient this test is exact.

In Section 7-3, we saw that the correlation coefficient between the pretest scores and final test scores was given by $r = 0.55$ for $N = 39$. For these data,

$$t_r = \frac{r\sqrt{N-2}}{\sqrt{1-r^2}} = \frac{0.55\sqrt{39-2}}{\sqrt{1-0.55^2}} = 4.01$$

From Table A-12, with $\alpha = .05$ and $v = 39 - 2 = 37$, we see that $t_{37:.975} = 2.02$, and so the decision rule for rejecting $H_0 : \rho = 0$ in favor of $H_1 : \rho \neq 0$ is as follows:

Decision Rule: Reject H_0 if $t < -2.02$ or if $t > 2.02$

Since $t = 4.01$ is in the rejection region of the test, the hypothesis of no association is rejected. Furthermore, we believe that the association is positive, and after an inspection of the scatter diagram of Figure 7-1, we conclude it is linear in form.

In this case, it would be highly unlikely to find pretest scores and final test scores negatively related; therefore, a one-tailed alternative, $H_1 : \rho_{pb} > 0$, is certainly reasonable. With a one-tailed test, the decision rule is given thus:

Decision Rule: Reject H_0 if $t > 1.69$

As before, H_0 is rejected.

32-8. EXERCISES

32-1. On a standardized reading test the mean score of $N = 25$ low-ability students is given by $\bar{Y} = 61.3$, and $S_Y = 10.2$. According to the publisher's manual, $\mu_Y = 70$. Is there reason to believe that the mean score for low-ability students is different from that of the standardizing population?

32-2. For the data of Exercise 32-1, is there reason to believe that $\mu_Y < 70$?

32-3. Find the 95 percent confidence interval for the data of Exercise 32-1.

32-4. Find the 95 percent confidence interval for the data of Exercise 32-2.

32-5. For your sample of 40 students, find the 95 percent confidence intervals around μ_Y for scores on the final test for
a. Students in program 1
b. Students in program 2

32-6. Split the risk of a type I error between the two groups in Exercise 32-5 and find the corresponding confidence intervals. Which method would you recommend: that of Exercise 32-5, or that of Exercise 32-6? Why?

32-7. For the data of Exercise 32-5, is there reason to believe that $\psi = \mu_1 - \mu_2 = 0$? Answer this question using
a. The assumption of equal variance
b. The assumption of unequal variance
Which method would you recommend? Why?

32-8. Find the 95 percent confidence interval for $\psi = \mu_1 - \mu_2$ for methods a and b of Exercise 32-7.

32-9. Use the matched-pair t test to analyze the data of Table 14-1. Which method would you recommend: the sign test, the matched-pair Wilcoxon test, or the matched-pair t test? Why?

32-10. Find the 95 percent confidence interval for $\psi = \mu_C - \mu_V$ for the data of Table 14-1. Compare it with the results obtained by using the
a. Sign test $-4 \le M_d \le +3$
b. Matched-pair
   Wilcoxon test $-3 \le M_d \le +1$
Note that the confidence intervals for the sign test and the matched-pair Wilcoxon test are the *median* difference and not the *mean* difference. How does this affect your answer to the question of Exercise 32-9?

32-11. Find the point biserial correlation coefficient for your sample of 40 students on the final. See Exercise 32-5. Test H_0: $\rho_{pb} = 0$ using $\alpha = .05$. Compare your result with the result of Exercise 32-7a.

32-12. Is there reason to believe that $\rho_{XY} = 0$ for your sample of 40 students for

$$X: \quad \text{score on pretest}$$

$$Y: \quad \text{score on final}$$

32-13. In the study of Exercise 21-10, the families were divided into two groups. The groups and their corresponding statistics were as follows.

	Yearly income	
Statistic	Less than $25,000	More than $25,000
N	28	52
$\bar{Y}$	$68.94	$89.41
S_Y	$8.39	$11.42

Is there a difference in food spending habits of the two groups? Answer the questions of Exercise 21-10, but find the confidence interval for the mean difference.

CHAPTER 33

Planned Pairwise Comparisons of Mean Values

33-1. MULTIPLE-SAMPLE INVESTIGATIONS

In Chapter 28, we introduced the notion of a contrast and showed how contrasts can be used to conduct a priori and post hoc investigations on sample proportions. As might be expected, the same models can be adapted to cover multiple-sample comparisons of mean values for quantitative variables. In this section, we illustrate procedures for a planned analysis.

As an example of a multiple-sample investigation where the dependent variable is quantitative, consider a researcher who wants to study the effects of alcohol consumption upon motor performance. For the study, suppose that a group of 63 healthy adults ranging in age from 25 to 35 years are interviewed concerning their daily use of alcohol. Upon completion of the interviews, the subjects are divided into two groups which can be classified as "nonusers" and "users" of alcohol. Each of these groups is then divided on the basis of a table of random numbers into three subgroups. Nonusers assigned to one of the subgroups are given three 1½-oz drinks that contain no alcohol. Subjects assigned to a second group are given three similar beverages, but this time each drink contains ½ oz of vodka. Finally, the members of the third group are given drinks containing a full ounce of vodka. These same beverages are also given to the three subgroups to which the users of alcohol have been assigned. Thus, six groups of subjects are generated that can be classified as nonusers or users of alcohol given zero, 1½ oz, or 3 oz of vodka to drink. For experimental control each subject has to complete the drinking of the three drinks in 30 minutes. After a rest period of 15 minutes, each subject is tested individually by an experimenter who does not know from which of the six groups the subject comes. The subjects are asked not to discuss their results with one another.

(If a researcher could disguise the beverages to make all of them smell, taste, and look the same and to make all of them produce the same sensations in the drinker, regardless of vodka content, this study would be classified as a *double-blind* study. In this kind of study, neither the experimenter nor the subject knows to which experimental group the subject belongs. With randomization, double-blind studies satisfy the requirements of internal validity, but not necessarily those of external validity. The study we are examining is, unfortunately, not a double-blind study, because it is unlikely that a researcher could produce three such drinks that could so mimic one another in taste, smell, and other factors.)

During the testing period, each subject is seated before a television screen on which appears a moving wavy line that is projected from the top to the bottom of the screen. The subject is given a hand-held device that projects a

Table 33-1. Sample statistics for 63 subjects classified according to normal use of alcohol and amount of alcohol administered before testing on a simple motor skill.

Type of subject	Nonuser			User		
Group number	1	2	3	4	5	6
Amount of vodka used	0 oz	1½ oz	3 oz	0 oz	1½ oz	3 oz
Sample size	10	8	9	12	9	15
Mean time	8.9	6.4	3.1	9.1	8.8	7.6
Standard deviation	1.6	2.2	2.7	1.4	1.9	2.3

beam of light. The subject is told to direct the light to a circular target that moves with the line. The movements of line and target are random. The testing period lasts 10 minutes. The dependent variable of the study is the number of minutes that the subject is able to stay on target. Results are as shown in Table 33-1.

33-2. DUNN'S METHOD FOR MULTIPLE PAIRWISE COMPARISONS OF MEANS

We can apply the Dunn method of multiple comparisons in situations other than the ones illustrated in Chapter 28 involving qualitative dependent variables. We will consider in this section a special case in which comparisons among the groups are restricted to two-sample t tests. In subsequent chapters, we will show how the Dunn method can be applied to other situations.

Upon examination of the design of the study of Table 33-1, suppose we wish to estimate the effect of alcohol on performance among those considered to be users. To do so, we could compare the zero- and three-ounce groups among users in a two-sample t test. We would, in this way, find out if 3 oz of vodka seems to have any effect on performance. But we might also like to know whether 1½ oz has any effect, whether this effect is smaller than that of 3 oz, whether 1½ or 3 oz has any effect on nonusers, whether the effects are the same for users and nonusers, and so on. Each of these questions can be answered by way of a two-sample t test.

The total number of possible two-sample t tests is equal to 15, but not all of them are of interest to the researcher or even interpretable. For example, the findings based on a t test of $\mu_{Y_1} - \mu_{Y_5}$ are hard to interpret, since the subjects in group 1 are nonusers, given no alcohol to drink, while the subjects in group 5 are users given 1½ oz of vodka. If this comparison were statistically significant, one would be hard-pressed to explain the source of the difference in terms of an independent variable. It is possible that alcohol users develop a tolerance to the alcohol and that 1½ oz of vodka will not impair their performance, but that impairment due to the use of alcohol over the years is the source of the significant difference. Other comparisons which would be hard to interpret are $\mu_{Y_1} - \mu_{Y_6}$, $\mu_{Y_2} - \mu_{Y_4}$, $\mu_{Y_2} - \mu_{Y_6}$, $\mu_{Y_3} - \mu_{Y_4}$, and $\mu_{Y_3} - \mu_{Y_5}$. The remaining nine comparisons are interpretable and interesting. For example, $\mu_{Y_1} - \mu_{Y_4}$ compares nonusers against users when both are given no alcohol. One would expect to find no difference in mean performance in these two groups. If a difference were to exist, the researcher might begin to suspect some systematic errors in the testing method. If no error could be detected, one might begin to look for other factors that would explain the difference, leading perhaps to an entirely new set of experiments. The comparison of μ_{Y_1} with μ_{Y_2} is also interesting, because it will show the effects of a small amount of alcohol on people who normally do not drink or drink small amounts.

Let us assume that we wish to perform all nine comparisons of interest. Were we to test each with a 5 percent risk of a type I error, the total probability of making at least one type I error would be approximately $9(.05) = .45$. Dunn's procedure, in this case, involves testing each of the comparisons at an alpha level that divides the desired total of 5 percent among the nine contrasts. Each comparison, then, would incur a risk of error equal to $.05/9$, or roughly $.0056$. In this way, we are assured that our total risk does not exceed 5 percent.

In general, if we wished to perform a certain number C of comparisons, we would perform each test at an alpha level of $.05/C$. We would then use a Z or t table, whichever was appropriate, to find the critical value corresponding to this alpha level. Since most tables were not designed with this procedure in mind, t tables have been prepared which specify the t values to use for certain values of C, α, and v. Such a table is presented as Table A-11. In addition, this table automatically divides the proper alpha values equally in two tails. Let us show how the values in the Dunn table are related to the critical values of the t distribution. Suppose $C = 5$, $\alpha = .05$, and $v = 24$. With these numbers, the critical value reported in Table A-11 is:

$$t_{\alpha:C,v}^{\text{Dunn}} = t_{.05:5,24}^{\text{Dunn}} = \pm 2.80$$

Let us now show that these values can be found in the t table for $v = 24$ and $\alpha = .05/5 = .01$. For a two-tailed critical value, we must enter Table A-12 to find $t_{v:\alpha/2} = t_{24:.005} = -2.80$ and $t_{v:1-\alpha/2} = t_{24:.995} = 2.80$. We cannot easily use Table A-12 if $C = 7$, however, because we would need to find the value of $t_{v:\alpha/2} = t_{24:.00357}$, which is not reported.

The Dunn method of planned comparisons is based upon the same assumptions as those of the two-sample t test. Recall from Chapter 32 that it is assumed that observations between and within samples are independent, that the sample sizes are large enough to ensure sufficient operation of the central limit theorem, and that the population variances or standard deviations are all equal. In this example, the experimental design guarantees the truth of the independence assumptions, since subjects have been tested individually and have not been allowed to report their experiences to other subjects. Further, the sample sizes are sufficiently large that the distributions of differences in sample means will be fairly close in form to the normal distribution, so long as the population distributions are not too far from normal.

The final assumption needed to justify the use of the t distribution is that the standard deviations of all of the populations are equal to a common, unknown value. Visual inspection of the sample standard deviations shows that they are not too different from one another. In Section 32-4, we saw that one could estimate the common value of an unknown population variance by combining the measures of variance from the individual samples, provided they were weighted by their degrees of freedom. The extension of this procedure to more than two groups yields an estimate of σ_Y^2 based on $\nu = (N_1 - 1) + (N_2 - 1) + \cdots + (N_K - 1)$ degrees of freedom. Specifically:

$$MS_W = \frac{(N_1 - 1)S_1^2 + (N_2 - 1)S_2^2 + \cdots + (N_K - 1)S_K^2}{(N_1 - 1) + (N_2 - 1) + \cdots + (N_K - 1)}$$

where K is the number of groups. Thus, for the six groups of Table 33-1:

$$MS_W = \frac{(10 - 1)(1.6)^2 + (8 - 1)(2.2)^2 + \cdots + (15 - 1)(2.3)^2}{(10 - 1) + (8 - 1) + \cdots + (15 - 1)}$$

$$= 4.2060$$

Once the number of comparisons C is known, one performs the resulting two-sample t tests. The nine tests of interest for our example are summarized in Table 33-2. For example, for the comparison between groups 1 and 2:

$$t = \frac{\bar{Y}_1 - \bar{Y}_2}{\sqrt{\dfrac{MS_W}{N_1} + \dfrac{MS_W}{N_2}}} = \frac{8.9 - 6.4}{\sqrt{\dfrac{4.2060}{10} + \dfrac{4.2060}{8}}} = \frac{2.5}{0.97} = 2.58$$

For this example, $\alpha = .05$, $C = 9$, and $\nu = 57$. With these values, we see that we must interpolate between $\nu = 40$ and $\nu = 60$. In this case, the critical values are given by $t_{.05:9,57}^{\text{Dunn}} = \pm 2.89$, so that the 95 percent decision rule for all nine comparisons is as follows:

Decision Rule: Reject H_0 if $t < -2.89$ or if $t > 2.89$

Table 33-2.   The $C = 9$ planned-comparison t tests for the data of Table 33-1.

Comparison	d	$\sqrt{\dfrac{MS_W}{N_k} + \dfrac{MS_W}{N_{k'}}}$	t
1 vs. 2	$8.9 - 6.4 = 2.5$	0.97	2.58
1 vs. 3	$8.9 - 3.1 = 5.8$	0.94	6.17[a,b]
2 vs. 3	$6.4 - 3.1 = 3.3$	1.00	3.30[a,b]
4 vs. 5	$9.1 - 8.8 = 0.3$	0.90	0.33
4 vs. 6	$9.1 - 7.6 = 1.5$	0.79	1.90
5 vs. 6	$8.8 - 7.6 = 1.2$	0.86	1.40
1 vs. 4	$8.9 - 9.1 = -0.2$	0.88	-0.23
2 vs. 5	$6.4 - 8.8 = -2.4$	1.00	-2.40
3 vs. 6	$3.1 - 7.6 = -4.5$	0.86	-5.23[a]

[a] Significant at $\alpha \leq .05$ for two tails.
[b] Significant at $\alpha \leq .05$ for one tail.

Box 33-1   Procedure for performing the Dunn method of multiple pairwise comparisons among means

Step 1. Compute the mean and standard deviation of each sample.

Step 2. Determine the value of the mean square within, which is used as an estimate of the common, unknown variance:

$$MS_W = \frac{(N_1 - 1)S_1^2 + (N_2 - 1)S_2^2 + \cdots + (N_K - 1)S_K^2}{(N_1 - 1) + (N_2 - 1) + \cdots + (N_K - 1)}$$

Step 3. List the comparisons of interest. Let the number of comparisons be denoted by C.

Step 4. Perform the two-sample t tests for the comparisons of interest, using the value of MS_W determined at step 2.

Step 5. Obtain the decision rule from Table A-11, using as parameters:

α: the probability of a type I error

C: the number of comparisons

v: the degrees of freedom associated with MS_W

Step 6. Make a decision.

As we see, three comparisons are significant: those involving groups 1 and 3, groups 2 and 3, and groups 3 and 6. Apparently, 3 oz of vodka given to nonusers has a strong influence upon their ability to keep on target. Subjects in group 3 score considerably below the nonusers given no vodka or $1\frac{1}{2}$ oz of vodka (those in groups 1 and 2) and are even less able to stay on target than regular users given the same large amount of 3 oz (group 6). For completeness, we summarize the Dunn procedure for comparisons on means in Box 33-1.

33-3. ONE-TAILED PLANNED COMPARISONS

The Dunn table of critical values can be modified to generate one-sided decision rules for directional alternatives. We will illustrate the method using the comparisons of Table 33-2. Of the nine planned comparisons, the following comparisons could have a directional alternative, because we expect increasing amounts of alcohol to produce increasing impairment in performance: 1 versus 2, 1 versus 3, 2 versus 3, 4 versus 5, 4 versus 6, and 5 versus 6. Unless one is familiar with related research, it is difficult to see how the test of 1 versus 4, 2 versus 5, and 3 versus 6 could be directional. The decision about direction must be made in advance of data collection. To determine the one-sided decision rule for these comparisons, we begin by noting that the table is set up for two-tailed decision rules. This means that for $C = 9$, the $\alpha = .05$ is divided equally among 18 tails.

Even though we have only six directional alternatives, we still have a total of nine comparisons, and so we still need to consider the spreading of $\alpha = .05$ over nine tests. In three of these, we will divide the alpha into two tails; in the other six, we will not. This means that for the six one-sided tests, we use the critical value associated with the nine tests which share $\alpha = .05$, but this time we assume that the shared alpha is not split into two tails. The remaining three tests — the two-sided tests — use the decision rule of Section 33-2. We now consider the generation of the decision rule for a one-tailed test with $\alpha = .05$ and $C = 9$. Placing all $\alpha = .05$ in one tail of nine tests results in the same per-comparison alpha rate as placing $\alpha = .05$ in each of 4.5 tests and then dividing it into two tails. This means that we wish to use $C = 4.5$ to enter the Dunn table, since the table automatically divides the alpha into two tails. With the parameters we have, we interpolate twice: once for $C = 4$ and once for $C = 5$. We find for $C = 4$ that $t = 2.59$ and for $C = 5$ that $t = 2.67$. We now interpolate between these values to obtain $t = 2.63$ as the appropriate critical value for the six one-sided alternatives. Thus, the one-sided decision rule is:

Decision Rule: Reject H_0 if $t > 2.63$

As can be seen, the same hypotheses are rejected.

33-4. PLANNED PAIRWISE COMPARISONS UNDER THE WELCH-ASPIN MODEL

The method described in Sections 33-2 and 33-3 for analyzing planned comparisons is based upon the assumption that the standard deviations in all of the populations sampled are equal. If this assumption is not satisfied, the two-sample t test model is not appropriate. Instead, the appropriate model is the Welch-Aspin model. The test procedure for the Welch-Aspin model is similar to that of the previous two sections, in that one identifies the comparisons of interest before collecting the data. Once the data are in, all desired two-sample Welch-Aspin tests are performed. The Dunn table of critical values can be used to obtain approximate decision rules. We will show how the table can be used to evaluate the nine comparisons of Table 33-2.

Consider comparing group 1 with group 2. The two-sample Welch-Aspin test for these two samples has

$$t^* = \frac{\bar{Y}_1 - \bar{Y}_2}{\sqrt{\dfrac{S_{\bar{Y}_1}^2}{N_1} + \dfrac{S_{\bar{Y}_2}^2}{N_2}}} = \frac{8.9 - 6.4}{\sqrt{\dfrac{1.6^2}{10} + \dfrac{2.2^2}{8}}} = \frac{2.5}{0.93} = 2.69$$

Table 33-3. The $C = 9$ planned comparisons for the unequal variance model.

Comparisons	$\bar{d}$	$\sqrt{\dfrac{S^2_{\bar{Y}_k}}{N_k} + \dfrac{S^2_{\bar{Y}_{k'}}}{N_{k'}}}$	t^*	v^*	Critical value
1 vs. 2	2.5	0.93	2.69	12	±3.33
1 vs. 3	5.8	1.03	5.63ª	12	±3.33
2 vs. 3	3.3	1.19	2.77	14	±3.28
4 vs. 5	0.3	0.75	0.40	14	±3.28
4 vs. 6	1.5	0.72	2.08	23	±3.06
5 vs. 6	1.2	0.87	1.38	19	±3.14
1 vs. 4	−0.2	0.65	−0.31	18	±3.16
2 vs. 5	−2.4	1.00	−2.40	13	±3.34
3 vs. 6	−4.5	1.08	−4.17ª	14	±3.28

ª Significant at $\alpha \le .05$ for two tails.

Box 33-2 Procedure for performing planned pairwise comparisons in the Welch-Aspin model

Step 1. Compute the mean and standard deviation of each sample.

Step 2. List the comparisons of interest. Let the number of comparisons be denoted by C.

Step 3. Perform the two-sample Welch-Aspin tests for the comparisons of interest.

Step 4. For the comparison $\bar{Y}_k - \bar{Y}_{k'}$ compute $v^*_{kk'}$:

$$\frac{1}{v^*_{kk'}} = \frac{1}{v_k}\left(1 - \frac{W_k}{W}\right)^2 + \frac{1}{v_{k'}}\left(1 - \frac{W_{k'}}{W}\right)^2$$

where

$$W = W_k + W_{k'}$$

$$W_k = \frac{N_k}{S^2_k}$$

$$W_{k'} = \frac{N_{k'}}{S^2_{k'}}$$

Step 5. Obtain the decision rule from Table A-11, using as parameters:

α: the probability of a type I error

C: the number of comparisons

v^*: the degrees of freedom calculated from step 4

Step 6. Make the decisions.

The $t*$ for the remaining comparisons are reported in Table 33-3. The degrees of freedom for this first comparison are given as follows:

$$\frac{1}{v*} = \frac{1}{v_1}\left(1 - \frac{W_1}{W}\right)^2 + \frac{1}{v_2}\left(1 - \frac{W_2}{W}\right)^2$$

where $W_1 = 10/1.6^2 = 3.9063$, $W_2 = 8/2.2^2 = 1.6529$, $W = W_1 + W_2 = 5.5592$, $v_1 = N_1 - 1 = 10 - 1 = 9$, and $v_2 = N_2 - 1 = 8 - 1 = 7$, so that

$$\frac{1}{v*} = \frac{1}{9}\left(1 - \frac{3.9063}{5.5592}\right)^2 + \frac{1}{7}\left(1 - \frac{1.6529}{5.5592}\right)^2$$
$$= 0.0804$$

and thus $v* = 12.44 \simeq 12$. Since we are making $C = 9$ tests, we enter the Dunn table of critical values with $\alpha = .05$, $C = 9$, and $v* = 12$. With these values, the critical values are given by

$$t_{.05:9,12}^{\text{Dunn}} = \pm 3.37$$

The remaining critical values are reported in Table 33-3. Note how much larger these critical values are than the critical values of $t = \pm 2.89$, which are based on the assumption that the population variances are equal. In this case μ_1 differs from μ_3 and μ_3 differs from μ_6, but μ_2 does not differ from μ_3, as was reported in Table 33-2. We provide directions for this model in Box 33-2.

33-5. PLANNED COMPARISONS UNDER THE WILCOXON MODEL

Both the multiple two-sample t test and the Welch-Aspin model presented in the previous sections are based upon the assumption that the original dependent variable of the study has a normal distribution or that the sample sizes are large enough to justify assuming that the distribution of the differences in sample means approaches the normal distribution through the central limit theorem. If either of these conditions is not satisfied, the previously described methods should not be used. A reasonable solution is to perform all possible two-sample Wilcoxon tests of interest. Unfortunately, this procedure has been shown to be of little utility if the sample sizes are small, since rejection regions may fail to exist when the risk of at least one type I error is split among the contrasts. Tables have been prepared of the appropriate decision rules, but only for the case in which the sample sizes are all equal. Because this is restrictive, and because each application of the test requires a reranking or a large-sample situation, the model is not presented. Instead, we will present an alternative model in Section 38-3.

33-6. TUKEY'S METHOD OF PAIRED COMPARISONS

Another method of pairwise comparisons that is encountered frequently in the literature is Tukey's method of paired comparisons (1953). This method is similar to the Dunn method, except that it requires an examination of all possible two-tailed pairwise comparisons. For that reason it is not a method that would be useful on the data of Table 33-1. When Tukey first proposed this method, it required the use of equal-sized samples. It can be used for unequal sample sizes provided they are not too dissimilar. This has been shown by Dunnett (1983). If an interest exists in all pairwise comparisons of the sample means, then it is known that the Tukey procedure is the best procedure, in that its critical values are smaller than those obtained for the Dunn procedure. However, the differences between the two methods are not large. As a demonstration of their nearly equal critical values, consider six groups and all 15 pairwise comparisons tested with $\alpha = .05$ and $\nu = 60$. The Dunn critical value is equal to 3.06, while the Tukey critical value is equal to 2.94.

The Tukey statistic is defined as follows:

$$t_T = \frac{\overline{Y}_{\text{largest}} - \overline{Y}_{\text{smallest}}}{\sqrt{MS_W(1/N_L + 1/N_S)}}$$

If t_T is not in the rejection region, then no other difference can be significantly different from zero. For the data of Table 33-1, we have:

$$t_T = \frac{9.1 - 3.1}{\sqrt{4.2060(1/12 + 1/9)}} = 6.63$$

The degrees of freedom for MS_W are given by $\nu = 57$ and the number of groups is $K = 6$. Critical values for Tukey's method are proportional to the values, q, read from Table A-13. This table is entered with the appropriate values of K and ν and with $\alpha = .05$ or $\alpha = .01$. For $\alpha = .05$, $K = 6$, and $\nu = 57$, we see that

$$q_{.05:6,57} = 4.16$$

This value is not on the same scale as the t distribution, but it can be placed on that scale by dividing it by $\sqrt{2}$. Thus, the critical value for comparing all $C = \binom{6}{2} = 15$ pairwise comparisons is given by:

$$t_{\alpha:K,\nu}^{\text{Tukey}} = t_{.05:6,57}^{\text{Tukey}} = \pm \frac{q_{.05:6,57}}{\sqrt{2}} = \pm \frac{4.16}{\sqrt{2}} = \pm 2.94$$

Hence, the Tukey statistic is significant. In addition, any other pairwise comparison with a t value smaller than -2.94 or greater than 2.94 is also

---

Box 33-3   Directions for Tukey's test

Step 1. To test

$$H_0: \quad \mu_{Y_k} - \mu_{Y_{k'}} = 0 \qquad \text{for all } k \text{ and } k'$$

against

$$H_1: \quad \text{at least one } \mu_{Y_k} - \mu_{Y_{k'}} \neq 0$$

compute

$$t_T = \frac{\overline{Y}_{\text{largest}} - \overline{Y}_{\text{smallest}}}{\sqrt{MS_W(1/N_L + 1/N_S)}}$$

Step 2. With α, K, and ν, reject H_0 if

$$t_T > t_{\alpha:K,\nu}^{\text{Tukey}} = \frac{q}{\sqrt{2}}$$

where q is read from Table A-13.

Step 3. If H_0 is rejected, compute

$$t_{k,k'} = \frac{\overline{Y}_k - \overline{Y}_{k'}}{\sqrt{MS_W(1/N_k + 1/N_{k'})}}$$

and compare each pairwise difference in means with $t_{\alpha:K,\nu}^{\text{Tukey}}$. Any difference that exceeds $t_{\alpha:K,\nu}^{\text{Tukey}}$ in absolute value represents a statistically significant difference.

---

significant. One undesirable property of the Tukey method is that it distributes the alpha across all pairwise comparisons—those that are interesting and those that are not—and, in this sense, the method might be wasteful of type I error control. Directions for Tukey's test are provided in Box 33-3.

The results of Tukey's method are often displayed graphically in the body of a manuscript or article. In these situations, the means are rank-ordered, and nonsignificant differences are underlined. For this example, one would convey the information as follows:

3.1   <u>6.4   7.6   8.8   8.9</u>   9.1

As indicated, the mean value 3.1 is significantly different from 6.4 and all other means. At the same time, 6.4 differs significantly from 9.1.

33-7. EXERCISES

33-1. In the study of Exercise 24-8 the sample means and standard deviations for groups of size 20 were as follows:

$$\bar{Y}_1 = 2000, \ \bar{Y}_2 = 2200, \ \bar{Y}_3 = 3300, \text{ and } \bar{Y}_4 = 3700$$
$$S_{Y_1} = 220, \ S_{Y_2} = 240, \ S_{Y_3} = 300, \text{ and } S_{Y_4} = 420$$

Make three pairwise analyses of the mean differences, using $\alpha = .05$, as follows:
a. Assuming all population variances are equal, use Dunn's method.
b. Assuming all population variances are equal, use Tukey's method.
c. Assuming population variances are not all equal, use the Welch-Aspin method.
Make a comparison of the three methods.

33-2. The study of Table 33-1 is modified and carried out on male and female college students over the age of 21. The results are as shown in the two tables at right. Apply Tukey's method to the eight means. Summarize the results in a short paragraph for a scholarly journal. Use $\alpha = .05$.

33-3. For the data of Exercise 33-2, list the pairwise contrasts of interpretable interest and apply Dunn's model to the data, assuming equal population variances. Use both one- and two-tailed tests in your study. Present the results in tabular form and in a short paragraph for a scholarly journal.

Males	Type of subject			
	Nonusers		Users	
Group number	1	2	3	4
Amount of vodka	0 oz	3 oz	0 oz	3 oz
Sample size	15	15	15	15
Mean time	12.2	6.1	13.2	11.4
Standard deviation	2.0	3.1	1.9	2.8

Females	Type of subject			
	Nonusers		Users	
Group number	5	6	7	8
Amount of vodka	0 oz	3 oz	0 oz	3 oz
Sample size	15	15	15	15
Mean time	10.3	4.1	11.6	8.7
Standard deviation	2.4	7.1	2.6	3.1

33-4. Repeat the analysis of Exercise 33-3 in terms of the Welch-Aspin model. Present the results in tabular form for a scholarly journal.

CHAPTER 34

Planned Multiple Comparisons Using Complex Contrasts

34-1. COMPLEX CONTRASTS

Let us reconsider the data of Table 33-1. In our presentation in Chapter 33, we examined certain pairwise comparisons that were of particular interest to us. A different investigation might focus on different comparisons in order to answer different questions of interest. Let us examine what some of these questions might be and see how we might generate tests to answer them. For example, another investigator might like to know whether the consumption of 1½ oz of vodka has an effect upon performance when compared with the no-alcohol condition. This would involve a comparison of the mean for all subjects given 1½ oz of vodka with the mean for all subjects drinking no alcohol.

As we saw in Section 4-6, the mean values in two samples can be combined to produce the mean of the combined group. To do so one weights each mean by its sample size, according to the formula

$$\bar{Y}_{(k,k')} = \frac{N_k\bar{Y}_k + N_{k'}\bar{Y}_{k'}}{N_k + N_{k'}}$$

Hence, to find the mean for all subjects receiving 1½ oz of vodka, one would calculate:

$$\bar{Y}_{(2,5)} = \frac{N_2\bar{Y}_2 + N_5\bar{Y}_5}{N_2 + N_5}$$

Similarly, the mean for all subjects given no alcohol is:

$$\bar{Y}_{(1,4)} = \frac{N_1\bar{Y}_1 + N_4\bar{Y}_4}{N_1 + N_4}$$

Therefore, the comparison of interest is given by

$$\begin{aligned}
\hat{\psi}_1 &= \bar{Y}_{(2,5)} - \bar{Y}_{(1,4)} \\
&= \frac{N_2\bar{Y}_2 + N_5\bar{Y}_5}{N_2 + N_5} - \frac{N_1\bar{Y}_1 + N_4\bar{Y}_4}{N_1 + N_4} \\
&= \frac{8(6.4) + 9(8.8)}{8 + 9} - \frac{10(8.9) + 12(9.1)}{10 + 12} \\
&= 7.67 - 9.01 = -1.34
\end{aligned}$$

The first element of this comparison is the average of the 17 people who have received 1½ oz of vodka. The mean number of minutes they stay on target is 7.67. The second element of this comparison is the average of the 22 people who have received no alcohol. For these 22 people, the mean value is 9.01 minutes. The difference between the two means, 1.34 minutes, is a comparison based on the means of four groups of people. Any contrast based on more than two means is called a *complex comparison*.

As another example of a comparison of interest, consider:

$$\begin{aligned}
\hat{\psi}_2 &= \frac{N_1\bar{Y}_1 + N_2\bar{Y}_2 + N_3\bar{Y}_3}{N_1 + N_2 + N_3} - \frac{N_4\bar{Y}_4 + N_5\bar{Y}_5 + N_6\bar{Y}_6}{N_4 + N_5 + N_6} \\
&= \frac{10(8.9) + 8(6.4) + 9(3.1)}{10 + 8 + 9} - \frac{12(9.1) + 9(8.8) + 15(7.6)}{12 + 9 + 15} \\
&= 6.23 - 8.40 = -2.17
\end{aligned}$$

This contrast represents the comparison of two means, the mean value for the 27 nonusers of alcohol (6.23 minutes), and the mean value for the 36 users

(8.40 minutes). The number of comparisons of three or more averages that one can generate from the data of Table 33-1 is large. In fact, if the number of groups exceeds two, the number of comparisons possible is infinite.

Let us take a further look at $\hat{\psi}_1$. Note that:

$$\hat{\psi}_1 = \tfrac{8}{17}\overline{Y}_2 + \tfrac{9}{17}\overline{Y}_5 - \tfrac{10}{22}\overline{Y}_1 - \tfrac{12}{22}\overline{Y}_4$$

can be written in terms of all of the six means of Table 33-1 as follows:

$$\hat{\psi}_1 = (-\tfrac{10}{22})\overline{Y}_1 + (\tfrac{8}{17})\overline{Y}_2 + (0)\overline{Y}_3 + (-\tfrac{12}{22})\overline{Y}_4 + (\tfrac{9}{17})\overline{Y}_5 + (0)\overline{Y}_6$$

In addition, note that the weights sum to zero:

$$(-\tfrac{10}{22}) + (\tfrac{8}{17}) + (0) + (-\tfrac{12}{22}) + (\tfrac{9}{17}) + (0) = 0$$

Further, this same summing to zero holds for the weights of $\hat{\psi}_2$. For this comparison:

$$\hat{\psi}_2 = (\tfrac{10}{27})\overline{Y}_1 + (\tfrac{8}{27})\overline{Y}_2 + (\tfrac{9}{27})\overline{Y}_3 + (-\tfrac{12}{36})\overline{Y}_4 + (-\tfrac{9}{36})\overline{Y}_5 + (-\tfrac{15}{36})\overline{Y}_6$$

and

$$(\tfrac{10}{27}) + (\tfrac{8}{27}) + (\tfrac{9}{27}) + (-\tfrac{12}{36}) + (-\tfrac{9}{36}) + (-\tfrac{15}{36}) = 0$$

Clearly, $\hat{\psi}_1$ and $\hat{\psi}_2$ represent contrasts, on sample means, similar to those examined in Chapter 28 for proportions. In previous chapters we established the theory that can be used to test these contrasts, and we will now apply it in the present context.

First it is known from Section 20-3 that the standard deviation of the linear combination

$$\hat{\psi} = W_1\overline{Y}_1 + W_2\overline{Y}_2 + \cdots + W_K\overline{Y}_K$$

is given by

$$\sigma_{\hat{\psi}} = \sqrt{W_1^2\mathrm{Var}(\overline{Y}_1) + W_2^2\mathrm{Var}(\overline{Y}_2) + \cdots + W_K^2\mathrm{Var}(\overline{Y}_K)}$$

We also know, from Section 32-1, that each variance can be estimated by

$$SE_{\overline{Y}_k}^2 = \frac{S_k^2}{N_k}$$

so that

$$SE_{\hat{\psi}} = \sqrt{W_1^2\frac{S_1^2}{N_1} + W_2^2\frac{S_2^2}{N_2} + \cdots + W_K^2\frac{S_K^2}{N_K}}$$

As seen in Section 33-2, if, in addition, all population variances are equal, the MS_W can be substituted for each sample variance to obtain:

$$SE_{\hat\psi} = \sqrt{MS_W \left(\frac{W_1^2}{N_1} + \frac{W_2^2}{N_2} + \cdots + \frac{W_K^2}{N_K} \right)}$$

This means that one can test the hypothesis $H_0 : \psi = 0$ against the alternative $H_1 : \psi \neq 0$ by computing:

$$t_{\hat\psi} = \frac{\hat\psi}{SE_{\hat\psi}}$$

The only thing lacking is the appropriate decision rule. From the previous chapter, we know that a researcher can define as many pairwise or complex contrasts as desired and determine critical values for $t_{\hat\psi}$ from the Dunn table, Table A-11. Under this formulation, the decision rule would read as follows:

Decision Rule: Reject H_0 if $t_{\hat\psi} < -t_{\alpha:C,\nu}^{\text{Dunn}}$ or if $t_{\hat\psi} > t_{\alpha:C,\nu}^{\text{Dunn}}$

where C is the total number of contrasts of interest and where ν is the degrees of freedom associated with MS_W. For completeness, directions for a planned analysis of means are given in Box 34-1.

Box 34-1   Procedure for a planned analysis on means

Step 1. Define all contrasts of interest as

$$\psi = W_1 \mu_{Y_1} + W_2 \mu_{Y_2} + \cdots + W_K \mu_{Y_K}$$

where, for each contrast:

$$W_1 + W_2 + \cdots + W_K = 0$$

Step 2. Under the assumption of equal variance, estimate the population value by MS_W.

Step 3. Test each contrast for statistical significance by using

$$t_{\hat\psi} = \frac{\hat\psi}{SE_{\hat\psi}} = \frac{W_1 \bar{Y}_1 + W_2 \bar{Y}_2 + \cdots + W_K \bar{Y}_K}{\sqrt{MS_W \left(\dfrac{W_1^2}{N_1} + \dfrac{W_2^2}{N_2} + \cdots + \dfrac{W_K^2}{N_K} \right)}}$$

Step 4. With the α of interest and $\nu = N - K$, determine the appropriate critical region from Table A-11.

Step 5. Make the decisions.

34-2. FAMILIES OF HYPOTHESES

We now wish to discuss a topic about which there is disagreement among applied researchers and theoretical statisticians. At this point, we will present results that make sense to us. As our presentation unfolds, our position will become clearer.

The study of Table 33-1 is based upon one dependent variable: the number of minutes subjects are able to stay on target. On the other hand, the study involves two independent variables, both of which vary across the random assignment of subjects. One of these variables is a *self-selected* characteristic; i.e., it is the *voluntary* matter of being a nonuser or user of alcohol. The remaining independent variable is one specified by the experimenters of the study, the amount of vodka consumed by each subject: 0, 1½, or 3 oz. These independent variables define *groups* of research questions that can be lumped together in discrete sets that make theoretical or practical sense. This grouping of hypotheses was hinted at in the presentation of results in Table 33-2, where related hypotheses were grouped together. For example, the comparisons 1 versus 2, 1 versus 3, and 2 versus 3 relate to comparisons among subjects who are nonusers of alcohol; comparisons 4 versus 5, 4 versus 6, and 5 versus 6 involve comparisons among users; and, finally, comparisons 1 versus 4, 2 versus 5, and 3 versus 6 involve contrasts between nonusers and users of alcohol. Such groups of conceptually related comparisons make up what are called *families of hypotheses*. The question that such families raise involves the manner of controlling the risk of a type I error. The procedure that seems to be gaining acceptance is to control the type I error rate according to family. If this were done using our convention of type I error control of $\alpha = .05$, the first three comparisons of Table 33-2 would be controlled at $\alpha_1 = .05$, the second set of three would be controlled at $\alpha_2 = .05$, and the last set of three would be controlled at $\alpha_3 = .05$.

This view is different from the way in which we presented the analysis in Chapter 33, and even there we provided options among which a researcher could choose. We first examined 9 contrasts that shared $\alpha = .05$ in the Dunn model, and later we considered all 15 pairwise contrasts in the Tukey model. In this section, we are presenting a third way of controlling type I errors, using the notion of a family of related hypotheses as the basis for this control. Which of these views to adopt must be decided by the researcher. Frequently, the choice can be guided by considering which questions are of primary importance in the study.

To help clarify the statistical issues involved, let us examine the type I error rates involved per contrast and per experiment in the three approaches just considered. In the Dunn model, each contrast is allotted $\alpha = .05/9 = .0056$, so that the overall type I error rate for the study is limited to 5 percent. Similarly, the error rate per contrast in the Tukey model is close to $\alpha = .05/15 = .0033$, and again the type I error rate for the experiment is held at $\alpha = .05$. On the other hand, for the three-family approach, using the family as the unit of control, each of the nine contrasts would receive $\alpha = .05/3 = 0.0167$. In addition, the *experimentwise* error rate under the Dunn and Tukey procedures would equal 5 percent, but under the three-family approach the experimentwise error rate would be 15 percent. Thus, the three views are not mutually consistent.

We use the family model here to continue our analysis of the data of Table 33-1. Contrasts $\hat{\psi}_1$ and $\hat{\psi}_2$ belong to different families. Contrast $\hat{\psi}_1$ belongs to a family in which there are an unlimited number of members. Contrast $\hat{\psi}_2$ involves a family consisting of only one member. Let us examine these families of hypotheses.

We see that $\hat{\psi}_1$ involves a comparison of subjects who have received either no vodka or 1½ oz of vodka. This is a contrast involving different amounts of alcohol *across* user type. This suggests that one family of related hypotheses would consist of all contrasts of interest that examine questions involving amounts of vodka. The members of this family of contrasts are $\hat{\psi}_{.1a}$, $\hat{\psi}_{.1b}$, and $\hat{\psi}_{.1c}$, where $\hat{\psi}_{.1a}$ compares the effects of zero and 1½ oz of vodka, $\hat{\psi}_{.1b}$ compares zero and 3 oz of vodka, and $\hat{\psi}_{.1c}$ compares 1½ and 3 oz of vodka. For the data of Table 33-1:

$$\hat{\psi}_{.1a} = \frac{10(8.9) + 12(9.1)}{22} - \frac{8(6.4) + 9(8.8)}{17}$$
$$= 9.01 - 7.67 = 1.34$$

and

$$SE_{\hat{\psi}.1a} = \sqrt{4.2060 \left(\frac{(^{10}/_{22})^2}{10} + \frac{(^{12}/_{22})^2}{12} + \frac{(-^8/_{17})^2}{8} + \frac{(-^9/_{17})^2}{9} \right)}$$
$$= \sqrt{\frac{4.2060}{20} + \frac{4.2060}{17}} = 0.66$$

In a similar way, $\hat{\psi}_{.1b} = 3.10$, $\hat{\psi}_{.1c} = 1.76$, $SE_{\hat{\psi}.1b} = 0.66$, and $SE_{\hat{\psi}.1c} = 0.65$. Finally:

$$t_{\hat{\psi}.1a} = \frac{1.34}{0.66} = 2.03$$

with $t_{\hat{\psi}.1b} = 5.08$ and $t_{\hat{\psi}.1c} = 2.70$. With $C = 3$, $\alpha = .05$, and $v = 57$, the critical values read from Table A-11 are given by $t_{.05:3,57}^{\text{Dunn}} = \pm 2.47$. Thus, differences associated with $\hat{\psi}_{.1b}$ and $\hat{\psi}_{.1c}$ are significant. Performance under the influence of 3 oz of vodka differs from that with zero or 1½-oz usage.

On the other hand, we see that $\hat{\psi}_2$ examines the difference between non-users and users regardless of the amount of alcohol consumed. This is the only contrast that can be defined between the combined means for the two types of users. Hence, the family has only $\hat{\psi}_2$ as a member. For this contrast:

$$\hat{\psi}_{2.} = [{}^{10}\!/_{27}(8.9) + {}^{8}\!/_{27}(6.4) + {}^{9}\!/_{27}(3.1)]$$
$$- [{}^{12}\!/_{36}(9.1) + {}^{9}\!/_{36}(8.8) + {}^{15}\!/_{36}(7.6)]$$
$$= 6.23 - 8.40 = -2.17$$

with

$$SE_{\hat{\psi}_{2.}} = \sqrt{4.2060 \left\{ \left[\frac{({}^{10}\!/_{27})^2}{10} + \frac{({}^{8}\!/_{27})^2}{8} + \frac{({}^{9}\!/_{27})^2}{9} \right] + \left[\frac{(-{}^{12}\!/_{36})^2}{12} + \frac{(-{}^{9}\!/_{36})^2}{9} + \frac{(-{}^{15}\!/_{36})^2}{15} \right] \right\}}$$

$$= \sqrt{\frac{4.2060}{27} + \frac{4.2060}{36}} = 0.52$$

so that

$$t_{\hat{\psi}_{2.}} = \frac{\hat{\psi}_{2.}}{SE_{\hat{\psi}_{2.}}} = \frac{-2.17}{0.52} = -4.17$$

We now determine the decision rule for this family, consisting of one hypothesis. When a family consists of only one member, $C = 1$. Dunn's critical values reduce to t test critical values, since the total α is distributed in one contrast among two tails. Therefore, the critical value for $v = 57$ is given by $t = \pm 2.00$. Thus, H_0 for the test of

$$H_0: \quad \psi_2 = 0$$

against

$$H_1: \quad \psi_2 \neq 0$$

is rejected. Nonusers of alcohol have a harder time staying on target than do users.

For a planned analysis based on the unequal-variance Welch-Aspin model, one must compute an effective number of degree-of-freedom values for *each* specific contrast. For the contrast,

$$\hat{\psi} = \sum_{k=1}^{K} W_k \bar{Y}_k$$

the squared standard error is given by

$$SE_{\hat{\psi}}^2 = \sum_{k=1}^{K} W_k^2 \frac{S_k^2}{N_k}$$

If we let $\hat{\theta}_k = W_k^2 S_k^2 / N_k$, then we can write the squared standard error as $SE_{\hat{\psi}}^2 = \hat{\theta}_1 + \hat{\theta}_2 + \cdots + \hat{\theta}_K$. In terms of the $\hat{\theta}_k$, the number of degrees of freedom associated with $\hat{\psi}$ is given by

$$v^* = \frac{(\hat{\theta}_1 + \hat{\theta}_2 + \cdots + \hat{\theta}_K)^2}{\hat{\theta}_1^2/v_1 + \hat{\theta}_2^2/v_2 + \cdots + \hat{\theta}_K^2/v_K} = \frac{1}{\hat{\theta}}(SE_{\hat{\psi}}^2)^2$$

where $\hat{\theta} = \sum_{k=1}^{K} \hat{\theta}_k^2/v_k$.

As an example, consider contrast $\psi_{.1a}$. For this contrast,

$$SE_{\hat{\psi}_{.1a}}^2 = (^{10}\!/_{22})^2 \frac{1.6^2}{10} + (^{12}\!/_{22})^2 \frac{1.4^2}{12} + (-^{8}\!/_{17})^2 \frac{2.2^2}{8} + (-^{9}\!/_{17})^2 \frac{1.9^2}{9}$$

$$= .0529 + .0486 + .1340 + .1124 = .3479$$

and so

$$t^* = \frac{\hat{\psi}_{.1a}}{SE_{\hat{\psi}_{.1a}}} = \frac{1.34}{\sqrt{.3479}} = 2.27$$

In addition

$$\hat{\theta} = \frac{(.0529)^2}{9} + \frac{(.0486)^2}{11} + \frac{(.1340)^2}{7} + \frac{(.1124)^2}{8} = .0047$$

and

$$v^* = \frac{(.3479)^2}{.0047} = 25.92 \approx 25$$

With this value, the critical value is found in Table A-11, with the α of interest and C the number of planned contrasts.

34-3. TESTS OF INTERACTION

Another important use of contrasts is made in identifying significant interactions among variables. The idea of an interaction is illustrated in the following four-group experiment. Consider taking 40 adults and dividing them into four groups. Let the groups be given the following experimental treatments:

Group 1. A glass of water and five sugar pills
Group 2. A glass of water and five barbiturate pills
Group 3. A glass of whiskey and five sugar pills
Group 4. A glass of whiskey and five barbiturate pills

After one hour, one would expect nothing to have happened to the subjects in group 1. The subjects in group 2 would be expected to be relaxed, groggy, or even asleep. Subjects in group 3 should be quite drunk, happy, or perhaps unconscious. Finally, the subjects in group 4 should be close to death, or else dead. Barbiturates by themselves are relaxing. Whiskey can also be relaxing. But when barbiturates and whiskey are brought together, the effect is devastating. One could say that the two drugs have a synergistic effect, or that the two drugs interact. An interaction is produced when the response to the joint appearance of two different factors differs from the simple sum of the responses obtained when the two factors are seen separately. It should be noted that not all interactions produce a magnified effect. In many cases, the factors might react to significantly decrease the response. In any case, the identification of significant interactions occupies a large part of the research activities of behavioral scientists.

A simple way to understand what is meant by an interaction is to know what is meant by the presence of no interaction. A graphic picture of a situation involving no interaction is provided in Figure 34-1.

Consider the two variables of our example, liquid and tablet. Let us denote the cell means for some physiological measure in Table 34-1 and in Figure 34-1 as follows:

$$\mu_{Y_{11}} = \text{mean given water and sugar}$$

$$\mu_{Y_{12}} = \text{mean given water and barbiturate}$$

$$\mu_{Y_{21}} = \text{mean given alcohol and sugar}$$

$$\mu_{Y_{22}} = \text{mean given alcohol and barbiturate}$$

We would estimate the effects of alcohol as the difference $\Delta_1 = \mu_{Y_{21}} - \mu_{Y_{11}}$

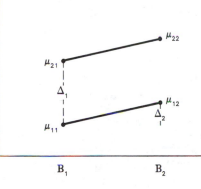

Figure 34-1.
A graphic representation of no interaction for a two-factor design with two levels on each factor.

Table 34-1. Mean values to study the interaction of liquid type and tablet type.

	Tablet	
Liquid	Sugar	Barbiturate
Water	$\mu_{Y_{11}}$	$\mu_{Y_{12}}$
Alcohol	$\mu_{Y_{21}}$	$\mu_{Y_{22}}$

and the effects of the barbiturate as $\Delta_2 = \mu_{Y_{12}} - \mu_{Y_{11}}$. The joint effects of alcohol and the barbiturate would be estimated by

$$\Delta_{12} = \mu_{Y_{22}} - \mu_{Y_{11}}$$

If there were no interaction, Δ_{12} should equal the sum of Δ_1 and Δ_2. That is:

$$\Delta_{12} = \Delta_1 + \Delta_2$$

or

$$\mu_{Y_{22}} - \mu_{Y_{11}} = (\mu_{Y_{21}} - \mu_{Y_{11}}) + (\mu_{Y_{12}} - \mu_{Y_{11}})$$

This equation for no interaction can also be written as follows:

$$\mu_{Y_{22}} - \mu_{Y_{21}} - \mu_{Y_{12}} + \mu_{Y_{11}} = 0$$

The sum on the left represents a contrast

$$\psi = \mu_{Y_{22}} - \mu_{Y_{21}} - \mu_{Y_{12}} + \mu_{Y_{11}}$$

whose value is zero for no interaction. Another way to examine this contrast is to note that by rearranging terms, we would indicate that no interaction occurs by writing:

$$\psi = (\mu_{Y_{11}} - \mu_{Y_{12}}) - (\mu_{Y_{21}} - \mu_{Y_{22}}) = 0$$
$$= (\text{change between sugar and barbiturate for water})$$
$$- (\text{change between sugar and barbiturate for alcohol})$$

When these changes are equal — i.e., when they can be graphed as the corresponding sides of a parallelogram as in Figure 34-1 — there is no interaction.

In like manner we can rearrange the terms, again, to show that

$$\psi = (\mu_{Y_{11}} - \mu_{Y_{21}}) - (\mu_{Y_{12}} - \mu_{Y_{22}}) = 0$$
= (change between water and alcohol for sugar)
− (change between water and alcohol for barbiturate)

represents a lack of interaction. When $\psi \neq 0$, it is said that the two factors interact.

Consider the following example, represented in Figure 34-2. In Figure 34-2a, we see an interaction that exists between sex and special training on how to make cream puffs. A group of 10 girls and 10 boys is divided at random into four groups in which five of the boys and five of the girls are given a recipe for cream puffs, together with the necessary ingredients, and are told to make the cream puffs as well as they can. The remaining five boys and five girls are given a demonstration by an experienced baker in the making of cream puffs. Particular attention is given to the appropriate methods for mixing ingredients, and the danger spots and other sticky problems are indicated. After all 20 subjects have completed their cream puff adventures, the results are rated for quality by 10 judges who score the work on a scale of 1 to 10. The results are as shown in Table 34-2. In this case, we see that the boys outperform the girls in the no-training condition by 3.5 points; however, given the training, the girls turn the tables on the boys. They are seen to have profited more from the training than have the boys, since they exceed the boys by 2.7 mean rating points. We would say that training and sex interact in his experiment.

Almost all tests of interaction are made within the model of equal population variances and equal sample sizes. However, this is not necessary, since

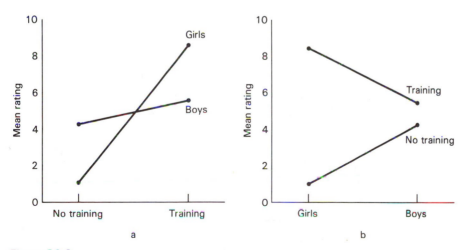

Figure 34-2.
Two examples of an interaction for a two-factor design with two levels on each factor.

Table 34-2. Mean ratings of quality of
workmanship in the making
of cream puffs by a group
of boys and girls.

	No training	Training
Girls	1.1	8.5
Boys	4.6	5.8

unequal sample sizes and unequal population variances can be handled under
the Welch-Aspin models. Nevertheless, we will illustrate only the method for
equal-sized samples and equal population variances. For the data of Table
34-2, the MS_W is given by 2.05. In terms of this measure of variation and
sample means, we go through the following steps:

$$\hat{\psi} = (1.1 - 4.6) - (8.5 - 5.8) = 6.2$$

$$SE_{\hat{\psi}} = \sqrt{2.05 \left[\frac{(1)^2}{5} + \frac{(-1)^2}{5} + \frac{(-1)^2}{5} + \frac{(1)^2}{5} \right]} = \sqrt{1.6400} = 1.28$$

$$t_{\hat{\psi}} = \frac{6.2}{1.28} = 4.84$$

$$\nu = 20 - 4 = 16$$

Decision Rule: Reject H_0 if $t_{\hat{\psi}} < -2.12$ or if $t_{\hat{\psi}} > 2.12$

Decision: Reject H_0. An interaction is observed.

Finally, let us point out that the set of interactions defines another family of
hypotheses for analyzing the data of Table 33-1. As we recall, this study is
based on two independent variables. One could ask whether these variables
interact. This could be investigated in terms of the three contrasts $\hat{\psi}_{12a}$, $\hat{\psi}_{12b}$,
and $\hat{\psi}_{12c}$. For the data of Table 33-1,

$$\hat{\psi}_{12a} = (\bar{Y}_1 - \bar{Y}_2) - (\bar{Y}_4 - \bar{Y}_5)$$
$$= (8.9 - 6.4) - (9.1 - 8.8) = 2.2$$

with

$$SE_{\hat{\psi}_{12a}} = \sqrt{4.2060 \left[\frac{(1)^2}{10} + \frac{(-1)^2}{8} + \frac{(-1)^2}{12} + \frac{(1)^2}{9} \right]} = 1.33$$

In addition, $\hat{\psi}_{12b} = 4.3$, $\hat{\psi}_{12c} = 2.1$, $SE_{\hat{\psi}_{12b}} = 1.23$, and $SE_{\hat{\psi}_{12c}} = 1.32$, so that

$$t_{\hat{\psi}_{12a}} = \frac{2.2}{1.33} = 1.65$$

$$t_{\hat{\psi}_{12b}} = \frac{4.3}{1.23} = 3.50$$

and

$$t_{\hat{\psi}_{12c}} = \frac{2.1}{1.32} = 1.59$$

With $\alpha = .05$, $C = 3$, and $v = 57$, the critical value reported in Table A-11 is $t_{.05:3,57}^{\text{Dunn}} = 2.47$. With this value, ψ_{12b} is different from zero. Directions for testing interactions are provided in Box 34-2.

Increasing the amount of vodka from 0 to 3 oz has a much greater impact on nonusers than on users. For users, the average time on target changes from 9.1 minutes to 7.6 minutes, while that for nonusers changes from 8.9 minutes to only 3.1 minutes. Alcohol clearly hinders the performance of nonusers of alcohol more than that of users.

Box 34-2   Procedure for testing interactions

Step 1. Determine the means of the four groups that involve the interaction of interest. Let the means be denoted in the same way the population values are in Table 34-1.

Step 2. Compute

$$\hat{\psi} = (\bar{Y}_{11} - \bar{Y}_{21}) - (\bar{Y}_{12} - \bar{Y}_{22})$$

Step 3. Under the assumption of equal variances, compute

$$SE_{\hat{\psi}} = \sqrt{MS_W \left[\frac{(1)^2}{N_{11}} + \frac{(-1)^2}{N_{12}} + \frac{(-1)^2}{N_{21}} + \frac{(1)^2}{N_{22}} \right]}$$

Step 4. Compute

$$t_{\hat{\psi}} = \frac{\hat{\psi}}{SE_{\hat{\psi}}}$$

Step 5. With $v = N - K$, determine the decision rule from Table A-12 or A-11, depending upon whether 1 or C contrasts are examined.

Step 6. Make a decision.

Occasionally, one sees the terms *ordinal* and *disordinal* used to describe interactions. In Figure 34-2a, the graph depicts what has been termed a disordinal interaction, because the lines cross. In Figure 34-2b, however, we have graphed the same interaction in another way, and here, because the lines do not cross, the interaction is termed ordinal. The terms have no unambiguous meaning, and we do not advise their use.

34-4. ORTHOGONAL CONTRASTS

The contrasts that many researchers in the social sciences prefer to use in their studies are those which do not contain redundant information. To see what this means, consider the three contrasts

$$\psi_1 = \mu_{Y_1} - \mu_{Y_2}$$
$$\psi_2 = \mu_{Y_1} - \mu_{Y_3}$$

and

$$\psi_3 = \mu_{Y_2} - \mu_{Y_3}$$

Notice that ψ_1 involves a comparison of μ_{Y_2} with μ_{Y_1} and that ψ_2 involves a comparison of μ_{Y_3} with μ_{Y_1}. These two contrasts are thereby restricted by their joint reference to μ_{Y_1}. Furthermore, ψ_3 is redundant, since

$$\psi_3 = \mu_{Y_2} - \mu_{Y_3} = (\mu_{Y_1} - \mu_{Y_3}) - (\mu_{Y_1} - \mu_{Y_2})$$
$$= \psi_2 - \psi_1$$

This means that the information concerning the difference between μ_{Y_2} and μ_{Y_3} is contained completely in the differences between μ_{Y_1} and μ_{Y_2} and between μ_{Y_1} and μ_{Y_3}. *Orthogonal* contrasts are free of this overlap in information about mean differences. It is for this reason that many researchers base their studies on orthogonal contrasts. Orthogonal contrasts are defined as follows.

Definition of orthogonal contrasts

Two contrasts,

$$\psi_1 = W_1^{(1)}\mu_{Y_1} + W_2^{(1)}\mu_{Y_2} + \cdots + W_K^{(1)}\mu_{Y_K}$$

and

$$\psi_2 = W_1^{(2)}\mu_{Y_1} + W_2^{(2)}\mu_{Y_2} + \cdots + W_K^{(2)}\mu_{Y_K}$$

are said to be orthogonal if, for equal sample sizes,

$$W_1^{(1)}W_1^{(2)} + W_2^{(1)}W_2^{(2)} + \cdots + W_K^{(1)}W_K^{(2)} = 0$$

The three contrasts ψ_1, ψ_2, and ψ_3 that we have used for illustration are not mutually orthogonal. But

$$\psi_1 = \mu_{Y_1} - \mu_{Y_2}$$

and

$$\psi_4 = \mu_{Y_1} + \mu_{Y_2} - 2\mu_{Y_3}$$

are mutually orthogonal, since:

$$(1)(1) + (-1)(1) + (0)(-2) = 0$$

Given three population means, one can identify two contrasts which are orthogonal. Given K population means, the number of mutually orthogonal contrasts that can be generated from the means can be shown to be given by $v = K - 1$, the number of degrees of freedom that exists between them. This notion of orthogonal contrasts provides another interpretation of v, the degrees of freedom associated with a sum of squares. It can be said that v represents the number of unique pieces of information in a collection of K sets of values. There are $K - 1$ unique pieces of information among K means that are associated with $v = K - 1$ degrees of freedom.

Even though the maximum number of orthogonal contrasts is known for a particular study, in a typical experiment not all of the orthogonal contrasts can be associated with meaningful research questions. It is not unusual to find that a researcher can define on a rational basis one or two meaningful orthogonal contrasts, only to find that the remaining contrasts possible under the restraints of orthogonality are not interpretable. We will, however, illustrate only the method of using *planned* orthogonal contrasts for studies in which the meaningful contrasts are essentially self-evident. Note the emphasis on *planned*. This is intentional. All studies using orthogonal contrasts are planned studies, since the decision to restrict one's contrasts to orthogonal contrasts is made in advance.

As an example, consider the data of Table 34-3. The data in this table were obtained from the records of a university. Students in six college majors, representing two professional programs—business administration and engineering—and four academic programs—chemistry, English, history, and mathematics—were sampled by a random process from currently enrolled students. On each sampled student, information was obtained about his or her score on a written composition test. Across the universe of entering

Table 34-3. Composition test scores for students from six college programs.

	Professional		Academic			
	Business	Engineering	Chemistry	English	History	Mathematics
	475	525	560	610	620	500
	600	385	410	505	460	480
	395	400	480	625	710	520
	460	515	720	685	690	535
	495	610	460	475	680	475
	415	650	480	560	450	395
	400	550	565	590	510	420
	395	525	590	640	580	460
	715	500	615	790	595	475
	600	510	460	730	675	520
Mean scores	495	517	534	621	597	478
Standard deviations	109.29	80.97	93.15	96.89	96.12	44.55

college freshmen, the test has been standardized to produce a score with $\mu_Y = 500$ and $\sigma_Y = 100$. As can be seen, mathematics and business administration majors obtained the lowest mean scores, while English and history majors obtained the highest mean scores. For these data, $MS_W = 7964.8$.

The study seems to have been set up to compare students in professional programs with those in academic programs. The contrast associated with this difference is:

$$\psi_1 = (\tfrac{1}{2})\mu_{Y_1} + (\tfrac{1}{2})\mu_{Y_2} + (-\tfrac{1}{4})\mu_{Y_3} + (-\tfrac{1}{4})\mu_{Y_4} + (-\tfrac{1}{4})\mu_{Y_5} + (-\tfrac{1}{4})\mu_{Y_6}$$

If we now consider the professional programs, the contrast that compares students in the business administration program with those in engineering is given by:

$$\psi_2 = (1)\mu_{Y_1} + (-1)\mu_{Y_2} + (0)\mu_{Y_3} + (0)\mu_{Y_4} + (0)\mu_{Y_5} + (0)\mu_{Y_6}$$

This contrast is orthogonal to ψ_1, since:

$$(\tfrac{1}{2})(1) + (\tfrac{1}{2})(-1) + (-\tfrac{1}{4})(0) + (-\tfrac{1}{4})(0) + (-\tfrac{1}{4})(0) + (-\tfrac{1}{4})(0) = 0$$

Within the academic programs, two different types are apparent. They are the humanities (English and history) students and the science (chemistry and mathematics) students. The comparison of students in the humanities with those in the scientific programs is given by:

$$\psi_3 = (0)\mu_{Y_1} + (0)\mu_{Y_2} + (\tfrac{1}{2})\mu_{Y_3} + (-\tfrac{1}{2})\mu_{Y_4} + (-\tfrac{1}{2})\mu_{Y_5} + (\tfrac{1}{2})\mu_{Y_6}$$

This contrast is orthogonal to ψ_1 and ψ_2.

Within the humanities programs, one can contrast the students in the English program with those in the history program by:

$$\psi_4 = (0)\mu_{Y_1} + (0)\mu_{Y_2} + (0)\mu_{Y_3} + (1)\mu_{Y_4} + (-1)\mu_{Y_5} + (0)\mu_{Y_6}$$

This contrast is orthogonal to ψ_1, ψ_2, and ψ_3.

Finally, within the scientific programs, the contrast involving chemistry and mathematics students is given by:

$$\psi_5 = (0)\mu_{Y_1} + (0)\mu_{Y_2} + (1)\mu_{Y_3} + (0)\mu_{Y_4} + (0)\mu_{Y_5} + (-1)\mu_{Y_6}$$

This contrast is orthogonal to ψ_1, ψ_2, ψ_3, and ψ_4.

For the first contrast,

$$
\begin{aligned}
\hat{\psi}_1 &= (\tfrac{1}{2})(495) + (\tfrac{1}{2})(517) + (-\tfrac{1}{4})(534) + (-\tfrac{1}{4})(621) \\
&\quad + (-\tfrac{1}{4})(597) + (-\tfrac{1}{4})(478) \\
&= -51.5
\end{aligned}
$$

The standard error for ψ_1 is given by:

$$
SE_{\hat{\psi}_1} = \sqrt{7964.8\left[\frac{(\tfrac{1}{2})^2}{10} + \frac{(\tfrac{1}{2})^2}{10} + \frac{(-\tfrac{1}{4})^2}{10} + \frac{(-\tfrac{1}{4})^2}{10} + \frac{(-\tfrac{1}{4})^2}{10} + \frac{(-\tfrac{1}{4})^2}{10}\right]}
$$

$$= 24.44$$

For the test of $H_0: \psi_1 = 0$ against $H_1: \psi_1 \neq 0$,

$$t_{\psi_1} = \frac{\hat{\psi}_1}{SE_{\hat{\psi}_1}} = \frac{-51.5}{24.44} = -2.11$$

The remaining four tests are reported in Table 34-4.

Since each contrast is examined as part of a planned analysis, Dunn's method is employed. The corresponding decision rule is determined with $C = 5$, $\alpha = .05$, and $\nu = 54$:

$$\text{Decision Rule:} \quad \text{Reject } H_0 \text{ if } t < -t^{\text{Dunn}}_{.05:5,54} = -2.68$$

$$\text{or if } t > t^{\text{Dunn}}_{.05:5,54} = 2.68$$

The only contrast that is different from zero is ψ_3.

Table 34-4. Table of orthogonal contrasts for the data of Table 34-3.

Contrast	Value of $\hat{\psi}$	$SE_{\hat{\psi}}$	$t_{\hat{\psi}}$
ψ_1	-51.5	24.44	-2.11
ψ_2	-22	39.91	-0.55
ψ_3	103	28.22	3.65[a]
ψ_4	24	39.91	0.60
ψ_5	56	39.91	1.40

[a] Significant at $\alpha \leq .05$.

34-5. TEST FOR MONOTONIC RELATIONSHIPS

The notion of a contrast serves as one of the major building blocks of experimental and observational investigations. This core position assumed by contrasts arises because of the great flexibility that a researcher has in selecting the weights to be applied to the sample means. As an example of how a contrast can be used to test for a monotonic relationship between two variables, consider the data of Table 34-5, measured on five groups of mentally retarded adults who were grouped according to mental age and who were given training on the conservation of volume. After the third training session, each subject was given a 16-item performance test to see how well he or she had learned the concepts related to the conservation of volume. The depen-

Table 34-5. Example of a monotonic relationship between the number of errors made in a concept-learning study and the number of trials given to learn the task.

	Mental age, years				
	6	7	8	9	10
Mean number of errors	13.2	12.8	8.1	7.0	3.1
Standard deviation	2.1	2.0	1.9	2.1	1.6
Number of subjects	6	5	7	6	7

dent variable was the number of errors made by the subject. We expect the mean number of errors to decrease with increases in average mental age. This expectation can be tested for statistical significance by use of a contrast. The appropriate weights for the contrast have been determined by statisticians and are summarized in Table A-14. The coefficients in the table have been generated to solve the problem of testing for orthogonal trends, which we will discuss in Section 38-5, but the coefficients in the rows denoted "linear" can be used in the present context. As can be seen, the weights vary with the number of samples. For this example, $K = 5$. The tabled weights for $K = 5$ are read to be:

$$W_1 = -2, \quad W_2 = -1, \quad W_3 = 0, \quad W_4 = 1, \quad \text{and} \quad W_5 = 2$$

Note that the weights increase in value. Since their sum is zero, we know that they define a contrast. In particular, the contrast is:

$$\hat{\psi} = -2\bar{Y}_1 - 1\bar{Y}_2 + 0\bar{Y}_3 + 1\bar{Y}_4 + 2\bar{Y}_5$$

If the means increase, $\hat{\psi}$ will be positive, but if the means decrease, $\hat{\psi}$ will be negative. For the data of Table 34-5, the value of $\hat{\psi}$ is given as follows:

$$\hat{\psi} = -2(13.2) - 1(12.8) + 0(8.1) + 1(7.0) + 2(3.1)$$
$$= -26.0$$

Under the assumption of equal population variances, $MS_W = 3.7354$, so that:

$$SE_{\hat{\psi}} = \sqrt{3.7354 \left[\frac{(-2)^2}{6} + \frac{(-1)^2}{5} + \frac{(0)^2}{7} + \frac{(1)^2}{6} + \frac{(2)^2}{7} \right]} = 2.45$$

With these figures,

$$t_{\hat{\psi}} = \frac{\hat{\psi}}{SE_{\hat{\psi}}} = \frac{-26.0}{2.45} = -10.61$$

In this example, a one-sided alternative is called for. Since the weights were devised to produce a positive value for $\hat{\psi}$ if the trend is increasing and a negative value for $\hat{\psi}$ if the trend is decreasing, we would expect t to be negative. This means we wish to place all of the α in the lower end of the critical region. The critical value read from Table A-12 with $v = N - K = 31 - 5 = 26$ is $t = -1.71$, so that the appropriate decision rule is as follows:

Decision Rule: Reject H_0 if $t_{\hat{\psi}} < -1.71$

Since $t_{\hat{\psi}} = -10.61 < -1.71$, the hypothesis of no monotonic decreasing trend is rejected.

Box 34-3   Procedure for testing for monotonicity

Step 1. Determine the value of K.

Step 2. Find the weights in Table A-14 for specifying the contrast ψ.

Step 3. Determine the value of $\hat{\psi}$ and $SE_{\hat{\psi}}$, and the value

$$t_{\hat{\psi}} = \frac{\hat{\psi}}{SE_{\hat{\psi}}}$$

Step 4. With the α of interest and $v = N - K$, determine the appropriate critical region from Table A-12.

Step 5. Make a decision.

Finally, it should be noted that in this example the spacings between the conditions of the independent variable were equal. Group 1 consisted of adults whose mental age was 6 years. Group 2 was defined for adults whose mental age was 7 years. The remaining groups are separated by one-year mental age ranges. The test for monotonicity does not require this equally spaced increase in the values of the independent variable. We could have performed the same sort of analysis on groups defined by 6, 8, 9, 10, and 13 years, and it would still have been justified. However, if the spacings are equal, and if the sample sizes are equal in each of the tested groups, the test for monotonic trend actually becomes one of linearity, a special case of the more general problem to be described in Chapter 38. In this example, the sample sizes are unequal, and so the test is one of monotonicity only. We close this section by describing in Box 34-3 the method for testing for monotonic relationships.

34-6. EXERCISES

34-1. Use the methods of this chapter, assuming equal group variances, on the data of Exercise 33-2. Compare:

a. Male nonusers with male users

b. Female nonusers with female users

c. The interaction of a and b

d. Among males, no alcohol and 3 oz of vodka

e. Among females, no alcohol and 3 oz of vodka

f. The interaction of d and e

Assign $\alpha = .05$ to each contrast.

34-2. In a study on the effects of length of psychotherapy, a group of male college students were rated according to how well they were able to function as rational human beings. High ratings signify emotional problems. Results are as shown:

Length in months	1 to 5	6 to 10	11 to 20	21 to 30
Mean rating	10.2	11.3	15.6	21.4
Standard deviation	8.3	9.1	12.6	12.4
Number	10	18	13	26

Test for monotonic trend.

34-3. A researcher has conducted a study to investigate different methods of teaching reading to sixth-grade students. The dependent variable Y is the score on a nationally normed standardized reading test for which $\mu_Y = 50$ and $\sigma_Y^2 = 10$. The independent variable X is defined as follows:

X_1: males taught by the old method
X_2: males taught by a phonics method
X_3: males taught by a linguistic method
X_4: females taught by the old method
X_5: females taught by a phonics method
X_6: females taught by a linguistic method

The data are as follows:

Group	1	2	3	4	5	6
	27	63	61	26	62	32
	52	60	50	29	69	40
	40	47	48	35	51	55
	36	55	50	40	58	60
	38	58	60	36	63	75
	51	60	61	47	47	76
	55	63	53	55	55	80
	58	47	38	60	65	67
	26	52	40	37	71	55
	40	60	51	40	62	71

Perform a planned, orthogonal study:
a. State the orthogonal contrasts to be tested and the appropriate decision rules.
b. Summarize your results in a short paragraph and provide the appropriate tables.

34-4. Consider again the data of Table 34-3. If a researcher views the contrasts examined in Section 34-4 as comprising three families (professional versus academic programs, the differences among professional programs, and the differences among the academic programs), what three critical values would be used to test contrasts in the three families?

PART VII

PROCEDURES BASED ON THE *F* DISTRIBUTION

As we have seen, the normal distribution is used primarily to make inferences about pairwise and complex contrasts involving proportions, and the chi-square (χ^2) distribution allows us to test omnibus hypotheses in the homogeneity model. Similarly, the *t* distribution is used primarily to make inferences about contrasts involving means. We now introduce a distribution that plays the same role in testing means as the chi-square distribution has in testing proportions. This distribution is called the *F distribution*. In the following chapters, we do not merely provide extensions of tests based on the *t* distribution. We also introduce techniques that are among the most important and flexible procedures for behavioral scientists, in that they can be used for multiple independent and dependent variables. The methods presented here focus on multiple qualitative independent variables and a single quantitative dependent variable.

The *F* Distribution and Test of Equal Variances

35-1. THE *F* DISTRIBUTION

As was mentioned in Chapter 5, the standard deviation satisfies our requirements for describing variation in samples and populations. But standard deviations are difficult to compare because of the complexity of their statistical distributions. Instead, for comparative purposes, variances are used. In performing tests of the equality of two population variances, the ratio of the sample estimates can be compared to critical values determined from a statistical distribution called *F*. This new distribution is generated in terms of two independent chi-square variables and is specified by the two parameters of the corresponding chi-square variables. We provide a definition of this variable here.

Definition of the F distribution

The F distribution is the distribution of the ratio of two independent chi-square variables, each divided by its degrees of freedom. Algebraically, let χ_1^2 and χ_2^2 denote the two independent chi-square variables with degrees of freedom v_1 and v_2, respectively. Then F_{v_1, v_2} is the distribution of the ratio:

$$F_{v_1, v_2} = \frac{\chi_1^2/v_1}{\chi_2^2/v_2}$$

Since each of the chi-square variables takes on only positive values, so does F. Further, each chi-square variable is completely specified by its number of degrees of freedom. Hence, F is specified by v_1 and v_2, the number of degrees of freedom in the numerator and denominator of F, respectively. In general, the distribution of F is skewed. Because we are unable to write F as a linear combination, we cannot rely on the central limit theorem to make the F distribution approach normality as the sample sizes increase.

However, the genesis of F variables arises naturally enough, since the F distribution was intended to examine the ratio of sample estimates of population variances. Thus, since each of the sample estimates is proportional to a chi-square variable, we obtain for the ratio of two chi-square variables

$$\frac{\chi_{v_1}^2}{\chi_{v_2}^2} = \frac{v_1 S_{Y_1}^2/\sigma_{Y_1}^2}{v_2 S_{Y_2}^2/\sigma_{Y_2}^2}$$

If we now divide the numerators of both sides by v_1 and the denominators by

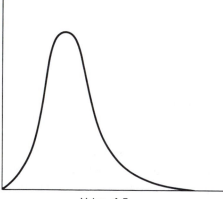

Value of F_{v_1, v_2}

Figure 35-1.
A typical F distribution.

v_2, we have

$$F_{v_1,v_2} = \frac{\chi^2_{v_1}/v_1}{\chi^2_{v_2}/v_2} = \frac{S^2_{Y_1}/\sigma^2_{Y_1}}{S^2_{Y_2}/\sigma^2_{Y_2}} = \frac{S^2_{Y_1}}{S^2_{Y_2}}\left(\frac{\sigma^2_{Y_2}}{\sigma^2_{Y_1}}\right)$$

Hence, the *F* distribution, as described above, involves the distribution of the ratios of variances. A typical *F* distribution is shown in Figure 35-1.

35-2. THE TEST OF $\sigma^2_{Y_1} = \sigma^2_{Y_2}$

The *F* distribution can be used to test whether the variances of two *normally* distributed populations are equal. We wish to determine whether the hypothesis

$$H_0: \sigma^2_{Y_1} = \sigma^2_{Y_2}$$

seems to be true. As usual, to do so, we assume that H_0 is true. If so, then the ratio $\sigma^2_{Y_2}/\sigma^2_{Y_1} = 1$, and we have

$$F = \frac{S^2_{Y_1}}{S^2_{Y_2}}\left(\frac{\sigma^2_{Y_2}}{\sigma^2_{Y_1}}\right) = \frac{S^2_{Y_1}}{S^2_{Y_2}}(1) = \frac{S^2_{Y_1}}{S^2_{Y_2}}$$

or the ratio of the two sample variances. If the sample variances are approximately equal, this ratio is close to unity. If the ratio of the sample variances is quite small, or quite large, we begin to question the null hypothesis. The test statistic can be compared to the percentiles of the *F* distribution in order to formulate a decision rule. With a type I error rate of .05, we would have

Decision Rule: Reject H_0 if $F < F_{v_1,v_2:.025}$ or if $F > F_{v_1,v_2:.975}$

where $v_1 = N_1 - 1$ and $v_2 = N_2 - 1$. Percentiles of the F_{v_1,v_2} distribution are shown in Table A-15. For example, $F_{6,24:.95} = 2.51$.

As an example of the use of the *F* distribution, consider the data of Table 32-2, based on $N_1 = 16$ and $N_2 = 23$. For these data, $S^2_{Y_1} = 8.54^2 = 72.93$ and $S^2_{Y_2} = 5.89^2 = 34.69$. Did the two samples come from populations with equal variances? To find out, we calculate the test statistic

$$F = \frac{S^2_{Y_1}}{S^2_{Y_2}} = \frac{72.93}{34.69} = 2.10$$

The hypotheses of interest are

$$H_0: \sigma^2_{Y_1} = \sigma^2_{Y_2}$$

and

$$H_1: \sigma_{Y_1}^2 \neq \sigma_{Y_2}^2$$

The decision rule for this test with $v_1 = 15$ and $v_2 = 22$, read from Table A-15, with interpolation, is

Decision Rule: Reject H_0 if $F < F_{v_1, v_2 : .025} = F_{15, 22 : .025} = 0.367$
or if $F > F_{v_1, v_2 : .975} = F_{15, 22 : .975} = 2.51$

Since the test statistic F does not lie in the rejection region, we do not reject H_0.

Suppose we had taken the ratio of $S_{Y_2}^2$ to $S_{Y_1}^2$. Then our test statistic would have been

$$F = \frac{S_{Y_2}^2}{S_{Y_1}^2} = \frac{34.69}{72.93} = 0.48$$

Since it is arbitrary which of the samples we label 1 and which we label 2, this test should yield the same results as the previous one. The first degree of freedom for the F ratio refers to the numerator of the above ratio, while the second refers to the denominator. Thus, we must enter the F table to find

$$F_{22, 15 : .025} = 0.400$$

Box 35-1   Procedure for testing $H_0: \sigma_{Y_1}^2 = \sigma_{Y_2}^2$

Step 1. Determine the values of $S_{Y_1}^2$ and $S_{Y_2}^2$.

Step 2. Compute

$$F = \frac{S_{Y_1}^2}{S_{Y_2}^2}$$

Step 3. In Table A-15, determine the values of

$$F_{v_1, v_2 : \alpha/2} \quad \text{and} \quad F_{v_1, v_2 : 1 - \alpha/2}$$

where

$$v_1 = N_1 - 1 \quad \text{and} \quad v_2 = N_2 - 1$$

Step 4. Reject H_0 if $F < F_{v_1, v_2 : \alpha/2}$
or if $F > F_{v_1, v_2 : 1 - \alpha/2}$

---

and

$$F_{22,15:.975} = 2.73$$

Again, because $F = 0.48$ lies within the acceptance region, we do not reject H_0, the same conclusion we reached previously. This must be the case. In Box 35-1, we provide directions for testing equality of two population variances.

We concluded that the two populations could have had equal variances. Our estimate of this common value is

$$MS_W = \frac{v_1 S_{Y_1}^2 + v_2 S_{Y_2}^2}{v_1 + v_2} = \frac{15(72.93) + 22(34.69)}{15 + 22} = 50.19$$

The 95 percent confidence interval for σ_Y^2 is given by

$$\frac{(v_1 + v_2)MS_W}{\chi^2_{v_1+v_2:1-\alpha/2}} < \sigma_Y^2 < \frac{(v_1 + v_2)MS_W}{\chi^2_{v_1+v_2:\alpha/2}}$$

$$\frac{37(50.19)}{55.63} < \sigma_Y^2 < \frac{37(50.19)}{22.14}$$

$$33.38 < \sigma_Y^2 < 83.88$$

35-3. CONFIDENCE INTERVAL FOR THE RATIO OF VARIANCES

As usual, a verbal statement of the acceptance region for the test of

$$H_0: \sigma_{Y_1}^2 = \sigma_{Y_2}^2$$

in terms of the F distribution and the test statistic would be that 95 percent of the time we expect that

$$F = \frac{S_{Y_1}^2}{S_{Y_2}^2}\left(\frac{\sigma_{Y_2}^2}{\sigma_{Y_1}^2}\right)$$

should lie between $F_{v_1,v_2:.025}$ and $F_{v_1,v_2:.975}$. This verbal statement provides us with two inequalities which can be turned into a confidence interval for the unknown variance ratio $\sigma_{Y_1}^2/\sigma_{Y_2}^2$. We expect that 95 percent of the time

$$\frac{S_{Y_1}^2}{S_{Y_2}^2}\left(\frac{\sigma_{Y_2}^2}{\sigma_{Y_1}^2}\right) > F_{v_1,v_2:.025}$$

and

$$\frac{S_{Y_1}^2}{S_{Y_2}^2}\left(\frac{\sigma_{Y_2}^2}{\sigma_{Y_1}^2}\right) < F_{v_1,v_2:.975}$$

Box 35-2   Procedure for setting up a $1 - \alpha$ percent confidence interval for $\sigma_{Y_1}^2 / \sigma_{Y_2}^2$.

Step 1. Compute $S_{Y_1}^2 / S_{Y_2}^2$.

Step 2. In Table A-15, determine the values of

$$F_{v_1, v_2 : \alpha/2} \quad \text{and} \quad F_{v_1, v_2 : 1 - \alpha/2}$$

Step 3. Determine the $1 - \alpha$ percent confidence interval as

$$\frac{S_{Y_1}^2 / S_{Y_2}^2}{F_{v_1, v_2 : 1 - \alpha/2}} < \frac{\sigma_{Y_1}^2}{\sigma_{Y_2}^2} < \frac{S_{Y_1}^2 / S_{Y_2}^2}{F_{v_1, v_2 : \alpha/2}}$$

These inequalities can be solved for $\sigma_{Y_1}^2 / \sigma_{Y_2}^2$ and then combined into a single confidence interval, yielding

$$\frac{S_{Y_1}^2 / S_{Y_2}^2}{F_{v_1, v_2 : .975}} < \frac{\sigma_{Y_1}^2}{\sigma_{Y_2}^2} < \frac{S_{Y_1}^2 / S_{Y_2}^2}{F_{v_1, v_2 : .025}}$$

For the samples of the previous section, we would have

$$\frac{2.10}{2.51} < \frac{\sigma_{Y_1}^2}{\sigma_{Y_2}^2} < \frac{2.10}{0.367}$$

or

$$0.84 < \frac{\sigma_{Y_1}^2}{\sigma_{Y_2}^2} < 5.73$$

According to this confidence interval, a ratio of 1 is a possibility. This means that the two population variances could be equal. This is the same conclusion as that made based on the test statistic. In addition, the confidence interval tells us the range of variance ratios we think likely to exist in the populations.

For completeness, we provide directions for establishing a confidence interval for $\sigma_{Y_1}^2 / \sigma_{Y_2}^2$ in Box 35-2.

35-4. ASSUMPTION OF NORMALITY FOR TESTING $\sigma_{Y_1}^2 = \sigma_{Y_2}^2$

Most of the statistical tests that we have described in previous sections are essentially distribution-free if the sample sizes are large. Thus for large samples, probability values of $\alpha = .05$, $\alpha = .01$, or any other value are attainable under H_0, even if the assumptions of the test are not satisfied. This convergence upon the true probability level occurs because of the operation of the central limit theorem. Unfortunately, it does not hold for tests of the equality of variances. The justification of the test of $\sigma_{Y_1}^2 = \sigma_{Y_2}^2$ is closely tied to the assumption of normality. Great deviations from normality render the test problematic. Thus, the test should be used only if the dependent variables have a normal or near normal distribution.

35-5. MULTIPLE-SAMPLE TESTS FOR HOMOGENEITY OF VARIANCE

We have presented a method for testing the equality of two population variances. We indicate in the exercises a strategy for using the two-sample test for examining multiple samples. Other procedures available for testing the equality of K population variances are Cochran's test, Hartley's F_{max} test, and the Bartlett-Box test. The first two tests require equal sample sizes. The Bartlett-Box test has the disadvantage of yielding too many false rejections of the hypothesis of equality when the distributions are long-tailed. Because of these limitations, we have not presented them here.

35-6. EXERCISES

35-1. Determine the variances on the final examination for your sample of 40 subjects who are

  1. Males in program 1
  2. Males in program 2
  3. Females in program 1
  4. Females in program 2

  a. Perform the four meaningful tests of equal variances between pairs of groups. Use a total risk of $\alpha = .05$.
  b. Examine all pairwise group differences in variance.

  c. Which do you prefer, model a or model b? Why?

35-2. For the data of Exercise 35-1, find the mean square within groups and determine the 95 percent confidence interval for σ^2. Under what condition is this procedure justified?

35-3. Determine the four confidence intervals of Exercise 35-1 for each population variance. Compare these four intervals to that of Exercise 35-2. What does this tell you about MS_w?

CHAPTER**36**

One-Factor Analysis of Variance

36-1. ANALYSIS OF VARIANCE

In the preceding chapters we have studied in detail one- and two-sample tests on measures of central tendency. In Section 32-4 we saw how to test H_0: $\mu_{Y_1} = \mu_{Y_2}$, assuming that the population variances were equal. We now wish to examine the extension of the test of equal means to the multiple-group situation. In particular, we wish to develop a method for testing the *omnibus* hypothesis

$$H_0: \mu_{Y_1} = \mu_{Y_2} = \cdots = \mu_{Y_K}$$

against an alternative that states

$$H_1: H_0 \text{ is false}$$

The method used to test H_0 was invented by Fisher and is called the *analysis of variance* (ANOVA). As will be seen, the only conclusion that could be made on the basis of a rejection of H_0 through Fisher's method is that the population means differ, but one cannot tell in what way they differ. This is the reason for H_1 being stated in so general a fashion.

Fisher's method for testing the hypothesis of equal means is based on a comparison of two separate estimates of the population variance. One of these estimates is insensitive to population mean differences, whereas the other is an overestimate of the population variance when the population means differ. Hence, if the two estimates are approximately equal in magnitude, it is concluded that the population means do not differ. If, however, the estimate that depends on mean differences is much larger than the other, it is concluded that the means must be different from each other.

In Section 9-4, we saw how a set of observations collected over a number of different samples could be used to obtain measures of explained and unexplained variation. Let us take another look at those measures and see what information they contain about the truth of the hypothesis H_0. Let us begin by examining the sum of squares of unexplained deviations. As we saw in the definition of the correlation ratio in Section 9-4 and in Box 9-1, the SS_U is computed as

$$SS_U = (N_1 - 1)S_{Y_1}^2 + (N_2 - 1)S_{Y_2}^2 + \cdots + (N_K - 1)S_{Y_K}^2$$

We also know that SS_U is based on

$$v = (N_1 - 1) + (N_2 - 1) + \cdots + (N_K - 1) = N - K$$

degrees of freedom and that

$$MS_W = \frac{SS_U}{N - K}$$

In the appendix to this chapter, we show that MS_W is an estimate of σ_Y^2 whether or not H_0 is true. Because MS_W is based on the deviations within each of the groups, SS_U is sometimes referred to as the *sum of squares within groups* and is denoted by SS_W.

Let us examine MS_W, but in terms of the pretest scores of Table 2-2. As we recall, the pretest scores were obtained before any differential treatment of the students took place. If we divide the 40 subjects at random into four groups of 10 subjects (and for convenience replace the one missing value by

Table 36-1. Pretest data of Table 2-2 presented as four samples of size 10 each

	Group 1	Group 2	Group 3	Group 4	Total
	10	25	28	14	77
	24	25	10	3	62
	28	10	17[a]	16	71
	23	18	30	17	88
	28	5	22	15	70
	17	13	16	13	59
	13	13	9	15	50
	16	20	13	16	65
	26	28	30	30	114
	29	8	17	17	71
$\sum\limits_{i=1}^{N} Y_i$	214	165	192	156	727
$\bar{Y}$	21.4	16.5	19.2	15.6	18.175
$\sum\limits_{i=1}^{N} Y_i^2$	5004	3285	4252	2814	15,355
S_Y^2	47.16	62.50	62.84	42.27	54.92

[a] Missing value replaced by median of the remaining nine observations.

its group median), then we have the four samples reported in Table 36-1. For these data, we have four independent sample estimates of the population σ_Y^2. They are given by $S_{Y_1}^2 = 47.16$, $S_{Y_2}^2 = 62.50$, $S_{Y_3}^2 = 62.84$, and $S_{Y_4}^2 = 42.27$. Each of these estimates is based on $v = 9$ degrees of freedom, and each is an equally valid estimate of σ_Y^2. The estimate of σ_Y^2 based on pooling the data from the four samples is

$$\text{MS}_W = \frac{9(47.16) + 9(62.50) + 9(62.84) + 9(42.27)}{9 + 9 + 9 + 9} = 53.69$$

This estimate is based on $v = 36$ degrees of freedom, and it is one way to estimate the common variance σ_Y^2 of the populations, regardless of whether these populations have the same mean.

Let us now examine the sum of squares of explained deviations. According to the definition of Section 9-4 and Box 9-1,

$$\text{SS}_E = N_1(\bar{Y}_1 - \bar{Y})^2 + N_2(\bar{Y}_2 - \bar{Y})^2 + \cdots + N_K(\bar{Y}_K - \bar{Y})^2$$

If each sample mean were to equal the mean of all the observations, that is, $\bar{Y}$, we would see that

$$SS_E = N_1(\bar{Y} - \bar{Y})^2 + N_2(\bar{Y} - \bar{Y})^2 + \cdots + N_K(\bar{Y} - \bar{Y})^2 = 0$$

If any set of means differed from $\bar{Y}$, then SS_E would not equal zero but would equal some number larger than zero, since all quantities are squared. Because SS_E is directly related to the variation between the means of the groups, SS_E is referred to as the *sum of squares between* the groups and is denoted by SS_B.

If we reflect a bit, we realize that there are two possible explanations for not all the $\bar{Y}_k$ values equaling $\bar{Y}$. One explanation is that the population means μ_{Y_k} may actually vary from population to population, and this variation will be reflected by the variation in the sample means. The other reason was described and examined in great detail in Chapter 21. There is was seen that even though samples are selected from one population, sample averages will vary from sample to sample. Furthermore, the variance of the distribution of means will equal $\sigma_{\bar{Y}}^2 = \sigma_Y^2 / N_0$, where σ_Y^2 is the variance of the original sample and N_0 is the size of each sample.

From this discussion, we see that if we are sampling from a single population, then

$$\sigma_Y^2 = N_0 \sigma_{\bar{Y}}^2$$

Therefore, if we estimate $\sigma_{\bar{Y}}^2$ by using the observed sample means and then multiply the result by N_0 we achieve an estimate of the population variance.

Since for K means

$$S_{\bar{Y}}^2 = \sum_{k=1}^{K} \frac{(\bar{Y}_k - \bar{Y})^2}{K - 1}$$

we can estimate S_Y^2 as

$$S_Y^2 = N_0 S_{\bar{Y}}^2 = N_0 \sum_{k=1}^{K} \frac{(\bar{Y}_k - \bar{Y})^2}{K - 1} = \frac{\sum_{k=1}^{K} N_0(\bar{Y}_k - \bar{Y})^2}{K - 1} = \frac{SS_B}{K - 1} = MS_B$$

where MS_B is called the *mean square between the groups*.

Let us compute $S_{\bar{Y}}^2$ for the four samples. In particular,

$$S_{\bar{Y}}^2 = \frac{1}{4 - 1} [(21.4 - 18.175)^2$$
$$+ (16.5 - 18.175)^2 + (19.2 - 18.175)^2 + (15.6 - 18.175)^2]$$
$$= 6.9625$$

If no difference exists among the population means, then $S_{\bar{Y}}^2$ measures the variation that exists between the sample means because of the vagaries of random sampling. From this value, we generate our between-group estimate of $\sigma_{\bar{Y}}^2$ as

$$\text{MS}_B = N_0 S_{\bar{Y}}^2 = 10(6.9625) = 69.63$$

Thus, MS_B and MS_W provide us with two different estimates of $\sigma_{\bar{Y}}^2$.

This example has been based on equal-size samples. We show in the chapter appendix that if H_0 is true, $E(\text{MS}_B) = \sigma_{\bar{Y}}^2$, regardless of equal or unequal sample sizes. If H_0 is false, MS_B will be large because it is affected both by sampling fluctuations among the sample means and by differences among the population means.

In Chapter 35 we saw that two different estimates of a population variance could be used to test population variances for equality using the F test. Here, if H_0 is true, we have two estimates of $\sigma_{\bar{Y}}^2$, that is, $\text{MS}_B = 69.63$ and $\text{MS}_W = 53.69$.

Fisher examined these two measures of variation and showed that the estimate not influenced by the truth of H_0 should be placed in the denominator of F. Thus, the test statistic for Fisher's analysis of variance is given as

$$F = \frac{\text{MS}_B}{\text{MS}_W}$$

We see that F will be large or small as MS_B is large or small. In addition, F can never be less than zero; $F = 0$ only if $\text{MS}_B = 0$, but this rarely happens. The expected value of F is a number close to 1. In particular, under H_0, $E(F) = \nu_2/(\nu_2 - 2)$. Because of the way F is defined for the analysis of variance, large values of F signify differences between population means, so that the critical region is one-tailed. Thus, the $1 - \alpha$ percent decision rule for the analysis of variance is always stated as

Decision Rule: Reject H_0 if $F > F_{\nu_1,\nu_2:1-\alpha}$

For our example,

$$F = \frac{\text{MS}_B}{\text{MS}_W} = \frac{69.63}{53.69} = 1.30$$

and with $\nu_1 = 3$ and $\nu_2 = 36$, the $\alpha = .05$ decision rule is given by

Decision Rule: Reject H_0 if $F > F_{3,36:.95} = 2.87$

In this case, H_0 is not rejected. This is not surprising; rather, it is expected. Since all samples come from the same population of values, the only source of variance between these samples must be that due to random sampling and not to differences in the four population means.

Table 36-2.   Typical ANOVA table

Source of variation	Degrees of freedom	Sum of squares	Mean square	F ratio	Measure of explained variation $\hat{\eta}^2$
Between groups	$K-1$	SS_B	MS_B	$\dfrac{MS_B}{MS_W}$	$\dfrac{SS_B}{SS_T}$
Within groups	$N-K$	SS_W	MS_W		
Total	$N-1$	SS_T			

$$\text{Reject } H_0 \text{ if } F > F_{K-1,N-K;1-\alpha}$$

The partitioning of the SS_T into SS_B and SS_W is usually summarized in an ANOVA table. A typical table is much like that presented in Table 36-2. Examination of the table shows how an analysis of variance is performed. Note that $\hat{\eta}^2$, which equals SS_B/SS_T, is included in the last column of the ANOVA table, in keeping with our discussion in Chapter 9.

A number of assumptions have been made and used in deriving the F statistic and its distribution. Because a violation of certain of these assumptions can have serious effects on type I and type II error rates of the F test, we would like to state the assumptions here. The assumption of independence of observations between and within groups is implicit in all the multiple-sample tests examined in this book. The assumptions of the equality of population variances and of the normality of the population distributions appear explicitly in our presentation of the F test, through the MS_W and the chi-square distributions used to define the F distribution. If these latter assumptions are violated, seriously inflated error rates can occur.

The methods described in this chapter are commonly referred to as the *one-way*, or *one-factor*, analysis of variance. This means that the null hypothesis specifies the equality of the means of populations whose characteristics distinguish levels of a single factor. Rejection of the null hypothesis indicates only that the means differ. We provide instructions for performing a one-factor ANOVA in Box 36-1.

We illustrate the analysis of variance for the data of Table 33-1. For these data, with $K = 6$ and $N = 63$, we have

$$v_1 = 6 - 1 = 5 \quad \text{and} \quad v_2 = 63 - 6 = 57$$

The weighted average of all the observations is

$$\overline{Y} = \frac{10(8.9) + 8(6.4) + \cdots + 15(7.6)}{10 + 8 + \cdots + 15} = 7.4683$$

Box 36-1   Procedure for performing a one-factor analysis of variance

Step 1. Let K = number of samples and N = total number of observations. Compute $v_1 = K - 1$ and $v_2 = N - K$.

Step 2. Determine the values of each sample mean and each sample variance.

Step 3. Determine the weighted average of the observations as

$$\bar{Y} = \frac{N_1 \bar{Y}_1 + N_2 \bar{Y}_2 + \cdots + N_K \bar{Y}_K}{N}$$

Step 4. Calculate the sum of the squares explained as

$$SS_B = N_1(\bar{Y}_1 - \bar{Y})^2 + N_2(\bar{Y}_2 - \bar{Y})^2 + \cdots + N_K(\bar{Y}_K - \bar{Y})^2$$

and the sum of squares unexplained as

$$SS_W = (N_1 - 1)S_{Y_1}^2 + (N_2 - 1)S_{Y_2}^2 + \cdots + (N_K - 1)S_{Y_K}^2$$

Step 5. Compute

$$MS_B = \frac{SS_B}{K - 1} \quad \text{and} \quad MS_W = \frac{SS_W}{N - K}$$

Step 6. Determine the value of the *F* ratio as

$$F = \frac{MS_B}{MS_W}$$

Step 7. Determine the alpha percent decision rule by selecting the appropriate critical value from Table A-15 with v_1 and v_2.

Step 8. Reject H_0 if F exceeds the critical value.

Step 9. Compute

$$\hat{\eta}^2 = \frac{SS_B}{SS_T}$$

The sum of squares between groups is given by

$$SS_B = 10(8.90 - 7.4683)^2 + 8(6.40 - 7.4683)^2$$
$$+ \cdots + 15(7.60 - 7.4683)^2$$
$$= 249.49$$

while the sum of squares within groups is equal to

$$SS_W = (10 - 1)(1.6)^2 + (8 - 1)(2.2)^2 + \cdots + (15 - 1)(2.3)^2$$
$$= 239.74$$

In terms of the two sums of squares and degrees of freedom,

$$MS_B = \frac{249.49}{6-1} = 49.8986$$

and

$$MS_W = \frac{239.74}{63-6} = 4.2060$$

The value of the F ratio is given simply as

$$F = \frac{49.8986}{4.2060} = 11.86$$

Finally, we see that 51 percent of the variation is explained by amount of alcohol consumed and user type, since

$$\hat{\eta}^2 = \frac{249.49}{249.49 + 239.74} = \frac{249.49}{489.23} = 0.51$$

The $\alpha = .05$ decision rule cannot be read directly from Table A-15, since $v_2 = 57$ is not in the table, so it will be necessary to interpolate between $v_2 = 40$ and $v_2 = 60$. The $\alpha = .05$ critical value is given by $F = 2.38$. Thus, the decision rule for rejecting H_0 is given by

Decision Rule: Reject H_0 if $F > 2.38$

Since $F = 11.86$, the hypothesis of equal mean values is rejected. The results are summarized in Table 36-3.

Table 36-3. ANOVA table for data of Table 33-1

Source of variation	Degrees of freedom	Sum of squares	Mean square	F ratio	Measure of explained variation $\hat{\eta}^2$
Between groups	5	249.49	49.90	11.86[a]	.51
Within groups	57	239.74	4.21		
Total	62	489.23			

[a] Reject H_0 if $F > F_{5,57:.95} = 2.38$.

36-2. CALCULATING FORMULAS FOR ANOVA

In practice, few researchers calculate SS_B, SS_W, and SS_T in terms of the definitions. Computing formulas for these sums of squares can be derived algebraically. Defining the quantities

$$I = \sum_{k=1}^{K} \sum_{i=1}^{N_k} Y_{ik}^2$$

$$II = \frac{1}{N} \left(\sum_{k=1}^{K} \sum_{i=1}^{N_k} Y_{ik} \right)^2 = \frac{1}{N} Y_{..}^2$$

$$III_B = \sum_{k=1}^{K} \frac{1}{N_k} \left(\sum_{i=1}^{N_k} Y_{ik} \right)^2 = \sum_{k=1}^{K} \frac{Y_{.k}^2}{N_k}$$

we can write

$$SS_B = III_B - II$$

$$SS_W = I - III_B$$

$$SS_T = I - II$$

We have adopted in these formulas a very compact and useful notation for summation that we have seen in previous chapters in terms of contingency tables. In this notation, a "dotted" subscript indicates that the values referred to by that subscript have been summed. For example,

$$Y_{.k} = \sum_{i=1}^{N_k} Y_{ik}$$

refers to the sum of the observations in the kth group, the sum extending over the subjects (indexed by the i subscript) in that group. Similarly,

$$Y_{..} = \sum_{k=1}^{K} \sum_{i=1}^{N_k} Y_{ik}$$

refers to the sum extending over both the i and k subscripts. This is the sum of all the observations. Then, with this notaion, $Y_{.k}^2$ is the square of the kth group's sum, and $Y_{..}^2$ is the square of the grand sum. For the data of Table 36-1,

$$I = 10^2 + 24^2 + \cdots + 17^2 = 15{,}355$$
$$Y_{..} = 10 + 24 + \cdots + 17 = 727$$

so that

$$II = \frac{727^2}{40} = 13{,}213.225$$

As shown in Table 36-1,

$$Y_{.1} = 214 \qquad Y_{.2} = 165 \qquad Y_{.3} = 192 \qquad Y_{.4} = 156$$

so that

$$III_B = \frac{214^2}{10} + \cdots + \frac{156^2}{10} = 13,422.1$$

With these values, we find

$$SS_B = III_B - II = 13,422.1 - 13,213.225 = 208.875$$

so that

$$MS_B = \frac{1}{4-1}(208.875) = 69.625$$

which agrees within rounding error with our previous result. Further,

$$SS_W = I - III_B = 15,355 - 13,422.1 = 1932.9$$

so that

$$MS_W = \frac{1}{40-4}(1932.9) = 53.69$$

as before. Finally

$$SS_T = I - II = 15,355 - 13,213.225 = 2141.775$$

Note that calculations based on these formulas are in general more accurate than those based on the definitional formulas.

36-3. CORRELATION RATIO AND ANALYSIS OF VARIANCE

By now, the similarity of the model presented in Chapter 9 for the correlation ratio and the model presented here for the analysis of variance should lead one to suspect a close connection between measuring the amount of variation explained by an independent variable and comparing the means among a number of populations. Since the two models are identical in all respects, the connection is not unexpected. The rejection of the hypothesis of equal means is identical to the rejection of the hypothesis that the correlation ratio is zero. As shown in the chapter appendix, another way to perform the analysis of variance is as shown in Box 36-2.

Box 36-2   Procedure for testing H_0: $\eta^2 = 0$ against H_1: $\eta^2 > 0$

Step 1. Compute the value of $\hat{\eta}^2$.

Step 2. Compute

$$F = \frac{N-K}{K-1}\left(\frac{\hat{\eta}^2}{1-\hat{\eta}^2}\right)$$

Step 3. Reject H_0 if

$$F > F_{K-1,N-K:1-\alpha}$$

As an illustration of the test, consider the data of Table 33-1. For these data, $\hat{\eta}^2 = .51$, so that

$$F = \frac{63-6}{6-1}\left(\frac{.51}{1-.51}\right) = 11.86$$

which is the value reported in Section 36-1.

36-4. THE TWO-SAMPLE *t* TEST AND THE ANALYSIS OF VARIANCE *F* TEST

The assumptions for the two-sample *t* test and the ANOVA *F* test are identical. Both models assume

1. The distributions of the dependent variables are normal, or the sample sizes are sufficiently large to guarantee normality of the sampling distribution of the means.
2. Population variances are equal.
3. Observations within samples are independent.
4. Observations between samples are independent.

The only difference between the two models is that the *t* test is a two-sample procedure, while the ANOVA *F* test is a two-or-more-sample procedure. Because of the similarity, one might think that the *t* test could be performed as a two-sample *F* test. It can be.

Consider the test of H_0: $\eta^2 = 0$, but for $K = 2$. In this case,

$$F = \frac{N-2}{2-1}\left(\frac{\hat{\eta}^2}{1-\hat{\eta}^2}\right) = \frac{\hat{\eta}^2(N-2)}{1-\hat{\eta}^2}$$

has an F distribution with $v_1 = 1$ and $v_2 = N - 2$. Suppose we take the square root of both sides of the equation. Thus,

$$\sqrt{F} = \frac{\hat{\eta}\sqrt{N-2}}{\sqrt{1-\hat{\eta}^2}}$$

which is very similar to the t test of Section 32-6. In fact, if we replace $\hat{\eta}$ by r_{pb}, we have

$$\sqrt{F} = \frac{r_{pb}\sqrt{N-2}}{\sqrt{1-r_{pb}^2}}$$

suggesting that $\sqrt{F} = t$. In fact, $\sqrt{F}$ is distributed as t, as we illustrate for the data of Table 4-1. For these data,

$$\text{SS}_T = \text{I} - \text{II} = 15{,}066 - \frac{710^2}{39} = 2140.36$$

$$\text{SS}_B = \text{III} - \text{II}$$

$$= \frac{343^2}{16} + \frac{367^2}{23} - \frac{710^2}{39} = 283.46$$

and

$$\hat{\eta}^2 = \frac{283.46}{2140.36} = .1324$$

so that

$$F = \frac{(39-2)(.1324)}{(2-1)(.8676)} = 5.6463$$

Finally,

$$\sqrt{F} = \sqrt{5.63} = 2.38$$

This agrees with the value of $t = 2.38$ reported in Section 32-6.

We have just illustrated an extremely important relationship between the t and F distributions, one which we use extensively in subsequent chapters. We now formally state this relationship.

Relationship between t_v and $F_{1,v}$

The distribution of t_v^2 is identical to the distribution of $F_{1,v}$. In particular,

$$F_{1,v:1-\alpha} = t_{v:\alpha/2}^2 = t_{v:1-\alpha/2}^2$$

Notice that this relationship between the t and the F distributions is analogous to that between the Z and χ_1^2 distributions. As we recall,

$$\chi_{1:1-\alpha}^2 = Z_{\alpha/2}^2 = Z_{1-\alpha/2}^2$$

36-5. APPENDIX

Here we show that MS_W is an estimate of σ_Y^2. For this, we begin with

$$SS_U = (N_1 - 1)S_{Y_1}^2 + (N_2 - 1)S_{Y_2}^2 + \cdots + (N_K - 1)S_{Y_K}^2$$

Suppose that we divide both sides of the equation for SS_U by σ_Y^2, the common value of the variances across all K groups. With this division,

$$\frac{SS_U}{\sigma_Y^2} = \frac{(N_1 - 1)S_{Y_1}^2}{\sigma_Y^2} + \frac{(N_2 - 1)S_{Y_2}^2}{\sigma_Y^2} + \cdots + \frac{(N_K - 1)S_{Y_K}^2}{\sigma_Y^2}$$

Each term on the right has a chi-square distribution with degrees of freedom given, respectively, by

$$v_1 = N_1 - 1, \qquad v_2 = N_2 - 1, \qquad \ldots, \qquad v_K = N_K - 1$$

Thus, the sum of these terms is also distributed as chi-square with

$$v = (N_1 - 1) + (N_2 - 1) + \cdots + (N_K - 1) = N - K$$

where $N = N_1 + N_2 + \cdots + N_K$, the total sample size. Because we saw in Section 25-2 that the mean of a chi-square distribution equals its degrees of freedom, we have

$$E\left(\frac{SS_U}{\sigma_Y^2}\right) = N - K$$

Using the scale theorem for population means of Section 20-2, we can see that

$$E\left(\frac{SS_U}{\sigma_Y^2}\right) = \frac{1}{\sigma_Y^2} E(SS_U) = N - K$$

Thus,

$$\frac{1}{N - K} E(SS_U) = \sigma_Y^2$$

and finally,

$$E\left(\frac{SS_U}{N - K}\right) = E(MS_W) = \sigma_Y^2$$

Therefore, the pooled variance estimate MS_W is an estimate of σ_Y^2, provided all samples come from populations with this variance. This measure serves as a single estimate of the common value of the population variances, regardless of the values of the various population means. Thus, the truth or falsity of H_0 has no influence whatsoever on the value of MS_W and measures of unexplained variation.

Let us now show that MS_B is also an estimate of σ_Y^2, but only if H_0 is true. In Section 9-4, we saw that

$$SS_T = SS_U + SS_E$$

which we now write in terms of ANOVA as

$$SS_T = SS_W + SS_B$$

Again, let us divide both sides of this equation by σ_Y^2, to yield

$$\frac{SS_T}{\sigma_Y^2} = \frac{SS_W}{\sigma_Y^2} + \frac{SS_B}{\sigma_Y^2}$$

We have seen that SS_W/σ_Y^2 is a chi-square variable with $N - K$ degrees of freedom, regardless of the truth of H_0. Note that the term on the left of the equation can be written as

$$\frac{SS_T}{\sigma_Y^2} = \frac{\sum_{i=1}^{N}(Y_i - \bar{Y})^2}{\sigma_Y^2} = \frac{(N-1)S_T^2}{\sigma_Y^2}$$

We have seen that the ratio on the left is distributed as a chi-square variable with $v = N - 1$ if the observations all came from a single population, that is, if H_0 is true. Hence, when H_0 is true,

$$\chi_{N-1}^2 = \chi_{N-K}^2 + \frac{SS_B}{\sigma_Y^2}$$

Therefore, by the additive property of the chi-square variables, SS_B/σ_Y^2 is distributed as a chi-square variable with $v = (N - 1) - (N - K) = K - 1$ degrees of freedom. Then again we see that

$$E\left(\frac{SS_B}{\sigma_Y^2}\right) = E(\chi_{K-1}^2) = K - 1$$

and so

$$E\left(\frac{SS_B}{K-1}\right) = E(MS_B) = \sigma_Y^2$$

if H_0 is true.

The connection between ANOVA and the correlation ratio is now demonstrated.

We begin with the ANOVA F test

$$F = \frac{MS_B}{MS_W} = \frac{SS_B/(K-1)}{SS_W/(N-K)} = \frac{N-K}{K-1}\left(\frac{SS_B}{SS_W}\right)$$

We now replace SS_W by $SS_T - SS_B$. This gives us

$$F = \frac{N-K}{K-1}\left(\frac{SS_B}{SS_T - SS_B}\right)$$

If we now divide the numerator and denominator by SS_T, we have

$$F \frac{[(N-K)/(K-1)](SS_B/SS_T)}{SS_T/SS_T - SS_B/SS_T}$$

Since $SS_B/SS_T = \hat{\eta}^2$, we have

$$F = \frac{N-K}{K-1}\left(\frac{\hat{\eta}^2}{1 - \hat{\eta}^2}\right)$$

We now wish to present a theoretical description of the ANOVA model and show its relationship to explained and unexplained measures of variability. We make this explicit connection because it can be generalized to multiple-factor ANOVA and to a regression model that involves multiple predictors. In Chapter 9, we introduced the notion of explained and unexplained deviations, and in Section 9-4 we examined them for a qualitative independent variable. The basic equation was written as

$$d_{T_i} = d_{E_i} + d_{U_i}$$

In terms of sample data and the notation of Section 36-2, we can write this as

$$Y_{ik} - \bar{Y}_{..} = (\bar{Y}_{.k} - \bar{Y}_{..}) + (Y_{ik} - \bar{Y}_{.k})$$

The mathematical model expresses the relationship for the corresponding population deviations. In particular, with $\mu_{.k}$ denoting the mean of the kth population and $\mu_{..}$ representing the mean of the combined populations, we have

$$Y_{ik} - \mu_{..} = (\mu_{.k} - \mu_{..}) + (Y_{ik} - \mu_{.k})$$

In ANOVA terminology, the explained deviation is called the *effect size* and is denoted by $\alpha_{.k}$, so that

$$\alpha_{.k} = \mu_{.k} - \mu_{..}$$

The unexplained deviation is called the *error*, or *residual*, and is denoted by e_{ik}, so that

$$e_{ik} = Y_{ik} - \mu_{.k}$$

In terms of this notation, the theoretical model is written

$$Y_{ik} - \mu_{..} = \alpha_{.k} + e_{ik}$$

Finally, if we transpose $\mu_{..}$ to the right side of the equation, we have what is referred to as the *hidden-structure equation* for one-factor ANOVA:

$$Y_{ik} = \mu_{..} + \alpha_{.k} + e_{ik}$$

It indicates that any observation differs from the overall population mean by an amount that is explained by being in the kth population, $\alpha_{.k}$, and an amount due to all factors not controlled in the design, e_{ik}.

These parameters can be estimated from the data as

$$\hat{\mu}_{..} = \overline{Y}_{..} \qquad \hat{\alpha}_{.k} = \overline{Y}_{.k} - \overline{Y}_{..} \qquad \hat{e}_{ik} = Y_{ik} - \overline{Y}_{.k}$$

So

$$SS_B = \sum_{k=1}^{K} N_k \hat{\alpha}_{.k}^2$$

and

$$SS_W = \sum_{i=1}^{N_k} \sum_{k=1}^{K} \hat{e}_{ik}^2$$

We now assume that $\hat{e}_{ik}$ are randomly selected from a normal distribution of errors for which

$$E(\hat{e}_{ik}) = 0 \qquad \text{and} \qquad \text{Var}(\hat{e}_{ik}) = \sigma^2$$

Under these conditions, MS_B/MS_W has an F distribution. Finally, we note that F can be written strictly in terms of the $\hat{\alpha}_{.k}$ and $\hat{e}_{ik}$ as

$$F = \frac{MS_B}{MS_W} = \frac{[1/(K-1)] \sum\limits_{k=1}^{K} N_k \hat{\alpha}_{.k}^2}{[1/(N-K)] \sum\limits_{i=1}^{N_k} \sum\limits_{k=1}^{K} \hat{e}_{ik}^2}$$

In this form we see that F is the ratio of two measures of variation, the numerator involving only explained components and the denominator containing only unexplained components. It is this insight that can be generalized to other statistical models. Thus, F is a test about the $\alpha_{.k}$ values, since $F = 0$ when all $\hat{\alpha}_{.k}$ equal zero. In addition, H_0 and H_1 can be written as

$$H_0: \alpha_{.1} = \alpha_{.2} = \cdots = \alpha_{.K} = 0$$

and

$$H_1: H_0 \text{ is false}$$

If we now consider the particular case of the two-sample t test, we have

$$\bar{Y}_{.1} - \bar{Y}_{.2} = (\bar{Y}_{.1} - \bar{Y}_{..}) - (\bar{Y}_{.2} - \bar{Y}_{..})$$
$$= \hat{\alpha}_{.1} - \hat{\alpha}_{.2}$$

Thus, we see that the difference in sample means is a sample estimate of the difference in population treatment effects. Let us now examine the mean square within (MS_W). We have

$$MS_W = \frac{SS_{U_1} + SS_{U_2}}{N_1 + N_2 - 2}$$

But

$$SS_{U_1} = \sum_{i=1}^{N_1} (Y_{i1} - \bar{Y}_{.1})^2 = \sum_{i=1}^{N_1} \hat{e}_{i1}^2$$

and

$$SS_{U_2} = \sum_{i=1}^{N_2} (Y_{i2} - \bar{Y}_{.2})^2 = \sum_{i=1}^{N_2} \hat{e}_{i2}^2$$

Thus,

$$MS_W = \frac{\sum\limits_{i=1}^{N_1} \hat{e}_{i1}^2 + \sum\limits_{i=1}^{N_2} \hat{e}_{i2}^2}{N_1 + N_2 - 2}$$

Therefore, MS_W combines the estimates of the errors from both samples. For this reason it is sometimes called the *mean square error*. Finally, in terms of the hidden structure components, we can write

$$t_{\bar{Y}_1 - \bar{Y}_2} = \frac{\bar{Y}_1 - \bar{Y}_2}{\sqrt{MS_W/N_1 + MS_W/N_2}}$$

$$= \frac{\hat{\alpha}_{.1} - \hat{\alpha}_{.2}}{\sqrt{\left(\dfrac{\sum\limits_{i=1}^{N_1} \hat{e}_{i1}^2 + \sum\limits_{i=1}^{N_2} \hat{e}_{i2}^2}{N_1 + N_2 - 2}\right)\left(\dfrac{1}{N_1} + \dfrac{1}{N_2}\right)}}$$

Thus, the test statistic $t_{\bar{Y}_1 - \bar{Y}_2}$ is clearly based on treatment effects and error estimates.

One advantage of our having specified the theoretical model for the analysis of variance is that the calculating formulas for sums of squares can be derived from it. We illustrate the procedure in detail here. The method is extremely useful for complex ANOVA designs not examined in his book. It is based on an examination of the subscripts and the means involved in the model.

Let us write the theoretical model in terms of the sample estimates as

$$Y_{ik} - \bar{Y}_{..} = (\bar{Y}_{.k} - \bar{Y}_{..}) + (Y_{ik} - \bar{Y}_{.k})$$

The term on the left is seen to be the total deviation, the first parenthetical expression on the right is seen to be $\hat{\alpha}_k$, the deviation explained by group membership, and the rightmost parenthetical term is the unexplained deviation. Each of the symbols Y_{ik}, $\bar{Y}_{.k}$, and $\bar{Y}_{..}$ represents an observation or a mean calculated from the sum $Y_{.k}$ or $Y_{..}$, with $Y_{.k}$ being the sum of N_k observations and $Y_{..}$ the sum of N observations. For consistency, we consider the observation Y_{ik} to be a mean based on one observation. We use the sums and the number of observations which have been summed in their calculation to define the Roman numerals I, II, and III$_B$ found in the calculating formulas. Recall that these are

$$I = \sum_{i=1}^{N} \sum_{k=1}^{K} Y_{ik}^2 \qquad II = \frac{Y_{..}^2}{N} \qquad III_B = \sum_{k=1}^{K} \frac{Y_{.k}^2}{N_k}$$

For each of these, when the sum upon which they are based has subscripts not dotted, the summation symbols indicate adding across these subscripts. For example, since Y_{ik} has two undotted subscripts, the summation for I requires adding across both i and k. Similarly, since $Y_{.k}$ has only k undotted, III$_B$ requires summing across k. Finally, since $Y_{..}$ has no undotted subscript, no summation is required.

Further, the quantity involved in the expression to be summed (or not, for II) always equals a sum squared and then divided by the number of observations used in calculating the sum. Again, for example, Y_{ik} is a "sum" of one observation, so the quantity used in calculating I equals $Y_{ik}^2/1$. Since $Y_{.k}$ is a sum of N_k observations, the quantity involved in III$_B$ equals $Y_{.k}^2/N_k$. Similarly, the quantity in the expression for II is $Y_{..}^2/N$, since $Y_{..}$ is calculated by adding N observations.

The computing formulas are then simply found by placing those quantities in the corresponding place in the theoretical model. For example, since the total deviation equals $Y_{ik} - \bar{Y}_{..}$, the sum of squares total equals

$$SS_T = \sum_{i=1}^{N} \sum_{k=1}^{K} Y_{ik}^2 - \frac{Y_{..}^2}{N} = I - II$$

Similarly, since the between groups deviation equals $\bar{Y}_{.k} - \bar{Y}_{..}$, the sum of squares between groups equals

$$SS_B = \sum_{k=1}^{K} \frac{Y_{.k}^2}{N_k} - \frac{Y_{..}^2}{N} = III_B - II$$

Finally, from the unexplained deviation $Y_{ik} - \bar{Y}_{.k}$, we derive

$$SS_W = \sum_{i=1}^{N} \sum_{k=1}^{K} Y_{ik}^2 - \sum_{k=1}^{K} \frac{Y_{.k}^2}{N_k} = I - III_B$$

The degrees of freedom for each of the terms can also be found from the model. For each Roman numeral, a certain number of terms must be summed, as described above. For I, the summation extends over all subjects and all groups, so that I equals the sum of N terms Y_{ik}^2. For II, the "sum" is only of the single term, $Y_{..}^2/N$. Finally, for III$_B$, we must sum K terms $Y_{.k}^2/N_k$. Then the degrees of freedom can be found by placing these values in the corresponding places in the theoretical model. For SS$_T$ =

I — II, the degrees of freedom are $N - 1$; for $SS_B = III_B - II$, the degrees of freedom are $K - 1$; and for $SS_W = I - III_B$, the degrees of freedom are $N - K$. We provide the following summary of these procedures.

Step 1. Write the theoretical model $d_T = d_E + d_U$ in terms of the Y values:

$$(Y_{ik} - \bar{Y}_{..}) = (\bar{Y}_{.k} - \bar{Y}_{..}) + (Y_{ik} - \bar{Y}_{.k})$$

$$\text{Total} \qquad \text{Between} \qquad \text{Within}$$

Step 2. Substitute the quantities to be summed and the minus signs:

$$\left(\sum_{i=1}^{N_k} \sum_{k=1}^{K} \frac{Y_{ik}^2}{1} - \frac{Y_{..}^2}{N} \right) = \left(\sum_{k=1}^{K} \frac{Y_{.k}^2}{N_k} - \frac{Y_{..}^2}{N} \right) + \left(\sum_{i=1}^{N_k} \sum_{k=1}^{K} \frac{Y_{ik}^2}{1} - \sum_{k=1}^{K} \frac{Y_{.k}^2}{N_k} \right)$$

Step 3. Write the sum of squares in terms of the Roman numerals:

$$I - II = (III_B - II) + (I - III_B)$$

$$SS_T \quad = \quad SS_B \quad + \quad SS_W$$

Step 4. Write down the degrees of freedom:

$$N - 1 = (K - 1) + (N - K)$$

$$\nu_T \quad = \quad \nu_B \quad + \quad \nu_W$$

Step 5. Write

$$MS_B = \frac{SS_B}{\nu_B} \qquad \text{and} \qquad MS_W = \frac{SS_W}{\nu_W}$$

36-6. EXERCISES

36-1. Perform a one-way ANOVA on the data of Exercise 35-1. State H_0 and H_1 in symbolic and verbal form. Use $\alpha = .05$ and specify the decision rule.

36-2. An experimenter was interested in determining the relationship between time spent per day in practicing a foreign language and the ability of the person to speak the language at the end of a 6-week period. Some 50 students were assigned at random among five experimental conditions that ranged from 15-min practice daily to 4-h practice per day. Then, at the end of 6 weeks, each student had a score for proficiency in the language. Perform a one-way ANOVA. The data follow:

36-3. Find $\hat{\eta}^2$ for Exercise 36-1, and test $H_0: \eta^2 = 0$.

36-4. Find $\hat{\eta}^2$ for Exercise 36-2, and test $H_0: \eta^2 = 0$.

36-5. Determine the errors for the data of Exercise 36-1. Plot them on normal probability paper. Is the distribution normal or near normal? Why?

Proficiency scores

Daily practice time

15 min	30 min	1 h	2 h	4 h
117	106	86	140	105
83	81	98	128	149
112	74	125	108	110
81	79	123	104	144
105	118	118	132	137
109	110	94	133	151
80	82	93	96	117
73	86	91	101	113
110	111	122	103	142
78	113	130	135	112

CHAPTER **37**

Alternative Models to the Analysis of Variance

37-1. ANALYSIS OF VARIANCE UNDER THE UNEQUAL VARIANCE MODEL

As mentioned previously, the F test assumes the equality of the population variances. When this assumption is violated, the sampling distribution of the F ratio no longer follows the F distribution under H_0. Fortunately, Welch has derived a test statistic, similar in nature to the two-sample Welch-Aspin statistic, whose distribution can be approximated by an F distribution with adjusted denominator degrees of freedom. Let us reexamine the F statistic:

$$F = \frac{MS_B}{MS_W} = \frac{1}{K-1} \sum_{k=1}^{K} \frac{N_k(\bar{Y}_k - \bar{Y})^2}{MS_W}$$

If the population variances are unequal, we do not compute MS_W. Rather, we would use each separate $S_{\bar{Y}_k}^2$ to estimate the variance of its own population. Let us make these substitutions into the F equation and denote the resulting statistic as F'. Thus, we have

$$F' = \frac{1}{K-1} \sum_{k=1}^{K} \frac{N_k(\bar{Y}_k - \bar{Y})^2}{S_{\bar{Y}_k}^2}$$

A statistic similar to F', denoted F^*, can be approximated by an F distribution with $K-1$ and v_2^* degrees of freedom, provided we replace $\bar{Y}$ with the estimate

$$\bar{Y}* = \frac{\sum_{k=1}^{K} W_k \bar{Y}_k}{\sum_{k=1}^{K} W_k}$$

where

$$W_k = \frac{N_k}{S_{\bar{Y}_k}^2}$$

and we divide F' by

$$C = 1 + \frac{2(K-2)}{3v_2^*}$$

where v_2^* is computed from

$$\frac{1}{v_2^*} = \frac{3}{K^2-1} \sum_{k=1}^{K} \frac{1}{v_k}\left(1 - \frac{W_k}{W}\right)^2$$

and where

$$v_k = N_k - 1$$

and

$$W = \sum_{k=1}^{K} W_k$$

With these substitutions,

$$F* = \frac{F'}{C}$$

We can conceptualize the use of $\bar{Y}*$ in place of $\bar{Y}$ in the following way. The samples in this situation come from populations with different variances, but under H_0 we assume that their means are equal. We want to combine the sample means to estimate their common population value. The precision of a sample mean depends on the sample size and the population variance. The precision is measured by the standard error. The larger the standard error, the more likely the sample mean is to be far from the population value. We can weight more heavily the sample means that are likely to be close to the population value if we use as weights measures that give greater emphasis to large sample sizes and small variances. We see that $W_k = N_k/S_{\bar{Y}_k}^2$ satisfies both requirements.

Let us apply this method to the data of Table 33-1. For these data,

$$W_1 = \frac{N_1}{S_1^2} = \frac{10}{1.6^2} = 3.9062, \qquad W_2 = \frac{N_2}{S_2^2} = \frac{8}{2.2^2} = 1.6529,$$

$$\cdots, \qquad W_6 = \frac{N_6}{S_6^2} = \frac{15}{2.3^2} = 2.8355$$

and

$$W = W_1 + W_2 + \cdots + W_6 = 18.2448$$

Furthermore:

$$\bar{Y}* = \frac{3.9062(8.9) + 1.6529(6.4) + \cdots + 2.8355(7.6)}{18.2448}$$

$$= 8.1324$$

With this value,

$$F' = \frac{1}{6-1}\left[\frac{10(8.9 - 8.1324)^2}{1.6^2} + \frac{8(6.4 - 8.1324)^2}{2.2^2} + \cdots\right.$$

$$\left. + \frac{15(7.6 - 8.1324)^2}{2.3^2}\right]$$

$$= 9.23$$

In addition,

$$\frac{1}{v_2^*} = \frac{3}{6^2 - 1}\left[\frac{1}{9}\left(1 - \frac{3.9062}{18.2448}\right)^2 + \frac{1}{7}\left(1 - \frac{1.6529}{18.2448}\right)^2 + \cdots\right.$$

$$\left. + \frac{1}{14}\left(1 - \frac{2.8355}{18.2448}\right)^2\right]$$

$$= 0.0411$$

so that

$$v_2^* = \frac{1}{0.0411} = 24.32 \simeq 24$$

Also

$$C = 1 + \frac{2(6-2)}{3(24.32)} = 1.1096 \quad \text{and} \quad F^* = \frac{9.23}{1.1096} = 8.32$$

Box 37-1 Procedure for testing equality of means when variances are unequal

Step 1. Compute the mean and variance of each sample.
Step 2. Compute

$$\frac{1}{v_2^*} = \frac{3}{K^2 - 1} \sum_{k=1}^{K} \frac{1}{v_k} \left(1 - \frac{W_k}{W}\right)^2$$

$$C = 1 + \frac{2(K-2)}{3v_2^*}$$

$$F' = \frac{1}{K - 1} \sum_{k=1}^{K} \frac{N_k(\bar{Y}_k - \bar{Y}^*)^2}{S_{\bar{Y}_k}^2}$$

and

$$F^* = \frac{F'}{C}$$

where

$$\bar{Y}^* = \frac{\sum\limits_{k=1}^{K} W_k \bar{Y}_k}{\sum\limits_{k=1}^{K} W_k}$$

$$W_k = \frac{1}{SE_{\bar{Y}_k}^2} = \frac{N_k}{S_{\bar{Y}_k}^2}$$

$$W = W_1 + W_2 + \cdots + W_K$$

Step 3. Reject H_0 if

$$F^* > F_{v_1, v_2^* : 1 - \alpha}$$

with

$$v_1 = K - 1$$

and v_2^* as computed.

Thus for $\alpha = .05$, $v_1 = K - 1 = 6 - 1 = 5$, and $v_2^* = 24$, the decision rule for rejecting

$$H_0: \mu_{Y_1} = \mu_{Y_2} = \cdots = \mu_{Y_K}$$

against

$$H_1: H_0 \text{ is false}$$

is given by

$$\text{Decision Rule: Reject } H_0 \text{ if } F^* > F_{5,24:.95} = 2.62$$

Thus, H_0 is rejected. Directions for testing H_0 are provided in Box 37-1.

37-2. KRUSKAL-WALLIS TEST

Both the analysis of variance and the Welch alternative are based on the assumption that the dependent variable has a normal distribution or that sample sizes are sufficiently large to apply the central limit theorem to approximate the distribution of sample means as normal. If either of these conditions cannot be satisfied, then one can use the Kruskal-Wallis model. This model is the simple extension of the two-sample Wilcoxon test to three or more populations where the original observations are replaced by ranks R_{ik}.

Thus, the hypothesis of the Kruskal-Wallis test is that the K distributions are identical. The alternative hypothesis is that the distributions are not identical. Rejection of the null hypothesis means that the distributions could differ in centers, variance, skewness, or kurtosis. Since we are most interested in centers, we must assume that the populations do not differ in variance or shape. If the distributions are identical, the expected values of the mean ranks for all samples are equal to a common value. Thus, the null hypothesis for this test can be written as

$$H_0: E(\overline{R}_{.1}) = E(\overline{R}_{.2}) = \cdots = E(\overline{R}_{.K})$$

where $\overline{R}_{.k}$ is the mean rank of the kth group.

The Kruskal-Wallis test is performed by assigning ranks to the original data in exactly the same fashion as that used for the two-sample Wilcoxon test. In addition, midranks are again assigned to tied observations. In this case, the test statistic is computed as

$$H = (N - 1)\hat{\eta}^2 = (N - 1)\left(\frac{\text{III}_B - \text{II}}{\text{I} - \text{II}}\right)$$

Box 37-2   Procedures for the Kruskal-Wallis test

Step 1. Rank-order the data in the total sample.

Step 2. Replace each observation by its rank value R_{ik}. Replace tied observations by midrank values.

Step 3. Compute I, II, and III_B:

$$I = \sum_{k=1}^{K} \sum_{i=1}^{N_k} R_{ik}^2$$

$$II = \frac{R_{..}^2}{N}$$

$$III_B = \sum_{k=1}^{K} \frac{R_{.k}^2}{N_k}$$

Step 4. Compute

$$\hat{\eta}^2 = \frac{III_B - II}{I - II} = \frac{SS_B}{SS_T}$$

and

$$H = (N - 1)\hat{\eta}^2$$

Step 5. Determine the critical value from Table A-10 for $v = K - 1$ and the α of interest as $\chi_{K-1:1-\alpha}^2$. Reject H_0 if $H > \chi_{K-1:1-\alpha}^2$.

Step 6. Make a decision.

---

where N = number of observations and $\hat{\eta}^2$, I, II, and III_B are computed from the ranks associated with each sample using the computing formulas of Section 36-2.

The sampling distribution of H was studied by Kruskal and Wallis in the late 1930s. They discovered that the sampling distribution of H could be adequately approximated by the chi-square distribution with $v = K - 1$ degrees of freedom. Directions for the test are provided in Box 37-2.

We illustrate the use of this test for the data of Table 9-2, which is reproduced in Table 37-1, along with the ranks. In terms of the rank totals,

$$I = 4^2 + 5^2 + \cdots + 39^2 = 22{,}130.50$$

$$II = \frac{(4 + 5 + \cdots + 39)^2}{40} = 16{,}810.00$$

$$III_B = \frac{252^2}{12} + \frac{147.5^2}{8} + \frac{128^2}{6} + \frac{160^2}{7} + \frac{132.5^2}{7} = 16{,}907.37$$

$$\hat{\eta}^2 = \frac{16{,}907.37 - 16{,}810.00}{22{,}130.50 - 16{,}810.00} = \frac{97.37}{5320.5} = .0183$$

Table 37-1. Data of Table 9-2 arranged for testing the Kruskal-Wallis hypothesis of identity of population distributions.

Humanities		Natural sciences		Social sciences		Other		Not known	
Score	Rank	Score	Rank	Score	Rank	Score	Rank	Score	Rank
21	4	19	1.5	19	1.5	42	14.5	35	9.5
24	5	20	3	30	6	42	14.5	35	9.5
31	7.5	31	7.5	45	19.5	43	17	37	11
38	12	39	13	59	32	47	23	45	19.5
43	17	50	27	64	34	47	23	46	21
43	17	54	29	67	35	52	28	47	23
48	25.5	57	30			80	40	71	39
48	25.5	68	36.5						
59	32								
59	32								
68	36.5								
69	38								
Rank total	252		147.5		128		160		132.5
Mean rank	21.0000		18.4375		21.3333		22.8571		18.9286

and

$$H = 39(.0183) = 0.71$$

We now determine the critical region from Table A-10 for $v = K - 1 = 5 - 1 = 4$. Since only small values of H are in agreement with the null hypothesis, the critical value is defined with the 95th percentile of the distribution. As indicated in Table A-10, $\chi^2_{4;.95} = 9.49$, so that the decision rule is given by

Decision Rule: Reject H_0 if $H > 9.49$

Since $H = 0.71 < 9.49$, the hypothesis of equal population centers is not rejected. We have reason to believe that scores on the pretest are unrelated to the college major of the students. The formulation of H in terms of $\hat{\eta}^2$ is shown in Serlin, Carr, and Marascuilo (1982).

37-3. EXERCISES

37-1. Repeat the analysis of Exercise 36-1, using the unequal-variance model.

37-2. Apply the Kruskal-Wallis model to the data of Exercise 36-1. What are the assumptions for this model? Which model would you recommend—that of Exercise 36-1, 37-1, or 37-2? Why?

Post Hoc and Planned Comparisons for One-Factor ANOVA

38-1. POST HOC COMPARISONS FOR THE ANALYSIS OF VARIANCE

A rejection of H_0 in the analysis of variance only tells us that the population means differ, but it does not tell us how the means differ. This is the problem that Scheffé encountered in the early 1950s. He examined the Fisher ANOVA model, and he noted that the hypothesis of equal mean values was not a complete statement of the hypothesis tested by the analysis of variance. The ANOVA F ratio is used to test the hypothesis that *all* population comparisons are equal to zero against the alternative that *at least one* comparison is statistically different from zero. In statistical terms, the most informative way to state the null and alternative hypotheses examined in analysis of variance is

$$H_0: \text{all } \psi = \sum_{k=1}^{K} W_k \mu_{Y_k} = 0$$

against

$$H_1: \text{at least one } \psi \neq 0$$

Scheffé was able to determine the critical value that could be used to test the entire universe of contrasts with an overall type I error rate preselected by the investigator. In particular, he showed that the $1 - \alpha$ percent critical value for testing $H_0: \psi = 0$ in terms of $t_{\hat{\psi}} = \hat{\psi}/\text{SE}_{\hat{\psi}}$ is given by

$$S = \sqrt{v_1 F_{v_1,v_2:1-\alpha}}$$

This critical value is associated with a strategy for identifying possible reasons for the rejection of the null hypothesis on the basis of the F test. If H_0 is rejected, there must exist *at least one* contrast that is statistically different from zero. In fact, there may be more. It is the investigator's job to identify the significant contrasts. Since this search is made only *following* a significant F test, the technique is referred to as *Scheffé's method for post hoc comparisons.* In practice, this means that a researcher who has a clear picture of what is interesting in a particular set of data will perform a planned analysis whereas a researcher who does not have a clear picture can proceed with the data analysis by simply performing the F test. If the test were significant, it would be followed with a post hoc set of comparisons that are interesting or suggested as statistically significant by the data. This strategy allows for the answering of an unlimited number of gut-level questions, hunches, poorly expressed ideas, clearly defined hypotheses, and a host of unthought-of research questions. It is a remarkable strategy.

Let us reexamine the data of Table 33-1 in light of Scheffé's model. In Table 38-1 are presented all the contrasts that were previously examined in a planned context. Assume that we had considered them on a post hoc basis after rejection of H_0 in Section 36-1. The post hoc critical value for all contrasts which could be constructed for the data, including these 22 contrasts, is given by

$$S = \sqrt{v_1 F_{v_1,v_2:1-\alpha}} = \sqrt{5 F_{5,57:.95}} = \sqrt{5(2.38)} = 3.45$$

The decision rule is then given by

Decision Rule: Reject $H_0: \psi = 0$ if $t_{\hat{\psi}} < -3.45$ or if $t_{\hat{\psi}} > 3.45$

On this basis, we would conclude that 7 contrasts out of the 22 examined are significant: ψ_2, ψ_{10}, ψ_{11}, ψ_{12}, ψ_{16}, ψ_{18}, and ψ_{21}.

Table 38-1. Complete list of contrasts for data of Table 33-1 examined in Chapters 33 and 34

ψ	G_1	G_2	G_3	G_4	G_5	G_6	$\hat{\psi}$	$SE_{\hat{\psi}}$	t
1	1	−1	0	0	0	0	2.50	0.97	2.58
2	1	0	−1	0	0	0	5.80	0.94	6.17[a]
3	1	0	0	−1	0	0	−0.20	0.88	−0.23
4	1	0	0	0	−1	0	0.10	0.94	0.11
5	1	0	0	0	0	−1	1.30	0.84	1.55
6	0	1	−1	0	0	0	3.30	1.00	3.30
7	0	1	0	−1	0	0	−2.70	0.94	−2.87
8	0	1	0	0	−1	0	−2.40	1.00	−2.40
9	0	1	0	0	0	−1	−1.20	0.90	−1.33
10	0	0	1	−1	0	0	−6.00	0.90	−6.67[a]
11	0	0	1	0	−1	0	−5.70	0.97	−5.88[a]
12	0	0	1	0	0	−1	−4.50	0.86	−5.23[a]
13	0	0	0	1	−1	0	0.30	0.90	0.33
14	0	0	0	1	0	−1	1.50	0.79	1.90
15	0	0	0	0	1	−1	1.20	0.86	1.40
16	10/27	8/27	9/27	−12/36	−9/36	−15/36	−2.17	0.52	−4.17[a]
17	10/22	−8/17	0	12/22	−9/17	0	1.34	0.66	2.03
18	10/22	0	−9/24	12/22	0	−15/24	3.10	0.61	5.08[a]
19	0	8/17	−9/24	0	9/17	−15/24	1.76	0.65	2.70
20	1	−1	0	−1	1	0	2.20	1.33	1.65
21	1	0	−1	−1	0	1	4.30	1.23	3.50[a]
22	0	1	−1	0	−1	1	2.10	1.32	1.59

[a] Significant as a post hoc comparison with $\alpha \leq .05$.

Even though contrasts ψ_{10} and ψ_{11} are found to be significant according to this method, these contrasts would probably not be considered of scientific interest to a researcher because they are *confounded*. The difference between μ_{Y_3} and μ_{Y_4}, while significant, could be attributed either to the differing amount of alcohol or to the different type of user. This is also true of the difference between μ_{Y_3} and μ_{Y_5}. Since the differences cannot be clearly ex-

---

Box 38-1   Procedures for a Scheffé post hoc analysis on means

Step 1. Perform the ANOVA F test.

Step 2. If the hypothesis H_0: all $\psi = 0$ is rejected, define contrasts to be tested. Test each contrast for significance by using

$$t_{\hat{\psi}} = \frac{\hat{\psi}}{SE_{\hat{\psi}}} = \frac{\displaystyle\sum_{k=1}^{K} W_k \bar{Y}_{.k}}{\sqrt{MS_W \displaystyle\sum_{k=1}^{K} (W_k^2 / N_k)}}$$

Reject H_0: $\psi = 0$ if $t_{\hat{\psi}} < -S$ or $t_{\hat{\psi}} > S$, where

$$S = \sqrt{v_1 F_{v_1, v_2 : 1-\alpha}}$$

---

plained in terms of the independent variables in the study, they were not examined in any of the planned analyses presented earlier.

For completeness, we indicate how to perform a post hoc analysis following a significant F test in Box 38-1.

38-2. POST HOC COMPARISONS FOR THE WELCH MODEL

Both the analysis of variance and the Scheffé method of post hoc comparisons are based on the assumption that the population variances are equal. If this assumption is not satisfied, those models are invalid and should not be used. One alternative is to adopt the Welch model which allows for difference in variances. For this model, one defines contrasts in exactly the same way as that used for the Scheffé model, except that instead of using MS_W in the determination of the corresponding standard errors, one uses the individual sample variances. In addition, the Scheffé coefficient S is replaced by an approximate Scheffé coefficient $S*$, which is defined as

$$S* = \sqrt{Cv_1 F_{v_1, v_2^* : 1-\alpha}}$$

where C and v_2^* are identical to the values used for the $F*$ test of Section 37-1. For completeness, directions for a post hoc analysis following rejection of a hypothesis using the $F*$ test are provided in Box 38-2.

We show how to evaluate the contrast $\hat{\psi}_{17}$ of Table 38-1 under this model. As before, $\hat{\psi}_{17} = 1.34$. However, $SE_{\hat{\psi}_{17}}$ is computed as

$$SE_{\hat{\psi}_{17}} = \sqrt{\left(\frac{10}{22}\right)^2 \frac{1.6^2}{10} + \left(\frac{12}{22}\right)^2 \frac{1.4^2}{12} + \left(-\frac{8}{17}\right)^2 \frac{2.2^2}{8} + \left(-\frac{9}{17}\right)^2 \frac{1.9^2}{9}}$$

$$= .5898$$

Box 38-2   Procedure for a post hoc analysis for the Welch model

Step 1. Perform the $F*$ test.
Step 2. If the hypothesis of the $F*$ test is rejected, define contrasts to be tested. Test each contrast for statistical significance by using

$$t_{\hat\psi} = \frac{\hat\psi}{SE_{\hat\psi}} = \frac{\sum_{k=1}^{K} W_k \bar Y_{.k}}{\sqrt{\sum_{k=1}^{K} W_k^2 (S_k^2/N_k)}}$$

Step 3. Determine $v*$ and C.
Step 4. Reject H_0: $\psi = 0$ if $t_{\hat\psi} < -S*$ or if $t_{\hat\psi} > S*$, where

$$S* = \sqrt{Cv_1 F_{v_1, v_2^*:1-\alpha}}$$

---

so that

$$t_{\hat\psi_{17}} = \frac{\hat\psi_{17}}{SE_{\hat\psi_{17}}} = \frac{1.34}{.5898} = 2.27$$

In Section 37-1, we saw that $v_2^* = 24$, $C = 1.1096$, and $F_{5,24:.95} = 2.62$. For this model, the critical value for testing each contrast is given by

$$S* = \sqrt{(1.1096)5(2.62)} = 3.81$$

a number larger than the ANOVA value $S = 3.45$. With $\alpha = .05$, the decision rule for testing each contrast is given by

Decision Rule: Reject H_0 if $t_{\hat\psi} < -3.81$ or if $t_{\hat\psi} > 3.81$

Hence, since $t_{\hat\psi_{17}} = 2.27$, this contrast would not be significant.

38-3. POST HOC PROCEDURES FOR THE KRUSKAL-WALLIS TEST

The Scheffé method is exceptionally flexible and can be used in many post hoc contexts following the rejection of an omnibus hypothesis of equal central values. A case in point is available for the Kruskal-Wallis test. If the hypothesis of the Kruskal-Wallis test is rejected, one can define contrasts as

$$\psi = W_1 E(\bar R_{.1}) + W_2 E(\bar R_{.2}) + \cdots + W_K E(\bar R_{.K})$$

and test them for significance by using

$$Z = \frac{\hat{\psi}}{\sigma_{\hat{\psi}}}$$

where

$$\sigma_{\hat{\psi}} = \sqrt{\frac{I - II}{N - 1} \sum_{i=1}^{K} \frac{W_k^2}{N_k}}$$

with I and II defined as in Section 37-2. In the appendix we show that the Scheffé coefficient for the Kruskal-Wallis test is

$$S^* = \sqrt{\chi_{\nu:1-\alpha}^2}$$

In Section 37-2, we analyzed the data of Table 37-1. Since the hypothesis of equal population centers was not rejected, we know that there is no contrast among mean ranks that will be significant. For illustrative purposes, however, we consider one such contrast here.

We examine how to contrast humanities majors and natural science majors, as a group, with social science majors. This contrast is defined by

$$\hat{\psi} = \frac{12\overline{R}_{.1} + 6\overline{R}_{.2}}{12 + 6} - \overline{R}_{.3}$$

The value of this contrast is

$$\hat{\psi} = \frac{12(21.0) + 6(21.3333)}{18} - 18.4375$$
$$= 21.1111 - 18.4375 = 2.6736$$

For the contrast of interest,

$$\sigma_{\hat{\psi}} = \sqrt{\frac{22{,}130.50 - 16{,}810.00}{39} \left[\frac{(12/18)^2}{12} + \frac{(-1)^2}{8} + \frac{(6/18)^2}{6} \right]}$$
$$= \sqrt{24.6319} = 4.9631$$

so that

$$Z = \frac{\hat{\psi}}{\sigma_{\hat{\psi}}} = \frac{2.6736}{4.9631} = 0.54$$

For this analysis,

$$S^* = \sqrt{\chi_{4:.95}^2} = \sqrt{9.49} = 3.08$$

Box 38-3   Procedure for a post hoc analysis on ranked data

Step 1. Perform the Kruskal-Wallis test.

Step 2. If the hypothesis of the *H* test is rejected, define contrasts to be tested. Test each contrast for statistical significance by using

$$Z_{\hat{\psi}} = \frac{\hat{\psi}}{\sigma_{\hat{\psi}}} = \frac{W_1 \bar{R}_1 + W_2 \bar{R}_2 + \cdots + W_K \bar{R}_K}{\sqrt{[(I - II)/(N - 1)](W_1^2/N_1 + W_2^2/N_2 + \cdots + W_K^2/N_K)}}$$

Step 3. Reject H_0: $\psi = 0$ if $Z_{\hat{\psi}} < -S^*$ or if $Z_{\hat{\psi}} > S^*$, where

$$S^* = \sqrt{\chi_{K-1:1-\alpha}^2}$$

---

so that the decision rule is given by

$$\text{Decision Rule: Reject } H_0 \text{ if } Z_{\hat{\psi}} < -3.08 \text{ or if } Z_{\hat{\psi}} > 3.08$$

Since $Z = 0.54$ is not in the rejection region, the comparison is not significant.

For completeness, procedures for a post hoc analysis following a significant Kruskal-Wallis test are provided in Box 38-3.

38-4. SUM OF SQUARES ASSOCIATED WITH A CONTRAST

We have seen in several chapters that the correlation ratio is an important descriptive statistic in the ANOVA model. Because we often examine the differences between population means in terms of contrasts, it is desirable to have a measure of explained variability associated with a contrast. In the appendix we show that

$$SS_{\hat{\psi}} = \frac{\hat{\psi}^2}{\sum\limits_{k=1}^{K} W_k^2/N_k}$$

For contrast $\hat{\psi}_{16}$ of Table 38-1,

$$SS_{\hat{\psi}} = \frac{(-2.1742)^2}{(10/27)^2(1/10) + (8/27)^2(1/8) + \cdots + (-15/36)^2(1/15)}$$

$$= \frac{(-2.1742)^2}{1/27 + 1/36} = 72.9264$$

so that

$$F = \frac{MS_{\hat{\psi}}}{MS_W} = \frac{72.9264}{4.2060} = 17.34$$

Box 38-4   Procedure for testing a two-tailed contrast for significance by using an F test

Step 1. Compute

$$MS_{\hat{\psi}} = \frac{\hat{\psi}^2}{\displaystyle\sum_{k=1}^{K} (W_k^2/N_k)}$$

Step 2. Reject H_0 if

$$F = \frac{MS_{\hat{\psi}}}{MS_W}$$

is in the rejection region defined by

$$F > S^2$$

for post hoc contrasts or by

$$F > (t_{\alpha:C,\nu}^{\text{Dunn}})^2$$

for planned contrasts

Step 3. If H_0 is rejected, estimate the strength of the association with

$$\hat{\eta}_{\hat{\psi}}^2 = \frac{SS_{\hat{\psi}}}{SS_T}$$

As we saw in Table 38-1, the corresponding t statistic was equal to -4.17 so that, except for rounding errors, $(-4.17)^2 = 17.34$. Since $SS_T = 489.28$, the contrast accounts for

$$\hat{\eta}_{\hat{\psi}}^2 = \frac{72.9264}{489.2800} = .1490$$

or 15 percent of the variation.

Note that in this example $\hat{\eta}_{\hat{\psi}}^2$ measures the variation in times on target as related to the two-sample status of being or not being a user of alcohol. In this sense, $\hat{\eta}_{\hat{\psi}}^2$ is in reality the square of the point biserial correlation coefficient. For completeness, we summarize the results of this section in Box 38-4.

38-5. TREND ANALYSIS

Commonly encountered designs in social science research involve an ordered quantitative independent variable. Examples of this kind of research would involve variables such as

1. One week, 2 weeks, 3 weeks, or 4 weeks of exposure to behavior modification
2. One trial, two trials, . . . , 10 trials of training in learning a list of 20 nonsense words
3. One hour, 4 h, 7 h, or 10 h of sleep deprivation
4. Ten decibels, 20 dB, 40 dB, or 80 dB of sound at 440 vibrations per second

Because of the numerical nature of the independent variable, hypotheses would typically be phrased in terms of a trend in the mean values of the dependent variable as a function of the levels of the independent variable. Contrasts can be constructed to examine trends, but the *distance* between adjacent levels of the conditions must be equal to a constant. In the first example, the periods of training changed by 1-week intervals. For the second example, the change is always equal to one trial. For the third example, changes occur in 3-h intervals. For the fourth example, the change is in the logarithm of the number of decibels. For example, $\log 10 = 1$, $\log 20 = 1.30313$, $\log 40 = 1.60626$, and $\log 80 = 1.90939$.

As an example in which trend analysis is of interest, consider the data of Table 38-2 where 40 subjects are classified according to their mental age. The dependent variable is the number of erroneous judgments of conservation of matter made by the subjects during a testing period. Since conservation of matter seems to represent a developmental process associated with age, one would expect the errors to decrease with age. However, the pattern of decrease in errors could take many forms. Some possible forms are illustrated in Figure 38-1. Whereas these four graphs illustrate the *most* typical relationships, others are possible. An example is provided in Figure 38-2, which has a linear increasing component, a decreasing quadratic component, and an increasing cubic component. As the illustration demonstrates, it is virtually impossible to describe the components of a curve in terms of the total graph. Although the graph is seen to be increasing, the influence of the

---

Table 38-2. Sample statistics for number of erroneous judgments as a function of mental age

Mental age, months	70	80	90	100	110
Mean $\bar{Y}_{.k}$	18	16	12	11.5	7.5
Variance S_k^2	35	25	30	35	25
Sample size N_k	8	8	8	8	8

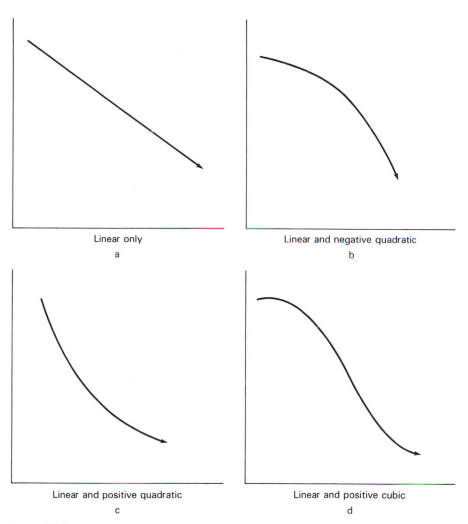

Figure 38-1.
Types of trend components possible for the data of Table 38-2.

$-0.2X^2$ component on the graph for small values of X could be overlooked. Trend analysis helps eliminate this problem.

Trend analysis is described in terms of contrasts. The problem for a researcher reduces to determining the weights to use in defining the contrasts. Fortunately, the weights for equal-sized samples have been determined and tabled. The weights are reported in Table A-14 for various values of K. For $K = 5$, the coefficients are given by the numbers reported in Table 38-3. Notice that the weights define orthogonal contrasts. Because we can associate sums of squares with each contrast and because we can test these contrasts with F ratios, the results of trend analyses are often reported in ANOVA tables. As we saw in Section 34-4, however, orthogonal contrasts must be

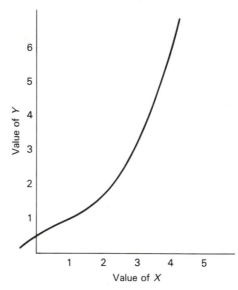

Figure 38-2.
Graph of the equation $Y = 0.5 + 0.6X - 0.2X^2 + 0.1X^3$ over the range $0 \leq X \leq 5$.

planned. The same is true of orthogonal trend contrasts. How these coefficients or weights relate to a trend analysis is demonstrated in Figure 38-3.

The linear (lin) weights trace out a straight line. If the relationship is positive or increasing, $\psi_{\text{lin}} > 0$ whereas if the relationship is negative or decreasing, $\psi_{\text{lin}} < 0$. The contrast is defined as

$$\psi_{\text{lin}} = -2\mu_1 - 1\mu_2 + 0\mu_3 + 1\mu_4 + 2\mu_5$$

The quadratic (quad) weights trace out a quadratic curve. In behavioral data, a negative quadratic component would contribute to the kneelike appearance of Figure 38-2(b). A positive quadratic component would contribute to the elbowlike appearance of Figure 38-2(c). For a quadratic compo-

Table 38-3.   Weights for a trend analysis for $K = 5$

			Group		
Contrast	1	2	3	4	5
Linear	−2	−1	0	1	2
Quadratic	2	−1	−2	−1	2
Cubic	−1	2	0	−2	1
Quartic	1	−4	6	−4	1

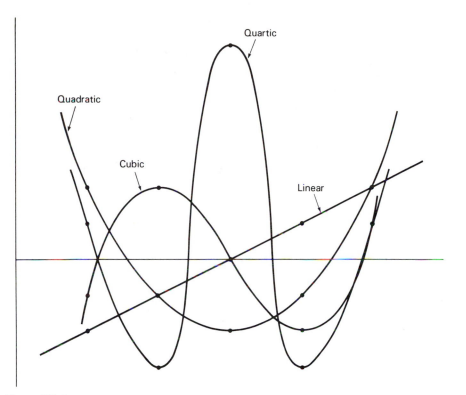

Figure 38-3.
The orthogonal curves defined by the trend analysis weights of Table 38-3.

nent,

$$\psi_{\text{quad}} = 2\mu_1 - 1\mu_2 - 2\mu_3 - 1\mu_4 + 2\mu_5$$

In Figure 38-2(b), $\psi_{\text{quad}} < 0$ whereas in Figure 38-2(c) $\psi_{\text{quad}} > 0$.

Cubic (cub) components are infrequently encountered. However, the curve represented in Figure 38-2(d) indicates the typical S-shaped nature of a cubic component. For a cubic component,

$$\psi_{\text{cub}} = -1\mu_1 + 2\mu_2 + 0\mu_3 - 2\mu_4 + 1\mu_5$$

Quartic (quar) relationships are almost never encountered in social science research; therefore, we ignore them. In our example, when calculating the sums of squares for each trend component, we consider SS_{lin}, SS_{quad}, and SS_{cub} and denote all remaining (rem) sum of squares as SS_{rem}.

For the data of Table 38-2,

$$SS_W = \sum_{k=1}^{K} (N_k - 1)S_k^2$$
$$= 7(35 + 25 + 30 + 35 + 25) = 1015$$

so that

$$MS_W = \frac{SSW}{N - K} = \frac{1015}{40 - 5} = \frac{1015}{35} = 29$$

Since

$$\bar{Y}_{..} = \frac{\sum\limits_{k=1}^{K} N_k \bar{Y}_{.k}}{N} = \frac{8(18) + 8(16) + \cdots + 8(7.5)}{40} = 13$$

it follows that

$$SS_B = \sum\limits_{k=1}^{K} N_k(\bar{Y}_k - \bar{Y}_{..})^2 = 540$$

so that

$$MS_B = \frac{SS_B}{K - 1} = \frac{540}{4} = 135$$

In addition,

$$\hat{\psi}_{\text{lin}} = -2(18) - 1(16) + 0(12) + 1(11.5) + 2(7.5) = -25.5$$

$$\hat{\psi}_{\text{quad}} = 2(18) - 1(16) - 2(12) - 1(11.5) + 2(7.5) = -0.5$$

$$\hat{\psi}_{\text{cub}} = -1(18) + 2(16) + 0(12) - 2(11.5) + 1(7.5) = -1.5$$

$$\hat{\psi}_{\text{quar}} = 1(18) - 4(16) + 6(12) - 4(11.5) + 1(7.5) = -12.5$$

So

$$SS_{\hat{\psi}_{\text{lin}}} = \frac{-25.5^2}{10/8} = 520.2000$$

$$SS_{\hat{\psi}_{\text{quad}}} = \frac{-0.5^2}{14/8} = 0.1429$$

$$SS_{\hat{\psi}_{\text{cub}}} = \frac{-1.5^2}{10/8} = 1.8000$$

$$SS_{\hat{\psi}_{\text{quar}}} = \frac{-12.5^2}{70/8} = 17.8571$$

Let us note that

$$520.2000 + 0.1429 + 1.8000 + 17.8571 = 540$$

Table 38-4. ANOVA table for data of Table 38-2

Source	df	Sum of squares	Mean square	F ratio	$\hat{\eta}^2$
Between groups	4	540.00	135.00	—	—
Linear	1	520.20	520.20	17.94	.33
Quad	1	0.14	0.14	0.01	—
Cubic	1	1.80	1.80	0.06	—
Remainder	1	17.86	17.86	0.62	—
Within groups	35	1015.00	29.00		
Total	39	1555.00			

so that

$$SS_{\hat{\psi}_{lin}} + SS_{\hat{\psi}_{quad}} + SS_{\hat{\psi}_{cub}} + SS_{\hat{\psi}_{quar}} = SS_B$$

The remainder of the analysis is presented in Table 38-4. A number of things are to be noted in the reporting of Table 38-4:

1. The F ratio for the overall between-group source of variation is calculated but not tested, since the interest is focused on the planned orthogonal contrasts associated with the nature of the trend in the mean scores.
2. The terms associated with the orthogonal trend component are indented, because they represent a decomposition of the overall sum of squares between groups.
3. Since in most cases no interest exists in terms above the cubic, they are lumped and termed *remainder*.
4. The probability of at least one type I error is usually distributed only across the contrasts for linear, quadratic, and cubic components. This means here that $C = 3$.
5. In this example, significant components are identified if $F > t_{Dunn}^2$, where t_{Dunn} is the value read from the Dunn table with $\alpha = .05$, $C = 3$, and $v_2 = 35$. In this example, $t_{Dunn}^2 = 2.52^2 = 6.35$.
6. $\hat{\eta}^2$ is computed only for the significant contrasts. In this case, $\hat{\eta}_{lin}^2 = .33$.

Finally, we recall that the Pearson product-moment correlation coefficient measures the linear association between two variables. We have just measured the linear relationship between an independent and a dependent variable, using the linear contrast. It is not surprising that

$$r^2 = \frac{SS_{\hat{\psi}\text{lin}}}{SS_T} = \hat{\eta}^2_{\text{lin}}$$

This statement is true only if the spaces between the independent variable are equal, as they are in this example, and if the sample sizes are equal.

38-6. APPENDIX

Here it is shown that $S^* = \sqrt{\chi^2 v_{\,\nu:1-\alpha}}$ for the Kruskal-Wallis test. As we know,

$$F_{\nu_1,\nu_2} = \frac{\chi^2_{\nu_1}/\nu_1}{\chi^2_{\nu_2}/\nu_2}$$

Let us see what happens to the denominator as ν_2 becomes exceedingly large. We know that

$$E(\chi^2_{\nu_2}) = \nu_2 \quad \text{and} \quad \text{Var}(\chi^2_{\nu_2}) = 2\nu_2$$

Then by the scale theorem, we have

$$E\left(\frac{\chi^2_{\nu_2}}{\nu_2}\right) = \frac{1}{\nu_2} E(\chi^2_{\nu_2}) = \frac{1}{\nu_2}(\nu_2) = 1$$

and

$$\text{Var}\left(\frac{\chi^2_{\nu_2}}{\nu_2}\right) = \frac{1}{\nu_2^2} \text{Var}(\chi^2_{\nu_2}) = \frac{1}{\nu_2^2}(2\nu_2) = \frac{2}{\nu_2}$$

Thus, regardless of ν_2, the mean of $\chi^2_{\nu_2}/\nu_2 = 1$. But as ν_2 becomes very large, $\text{Var}(\chi^2_{\nu_2}/\nu_2)$ becomes very small. For $\nu_2 = \infty$, $\text{Var}(\chi^2_{\nu_2}/\nu_2) = 0$. This means that for infinite degrees of freedom, when we sample from a $\chi^2_{\nu_2}$ distribution and calculate $\chi^2_{\nu_2}/\nu_2$, we get the value of unity, and it is never anything else because the variance is zero. Hence,

$$F_{\nu_1,\infty} = \frac{\chi^2_{\nu_1}/\nu_1}{1} = \frac{\chi^2_{\nu_1}}{\nu_1}$$

and

$$\nu_1 F_{\nu_1,\infty} = \chi^2_{\nu_1}$$

Therefore, the Scheffé coefficient for the Kruskal-Wallis test is given by

$$S^* = \sqrt{\nu F_{\nu,\infty:1-\alpha}} = \sqrt{\chi^2_{\nu:1-\alpha}}$$

We now show that

$$SS_{\hat{\psi}} = \frac{\hat{\psi}^2}{\sum_{k=1}^{K} W_k^2 / N_k}$$

The general ANOVA hypothesis is tested in terms of an F ratio with ν_1 and ν_2 degrees of freedom. We have seen that

$$t_{\nu_2}^2 = F_{1,\nu_2}$$

This means that all two-tailed t tests can be performed as F tests. With this in mind, consider the test of $H_0 : \psi = 0$ against $H_1 : \psi \neq 0$. As a t test, with ν_2 degrees of freedom, we would write

$$t = \frac{\hat{\psi}}{SE_{\hat{\psi}}}$$

As an F test with $\nu_1 = 1$ and ν_2 degrees of freedom, we have

$$F = t^2 = \frac{\hat{\psi}^2}{SE_{\hat{\psi}}^2}$$

Let us examine this ratio in terms of sample statistics. Since

$$\hat{\psi} = W_1 \overline{Y}_{.1} + W_2 \overline{Y}_{.2} + \cdots + W_K \overline{Y}_{.K} = \sum_{k=1}^{K} W_k \overline{Y}_{.k}$$

we have

$$\hat{\psi}^2 = \left(\sum_{k=1}^{K} W_k \overline{Y}_{.k} \right)^2$$

In a similar fashion, we know that

$$SE_{\hat{\psi}}^2 = MS_W \left(\frac{W_1^2}{N_1} + \frac{W_2^2}{N_2} + \cdots + \frac{W_K^2}{N_K} \right) = MS_W \sum_{k=1}^{K} \frac{W_k^2}{N_k}$$

Therefore,

$$F = \frac{\left(\sum_{k=1}^{K} W_k \overline{Y}_{.k} \right)^2}{MS_W \sum_{k=1}^{K} W_k^2 / N_k}$$

Because an F ratio is written as the ratio of two mean squares, we can write F as

$$F = \frac{MS_{\hat{\psi}}}{MS_W}$$

By comparing the two expressions for F, we can identify the $MS_{\hat{\psi}}$ as

$$MS_{\hat{\psi}} = \frac{\left(\sum_{k=1}^{K} W_k \bar{Y}_{.k}\right)^2}{\sum_{k=1}^{K} W_k^2 / N_k}$$

Since this F has a distribution with $\nu_1 = 1$, we also know that

$$MS_{\hat{\psi}} = \frac{SS_{\hat{\psi}}}{1} = SS_{\hat{\psi}} = \frac{\left(\sum_{k=1}^{K} W_k \bar{Y}_{.k}\right)^2}{\sum_{k=1}^{K} W_k^2 / N_k} = \frac{\hat{\psi}^2}{\sum_{k=1}^{K} W_k^2 / N_k}$$

This means that each contrast has an associated sum of squares and a corresponding mean square. It also indicates that a measure of explained variation can be computed for a single contrast as

$$\hat{\eta}_{\hat{\psi}}^2 = \frac{SS_{\hat{\psi}}}{SS_T}$$

EXERCISES

38-1. Find the $\alpha = .05$ post hoc critical value for the data of Table 9-2. Determine the value of C, the number of planned contrasts, that could have been examined using the same critical value. What does this suggest to you?

38-2. For the data of Table 33-1, find the values of ν_1 and ν_2^* for the Welch model. Determine the value of S^* for $\alpha = .05$.

38-3. Do a planned trend analysis on the data of Exercise 36-2. To do so, use as the spacing of the independent variable the logarithm of the practice time. Use $\alpha = .05$.

38-4. Some researchers analyze the data of Exercise 38-2 in terms of a post hoc analysis. Would you recommend a post hoc analysis or a planned analysis? Why?

38-5. Make a post hoc analysis for the data of Exercise 36-1, using $\alpha = .05$.

38-6. Examine the five contrasts of Table 34-4, described in Section 34-4. Report the results in an ANOVA table.

38-7. Report the results of Exercise 34-3 in an ANOVA table.

CHAPTER 39

Two-Factor Analysis of Variance
— Crossed and Nested Designs

39-1. FULLY CROSSED INTERACTION AND NESTED DESIGNS

Until now, our discussion of the analysis of variance has dealt mainly with one independent variable, group membership, and one dependent variable. This is in keeping with the goals outlined in Chapter 2, where we stressed the importance of internal and external validity for behavioral research. To achieve these goals, studies should be designed so that none of the independent variables could be confounded with one another. We now begin a formal investigation of studies with multiple independent variables. As we shall now see, there are ways to examine the effects of more than one independent variable at a time and still feel secure that a study has internal validity and, under appropriate conditions, external validity.

We have already encountered studies that involve the operation of more than one independent factor. Consider, for example, the experiment presented in Section 34-3 involving alcohol, water, sugar, and barbiturates. In this study there are two possible sources for the observed effect: the liquid and/or the medication. Such an experiment is often referred to as a *two-way layout,* since it involves two main sources for the observed effects. This design is to be contrasted with the *one-way layouts* we have, so far, examined in depth. A second example of a two-way layout was considered in Section 33-1, where we looked at the experiment on motor skills as they were affected by alcohol intake by users and nonusers. Even though we treated the data in terms of a one-factor experiment, we were very careful in identifying the possible families of hypotheses that could be generated in the analysis.

A further distinction should be made among two-way layouts. In the liquid/drug example, each kind of drug was administered with each kind of liquid. Such layouts, in which all levels of one variable are observed at all levels of the second variable, are called *fully crossed,* or *factorial,* designs. Similarly, both users and nonusers of alcohol were observed at one of the three amounts of alcohol administered to the subjects. This experiment, too, involves a fully crossed design.

As an example of a design that is not crossed, consider an experiment conducted with six teachers, three at each of two schools. If the dependent variable is student test scores, we could isolate two sources of variation, one due to school differences and the other due to teacher differences. In this case, however, the three teachers at the first school are not identical to, or equivalent to, the three teachers at the other school. The teacher source of variation, if it should exist, is said to be nested within the schools. As we shall see, the analysis of a *nested design* proceeds as if there were two separate experiments performed, one at each school.

Figure 39-1 depicts the differences between crossed and nested designs. Figure 39-1a represents the liquid-drug example. The two kinds of drug are drug 1 and drug 2, while the two liquids are liquid 1 and liquid 2. Each kind of drug is measured with each kind of liquid. In Figure 39-1b, the motor skill study is shown to involve two levels of user, user 1 and user 2, and three amounts of alcohol, amounts 1, 2, and 3. Again, each amount is observed with each type of user. However, Figure 39-1c shows the six teachers, T_1 through T_6, and the two schools, school 1 and school 2. Notice here that school 1 appears only with T_1, T_2, and T_3. School 1 is not, and cannot be, observed with T_4, T_5, and T_6. Hence, between-teacher differences can be examined only *within* school 1 or *within* school 2. Since the three teachers at each school are not identical, we cannot consider this to be a crossed design. It is because the three amounts of alcohol administered to the two types of users are biochemically identical in all respects that the alcohol user experiment is considered fully crossed.

Although it is incorrect to view a nested design as fully crossed, the converse is not true. In certain instances, the hypothesis of interest can compel us

	Liquid 1	Liquid 2
Drug 1	$L_1 \times D_1$	$L_2 \times D_1$
Drug 2	$L_1 \times D_2$	$L_2 \times D_2$

a Liquid-drug example of crossed design

	User 1	User 2
Amount 1	$U_1 \times A_1$	$U_2 \times A_1$
Amount 2	$U_1 \times A_2$	$U_2 \times A_2$
Amount 3	$U_1 \times A_3$	$U_2 \times A_3$

b User-amount example of crossed design

	T_1	T_2	T_3	T_4	T_5	T_6
School 1	$T_1 \times S_1$	$T_2 \times S_1$	$T_3 \times S_1$			
School 2				$T_4 \times S_2$	$T_5 \times S_2$	$T_6 \times S_2$

c Teacher-school example of nested design

Figure 39-1.
Crossed and nested designs.

to view a crossed design in a nested fashion. This is especially true when we are interested in the effects of a treatment on certain kinds of individuals only. Consider an experiment that seeks to examine a new teaching program designed for certain kinds of students, and let us assume that the students have been classified on the basis of some criterion as fast and slow learners. Each type of student learner is assigned to one of two subgroups at random, and one subgroup is given the old program, while the other is given the new program. Each program type is combined with each student type, so we could view this as a fully crossed design. Suppose, however, that we have designed the new program to be especially helpful for slow learners so that we are most interested in the difference between the programs for slow learners. Of course, we would not neglect the fast learners, because we would hope that the new program does as well as the old for these students, while being particularly effective for slow learners.

Under these conditions it would make sense to view this fully crossed design as if it involved program differences within each student type, a nested design. We shall see that the methods used for analyzing nested designs can also be applied to crossed designs to answer questions of interest. But unfortunately we cannot analyze a design in both ways because the hypotheses of interest and the hidden structure of the data must be stated in advance. These prestated hypotheses and structure assumptions dictate the proper kind of analysis to apply. The meaning of this will become clearer in later sections.

39-2. TWO-WAY ANALYSIS OF VARIANCE—CROSSED DESIGNS

As for the one-way layout, the ANOVA procedure is an attempt to detect differences among population means. The same is true of the two-way case. With two sources of effects, however, the analysis detects differences among two separate sets of population means. For example, in the liquid-drug experiment, interest exists in determining whether there is a difference in the effects due to water (wat) and to alcohol (alc). The null hypothesis in this case would then be

$$H_0: \mu_{\text{wat}} = \mu_{\text{alc}}$$

At the same time, of course, we want to examine the difference in the effects of sugar (sug) and barbiturates (barb). This null hypothesis is

$$H_0: \mu_{\text{sug}} = \mu_{\text{barb}}$$

We can examine both hypotheses, often called *main-effects hypotheses*, with ease if we restrict ourselves to equal numbers of subjects being given each combination of treatments. In this example, 10 people are given each of the treatment combinations, so the equal-cell-size restriction is satisfied. We consider only the equal-size-sample cases in these chapters for two- and multiple-factor ANOVA designs. The problem of unequal sample size is examined in Chapter 47.

As mentioned in Chapter 34, this experiment provides a good example of an interaction between different treatments. There, we saw that an interaction is measured by a difference in mean differences. The two-way design allows us to detect interactions as well as main effects. The null hypothesis examining whether an interaction exists is, as we saw,

$$H_0: \mu_{\text{wat}+\text{sug}} - \mu_{\text{wat}+\text{barb}} = \mu_{\text{alc}+\text{sug}} - \mu_{\text{alc}+\text{barb}}$$

All three null hypotheses are tested by using F ratios.

Consider the data of Table 39-1. The data were generated from a study in which 30 males and 30 females were divided equally among three experimental conditions. The three experimental conditions involved listening to one version of a song from three versions sung by a group. In one version a lead

Table 39-1. Scores obtained by 30 male and 30 female
subjects on a musical preference measure

Sex of subjects	Subject number	Male lead	Female lead	No lead
Males	1	77	60	57
	2	77	60	59
	3	77	62	60
	4	80	67	61
	5	82	68	62
	6	83	70	62
	7	83	72	63
	8	88	75	64
	9	90	78	67
	10	97	80	67
Females	1	82	78	59
	2	83	78	62
	3	87	79	62
	4	88	79	65
	5	90	85	66
	6	96	86	67
	7	96	89	67
	8	96	90	67
	9	99	93	69
	10	99	94	70

vocal was sung by a male, in another the lead singer was female, and in a third version the lines were sung by the entire group. The dependent measure was a rating by the subjects on a scale of 0 to 100 of how well they liked the song. The experiment was intended to provide information about the relationship between sex of listener (L) and sex of singer (S) in the performance.

In practice, this analysis would normally be performed with a computer. We have provided the theory and computation formulas in the appendix to this chapter. As with the one-way ANOVA, each hypothesis is tested with an F ratio where the denominator is the mean square within groups. For each of the hypotheses, the numerator is the mean square explained by the particular factor. The mean scores are reported in Table 39-2. We note that there are mean scores for each level of listener, each level of singer, and each cell of the combinations of listener and singer. Let the two levels of listener be denoted by L, where l_1 = male and l_2 = female. Let the three levels of singers be denoted S, where s_1 = male lead singer, s_2 = female lead singer, and s_3 = no lead singer.

The two-factor model must contain parameters associated with three sources of variation, the main effects for listener and singer as well as the interaction of the two. If we let $i = 1, 2, \ldots, n$ represent the ith subject in a specific group, we can postulate that the observation for the ith subject of the lth sex hearing the sth singer is composed of parts due to the listener effect,

Table 39-2. Mean scores for data of Table 39-1

Sex	Male lead	Female lead	No lead	Total
Males	83.40	69.20	62.20	71.60
Females	91.60	85.10	65.40	80.70
Total	87.50	77.15	63.80	76.15

the singer effect, and the interaction of the two, plus a part unexplained by these factors. In terms of the explained, unexplained, and total deviations introduced in Chapter 9, we have

$$d_T = d_L + d_S + d_{L \times S} + d_U$$

If these deviations are squared and summed across the entire sample of $N = LSn$ observations, we have

$$SS_T = SS_L + SS_S + SS_{L \times S} + SS_W$$

Again applying the methods of the appendix to Chapter 36 and the appendix of this chapter, we find

$$SS_T = 9075.65 \qquad v_T = 59$$
$$SS_L = 1242.15 \qquad v_L = 1$$
$$SS_S = 5646.90 \qquad v_S = 2$$
$$SS_{L \times S} = 409.30 \qquad v_{L \times S} = 2$$
$$SS_W = 1777.30 \qquad v_W = 54$$

Table 39-3. ANOVA table for data of Table 39-1

Source	df	SS	MS	F	$\hat{\eta}^2$
Between listeners	1	1242.15	1242.15	37.74[a]	.14
Between singers	2	5646.90	2823.45	85.79[b]	.62
$L \times S$	2	409.30	204.65	6.22[b]	.05
Within	54	1777.30	32.91		
Total	59	9075.65			

[a] Significant at $\alpha = .05$, critical value is $F_{1,54;.95} = 4.02$
[b] Significant at $\alpha = .05$, critical value is $F_{2,54;.95} = 3.17$

As shown in the appendix, these values can be calculated by hand. Because of the opportunity for making errors, the computation can be quite time-consuming. Most of the time, a computer would perform the calculations for us. With these values,

$$MS_L = \frac{1242.15}{1} = 1242.15$$

$$MS_S = \frac{5646.90}{2} = 2823.45$$

$$MS_{L\times S} = \frac{409.30}{2} = 204.65$$

$$MS_W = \frac{1777.30}{54} = 32.91$$

Finally,

$$F_L = \frac{MS_L}{MS_W} = \frac{1242.15}{32.91} = 37.74$$

$$F_S = \frac{MS_S}{MS_W} = \frac{2823.45}{32.91} = 85.79$$

$$F_{L\times S} = \frac{MS_{L\times S}}{MS_W} = \frac{204.65}{32.91} = 6.22$$

The complete ANOVA table is shown in Table 39-3.

This table involves three families of hypotheses associated with listeners, singers, and the interaction of listeners with singers. If these families had been investigated by three separate ANOVAs, each would be tested with $\alpha_L = \alpha_S = \alpha_{L\times S} = .05$, so that the total risk of at least one type I error across the entire study is given by

$$\alpha_T \leq \alpha_L + \alpha_S + \alpha_{L\times S} = .05 + .05 + .05 = .15$$

We adopt this model and use it in the remaining examples in this and later chapters. With this model, we now set up our three decision rules, one for each family of hypotheses. The three decision rules are given by

1. Reject $H_{0(L)}$ if $F > F_{1,54:.95} = 4.02$.
2. Reject $H_{0(S)}$ if $F > F_{2,54:.95} = 3.17$.
3. Reject $H_{0(L\times S)}$ if $F > F_{2,54:.95} = 3.17$.

All three hypotheses are rejected.

39-3. TWO-FACTOR NESTED COMPARISONS WITH n OBSERVATIONS PER CELL

Not all two-factor fully crossed designs are interpretable or interesting in terms of two main effects and an interaction. As an example, consider the data of Table 39-4. These data are based on a survey conducted by a political action committee using a large group of registered voters who were sent a four-item questionnaire designed to measure their attitude toward financial support of private and church schools by local, state, and federal government grants and funds. High scores represent opposition.

The committee was interested in supplying pamphlets to various religious groups whose views differed, to help them understand one another's views. It was expected that persons of a particular educational level might be more like one another than people with different amounts of education. So that the committee would not have to distribute pamphlets to people who already agree, the interest centered on each level of education separately, to find religions whose views differed for each individual level. In this study, the religious groups are identified as: R_1, none; R_2, Catholic; R_3, Jewish; R_4,

Table 39-4. Attitude toward financial support of private and church schools by education and religion

Religion	Educational level			
	E_1	E_2	E_3	E_4
R_1	2	1	0	0
	6	3	2	0
	7	4	2	0
	7	5	4	2
R_2	10	9	8	12
	15	11	10	12
	16	12	11	13
	16	16	11	16
R_3	8	8	0	0
	10	11	4	1
	12	11	4	3
	16	16	5	4
R_4	10	8	1	1
	10	8	3	2
	11	10	4	4
	12	12	5	4
R_5	6	11	8	9
	10	12	10	10
	15	13	10	12
	16	14	13	16

liberal Protestant; and R_5, conservative Protestant. The education groups consist of people whose education is: E_1, less than eighth grade; E_2, some high school; E_3, high school graduate; and E_4, some college.

Although we could start with a model that included the two main effects of religion and education and an interaction effect, we find that examining interactions does not answer the questions of interest, which compare religions for each educational level. One solution would be to perform a series of one-factor ANOVAs within each level of education.

With this point of view, the hypotheses of interest are

$$H_{0R(E_1)}: \mu_{11.} = \mu_{21.} = \cdots = \mu_{R1.}$$

$$H_{0R(E_2)}: \mu_{12.} = \mu_{22.} = \cdots = \mu_{R2.}$$

$$\cdots\cdots\cdots\cdots\cdots\cdots\cdots\cdots\cdots\cdots\cdots$$

$$H_{0R(E_E)}: \mu_{1E.} = \mu_{2E.} = \cdots = \mu_{RE.}$$

Note that each of the religion hypotheses is similar to the hypothesis of a one-factor ANOVA. Such hypotheses are referred to as *nested*, or *simple main-effect, hypotheses*. In addition, one can test a main-effect hypothesis concerning differences among the education levels, which could also be approached as a one-factor ANOVA, by examining

$$H_0: \mu_{.1.} = \mu_{.2.} = \cdots = \mu_{.E.}$$

Each of the one-factor ANOVAs would have its own mean square within. As shown in the chapter appendix, the combined sum of squares within is used in testing all the hypotheses. It is computed from all the cells of the design, not just from the cells associated with a specific hypothesis. The reason for doing so is that the probability of rejecting a particular H_0 when it is false is increased.

For the data of Table 39-4, the decision rule for education is given by

$$\text{Decision Rule: Reject } H_0 \text{ if } F > F_{3,60:.95} = 2.76$$

The appropriate decision rule for religion (R) nested in education (E) is a bit more problematic, and the model we propose would not be subscribed to by all researchers. We offer an argument for our model and will let each researcher decide which is the more valid model. In the interaction model for this experiment, the experimentwise error rate is

$$\alpha_T \le \alpha_E + \alpha_R + \alpha_{R \times E} = .05 + .05 + .05 = .15$$

In the nested model, we again assign the education main effect to be allotted $\alpha_E = .05$. Therefore, the tests of the remaining hypotheses should be based on

$$\alpha_{R(E)} = \alpha_R + \alpha_{R \times E} = .05 + .05 = .10$$

With this risk of a type I error, both analyses are made with an identical experimentwise error rate. Now, however, the appropriate decision rule for *each* of the nested hypotheses is not clear. We propose that each of the E nested hypotheses be tested with

$$\alpha_{R(E_e)} = \frac{1}{E}(.10) = \frac{1}{4}(.10) = .025$$

For this example, each nest is allotted an alpha of $\alpha_{R(E_e)} = .025$. With this risk of a type I error, each nested hypothesis should be tested with the decision rule

Decision Rule: Reject H_0 if $F > F_{4,60:.975} = 3.01$

For the data of Table 39-4 and the formulas derived in the appendix,

$$SS_T = 1953.55 \qquad v_T = 79$$
$$SS_W = 337.50 \qquad v_W = 60$$
$$SS_E = 389.35 \qquad v_E = 3$$
$$SS_{R(1)} = 165.50 \qquad v_{R(1)} = 4$$
$$SS_{R(2)} = 232.00 \qquad v_{R(2)} = 4$$
$$SS_{R(3)} = 259.50 \qquad v_{R(3)} = 4$$
$$SS_{R(4)} = 569.70 \qquad v_{R(4)} = 4$$

Table 39-5. ANOVA table for religion nested in each level of education

Source	df	SS	MS	F	$\hat{\eta}^2$
Education	3	389.35	129.78	23.09[a]	.20
Religion in education	16	1226.70			
R in E_1	4	165.50	41.38	7.36[b]	.08
R in E_2	4	232.00	58.00	10.31[b]	.12
R in E_3	4	259.50	64.75	11.51[b]	.13
R in E_4	4	569.70	142.43	25.32[b]	.29
Within	60	337.50	5.63		
Total	79	1953.55			

[a] Significant at $\alpha = .05$, critical value is $F_{3,60:.95} = 2.76$.
[b] Significant at $\alpha = .025$, critical value is $F_{4,60:.975} = 3.01$.

These values are summarized in Table 39-5. We see that all five hypotheses are rejected. As is always the case with an omnibus test, we still do not know in what manner the means differ. We examine this in Chapter 40.

39-4. TWO-FACTOR CELL MEANS MODEL WITH n OBSERVATIONS PER CELL

As might be expected, in many research studies both nested comparisons and interaction comparisons are of interest. Unfortunately, only one type of comparison can be investigated in a particular context because of the restrictions imposed on the data by the assumed latent structure of the model. To get around this problem, consider an alternate model that permits an evaluation of both nested and interaction effects. This model is called the *cell means model*. The cell means model analyzes the data as a one-factor ANOVA. For the data of Table 39-4, we find

$$SS_{cells} = 1616.05 \qquad v_{cells} = 19$$
$$SS_W = 337.50 \qquad v_W = 60$$
$$SS_T = 1953.55 \qquad v_T = 79$$

The analysis is summarized in Table 39-6.

When we examined the interaction and nested models, we allowed the total experiment error rates to equal .15. For the two models, this was achieved with

$$\alpha_T \le \alpha_R + \alpha_E + \alpha_{R \times E} = .05 + .05 + .05 = .15$$

and

$$\alpha_T \le \alpha_R + \alpha_{(E)R} = .05 + .10 = .15$$

Since the present model should have an equivalent type I error rate, we

Table 39-6.   ANOVA table for cell means model for data of Table 39-4

Source	df	SS	MS	F	$\hat{\eta}^2$
Between cells	19	1616.05	85.06	15.11[a]	.83
Within cells	60	337.50	5.63		
Total	79	1953.55			

[a] Significant at $\alpha = .15$, critical value is $F_{19,60;.85} = 1.45$.

propose to let

$$\alpha_T = \alpha_{\text{cells}} = .15$$

With this decision rule, we know that

$$H_0: \mu_{11} = \mu_{12} = \mu_{13} = \cdots = \mu_{RE}$$

should be rejected if $F > F_{19,60:.85} = 1.45$. Thus, H_0 is rejected, and we know that at least one contrast in the μ_{re} is different from zero.

39-5. APPENDIX

In this section, we specify the hidden-structure equation for the two-factor design with interactions and for the nested model. From these equations, we derive formulas for sums of squares and degrees of freedom. For the interaction model, the equation must contain parameters associated with the two main effects and the interaction, which supply the "explained" parts of the equation, and we must also have an unexplained, error component. These are denoted $\alpha_{a..}$, $\alpha_{.b.}$, $\gamma_{ab.}$, and e_{abi}, respectively. With this notation, the hidden-structure equation becomes

$$Y_{abi} = \mu_{...} + \alpha_{a..} + \alpha_{.b.} + \gamma_{ab.} + e_{abi}$$

With this notation the three hypotheses of interest are

$$H_{0(A)}: \quad \alpha_{1..} = \alpha_{2..} = \cdots = \alpha_{A..} = 0$$

$$H_{0(B)}: \quad \alpha_{.1.} = \alpha_{.2.} = \cdots = \alpha_{.B.} = 0$$

$$H_{0(A \times B)}: \gamma_{11.} = \gamma_{12.} = \cdots = \gamma_{AB.} = 0$$

As before, $\mu_{...}$, $\alpha_{a..}$, $\alpha_{.b.}$, and e_{abi} can be estimated as

$$\hat{\mu}_{...} = \bar{Y}_{...} \qquad\qquad \hat{\alpha}_{.b.} = \bar{Y}_{.b.} - \bar{Y}_{...}$$

$$\hat{\alpha}_{a..} = \bar{Y}_{a..} - \bar{Y}_{...} \qquad \hat{e}_{abi} = Y_{abi} - \bar{Y}_{ab.}$$

We recall that the interaction is measured by how much the joint effect of the two variables differs from the simple sum of the effects when the variables appear separately. The magnitude of the joint effect is indicated by the difference between the cell mean and the grand mean $\mu_{ab.} - \mu_{...}$; the individual effects are given by $\mu_{a..} - \mu_{...}$ and $\mu_{.b.} - \mu_{...}$. Therefore the interaction is

$$\gamma_{ab.} = (\mu_{ab.} - \mu_{...}) - (\mu_{a..} - \mu_{...}) - (\mu_{.b.} - \mu_{...})$$
$$= \mu_{ab.} - \mu_{a..} - \mu_{.b.} + \mu_{...}$$

Therefore, in the sample, the interaction deviation is estimated by

$$\hat{\gamma}_{ab.} = (\overline{Y}_{ab.} - \overline{Y}_{...}) - (\overline{Y}_{a..} - \overline{Y}_{...}) - (\overline{Y}_{.b.} - \overline{Y}_{...})$$
$$= \overline{Y}_{ab.} - \overline{Y}_{a..} - \overline{Y}_{.b.} + \overline{Y}_{...}$$

As in the one-factor ANOVA model, the parameters must satisfy certain restrictions. For the two-factor model, these are

$$\sum_{a=1}^{A} \alpha_{a..} = 0 \qquad \sum_{b=1}^{B} \alpha_{.b.} = 0$$

$$\sum_{a=1}^{A} \gamma_{ab.} = 0 \qquad \text{for each } b$$

$$\sum_{b=1}^{B} \gamma_{ab.} = 0 \qquad \text{for each } a$$

To continue, we now assume that each $\hat{e}_{abi}$ is selected at random from a normal population for which

$$E(\hat{e}_{abi}) = 0 \qquad \text{and} \qquad \text{Var}\,(\hat{e}_{abi}) = \sigma^2$$

In terms of the hidden-structure equation,

$$Y_{abi} - \mu_{...} = \alpha_{a..} + \alpha_{.b.} + \gamma_{ab.} + e_{abi}$$

so that in the sample the hidden-structure equation is

$$\overline{Y}_{abi} - \overline{Y}_{...} = (\overline{Y}_{a..} - \overline{Y}_{...}) + (\overline{Y}_{.b.} - \overline{Y}_{...}) + (\overline{Y}_{ab.} - \overline{Y}_{a..} - \overline{Y}_{.b.} + \overline{Y}_{...}) + (Y_{abi} - \overline{Y}_{ab.})$$

If we follow the steps described in the appendix to Chapter 36, we get the computing formulas for the sums of squares and degrees of freedom, which are now summarized:

$$\text{I} = \sum_a \sum_b \sum_i Y_{abi}^2$$

$$\text{II} = \frac{Y_{...}^2}{N} = \frac{1}{N}\left(\sum_a \sum_b \sum_i Y_{abi}\right)^2$$

$$\text{III}_A = \frac{1}{Bn} \sum_a Y_{a..}^2 = \frac{1}{Bn} \sum_a \left(\sum_b \sum_i Y_{abi}\right)^2$$

$$\text{III}_B = \frac{1}{An} \sum_b Y_{.b.}^2 = \frac{1}{An} \sum_b \left(\sum_a \sum_i Y_{abi}\right)^2$$

$$\text{III}_{A \times B} = \frac{1}{n} \sum_a \sum_b Y_{ab.}^2 = \frac{1}{n} \sum_a \sum_b \left(\sum_i Y_{abi}\right)^2$$

so that

$$SS_T = \sum_a \sum_b \sum_i (Y_{abi} - \bar{Y}_{...})^2 = I - II$$

$$SS_A = Bn \sum_a (\bar{Y}_{a..} - \bar{Y}_{...})^2 = III_A - II$$

$$SS_B = An \sum_b (\bar{Y}_{.b.} - \bar{Y}...)^2 = III_B - II$$

$$SS_{A \times B} = n \sum_a \sum_b (\bar{Y}_{ab.} - \bar{Y}_{a..} - \bar{Y}_{.b.} + \bar{Y}_{...})^2$$
$$= III_{A \times B} - III_A - III_B + II$$

$$SS_W = \sum_a \sum_b \sum_i (Y_{abi} - \bar{Y}_{ab.})^2 = I - III_{A \times B}$$

The corresponding degrees of freedom are given by

$$ABn - 1 = (A - 1) + (B - 1) + (AB - A - B + 1) + (ABn - AB)$$

or

$$v_T = v_A + v_B + v_{A \times B} + v_W$$

Also, we note that if we had a fully crossed design with one subject per cell, we could not test an interaction, since none of the $\gamma_{ab.}$ could be estimated from the data. The estimation of $\gamma_{ab.}$ would require $\bar{Y}_{ab.}$, but these represent single observations. Thus, a two-way ANOVA with $n = 1$ should be considered only if there are good reasons for believing that all $\gamma_{ab.} = 0$. Performing a two-way ANOVA with $n = 1$, when interactions exist, reduces the power for the main-effect tests. The reduction in power comes about by an inflation of MS_W, which contains both error and interaction components. Thus, a large MS_W in a two-way design with $n = 1$ serves as a warning that the two factors may be interacting.

We now derive formulas for sums of squares and degrees of freedom for the model in which factor A is nested within levels of factor B. Let us begin by defining $\alpha_{a(b).}$ the effect of level a nested in level b. From the hidden-structure equation, we see that

$$\alpha_{a(b).} = (Y_{abi} - \mu_{...}) - \alpha_{a..} - e_{abi}$$
$$= (Y_{abi} - \mu_{...}) - (\mu_{a..} - \mu_{...}) - (Y_{abi} - \mu_{ab.})$$
$$= \mu_{ab.} - \mu_{a..}$$

In the sample,

$$\hat{\alpha}_{a(b).} = \bar{Y}_{ab.} - \bar{Y}_{a..}$$

Thus, $\hat{\alpha}_{a(b).}$ measures the difference between the mean for level a in level b and the total mean for level b. It is referred to as a *nested* main effect or a *simple* main effect.

As with the interaction model, we assume that each $\hat{e}_{abi}$ is selected at random from a normal distribution for which

$$E(\hat{e}_{abi}) = 0 \quad \text{and} \quad \text{Var}\,(\hat{e}_{abi}) = \sigma^2$$

If we examined the individual treatment effects, we would find that they satisfy restrictions which parallel those of the interaction model. In particular, we would see that

$$\sum_b \alpha_{.b.} = 0$$

and for each b

$$\sum_a \alpha_{a(b).} = 0$$

In terms of the hidden-structure equation,

$$Y_{abi} - \mu_{...} = \alpha_{.b.} + \alpha_{a(b).} + e_{abi}$$

so that in the sample

$$\begin{aligned} Y_{abi} - \bar{Y}_{...} &= \hat{\alpha}_{.b.} + \hat{\alpha}_{a(b).} + \hat{e}_{abi} \\ &= (\bar{Y}_{.b.} - \bar{Y}_{...}) + (\bar{Y}_{ab.} - \bar{Y}_{.b.}) + (Y_{abi} - \bar{Y}_{ab.}) \end{aligned}$$

Squaring and adding across all subjects, we would have

$$SS_T = SS_B + SS_{A(B)} + SS_W$$

and

$$I - II = (III_B - II) + (III_{A \times B} - III_B) + (I - III_{A \times B})$$

with degrees of freedom given by

$$ABn - 1 = (B - 1) + (AB - B) + (ABn - AB)$$

so that

$$v_T = v_B + v_{A(B)} + v_E$$

We can examine the hidden-structure equation for the nested model to learn how to calculate the sum of squares due to effect A within a specific level of factor B. This effect is measured by the deviation

$$d_{a(b)} = \bar{Y}_{ab.} - \bar{Y}_{.b.}$$

which is the difference between the mean of a certain A level in a specific B level and the overall mean of that B level. As we have seen, it is a deviation expressing the main effect due to *A within a given level of B*. Thus, we consider each nest to be a one-way ANOVA within the levels of *B*. To calculate the sum of squares due to *A* within each *B* level, we would need Roman numerals III_A and II, but *specific* to each level of *B*. We label these $III_{A(b)}$ and II_b, respectively, where

$$III_{A(b)} = \sum_{a=1}^{A} \frac{Y_{ab.}^2}{n} \qquad \text{and} \qquad II_b = \frac{Y_{.b.}^2}{An}$$

Then we have $SS_{A(b)} = III_{A(b)} - II_b$.

39-6. EXERCISES

39-1. Define the following terms:
  a. Fully crossed design
  b. Nested design
  c. Main effect
  d. Interaction effect
  e. Nested or simple effect
  f. Level
  g. Cell
  h. Family of hypotheses

39-2. Perform a two-way ANOVA on the males of Exercise 33-2, testing for an interaction.

39-3. Examine the males of Exercise 33-2 in terms of a nested design. Which design makes the most sense, users nested in amounts of alcohol or alcohol nested in users? Why? Carry out the most meaningful analysis.

39-4. Repeat Exercise 39-2 on the females.

39-5. Repeat Exercise 39-3 on the females.

39-6. Analyze the data of Exercise 34-3 as a fully crossed design.

39-7. Analyze the data of Exercise 34-3 as a nested design where
  a. Sex is nested in method.
  b. Method is nested in sex.

39-8. Analyze the religion and education example as a fully crossed design with interactions. Compare and contrast the hypotheses involved and the conclusions drawn.

CHAPTER 40

Post Hoc and Planned Comparisons for Two-Factor ANOVA Designs

40-1. COMPARISONS IN TWO-FACTOR DESIGNS

In this chapter we examine the designs of Chapter 39 and show how planned and post hoc comparisons can be examined so as to preserve the type I error rates of the various omnibus tests. We discuss these contrasts in the two-way ANOVA model for crossed designs with interactions, for the nested model, and for the cell means model. For conciseness of presentation and for purposes of comparing the models, we analyze one set of data from more than one of these perspectives. This, of course, is theoretically inappropriate. The research questions determine which of the models to use and whether the analysis will proceed as planned or post hoc. Once the model is selected, the data are analyzed and the results reported.

40-2. POST HOC CONTRASTS FOR TWO-FACTOR INTERACTION DESIGNS WITH n OBSERVATIONS PER CELL

For this exposition, consider the data of Table 39-1, for which the mean values are shown in Table 39-2 and for which the ANOVA table is reported in Table 39-3. Assuming the researcher had no contrasts of interest to compose a planned approach to the analysis, we see that the questions must be addressed by using a post hoc method for testing contrasts. Consistent with our familywise apportionment of the type I error rates, we conduct our post hoc analyses by examining contrasts within each family of hypotheses. The three post hoc Scheffé coefficients are thus given by

Listener (L):

$$S_L = \sqrt{\nu_L F_{\nu_L, \nu_W : 1-\alpha}} = \sqrt{1(4.02)} = 2.00$$

Singer (S):

$$S_S = \sqrt{\nu_S F_{\nu_S, \nu_W : 1-\alpha}} = \sqrt{2(3.17)} = 2.52$$

Listener $\times$ singer ($L \times S$):

$$S_{L \times S} = \sqrt{\nu_{L \times S} F_{\nu_{L \times S}, \nu_W : 1-\alpha}} = \sqrt{2(3.17)} = 2.52$$

For the listener family, since there are only two groups, there is only one possible comparison of male versus female listeners. Thus, the significant F indicates that the two groups differ. In fact, the Scheffé coefficient is equivalent to $t_{\nu_W : 1-\alpha/2}$. At this point, it makes sense to calculate a confidence interval for the difference. The 95 percent confidence interval for the one comparison is given by

$$\psi_1 = \bar{Y}_{1..} - \bar{Y}_{2..} \pm S_L \sqrt{MS_W[(+1)^2/Sn + (-1)^2/Sn]}$$
$$= 71.60 - 80.60 \pm 2.00 \sqrt{32.91 \left(\tfrac{1}{30} + \tfrac{1}{30}\right)}$$
$$= -9.10 \pm 2.96$$

Thus, males give lower ratings than females. With a 95 percent confidence interval, the mean difference can extend from a low of $-9.10 - 2.96 = -12$ to a high of $-9.10 + 2.96 = -6$.

For the singer effect, if the contrasts that make most sense are all possible pairwise contrasts, these should have been examined by using a planned Tukey approach. In this case, another contrast that makes sense, and is interesting, compares the song with a lead singer, male or female, with the song sung by the group without a lead. Let us assume that these four contrasts, listed in Table 40-1, were not planned.

Since the main effect for singer tests a hypothesis about the $\mu_{.s.}$, the contrasts must compare the $\bar{Y}_{.s.}$. For example, to compare male lead to female

Table 40-1. Four contrasts for singer main effect

Contrast	Weights for group			Value of contrast $\hat{\psi}$	$SE_{\hat{\psi}}^2$	$t = \dfrac{\hat{\psi}}{SE_{\hat{\psi}}}$
	S_1	S_2	S_3			
ψ_1	1	-1	0	10.35	3.2913	5.71[a]
ψ_2	1	0	-1	23.70	3.2913	13.06[a]
ψ_3	0	1	-1	13.35	3.2913	7.36[a]
ψ_4	½	½	-1	18.525	2.4685	11.79[a]

[a] Significant at $\alpha = .05$, post hoc critical value is $S_s = 2.52$.

lead, we would have

$$\hat{\psi}_1 = (1)\overline{Y}_{.1.} + (-1)\overline{Y}_{.2.} + (0)\overline{Y}_{.3.}$$

The remaining three contrasts and the appropriate weights are shown in Table 40-1. The squared standard error for $\hat{\psi}_1$ is calculated in the same manner as that for contrasts in one-way ANOVA. In particular,

$$SE_{\hat{\psi}_1}^2 = MS_W \left(\frac{(1)^2}{Ln} + \frac{(-1)^2}{Ln} + \frac{(0)^2}{Ln} \right)$$

These are also reported in Table 40-1. For the complex contrast $\hat{\psi}_4$, these are calculated as

$$\hat{\psi}_4 = \tfrac{1}{2}\overline{Y}_{.1.} + \tfrac{1}{2}\overline{Y}_{.2.} + (-1)\overline{Y}_{.3.}$$
$$= \tfrac{1}{2}(87.50) + \tfrac{1}{2}(77.15) + (-1)(63.80)$$
$$= 18.525$$

and

$$SE_{\hat{\psi}_4}^2 = 32.91 \left(\frac{(\tfrac{1}{2})^2}{20} + \frac{(\tfrac{1}{2})^2}{20} + \frac{(-1)^2}{20} \right)$$
$$= 2.4685$$

We see from the table that all four contrasts are significant. Thus, male singers are different from female singers and from no lead singer, female singers are different from no lead singer, and songs with a lead singer differ from those with no lead singer. Each conclusion specifies a difference but does not state which were preferred. Technically speaking, this is the only conclusion allowed from a two-tailed test. One would have to compute confidence intervals to determine which were preferred. But from our experiences in the past, we know that for a significant contrast, the confidence interval will not cover zero and will fall in the direction of $\hat{\psi}$. On this basis, we conclude, for example, that male singers were preferred to female singers. We draw this type of conclusion throughout the remainder of the book.

There is a tendency among some researchers to view a contrast such as

$$\psi^{(1)} = \mu_{11.} - \mu_{12.}$$

as representing an interaction comparison. Unfortunately, to examine this kind of pairwise contrast as an interaction is an error because it confounds a main effect with the interaction. As pointed out in Section 34-3, an interaction contrast involves at least four cell means. Thus, in this case, an example of an interaction contrast is given by

$$\psi_{(12)(12)} = (\mu_{11} - \mu_{12}) - (\mu_{21} - \mu_{22})$$

a difference of differences.

To examine an inappropriate contrast under the interaction model is to commit a type IV error in the sense described by Marascuilo and Levin (1970). In particular, a type IV error is committed whenever a researcher does the correct omnibus test of a hypothesis but performs a post hoc analysis on contrasts that are not members of the family of contrasts defined by the model. The contrast $\psi^{(1)}$ is not definable under the interaction model. To examine it in the context of this model is to commit a type IV error. We now define this important concept.

Definition of a type IV error

Consider a test of the omnibus hypothesis

$$H_0: \text{all } \psi = 0$$

against the alternate hypothesis

$$H_1: \text{at least one } \psi \neq 0$$

If the omnibus test leads to rejection and if a contrast is examined that is not defined as an element of the set of contrasts defined by H_0, then a type IV error has been committed.

Level of A \ B	1	2	$\cdots$	b	$\cdots$	b'	$\cdots$	B
1	μ_{11}	μ_{12}	$\cdots$	μ_{1b}	$\cdots$	$\mu_{1b'}$	$\cdots$	μ_{1B}
2	μ_{21}	μ_{22}	$\cdots$	μ_{2b}	$\cdots$	$\mu_{2b'}$	$\cdots$	μ_{2B}
.	.	.	.	.	.	.	.	.
.	.	.	.	.	.	.	.	.
.	.	.	.	.	.	.	.	.
a				μ_{ab}	$\cdots$	$\mu_{ab'}$		
.				.		.		
.				.		.		
.				.		.		
a'				$\mu_{a'b}$	$\cdots$	$\mu_{a'b'}$		
.	.	.	.	.	.	.	.	.
.	.	.	.	.	.	.	.	.
.	.	.	.	.	.	.	.	.
A	μ_{A1}	μ_{A2}	$\cdots$	μ_{Ab}	$\cdots$	$\mu_{Ab'}$	$\cdots$	μ_{AB}

Figure 40-1.
Example of a tetrad difference admissible as an interaction contrast.

Later we see some examples of contrasts involving more than four cells. Contrasts involving only four cells are called *tetrad differences* and are denoted

$$\psi_{(ll')(ss')} = \mu_{ls} - \mu_{ls'} - \mu_{l's} + \mu_{l's'}$$

The four cells are not selected at random. The rows and columns must be coordinated in the matter illustrated in Figure 40-1. We now define interaction contrasts that are tetrad differences, and we provide a definition of their standard errors.

Definition of a tetrad difference and associated standard errors

Consider two factors A and B measured on levels a and a' and b and b', respectively. A tetrad interaction contrast is defined as

$$\psi_{(aa')(bb')} = \mu_{ab} - \mu_{a'b} - \mu_{ab'} + \mu_{a'b'}$$

Also $\psi_{(aa')(bb')}$ can be written as

$$\psi_{(aa')(bb')} = (\mu_{ab} - \mu_{a'b}) - (\mu_{ab'} - \mu_{a'b'})$$

or as

$$\psi_{(aa')(bb')} = (\mu_{ab} - \mu_{ab'}) - (\mu_{a'b} - \mu_{a'b'})$$

For n observations in each cell of a two-factor design, the standard error of $\hat{\psi}_{(aa')(bb')}$ is defined as

$$SE_{\hat{\psi}_{(aa')(bb')}} = \sqrt{MS_W \left[\frac{(+1)^2}{n} + \frac{(-1)^2}{n} + \frac{(-1)^2}{n} + \frac{(+1)^2}{n} \right]}$$

$$= \sqrt{\frac{4MS_W}{n}}$$

For the data of Table 39-2 the possible tetrad differences are represented by the three tables shown in Table 40-2. The interaction contrasts for these three 2×2 tables are given by

$$\hat{\psi}_{(12)(12)} = 83.40 - 69.20 - 91.60 + 85.10 = 7.70$$

$$\hat{\psi}_{(12)(13)} = 83.40 - 62.20 - 91.60 + 65.40 = -5.00$$

$$\hat{\psi}_{(12)(23)} = 69.20 - 62.20 - 85.10 + 65.40 = -12.70$$

for which the squared standard errors are given by

$$SE^2_{\hat{\psi}_{(12)(12)}} = SE^2_{\hat{\psi}_{(12)(13)}} = SE^2_{\hat{\psi}_{(12)(23)}}$$

$$= MS_W \left[\frac{(+1)^2}{n} + \frac{(-1)^2}{n} + \frac{(-1)^2}{n} + \frac{(+1)^2}{n} \right]$$

$$= MS_W \left(\frac{4}{n} \right) = 32.91 \left(\frac{4}{10} \right) = 13.164$$

Table 40-2. All possible tetrad tables that can be generated from Table 39-2

Listener	Singer	
	Male	Female
Male	83.40	69.20
Female	91.60	85.10
	Male	None
Male	83.40	62.20
Female	91.60	65.40
	None	Female
Male	62.20	69.20
Female	65.40	85.10

Table 40-3. Four contrasts for interaction effect

Contrast	L_1S_1	L_1S_2	L_1S_3	L_2S_1	L_2S_2	L_2S_3	Value of contrast $\hat{\psi}$	$SE^2_{\hat{\psi}}$	$t = \dfrac{\hat{\psi}}{SE_{\hat{\psi}}}$
ψ_5	1	-1	0	-1	1	0	7.70	13.164	2.12
ψ_6	1	0	-1	-1	0	1	-5.00	13.164	-1.38
ψ_7	0	1	-1	0	-1	1	-12.70	13.164	-3.50[a]
ψ_8	½	½	-1	$-½$	$-½$	1	-8.85	9.873	-2.82[a]

[a] Significant at $\alpha = .05$, post hoc critical value is $S_{L \times S} = 2.52$.

A confidence interval for any tetrad difference is given by

$$\psi = \hat{\psi} \pm \Delta$$

where

$$\Delta = S_{L \times S} SE_{\hat{\psi}}$$

Thus, to determine the significance of any contrast, we can compare any $\hat{\psi}$ to Δ. If $\hat{\psi} < -\Delta$ or $\hat{\psi} > \Delta$, then the confidence interval does not include zero. Therefore, any tetrad contrast that exceeds in magnitude

$$\Delta = S_{L \times S} SE_{\hat{\psi}} = 2.52 \sqrt{13.164} = 9.14$$

represents a significant source of variation. Results are summarized in Table 40-3. The third tetrad contrast is significant, indicating that male and female listeners are in more agreement on songs with no lead singer than they are on songs with female lead singers.

Other interaction contrasts are possible. Visual inspection of the data can guide our choices in a post hoc analysis. The most general definition of an interaction involves a contrast of a contrast. For example, we have examined the main-effect contrast for listener, and we have also tested the complex main-effect contrast for lead singer versus no lead singer. The appropriate interaction that combines these would involve a comparison of the lead singer versus no lead singer in male listeners to the same contrast in females. That is,

$$\hat{\psi}_{L \times \hat{\psi}_4} = (½\bar{Y}_{11.} + ½\bar{Y}_{12.} - \bar{Y}_{13.}) - (½\bar{Y}_{21.} + ½\bar{Y}_{22.} - \bar{Y}_{23.})$$
$$= [½(83.40) + ½(69.20) - 62.20] - [½(91.60) + ½(85.10) - 65.40]$$
$$= 14.10 - 22.95 = -8.85$$

The appropriate squared standard error is

$$SE^2_{\psi_{L \times \hat{\psi}_4}} = 32.91 \left[\frac{(½)^2}{10} + \frac{(½)^2}{10} + \frac{(-1)^2}{10} + \frac{(-½)^2}{10} + \frac{(-½)^2}{10} + \frac{1^2}{10} \right]$$
$$= 9.873$$

Box 40-1   Procedure for testing post hoc contrasts in an interaction model

Step 1. Set up an ANOVA table and test the three omnibus hypotheses.

Step 2. For rejected main-effect hypotheses, define the contrasts of interest. In terms of the notation of Section 39-2, contrasts for the *A* effect are

$$\hat{\psi}_A = \sum_{a=1}^{A} W_{a.}\overline{Y}_{a..}$$

and for the *B* effect are

$$\hat{\psi}_B = \sum_{b=1}^{B} W_{.b}\overline{Y}_{.b.}$$

Step 3. Calculate the corresponding squared standard errors as

$$SE^2_{\hat{\psi}_A} = MS_W \sum_{a=1}^{A} \frac{W^2_{a.}}{Bn}$$

and

$$SE^2_{\hat{\psi}_B} = MS_W \sum_{b=1}^{B} \frac{W^2_{.b}}{An}$$

Step 4. For each contrast, compute $t_{\hat{\psi}_A}$ and $t_{\hat{\psi}_B}$.

Step 5. Determine the decision rules as

Decision Rule, *A*: Reject H_{0A} if $t_{\hat{\psi}_A} < -\sqrt{v_A F_{v_A, v_W : 1-\alpha}}$ or if $t_{\hat{\psi}_A} > +\sqrt{v_A F_{v_A, v_W : 1-\alpha}}$

and

Decision Rule, *B*: Reject H_{0B} if $t_{\hat{\psi}_B} < -\sqrt{v_B F_{v_B, v_W : 1-\alpha}}$ or if $t_{\hat{\psi}_B} > +\sqrt{v_B F_{v_B, v_W : 1-\alpha}}$

Step 6. For a rejected interaction hypothesis, define and calculate tetrad contrasts of interest and their standard errors.

Step 7. For each contrast compute $t_{(aa')(bb')}$.

Step 8. Determine the decision rule as

Decision Rule, *AB*: Reject H_{0AB} if $t_{(aa')(bb')} < -\sqrt{v_{A \times B} F_{v_{A \times B}, v_W : 1-\alpha}}$

or if $t_{(aa')(bb')} > +\sqrt{v_{A \times B} F_{v_{A \times B'}, v_W : 1-\alpha}}$

Step 9. Test any complex interaction contrasts of interest.

and the test statistic is

$$t_{\hat{\psi}} = \frac{\hat{\psi}}{\text{SE}_{\hat{\psi}}} = \frac{-8.85}{\sqrt{9.873}} = -2.82$$

Since $t_{\hat{\psi}} < -2.52$, this interaction is significant, revealing that females are more disparate in their ratings of lead versus no lead singer than are males. Directions are provided for testing post hoc contrasts in Box 40-1.

40-3. PLANNED CONTRASTS FOR TWO-FACTOR INTERACTION DESIGNS WITH n OBSERVATIONS PER CELL

Let us now examine the data of Table 39-1 from a planned analysis point of view, to see how a planned analysis would proceed differently. Since $v_L = 1$, we know that one, and only one, contrast can be defined for listener. This contrast is identical to the post hoc contrast of Section 40-2. Whenever a family of hypotheses are tested with $v = 1$, planned and post hoc comparisons are identical and give the same results as the overall F test.

For a planned analysis on the singer main effect, the contrasts listed in Table 40-1 are the ones likely to have been considered. If we did not plan to examine ψ_4, the Tukey method would be appropriate. In the Tukey analysis, the critical value equals

$$t_{.05:3,54}^{\text{Tukey}} = 2.41$$

We can compare this to the Scheffé coefficient for the post hoc analysis $S = 2.52$ and to the Dunn critical value for $C = 3$, which is 2.48. Thus, if only the three pairwise comparisons are planned, the Tukey procedure is optimum.

However, let us assume that we planned to test the four contrasts listed in Table 40-1. For four planned contrasts the Dunn critical value equals 2.59. Notice that this value exceeds the Scheffé coefficient. As pointed out in many of the exercises, beyond a certain number of planned comparisons, the Dunn critical value exceeds the Scheffé coefficient. In such cases, if the Scheffé coefficient is smaller than the appropriate Dunn value, the analysis is best handled as if the comparisons were tested post hoc.

On the basis of this discussion, let us examine how we would test all four contrasts. The calculation of the $t_{\hat{\psi}}$ are the same, regardless of whether the analysis is planned or post hoc. The only change, in general, is that the test statistics of the planned contrasts would be compared to the smallest appropriate critical value, whereas the test statistics of post hoc contrasts could be compared only to the Scheffé coefficient. Usually, if one desires only to examine all pairwise contrasts, the Tukey critical value is the smallest, as we have seen. If other contrasts are planned, or if fewer than all the pairwise contrasts are desired, then the Dunn critical value is usually smaller than the Scheffé coefficient. If this is so, the test statistics are compared to the Dunn critical value. There are cases, as we see here, where the Scheffé coefficient provides the best test.

For planned interaction contrasts, again the only change required involves the appropriate critical value. The Tukey method is not recommended for examining interactions. The test statistics of the planned interaction contrasts would be compared to the smaller of the Dunn and Scheffé critical values. In most cases, the Dunn value is smaller. For example, suppose one had planned to test only the three tetrad contrasts in Table 40-2, ψ_5, ψ_6, and ψ_7. The Dunn value for $C = 3$ equals

$$t^{\text{Dunn}}_{.05:3,54} = 2.48$$

Thus we see that only ψ_7 is significant. Also apparent is the fact that in planning only ψ_5, ψ_6, and ψ_7 to be tested, an examination of ψ_8 is inadmissible.

40-4. GENERATING INTERACTION CONTRASTS FROM MAIN-EFFECT CONTRASTS

In the analysis of variance examined to this point, we have been able fairly easily to specify contrast weights to use in testing contrasts of interest. This has been particularly true in one-way ANOVA and in testing main-effects contrasts in two-way ANOVA. Sometimes it may be more difficult to generate the contrast weights for interaction contrasts, even when they have been successfully conceptualized as contrasts of contrasts. In this section, we provide a method for generating weights for interaction contrasts from the main-effect contrast weights.

For this demonstration, consider the following two contrasts defined for the data of Table 39-4 viewed as one in which interactions are of interest:

$$\psi_{1.} = 0\mu_{1..} + \tfrac{1}{2}\mu_{2..} - \tfrac{1}{2}\mu_{3..} - \tfrac{1}{2}\mu_{4..} + \tfrac{1}{2}\mu_{5..}$$

and

$$\psi_{.1} = -\tfrac{1}{2}\mu_{.1.} - \tfrac{1}{2}\mu_{.2.} + \tfrac{1}{2}\mu_{.3.} + \tfrac{1}{2}\mu_{.4.}$$

The weights that define the contrast of $\psi_{11.} = \psi_{1.} \times \psi_{.1}$ are generated from the weights of these contrasts. Since an interaction can be viewed as a contrast of two different contrasts, we would have to apply the weights of $\psi_{1.}$ to the weights of $\psi_{.1}$. If we view an interaction of two variables as a multiplication of effects, we could find the coefficients for $\psi_{11.}$ by multiplying the weights of $\psi_{1.}$

by the weights of $\psi_{.1}$. In this case we would have the following table:

		Educational level			
		E_1	E_2	E_3	E_4
Religion	$\psi_{1.} \times \psi_{.1}$	$-\tfrac{1}{2}$	$-\tfrac{1}{2}$	$\tfrac{1}{2}$	$\tfrac{1}{2}$
R_1	0	0	0	0	0
R_2	$\tfrac{1}{2}$	$-\tfrac{1}{4}$	$-\tfrac{1}{4}$	$\tfrac{1}{4}$	$\tfrac{1}{4}$
R_3	$-\tfrac{1}{2}$	$\tfrac{1}{4}$	$\tfrac{1}{4}$	$-\tfrac{1}{4}$	$-\tfrac{1}{4}$
R_4	$-\tfrac{1}{2}$	$\tfrac{1}{4}$	$\tfrac{1}{4}$	$-\tfrac{1}{4}$	$-\tfrac{1}{4}$
R_5	$\tfrac{1}{2}$	$-\tfrac{1}{4}$	$-\tfrac{1}{4}$	$\tfrac{1}{4}$	$\tfrac{1}{4}$

This complex contrast reduces to

$$\psi_{11} = \tfrac{1}{4}[(\mu_{23} + \mu_{24} + \mu_{53} + \mu_{54}) - (\mu_{21} + \mu_{22} + \mu_{51} + \mu_{52})]$$
$$- \tfrac{1}{4}[(\mu_{33} + \mu_{34} + \mu_{43} + \mu_{44}) - (\mu_{31} + \mu_{32} + \mu_{41} + \mu_{42})]$$

At this point ψ_{11} reduces to a tetrad difference contrast involving four means. For the mean values reported in Table 40-4,

$$\overline{Y}_{cons/hi} = \tfrac{1}{4}(\overline{Y}_{23} + \overline{Y}_{24} + \overline{Y}_{53} + \overline{Y}_{54})$$
$$= \tfrac{1}{4}(10.00 + 13.25 + 10.25 + 11.75)$$
$$= 11.3125$$

$$\overline{Y}_{cons/lo} = \tfrac{1}{4}(\overline{Y}_{21} + \overline{Y}_{22} + \overline{Y}_{51} + \overline{Y}_{52})$$
$$= \tfrac{1}{4}(14.25 + 12.00 + 11.75 + 12.50)$$
$$= 12.6250$$

$$\overline{Y}_{lib/hi} = \tfrac{1}{4}(\overline{Y}_{33} + \overline{Y}_{34} + \overline{Y}_{43} + \overline{Y}_{44})$$
$$= \tfrac{1}{4}(3.25 + 2.00 + 3.25 + 2.75)$$
$$= 2.8125$$

$$\overline{Y}_{lib/lo} = \tfrac{1}{4}(\overline{Y}_{31} + \overline{Y}_{32} + \overline{Y}_{41} + \overline{Y}_{42})$$
$$= \tfrac{1}{4}(11.50 + 11.50 + 10.75 + 9.50)$$
$$= 10.8125$$

In terms of these mean values,

$$\hat{\psi}_{1.\times.1} = (11.3125 - 12.6250) - (2.8125 - 10.8125)$$
$$= 6.6875$$

These four means are reported in Table 40-5. We see, then, that ψ_{11} can be interpreted as a tetrad difference involving the conservative (cons) and liberal (lib) religions and low (lo) and high (hi) levels of education.

Table 40-4. Table of mean values for the data of Table 39-4

		Education			
Religion	1	2	3	4	Total
1	5.50	3.25	2.00	0.50	2.8125
2	14.25	12.00	10.00	13.25	12.3750
3	11.50	11.50	3.25	2.00	7.0625
4	10.75	9.50	3.25	2.75	6.5625
5	11.75	12.50	10.25	11.75	11.5625
Total	10.75	9.75	5.75	6.05	8.0750

The squared standard error for this contrast is given by

$$SE^2_{\hat{\psi}_{11}} = MS_W \sum_{r=1}^{R} \sum_{e=1}^{E} \frac{W^2_{re}}{n}$$
$$= 5.62[16(\tfrac{1}{4})^2] = 5.62$$

Thus, the test statistic for testing $H_0: \psi_{11} = 0$ is given by

$$t_{\hat{\psi}_{11}} = \frac{\hat{\psi}_{11}}{SE_{\hat{\psi}_{11}}} = \frac{6.6875}{\sqrt{5.62}} = 2.82$$

Other interaction contrasts, standard errors, and test statistics can be calculated in a similar fashion. For a post hoc analysis

$$S_. = \sqrt{\nu_{E \times R} F_{\nu_{E \times R}, \nu_W : 1-\alpha}} = \sqrt{12 F_{12,60:.95}} = \sqrt{12(1.92)} = 4.80$$

and so the contrast is not different from zero.

Table 40-5. Interaction of $\psi_{1.}$ and $\psi_{.2}$ represented as a tetrad table

	Education	
Religion	Low	High
Conservative	12.6250	11.3125
Liberal	10.8125	2.8125

Box 40-2   Procedure for calculating contrast coefficients for an interaction of two contrasts defined on the two main effects

Step 1. Define the two main-effects contrasts of interest. Let

$$\hat{\psi}_{A.} = \sum_{a=1}^{A} W_{a.}\bar{Y}_{a.}$$

represent the specified contrast among the A row means, and let

$$\hat{\psi}_{.B} = \sum_{b=1}^{B} W_{.b}\bar{Y}_{.b}$$

represent the specified contrast among the B column means.

Step 2. Set up a table as shown below. Along the top margin write the B column coefficients $W_{.b}$, and along the left-side margin write the A row coefficients $W_{a.}$.

Step 3. Fill in the table by multiplying each $W_{a.}$ by each $W_{.b}$, putting the product in the ath row and bth column position inside the table, as shown.

	$W_{.1}$	$W_{.2}$	$\cdots$	$W_{.b}$	$\cdots$	$W_{.B}$
$W_{1.}$	$W_{1.}W_{.1}$	$W_{1.}W_{.2}$	$\cdots$	$W_{1.}W_{.b}$	$\cdots$	$W_{1.}W_{.B}$
$W_{2.}$	$W_{2.}W_{.1}$	$W_{2.}W_{.2}$	$\cdots$	$W_{2.}W_{.b}$	$\cdots$	$W_{2.}W_{.B}$
$\cdots$						
$W_{a.}$	$W_{a.}W_{.1}$	$W_{a.}W_{.2}$	$\cdots$	$W_{a.}W_{.b}$	$\cdots$	$W_{a.}W_{.B}$
$\cdots$						
$W_{A.}$	$W_{A.}W_{.1}$	$W_{A.}W_{.2}$	$\cdots$	$W_{A.}W_{.b}$	$\cdots$	$W_{A.}W_{.B}$

Step 4. Denote the desired interaction contrast as

$$\hat{\psi}_{A.\times.B} = \sum_{a=1}^{A}\sum_{b=1}^{B} W_{ab}\bar{Y}_{ab}$$

The coefficients W_{ab} can be found in the ath row and bth column inside the table. That is,

$$W_{ab} = W_{a.}W_{.b}$$

Step 5. Compute the squared standard error:

$$\text{SE}^2_{\hat{\psi}_{A.\times.B}} = \frac{\text{MS}_W}{n}\sum_{a=1}^{A}\sum_{b=1}^{B} W_{ab}^2$$

We provide directions in Box 40-2 for calculating the contrast coefficients for examining the interaction of two contrasts defined on two main effects. If we assume, for example, that the researchers had planned to examine four orthogonal main-effect contrasts among religions and three orthogonal main-effect contrasts among education levels, then they could have generated 12 orthogonal interaction contrasts with the present method. For a planned orthogonal analysis with 12 contrasts, the critical value is given by

$$t_{.05:12,60}^{\text{Dunn}} = 2.98$$

Even here, ψ_{11} is not significant.

40-5. POST HOC AND PLANNED CONTRASTS FOR THE NESTED MODEL

For this discussion, consider the nested analysis summarized in Table 39-5. By now, we hope that the differences between planned and post hoc analyses have become understood. We briefly summarize these differences in the nested analysis. We recall that the four nested hypotheses are tested with

$$\alpha = \tfrac{1}{4}(.10) = .025$$

With this risk of a type I error, each nested hypothesis should be tested with the decision rule

Decision Rule: Reject H_0 if $F > F_{4,60:.975} = 3.01$

Thus, all four hypotheses are rejected. Post hoc analysis can be performed by examining contrasts in *each* level of E, with

$$S = \sqrt{4F_{4,60:.975}} = \sqrt{4(3.01)} = 3.47$$

Planned analyses are carried out within each level of E by using the smallest appropriate critical value. If all 10 pairwise comparisons are desired, the Tukey value for $\alpha = .025$ can be obtained by interpolation to equal

$$t_{.025:5,60}^{\text{Tukey}} = 3.18$$

If other or different contrasts were planned, we would use the Dunn critical value. Let us assume that we planned to examine four orthogonal contrasts, as mentioned in the previous section. To find this value from the Dunn table, we realize that dividing $\alpha_{R(E)} = .025$ into four contrasts yields the same alpha per contrast as dividing .05 into eight contrasts. Since the Dunn table divides

$\alpha = .05$ into C contrasts, we find the necessary Dunn critical value for each set of nested contrasts to equal

$$t^{\text{Dunn}}_{.025:4,60} = t^{\text{Dunn}}_{.05:8,60} = 2.84$$

This is smaller than the Tukey and Scheffé critical values.

40-6. CONTRASTS FOR TWO-FACTOR CELL MEANS MODEL WITH n OBSERVATIONS PER CELL

From a post hoc point of view, we can examine any contrast in the cell means example summarized in Table 40-4 with

$$S = \sqrt{19(1.45)} = \sqrt{27.55} = 5.25$$

Let us examine the cost in using this model. Confidence intervals and tests will have much lower power.

In the interaction analysis, post hoc comparisons for the three sources of variation are based on the following Scheffé coefficients:

Religion: $S_R = \sqrt{4F_{4,60:.95}} = 3.19$

Education: $S_E = \sqrt{3F_{3,60:.95}} = 2.89$

$R \times E$: $S_{R \times E} = \sqrt{12F_{12,60:.95}} = 4.82$

so that the power of the interaction model, relative to the cell means model, would clearly be greater because of the smaller Scheffé coefficients.

In the nested analysis of Table 39-5, post hoc comparisons for the two sources of variation are based on the following Scheffé coefficients, found previously:

Education: $S_E = 2.89$

Religion in education: $S_{R(E)} = 3.48$

so that the power of the nested model, relative to the cell means model for each family of hypotheses, is again greater. Unless a researcher can obtain a large sample for a study to increase the degrees of freedom for the within source of variation to provide a smaller critical value for F, the thoughts of investigating both interaction and nested hypotheses on a post hoc basis should be eliminated immediately from consideration. To examine both types of contrasts requires large financial investment, so that with small samples only one type can be examined efficiently. Careful thought should be given to which model is the most appropriate from either a theoretical or a practical point of view.

40-7. EXERCISES

40-1. Repeat Exercises 39-7a and 39-7b in terms of a planned orthogonal study, using the methods of this chapter.

40-2. Analyze the data of Exercise 34-3 as a cell means model for:
a. Planned analysis
b. Post hoc analysis

CHAPTER 41

Higher-Order Factorial Designs

41-1. MULTIPLE-FACTOR DESIGNS

Studies with multiple independent variables are quite common in social science research. Previous chapters have presented the techniques used for studies involving one or two independent variables. Not surprisingly, these same techniques are applicable to the study of three, four, five, or more factors. The arithmetic becomes more complicated, even though the logic remains the same. Thus, in higher-order factorial designs, a researcher, guided by the research questions, must still choose an interaction, nested, or cell means model. Once this decision has been made, the researcher still must decide between planned and post hoc comparisons, choosing among

1. Tukey's method for all possible pairwise comparisons
2. Dunn's method for planned contrasts
3. Scheffé's method for data-suggested post hoc comparisons
4. Orthogonal contrasts
5. Trend analysis via orthogonal polynomial components
6. A test for monotonic relationship in mean values
7. Interaction contrasts, testing a difference of differences
8. Contrasts defined through nested comparisons

The questions that arise for one- and two-factor designs reappear for three, four, five, or more factors. Nothing new needs to be learned to analyze these designs successfully.

41-2. EXAMPLE OF A TWO-FACTOR DESIGN

Consider the following two-factor design, which we generalize in Sections 41-3 and 41-4 to three and four factors. The design is diagrammed in Figure 41-1. It is the same design examined in Chapters 39 and 40. Here E is represented by

E_1: less than an eighth-grade education
E_2: some high school
E_3: high school graduate
E_4: some college

and R is represented by

R_1: none
R_2: Catholic
R_3: Jewish
R_4: Protestant (liberal)
R_5: Protestant (conservative)

	Religion
Education	$R_1\ R_2\ R_3\ R_4\ R_5$
E_1	
E_2	
E_3	
E_4	

Figure 41-1.
An example of a fully-crossed two-factor design with religion at five levels and education at four levels with $N = 10$ subjects per crossed levels of R and E.

Assume that $n = 10$ subjects are observed in each cell of the $E \times R = 4 \times 5 = 20$-cell layout and that the dependent variable is a measure of attitude toward public funding of private schools.

Three possible ANOVA models for this design are presented in Table 41-1. Let us examine each of these models and see how they can be analyzed.

Table 41-1.   Three possible models for design of Figure 41-1

	Degrees of freedom	
Source	In general	For the example

Model 1: Interaction for education and religion

Education	$E - 1$	3
Religion	$R - 1$	4
$E \times R$	$(E - 1)(R - 1)$	12
Within	$ER(n - 1)$	180
Total	$ERn - 1$	199

Model 2: Education nested in religion

Religion	$R - 1$	4	
Education in Religion	$R(E - 1)$	15	
E in R_1	$E - 1$		3
E in R_2	$E - 1$		3
E in R_3	$E - 1$		3
E in R_4	$E - 1$		3
E in R_5	$E - 1$		3
Within	$ER(n - 1)$	180	
Total	$ERn - 1$	199	

Model 3: Religion nested in education

Education	$E - 1$	3	
Religion in Education	$E(R - 1)$	16	
R in E_1	$R - 1$		4
R in E_2	$R - 1$		4
R in E_3	$R - 1$		4
R in E_4	$R - 1$		4
Within	$ER(n - 1)$	180	
Total	$ERn - 1$	199	

The first design pays particular attention to the $E \times R$ interaction; the second design emphasizes education by nesting in religion; and the third focuses on religion by nesting in education.

For model 1, differences among the four educational groups can be examined by

1. Tukey's method of all pairwise comparisons
2. Scheffé's method for post hoc comparisons
3. A test of monotonicity for increasing levels of education
4. Three planned orthogonal contrasts

$$\psi_{1E} = (\mu_{1.} + \mu_{2.}) - (\mu_{3.} + \mu_{4.})$$

$$\psi_{2E} = (\mu_{1.} - \mu_{2.})$$

$$\psi_{3E} = (\mu_{3.} - \mu_{4.})$$

where ψ_{1E} compares low levels of education to high levels; ψ_{2E} compares the two low levels of education, and ψ_{3E} compares the two high levels of education.

Differences among the five religion groups can be examined by

1. Tukey's method of all pairwise comparisons
2. Scheffé's method for post hoc comparisons
3. Four planned orthogonal comparisons

$$\psi_{1R} = \tfrac{1}{2}(\mu_{.2} + \mu_{.5}) - \tfrac{1}{2}(\mu_{.3} + \mu_{.4})$$

$$\psi_{2R} = \mu_{.2} - \mu_{.5}$$

$$\psi_{3R} = \mu_{.3} - \mu_{.4}$$

$$\psi_{4R} = \tfrac{1}{4}(\mu_{.2} + \mu_{.3} + \mu_{.4} + \mu_{.5}) - \mu_{.1}$$

where ψ_{1R} measures the difference between the conservative and the liberal religions, ψ_{2R} compares the two conservative religions, ψ_{3R} compares the two liberal religions, and ψ_{4R} compares religious group against no religion.

The interaction of $E \times R$ can be investigated (1) in terms of tetrad differences in either a planned or a post hoc mode and (2) by examining contrasts of contrasts through the 12 interaction contrasts defined by $\psi_{1E} \times \psi_{1R}$, $\psi_{1E} \times \psi_{2R}$, . . . , and $\psi_{3E} \times \psi_{4R}$.

In model 2, the effects of increased levels of education upon *each* religion can be examined in detail. For example, increasing levels of education may have little impact on attitudes toward public funding of private education for Catholic subjects, but the relationship could be dramatically different for one of the liberal religions. This could not be learned if model 1 or model 3 were adopted. Each level of education could be examined in terms of ψ_{1E}, ψ_{2E}, and ψ_{3E} nested within each level of religion.

Differences in levels of religion for model 2 would be best examined through the four contrasts ψ_{1R}, ψ_{2R}, ψ_{3R}, and ψ_{4R} of model 1.

Model 3 has been examined in Chapters 39 and 40. Tests across levels of education would proceed as for model 1. Religious differences could be investigated in each level of education by examining the four contrasts of model 1. We have discussed this model in detail.

As indicated, there are many ways to analyze these data. Perhaps the more interesting of the two models we have not analyzed is model 2, since it allows us to study the impact of increasing levels of education on attitudes for five very dissimilar religious groups.

41-3. THREE-FACTOR DESIGN

Suppose the design of Figure 41-1 is replicated on males and females, so as to generate the study shown in Figure 41-2. If we exclude model 3 of Section 41-2 because it is conceptually the same as model 2, some possible extensions for these three factors are shown in Table 41-2. Many more can be generated, but by examining the most meaningful designs we should be able to construct useful designs for other situations.

Model 4 is the most commonly seen design for fully crossed factorial studies involving three factors. It appears more frequently than any other design, perhaps because researchers often fail to ask the right questions of their data and because most computer programs are set up to analyze three-factor designs in this way, unless programmed to do otherwise.

Designs are not chosen in a vacuum, but are decided upon by a researcher in terms of the questions that need to be answered. We analyzed the two-factor design of Figure 41-1 and of Chapters 39 and 40 as a nested design because it provided answers pertinent to the goals of the political action group. We have to provide different contexts to justify the adoption of different designs.

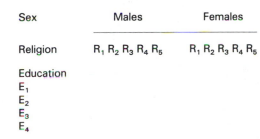

Figure 41-2.
The design of Figure 41-1 augmented by two levels of sex.

Table 41-2. Four possible models for design of Figure 41-2

| | Degrees of freedom | |
Source	In general	For the example
Model 4: All possible interactions		
Sex	$S - 1$	1
Education	$E - 1$	3
Religion	$R - 1$	4
$S \times E$	$(S - 1)(E - 1)$	3
$S \times R$	$(S - 1)(R - 1)$	4
$E \times R$	$(E - 1)(R - 1)$	12
$S \times E \times R$	$(S - 1)(E - 1)(R - 1)$	12
Within	$SER(n - 1)$	360
Total	$SERn - 1$	399
Model 5: Education × religion nested in sex		
Sex	$S - 1$	1
In Males	$ER - 1$	19
Education	$E - 1$	3
Religion	$R - 1$	4
$E \times R$	$(E - 1)(R - 1)$	12
In Females	$ER - 1$	19
Education	$E - 1$	3
Religion	$R - 1$	4
$E \times R$	$(E - 1)(R - 1)$	12
Within	$SER(n - 1)$	360
Total	$SERn - 1$	399
Model 6: Education nested in religion nested in sex		
Sex	$S - 1$	1
In Males	$ER - 1$	19
Religion	$R - 1$	4
Education in Religion	$R(E - 1)$	15
E in R_1	$E - 1$	3
E in R_2	$E - 1$	3
E in R_3	$E - 1$	3

Table 41-2 (*Continued*).

Source	Degrees of freedom	
	In general	*For the example*

Model 6: Education nested in religion nested in sex

Source	In general	For the example
E in R_4	$E - 1$	3
E in R_5	$E - 1$	3
In Females	$ER - 1$	19
Religion	$R - 1$	4
Education in Religion	$R(E - 1)$	15
E in R_1	$E - 1$	3
E in R_2	$E - 1$	3
E in R_3	$E - 1$	3
E in R_4	$E - 1$	3
E in R_5	$E - 1$	3
Within	$SER(n - 1)$	360
Total	$SERn - 1$	399

Model 7: Education × sex nested in religion

Source	In general	For the example	
Religion	$R - 1$	4	
In Religion 1	$ES - 1$	7	
Sex	$S - 1$		1
Education	$E - 1$		3
$S \times E$	$(S - 1)(E - 1)$		3
In Religion 2	$ES - 1$	7	
Sex	$S - 1$		1
Education	$E - 1$		3
$S \times E$	$(S - 1)(E - 1)$		3
In Religion 3	$ES - 1$	7	
Sex	$S - 1$		1
Education	$E - 1$		3
$S \times E$	$(S - 1)(E - 1)$		3
In Religion 4	$ES - 1$	7	
Sex	$S - 1$		1
Education	$E - 1$		3
$S \times E$	$(S - 1)(E - 1)$		3
In Religion 5	$ES - 1$	7	
Sex	$S - 1$		1
Education	$E - 1$		3
$S \times E$	$(S - 1)(E - 1)$		3
Within	$SER(n - 1)$	360	
Total	$SERn - 1$	399	

Let us assume that this three-factor study was adopted by a political scientist. Research questions of interest might include

1.   Do views toward public aid to private education vary according to sex, education, or religion?
2.   Does the difference between males and females change with education or religion?
3.   Do the differences between religions vary according to education?
4.   Do education and religion, jointly, have an effect on the differences between males and females?

If answers to these questions are desired, then model 4 is preferred. Question 1 is answered by means of the main-effect tests and associated contrasts. Questions 2 and 3 are answered by examining the $S \times E$, $S \times R$, and the $E \times R$ interactions. Finally, question 4 is examined in the three-factor interaction $S \times E \times R$. However, this design may be wasteful of information in that answers to questions 3 and 4 may be of little interest. One reason why question 4 might be of little interest is that three-factor and higher-order interactions are extremely difficult to interpret. We can illustrate this for a particular three-factor interaction contrast, sex $\times \psi_{11}$ from Chapter 40. As we recall, ψ_{11} contrasted the difference between low and high levels of education for subjects with a conservative religion with the same difference among people with a liberal religion. The three-factor interaction involving sex asks whether this complex interaction contrast is the same or different for males and females. It is a contrast in interaction contrasts, and it is very difficult to determine the practical or theoretical meaning of the interaction.

In addition, one or more of the two-factor interactions may be difficult to interpret. In this study, if the gender differences are of primary interest, $S \times E$ and $S \times R$ are interpretable. The $E \times R$ interaction, which does not involve sex, may not be interpretable unless clearly defined main effects of education and religion are involved in an interaction contrast using the methods of Section 40-4. Thus, model 4 provides answers to many questions of minimal interest.

The distinguishing feature of model 5 is that it treats the sexes as two distinct populations by nesting in sex. It focuses on questions relating to education, religion, and their interaction for each sex separately. Model 6 is similar, in that we again nest in sex, but education is, in addition, nested in religion for each sex. For both models 5 and 6, the major questions involve education and religion, and the sexes are compared globally and only once.

Assume a researcher would like answers to the following questions:

1.   Does a gender difference exist in a particular religion?
2.   Does education change opinions in a particular religion?
3.   Does education affect the gender gap in a particular religion?

If answers to these questions are of interest, then model 7 is preferred. Question 1 is answered via the simple effect of sex in each religion. Question

2 is answered by the simple effect of education nested in each religion. Finally, question 3 is answered by the $S \times E$ interaction in each religion.

This design is actually a series of five two-factor $S \times E$ analyses. The advantage to analyzing them as a three-factor nested design is that the error degrees of freedom are increased in the latter by combining the separate error terms. The assumptions for these designs are the usual ones of independence of observations, normality, and equal error variances. Occasionally, the error variances may differ from nest to nest. If so, combining the error terms is inappropriate, and one should perform a set of separate two-factor ANOVAs.

41-4. DISTRIBUTION OF THE RISK OF TYPE I ERRORS FOR NESTED DESIGNS

In a three-factor design with the inclusion of each of the two-factor interactions and the one three-factor interaction, the total risk of a type I error is

$$\alpha_T \leq \alpha_A + \alpha_B + \alpha_C + \alpha_{AB} + \alpha_{AC} + \alpha_{BC} + \alpha_{ABC}$$

If each source of variation is tested at .05, then $\alpha_T \leq .35$. If a model is used where some factors are nested in others, then we maintain an overall $\alpha_T \leq .35$ by apportioning the risk of a type I error appropriately. For example, consider model 7.

We begin by assigning $\alpha_R = .05$ to religion. The remaining $\alpha = .30$ is divided equally among the five religions, so that each nest receives $\alpha_{SE(R)} = 0.06$. Within each nest, the three sources of variation—$S(R)$, $E(R)$, and $S \times E(R)$—divide $\alpha_{SE(R)} = .06$ equally, giving $\alpha_{S(R)} = .02$, $\alpha_{E(R)} = .02$, and $\alpha_{S \times E(R)} = .02$.

41-5. FOUR-FACTOR DESIGN

The principles used to construct fourth- or higher-order designs are similar to those used for three factors. We do not provide directions for the many designs possible in such situations. Instead, we show in Table 41-3 the most commonly encountered design, model 8, and an extension of model 7 to model 9. Model 8 is a weak design since it focuses on the three- and four-factor interactions. Very rarely are they interpretable. The design is represented in Figure 41-3. It is the extension of the design represented in Figure 41-2, across three cities.

Table 41-3.   Two possible models for a four-factor fully crossed design

Source	Degrees of freedom	
	In general	For the example

Model 8: All possible interactions

Source	In general	For the example
Cities	$C-1$	2
Sex	$S-1$	1
Education	$E-1$	3
Religion	$R-1$	4
$C \times S$	$(C-1)(S-1)$	2
$C \times E$	$(C-1)(E-1)$	6
$C \times R$	$(C-1)(R-1)$	8
$S \times E$	$(S-1)(E-1)$	3
$S \times R$	$(S-1)(R-1)$	4
$E \times R$	$(E-1)(R-1)$	12
$C \times S \times E$	$(C-1)(S-1)(E-1)$	6
$C \times S \times R$	$(C-1)(S-1)(R-1)$	8
$C \times E \times R$	$(C-1)(E-1)(R-1)$	24
$S \times E \times R$	$(S-1)(E-1)(R-1)$	12
$C \times S \times E \times R$	$(C-1)(S-1)(E-1)(R-1)$	24
Within	$CSER(n-1)$	1080
Total	$CSERn-1$	1199

Model 9: Education and sex nested in religion and city

Source	In general	For the example			
Cities	$C-1$	2			
In City 1	$SER-1$	39			
Religions	$R-1$		4		
In Religion 1	$ES-1$		7		
Sex	$S-1$			1	
Education	$E-1$			3	
$S \times E$	$(S-1)(E-1)$			3	
In Religion 2	$ES-1$		7		
Sex	$S-1$			1	
Education	$E-1$			3	
$S \times E$	$(S-1)(E-1)$			3	

Table 41-3   *(Continued)*.

Source	Degrees of freedom	
	In general	*For the example*

Model 9: Education and sex nested in religion and city

Source	In general	For the example
In Religion 3	$ES - 1$	7
Sex	$S - 1$	1
Education	$E - 1$	3
$S \times E$	$(S - 1)(E - 1)$	3
In Religion 4	$ES - 1$	7
Sex	$S - 1$	1
Education	$E - 1$	3
$S \times E$	$(S - 1)(E - 1)$	3
In Religion 5	$ES - 1$	7
Sex	$S - 1$	1
Education	$E - 1$	3
$S \times E$	$(S - 1)(E - 1)$	3
In City 2 (see city 1)	$SER - 1$	39
In City 3 (see city 1)	$SER - 1$	39
Within	$CRSE(n - 1)$	1080
Total	$CRSEn - 1$	1199

	San Francisco		Toledo		New York	
	Males $R_1\,R_2\,R_3\,R_4\,R_5$	Females $R_1\,R_2\,R_3\,R_4\,R_5$	Males $R_1\,R_2\,R_3\,R_4\,R_5$	Females $R_1\,R_2\,R_3\,R_4\,R_5$	Males $R_1\,R_2\,R_3\,R_4\,R_5$	Females $R_1\,R_2\,R_3\,R_4\,R_5$
E_1						
E_2						
E_3						
E_4						

Figure 41-3.
The design of Figure 41-2 augmented by three cities.

41-5. EXERCISES

41-1. A researcher was interested in studying how students varying in ability would be affected by different methods of teaching reading to sixth-grade students. She obtained 90 male and 90 female sixth graders. Of each sex 30 were determined as being low in reading ability, and an equal number of each sex were classified as having average and high ability in reading. Within each ability and sex category, 10 subjects were randomly assigned to one of the three reading methods. The final design was as follows with 10 subjects per cell.

Sex	Ability	Method		
		Old	Phonics	Linguistic
Female	Low			
	Average			
	High			
Male	Low			
	Average			
	High			

Set up the ANOVA table for the fully crossed design involving all two-factor and three-factor interactions.

41-2. For Exercise 41-1, assign $\alpha = .05$ to each family, and describe how you would analyze the contrasts for each family.

41-3. Nest two of the factors in the third factor for the design of Exercise 41-1, and redesign the

study by showing the ANOVA table you would use to describe the model.

41-4. Distribute Type I error rates in the model of Exercise 41-3, and describe how you would analyze contrasts.

41-5. What conditions could invalidate the study of Exercise 41-1 with respect to internal and external validity?

41-6. A survey was conducted to investigate attitudes concerning whether gay teachers should be permitted to teach in the elementary and secondary public schools. The attitude inventory consisted of 10 items, each scored on a Likert scale from 1 to 5. A score of 10 represents maximum opposition to the employment of gay teachers, and a score of 50 represents unreserved approval of the employment of gay teachers. Analyze the data on page 561 as a full factorial model. Test each family of hypotheses at $\alpha = .05$.

41-7. Reanalyze the data of Exercise 41-6 in terms of a more meaningful design.

41-8. For the significant sources of variation of Exercise 41-7, perform a post hoc analysis with each family of hypotheses controlled to give an experiment error rate equal to that of Exercise 41-6.

41-9. Perform a planned analysis on the data of Exercise 41-7.

41-10. Write up the results of Exercise 41-6, 41-7, 41-8, or 41-9 for the results section of a scholarly journal.

	Education							
	8 or less years		Some high school		High school graduate		Some college	
Religion	Male	Female	Male	Female	Male	Female	Male	Female
None	28	26	16	16	39	41	38	40
	29	28	16	28	40	42	42	49
	30	30	40	29	41	44	47	49
	35	42	47	49	50	49	50	50
Catholic	20	14	10	13	20	22	10	30
	23	18	17	21	25	26	30	36
	24	19	20	22	25	30	40	37
	28	29	23	29	39	38	47	41
Jewish	18	10	42	40	48	47	40	49
	26	29	47	41	49	47	47	50
	29	41	47	44	50	50	50	50
	40	46	50	49	50	50	50	50
Protestant liberal	11	10	12	12	40	40	47	45
	20	10	15	13	41	41	47	45
	21	12	17	18	45	49	50	47
	22	17	36	22	47	50	50	50
Protestant conservative	10	10	11	10	10	18	15	17
	10	10	11	10	23	18	28	29
	12	10	14	13	26	29	30	29
	13	11	30	20	27	30	33	35

CHAPTER 42

Randomized Block Designs and Repeated Measures

42-1. STATISTICAL CONTROL

The ideal research design using human subjects, if it could be produced, would be one in which all the subjects were identical in all respects except for the differences associated with the independent variable and the natural variation that exists between people even when they are observed under the same condition. Under this model, all variation would be attributed to explained and unexplained components. Although this kind of control is not feasible in most cases, one can, instead, often achieve *statistical control*. We have seen some examples in which statistical control was used to approximate more closely the ideal situation resulting from the use of identical subjects. The method discussed in Section 2-4 was purposely designed to achieve that goal. As we recall, NK subjects are rank-ordered on the basis of a variable believed to be correlated with the dependent measure. Next, the subjects are divided into N groups of K subjects. The first K subjects are assigned to the K conditions by using a table of random numbers. This process is repeated N times to produce a two-factor design in which one of the main factors is treatment and the other represents the N levels on which the subjects are divided. Other examples appeared in applications of the matched-pair Wilcoxon test and the matched-pair t test. In these examples, the subjects could be considered matched with themselves. Designs in which subjects are paired or grouped into subsets on the basis of common characteristics are generally referred to as *randomized block designs*, whereas designs in which the same subjects are observed in a before-after paradigm or across a series of similar experimental trials are called *repeated-measures designs*. The statistical analyses of both designs follow the same arithmetic computations, and so they can be studied under one model. In both cases the hypothesis under test is given by

$$H_0: \mu_{.1} = \mu_{.2} = \cdots = \mu_{.K}$$

or by

$$H_0: \text{all } \psi = \sum_{k=1}^{K} W_k \mu_{.k} = 0 \qquad \text{where} \qquad \sum_{k=1}^{K} W_k = 0$$

In repeated-measures designs, subjects may be observed at time 1, time 2, . . . , time K. Because the times of measurement are often equally spaced, H_0 could be replaced by a set of $K - 1$ orthogonal hypotheses

$$H_{01}: \psi_{\text{lin}} = 0$$

$$H_{02}: \psi_{\text{quad}} = 0$$

and so on. This analysis may be useful if the ordered nature of the time variable is important to the researcher.

42-2. STATISTICAL CONTROL ACHIEVED THROUGH RANDOMIZED BLOCKS

If a researcher knows that the dependent variable of a study can be affected by another variable, the effects of the nuisance variable can be minimized by means of a randomized block design. In the ideal situation, a researcher has a pool of subjects on whom previously recorded measurements are available on a variable believed to have a possible relationship with the dependent variable. The subjects are rank-ordered on the basis of this variable and are assigned to the K treatments (tr), K at a time, on the basis of a table of random numbers. Then the experiment is performed. At the end of the experiment, scores on the dependent variable are found for each subject. The purpose of the blocking procedure is to create K groups of subjects that initially are very much alike, so that the within-block variation is reduced.

The model is described in the appendix to this chapter, where the F statistic is shown to be

$$F = \frac{MS_{tr}}{MS_R}$$

where

$$MS_{tr} = \frac{1}{K-1} \sum_{k=1}^{K} B(\bar{Y}_{.k} - \bar{Y}_{..})^2$$

$$MS_R = \frac{1}{(K-1)(B-1)} \sum_{k=1}^{K} \sum_{b=1}^{B} (Y_{bk} - \bar{Y}_{b.} - \bar{Y}_{.k} + \bar{Y}_{..})^2$$

$K =$ number of treatments

$B =$ number of blocks

The results can be summarized as shown in Table 42-1. Remember that henceforth the subscript R refers to *residual*, not religion. Likewise, subscript T refers to *total*.

Note that the MS between blocks is not computed. In most situations it has no clear interpretation. Blocks are placed in the study to serve as a statistical control. If the dependent variable is indeed correlated with the blocking variable, the sum of squares between blocks will be large. If blocks are not a major source of variations, then SS_B will be small. In addition, the treatment effects are nested within each block. That is the reason for the indentation in Table 42-1 of the between-treatment and residual sources of variability.

Table 42-1. ANOVA table for randomized block design

Source	df	SS	MS	F ratio	$\hat{\eta}^2$
Between blocks	$B - 1$	$III_B - II$			
Within blocks	$B(K - 1)$	$I - III_B$			
Between treatments	$K - 1$	$III_{Tr} - II$	MS_{Tr}	$\dfrac{MS_{Tr}}{MS_R}$	$\dfrac{III_{Tr} - II}{I - II}$
Residual	$(B - 1)(K - 1)$	$I - III_B - III_{Tr} + II$	MS_R		
Total	$BK - 1$	$I - II$			

Finally, for the treatment effect

$$\hat{\eta}^2 = \frac{SS_{tr}}{SS_T}$$

The major reason for using a randomized block design is that one believes that an association exists among the observations in a block which, if taken into account, reduces the residual variance and increases power. For example, we should find a correlation between treatment 1 and treatment 2 scores across blocks. For the randomized block design, in addition to the usual assumptions of independence between blocks, normality of errors, and equal variances, an additional assumption is required to justify the model. It must be assumed that:

$$\rho_{12} = \rho_{13} = \cdots = \rho_{1K} = \rho_{23} = \cdots = \rho_{(K-1)K}$$

or that all pairwise correlations between columns are equal. In many cases, this assumption is difficult to justify. This is especially true in learning studies involving repeated measures, in which each block represents a specific person.

As an example of a *pseudo*randomized block design, consider the data of Table 42-2. These data were obtained by searching test records for six different educational programs and selecting one subject at random from each program to fill 13 blocks, defined in terms of equal-interval verbal test scores on an entering first-year student test. Although the intervals are of equal width, this is not a requirement to justify a randomized block design. The intervals could be of unequal width, and the analysis would proceed in exactly the same manner.

We call this a pseudorandomized block design because the subjects were not rank-ordered on the basis of the verbal test score and then randomly assigned to programs. Instead, the educational program of each student is known, and the records are searched so as to make six groups of students who are identical on their verbal test scores. In general, this kind of matching is a real threat to both external and internal validity, and it permits a confounding from *regression to the mean* to arise in the final outcomes. We suggest that Section 8-4 be reviewed to see how it could affect the outcomes of this study.

The hypothesis can be stated in its most general form as

$$H_0: \text{all } \psi = \sum_{k=1}^{K} W_k \mu_{.k} = 0$$

and this would be tested against

$$H_1: \text{at least one } \psi \neq 0$$

Table 42-2. Randomized block design with blocks defined by equal-width verbal
scores on SAT

Block on verbal score	Educational program					
	Business administration	Engineering	Chemistry	English	History	Math
280	400	435	415	455	450	395
320	410	390	550	445	475	560
360	420	480	440	415	460	380
400	470	410	460	535	510	470
440	415	490	520	530	500	450
480	600	525	480	640	710	520
520	460	500	490	510	480	620
560	600	610	590	500	680	520
600	500	500	565	560	630	570
640	530	600	615	680	640	600
680	540	650	720	765	690	610
720	690	750	680	780	740	715
760	650	710	690	740	690	680

Note: Dependent variable is score on composition test.

For the data of Table 42-2,

$$Y_{1.} = 400 + 435 + 415 + 455 + 450 + 395 = 2550$$

In like manner, $Y_{2.} = 2830$, $Y_{3.} = 2595$, . . . , $Y_{13.} = 4160$. For the education groups,

$$Y_{.1} = 400 + 410 + \cdots + 650 = 6685$$

with $Y_{.2} = 7050$, $Y_{.3} = 7215$, $Y_{.4} = 7555$, $Y_{.5} = 7655$, and $Y_{.6} = 7090$. In addition,

$$Y_{..} = 400 + 410 + \cdots + 680 = 43{,}250$$

In terms of these totals and the original data,

$$I = \sum_{b=1}^{B} \sum_{k=1}^{K} Y_{bk}^2 = 400^2 + 435^2 + \cdots + 680^2 = 24{,}877{,}950$$

$$II = \frac{Y_{..}^2}{N} = \frac{1}{78}(400 + 435 + \cdots + 680)^2 = \frac{(43{,}250)^2}{78} = 23{,}981{,}570$$

$$III_B = \sum_{b=1}^{B} \frac{Y_{b.}^2}{K} = \frac{1}{6}(2550^2 + \cdots + 4160^2) = 24{,}680{,}798$$

$$III_E = \sum_{k=1}^{K} \frac{Y_{.k}^2}{B} = \frac{1}{13}(6685^2 + \cdots + 7090^2) = 24{,}030{,}238$$

$$SS_B = III_B - II = 24{,}680{,}798 - 23{,}981{,}570 = 699{,}228$$

$$SS_W = I - III_B = 24{,}877{,}950 - 24{,}680{,}798 = 197{,}152$$

$$SS_T = I - II = 24{,}877{,}950 - 23{,}981{,}570 = 896{,}380$$

$$SS_E = III_E - II = 24{,}030{,}238 - 23{,}981{,}570 = 48{,}668$$

$$SS_R = I - III_B - III_E + II$$
$$= 24{,}877{,}950 - 24{,}680{,}798 - 24{,}030{,}238 + 23{,}981{,}570 = 148{,}484$$

$$v_E = K - 1 = 6 - 1 = 5$$

$$v_R = (B - 1)(K - 1) = (13 - 1)(6 - 1) = 60$$

Then we have

$$MS_E = \frac{SS_E}{v_E} = \frac{48{,}668}{5} = 9733.4$$

$$MS_R = \frac{148{,}484}{60} = 2474.7$$

so that

$$F = \frac{MS_E}{MS_R} = \frac{9733.4}{2474.7} = 3.93$$

The ANOVA table is presented in Table 42-3.

Suppose that these data were to be analyzed as a planned orthogonal analysis, by examining the contrasts of Table 42-4. Then ψ_1 examines the difference between the professional programs and the liberal arts programs, and ψ_2 contrasts the two professional programs. If we view chemistry and mathematics to represent scientific programs and English and history to represent humanities, then ψ_3 compares scientific programs to humanities, ψ_4

Table 42-3. ANOVA table for data of Table 42-2

Source	df	SS	MS	F ratio	$\hat{\eta}^2$
Between blocks	12	699,228			.780
Within blocks	65	197,152			
Between programs	5	48,668	9733.4	3.93[a]	.054
Residual	60	148,484	2474.7		
Total	77	896,380			

[a] $F_{5,60:.95} = 2.38$.

compares the two sciences, and ψ_5 contrasts the humanities. With $\bar{Y}_{.1} = 514.2308$, $\bar{Y}_{.2} = 542.3077$, $\bar{Y}_{.3} = 555.0000$, $\bar{Y}_{.4} = 581.1539$, $\bar{Y}_{.5} = 588.8462$, and $\bar{Y}_{.6} = 545.3846$, we have

$$\hat{\psi}_1 = \tfrac{1}{2}(514.2308) + \tfrac{1}{2}(542.3077) - \tfrac{1}{4}(555.0000) - \tfrac{1}{4}(581.1539)$$
$$- \tfrac{1}{4}(588.8462) - \tfrac{1}{4}(545.3846)$$
$$= -39.3269$$

with

$$SS_{\hat{\psi}_1} = \frac{13(-39.3269)^2}{(\tfrac{1}{2})^2 + (\tfrac{1}{2})^2 + (-\tfrac{1}{4})^2 + (-\tfrac{1}{4})^2 + (-\tfrac{1}{4})^2 + (-\tfrac{1}{4})^2}$$
$$= 26,807.86$$

Table 42-4. Weights for planned analysis for data of Table 42-2 with $C = 5$ contrasts

Con-trast	Business admin-istration	Engi-neering	Chem-istry	English	His-tory	Math
1	$\tfrac{1}{2}$	$\tfrac{1}{2}$	$-\tfrac{1}{4}$	$-\tfrac{1}{4}$	$-\tfrac{1}{4}$	$-\tfrac{1}{4}$
2	1	-1	0	0	0	0
3	0	0	$\tfrac{1}{2}$	$-\tfrac{1}{2}$	$-\tfrac{1}{2}$	$\tfrac{1}{2}$
4	0	0	1	0	0	-1
5	0	0	0	1	-1	0

In like manner, $\hat{\psi}_2 = -28.0769$, $\hat{\psi}_3 = -34.8078$, $\hat{\psi}_4 = 9.6154$, and $\hat{\psi}_5 = -7.6923$, with $SS_{\hat{\psi}_2} = 5124.03$, $SS_{\hat{\psi}_3} = 15{,}750.53$, $SS_{\hat{\psi}_4} = 600.96$, and $SS_{\hat{\psi}_5} = 384.61$. The results of the analysis are summarized in Table 42-5. With $C = 5$, $\alpha = .05$, and $v_2 = 60$, the decision rule is

Decision Rule: Reject H_0: $\psi_C = 0$ if $F_{\hat{\psi}_C} > t^2_{\text{Dunn}} = 2.66^2 = 7.08$

As we see, ψ_1, the contrast involving the comparison of liberal arts to professional programs, is significant. None of the other contrasts is significant.

The application of blocking to control *extraneous* or *nuisance* variables is quite general in behavioral research. In the example of Table 42-2, an exceedingly deliberate type of blocking was instituted, whereby a quantitative variable was divided into 13 equal-width intervals for which the interval width was set arbitrarily at 40 test score points. With such a deliberate selection, tests for linear, quadratic, and cubic trend could be performed on the blocking variable, since it actually represents 13 equally spaced levels of verbal ability. This does not mean that all blocking variables must represent a partitioning of a quantitative variable into B mutually exclusive, exhaustive, and ordered classes. In most studies, the blocking is done on different dimensions.

It is quite unusual to encounter blocking variables in which only *one* subject is observed at each condition, examined within blocks. The typical situation is to encounter multiple observations per treatment condition. When this happens, however, designs similar to those of Chapter 41 are called upon. With these designs, block $\times$ treatment interactions can be examined, as well as treatment-within-block differences. For completeness, we provide directions

Table 42-5. ANOVA table for data of Table 42-2, with orthogonal contrasts defined in Table 42-3

Source	df	SS	MS	F ratio	$\hat{\eta}^2$
Between blocks	12	699,228			
Within blocks	65	197,152			
Between programs	5	48,668			
ψ_1	1	26,807.9	26,807.9	10.83[a]	.03
ψ_2	1	5,124.0	5,124.0	2.07	
ψ_3	1	15,750.5	15,750.5	6.30	
ψ_4	1	601.0	601.0	0.24	
ψ_5	1	384.6	384.6	0.16	
Residual	60	148,484	2,474.7		
Total	77	896,380			

[a] $F_{1,60;.01} = 7.08$.

Box 42-1   Procedure for a one-factor repeated-measures or randomized block design

Step 1. Compute I, II, III_B, and III_{Tr} as described in this section.

Step 2. With these values determine

$$SS_T = I - II \qquad SS_W = I - III_B$$

$$SS_B = III_B - II \qquad SS_{Tr} = III_{Tr} - II$$

and

$$SS_R = I - III_B - III_{Tr} + II$$

Step 3. Complete the ANOVA table as illustrated in Table 42-1.

Step 4. Reject H_0: all $\psi = \sum_{k=1}^{K} W_k \mu_{.k} = 0$ if $F > F_{K-1,(K-1)(B-1):1-\alpha}$

Step 5. Make post hoc comparisons, using

$$S = \sqrt{(K-1)F_{K-1,(K-1)(B-1):1-\alpha}}$$

and

$$SE_{\psi}^2 = MS_R \sum_{k=1}^{K} \frac{W_k^2}{B}$$

For a planned analysis, replace S by $t_{\alpha:C,\nu}^{\text{Dunn}}$ values read from Table A-11. For pairwise comparisons only, replace F by

$$t^{\text{Tukey}} = \frac{\bar{Y}_{\max} - \bar{Y}_{\min}}{\sqrt{MS_R(2/B)}}$$

and use the corresponding critical value defined by $t_{\alpha:K,\nu_2}^{\text{Tukey}} = q/\sqrt{2}$, where q is read from Table A-13.

---

for a one-factor repeated-measures, or randomized block, design in Box 42-1.

42-3. REPEATED-MEASURES DESIGN FOR TWO FULLY CROSSED FACTORS

As an example of a two-factor repeated-measures design, consider the data of Table 42-6. Twelve subjects were divided at random into three groups of four subjects each. A complicated stylus maze was constructed on a large

Table 42-6. Number of errors made by three groups of subjects on five trials of a repeated-measures investigation

| | Subject | \multicolumn{5}{c}{Trial} |
		1	2	3	4	5
Intelligence group	11	40	39	33	33	20
	12	40	33	31	23	22
	13	38	34	30	28	26
	14	31	29	26	21	20
Average 20 group	21	28	28	24	21	20
	22	39	25	23	23	17
	23	32	32	28	31	26
	24	34	27	26	25	23
Few-errors group	31	40	40	30	30	29
	32	35	31	25	22	22
	33	39	38	36	36	23
	34	36	24	21	23	21

board. On the face of the board were small brass disks arranged in columns and rows, with a small space separating each disk. The back of the board was wired so that an electric circuit would operate if particular disks were touched with the stylus. The subjects were instructed to take the stylus and to start at the upper left corner of the board, moving it from disk to disk, one at a time, to the lower right corner. Only one path could be taken without operating the circuit. One group of subjects was told that ability to learn the maze was closely related to intelligence. Another group was told that the average college student made only 20 errors by the fifth trial. The third group was told that they were simply to make as few errors as possible. Each group of subjects was given five trials. The number of errors are shown in Table 42-6. In this study, if the interactions are of interest, there are three families of hypotheses to test. Let G represent group; T, trial (*not*, as earlier, *total*); and S, subject number. Then we have

$$H_{01}: \text{all } \psi_G = \sum_{g=1}^{3} W_{g.} \mu_{g.} = 0$$

$$H_{02}: \text{all } \psi_T = \sum_{t=1}^{5} W_{.t} \mu_{.t} = 0$$

$$H_{03}: \text{all } \psi_{G \times T} = \sum_{g=1}^{3} \sum_{t=1}^{5} W_{gt} \mu_{gt} = 0$$

We begin with a one-way ANOVA, treating subjects as blocks and as a source of variability. Under this approach the total deviation is decomposed into a between subject deviation and an unexplained deviation

$$Y_{gts} - \overline{Y}_{...} = (\overline{Y}_{g.s} - \overline{Y}_{...}) + (Y_{gts} - \overline{Y}_{g.s})$$

with degrees of freedom given by

$$GTS - 1 = (GS - 1) + (GTS - GS)$$

and the sum of squares defined by

$$I - II = (III_{GS} - II) + (I - III_{GS})$$

The deviation $\overline{Y}_{g.s} - \overline{Y}_{...}$ is actually the deviation due to subjects or blocks, but we need the two subscripts to distinguish a particular subject (subj) in a given group (grp). For this reason the deviation is said to be due to *subjects in groups*.

For the data of Table 42-6, $Y_{1.1} = 40 + 39 + 33 + 33 + 20 = 165$, with $Y_{1.2} = 149$, $Y_{1.3} = 156$, and $Y_{1.4} = 127$. From these totals, $Y_{1..} = 165 + 149 + 156 + 127 = 597$. In like manner, $Y_{2.1} = 121, Y_{2.2} = 127, Y_{2.3} = 149$, and $Y_{2.4} = 135$, with $Y_{2..} = 532$. Finally, $Y_{3.1} = 169$, $Y_{3.2} = 135$, $Y_{3.3} = 172$, and $Y_{3.4} = 125$, with $Y_{3..} = 601$. With these data

$$I = 40^2 + 39^2 + \cdots + 21^2 = 52,292$$

$$II = \frac{(40 + 39 + \cdots + 21)^2}{3(5)(4)} = \frac{1730^2}{60} = 49,881.6667$$

$$III_{GS} = \frac{165^2 + 149^2 + \cdots + 125^2}{5} = 50,616.4000$$

$$SS_{tot} = I - II = 52,292 - 49,881.6667 = 2410.3333$$

$$\begin{aligned} SS_{subj\,in\,grp} &= III_{GS} - II \\ &= 50,616.4000 - 49,881.6667 = 734.7333 \end{aligned}$$

$$SS_{within\,subj} = I - III_{GS} = 52,292 - 50,616.4000 = 1675.6000$$

so that

$$MS_{GS} = \frac{III_{GS} - II}{GS - 1} = \frac{734.7333}{3(4) - 1} = 66.79$$

$$MS_W = \frac{I - III_{GS}}{GTS - GS} = \frac{1675.6000}{3(5)(4) - 3(4)} = 34.91$$

$$F = \frac{MS_{GS}}{MS_W} = \frac{66.79}{34.91} = 1.91$$

Even though $F = 1.91$ is not in the critical region defined by $F_{11,48:.95} = 2.00$, the amount of variation explained by subject differences is

$$\hat{\eta}_s^2 = \frac{734.7333}{2410.3333} = .30$$

which is a large proportion of the total variability. These values are reported in Table 42-7, except for the F ratio and $\hat{\eta}^2$. Generally, these are not reported in the ANOVA table, since the subjects who enter the study may not represent a random sample of subjects from the universe of all possible subjects. If, however, they do represent a true random sample, this corresponding F ratio can be reported, if desired.

As a second step, we decompose the between subject deviation. This gives rise to a difference between the groups and a residual based on the differences between the subjects. In this case,

$$d_{GS} = d_G + d_{S(G)}$$
$$(\overline{Y}_{g.s} - \overline{Y}_{...}) = (\overline{Y}_{g..} - \overline{Y}_{...}) + (\overline{Y}_{g.s} - \overline{Y}_{g..})$$
$$(III_{GS} - II) = (III_G - II) + (III_{GS} - III_G)$$

with degrees of freedom

$$(GS - 1) = (G - 1) + (GS - G)$$

The deviation $d_{S(G)}$ is the residual deviation due to the within-group variability of the subjects. It is analogous to the within-group deviation in standard ANOVA, but it is based on subject totals and not individual scores. For the

---

Table 42-7.   ANOVA table for data of Table 42-6

Source	df	SS	MS	F ratio	$\hat{\eta}^2$
Between subjects	11	734.73	67.79		
Groups	2	150.03	75.02	1.15	
S(G)	9	584.70	64.97		
Within subjects	48	1675.60	34.91		
Trials	4	1295.83	323.96	35.20[a]	.54
Groups × trials	8	48.46	6.06	0.67	
Residual	36	331.31	9.20		
Total	59	2410.33			

[a] Significant at $\alpha = .05$ for $F_{4,36;.95} = 2.64$.

data of Table 42-6,

$$\text{III}_G = \frac{597^2 + 532^2 + 601^2}{20} = 50,031.7000$$

so that

$$\text{SS}_G = \text{III}_G - \text{II} = 50,031.7000 - 49,881.6667 = 150.0333$$

$$\text{SS}_{SG} = \text{III}_{GS} - \text{III}_G = 50,616.4000 - 50,031.7000 = 584.7000$$

$$\text{MS}_G = \frac{150.0333}{2} = 75.0167$$

$$\text{MS}_{S(G)} = \frac{584.7000}{9} = 64.9667$$

Finally,

$$H_{01}: \text{all } \psi_G = W_{1.}\mu_{1..} + W_{2.}\mu_{2..} + W_{3.}\mu_{3..} = 0$$

is tested with

$$F = \frac{\text{MS}_G}{\text{MS}_{S(G)}} = \frac{75.0167}{64.9667} = 1.15$$

In this case, H_0 is not rejected since $F = 1.15$ is less than $F_{2,9:.95} = 4.26$. If H_0 had been rejected, contrasts could have been investigated with

$$S = \sqrt{2(4.26)} = 2.92$$

and

$$\text{SE}_\psi^2 = 64.9667 \sum_{g=1}^{3} \frac{W_{g.}^2}{20}$$

As a third step, we now decompose the variation within subjects:

$$d_U = d_T + d_{G \times T} + d_R$$

$$Y_{gts} - \bar{Y}_{g.s} = (\bar{Y}_{.t.} - \bar{Y}_{...}) + (\bar{Y}_{gt.} - \bar{Y}_{.t.} - \bar{Y}_{g..} + \bar{Y}_{...})$$
$$+ (Y_{gts} - \bar{Y}_{gt.} - \bar{Y}_{g.s} + \bar{Y}_{g..})$$

$$\text{I} - \text{III}_{GS} = (\text{III}_T - \text{II}) + (\text{III}_{GT} - \text{III}_T - \text{III}_G + \text{II})$$
$$+ (\text{I} - \text{III}_{GT} - \text{III}_{GS} + \text{III}_G)$$

with degrees of freedom

$$GTS - GS = (T - 1) + (GT - T - G + 1) + (GTS - GT - GS + G)$$

For this analysis we need the totals for each cell of the design. They are reported in Table 42-8. With these figures

$$\text{III}_T = \frac{432^2 + 380^2 + \cdots + 269^2}{12} = 51{,}177.5000$$

$$\text{III}_{G \times T} = \frac{149^2 + 135^2 + \cdots + 95^2}{4} = 51{,}376$$

so that

$$SS_T = \text{III}_T - \text{II} = 51{,}177.5000 - 49{,}881.6667 = 1295.8333$$

$$\begin{aligned}
SS_{G \times T} &= \text{III}_{GT} - \text{III}_G - \text{III}_T + \text{II} \\
&= 51{,}376 - 50{,}031.7000 - 51{,}177.5000 + 49{,}881.6667 = 48.4667
\end{aligned}$$

$$\begin{aligned}
SS_R &= \text{I} - \text{II}_{GT} - \text{III}_{GS} + \text{III}_G \\
&= 52{,}292 - 51{,}376 - 50{,}614.4000 + 50{,}031.7000 = 331.3000
\end{aligned}$$

with

$$MS_T = \frac{1295.8333}{4} = 323.9583$$

$$MS_{G \times T} = \frac{48.4667}{8} = 6.0583$$

$$MS_R = \frac{331.3000}{36} = 9.2028$$

Table 42-8. Totals for each of $G \times T$ cells of design for data of Table 42-6

| Group | Trial | | | | | |
	1	2	3	4	5	Total
1	149	135	120	105	88	597
2	133	112	101	100	86	532
3	150	133	112	111	95	601
Total	432	380	333	316	269	1730

Thus, the hypothesis

$$H_{02}: \text{all } \psi_T = W_{.1}\mu_{.1} + W_{.2}\mu_{.2} + W_{.3}\mu_{.3} + W_{.4}\mu_{.4} + W_{.5}\mu_{.5} = 0$$

is tested with

$$F = \frac{\text{MS}_T}{\text{MS}_R} = \frac{323.9583}{9.2028} = 35.20$$

And the hypothesis

$$H_{03}: \text{all } \psi_{G \times T} = W_{11}\mu_{11} + W_{12}\mu_{12} + \cdots + W_{35}\mu_{35} = 0$$

is tested with

$$F = \frac{\text{MS}_{G \times T}}{\text{MS}_R} = \frac{6.0583}{9.2028} = 0.66$$

Thus, the trial source of variation is significant, since $F = 35.20$ is greater than $F_{4,36:.95} = 2.64$. The two-factor interaction is not significant. No tetrad differences are significantly different from zero, nor are any other post hoc contrasts.

In general, the trials source of variation is examined with set of planned orthogonal contrasts, since researchers are interested in the learning curve across trials. This means that one would test

$$H_{02,1}: \psi_{\text{lin}} = 0 \qquad H_{02,3}: \psi_{\text{cub}} = 0$$

$$H_{02,2}: \psi_{\text{quad}} = 0 \qquad H_{02,4}: \psi_{\text{quar}} = 0$$

by decomposing

$$SS_T = 1295.8333$$

so that

$$SS_{\text{lin}} + SS_{\text{quad}} + SS_{\text{cub}} + SS_{\text{quar}} = 1295.8333$$

In addition,

$$SS_{G \times T} = 48.4667$$

would be decomposed so that

$$SS_{\text{lin} \times G} + SS_{\text{quad} \times G} + SS_{\text{cub} \times G} + SS_{\text{quar} \times G} = 48.4667$$

The $SS_{lin \times G}$ indicates whether the linear trends in the three groups are equal. Let us see how to calculate this sum of squares.

If the linear trends were all equal, then we could treat the combined group as one large sample and determine the sum of squares explained by the linear trend in the total sample. This latter sum of squares, however, is exactly SS_{lin}, the sum of squares due to the linear trend for the trial main effect. As the separate group linear trends become more disparate, the best-fitting lines in the individual groups explain more variation than the line in the combined group. Therefore, if we compare the sum of squares explained in the separate groups to that explained in the combined group, we have an indication of how much the separate-group slopes differ from one another. For the overall three-group case, for example, $SS_{lin \times G}$ would be computed as

$$SS_{lin(G_1)} + SS_{lin(G_2)} + SS_{lin(G_3)} - SS_{lin(G_1 + G_2 + G_3)}$$

This quantity is zero when the lines are parallel and is large when they are not. The three remaining components are computed in a similar fashion.

The $SS_{lin \times G}$ would be used to test the hypothesis that the linear components in each of the G groups are the same. This would be tested with $v = G - 1$. For our example, $v = 3 - 1 = 2$, since three lines are being tested for parallelism.

In terms of the totals of Table 42-8, $SS_{lin} = 1267.5$. The linear sums of

Table 42-9. ANOVA table for repeated-measures design of treatment $\times$ trials with orthogonal tests for trend

Source	df	SS		MS	F ratio
Between Subjects	11	734.73			
Group	2		150.03	75.02	1.15
S(G)	9		584.70	64.97	
Within Subjects	48	1675.60			
Trials	4		1295.83		
Linear	1		1267.50	1267.50	137.77[a]
Quadratic	1		9.52	9.52	1.03
Cubic	1		10.21	10.21	1.11
Quartic	1		8.60	8.60	<1.00
G $\times$ T	8		48.46		
G $\times$ lin	2		26.60	13.30	1.45
G $\times$ quad	2		10.04	5.02	<1.00
G $\times$ cub	2		6.07	3.04	<1.00
G $\times$ quar	2		5.75	2.88	<1.00
Residual	36		331.31	9.10	
Total	59	2410.33			

[a] Significant at $\alpha = .05$.

squares for the three treatment conditions are given by

$$SS_{\text{lin}(G_1)} = 577.6 \qquad SS_{\text{lin}(G_2)} = 280.9 \qquad SS_{\text{lin}(G_3)} = 435.6$$

so that

$$SS_{\text{lin}\times G} = 577.6 + 280.9 + 435.6 - 1267.5 = 26.6$$

The values for SS_{lin} and $SS_{\text{lin}\times G}$ are reported in Table 42-9. Also reported are the sums of squares for the quadratic, cubic, and quartic components. As indicated, the only significant trend component is the main-effect linear component. The critical value for the main-effect contrast is given by $(t^{\text{Dunn}}_{.05:4,36})^2 = 2.64^2 = 6.97$ and for the interaction contrasts by $F_{2,36:.9875} = 5.07$. For completeness, in Box 42-2, we provide directions for the analysis of fully crossed repeated-measures or randomized block designs.

42-4. FRIEDMAN TEST

One of the major assumptions of the randomized block and repeated-measures designs is that the unexplained deviations have a normal distribution. If this assumption is violated, one can replace the corresponding F statistic by a statistic whose distribution is approximately chi-square. Although this test is frequently referred to as a *two-way analysis of variance on ranks,* it is best illustrated for the situation where it is the optimal test. For this optimum case, the actual data consist of ratings.

Consider a study in which 10 judges were asked to rate five different wines for excellence, where a rank of 1 is assigned to the best wine and a rank of 5 is assigned to the poorest. For the general case, let the wines be denoted A_1, A_2, . . . , A_K, and let the judges be denoted B_1, B_2, . . . , B_J. Consider the ranks assigned to the K wines by judge j:

$$r_{j1}, r_{j2}, \ldots, r_{jK}$$

Across all J judges the mean rank for each wine is

$$\overline{R}_{.1}, \overline{R}_{.2}, \ldots, \overline{R}_{.K}$$

If the wines are of equal quality, then

$$\mu_{\overline{R}_{.k}} = \frac{1}{JK} \sum_{j=1}^{J} \sum_{k=1}^{K} r_{jk} = \frac{1}{JK} \sum_{j=1}^{J} R_{j.} = \overline{R}_{..}$$

Since the average of the numbers $1, 2, \ldots, K$ is $(K + 1)/2$, the null form of

---

Box 42-2   Procedure for a fully crossed repeated-measures or randomized block design

Step 1. Compute I, II, III_G, III_T, III_{GS}, and III_{GT}, described in this section.

Step 2. Compute

$$SS_G = III_G - II$$

$$SS_T = III_T - II$$

$$SS_{G \times T} = III_{GT} - III_G - III_T + II$$

$$SS_{S(G)} = III_{GS} - III_G$$

$$SS_R = I - III_{GT} - III_{GS} + III_G$$

Step 3. Complete the ANOVA table, using as a model Table 42-7.

Step 4. For contrasts between groups use

$$SE_{\hat{\psi}}^2 = MS_{S(G)} \sum_{g=1}^{G} \frac{W_{g\cdot}^2}{ST}$$

with

$$S_G = \sqrt{(G-1)F_{(G-1),(GS-G):1-\alpha}}$$

For contrasts between trials and for the groups × trials interaction, use

$$SE_{\hat{\psi}}^2 = MS_R \sum_{t=1}^{T} \frac{W_{\cdot t}^2}{SG}$$

or

$$SE_{\hat{\psi}}^2 = MS_R \sum_{t=1}^{T} \sum_{g=1}^{G} \frac{W_{gt}^2}{S}$$

respectively, with

$$S_T = \sqrt{(T-1)F_{(T-1),G(S-1)(T-1):1-\alpha}}$$

and:

$$S_{G \times T} = \sqrt{(S-1)(T-1)F_{(T-1)(S-1),G(S-1)(T-1):1-\alpha}}$$

For planned analysis, replace the Scheffé coefficients by Dunn critical values read from Table A-11.

H_0 can be stated as

$$H_0: \mu_{\bar{R}_{.1}} = \mu_{\bar{R}_{.2}} = \cdots = \mu_{\bar{R}_{.K}} = \frac{K+1}{2}$$

or

$$H_0: \text{all } \psi = \sum_{k=1}^{K} W_k \mu_{\bar{R}_{.k}} = 0$$

with H_1 defined as

$$H_1: H_0 \text{ is false}$$

The test statistic for evaluating H_0 can be written as

$$\chi_r^2 = J(K-1)\left(\frac{\text{III}_T - \text{II}}{\text{I} - \text{II}}\right) = J(K-1)\hat{\eta}^2$$

When H_0 is true, χ_r^2 has a distribution that can be approximated by a chi-square variable with $v = K - 1$ degrees of freedom. In this case, $\hat{\eta}^2$ is called *Kendall's coefficient of concordance*. In the literature it is usually denoted as W.

As an example of this test, consider the data of Table 42-10 for $K = 5$ wines and $J = 10$ judges:

$$\bar{R}_{.1} = 4.1 \qquad \bar{R}_{.2} = 1.4 \qquad \bar{R}_{.3} = 2.0 \qquad \bar{R}_{.4} = 2.9 \qquad \bar{R}_{.5} = 4.6$$

Table 42-10.   Ratings given to five wines by 10 judges

	Wine				
Judge	A_1	A_2	A_3	A_4	A_5
J_1	4	1	2	3	5
J_2	5	1	4	2	3
J_3	5	2	3	1	4
J_4	5	1	2	3	4
J_5	3	1	2	4	5
J_6	4	2	1	3	5
J_7	4	2	1	3	5
J_8	3	1	2	4	5
J_9	4	2	1	3	5
J_{10}	4	1	2	3	5
Total	41	14	20	29	46
Mean rank	4.1	1.4	2.0	2.9	4.6

Thus, wine A_2 is rated the best and wine A_5 is rated the worst. For the test of no difference in mean ratings, $I = 550$, $II = 450$, and $III_T = 523.4$, so that

$$\hat{\eta}^2 = \frac{523.4 - 450}{550 - 450} = \frac{73.4}{100} = .734$$

and

$$\chi_r^2 = 10(4)(0.734) = 29.36$$

With $\nu = 5 - 1 = 4$ degrees of freedom, H_0 is rejected at $\alpha = .05$ since $\chi_{4:.95}^2 = 9.49$. We know that some contrast in $\overline{R}_{.k}$ is significantly different from zero. In this case the $\text{SE}_{\hat{\psi}}^2$ of any contrast is given by

$$\text{SE}_{\hat{\psi}}^2 = \frac{I - II}{J(K - 1)} \sum_{k=1}^{K} \frac{W_k^2}{J}$$

In this sort of study, one would want to know only which wines differ from one another. Usually this means that only pairwise comparisons are of direct interest. For a post hoc analysis, any mean difference that is more extreme than $\pm\Delta_S$, where

$$\Delta_S = S^*\text{SE}_{\hat{\psi}}$$

would be declared significant for $\hat{\psi}_{kk'} = \overline{R}_{.k} - \overline{R}_{.k'}$. For these data

$$S^* = \sqrt{\chi_{K-1:1-\alpha}^2} = \sqrt{9.49} = 3.08$$

and

$$\text{SE}_{\hat{\psi}}^2 = \frac{I - II}{J(K - 1)} \left(\frac{1}{J} + \frac{1}{J}\right)$$
$$= \frac{550 - 450}{10(4)} \left(\frac{2}{10}\right) = .50$$

so that

$$\Delta_S = 3.08(0.7071) = 2.18$$

If we rank-order the wines by mean ranks, we have

Wine	A_2	A_3	A_4	A_1	A_5
Mean rank	1.4	2.0	2.9	4.1	4.6

Box 42-3   Procedure for the Friedman test

Step 1. Rank-order the treatments, objects, etc., in each block for a randomized block model or within each subject for a repeated-measures design.

Step 2. Compute the rank total for each treatment, object, etc. Denote the totals and mean ranks by

$$R_{.1}, R_{.2}, \ldots, R_{.K}$$

and

$$\overline{R}_{.1}, \overline{R}_{.2}, \ldots, \overline{R}_{.K}$$

Step 3. For an omnibus test of

$$H_0: \text{all } \psi = \sum_{k=1}^{K} W_k \mu_{\overline{R}_{.k}} = 0$$

compute

$$\chi_r^2 = J(K-1)\hat{\eta}^2$$

where $\hat{\eta}^2 = (\text{III}_T - \text{II})/(\text{I} - \text{II})$, and reject H_0 if $\chi_r^2 > \chi_{K-1:1-\alpha}^2$.

Step 4. If H_0 is rejected, examine contrasts in terms of

$$Z = \frac{\hat{\psi}}{\text{SE}_{\hat{\psi}}}$$

where

$$\hat{\psi} = \sum_{k=1}^{K} W_k \overline{R}_{.k}$$

$$\text{SE}_{\hat{\psi}}^2 = \frac{\text{I} - \text{II}}{J(K-1)} \sum_{k=1}^{K} \frac{W_k^2}{J}$$

$$S^* = \sqrt{\chi_{K-1:1-\alpha}^2}$$

Step 5. For testing H_0: all $\psi_{kk'} = \mu_{\overline{R}_{.k}} - \mu_{\overline{R}_{.k'}} = 0$, use

$$t^{\text{Tukey}} = \frac{\overline{R}_{\max} - \overline{R}_{\min}}{\sqrt{\dfrac{(\text{I} - \text{II})}{J(K-1)}\left(\dfrac{2}{J}\right)}}$$

and reject H_0 if $t^{\text{Tukey}} > t_{.05:K,\infty}^{\text{Tukey}} = q/\sqrt{2}$. Test rejected hypotheses, using

$$Z = \frac{\overline{R}_k - \overline{R}_{k'}}{\sqrt{\dfrac{(\text{I} - \text{II})}{J(K-1)}\left(\dfrac{2}{J}\right)}}$$

and

$$t_{.05:K,\infty}^{\text{Tukey}} = q/\sqrt{2}$$

We see that A_2 differs from A_1 and A_5 and that A_3 differs from A_5. We summarize the results as follows:

A_2	A_3	A_4	A_1	A_5
1.4	2.0	2.9	4.1	4.6

In practice, one can increase the power of the analysis by replacing the omnibus χ_r^2 test with a Tukey test, provided that comparisons are restricted to pairwise comparisons only. For this improved model

$$t^{\text{Tukey}} = \frac{\overline{R}_{\max} - \overline{R}_{\min}}{\sqrt{\frac{(I - II)}{J(K - 1)}\left(\frac{2}{J}\right)}}$$

For these data

$$t^{\text{Tukey}} = \frac{4.6 - 1.4}{\sqrt{\frac{(550 - 450)}{10(4)}\left(\frac{2}{10}\right)}} = \frac{3.2000}{0.7071} = 4.52$$

With $\alpha = .05$, $K = 5$, and $v = \infty$, the critical value for rejecting H_0: all $\psi_{kk'} = \mu_{\overline{R}.k} - \mu_{\overline{R}.k'} = 0$ is given by

$$t^{\text{Tukey}}_{.05:5,\infty} = \frac{q}{\sqrt{2}} = \frac{3.86}{\sqrt{2}} = 2.73$$

With this critical value any difference more extreme than

$$\Delta_T = t^{\text{Tukey}}_{.05:5,\infty} = 2.73(0.7071) = 1.93$$

is significant. For this model, A_2 differs from A_1 and A_5, and A_3 differs from A_1 and A_5. We summarize the results as follows:

A_2	A_3	A_4	A_1	A_5
1.4	2.0	2.9	4.1	4.6

We provide directions for the Friedman test in Box 42-3.

42-5. COCHRAN'S Q TEST

Cochran's Q test is a test of equality of correlated proportions. It is a special case of the Friedman test, where the dependent variable is dichotomous. It is also the extension of the McNemar test to three or more measures. As an example of where it might be used, consider the study of Section 42-4 but where the judges are asked to rate the wines as good or poor. If the wine is rated good, it is scored 1; if it is rated poor, it is scored 0. Suppose the scoring is as shown in Table 42-11. As we see, the mean values are actually proportions of good ratings. Thus, the form of H_0 is

$$H_0: p_{.1} = p_{.2} = \cdots = p_{.K}$$

or

$$H_0: \text{all } \psi = \sum_{k=1}^{K} W_k p_{.k} = 0$$

with H_1 defined as

$$H_1: H_0 \text{ is false}$$

Note that the hypothesis is similar to that of the Karl Pearson test of homogeneity. However, the assumptions are different. For this test, observations are correlated within a judge. In the Karl Pearson test, all observations are independent. If we let the wine totals be represented by $T_{.1}, T_{.2}, \ldots, T_{.K}$ and the judges' totals by $T_{1.}, T_{2.}, \ldots, T_{J.}$, and with $\text{III}_T = (1/J)\Sigma T_{.k}^2$ and $\text{III}_J = (1/K)\Sigma T_{j.}^2$, Cochran's test statistic is

$$Q = J(K-1)\left(\frac{\text{III}_T - \text{II}}{\text{I} - \text{III}_J}\right)$$

Table 42-11. Judgments of good or poor assigned to five wines by 10 judges

			Wine			
Judge	A_1	A_2	A_3	A_4	A_5	Total
J_1	0	1	1	0	0	2
J_2	0	1	0	1	1	3
J_3	0	1	0	1	0	2
J_4	0	1	1	0	0	2
J_5	1	1	1	0	0	3
J_6	0	1	1	0	0	2
J_7	0	1	1	0	0	2
J_8	0	1	0	0	0	1
J_9	0	1	1	0	0	2
J_{10}	0	1	1	1	0	3
Total	1	10	7	3	1	22
Percent	10	100	70	30	10	

which can be approximated by a chi-square variable with $v = K - 1$ degrees of freedom.

As we mentioned, Cochran's Q is a special case of the Friedman test, although the formulas appear different. If one ranked the dichotomous values within subject, assigning midranks to ties, and then calculated χ_r^2, the results would be identical. The formula for Q is derivable from χ_r^2, but the algebra is tedious.

For the data of Table 42-11, $I = 22$, $II = 9.68$, $III_T = 16$, $III_J = 10.4$, and

$$Q = 10(5 - 1)\left(\frac{16 - 9.68}{22 - 10.4}\right) = 21.79$$

With $\alpha = .05$, H_0 is rejected since $\chi_{4:.95}^2 = 9.49$. Note that $Q < \chi_r^2$. The reason is that under the Friedman model judges are asked to make finer distinctions than they make under the Cochran Q model.

For this model, contrasts can be examined with

$$\hat{\psi} = \sum_{k=1}^{K} W_k \hat{p}_{.k}$$

$$SE_{\hat{\psi}} = \frac{I - III_J}{J(K - 1)} \sum_{k=1}^{K} \frac{W_{.k}^2}{J}$$

$$S^* = \sqrt{\chi_{K-1:1-\alpha}^2}$$

For these data and pairwise comparisons, any difference more extreme than $\pm \Delta_S$, where

$$\Delta_S = S^* SE_{\hat{\psi}} = 3.08 \sqrt{\frac{22 - 10.4}{10(4)}\left(\frac{2}{10}\right)} = 0.74$$

is significant. Thus, wine A_2 differs from wines A_1 and A_5.

If only pairwise comparisons are of interest, Q should be replaced by

$$t^{\text{Tukey}} = \frac{\hat{p}_{\max} - \hat{p}_{\min}}{\sqrt{\frac{I - III_J}{J(K - 1)}\left(\frac{2}{J}\right)}}$$

For these data

$$t^{\text{Tukey}} = \frac{1.00 - 0.10}{\sqrt{\frac{22 - 10.4}{10(4)}\left(\frac{2}{10}\right)}} = \frac{0.9000}{0.2408} = 3.74$$

With $\alpha = .05$, H_0 is rejected since $t^{\text{Tukey}} > t_{.05:5,\infty}^{\text{Tukey}} = 2.73$. Any pairwise con-

---

Box 42-4   Procedure for Cochran's Q test

Step 1. Assign 1 and 0 to the treatments, objects, etc., in each block for a randomized block model or within each subject for a repeated-measures design.

Step 2. Follow steps 2 through 5 for the Friedman test, but replace χ_r^2, SE_ψ^2, and t^{Tukey} by

$$Q = J(K-1)\frac{\text{III}_T - \text{II}}{\text{I} - \text{III}_J}$$

$$SE_\psi^2 = \frac{\text{I} - \text{III}_J}{J(K-1)}\sum_{k=1}^{K}\frac{W_k^2}{J}$$

and

$$t^{\text{Tukey}} = \frac{\hat{p}_{\max} - \hat{p}_{\min}}{\sqrt{\dfrac{(\text{I} - \text{III}_J)}{J(K-1)}\left(\dfrac{2}{J}\right)}}$$

---

trast more extreme than $\pm\Delta_T$, where:

$$\Delta_T = 2.73(0.2408) = 0.66$$

is significant. Thus, wine A_2 differs from wines A_4, A_1, and A_5. We provide directions for the Cochran test in Box 42-4.

42-6. ASSUMPTIONS FOR THE RANDOMIZED BLOCK AND REPEATED-MEASURES DESIGNS

As mentioned in Section 42-2, the assumptions underlying the single-factor randomized block design are somewhat different from the assumptions that underlie the tests previously encountered. For example, to perform the classical ANOVA *F* test, we must assume

1. The populations are normally distributed.
2. The observations between groups are independent.
3. The observations within groups are independent.
4. The populations have equal variances.

Because of the nature of the randomized block design, these assumptions are modified somewhat. We still require the dependent variable to be normally distributed. Further, the observations between blocks must be independent of one another. Since the act of setting up blocks generates a correlation between the observations, we cannot assume the observations within the block to be independent; rather, we assume that a very particular correlation pattern exists. Specifically, if all the pairwise correlations between columns are equal in the population to a common value and if all the column variances in the population are equal to one another, then the randomized block (and repeated-measures) analysis examined in Section 42-2 is justified. If these assumptions are met, then the data are said to have *compound symmetry,* and the single-factor randomized block F tests can be compared to the appropriate critical values read from the percentiles of the F distribution.

Similar requirements apply in the two-factor design. In addition, in such a design, there are several groups of subjects. Before considering the compound symmetry problem, one must ensure that the respective variances and correlations are equal across the groups. If this homogeneity assumption is met, then one can combine the within-sample variances and correlations and examine the compound symmetry assumption.

The assumptions underlying those designs are very stringent and may be difficult to justify. The result of violating the assumptions is an inflated type I error rate. We cannot be sure that we will reject only 5 percent of the correct null hypotheses in the long run. There are two ways of dealing with a design in which compound symmetry does not exist. The first, called the *Geisser-Greenhouse conservative F test,* tends, as the name implies, to make the test overly conservative, adversely affecting power. However, the correction is very easy to apply. The second, called the *adjusted F test,* yields close to a 5 percent type I error rate, but it is computationally more complex. We illustrate both procedures, using the data of Table 42-2 and the analysis presented in Table 42-4.

Both procedures change only the tabled critical value against which the randomized block F tests are compared. The F ratios themselves are not changed. For the present example, the F ratio of 3.80 would still be used. Different degrees of freedom would be used, however, in the table of F distribution percentiles. These adjustments apply only to tests of the within-block (or within-subject) effects. The conservative F test procedure uses as degrees of freedom

$$v_{1(GG)} = \frac{v_{\text{treat}}}{v_{\text{treat}}} = 1$$

and

$$v_{2(GG)} = \frac{v_R}{v_{\text{treat}}}$$

Since $v_{\text{treat}} = 5$, $v_{2(GG)} = \frac{58}{5} = 11.6 \approx 11$; as usual, we round down. Since $F_{1,11:.95} = 4.84$, the observed F ratio no longer indicates that H_0 should be rejected.

As can be seen, the Geisser-Greenhouse conservative F test can cause a large change in the critical values for the ANOVA. Typically, there is a smaller change when the adjusted F test is used. For this procedure, the variances of and covariances among all the measures are used to compute a quantity called $\hat{\theta}$, which is most easily obtained from widely available computer packages. For the data of Table 42-2, $\hat{\theta} = 0.7184$. This value is used to adjust the degrees of freedom as

$$v_{1(\text{adj})} = v_{\text{treat}} \cdot \hat{\theta} \quad \text{and} \quad v_{2(\text{adj})} = v_R \cdot \hat{\theta}$$

For our example,

$$v_{1(\text{adj})} = 5(.7184) = 3.59 \approx 3$$

$$v_{2(\text{adj})} = 58(.7184) = 41.67 \approx 41$$

Since $F_{3,41:.95} = 2.83$, we conclude on the basis of the adjusted F test that a significant difference exists among the educational programs.

The conservative and the adjusted F tests are related in the following way. If the sample variances and covariances exhibit exact compound symmetry, then the value of $\hat{\theta}$ will equal unity and the degrees of freedom used to enter the F table remain unchanged. If, however, there is a lack of compound symmetry, then the smallest possible value of $\hat{\theta}$ is $1/(K-1)$, the actual value used for the Geisser-Greenhouse conservative F test. Hence, the conservative test examines the significance of the F ratio in the worst possible case, that is, having the greatest reduction in degrees of freedom.

This fact allows us a practical testing strategy that may avoid the necessity for calculating $\hat{\theta}$. We begin by testing the F ratio as originally presented, using the original degrees of freedom and assuming compound symmetry. If this procedure does not produce a significant result, then we may stop at this point, concluding nonsignificance. If, however, this original test is significant, then we compare the F ratio to the critical value found by using the Giesser-Greenhouse conservative procedure. If the conservative F test is also significant, then we may stop and conclude significance. Finally, if the original F test yields significance but the conservative test does not, then the matter can be resolved only by using the adjusted F test.

42-7. APPENDIX

To analyze the data for a randomized block design, we begin with a one-way analysis of variance on the blocks. According to the principles discussed in Section 9-4, we know that the total, block, and unexplained deviations can be related to the sample Y values as

$$Y_{bk} - \bar{Y}_{..} = (\bar{Y}_{b.} - \bar{Y}_{..}) + (Y_{bk} - \bar{Y}_{b.})$$

where

Y_{bk} = value of Y for subject assigned to kth treatment in bth block

$\bar{Y}_{.k}$ = mean on kth treatment

$\bar{Y}_{b.}$ = mean on bth block

$\bar{Y}_{..}$ = grand mean

According to the methods of Chapter 36, the corresponding degrees of freedom are

$$BK - 1 = (B - 1) + (BK - B)$$

The sum of squares is

$$\text{I} - \text{II} = (\text{III}_B - \text{II}) + (\text{I} - \text{III}_B)$$

The unexplained deviation is a within-block deviation. However, in this case, the unexplained (within-block) component can be further decomposed into a deviation explained by treatment effect and a residual unexplained by both block and treatment effects

$$Y_{bk} - \bar{Y}_{b.} = (\bar{Y}_{.k} - \bar{Y}_{..}) + (Y_{bk} - \bar{Y}_{b.} - \bar{Y}_{.k} + \bar{Y}_{..})$$

for which the corresponding degrees of freedom are

$$BK - B = (K - 1) + (BK - B - K + 1)$$

and the sum of squares is

$$\text{I} - \text{III}_B = (\text{III}_K - \text{II}) + (\text{I} - \text{III}_B - \text{III}_K + \text{II})$$

Under this partitioning, the hypothesis of general interest is

$$H_0: \mu_{.1} = \mu_{.2} = \cdots = \mu_{.K} = 0$$

or

$$H_0: \text{all } \psi = \sum_{k=1}^{K} W_k \mu_{.k} = 0$$

In both cases, H_1 is simply that H_0 is false.

As we see, the model is best analyzed in two steps. Step 1 consists of a between-block analysis of variance, and step 2 consists of a within-block analysis of variance. Putting all these pieces together, we have

$$Y_{bk} - \bar{Y}_{..} = (\bar{Y}_{b.} - \bar{Y}_{..}) + (\bar{Y}_{.k} - \bar{Y}_{..}) + (Y_{bk} - \bar{Y}_{b.} - \bar{Y}_{.k} + \bar{Y}_{..})$$

42-8. EXERCISES

42-1. Fifteen male and fifteen female third graders were assigned at random to be taught reading by one of three methods: the old method, a phonics method, and a linguistic method. They were then tested on three different occasions to determine whether the treatment effects were sustained over the summer break equally for the three methods. The three testings were at three times:

1. At the end of the school year
2. Just before the end of July
3. At the beginning of the next school year

The results were as follows:

Sex	Old			Phonics			Linguistic		
	1	2	3	1	2	3	1	2	3
Males	55	45	46	68	62	60	75	66	57
	48	50	48	67	69	57	60	45	58
	45	40	37	60	57	45	55	51	49
	42	42	36	56	59	61	58	56	50
	43	35	37	61	63	46	55	59	54
Females	55	58	50	67	65	67	70	65	62
	56	56	49	65	62	65	59	65	66
	50	49	40	58	65	59	58	69	59
	47	48	40	60	59	40	56	50	50
	45	49	49	58	65	46	59	52	58

Analyze the data for only the males in the old method. Remember that 55, 45, and 46 refer to the data for one subject measured at three different times.

42-2. Analyze the data for all the males in the table. Note that this is a two-factor design with factors being method and time. This design is described in the text.

42-3. The overall design has three factors: sex, method, and time. Present the ANOVA table that includes the three-factor interactions. Set $\alpha = .05$ for each family of hypotheses. The design is not in the text.

42-4. Analyze the data of Exercise 42-3 nesting in gender, and present the ANOVA table that uses all degrees of freedom. Redistribute the risk of a type I error, and provide the directions for examining each family of hypotheses. Do the analyses and present the results in a short paper suitable for a scholarly journal.

42-5. Define the following terms:
a. Statistical control
b. Randomized block design
c. Repeated-measures design

42-6. What are the purposes of a randomized block design?

42-7. Apply the Friedman test to the 10 subjects in the old method, combining the males and females into one group.

42-8. Dichotomize the scores for the 10 subjects assigned to the old method. Let $Y = 0$ if the score on the test is 49 or less. Let $Y = 1$ if the score on the test is 50 or more. Apply Cochran's Q to the data.

42-9. The following study was conducted in which the effects of visual and verbal mediation on the learning of paired-associate nouns were investigated. Eighteen children in three grades — 1, 4, and 7 — participated in the study. Within each grade there were three low SES children and three high SES children. Each subject learned four sets of paired-associate lists, each containing 15 pairs. All lists were equated for frequency of occurrence and meaningfulness. Each of the four lists was learned under one of the visual mediation conditions A_1 and A_2 with one of the verbal mediation conditions B_1 and B_2. Those conditions are as follows:

A_1: An action picture, used to mediate between the two nouns, is shown to the subject after the presentation of each pair.

A_2: A static picture with juxtaposed representations of the two nouns is shown to the subject after the presentation of each pair.

B_1: The experimenter says the noun pair is connected by a verb (the same verb as the action pictures depict).

B_2: The experimenter says the noun pair is connected by the word *and*.

The following table shows the number of correct associations out of 15 made on the fifth trial. Analyze these data.

		Grade 1						Grade 4						Grade 7					
		Low SES			High SES			Low SES			High SES			Low SES			High SES		
		S_1	S_2	S_3	S_4	S_5	S_6	S_7	S_8	S_9	S_{10}	S_{11}	S_{12}	S_{13}	S_{14}	S_{15}	S_{16}	S_{17}	S_{18}
A_1	B_1	4	4	5	6	7	5	4	8	6	10	9	6	11	13	8	14	12	11
	B_2	3	4	4	5	5	3	5	5	6	7	7	4	8	8	5	12	11	10
A_2	B_1	2	3	3	4	5	2	3	6	6	9	7	8	9	9	7	12	13	12
	B_2	1	2	2	2	3	1	2	4	5	4	6	6	6	5	6	12	10	11

42-10. In a study of the rate of acquisition of paired associates as a function of the meaningfulness of the stimulus and response items, 32 subjects were divided into four groups:

Group 1. Both stimulus and response words were high-meaningfulness words.

Group 2. The stimulus word was of low meaningfulness; the response word was of high meaningfulness.

Group 3. The stimulus word was of high meaningfulness; the response word was of low meaningfulness.

Group 4. Both stimulus and response words were of low meaningfulness.

Subjects were given 10 paired associates to learn in four test trials. Each subject had 15 s to study the 10 pairs before the test trials began. The following are the number of correct responses given when the 10 stimulus words were presented, for 6 s each, 1 min for the whole trial. Analyze the data in the table below.

42-11. Verify the figures in Table 42-9.

Subject	Group 1								Group 2								Group 3								Group 4							
	1	2	3	4	5	6	7	8	9	10	11	12	13	14	15	16	17	18	19	20	21	22	23	24	25	26	27	28	29	30	31	32
Trial 1	2	1	0	0	1	2	2	1	0	0	1	0	0	1	2	0	0	0	0	1	1	0	0	1	0	0	0	1	0	0	0	0
2	4	3	1	2	3	3	2	3	3	2	2	1	2	4	4	2	1	2	1	2	1	2	1	2	0	1	1	1	0	1	1	0
3	7	6	3	5	5	6	5	4	5	5	5	3	4	6	7	4	3	4	2	3	2	4	3	4	2	2	1	2	1	2	3	2
4	8	9	6	8	7	8	7	7	7	6	8	5	6	7	9	5	5	6	4	4	3	6	4	5	2	3	2	3	2	2	3	3

Statistical Control — Adjusted Averages and Analysis of Covariance

43-1. STATISTICAL CONTROL

In Chapter 42, two statistical control models were described that could be used to reduce the effects of confounding variables on the dependent variable of a study utilizing human subjects. The methods were based on the use of either randomized blocks on groups of similar subjects or the same subject in a repeated-measures design. Unfortunately, these designs are not always easy to execute, especially if the subjects appear in already consolidated groups. When this happens, a researcher can approximate the statistical control achieved by a randomized block design by using the method of adjusted averages or the analysis of covariance. The method of adjusted averages makes use of a blocking variable, similar to the randomized block design, except that the blocking is usually done after the fact. However, the analysis of covariance (ANCOVA) uses a variable correlated with the dependent variable to reduce the residual variance through linear regression. The variable used in ANCOVA is usually the same kind as that used in the randomized block design and must be selected in advance of treatment.

43-2. METHOD OF ADJUSTED AVERAGES

One of the major problems faced in program evaluation and research in education or related disciplines is the creation of an experimental design that ensures high levels of internal and external validity. Often, as a result of social or political pressures, class scheduling, school facilities, and numerous other limitations, investigators are prevented from assigning students or subjects at random to different programs or treatment groups in order to conduct a sound, planned study. As a consequence, groups cannot be viewed as equivalent at the beginning of a study.

One way to achieve a reasonable design in practice is to *create* an artificial sample that is used as a *standard* to which all groups are compared. As an example of how a standard sample can be established, consider the data of Table 43-1 which are taken from the annual testing of sixth-grade students in a California unified school district. The purpose of this study was to evaluate

Table 43-1. Mean scores and sample sizes on arithmetic application of mathematics test

School	IQ score level (sample size)					Unadjusted means (sample size)
	L_1	L_2	L_3	L_4	L_5	
1	6.36 (25)	8.59 (22)	17.80 (5)			8.40 (52)
2	7.34 (32)	9.54 (35)	16.92 (24)	17.75 (4)		11.01 (95)
3	9.20 (5)	9.89 (19)	19.55 (20)	28.33 (6)		15.90 (50)
4		8.77 (13)	17.30 (10)	26.40 (10)	30.17 (12)	20.29 (45)
Mean value	7.09	9.27	17.95	25.25	30.17	13.18
Sample size	62	89	59	20	12	242
Variance[a]	86	41	45	54	16	

[a] Reported to the nearest whole number.

how well students in the schools were performing on a standardized mathematics test. Because the characteristics of the students entering the schools may differ greatly, a simple comparison of mean scores may not reveal how much the students are improving.

Sample sizes and mean scores on the arithmetic application section of the test are reported for five IQ score levels of the Lorge-Thorndike Test of Mental Abilities. The IQ test was administered in the spring, and the achievement test was administered a year later. Level 1 consists of sixth-grade students who scored 84 or less on the IQ test. Level 2 is defined for the students who scored in the range from 85 through 99. Level 3 is defined for students whose IQ scores cover the midrange of 100 through 115. Level 4 is defined by IQ scores from 116 through 131. Finally, level 5 contains all students who scored more than 131 on the IQ test. These levels are denoted $L_1, L_2, L_3, L_4,$ and L_5, respectively. Note that the levels are being used as if they constituted a blocking variable, since it is reasonable to assume that the mathematics scores should be positively correlated with IQ. Thus, students within a block are comparable within a specified range of IQ scores.

The schools are presented in the rank order determined from the school averages on the arithmetic application part of the test. The mean school scores range from a low of 8.40 to a high of 20.29. This clearly represents a large range in performance across schools.

Closer inspection of the data for the two schools farthest apart in mean value suggests that the school averages may not be appropriate measures for comparison of actual performance of students in these apparently extreme schools. School 1 has 25 students in L_1, 22 in L_2, and 5 in L_3. School 4, however, has 12 students in L_5 and 10 in L_4. Certainly these schools are not comparable with respect to these measures of achievement. One would expect the average arithmetic application score at school 1 to be low and the corresponding average at school 4 to be high on this basis alone, and not simply because instruction at school 4 is superior to that at school 1. The student input into the schools, as measured by the verbal ability scores, is different, and the difference in the mean mathematics scores should reflect this basic difference. To overcome this problem in initial differences, we create an artificial school, which we call the *standard school*, that closely resembles the makeup of the school district as a whole. Then we compare each school to the standard school, level by level.

If we now return to the data of Table 43-1 and sum across the four schools, 62 students have Lorge-Thorndike IQ scores in the low IQ group L_1. The remaining frequencies are 89 in L_2, 59 in L_3, 20 in L_4, and 12 in L_5. If each of the four schools had a group of students identical to the total population of the school district, then differences in means would certainly reflect the teaching programs in the various schools, provided that all other factors were equal. Thus, to control student input, we can create a standard school of 100 students consisting of five blocks with the same proportion of students in each block as in the school district. The school with this property has block sizes given by

$$N_1 = \frac{n_1}{n}(100) = \frac{62}{242}(100) = 26$$

$$N_2 = \frac{n_2}{n}(100) = \frac{89}{242}(100) = 37$$

$$N_3 = \frac{n_3}{n}(100) = \frac{59}{242}(100) = 24$$

$$N_4 = \frac{n_4}{n}(100) = \frac{20}{242}(100) = 8$$

$$N_5 = \frac{n_5}{n}(100) = \frac{12}{242}(100) = 5$$

We apply the rules for calculating combined group means by acting as though each school had the same composition as the school district. This *adjusted mean* $\bar{Y}_g^A$ is a weighted average of the school's block means. It is defined as

$$\bar{Y}_g^A = \frac{N_1}{N}\bar{Y}_{g1} + \frac{N_2}{N}\bar{Y}_{g2} + \cdots + \frac{N_K}{N}\bar{Y}_{gK}$$

This formula is valid for a school that has students in each stratum. Consider school 1, which has no students in L_4 or L_5. For this school, the adjusted mean is calculated by including only strata L_1, L_2, and L_3 of the standard population. Since the standard population has 26, 37, and 24 of its 87 students in these respective strata, these are the weights used. Under this model

$$\begin{aligned}
\bar{Y}_1^A &= {}^{26}\!/\!_{87}\bar{Y}_{11} + {}^{37}\!/\!_{87}\bar{Y}_{12} + {}^{24}\!/\!_{87}\bar{Y}_{13} \\
&= {}^{26}\!/\!_{87}(6.36) + {}^{37}\!/\!_{87}(8.59) + {}^{24}\!/\!_{87}(17.80) \\
&= 10.46
\end{aligned}$$

For the other schools $\bar{Y}_2^A = 11.49$, $\bar{Y}_3^A = 13.69$, and $\bar{Y}_4^A = 14.89$. Whereas the range in the unadjusted means was 8.40 to 20.29, the range in the adjusted means is reduced, from a low of 10.46 to a high of 14.89. This is more in agreement with the strata mean comparisons which are a truer reflection of performance.

We would like to compare how well each school is performing with how we would *expect* it to perform if the students in each of its levels were like those of the entire school district. To do this, we weight the population means by the proportions of students in each level of the standard school. Because the population means are unknown, we estimate the population strata means by using the data of each school. Thus, for each school

$$\mu_g^A = \frac{N_1}{N}\mu_{.1} + \frac{N_2}{N}\mu_{.2} + \cdots + \frac{N_K}{N}\mu_{.K}$$

Under this model

$$\mu_1^A = {}^{26}\!/_{87}(7.09) + {}^{37}\!/_{87}(9.27) + {}^{24}\!/_{87}(17.95)$$
$$= 11.01$$

with $\mu_2^A = 12.21$, $\mu_3^A = 12.21$, and $\mu_4^A = 15.22$.

To determine whether each school is performing to expectation or as well as another school, we need to calculate the standard errors of the adjusted means. Because each adjusted mean is a linear combination of the level means of each school, we can use our rules for the variance of a linear combination to find

$$\text{SE}_{\bar{Y}^A}^2 = \left(\frac{N_1}{N}\right)^2 \left(\frac{\sigma_1^2}{n_1}\right) + \left(\frac{N_2}{N}\right)^2 \left(\frac{\sigma_2^2}{n_2}\right) + \cdots + \left(\frac{N_K}{N}\right)^2 \left(\frac{\sigma_K^2}{n_K}\right)$$

where n_k is the number of students in level k, for a particular school. Under this model,

$$\text{SE}_{\bar{Y}_1^A}^2 = ({}^{26}\!/_{87})^2({}^{86}\!/_{25}) + ({}^{37}\!/_{87})^2({}^{41}\!/_{22}) + ({}^{24}\!/_{87})^2({}^{45}\!/_5) = 1.33$$

with $\text{SE}_{\bar{Y}_2^A}^2 = 0.59$, $\text{SE}_{\bar{Y}_3^A}^2 = 1.82$, and $\text{SE}_{\bar{Y}_4^A}^2 = 1.33$.

Because the school sample sizes are relatively large, the sampling distribution of $\bar{Y}^A$ tends to be normal in form as a result of the central limit theorem. Thus, the hypothesis $H_0: E(\bar{Y}^A) = \mu^A$ can be tested by referring

$$Z = \frac{\bar{Y}^A - \mu^A}{\text{SE}_{\bar{Y}^A}^2}$$

to the standard normal distribution. The null hypothesis of no difference for a single hypothesis test is rejected if $Z < Z_{\alpha/2}$ or if $Z > Z_{1-\alpha/2}$, where the critical values are read from tables of the standard normal distribution. When there is more than one test, alpha is split equally among the hypotheses.

For school 1, the test of $H_0: E(\bar{Y}_1^A) = 11.01$ indicates that, as a group, students are performing slightly, but not statistically significantly, below average, since

$$Z_1 = \frac{10.46 - 11.01}{\sqrt{1.33}} = -0.48$$

Remaining Z values for the other schools are

$$Z_2 = -0.94 \qquad Z_3 = 1.10 \qquad Z_4 = -0.29$$

None of the schools seems to be performing far from expectation. We provide directions for comparing adjusted mean values in Box 43-1.

Box 43-1   Procedure for comparing adjusted means

Step 1. Select a standard sample for the K levels. Denote the level sizes $N_1, N_2, \ldots, N_K$.

Step 2. Compute the means and variances of each level for each sample. Denote the values for group g by

$$\bar{Y}_{g1}, \bar{Y}_{g2}, \ldots, \bar{Y}_{gK}$$

and

$$S_{g1}^2, S_{g2}^2, \ldots, S_{gK}^2$$

Estimate the mean for each level from the entire set of data. Denote these means

$$\mu_{.1}, \mu_{.2}, \ldots, \mu_{.K}$$

For each level, determine the within-group variance, using a one-factor ANOVA model for each stratum. Denote these variances

$$\sigma_1^2, \sigma_2^2, \ldots, \sigma_K^2$$

Step 3. Compute the adjusted and expected means for group g:

$$\bar{Y}_g^A = \frac{1}{N} \sum_{k=1}^{K} N_k \bar{Y}_{gk}$$

$$\mu_g^A = \frac{1}{N} \sum_{k=1}^{K} N_k \mu_{.k}$$

If a group has zero frequencies at some level, adjust N to reflect the strata actually used.

Step 4. Compute the squared standard errors as

$$SE_{\bar{Y}_g^A}^2 = \sum_{k=1}^{K} \left(\frac{N_k}{N} \right)^2 \frac{\sigma_k^2}{n_{gk}}$$

where $n_{g1}, n_{g2}, \ldots, n_{gK}$ are the sample sizes for each group in each stratum.

Step 5. Test $H_0: E(\bar{Y}_g^A) = \mu_g^A$ with

$$Z = \frac{\bar{Y}_g^A - \mu_g^A}{SE_{\bar{Y}_g^A}}$$

Step 6. Reject H_0, using critical values selected from Table A-11.

43-3. ADJUSTED VALUES IN A SINGLE SAMPLE

For the method of adjusted averages described in Section 43-2, adjustment was made directly to the mean of the sample. Another way to adjust the sample average is first to adjust the individual scores and then to compute the average of the adjusted scores, to obtain an adjusted average. The method used for this type of adjustment employs the correlation between the stratifying variable and the dependent variable directly, through the corresponding linear regression equation. The resulting procedure is commonly referred to as the *analysis of covariance,* and the variable used for stratification in the model of Section 43-2 is called a *covariate.*

The analysis of covariance is based on a type of statistical control achieved by trying to predict what each person's score would be if each person were like the average person in the study. The predicted value is called the *adjusted value.* The model for obtaining an adjusted score for an individual subject is shown in Figure 43-1. In obtaining this adjusted score, it is assumed that a straight-line relationship exists between the dependent variable Y and the covariate X. In particular, we know that in the sample

$$\hat{Y} = \bar{Y} + B_1(X - \bar{X})$$

where

$$B_1 = r\left(\frac{S_Y}{S_X}\right)$$

If we now consider an individual whose X value is given by $X = X_0$, the corresponding predicted value is given by

$$\hat{Y}_{X_0} = \bar{Y} + B_1(X_0 - \bar{X})$$

For this individual, let the deviation between the observed $Y = Y_0$ and the predicted $\hat{Y}_{X_0}$ value be denoted as the unexplained deviation:

$$d_U = Y_0 - \hat{Y}_{X_0} = Y_0 - \bar{Y} - B_1(X_0 - \bar{X})$$

This deviation measures how much the individual's performance differs from what is expected. If we assume that the most typical individual of the group has an $X = \bar{X}$, then the predicted score for this average, or ideal, subject is given by

$$\hat{Y}_I^A = \bar{Y} + B_1(\bar{X} - \bar{X}) = \bar{Y}$$

The adjusted value for the individual whose $X = X_0$ is calculated by assuming that the person would deviate by the same amount d_U from what would be

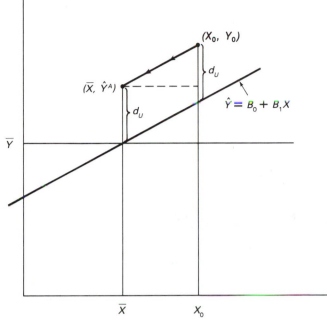

Figure 43-1.
The model for determining an adjusted score.

predicted had the individual's X score equaled that of the ideal subject $\overline{X}$. Thus,

$$\begin{aligned}
\hat{Y}^A &= \hat{Y}_I + d_U \\
&= \overline{Y} + Y_0 - \overline{Y} - B_1(X_0 - \overline{X}) \\
&= Y_0 - B_1(X_0 - \overline{X})
\end{aligned}$$

In terms of the geometry of Figure 43-1, we note that Y_0 is projected parallel to the regression line to the point $X = \overline{X}$. For completeness, we provide directions in Box 43-2 for computing the adjusted value for each subject in a given sample.

As an example of how one would estimate adjusted scores, consider the

Box 43-2   **How to compute an adjusted score for a typical subject whose observed values are $X = X_0$ and $Y = Y_0$**

Step 1. Determine $\overline{X}$ and B_1 for the group of N subjects.
Step 2. Estimate an individual's adjusted score as

$$\hat{Y}^A = Y_0 - B_1(X_0 - \overline{X})$$

Table 43-2. Adjusted test scores[a] for 11 business administration students

Student	X	Y	Adjusted Y	Y^A − Y
1	610	475	400	−75
2	590	600	535	−65
3	300	395	469	+74
4	520	460	428	−22
5	610	495	420	−75
6	300	415	489	+74
7	280	400	484	+84
8	285	395	476	+81
9	520	715	683	−32
10	500	600	578	−22
11	480	480	468	−22
Mean value	454	494	494	0

[a] All values have been rounded to the nearest integer.

data for the 11 subjects of Table 43-2, whose major is business administration. For these 11 subjects

$$\bar{Y} = 494 \qquad \bar{X} = 454 \qquad B_1 = (0.63)(^{104}/_{136}) = 0.48$$

so that the equation for an adjusted score is given by

$$\hat{Y}^A = Y_0 - 0.48(X_0 - 454)$$

For the subject with $X_0 = 610$ and $Y_0 = 475$,

$$\hat{Y}^A = 475 - 0.48(610 - 454) = 475 - 75 = 400$$

Notice that this subject has a relatively high verbal score of 610. It is $610 - 454 = 156$ points above the average of the business administration students. However, this subject falls far below the predicted score of

$$\hat{Y}_0 = 494 + 0.48(610 - 454) = 569$$

by

$$d_U = Y_0 - \hat{Y}_0 = 475 - 569 = -94$$

points. Thus, in terms of the average student for whom $\bar{Y} = 494$, this student has an adjusted score of only

$$\hat{Y}^A = 494 - 94 = 400$$

Given the relatively high verbal test score, the adjusted score on the composition test is quite low. The remaining adjusted scores are shown in Table 43-2. Notice that subjects 3, 6, 7, and 8 have adjusted scores that are high relative to their observed scores. These subjects scored higher than expected. On the other hand, subjects 1, 2, and 5 scored considerably lower than expected. Notice that their verbal scores of 610, 590, and 610 are quite high relative to the mean value of 454, but their observed performance scores of 475, 600, and 495 are lower than expected, respectively. For this reason they have low adjusted scores.

We again note that the mean adjusted score is

$$\bar{Y}^A = \bar{Y} - B_1(\bar{X} - \bar{X}) = \bar{Y}$$

Although the mean adjusted score is equal to the mean Y score, the variance of the adjusted scores is considerably smaller than the variance of the unadjusted scores. For the original data

$$S_Y^2 = 104^2 = 10{,}816$$

while for the adjusted data

$$S_{Y^A}^2 = 6487$$

As we see, removing the variation attributable to the verbal test scores reduces the variance of the adjusted scores by a considerable amount. This reduction of variance can be used to advantage in the analysis of covariance to increase the power of the corresponding statistical tests.

43-4. ANALYSIS OF COVARIANCE

The analysis of covariance is based on the adjustment procedure described in Section 43-3 as applied to multiple samples. As we have seen, if a covariate is available, we can adjust the Y scores of a sample so that they can be compared to one another, because each person is conceived as having equal ability on the covariate. This procedure is similar to our having created a hypothetical *standard school* in Section 43-2. One purpose of analysis of covariance is to use the adjustment method so as to make groups of subjects more easily compared on a Y variable, by equating the abilities of the groups on the covariate. As we have also seen, an outcome of the adjustment procedure is to make the

Table 43-3. Composition and verbal test scores for entering first-year students[a]

Business administration		Engineering		Chemistry		English		History		Math		Total	
X	Y	X	Y	X	Y	X	Y	X	Y	X	Y	X	Y
610[a]	475	500	525	480	560	710	610	500	620	610	500		
590	600	520	385	280	410	480	505	600	460	470	480		
300	395	400	400	495	480	795	625	510	710	580	520		
520	460	460	515	690	720	710	685	700	430	600	535		
610	495	580	610	470	460	500	475	700	680	500	475		
300	415	700	650	395	480	600	560	310	450	300	395		
280	400	420	550	600	565	650	590	600	510	510	420		
285	395	480	525	590	590	500	640	610	580	630	460		
520	715	620	500	670	615	760	790	635	595	490	475		
500	600	500	510	480	460	700	730	705	675	480	520		
480	480					700	765	700	690	610	605		
						650	650	715	760				
						650	600						
						690	680						
($\bar{X}_k, \bar{Y}_k$) 454	494	518	517	515	564	600	636	577	597	525	490	541	554
(S_{X_k}, S_{Y_k}) 136	104	92	81	126	93	97	91	120	112	96	57	127	105
$r_{XY(k)}$ 0.63		0.57		0.89		0.69		0.39		0.64		0.64	
N_k 11		10		10		14		12		11		68	

[a] Except for the correlation coefficients, all statistics in this table have been rounded to the nearest integer.

variability of the adjusted scores smaller than that of the original scores. Reducing this variability, which is the major goal of ANCOVA, will make our analysis more powerful, just as was achieved in the randomized block design.

Let us consider the following example. All entering first-year students at a university are required to take a course in composition. The instructor wishes to know if the course is equally effective for students in six programs: business administration, engineering, chemistry, English, history, and mathematics. The difficulty in merely comparing their scores on a final examination is that the students enter the course with different verbal abilities. Since the students verbal SAT scores are available for use as a covariate, the instructor will compare the groups' composition means after they have been adjusted for incoming verbal ability. The data for the verbal SAT scores and the scores on a final composition examination are indicated by program in Table 43-3.

As a first step, we need to find the adjusted averages for the groups $\overline{Y}_k^A$. If we apply the adjustment procedure of the previous section to each group, and if the relationship between Y and X in each group is different, then we will not be able to make the scores comparable. Some group's scores will be unfairly adjusted compared to another's. So we must assume that the population slopes are equal, that is, that the regression lines are parallel. We combine the separate group slopes to form a *pooled* estimate of the common population slope, which is then used to adjust all the groups' scores. In the appendix, we show that the pooled slope is given by

$$B_{1(W)} = \frac{\sum\limits_{k=1}^{K} W_k B_{1(k)}}{W}$$

where

$$W_k = (N_k - 1)S_{X(k)}^2 \qquad \text{and} \qquad W = \sum_{k=1}^{K} W_k$$

For the data of Table 43-3, the regression equations are given by

$$\hat{Y}_k = \overline{Y}_{.k} + B_{1(k)}(X - \overline{X}_{.k})$$

and

Group 1: $\qquad \hat{Y}_1 = 494 + 0.4810(X - 454)$

Group 2: $\qquad \hat{Y}_2 = 517 + 0.5021(X - 518)$

Group 3: $\qquad \hat{Y}_3 = 564 + 0.6595(X - 515)$

Group 4: $\qquad \hat{Y}_4 = 636 + 0.6427(X - 600)$

Group 5: $\qquad \hat{Y}_5 = 597 + 0.3676(X - 577)$

Group 6: $\qquad \hat{Y}_6 = 490 + 0.3813(X - 525)$

These regression equations are presented graphically in Figure 43-2. With the pooled within group slope given in terms of the W_k we have

$$W_1 = (11 - 1)136^2 = 184{,}960$$

with $W_2 = 76{,}176$, $W_3 = 142{,}884$, $W_4 = 122{,}317$, $W_5 = 158{,}400$, and

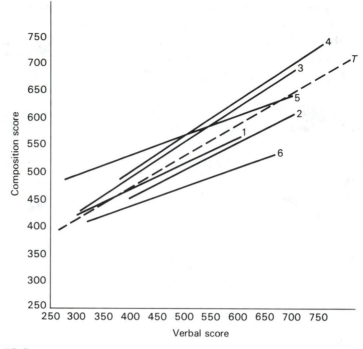

Figure 43-2.
The regression lines for the six education groups and the total regression line.

$W_6 = 92{,}160$, and with $W = 184{,}960 + \cdots + 92{,}160 = 776{,}897$. Thus,

$$B_{1(W)} = \frac{184{,}960(0.4810) + 76{,}176(0.5021) + \cdots + 92{,}160(0.3813)}{184{,}960 + 76{,}176 + \cdots + 92{,}160}$$

$$= \frac{393{,}427}{776{,}897} = 0.5064$$

We use $B_{1(W)}$ to estimate the predicted score that each observation in the study would have if its X value were the overall X mean of the combined samples:

$$\hat{Y}^A_{ik} = Y_{ik} - B_{1(W)}(X_{ik} - \overline{X}_{..})$$

in the kth group. By averaging these values in each group, we get the adjusted mean $\overline{Y}^A_{.k}$:

$$\overline{Y}^A_{.k} = \overline{Y}_{.k} - B_{1(W)}(\overline{X}_{.k} - \overline{X}_{..})$$

For the data of Table 43-3, the adjusted averages are

$$\overline{Y}^A_{.1} = 494 - 0.5064(454 - 541) = 538$$

with $\overline{Y}^A_{.2} = 529$, $\overline{Y}^A_{.3} = 577$, $\overline{Y}^A_{.4} = 606$, $\overline{Y}^A_{.5} = 579$, and $\overline{Y}^A_{.6} = 498$.

Note how different the adjusted averages are from the unadjusted values. By treating all subjects as if their verbal test scores were given by $X = \overline{X}_{..} = 541$, we see that business administration students have their mean value increased from 494 to 538. This reflects the fact that they are performing better on the composition final that would be expected based on their incoming verbal ability. This is similar to the discussion of Section 43-2, where we saw that the school with low-ability students was actually performing closer to its expected performance than was measured by the school's unadjusted mean.

Now that we have the adjusted means, we would like to know whether the corresponding population adjusted means are equal. Thus, we would like to test

$$H_0: \mu_{Y(1)}^A = \mu_{Y(2)}^A = \cdots = \mu_{Y(K)}^A$$

against

$$H_1: H_0 \text{ is false}$$

where

$$\mu_{Y(k)}^A = \mu_{Y(k)} - \beta_{1(W)}(\mu_{X(k)} - \mu_X)$$

Here $\beta_{1(W)}$ is the population pooled slope relating Y and X, and μ_X is the X mean in the combined populations.

We have adjusted scores Y_{ik}^A and adjusted means $\overline{Y}_{.k}^A$, so it would seem possible simply to perform ANOVA on these to detect differences in the population. Unfortunately, this leads to statistical complications. The adjusted means would yield an adjusted MS_B, and the scores would lead to an adjusted MS_W, but these would not be *independent,* because they have both been adjusted by using the same $B_{1(W)}$. For their ratio to follow the F distribution under H_0, they must have independent χ^2 distributions.

The appropriate procedure follows the same logic as in Section 43-2. Instead of comparing the adjusted means, we compare each to the total sample, which we treat as a standard comparison group. In the *total* (T) sample, the regression equation is

$$\hat{Y}_T = \overline{Y}_{..} + B_{1(T)}(X - \overline{X}_{..})$$

where $B_{1(T)}$ is the slope calculated from the entire set of subjects treated as a single sample. From the values given in Table 43-3, this equation is

$$\hat{Y}_T = 554 + 0.5681(X - 541)$$

If H_0 were true, then all the separate regression lines would fall close to this standard line, whereas the separate lines falling far from the standard line would suggest that H_0 may be false. If we examine the deviations of each Y value from the standard line, we can find the total amount of variability. If the separate lines are far from the total line, then the deviation of each Y value from its *own group's* line should be much smaller than the total deviation. Thus, a comparison of the sums of squares of these respective deviations indicates how close the separate lines are to the total line and, hence, whether H_0 should be rejected.

In the appendix, we show that the adjusted total, unexplained, and explained sums of squares, respectively, can be calculated as

$$SS_T^A = SS_{T(Y)} - B_{1(T)}^2 SS_{T(X)}$$

$$SS_U^A = SS_{W(Y)} - B_{1(W)}^2 SS_{W(X)}$$

$$SS_E^A = SS_T^A - SS_U^A$$

The sums of squares on the right-hand side of these equations are obtained from separate one-way ANOVAs on the X and Y variables.

For our example, the ANOVA results for the Y and X variables are shown in Tables 43-4 and 43-5, respectively. In terms of $B_{1(W)}$, $B_{1(T)}$, and these figures,

$$SS_T^A = 738{,}363 - (0.5681)^2(936{,}858) = 436{,}004$$

$$SS_U^A = 521{,}753 - (0.5064)^2(775{,}670) = 322{,}839$$

$$SS_E^A = 436{,}004 - 322{,}839 = 113{,}165$$

As usual, the degrees of freedom between groups are given by $v_E = K - 1$. The mean square within groups in ANOVA has $v_W = N - K$ degrees of freedom. However, the mean square unexplained in ANCOVA has only $v_U = N - K - 1$ degrees of freedom, because 1 degree of freedom is used to estimate $B_{1(W)}$. With these degrees of freedom, we calculate the adjusted mean squares as

$$MS_E^A = \frac{SS_E^A}{K - 1} \quad \text{and} \quad MS_U^A = \frac{SS_U^A}{N - K - 1}$$

Table 43-4. ANOVA table for composition scores

Source	df	SS	MS	F ratio	$\hat{\eta}^2$
Between	5	216,610	43,322	5.15	.29
Within	62	521,753	8,415		
Total	67	738,363			

$F_{5,62:.95} = 2.37.$

Table 43-5. Analysis of variance on verbal test scores

Source	df	SS	MS	F ratio	$\hat{\eta}^2$
Between	5	161,187	32,237	2.58	.17
Within	62	775,670	12,511		
Total	67	936,858			

$F_{5,02:.95} = 2.37.$

The ANCOVA F ratio is defined as the ratio of these mean squares. That is,

$$F = \frac{MS_E^A}{MS_U^A}$$

For the data of Table 43-3, these values are

$$MS_E^A = \frac{113,165}{5} = 22,633$$

$$MS_U^A = \frac{322,839}{61} = 5292$$

$$F = \frac{22,633}{5292} = 4.28$$

These values are inserted into an ANCOVA table, as in Table 43-6.

Under H_0, this F ratio is distributed as an F variable with v_E and v_U degrees of freedom. The decision rule is

Decision Rule: Reject H_0 if $F > F_{v_E, v_U : 1-\alpha}$

For our example, this becomes

Decision Rule: Reject H_0 if $F > F_{5,61:.95} = 2.37$

Table 43-6. Analysis of covariance for data of Table 43-3

Source	df	SS	MS	F ratio
Between adjusted means	5	113,165	22,633	4.28
Within	61	322,839	5,292	
Total	66	436,004		

$F_{5,61:.95} = 2.37.$

Hence, H_0 is rejected. The population adjusted means are not equal. For completeness, we provide directions in Box 43-3 for performing an analysis of covariance.

Let us compare the results of ANOVA and ANCOVA for the data of Table 43-3. The F values of the two procedures, 5.15 and 4.28, respectively, are not equal. It may not seem that ANCOVA has helped us at all. This is not the case. The ANOVA of the composition scores merely told us that the population means differ. We could almost have predicted as much by seeing that the verbal abilities of the groups differ widely. The analysis of covariance attempts to determine whether the composition means would have differed, assuming the verbal abilities of the groups were equal to a common value. A second important outcome from ANCOVA is that the unexplained variability is greatly reduced, compared to ANOVA. Notice that

$$MS_{W(Y)} = 8415$$

whereas

$$MS_U^A = 5292$$

This represents a considerable reduction in the unexplained variation. Perhaps the most important reason for using ANCOVA is its ability to reduce the unexplained variability, thus increasing its power over ANOVA.

To close this section, we list the assumptions underlying the analysis of covariance. Violations of these assumptions can have serious effects on the type I and type II error rates of the procedure. Analysis of covariance is based on seven assumptions:

1. The K regressions between X and Y are linear.
2. The K regression lines are parallel.
3. The variances about each regression line satisfy the condition of homoscedasticity.
4. The residual variance about all regression lines should equal a common value.
5. The pairs of observations between and within samples are completely independent.
6. The residuals are normally distributed.
7. The values of the covariate cannot depend on the conditions defining the groups.

43-5. CONTRASTS FOR THE ANALYSIS OF COVARIANCE

In the previous example, the hypothesis of no differences in adjusted means was rejected. Just as in the analysis of variance, the ANCOVA F test is used to

Box 43-3   Procedures for analysis of covariance

Step 1. Perform a regression analysis on each sample to obtain

$$B_{1(1)}, B_{1(2)}, \ldots, B_{1(K)}$$

and the corresponding

$$W_1 = (N_1 - 1)S_{X(1)}^2, W_2 = (N_2 - 1)S_{X(2)}^2, \ldots, W_K = (N_K - 1)S_{X(K)}^2$$

Step 2. Perform an analysis of variance on the X variables to obtain $SS_{B(X)}$, $SS_{W(X)}$, and $SS_{T(X)}$.

Step 4. Estimate $\beta_{1(W)}$ by

$$B_{1(W)} = \frac{\sum\limits_{k=1}^{K} W_k B_{1(k)}}{\sum\limits_{k=1}^{K} W_k}$$

Step 5. Obtain an estimate of $\beta_{1(T)}$ by

$$B_{1(T)} = r_{XY(T)} \frac{S_{Y(T)}}{S_{X(T)}}$$

by treating the K samples as one sample of size N.

Step 6. Compute

$$SS_U^A = SS_{W(Y)} - B_{1(W)}^2 SS_{W(X)}$$

$$SS_T^A = SS_{T(Y)} - B_{1(T)}^2 SS_{T(X)}$$

$$SS_E^A = SS_T^A - SS_U^A$$

and complete the ANCOVA table as shown in Table 43-6, using

$$v_E^A = K - 1 \qquad v_U^A = N - K - 1 \qquad v_T^A = N - 2$$

Step 7. Compute

$$MS_E^A = \frac{SS_E^A}{v_E^A} \qquad \text{and} \qquad MS_U^A = \frac{SS_U^A}{v_U^A}$$

Step 8. Compute

$$F = \frac{MS_E^A}{MS_U^A}$$

and reject

$$H_0: \mu_{Y(1)}^A = \mu_{Y(2)}^A = \cdots = \mu_{Y(K)}^A$$

if

$$F > F_{v_1, v_2 : 1-\alpha}$$

where $v_1 = K - 1$ and $v_2 = N - K - 1$.

test the hypothesis that all contrasts in the adjusted population means are zero, against the alternative which states that at least one contrast is not zero. Therefore complex as well as simple contrasts can be examined, and standard contrast procedures may be applied to the adjusted means. This generalization is, indeed, valid for all the models presented except for Tukey's method. Tukey's method is excluded, because the standard errors for pairwise com-

---

Box 43-4 Procedure for analyzing contrasts among covariate adjusted means

Step 1. Compute

$$\bar{Y}^A_{.1}, \bar{Y}^A_{.2}, \ldots, \bar{Y}^A_{.K}$$
$$\bar{X}_{.1}, \bar{X}_{.2}, \ldots, \bar{X}_{.K}$$

and

$$MS^A_U$$

Step 2. Compute

$$\hat{\psi} = \sum_{k=1}^{K} W_k \bar{Y}^A_{.k}$$

and

$$SE^2_{\hat{\psi}} = MS^A_U \left[\sum_{k=1}^{K} \frac{W_k^2}{N_k} + \frac{\hat{\psi}_X^2}{SS_{W(X)}} \right]$$

where

$$\hat{\psi}_X = \sum_{k=1}^{K} W_k \bar{X}_{.k}$$

Step 3. Reject

$$H_0: \psi = 0$$

if

$$t = \frac{\hat{\psi}}{SE_{\hat{\psi}}}$$

is in the critical region defined by the value of Table A-11, if C comparisons are planned, or by S, if the contrasts are performed post hoc, where $S = \sqrt{(K-1)F_{K-1,N-K-1:1-\alpha}}$.

parisons are not equal across all comparisons. We provide directions in Box 43-4 for performing comparisons of adjusted averages.

As an example, an examination of the data suggests that the adjusted means of English and history differ from those of business administration and engineering. Thus, the contrast of interest would be given by

$$\hat{\psi} = (^{11}\!/\!_{21}\overline{Y}^A_{.1} + ^{10}\!/\!_{21}\overline{Y}^A_{.2}) - (^{14}\!/\!_{26}\overline{Y}^A_{.4} + ^{12}\!/\!_{26}\overline{Y}^A_{.5})$$

We need to calculate the value of this contrast as well as the value of the same contrast on the X means. Thus,

$$\hat{\psi} = {}^{11}\!/\!_{21}(538) + {}^{10}\!/\!_{21}(529) - {}^{14}\!/\!_{26}(606) - {}^{12}\!/\!_{26}(579) = -59.82$$

and

$$\hat{\psi}_X = {}^{11}\!/\!_{21}(454) + {}^{10}\!/\!_{21}(518) - {}^{14}\!/\!_{26}(600) - {}^{12}\!/\!_{26}(577) = -104.91$$

Using the value of MS^A_U and $\mathrm{SS}_{X(W)}$, we get for the squared standard error

$$\mathrm{SE}^2_{\hat{\psi}} = 5292\left(\frac{(^{11}\!/\!_{21})^2}{11} + \frac{(^{10}\!/\!_{21})^2}{10} + \frac{(-^{14}\!/\!_{26})^2}{14} + \frac{(-^{12}\!/\!_{26})^2}{12} + \frac{(-104.91)^2}{775,670}\right)$$

$$= 530.6275$$

Hence

$$t = \frac{-59.82}{\sqrt{530.6275}} = -2.60$$

Thus, since

$$S = \sqrt{5(2.37)} = 3.44$$

we do not reject the null hypothesis that the adjusted population means are equal.

43-6. ANALYSIS OF COVARIANCE AND BLOCKING

One often hears that the analysis of covariance should not be used whenever the covariate means $\overline{X}_1, \overline{X}_2, \ldots, \overline{X}_K$ are essentially equal, since adjustment to a common value accomplishes little, and that it should be used whenever there are large differences in the covariate means for the converse reason. These situations are illustrated in Figures 43-3 and 43-4. In fact, just the opposite is true. This is easy to show by examining the squared standard error

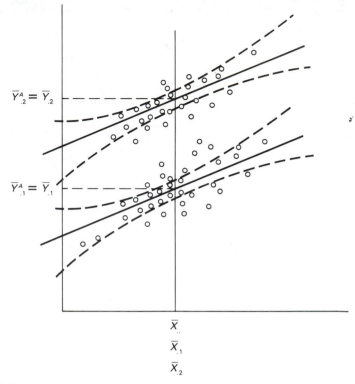

Figure 43-3.
Case where ANCOVA is most favorable: $\overline{X}_1 = \overline{X}_2$.

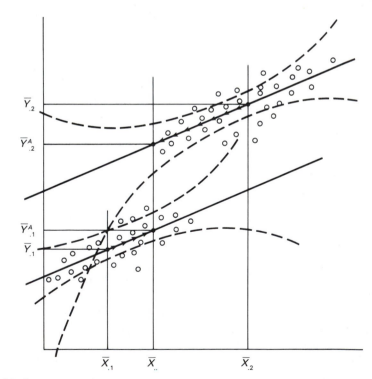

Figure 43-4.
Case where ANCOVA is least favorable: $\overline{X}_1 \neq \overline{X}_2$.

of the difference in two adjusted values. For $\psi = \mu_{.1}^A - \mu_{.2}^A$, we know that

$$\text{SE}_\psi^2 = \text{MS}_U^A \left[\frac{1}{N_1} + \frac{1}{N_2} + \frac{(\overline{X}_1 - \overline{X}_2)^2}{\text{SS}_{W(X)}} \right]$$

We see that SE_ψ^2 increases as MS_U^A and $(\overline{X}_1 - \overline{X}_2)^2$ increase.

Thus, the squared standard error will be smallest for situations in which both MS_U^A and $(\overline{X}_1 - \overline{X}_2)^2$ are small. Most important, MS_U^A will be small if a substantial correlation exists between Y and X. This was true in our example, and we saw that MS_U^A was approximately 63 percent of $\text{MS}_{W(Y)}$. As we saw, however, the F ratio did not increase accordingly. This was due to the large differences among the X means.

Another point needs to be made about the relationship of the covariate and the independent variable. The covariate cannot be dependent on the independent variable. For example, suppose a researcher decides to compare the weight loss of male and female subjects. Both groups are given the same diet. The subjects would be weighed at the beginning and end of the study. We wish to test whether the adjusted means of the men and women on the posttest are the same, after we adjust for pretest differences.

Since men are generally heavier than women, we would not be a bit surprised to learn that, on the pretest, $\overline{X}_M > \overline{X}_F$. To some, this would signal the need for an ANCOVA. To perform it would be wrong, because the covariate, pretest weight, is highly correlated with the independent variable, sex. In the context of this example, several outcomes could arise, depending on how pretest weight is related to sex and on how the posttest weight relates to pretest weight within the male and female groups. In the analysis of this design, ANCOVA could indicate a spuriously large effect, even when there is none. Let us assume that the results of this experiment are as shown in Figure 43-5. The fact that the points lie along the line $Y = X$ indicates that there was *no* weight loss, and the diet would be considered equally ineffective for both groups. The adjusted means, however, seem to indicate otherwise. One might be tempted to conclude, invalidly, that the females, weighing less than the males after correction, lost much more weight than the males. The correct solution is to analyze the data as a gender $\times$ diet two-factor ANOVA, discussed in Chapter 40, involving the two genders (male, female) and two experimental conditions (diet, no diet) and to use *weight loss* as the dependent variable.

If the regression lines are not linear, if they are not parallel, if homoscedasticity is not satisfied, and if the residuals are not normal, then the ANCOVA model cannot be justified. These assumptions are used to obtain the sampling distribution of F under H_0. The homoscedasticity and normality assumptions are still required to justify the use of randomized blocks. Blocking, however, is appropriate for nonlinear regressions and for the case in which the lines are not parallel. Note that the method of adjusted averages can be applied with unequal sample sizes. In addition, it is valid for unequal cell variances and

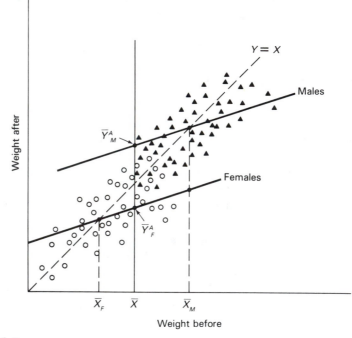

Figure 43-5.
Invalid use of ANCOVA.

might, in some cases, be usable when homoscedasticity is violated in ANCOVA. If one has a choice between covariance analysis and blocking, the choice should favor covariance if r_{XY} is greater than 0.6, for in those cases the analysis of covariance will exhibit greater power. When r_{XY} is less than 0.4, the randomized block design is preferred. Between these two values, the choice is unclear; both methods seem to do equally well.

43-7. CHANGE SCORE ANALYSIS

Another model used to achieve statistical control is to use difference scores similar to those of the matched-pair sign, Wilcoxon, or *t* test, provided the first and second measurements use the same metric. The analysis reduces to an analysis of variance on the difference, or *change, scores.* Planned and post hoc procedures can be used on the change scores directly. The diet study of Section 43-8 is best analyzed in terms of change scores; however, it can also be treated as a repeated-measures design in which the between-group factor is gender and the within-group factor is trial. The test of the gender effect is given by the interaction test of gender and trials. [See Levin and Marascuilo (1972) for a discussion of this similarity.]

43-8. APPENDIX

To obtain the formula for the within-group slope, recall that for the kth group the slope can be written as

$$B_{1(k)} = r_{XY(k)} \frac{S_{Y(k)}}{S_{X(k)}}$$

If we multiply the right side of this equation by $S_{X(k)}/S_{X(k)}$, we have

$$B_{1(k)} = \frac{r_{XY(k)} S_{Y(k)} S_{X(k)}}{S_{X(k)}^2} = \frac{S_{XY(k)}}{S_{X(k)}^2}$$

or the ratio of the covariance between Y and X to the variance of X. If we multiply the numerator and denominator by $N_k - 1$, we see that $B_{1(k)}$ can be written as

$$B_{1(k)} = \frac{(N_k - 1)S_{XY(k)}}{(N_k - 1)S_{X(k)}^2}$$

We have seen the denominator many times; it is the sum of the squared X deviations in the sample. Similarly, recalling that the covariance $S_{XY(k)}$ can be written as

$$S_{XY(k)} = \frac{\sum_{i=1}^{N_k} (X_{ik} - \overline{X}_{.k})(Y_{ik} - \overline{Y}_{.k})}{N_k - 1}$$

we see that the numerator is the sum of the product of the X and Y deviations in the sample, called the *sum of cross products*. Thus, the slope equals the ratio of the sum of cross products to the sum of squared X deviations.

Finally, recall that when we defined the combined estimate of the common population variance, the numerator was the combined sum of squared deviations and the denominator was the combined degrees of freedom. With a similar logic, it makes sense in the present context to estimate the common population slope as the ratio of the *pooled* sum of cross products to the pooled sum of squared X deviations. This estimate is called the *pooled within-group slope $B_{1(W)}$*. This weighted slope is given by

$$B_{1(W)} = \frac{\sum_{k=1}^{K} (N_k - 1)S_{XY(k)}}{\sum_{k=1}^{K} (N_k - 1)S_{X(k)}^2} = \frac{\sum_{k=1}^{K} W_k B_{1(k)}}{\sum_{k=1}^{K} W_k}$$

where $W_k = (N_k - 1)S_{X(k)}^2$. The pooled within-group slope is a weighted average of the $B_{1(k)}$. Notice that these weights involve both the sample size and the variance for each group. It is reasonable to weight more heavily a slope we think is more accurate than one that is less accurate. The larger the sample size and the more widely spread the X values, the more accurate the line is in estimating the population line. This is reflected in our weights.

To obtain the sum of squares for ANCOVA, consider the total deviation $d_{T(ik)}$ for the ith observation in group k, as computed with respect to the value predicted by the total line, defined by $\hat{Y}_{T(ik)}$. This deviation is

$$d_{T(ik)} = Y_{ik} - \hat{Y}_{T(ik)} = Y_{ik} - \overline{Y}_{..} - B_{1(T)}(X_{ik} - \overline{X}_{..})$$

If we square these deviations and add across the entire set of samples, we have the *adjusted sum of squares total* SS_T^A:

$$SS_T^A = \sum_{k=1}^{K} \sum_{i=1}^{N_k} (Y_{ik} - \overline{Y}_{..})^2 - B_{1(T)}^2 \sum_{k=1}^{K} \sum_{i=1}^{N_k} (X_{ik} - \overline{X}_{..})^2$$
$$= SS_{T(Y)} - B_{1(T)}^2 SS_{T(X)}$$

In the analysis of variance, we determine the unexplained deviations for an observation by comparing each value to the mean of its own group. Here, we find the unexplained deviation $d_{U(ik)}$ by comparing the observation to the regression line in its own group, under the assumption that the lines are parallel. This latter deviation is given by

$$d_{U(ik)} = Y_{ik} - \hat{Y}_{ik} = Y_{ik} - \overline{Y}_{.k} - B_{1(W)}(X_{ik} - \overline{X}_{.k})$$

If we square these deviations and add across the entire set of samples, we have the *adjusted sum of squares unexplained* SS_U^A:

$$SS_U^A = \sum_{k=1}^{K} \sum_{i=1}^{N_k} (Y_{ik} - \overline{Y}_{.k})^2 - B_{1(W)}^2 \sum_{k=1}^{K} \sum_{i=1}^{N_k} (X_{ik} - \overline{X}_{.k})^2$$
$$= SS_{W(Y)} - B_{1(W)}^2 SS_{W(X)}$$

Finally, in a similar way, we could define the explained deviation and the *adjusted sum of squares explained* SS_E^A. It is much simpler, however, to obtain this value by subtraction:

$$SS_E^A = SS_T^A - SS_U^A$$

Examining the formulas for SS_T^A and SS_U^A, we see that the remaining values needed to complete our calculations may be obtained by performing a one-factor ANOVA on the Y and X variables.

43-9. EXERCISES

In a study in which a new reading program was tested in five different schools, a pretest for which the mean score was 50 and the standard deviation was 10 was given to all students. After 30 weeks of training, all students were given a posttest. The results are as shown :

| | Control program | | Experimental program | | |
| | School 1 | School 2 | School 3 | School 4 | School 5 |
Pretest	Mean Number SD	Mean Number SD	Mean Number SD	Mean Number SD	Mean Number SD
Less than 40	38.2 10 3.6	37.6 20 2.9	39.3 15 1.9	40.1 6 3.6	40.6 7 6.1
40 to 49	46.3 6 4.2	49.1 8 4.3	50.2 20 2.3	49.8 12 3.0	50.3 13 5.2
50 to 59	55.6 8 4.7	53.7 3 5.1	52.6 12 4.4	59.9 15 3.9	59.3 14 3.9
60 and over	60.2 13 5.8	58.7 7 6.2	63.6 9 6.9	64.5 8 4.2	66.2 10 6.2

43-1. Determine the unadjusted mean for each school. Explain what is seen.

43-2. Set up a standard population with $N_1 = 16$, $N_2 = 34$, $N_3 = 34$, and $N_4 = 16$. Determine the adjusted mean for each school. Explain what is seen.

43-3. Determine the standard error for the adjusted means for each school.

43-4. Set up five meaningful contrasts, and test them for significance with a family error rate of $\alpha = .05$.

43-5. Perform a nested ANOVA on these data in which program is nested in each level of pre-test grouping. In each nest examine the five contrasts of Exercise 43-4.

43-6. Of these models, which do you prefer? Why?

43-7. In Section 8-2 the regression line for the data of Table 7-1 was found to be given by $\hat{Y} = 25.08 + 1.15X$. In deviation form, $Y = \bar{Y} + B(X - \bar{X}) = 46.05 + 1.15(X - 18.20)$. Find the adjusted score for subjects whose $X = 10, 20,$ or 30.

43-8. For your sample of $N = 40$ subjects, perform an analysis of covariance on major with final used as the dependent variable and pretest score used as the covariate. Eliminate the other and unknown responses.

43-9. Even if H_0 of Exercise 43-8 is not rejected, perform a post hoc analysis on the adjusted means.

43-10. A study was designed to determine the effects of a modified programmed lecture (treatment A) and a mathematical game approach (treatment B) in instructing the summer school underperformer in ninth-grade general mathematics. The following statistical hypothesis was subjected to statistical test.

Alternative hypothesis: Summer school underperformers in ninth-grade mathematics will show greater gains in performance on the cooperative arithmetic test when their instructional program has used a mathematical game approach than when it has used a modified programmed lecture approach.

Thirty-four students were used as subjects. These students were told only that they were attending summer school to make up their academic deficiencies. The students were randomly assigned to treatment groups $A(n_A = 17)$ and $B(n_B = 17)$. The grade placement score (GPS) data on the cooperative arithmetic test (national norms) were used to evaluate academic gain during the summer session. The data are shown at right.

a. Submit these data to a group × trial repeated-measures analysis.
b. Submit these data to an analysis of covariance where the covariate is the pretest.
c. Compute difference scores and perform a two-sample t test. Compare and contrast the three methods.
d. Which method would you recommend? Why?

43-11. Analyze the data of Table 43-3, using as planned contrasts the comparisons of Section 42-2. Use the verbal scores as a covariate.

GPS data for classroom A		GPS data for classroom B	
Pretest	Posttest	Pretest	Posttest
6.1	5.8	6.2	8.3
6.2	6.2	6.2	9.0
6.2	7.7	6.2	9.0
6.2	6.4	6.2	8.8
6.3	7.6	6.2	8.6
6.3	6.3	6.3	7.7
6.3	7.7	6.5	9.5
6.5	6.2	6.5	7.7
6.5	7.6	7.0	9.5
6.5	8.0	7.0	10.8
6.5	8.0	7.0	7.7
7.0	8.0	7.0	9.8
7.4	8.5	7.0	10.5
7.5	8.5	7.4	7.4
7.7	8.5	7.6	9.9
8.3	9.5	8.3	11.7
8.5	10.2	8.6	13.0

CHAPTER 44

Procedures for Linear Regression Coefficients

44-1. METHODS FOR THE SLOPE OF A LINEAR REGRESSION EQUATION

We saw in Chapter 8 that the sample correlation coefficient and the slope of a regression line were related by

$$B_1 = r_{XY} \frac{S_Y}{S_X}$$

The population parameters that these sample statistics estimate are related to one another in a parallel fashion; that is,

$$\beta_1 = \rho_{XY} \frac{\sigma_Y}{\sigma_X}$$

Because of this relationship, the only way (except for the unlikely case that we have a zero population standard deviation) that β_1 could equal zero would be if ρ_{XY} equaled zero. Hence, we see that a test of $H_0: \rho_{XY} = 0$ must be identical to the test of $H_0: \beta_1 = 0$.

In Section 32-7, we saw that the test of $H_0: \rho_{XY} = 0$ was performed by using the t distribution and the test statistic

$$t = \frac{r_{XY}\sqrt{N-2}}{\sqrt{1-r_{XY}^2}}$$

which, under H_0, was distributed as a t variable with $\nu = N - 2$ degrees of freedom. Because of the identity of the two hypotheses involving β_1 and ρ_{XY}, we could use this one test statistic to examine both hypotheses. Nevertheless, the test of $H_0: \beta_1 = 0$ is often performed by using the sample B_1 directly. This test is easy to derive, and we will do so. In addition, through this derivation we also derive the standard error of B_1, which is useful in setting up confidence intervals for β_1 and in testing the equality of two or more population slopes, one of the major assumptions of the analysis of covariance.

The test statistic for $H_0: \rho_{XY} = 0$ can be manipulated to yield an expression involving B_1. Beginning with

$$t = \frac{r_{XY}\sqrt{N-2}}{\sqrt{1-r_{XY}^2}}$$

we see that the slope of B_1 can be introduced by multiplying numerator and denominator by S_Y/S_X:

$$t = \frac{\sqrt{N-2}\; r_{XY}\, S_Y/S_X}{\sqrt{1-r_{XY}^2}\, S_Y/S_X} = \frac{\sqrt{N-2}\; B_1}{\sqrt{1-r_{XY}^2}\, S_Y/S_X}$$

Because t can be written as the value of a variable divided by its standard error, we have

$$SE_{B_1} = \frac{S_Y}{S_X}\sqrt{\frac{1-r_{XY}^2}{N-2}}$$

We apply this statistic to test $H_0: \beta_1 = 0$ for the data of Table 7-1, whose summary statistics appear in Table 44-1.

For these data

$$B_1 = 1.15 \qquad S_Y = 15.60 \qquad S_X = 7.51 \qquad r_{XY} = 0.55 \qquad N = 39$$

With these values,

$$SE_{B_1} = \frac{15.60}{7.51}\sqrt{\frac{1-0.55^2}{39-2}} = 0.2852$$

Table 44-1. Statistics based on data of Table 7-1

Statistic	X	Y
Sum	710	1,796
Sum of squares	15,066	91,952
Mean	18.21	46.05
Standard deviation	7.51	15.60
Correlation coefficient	.55	

so that

$$t = \frac{1.15}{0.2852} = 4.03$$

Except for rounding errors, this is the same value as that reported in Section 32-7.

A $1 - \alpha$ percent confidence interval for β_1 is given by

$$B_1 + t_{v:\alpha/2}SE_{B_1} < \beta_1 < B_1 + t_{v:1-\alpha/2}SE_{B_1}$$

Box 44-1 **Procedure for testing $H_0: \beta_1 = 0$ and $H_0: \beta_1 = \beta_{10}$**

Step 1. Determine B_1, S_Y, S_X, N, and r_{XY}, and compute

$$SE_{B_1} = \frac{S_Y}{S_X}\sqrt{\frac{1 - r_{XY}^2}{N - 2}}$$

Step 2. To test $H_0: \beta_1 = 0$, determine

$$t = \frac{B_1}{SE_{B_1}}$$

Step 3. Reject H_0 if $t < t_{v:\alpha/2}$ or if $t > t_{v:1-\alpha/2}$, where $v = N - 2$. If the alternative hypothesis is directional, place the entire risk of a type I error in the appropriate tail of the t distribution.

Step 4. If H_0 is rejected, determine a $1 - \alpha$ percent confidence interval for β_1 as

$$\beta_1 = B_1 \pm t_{v:\alpha/2}SE_{B_1}$$

Step 5. To test $H_0: E(B_1) = \beta_{10}$, replace the test statistic of step 2 with

$$t = \frac{B_1 - \beta_{10}}{SE_{B_1}}$$

For this example, $v = N - 2 = 39 - 2 = 37$, with $t_{37:.025} = -2.02$ and $t_{37:.975} = 2.02$, so that

$$1.15 - 2.02(0.2852) < \beta_1 < 1.15 + 2.02(0.2852)$$

$$0.57 < \beta_1 < 1.73$$

In Box 44-1, we provide directions for testing $H_0: \beta_1 = 0$ and for testing $H_0: \beta_1 = \beta_{10}$, where β_{10} is specified in advance of data collection and represents a value of theoretical or practical interest. The test described in step 5 is not encountered too frequently and is presented only for completeness.

44-2. METHODS FOR THE INTERCEPT OF A LINEAR REGRESSION EQUATION

The tests of $H_0: \beta_0 = 0$ and $H_0: E(B_0) = \beta_{00}$ parallel those of the previous section for β_1. For these tests one uses

$$t = \frac{B_0}{SE_{B_0}} \quad \text{or} \quad t = \frac{B_0 - \beta_{00}}{SE_{B_0}}$$

Since $B_0 = \overline{Y} - B_1\overline{X}$, it is not surprising that the standard errors of B_0 and B_1 are related. In particular,

$$SE_{B_0} = \sqrt{\frac{\sum_{i=1}^{N} X_i^2}{N}} \, SE_{B_1}$$

For these tests, $v = N - 2$. We provide directions in Box 44-2 for testing $H_0: \beta_0 = 0$ and $H_0: E(B_0) = \beta_{00}$, where β_{00} is some particular value of interest. For the data of Table 44-1, $B_0 = 25.08$ and

$$\sum_{i=1}^{N} X_i^2 = 15,066$$

so that

$$SE_{B_0} = \sqrt{\frac{15,066}{39}} \, (0.2852) = 5.6055$$

and a test of $H_0: \beta_0 = 0$ yields a test statistic

$$t = \frac{25.08}{5.6055} = 4.47$$

Box 44-2   Procedure for testing $H_0 : \beta_0 = 0$ and $H_0 : E(B_0) = \beta_{00}$

Step 1. Determine B_0, N, SE_{B_1}, and $\sum_{i=1}^{N} X_i^2$, and compute

$$SE_{B_0} = \sqrt{\frac{\sum_{i=1}^{N} X_i^2}{N}} \, (SE_{B_1})$$

Step 2. To test $H_0 : \beta_0 = 0$, determine

$$t = \frac{B_0}{SE_{B_0}}$$

Step 3. Reject H_0 if $t < t_{v:\alpha/2}$ or if $t > t_{v:1-\alpha/2}$, where $v = N - 2$. If the alternative is directional, place the entire risk of a type I error in the appropriate tail of the t distribution.

Step 4. If H_0 is rejected, determine a $1 - \alpha$ percent confidence interval for β_0 as

$$\beta_0 = B_0 \pm t_{v:\alpha/2} SE_{B_0}$$

Step 5. To test $H_0 : E(B_0) = \beta_{00}$, replace the test statistic of step 2 with

$$t = \frac{B_0 - \beta_{00}}{SE_{B_0}}$$

Since $t > 2.02$, H_0 is rejected and the 95 percent confidence interval for β_0 is given by

$$\beta_0 = 25.08 \pm 2.02(5.6055)$$
$$= 25.08 \pm 11.32$$

44-3. MULTIPLE COMPARISONS AMONG THE SLOPES OF K REGRESSION LINES

In Section 34-3 we defined an interaction between two qualitative variables in terms of a contrast involving four mean values. If one takes a second look at Figure 34-1, clearly the existence of no interaction implies that the two line segments are *parallel*. If the line segments are not parallel, then an interaction is said to exist. This same model applies to interactions involving a qualitative variable with a quantitative variable.

Consider the data of Table 44-2, shown graphically in Figure 44-1. In this study a group of children were randomly assigned to three teaching conditions, which constitute levels of the independent variable in the study. The conditions are as follows:

Table 44-2. Sample statistics based on three independent groups of students given three different training models

Statistic	Group 1		Group 2		Group 3	
	X	Y	X	Y	X	Y
Mean	56.1	58.3	52.3	57.6	51.7	69.2
Standard deviation	8.3	10.1	7.9	11.3	8.2	12.2
Correlation coefficient	.47		.56		.71	
Slope	0.57		0.80		1.06	
Intercept	26.32		15.76		14.40	
MS_R	81.81		91.02		76.35	
Sample size	36		28		31	

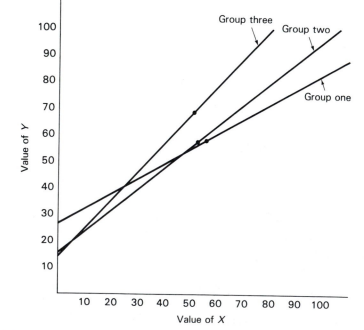

Figure 44-1.
Regression lines for the data of Table 44-2.

1. Thirty-six subjects were trained by using a traditional method of teaching the addition of fractions.
2. Twenty-eight subjects were trained by using hand calculators, again with the traditional method.
3. Thirty-one subjects were trained by using hand calculators and a new method employing colored pictures and diagrams as teaching aids.

The dependent variable of the study is defined as

$$Y = \text{scores on an arithmetic test given 10 weeks after the}$$
$$\text{introduction of training}$$

A second independent variable in this study is an aptitude measure defined as

$$X = \text{scores on an arithmetic test given before training}$$

The hypothesis of the study, stated in its null form, involves the interaction of training with aptitude and is given by

$$H_0: \text{initial level of performance does not interact with training}$$

In other words, the null hypothesis states that the difference in subjects' performances from one treatment to another will not depend on their initial performance level. In its statistical form, H_0 can be stated as

$$H_0: \beta_{1(1)} = \beta_{1(2)} = \beta_{1(3)}$$

where $\beta_{1(k)}$ is the slope relating Y to X in the kth population. This is an omnibus hypothesis for which the correct alternative is

$$H_1: H_0 \text{ is false}$$

As with all omnibus hypotheses, there are an infinite number of contrasts of the form

$$\psi = W_1 \beta_{1(1)} + W_2 \beta_{1(2)} + W_3 \beta_{1(3)}$$

where $W_1 + W_2 + W_3 = 0$, which can be investigated for significance. In this study, it makes sense to examine only a small subset of the possible contrasts, such as

$$\psi_{12} = \beta_{1(1)} - \beta_{1(2)}$$
$$\psi_{13} = \beta_{1(1)} - \beta_{1(3)}$$
$$\psi_{23} = \beta_{1(2)} - \beta_{1(3)}$$

for significance. These planned contrasts can be examined under one of two models, depending on which seems appropriate. The two models assume either equal or unequal variances among the groups. The equal-variance model leads to the use of multiple *t* tests, while the unequal-variance model leads to the use of multiple Welch-Aspin tests. We illustrate both models.

For the equal-variance model, we begin by estimating the common value of the unexplained variance. In regression analysis, it is customary to refer to this measure of unexplained variance as the *residual variance,* or the *mean square residual.* We denote this MS_R. It is called a *residual variance* because it represents the variance in Y that is not explainable by the relationship between Y and X. In this sense, MS_R is referred to as the variance in Y with effects of X partialed out. As shown in Section 9-2, each $d_{Ui} = Y_i - \hat{Y}_i$ represents a deviation between an observed Y value and its predicted value, where the predicted value represents an estimate of the average Y for people with a particular X score. Thus SS_U represents a sum of squared deviations about an average, similar to that used to define the variance of a sample. In this case the average is the line. Thus, if SS_U were to be divided by its appropriate degrees of freedom, we could compute the variance of the Y values in terms of their fluctuations about the best-fitting straight line.

As we recall, each $Y_i - \hat{Y}_i$ was computed after B_0 and B_1 were estimated from the data. Therefore the complete set of $Y_i - \hat{Y}_i$ values are restricted by the specific values taken on by B_0 and B_1. Change B_0 and B_1, and each $Y_i - \hat{Y}_i$ changes, because each depends on the values assumed by B_0 and B_1. This implies that MS_R is based on $v = N - 2$ degrees of freedom and not $N - 1$, as is the case for S_Y^2, where the deviations depend only on the single value of $\bar{Y}$. For the data of Table 44-1, based on Table 9-7, SS_U was reported in Section 9-2 as 6402.51, so that $MS_R = 6402.51/(39 - 2) = 173.04$. In terms of MS_R, the squared standard error of B_1 can be written as

$$SE_{B_1}^2 = \frac{MS_R}{SS_X} = \frac{MS_R}{(N-1)S_X^2} = \frac{MS_R}{W}$$

In the case of *multiple* linear regressions, and under the assumption of equal variances, the pooled MS_R is

$$MS_R = \frac{SS_{U(1)} + SS_{U(2)} + \cdots + SS_{U(K)}}{(N_1 - 2) + (N_2 - 2) + \cdots + (N_K - 2)}$$
$$= \frac{(N_1 - 2)MS_{R(1)} + (N_2 - 2)MS_{R(2)} + \cdots + (N_K - 2)MS_{R(K)}}{(N_1 - 2) + (N_2 - 2) + \cdots + (N_K - 2)}$$

We see that the numerator of the pooled MS_R is the sum of the unexplained sums of squares from the separate groups, whereas the denominator equals the sum of the separate groups' degrees of freedom. For our example, with

$K = 3$,

$$MS_R = \frac{34(81.81) + 26(91.02) + 29(76.35)}{34 + 26 + 29} = 83.72$$

This estimate is based on

$$\nu = \nu_1 + \nu_2 + \nu_3 = 34 + 26 + 29 = 89$$

degrees of freedom. With $\alpha = .05$, $C = 3$, and $\nu = 89$, the critical values for the three planned contrasts are given by $t_{.05:3,89}^{\text{Dunn}} = 2.45$. With the pooled estimate of the variance, the test of $H_0: \beta_{1(1)} = \beta_{1(2)}$ is given by

$$t_{12} = \frac{\hat{\psi}_{12}}{SE_{\hat{\psi}_{12}}} = \frac{B_{1(1)} - B_{1(2)}}{\sqrt{SE_{B_{1(1)}}^2 + SE_{B_{1(2)}}^2}}$$

$$= \frac{B_{1(1)} - B_{1(2)}}{\sqrt{MS_R/W_1 + MS_R/W_2}}$$

where

$$W_1 = (N_1 - 1)S_{X(1)}^2 \text{ and } W_2 = (N_2 - 1)S_{X(2)}^2$$

For these data, $W_1 = (36 - 1)(8.3)^2 = 2411.15$ and $W_2 = (28 - 1)(7.9)^2 = 1685.07$, so that

$$t_{12} = \frac{0.57 - 0.80}{\sqrt{83.72/2411.15 + 83.72/1685.07}} = \frac{-0.23}{0.29} = -0.79$$

The hypothesis $H_0: \beta_{1(1)} - \beta_{1(2)} = 0$ is not rejected. For the remaining two contrasts, $W_3 = (31 - 1)(8.2)^2 = 2017.20$, so that $t_{13} = -1.75$ and $t_{23} = -0.87$ are not in the critical region, and the hypotheses $H_0: \beta_{1(1)} - \beta_{1(3)} = 0$ and $H_0: \beta_{1(2)} - \beta_{1(3)} = 0$ are not rejected.

Because there is no evidence of a treatment by aptitude interaction, we might wish to estimate the *pooled within-group slope*. This was defined in Chapter 43 as

$$B_{1(W)} = \frac{W_1 B_{1(1)} + W_2 B_{1(2)} + W_3 B_{1(3)}}{W_1 + W_2 + W_3}$$

For these data

$$B_{1(W)} = \frac{(2411.15)(0.57) + (1685.07)(0.80) + (2017.20)(1.06)}{2411.15 + 1685.07 + 2017.20}$$

$$= \frac{4860.64}{6113.42} = 0.79$$

The squared standard error of this estimate is

$$SE^2_{B_{1(W)}} = \frac{MS_R}{W_1 + W_2 + W_3} = \frac{MS_R}{W}$$

where W is the pooled within-group sum of squares for the covariate. Here

$$SE^2_{B_{1(W)}} = \frac{83.72}{6113.42} = 0.0137$$

With these values,

$$t = \frac{B_{1(W)}}{SE_{B_{1(W)}}} = \frac{0.79}{0.12} = 6.58$$

With $v = 89$ degrees of freedom at $\alpha = .05$, the hypothesis $H_0: \beta_{1(W)} = 0$ is rejected.

The 95 percent confidence interval for $\beta_{1(W)}$ is

$$\begin{aligned} \beta_{1(W)} &= B_{1(W)} \pm t_{v:\alpha/2} SE_{B_{1(W)}} \\ &= 0.79 \pm 1.99 \sqrt{0.0137} \\ &= 0.79 \pm 0.23 \end{aligned}$$

For the Welch-Aspin model, the t^* statistic for the test of $H_0: \beta_{1(1)} - \beta_{1(2)} = 0$ is given by

$$\begin{aligned} t^*_{12} &= \frac{B_{1(1)} - B_{1(2)}}{\sqrt{MS_{R(1)}/W_1 + MS_{R(2)}/W_2}} \\ &= \frac{0.57 - 0.80}{\sqrt{81.81/2411.15 + 91.02/1685.07}} = \frac{-0.23}{0.30} = -0.77 \end{aligned}$$

The remaining values are given by $t^*_{13} = -1.81$ and $t^*_{23} = -0.87$. The degrees of freedom for t^*_{12} are found from

$$\frac{1}{v^*_{12}} = \frac{1}{v_1}\left(1 - \frac{W^*_1}{W^*}\right)^2 + \frac{1}{v_2}\left(1 - \frac{W^*_2}{W^*}\right)^2$$

where

$$W^*_1 = \frac{W_1}{MS_{R(1)}} \qquad W^*_2 = \frac{W_2}{MS_{R(2)}} \qquad W^* = W^*_1 + W^*_2$$

For these data

$$W_1^* = \frac{2411.15}{81.81} = 29.47$$

$$W_2^* = \frac{1685.07}{91.02} = 18.51$$

$$W^* = 29.47 + 18.51 = 47.98$$

so that

$$\frac{1}{v_{12}^*} = \frac{1}{34}\left(1 - \frac{29.47}{47.98}\right)^2 + \frac{1}{26}\left(1 - \frac{18.51}{47.98}\right)^2 = 0.0189$$

and

$$v_{12}^* = 52.9 \approx 52$$

The remaining values are $v_{13}^* = 61$ and $v_{23}^* = 52$. With these values, critical values for $\alpha = .05$ and $C = 3$ are read from Table A-11. The corresponding decision rules are as follows:

1. Reject H_0 if $t_{12}^* < -2.49$ or if $t_{12}^* > 2.49$.
2. Reject H_0 if $t_{13}^* < -2.47$ or if $t_{13}^* > 2.47$.
3. Reject H_0 if $t_{23}^* < -2.49$ or if $t_{23}^* > 2.49$.

None of the hypotheses is rejected. We provide directions in Box 44-3 for making pairwise comparisons among slopes of K regression lines.

Box 44-3   Procedure for making multiple comparisons among K regression slopes

Step 1. Count the number of comparisons to be made. Let the number be C.
Step 2. Decide upon the equal-variance model or the unequal-variance model.
Step 3. For the equal-variance model, compute

$$MS_R = \frac{(N_1 - 2)MS_{R(1)} + (N_2 - 2)MS_{R(2)} + \cdots + (N_K - 2)MS_{R(K)}}{(N_1 - 2) + (N_2 - 2) + \cdots + (N_K - 2)}$$

Step 4. Compute

$$W_1 = (N_1 - 1)S_{X(1)}^2, \ldots, W_K = (N_K - 1)S_{X(K)}^2$$

and

$$W = W_1 + W_2 + \cdots + W_K$$

Step 5. Compute, for $k < k'$,

$$t_{kk'} = \frac{B_{1(k)} - B_{1(k')}}{\sqrt{MS_R/W_k + MS_R/W_{k'}}}.$$

or

$$t_{kk'}^{*} = \frac{B_{1(k)} - B_{1(k')}}{\sqrt{MS_{R(k)}/W_k + MS_{R(k')}/W_{k'}}}$$

depending on the model adopted.

Step 6. For the equal-variance model, use $\nu = (N_1 - 2) + (N_2 - 2) + \cdots + (N_K - 2)$ degrees of freedom to enter Table A-11. Reject the hypotheses associated with $t_{kk'}$ if

$$t_{kk'} < t_{\alpha : C, \nu}^{\text{Dunn}} \qquad \text{or} \qquad t_{kk'} > t_{\alpha : C, \nu}^{\text{Dunn}}$$

For the Welch-Aspin model, compute ν^{*} from

$$\frac{1}{\nu_{kk'}^{*}} = \frac{1}{\nu_k}\left(1 - \frac{W_k^{*}}{W^{*}}\right)^2 + \frac{1}{\nu_{k'}}\left(1 - \frac{W_k^{*}}{W^{*}}\right)^2$$

where

$$W_k^{*} = \frac{W_k}{MS_{R(k)}}$$

and

$$W^{*} = W_k^{*} + W_{k'}^{*}$$

Use $\nu_{kk'}^{*}$ to enter Table A-11. Reject the hypothesis associated with $t_{kk'}^{*}$ if

$$t_{kk'}^{*} < t_{\alpha : C, \nu_{k,k'}^{*}}^{\text{Dunn}} \qquad \text{or} \qquad t_{kk'}^{*} > t_{\alpha : C, \nu_{k,k'}^{*}}^{\text{Dunn}}$$

Step 7. Determine confidence intervals of interest as

$$\beta_{1(k)} - \beta_{1(k')} = B_{1(k)} - B_{1(k')} \pm t_{\alpha : C, \nu}^{\text{Dunn}} \sqrt{\frac{MS_R}{W_k} + \frac{MS_R}{W_{k'}}}$$

for the equal-variance model or

$$\beta_{1(k)} - \beta_{1(k')} = B_{1(k)} - B_{1(k')} \pm t_{\alpha : C, \nu_{kk'}^{*}}^{\text{Dunn}} \sqrt{\frac{MS_{R(k)}}{W_k} + \frac{MS_{R(k')}}{W_{k'}}}$$

for the Welch-Aspin model.

44-4. CONFIDENCE INTERVAL FOR A REGRESSION LINE

Sometimes a researcher may want a $1 - \alpha$ percent confidence interval for the regression line, in order to specify the limits for the population line. We derive this confidence interval by first examining the confidence interval for Y at a particular value of $X = X_0$. The point estimate of Y_{X_0} is given from the regression equation as

$$\hat{Y}_{X_0} = B_0 + B_1 X_0 = \bar{Y} + B_1(X_0 - \bar{X})$$

The squared standard error of $\hat{Y}_{X_0}$ is given by

$$SE^2_{\hat{Y}_{X_0}} = SE^2_{\bar{Y}} + (X_0 - \bar{X})^2(SE^2_{B_1})$$
$$= \frac{MS_R}{N} + (X_0 - \bar{X})^2 \frac{MS_R}{W} = MS_R\left[\frac{1}{N} + \frac{(X_0 - \bar{X})^2}{W}\right]$$

where $W = (N - 1)S^2_X$.

When $X_0 = \bar{X}$, $SE^2_{\hat{Y}_{X_0}}$ reduces to MS_R/N which, for $r_{YX} \neq 0$, is less than S^2_Y/N; the confidence interval is narrower than that for the sample mean. Thus, a $1 - \alpha$ percent confidence interval for $E(\hat{Y}_{X_0})$ is

$$E(\hat{Y}_{X_0}) = B_0 + B_1 X_0 \pm t_{v:\alpha/2} SE_{\hat{Y}_{X_0}}$$

where $v = N - 2$ degrees of freedom.

For the data of Table 44-1, the standard error on the final for all students who earned a score of $X = 20$ on the pretest is

$$SE_{\hat{Y}_{20}} = 13.15 \sqrt{\frac{1}{39} + \frac{(20 - 18.21)^2}{15,066}} = 2.11$$

For $\alpha = .05$ and $t_{37:.025} = -2.02$, we have

$$E(\hat{Y}_{20}) = 25.08 + 1.15(20) \pm 2.02(2.11)$$
$$= 48.04 \pm 4.26$$

In Section 8-3, 10 students in the population had a score of $X_0 = 20$ on the pretest. Their mean on the final, for which the above is a confidence interval, was 49.7; this is a rare instance in which we can *know* that our confidence interval is true. We provide directions in Box 44-4 for obtaining a $1 - \alpha$ percent confidence interval for the expected value of Y at a fixed value of X.

Of greater interest, of course, is the evaluation of a confidence interval for the regression line over its entire range of values. We know that the position of the line is affected by changes in both B_0 and B_1. To specify the confidence interval for the population line, we have to try to capture the population's β_0 and β_1, simultaneously. Thus, a simple confidence interval based on the t

---

Box 44-4   Confidence interval for expected value of Y at $X = X_0$

Step 1. Estimate the mean value as

$$\hat{Y}_{X_0} = B_0 + B_1 X_0$$

Step 2. Determine the squared standard error as

$$SE^2_{\hat{Y}_{X_0}} = MS_R \left[\frac{1}{N} + \frac{(X_0 - \bar{X})^2}{W} \right]^2$$

Step 3. The $1 - \alpha$ percent confidence interval for the expected value of Y at X_0 is

$$E(\hat{Y}_{X_0}) = B_0 + B_1 X_0 \pm t_{\nu:\alpha/2} SE_{\hat{Y}_{X_0}}$$

where $\nu = N - 2$.

---

distribution will not work with two parameters. The Scheffé coefficient, however, based on the F distribution with 2 numerator degrees of freedom, yields the appropriate control of type I error rate. Thus, the $1 - \alpha$ percent confidence interval for the population regression line $\beta_0 + \beta_1 X$ is

$$\beta_0 + \beta_1 X = B_0 + B_1 X \pm S(SE_{\hat{Y}_X})$$

where

$$S = \sqrt{2F_{2,N-2:1-\alpha}}$$

and

$$SE^2_{\hat{Y}_X} = MS_R \left[\frac{1}{N} + \frac{(X - \bar{X})^2}{W} \right]$$

For the data of Table 44-1, we find

$$SE^2_{\hat{Y}_X} = 173.04 \left[\frac{1}{39} + \frac{(X - 18.21)^2}{15,066} \right]$$

and

$$S = \sqrt{2F_{2,37:.95}} = \sqrt{2(3.26)} = 2.55$$

so that

$$\beta_0 + \beta_1 X = 25.08 + 1.15X \pm 33.54 \sqrt{\frac{1}{39} + \frac{(X - 18.21)^2}{15,066}}$$

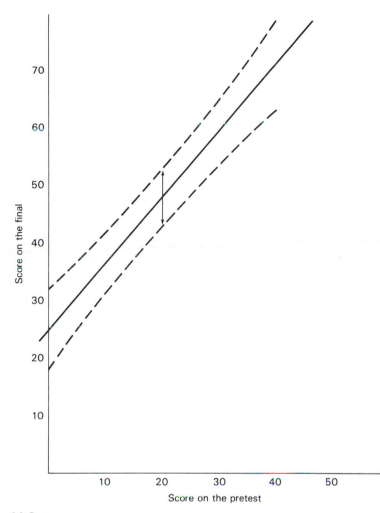

Figure 44-2.
The 95 percent confidence interval for the regression line based on the data of Table 44-1. Also shown is the 95 percent confidence interval for $X = 20$.

For $X = 0$, the limits for the confidence interval are given by

$$Y = \beta_0 + \beta_1 X = 25.08 + 1.15(0) \pm 33.54 \sqrt{\frac{1}{39} + \frac{(0 - 18.21)^2}{15{,}066}}$$

$$= 25.08 \pm 7.16$$

In like fashion, the limits for $X = 10$ are 36.58 ± 5.82; for $X = 18.21$, they are 46.05 ± 5.37; for $X = 30$, the limits are 59.58 ± 6.26; and for $X = 40$, the limits are 71.08 ± 8.02. These limits are shown in Figure 44-2, along with the curved lines that define the 95 percent confidence interval for the unknown population regression line. Note that the confidence band is at its narrowest point at $X = \overline{X} = 18.21$.

Box 44-5   Procedure for determining a $1 - \alpha$ percent confidence interval for a regression line

Step 1. Follow the steps for finding the confidence interval for Y at $X = X_0$, but do this for four or five values of X that cover the range of X values observed in the sample.

Step 2. Replace the t critical value by

$$S = \sqrt{2F_{2,N-2:1-\alpha}}$$

and plot the resulting limits:

$$Y = B_0 + B_1X + S(\text{SE}_{\hat{Y}_X})$$

where

$$\text{SE}^2_{\hat{Y}_X} = \text{MS}_R \left[\frac{1}{N} + \frac{(X - \overline{X})^2}{W} \right]$$

Step 3. Join the points to make a continuous curve extending over the range of interest.

Also, the band gets increasingly wider as X gets farther from $\overline{X}$. Beyond the observed range in the sample, the confidence intervals can become exceedingly wide. Finally, notice that the single confidence interval for a *fixed* value of $X = 30$ is contained within the simultaneous confidence interval. We provide directions in Box 44-5 for calculating a confidence interval for the regression line.

44-5. EXERCISES

44-1. Find the regression equation for your sample of 40 students for X: pretest and Y: final.

44-2. For the data of Exercise 44-1, test the hypotheses:
a. $H_0: \beta_0 = 0$
b. $H_0: \beta_1 = 1$
Use $\alpha = .05$ for each hypothesis. What interpretations can you give to these hypotheses? Are they meaningful for this situation? Why?

44-3. Find the 95 percent confidence intervals for β_0 and β_1 of Exercise 44-1.

44-4. How are the following hypotheses related to one another?
a. $\rho_{XY} = 0$
b. $\beta_1 = 0$
c. $\beta_1 = 1$

44-5. What are the assumptions for the tests of Exercise 44-4? How important is it that you adhere to the assumptions for the analysis of Exercises 44-2 and 44-3?

44-6. Estimate the value of Y from the regression line $\hat{Y}$ at $X_0 = \bar{X} + S_X$ for the data of Exercise 44-1. In addition, find the 95 percent confidence interval for Y at X_0.

44-7. The confidence interval for μ_Y can be obtained under two different models:
a. $\mu_Y = \bar{Y} \pm t_{N-1:\alpha/2} S_Y / \sqrt{N}$
b. $\mu_Y = \bar{Y} \pm t_{N-2:\alpha/2} \sqrt{MS_R} / \sqrt{N}$
Use these two models on the data of Exercise 44-1. Which model do you prefer? Why?·What are the assumptions for each model?

44-8. From your sample regression line, find the 95 percent simultaneous confidence interval for the population line. Graph the interval.

44-9. For the data of Table 43-3, test the six slopes for parallelism, using planned pairwise comparisons under
a. Equal-variance assumption
b. Unequal-variance assumption
You can save effort by testing the two most disparate slopes first.

PART VIII

PROCEDURES FOR MULTIPLE INDEPENDENT VARIABLES

In the previous chapters, we examined methods for treating multiple qualitative independent variables and a single quantitative dependent variable. In the next chapters, we introduce methods for handling multiple quantitative independent variables. These procedures make use of multiple regression theory, which is perhaps the most powerful of the statistical methods in use by behavioral scientists, because analysis of variance and analysis of covariance can be treated as special cases of this more flexible model. In the models to be presented, multiple qualitative and quantitative independent variables can be analyzed together, and the dependent variable can be either quantitative or qualitative.

CHAPTER 45

Multiple Regression Theory

45-1. MULTIPLE REGRESSION

In Chapters 7, 8, and 9, the discussion focused on the linear relationship between one independent variable and one dependent variable. Techniques appropriate for this model were described in terms of simple correlation theory and simple linear regression analysis. As soon as a researcher employs two or more predictor variables $X_1, X_2, \ldots, X_P$, the models expand to what are generally referred to as *multiple correlation* and *multiple regression theory*. As will be seen, these extended procedures generate a new variable which is simply a linear combination of the predictor variables. Once the composite of the predictor variables has been established, the model may be interpreted in the same way as in the single-predictor-variable model. This means that one can continue to examine and evaluate best-fitting straight-line relationships, regression slopes and intercepts, the proportion of the total amount of variability in Y explained by the predictors, and other related characteristics. These relationships now refer to multiple predictors taken collectively, however, and not to a single independent variable.

The rationale behind the multiple-predictor approach is intuitively appealing, in that having more detailed information about individuals or sampling units typically permits more precision in prediction of performance than could be done with only one piece of information.

The simplest model that could be used to predict Y from X_1 and X_2 is given as

$$\hat{Y} = B_0 + B_1 X_1 + B_2 X_2$$

where B_0, B_1, and B_2 are sample estimators of the unknown parameters β_0, β_1, and β_2, respectively. As indicated, this represents the simple extension of the one-predictor model to two predictors. Moreover, this model assumes that the two variables X_1 and X_2 do not "interact" with respect to predicting Y. If we wished to include possible interactions of X_1 and X_2 in our model, we could follow the procedures for calculating interaction contrast coefficients shown in Chapter 40. There, we obtained the coefficients by multiplying the main-effects contrast coefficients. Here, we achieve the same effect by multiplying X_1 and X_2. Thus, a simple model that would build in a possible interaction between X_1 and X_2 is given by

$$\hat{Y} = B_0 + B_1 X_1 + B_2 X_2 + B_3 X_1 X_2$$

If we let $X_3 = X_1 X_2$, then this model reduces to

$$\hat{Y} = B_0 + B_1 X_1 + B_2 X_2 + B_3 X_3$$

which is similar to the first model except that three predictor variables are used to describe the relationship with Y.

Let us return to the two-predictor equation. To examine the relationship between Y and the predictors X_1 and X_2 in detail, it is desirable that B_1 and B_2 reflect the unique contributions of each predictor to the equation. Unfortunately, this is impossible. The best that can be done is to determine the relationship between Y and X_1, with X_2 "controlled," and the relationship between Y and X_2, with X_1 "controlled." How this statistical control is achieved is described in the next sections on partial correlation theory.

45-2. PARTIAL CORRELATION THEORY

Perhaps the easiest way to introduce partial correlation theory is through an example. For the example, consider the data of Table 45-1. These data

Table 45-1. Mental age and reading test scores used to predict arithmetic test score

	X_1 = mental age	X_2 = reading test	Y = arithmetic test
	9.2	61	126
	10.0	47	60
	8.0	79	117
	7.4	40	96
	9.7	60	79
	10.7	59	99
	9.2	61	92
	9.2	79	91
	11.9	83	146
	9.8	67	110
	10.9	74	116
	7.1	40	69
	10.2	71	107
	8.7	40	82
	8.5	57	64
	10.9	58	100
	11.8	66	138
	8.8	58	63
	9.5	59	82
	8.7	48	73
	10.4	100	142
	9.5	83	87
	8.1	70	89
	8.9	48	99
	11.7	85	119
	8.0	80	100
	6.9	55	84
	12.1	100	140
	13.0	88	131
	9.7	45	110
	9.6	58	93
	10.9	90	141
	9.8	84	99
	11.8	81	114
	9.3	49	96
	8.1	54	39
	11.4	87	149
	6.9	36	53
	9.3	51	49
	7.0	55	91
Mean value	9.5650	65.1500	98.3750
Standard deviation	1.5575	17.2810	27.8820
Correlation coefficient X_1	1.0000	.6300	.6700
X_2	.6300	1.0000	.7080
Y	.6700	.7080	1.0000

represent the following three variables collected on 40 children: Y = number of items answered correctly on an arithmetic test, X_1 = mental age in years, and X_2 = score on a reading test.

If we consider the arithmetic test scores of Table 45-1, we can show that they are correlated with both the mental ages X_1 and reading scores X_2, with r_{YX_1} = .6700 and r_{YX_2} = .7080. At the same time, the mental ages and reading scores are also correlated, with $r_{X_1X_2}$ = .6300. This latter high correlation suggests that part of the correlation between Y and X_1 could arise because of the association that X_1 has with X_2. If the associations that Y and X_1 have with X_2 could be taken into account and adjusted for, then we would have a purer, or more refined, measure of the association between Y and X_1. Such a measure of association is called a *partial correlation coefficient*. It measures the association between two variables, after the linear relationship with a third variable has been taken into consideration. We now develop the concept of partial correlation.

For this development, let the three variables be denoted by X_1, X_2, and X_3, and let us examine the relationships between X_1 and X_3 and between X_2 and X_3. Because a variety of independent and dependent variables are involved in the regression equations to follow, we need to introduce notation to distinguish among them. Conventionally, the dependent variable's subscript is separated from those of the independent variables by a center dot. Thus, if we predict X_1 from X_3, we write

$$\hat{X}_{1\cdot 3} = \overline{X}_1 + B_{1\cdot 3}(X_3 - \overline{X}_3)$$

and for the regression of X_2 on X_3, we write

$$\hat{X}_{2\cdot 3} = \overline{X}_2 + B_{2\cdot 3}(X_3 - \overline{X}_3)$$

With this notation, we can write the deviation equations as

$$X_1 - \overline{X}_1 = (X_1 - \hat{X}_{1\cdot 3}) + (\hat{X}_{1\cdot 3} - \overline{X}_1)$$
$$X_2 - \overline{X}_2 = (X_2 - \hat{X}_{2\cdot 3}) + (\hat{X}_{2\cdot 3} - \overline{X}_2)$$

These latter equations correspond to

$$d_{TX_1} = d_{UX_1} + d_{EX_1} \quad \text{and} \quad d_{TX_2} = d_{UX_2} + d_{EX_2}$$

As we know, the explained deviations d_{EX_1} and d_{EX_2} involve X_3, in that they are the deviations explained by X_3. And the unexplained deviations d_{UX_1} and d_{UX_2} are those parts of X_1 and X_2 that cannot be related to X_3.

We now show that the unexplained deviation is uncorrelated with the predictor variable. The zero correlation between the unexplained portion of a variable and the variable itself can be proved algebraically; instead, we wish to demonstrate this relationship by an example using the data of Table 7-1 and Table 9-1, which give us predictor values and unexplained deviations in a regression of a final test score on a pretest score. The correlation between d_U and X is given, with four-decimal-place accuracy, by

$$r_{d_U,X} = \frac{N \sum d_U X - \sum d_U \sum X}{\sqrt{N \sum d_U^2 - \left(\sum d_U \right)^2} \sqrt{N \sum X^2 - \left(\sum X \right)^2}}$$

$$= \frac{39(0.6037) - 0.0271(710)}{\sqrt{39(6403.6576) - 0.0271^2} \sqrt{39(15,066) - 710^2}}$$

$$= .00003$$

Except for rounding errors, this value is equal to zero. This indicates that the unexplained deviations have no overlap with the predictor variable, since the corresponding r^2 is also zero. It follows from this example, then, that $d_{U_{X_1}}$ and $d_{U_{X_2}}$ represent the parts of the original variables that are unrelated to X_3. We usually say that X_3 is *removed, controlled,* or *partialed out* of X_1 and X_2.

Let us now return to our original problem of correlating X_1 and X_2 with the effects of X_3 partialed out. If we computed $d_{U_{X_1}}$ and $d_{U_{X_2}}$ for each of the N subjects and then found a correlation coefficient based on them, we would have estimated the correlation between X_1 and X_2 after the effects of X_3 have been removed from each. If we denote this correlation coefficient as $r_{X_1 X_2 \cdot X_3}$, then

$$r_{X_1 X_2 \cdot X_3} = \frac{N \sum d_{U_{X_1}} d_{U_{X_2}} - \sum d_{U_{X_1}} \sum d_{U_{X_2}}}{\sqrt{N \sum d_{U_{X_1}}^2 - \left(\sum d_{U_{X_1}} \right)^2} \sqrt{N \sum d_{U_{X_2}}^2 - \left(\sum d_{U_{X_2}} \right)^2}}$$

If we now substitute sample statistics into this definition and perform the resulting algebra, we obtain the following computing formula for $r_{X_1 X_2 \cdot X_3}$:

Computing formula for $r_{X_1 X_2 \cdot X_3}$

The computing formula for the sample partial correlation coefficient between variables X_1 and X_2, with the effects of X_3 removed, is

$$r_{X_1 X_2 \cdot X_3} = \frac{r_{X_1 X_2} - r_{X_1 X_3} r_{X_2 X_3}}{\sqrt{1 - r_{X_1 X_3}^2} \sqrt{1 - r_{X_2 X_3}^2}}$$

We now return to our original notation in which Y represents a dependent variable and X_1 and X_2 represent independent variables. Although correlation coefficients are usually reported to two decimal places, the computations underlying them should be based on as many significant digits as possible. This reduces the chances of error from rounding decimal values. Thus, for four-decimal-place accuracy, we have for the data of Table 45-1

$$r_{YX_1 \cdot X_2} = \frac{r_{YX_1} - r_{YX_2} r_{X_1 X_2}}{\sqrt{1 - r_{YX_2}^2}\sqrt{1 - r_{X_1 X_2}^2}} = \frac{.6700 - (.7080)(.6300)}{\sqrt{1 - .7080^2}\sqrt{1 - .6300^2}}$$

$$= .4084$$

and, similarly, $r_{YX_2 \cdot X_1} = .4959$.

The partial correlation coefficients are somewhat smaller than the simple, or *zero-order*, correlations of the dependent variable with each of the two independent variables. For mental age, $r_{YX_1} = .6700$, whereas $r_{YX_1 \cdot X_2} = .4084$; for the reading scores, $r_{YX_2} = .7080$, whereas $r_{YX_2 \cdot X_1} = .4959$. These "purer" measures of association represent another form of statistical control, similar to those described in the previous chapters.

This reduction in the partial correlation coefficients happens because, in this example, all three variables are positively correlated and, thus, some of the covariance between any two variables is shared with the third variable. When this shared relationship is removed statistically, the unique relationship that remains is smaller. In some cases, however, a partial correlation may be larger than its zero-order correlation; in still other cases, it may even be different in sign.

Partial correlations that involve the removal of two or more independent variables are often encountered in behavioral research. Since the arithmetic involved in determining higher-order partial correlation coefficients is tedious, such correlations are usually found by means of computers. The reason is easy to appreciate if one considers the partial correlation between two variables X_1 and X_2 after the effects of two other variables X_3 and X_4 are removed. This is denoted $r_{X_1 X_2 \cdot X_3 X_4}$. The appropriate formula is

$$r_{X_1 X_2 \cdot X_3 X_4} = \frac{r_{X_1 X_2 \cdot X_3} - r_{X_1 X_4 \cdot X_3} r_{X_2 X_4 \cdot X_3}}{\sqrt{1 - r_{X_1 X_4 \cdot X_3}^2}\sqrt{1 - r_{X_2 X_4 \cdot X_3}^2}}$$

and it requires that $r_{X_1 X_2 \cdot X_3}$, $r_{X_1 X_4 \cdot X_3}$, and $r_{X_2 X_4 \cdot X_3}$ be computed first. Alternatively, the equivalent formula

$$r_{X_1 X_2 \cdot X_3 X_4} = \frac{r_{X_1 X_2 \cdot X_4} - r_{X_1 X_3 \cdot X_4} r_{X_2 X_3 \cdot X_4}}{\sqrt{1 - r_{X_1 X_3 \cdot X_4}^2}\sqrt{1 - r_{X_2 X_3 \cdot X_4}^2}}$$

requires that $r_{X_1 X_2 \cdot X_4}$, $r_{X_1 X_3 \cdot X_4}$, and $r_{X_2 X_3 \cdot X_4}$ be computed first. In either case, it is apparent why a computer should be used to perform the necessary calculations.

The concept of partialing out one variable can be extended to the removal of the influences of many variables $X_2, X_3, \ldots, X_P$ from the correlation between Y and X_1. The symbols for this partial correlation coefficient in the sample and population would be, by extension, $r_{YX_1 \cdot X_2 X_3 \ldots X_P}$ and $\rho_{YX_1 \cdot X_2 X_3 \ldots X_P}$, respectively.

45-3. TESTING PARTIAL CORRELATION COEFFICIENTS FOR STATISTICAL SIGNIFICANCE

In Section 32-7, we saw that the test of $H_0: \rho_{XY} = 0$ was based on a t statistic with $\nu = N - 2$ degrees of freedom. Also, in Chapter 24, we saw that the tests of $H_0: \rho_{XY} = \rho_0$ and $H_0: \rho_{XY}^{(1)} = \rho_{XY}^{(2)}$ could be performed in terms of the Fisher z transformation. For tests on partial correlations, exactly the same theory is called upon. With advanced methods, one can show that with V variables partialed out, for the test of $H_0: \rho_{YX_1 \cdot X_2 X_3 \ldots X_P} = 0$, the test statistic with $\nu = N - 2 - V$ degrees of freedom is given by

$$t = \frac{r_{YX_1 \cdot X_2 X_3 \ldots X_P} \sqrt{N - 2 - V}}{\sqrt{1 - r_{YX_1 \cdot X_2 X_3 \ldots X_P}^2}}$$

And for the tests of $H_0: \rho_{YX_1 \cdot X_2 X_3 \ldots X_P} = \rho_0$ and $H_0: \rho_{YX_1 \cdot X_2 X_3 \ldots X_P}^{(1)} = \rho_{YX_1 \cdot X_2 X_3 \ldots X_P}^{(2)}$, the corresponding test statistics are given, respectively, by

$$Z = \frac{z_{r_{YX_1 \cdot X_2 \ldots X_P}} - z_0}{1/\sqrt{N - 3 - V}}$$

and

$$Z = \frac{z_{r_{YX_1 \cdot X_2 \ldots X_P}}^{(1)} - z_{r_{YX_1 \cdot X_2 \ldots X_P}}^{(2)}}{\sqrt{1/(N_1 - 3 - V) + 1/(N_2 - 3 - V)}}$$

where V = number of variables partialed out of Y. Notice that when $V = 0$, we obtain the formulas for testing ρ_{YX}.

For the data of Table 45-1, one could test the hypothesis that there is no linear relationship between reading scores X_2 and arithmetic scores Y when the effect of mental age X_1 has been removed. Thus, for the test of

$$H_0: \rho_{YX_2 \cdot X_1} = 0$$

the value of the test statistic is

$$t = \frac{0.4959 \sqrt{40 - 3}}{\sqrt{1 - 0.4959^2}} = 3.47$$

Box 45-1 **Procedure for testing a partial correlation coefficient for significance where the number of partialed variables equals V**

Step 1. Compute the partial correlation coefficient of interest. Let r represent the sample partial correlation with V variables partialed out, and let ρ represent the corresponding population value.

Step 2a. To test $H_0: \rho = 0$, compute

$$t = \frac{r\sqrt{N - 2 - V}}{\sqrt{1 - r^2}}$$

Step 3a. Reject H_0 if

$$t < t_{N-2-V:\alpha/2} \qquad \text{or} \qquad t > t_{N-2-V:1-\alpha/2}$$

or:

Step 2b. To test $H_0: \rho = \rho_0$, use the Fisher z transformation, with the variance of z given by

$$\text{var}(z) = \frac{1}{N - 3 - V}$$

Step 3b. Reject H_0 if

$$Z = \frac{z_r - z_0}{1/\sqrt{N - 3 - V}}$$

is in the rejection region defined by

$$Z < Z_{\alpha/2} \qquad \text{or} \qquad Z > Z_{1-\alpha/2}$$

or:

Step 2c. To test $H_0: \rho_1 = \rho_2$, use the Fisher z transformation and compute

$$Z = \frac{z_1 - z_2}{\sqrt{1/(N_1 - 3 - V) + 1/(N_2 - 3 - V)}}$$

Step 3c. Reject H_0 if Z is in the rejection region defined by

$$Z < Z_{\alpha/2} \qquad \text{or} \qquad Z > Z_{1-\alpha/2}$$

With $\alpha = .05$, $V = 1$, $N = 40$, and $v = N - 2 - V = 40 - 2 - 1 = 37$, the two-tailed decision rule for rejecting H_0 is

Decision Rule: Reject H_0 if $t < -2.03$ or if $t > +2.03$.

One would conclude that reading and arithmetic scores were correlated, even when the mental ages were controlled.

We do not provide examples of the tests using the Fisher z transformations as specified in steps 2b or 2c of the procedure for testing partial correlation coefficients. We do provide, however, in Box 45-1, directions for performing tests on partial correlation coefficients.

45-4. PART CORRELATION

Closely tied to the concept of a partial correlation coefficient is a measure of association called a *part*, or *semipartial, correlation coefficient*. Whereas a partial correlation coefficient measures the correlation between two variables X_1 and X_2, both of which have the respective linear relationships with a third variable X_3 removed, a part correlation refers to the correlation between X_1 and X_2 where the linear relationship with X_3 has been removed from either X_1 or X_2 but not from both.

For the special case in which $P = 2$, the partial correlation between Y and X_1, after the effects of X_2 have been removed from both variables, is given simply as the correlation between the residuals $Y - \hat{Y}$ and $X_1 - \hat{X}_1$. In like manner, the part correlation between Y and X_1, after the effects of X_2 have been removed from X_1 alone, is given simply as the correlation between Y and the residual $X_1 - \hat{X}_1$. This correlation is computed as

$$r_{Y(X_1 \cdot X_2)} = \frac{r_{YX_1} - r_{YX_2} r_{X_1 X_2}}{\sqrt{1 - r_{X_1 X_2}^2}} = r_{YX_1 \cdot X_2} \sqrt{1 - r_{YX_2}^2}$$

We do not provide the generalization to more variables at this point; however, we do offer it in the next chapter.

Note that $r_{YX_1 \cdot X_2}$ and $r_{Y(X_1 \cdot X_2)}$ differ only by the factor $\sqrt{1 - r_{YX_2}^2}$, which is less than or equal to 1. Thus,

$$r_{Y(X_1 \cdot X_2)} \leq r_{YX_1 \cdot X_2}$$

Also, we see that $r_{Y(X_1 \cdot X_2)}$ can equal zero only if $r_{YX_1 \cdot X_2} = 0$.

For our present three-variable example, we recall that $r_{YX_1} = .6700$, $r_{YX_2} = .7080$, and $r_{X_1 X_2} = .6300$, yielding $r_{YX_1 \cdot X_2} = .4084$ and $r_{YX_2 \cdot X_1} = .4959$. In terms of the computational formula, the part correlations are

$$r_{Y(X_1 \cdot X_2)} = .4084 \sqrt{1 - .7080^2} = .2881$$

$$r_{Y(X_2 \cdot X_1)} = .4959 \sqrt{1 - .6700^2} = .3681$$

As indicated, both of these part correlations are less than their respective partials.

The interpretive difference between $r_{YX_1 \cdot X_2}$ and $r_{Y(X_1 \cdot X_2)}$ is quite subtle and, thus, should be understood and appreciated. The squared part correlation coefficient $r^2_{Y(X_1 \cdot X_2)}$ may be interpreted as the percentage of Y variation explained by the portion of X_1 that is free of X_2. In contrast, the squared partial correlation coefficient $r^2_{YX_1 \cdot X_2}$, may be interpreted as the percentage of the portion of Y free of X_2 that is explained by the portion of X_1 that is also free of X_2. In this sense, a squared part correlation reflects the percentage of the *total* Y variability that is explained by a *portion* of X_1, whereas a squared partial correlation reflects a percentage of a portion of the Y variation that is explained by a similar portion of X_1.

In the present example, the part correlation is perhaps the correlation of choice. We expect a high correlation between arithmetic scores and reading ability scores, especially if the arithmetic test contains word problems. Thus, to see whether arithmetic ability improves with mental age, it would make sense to measure the correlation of mental age with a "pure" arithmetic measure. This would yield $r_{X_1(Y \cdot X_2)}$. For our data,

$$
\begin{aligned}
r_{X_1(Y \cdot X_2)} &= r_{X_1 Y \cdot X_2} \sqrt{1 - r^2_{X_1 X_2}} \\
&= .4084 \sqrt{1 - .6300^2} \\
&= .3172
\end{aligned}
$$

Thus, only about $.3172^2$ or 10 percent, of the variability in the test of arithmetic, from which reading ability has been removed, is shared with mental age. Since a large part of a mental age test is composed of reading ability items, it would not make sense to remove reading ability from mental age.

45-5. ESTIMATE OF POPULATION BETA WEIGHTS

The estimates B of the population beta weights, β, as the regression coefficients are referred to in multiple regression theory, are relatively simple, once the partial correlation coefficients are known. For two independent variables, the formula for the sample estimate of the population beta weights is a simple extension of the equations given in Section 8-1 for estimating β_0 and β_1 for one independent variable.

As shown in Chapter 8

$$
B_1 = r_{YX} \frac{S_Y}{S_X} = r_{YX} \sqrt{\frac{S_Y^2}{S_X^2}}
$$

The formulas for multiple regression coefficients for two independent variables can be similarly defined. Because the regression coefficients are proportional to partial correlation coefficients, they are sometimes referred to as *partial regression coefficients.* Computational formulas are given by

$$B_{YX_1 \cdot X_2} = r_{YX_1 \cdot X_2} \frac{S_Y \sqrt{1 - r_{YX_2}^2}}{S_{X_1} \sqrt{1 - r_{X_1 X_2}^2}}$$

$$B_{YX_2 \cdot X_1} = r_{YX_2 \cdot X_1} \frac{S_Y \sqrt{1 - r_{YX_1}^2}}{S_{X_2} \sqrt{1 - r_{X_2 X_1}^2}}$$

and

$$B_0 = \bar{Y} - B_{YX_1 \cdot X_2}\bar{X}_1 - B_{YX_2 \cdot X_1}\bar{X}_2$$

For the data of Table 45-1,

$$B_{YX_1 \cdot X_2} = .4084 \frac{27.8820}{1.5575} \frac{\sqrt{1 - .7080^2}}{\sqrt{1 - .6300^2}} = 6.6485$$

Similarly, $B_{YX_2 \cdot X_1} = .7648$. With these values:

$$B_0 = 98.3750 - 6.6485(9.5650) - 0.7648(65.1500) = -15.04$$

Therefore, the equation relating the arithmetic test scores to the two predictors is given to two decimal places by

$$\hat{Y} = -15.04 + 6.65X_1 + 0.76X_2$$

Sometimes the results are reported in deviation form as

$$\hat{Y} = \bar{Y} + B_{YX_1 \cdot X_2}(X_1 - \bar{X}_1) + B_{YX_2 \cdot X_1}(X_2 - \bar{X}_2)$$

With two-decimal-place accuracy,

$$\hat{Y} = 98.38 + 6.65(X_1 - 9.56) + 0.76(X_2 - 65.15)$$

The negative intercept for the more familiar form, $B_0 = -15.04$, indicates that for persons whose mental age is zero and whose reading score is zero, their predicted score on the arithmetic test would be -15. Of course, this is nonsense. Note that no one in the sample has a mental age below 6 or has a reading score less than 30. This example illustrates the danger of trying to estimate values of Y whose X values are beyond the range of the observed sample X values. Extrapolations beyond the observed data must be made with caution. For the deviation form, the intercept value of 98.38 represents the mean value for subjects with $X_1 = \bar{X}_1$ and $X_2 = \bar{X}_2$.

In most studies in the behavioral sciences, the slopes have more meaning than the intercepts. Here, $B_{YX_1 \cdot X_2} = 6.6485$ indicates that for students with the same reading ability, an increase in mental age of 1 year would be associated with a mean increase in the arithmetic scores of 6.65 points. Similarly, for students with the same mental age, an increase of 1 point on the reading test would be associated with a mean increase of $B_{YX_2 \cdot X_1} = 0.76$ point on the arithmetic test.

Sometimes, it is useful to conceive of a multiple regression analysis in terms of standard scores, so that the regression coefficients would be on the same scale and comparable. If we denote the standard scores for an individual on Y, X_1, and X_2 as Z_Y, Z_1, and Z_2, respectively, then we can define a regression equation as

$$\hat{Z}_Y = b_1 Z_1 + b_2 Z_2$$

where b_1 and b_2 are called the *standardized* regression coefficients. They can be calculated by the methods outlined for B_1 and B_2 above. It is easier, however, to calculate b_1 and b_2 from B_1 and B_2, respectively, as follows:

$$b_1 = B_1 \frac{S_{X_1}}{S_Y} \quad \text{and} \quad b_2 = B_2 \frac{S_{X_2}}{S_Y}$$

For the data of Table 45-1,

$$b_1 = 6.6485 \frac{1.5575}{27.8820} = 0.3714$$

$$b_2 = 0.7648 \frac{17.2810}{27.8820} = 0.4740$$

Thus, in terms of standard scores,

$$\hat{Z}_Y = 0.3714 Z_1 + 0.4740 Z_2$$

This equation is reexamined in Section 45-8, where its connection with measures of explained variability is demonstrated.

For completeness, we define standardized regression weights and regression equations for P predictors. B_1, B_2, . . . , B_P are defined explicitly in Section 45.6.

Definition of sample standardized regression coefficients

Let B_1, B_2, . . . , B_P be the estimates for

$$\hat{Y} = B_0 + B_1 X_1 + B_2 X_2 + \cdots + B_P X_P$$

The sample standardized regression coefficients for the standard score regression equation

$$\hat{Z}_Y = b_1 Z_{X_1} + b_2 Z_{X_2} + \cdots + b_P Z_{X_P}$$

are defined as

$$b_1 = B_1 \frac{S_{X_1}}{S_Y}, \qquad b_2 = B_2 \frac{S_{X_2}}{S_Y}, \qquad \ldots, \qquad b_P = B_P \frac{S_{X_P}}{S_Y}$$

The value of B or b estimates the average increase in Y for every unit increase in X. For B, these values are given in raw scale units, whereas for b they are given in standard deviation units.

45-6. VARIATIONS FROM PREDICTION AND SLOPE ESTIMATION

As we saw in the one-predictor case in Chapter 9, one goal in regression analysis is to assess how well the predicted Y values fit the observed Y values. In Chapter 44, we were able to use the sums of squared unexplained deviations to generate an estimate of the unexplained, or error, variance. We can easily use the same concepts in multiple regression. Again, we define the unexplained deviation as

$$d_U = Y - \hat{Y}$$

For the first subject of Table 45-1, whose X_1 and X_2 values are 9.2 and 61, respectively, we find

$$\hat{Y} = -15.04 + 6.65(9.2) + 0.76(61) = 92.50$$

Since the actual score on the test for this subject is $Y = 126$, the deviation between Y and $\hat{Y}$ is given by $d_U = Y - \hat{Y} = 126 - 92.5 = 33.5$. The remaining estimated scores and residuals are reported in Table 45-2 with two-decimal-place accuracy.

The unexplained variance can be computed directly from the residuals. Since the $\hat{Y}$ values are here restricted by the three estimates B_0, B_1, and B_2, the residual (R) variance is defined with $v = N - 3$ degrees of freedom as

$$MS_{R(Y \cdot X_1 X_2)} = \sum_{i=1}^{N} \frac{(Y_i - \hat{Y}_i)^2}{N - 3}$$

$$= \frac{1}{40 - 3} [(33.50)^2 + (-27.18)^2 + \cdots + (17.69)^2]$$

$$= (\tfrac{1}{37})(12{,}624.10) = 341.19$$

Table 45-2.　Residuals for 40 subjects of Table 45-1

Y_i	$\hat{Y}_i$	$Y_i - \hat{Y}_i$
126	92.50	33.50
60	87.18	−27.18
117	98.20	18.80
96	64.57	31.43
79	95.06	−16.06
99	100.96	−1.96
92	92.50	−0.50
91	106.18	−15.18
146	127.18	18.82
110	101.05	8.95
116	113.69	2.31
69	62.58	6.42
107	106.75	0.25
82	73.22	8.78
64	84.81	−20.81
100	101.53	−1.53
138	113.59	24.41
63	87.56	−24.56
82	92.98	−10.98
73	79.30	−6.30
142	130.12	11.88
87	111.22	−24.22
89	92.03	−3.03
99	80.63	18.37
119	127.37	−8.37
100	98.96	1.04
84	72.65	11.35
140	141.43	−1.43
131	138.29	−7.29
110	83.67	26.33
93	92.88	0.12
141	125.85	15.15
99	113.97	−14.97
114	124.99	−10.99
96	84.05	11.95
39	79.87	−40.87
149	126.89	22.11
53	58.21	−5.21
49	85.57	−36.57
91	73.31	17.69

To reduce the problem of an unwieldly subscript notation, we define, for P predictor variables, the MS_R as follows:

Definition of mean square residual for P predictors

The estimate of the residual variance about the regression equation for P predictor variables is

$$MS_R = \frac{1}{N - P - 1} \sum_{i=1}^{N} (Y_i - \hat{Y}_i)^2$$

Using the MS_R notation to represent variance in one variable that is unexplained in its linear relationship with another variable, we can make the formulas for $B_{YX_1 \cdot X_2}$ and $B_{YX_2 \cdot X_1}$ resemble the definition of a one-predictor-variable regression coefficient given in Chapter 8.

Sample regression coefficients B for two independent variables

The sample regression coefficients for two independent variables are defined as

$$B_{YX_1 \cdot X_2} = r_{YX_1 \cdot X_2} \sqrt{\frac{MS_{R(Y \cdot X_2)}}{MS_{R(X_1 \cdot X_2)}}}$$

$$B_{YX_2 \cdot X_1} = r_{YX_2 \cdot X_1} \sqrt{\frac{MS_{R(Y \cdot X_1)}}{MS_{R(X_2 \cdot X_1)}}}$$

and

$$B_0 = \bar{Y} - B_{YX_1 \cdot X_2} \bar{X}_1 - B_{YX_2 \cdot X_1} \bar{X}_2$$

The formulas for two predictors can be extended to the case where Y is predicted from $X_1, X_2, \ldots, X_P$. These are given as follows.

Sample regression coefficients for P independent variables

The sample regression coefficients for predicting Y from $X_1, X_2, \ldots, X_P$ are computed as

$$B_{YX_1 \cdot X_2 X_3 \ldots X_P} = r_{YX_1 \cdot X_2 X_3 \ldots X_P} \sqrt{\frac{MS_{R(Y \cdot X_2 X_3 \ldots X_P)}}{MS_{R(X_1 \cdot X_2 \ldots X_P)}}}$$

Clearly the subscript notation can become overwhelming. We have preserved it to this point to emphasize that the regression coefficients are based on partial correlations and to denote which variables are partialed from which other variables. In the future, where the variables in an equation are clearly delineated, this notation is simplified. Instead of writing

$$\hat{Y} = B_0 + B_{YX_1 \cdot X_2 X_3 \ldots X_P} X_1 + B_{YX_2 \cdot X_1 X_3 \ldots X_P} X_2 + \cdots + B_{YX_P \cdot X_1 X_2 \ldots X_{P-1}} X_P$$

we write

$$\hat{Y} = B_0 + B_1 X_1 + B_2 X_2 + \cdots + B_P X_P$$

Remember that all the B's are partial regression coefficients.

45-7. MULTIPLE CORRELATION COEFFICIENT

At this point, we introduce a statistic that will prove useful in understanding the rationale behind multiple regression. For the Y variable in the one-predictor model,

$$SS_{Explained} + SS_{Unexplained} = SS_{Total}$$

and

$$r_{YX}^2 = \frac{SS_E}{SS_T}$$

This partitioning of a sum of squares and the determination of a measure of association can be extended to the case where there is more than one predictor variable, so that one can similarly compute SS_E, SS_U, and SS_T on the basis of all P predictor variables. In regression analysis, the sum of squares explained is called the *sum of squares regression*.

For our example with $P = 2$, we have seen that

$$SS_U = SS_R = 12,624.10$$

In addition, the total sum of squares for Y is

$$SS_T = (N - 1)S_Y^2 = 39(27.8820)^2 = 30,318.80$$

Accordingly (reg = regression),

$$SS_E = SS_{reg} = SS_T - SS_R = 30,318.80 - 12,624.10 = 17,694.70$$

Finally

$$\frac{SS_E}{SS_T} = \frac{SS_{reg}}{SS_T} = \frac{17,694.70}{30,318.80} = .5836$$

This ratio is called the *squared multiple correlation coefficient* $\hat{R}^2_{Y \cdot X_1 X_2}$, and it is interpreted exactly as the squared correlation coefficient of the one-predictor situation. Thus, we see that about 58 percent of the variability in the arithmetic test scores can be explained in terms of the joint effects of the variation in mental age and reading ability. For completeness, we note the following definition.

Definition of multiple correlation coefficient

The square of the multiple correlation coefficient is defined as

$$\hat{R}^2 = \frac{SS_E}{SS_T} = \frac{SS_{reg}}{SS_T}$$

We have seen that $MS_{R(Y \cdot X_1 X_2)} = 341.19$ when it is computed from the individual unexplained deviations. In the multiple-predictor case, MS_R can be calculated from the Y variance and the squared multiple correlation coefficient as

$$MS_R = \frac{N-1}{N-P-1} S_Y^2 (1 - \hat{R}^2_{Y \cdot X_1 X_2 \dots X_P})$$

For our example,

$$MS_R = \frac{40-1}{40-2-1} (27.8820)^2 (1 - .5836) = 341.21$$

is within rounding errors of the result found from the deviations. For completeness, we provide a formula for the residual variance in multiple regression theory.

Residual variance for predicting Y from $X_1, X_2, \dots, X_P$

The residual variance for predicting Y from $X_1, X_2, \dots, X_P$ can be computed as

$$MS_R = \frac{N-1}{N-P-1} S_Y^2 (1 - \hat{R}^2_{Y \cdot X_1 X_2 \dots X_P})$$

45-8. LINEAR COMBINATIONS FOR CORRELATED VARIABLES

Let us define a linear combination of the X variables as

$$L = W_1 X_1 + W_2 X_2 + \cdots + W_P X_P$$

In Section 20-3 we stated that the variance of this linear combination would be given by

$$\mathrm{var}(L) = W_1^2 \sigma_1^2 + W_2^2 \sigma_2^2 + \cdots + W_P^2 \sigma_P^2$$

provided that the X_p values are uncorrelated. We now need to extend this notion to the case in which the X_p and $X_{p'}$ are correlated. To do this, it is convenient to recall the notion of a covariance. The covariance of X_p and $X_{p'}$ is

$$S_{X_p X_{p'}} = r_{X_p X_{p'}} S_{X_p} S_{X_{p'}}$$

This form is very convenient for use in multiple regression analysis, and it permits an extension of the theory of linear combinations for correlated variables.

We now formulate the variance of a linear combination of variables.

Variance of a linear combination

If we let $X_1, X_2, \ldots, X_P$ be P variables which may or may not be correlated, we define the sample variance of

$$L = \sum_{p=1}^{P} W_p X_p$$

as

$$S_L^2 = \sum_{p=1}^{P} W_p^2 S_{X_p}^2 + 2 \sum_{p=1}^{P} \sum_{\substack{p'=1 \\ p < p'}}^{P} W_p W_{p'} r_{X_p X_{p'}} S_{X_p} S_{X_{p'}}$$

and in the population as

$$\sigma_L^2 = \sum_{p=1}^{P} W_p^2 \sigma_{X_p}^2 + 2 \sum_{p=1}^{P} \sum_{\substack{p'=1 \\ p < p'}}^{P} W_p W_{p'} \rho_{X_p X_{p'}} \sigma_{X_p} \sigma_{X_{p'}}$$

45-9. COMPUTING FORMULA FOR $\hat{R}^2_{Y \cdot X_1 X_2 \ldots X_P}$

As we saw in Section 45-6, the regression equation describing our present example can be written in standard form as the linear combination

$$\hat{Z}_Y = 0.3714 Z_1 + 0.4740 Z_2$$

If we compute the variance of $\hat{Z}_Y$, we have

$$S^2_{\hat{Z}_Y} = (0.3714)^2 S^2_{Z_1} + (0.4740)^2 S^2_{Z_2} + 2(0.3714)(0.4740) S_{Z_1} S_{Z_2} r_{Z_1 Z_2}$$

where $S_{Z_1} S_{Z_2} r_{Z_1 Z_2}$ is simply the covariance between Z_1 and Z_2. Because the correlation between X_1 and X_2 is scale-free and location-free, $r_{Z_1 Z_2} = r_{X_1 X_2}$. For this example, $r_{X_1 X_2} = .6300$. Recalling that $S^2_{Z_1} = S^2_{Z_2} = 1.00$, we find

$$S^2_{\hat{Z}_Y} = .3714^2 + .4740^2 + 2(0.3714)(0.4740)(0.6300)$$
$$= .5840 = \hat{R}^2_{Y \cdot X_1 X_2}$$

We have found, then, that for $P = 2$

$$\hat{R}^2_{Y \cdot X_1 X_2} = b_1^2 + b_2^2 + 2 b_1 b_2 r_{X_1 X_2}$$

This result generalizes to the case in which there are $P \geq 2$ predictors:

$$\hat{R}^2_{Y \cdot X_1 X_2 \ldots X_P} = \sum_{p=1}^{P} b_p^2 + 2 \sum_{p=1}^{P} \sum_{\substack{p'=1 \\ p < p'}}^{P} b_p b_{p'} r_{X_p X_{p'}}$$

We now provide two other formulas for $\hat{R}^2_{Y \cdot X_1 X_2 \ldots X_P}$ which may prove useful under different circumstances. These can be developed algebraically by substituting equivalent terms for b_1 and b_2 into the above equation for $\hat{R}^2_{Y \cdot X_1 X_2 \ldots X_P}$. For $P = 2$, convenient formulas are given by

$$\hat{R}^2_{Y \cdot X_1 X_2} = r_{Y X_1} b_1 + r_{Y X_2} b_2$$
$$\hat{R}^2_{Y \cdot X_1 X_2} = r^2_{Y X_1} + r^2_{Y(X_2 \cdot X_1)}$$

or

$$\hat{R}^2_{Y \cdot X_1 X_2} = r^2_{Y X_2} + r^2_{Y(X_1 \cdot X_2)}$$

For our example,

$$\hat{R}^2_{Y \cdot X_1 X_2} = (.6700)(.3714) + (.7080)(.4740) = .5840$$
$$\hat{R}^2_{Y \cdot X_1 X_2} = .6700^2 + .3681^2 = .5840$$
$$\hat{R}^2_{Y \cdot X_1 X_2} = .7080^2 + .2881^2 = .5840$$

Box 45-2   Procedures for computing $\hat{R}^2_{Y \cdot X_1 X_2 \ldots X_P}$

Step 1. Determine the correlation coefficients among predictor variables X_1, $X_2, \ldots, X_P$, and determine the correlation coefficients of each X_p and Y.

Step 2. Determine the P standardized regression weights $b_1, b_2, \ldots, b_P$.

Step 3. Compute $\hat{R}^2_{Y \cdot X_1 X_2 \ldots X_P}$:

$$\hat{R}^2_{Y \cdot X_1 X_2 \ldots X_P} = \sum_{p=1}^{P} b_p^2 + 2 \sum_{p=1}^{P} \sum_{\substack{p'=1 \\ p < p'}}^{P} b_p b_{p'} r_{X_p X_{p'}}$$

$$\hat{R}^2_{Y \cdot X_1 X_2 \ldots X_P} = r_{YX_1} b_1 + r_{YX_2} b_2 + \cdots + r_{YX_P} b_P$$

or

$$\hat{R}^2_{Y \cdot X_1 X_2 \ldots X_P} = r^2_{YX_1} + r^2_{Y(X_2 \cdot X_1)} + \cdots + r^2_{Y(X_P \cdot X_1 X_2 \ldots X_{P-1})}$$

These formulas extend directly to the multiple-predictor case. For the first formula,

$$\hat{R}^2_{Y \cdot X_1 X_2 \ldots X_P} = \sum_{p=1}^{P} r_{YX_p} b_p$$

Since the others are variations of one another, we present only one example:

$$\hat{R}^2_{Y \cdot X_1 X_2 \ldots X_P} = r^2_{YX_1} + r^2_{Y(X_2 \cdot X_1)} + r^2_{Y(X_3 \cdot X_1 X_2)} + \cdots + r^2_{Y(X_P \cdot X_1 X_2 \ldots X_{P-1})}$$

Notice that $r^2_{Y(X_1 \cdot X_2 X_3 \ldots X_{P-1})}$ indicates the increase in $\hat{R}^2$ due to adding the Pth variable to an equation containing predictors $X_1 X_2 \cdots X_{P-1}$. This property will be very useful in other contexts described later.

At this point there is only one way for $\hat{R}^2_{Y \cdot X_1 X_2 \ldots X_P}$ to equal zero. This can happen only if $b_1 = b_2 = \cdots = b_P = 0$. For completeness, in Box 45-2 we give methods for computing $\hat{R}^2_{Y \cdot X_1 X_2 \ldots X_P}$.

45-10. TESTING THE MULTIPLE CORRELATION COEFFICIENT FOR STATISTICAL SIGNIFICANCE

In the one-predictor model, the hypothesis $H_0: \rho_{YX} = 0$ is equivalent to the hypothesis $H_0: \beta_1 = 0$. For $p > 1$, this equivalence extends in a direct fashion. Let us define the population squared correlation coefficient as $R^2_{Y \cdot X_1 X_2 \ldots X_P}$. The hypothesis $H_0: R^2_{Y \cdot X_1 X_2 \ldots X_P} = 0$ is equivalent to the hypothesis H_0: all $\beta_p = 0$, since the only way that $R^2_{Y \cdot X_1 X_2 \ldots X_P}$ could equal zero would be if each constituent β_p were also equal to zero.

The test statistic for this hypothesis is

$$F = \frac{N - P - 1}{P} \frac{\hat{R}^2}{1 - \hat{R}^2}$$

Critical values are read from the F distribution with P and $N - P - 1$ degrees of freedom. For the data of Table 45-1,

$$F = \frac{40 - 2 - 1}{2} \left(\frac{0.5840}{1 - 0.5840} \right) = 25.97$$

Since $F = 25.97 > F_{2,37:.95} = 3.26$, one can reject the hypothesis that $R^2_{Y \cdot X_1 X_2} = 0$, with $\alpha = .05$. When $P = 1$, the test statistic reduces to

$$F = \frac{N - 2}{1} \left(\frac{r^2_{XY}}{1 - r^2_{XY}} \right)$$

By taking the square root of both sides,

$$\sqrt{F} = t = \frac{\sqrt{N - 2} \; r_{XY}}{\sqrt{1 - r^2_{XY}}}$$

the same formula we reported in Section 32-7 for testing $H_0: \rho_{XY} = 0$. Again, we see that multiple regression analysis is an extension of the concepts of simple regression.

For completeness, we provide the procedure for testing $H_0: R^2_{Y \cdot X_1 X_2 \ldots X_P} = 0$ and $H_0: \beta_1 = \beta_2 = \cdots = \beta_P = 0$ in Box 45-3.

Results of this test are usually summarized in an ANOVA table similar to that of Table 45-3. The ANOVA table for the data of Table 45-1 is shown as Table 45-4. The numbers in Table 45-4 are

$$SS_T = (N - 1)S_Y^2 = (40 - 1)(27.8820^2) = 30{,}318.80$$

$$SS_{reg} = (N - 1)S_Y^2 \hat{R}^2 = (40 - 1)(27.8820^2)(0.5840)$$
$$= 17{,}706.20$$

Box 45-3   Procedure for testing $H_0: R^2_{Y \cdot X_1 X_2 \ldots X_P}$ and $H_0: \beta_1 = \beta_2 = \cdots = \beta_P = 0$

Step 1. Compute

$$\hat{R}^2_{Y \cdot X_1 X_2 \ldots X_P} \quad \text{and} \quad F = \frac{N - P - 1}{P} \left(\frac{\hat{R}^2}{1 - \hat{R}^2} \right)$$

Step 2. Reject H_0 if $F > F_{P,N-P-1:1-\alpha}$.

Table 45-3. ANOVA table for multiple regression

Source	df	Sum of squares	Mean square	F
Regression P		$(N-1)S_Y^2\hat{R}^2$	$\dfrac{N-1}{P}S_Y^2\hat{R}^2$	$\left(\dfrac{N-P-1}{P}\right)\left(\dfrac{\hat{R}^2}{1-\hat{R}^2}\right)$
Residual	$N-P-1$	$(N-1)S_Y^2(1-\hat{R}^2)$	$\dfrac{N-1}{N-P-1}S_Y^2(1-\hat{R}^2)$	
Total	$N-1$	$(N-1)S_Y^2$		

Table 45-4. ANOVA table for data of Table 45-1

Source	df	Sum of squares	Mean square	F	$\hat{R}^2$
Regression	2	17,694.7	8847.4	25.93[a]	.58
Residual	37	12,624.1	341.19		
Total	39	30,318.8			

[a] Significant at $\alpha = .05$ for $F_{2,37:.95} = 3.26$.

and

$$SS_R = (N-1)S_Y^2(1-\hat{R}^2) = (40-1)(27.8820^2)(0.4160)$$
$$= 12,612.60$$

with

$$v_T = N - 1 = 39$$

$$v_{\text{reg}} = P = 2$$

and

$$v_R = N - P - 1 = 37$$

45-11. COMMENTS ABOUT $\hat{R}^2$ AND $S_{Y \cdot x_1 x_2 \ldots x_P}^2$

Although it is standard practice to test the hypothesis that R^2 in the population is equal to zero, a comment is in order when it comes to interpreting the magnitude of $\hat{R}^2$ in a sample. The more predictor variables P that one includes in a particular multiple regression analysis involving N individuals or sample units, the larger $\hat{R}^2$ can be expected to be, even when the population R^2 equals zero. This increase in $\hat{R}^2$ as P increases can be illustrated through the formula for $\hat{R}^2$. As we saw,

$$\hat{R}^2_{Y \cdot X_1 X_2 \ldots X_P} = r_{YX_1} b_1 + r_{YX_2} b_2 + \cdots + r_{YX_P} b_P$$

where $b_1, b_2, \ldots, b_P$ are the standardized regression coefficients. Because the equation for $\hat{Y}$ is that of the best-fitting line, some of the sample fit can be merely due to chance fluctuations, and a large correlation can be generated from small b_p and r_{YX_p} values. For example, suppose $P = 10$, $b_p = .08$, and $r_{YX_p} = .25$ for each p. For this case, $\hat{R}^2 = 10(.08)(.25) = .20$. This means that small, but not statistically significant, correlations can greatly increase the magnitude of $\hat{R}^2_{Y \cdot X_1 X_2 \ldots X_P}$.

Assuming that $R^2 = 0$, the expected value of $\hat{R}^2$ can be shown to equal

$$E(\hat{R}^2_{Y \cdot X_1 X_2 \ldots X_P}) = \frac{P}{N - 1}$$

Thus, whenever P is large, relative to N, $\hat{R}^2$ can be expected to be large by chance alone. In the present example, with $P = 2$ and $N = 40$, $E(\hat{R}^2_{Y \cdot X_1 X_2}) = $ $2/39 = .0513$ if H_0 is true. If $P = 10$ predictor variables were used instead, $E(\hat{R}^2_{Y \cdot X_1 X_2 \ldots X_{10}}) = 10/39 = .2564$. That is, on average one would expect to obtain a sample $\hat{R}^2$ of .2564 even if R^2 in the population were equal to zero.

In interpreting a particular $\hat{R}^2$, one is advised to *correct* it with regard to its chance value, such as one might do when correcting a multiple-choice test score for guessing. This adjusted $\hat{R}^2$ may be computed according to the formula

$$\hat{R}^2_A = 1 - (1 - \hat{R}^2) \left(\frac{N - 1}{N - P - 1} \right)$$

where $\hat{R}^2_A$ represents the adjusted squared multiple correlation coefficient. This formula makes $\hat{R}^2_A$ equal to 0 when $\hat{R}^2$ equals its expected value and $\hat{R}^2_A$ equal to 1 when $\hat{R}^2 = 1$. For our example,

$$\hat{R}^2_A = 1 - (1 - .5840)(39/37) = 1 - .4385 = .5615$$

45-12. ASSUMPTIONS UNDERLYING HYPOTHESIS TESTING IN MULTIPLE REGRESSION ANALYSIS

In Section 7-6, we specified four criteria to be satisfied for a valid interpretation of r_{XY} to be possible. The relationship between Y and X had to be linear, variability about the line had to be homoscedastic, and no trunction of the variables or outliers in the sample was allowed. These criteria must still be met for each predictor for a proper interpretation of $\hat{R}^2$. The assumptions to be met for appropriate hypothesis testing in the multiple regression model parallel those required in analysis of variance, and we now discuss these in the present context.

In multiple regression analysis, each set of scores on the ith individual constitutes an observation; that is, we observe on each person the values Y_i, $X_{i1}, X_{i2}, \ldots, X_{iP}$. Between individuals, these sets of data must be independent. In addition, we require that the error or residual deviations be normally distributed, with a mean of zero and a variance of $\sigma^2_{Y \cdot x_1 x_2 \ldots x_P}$. The variance about the regression must be homoscedastic.

One of two assumptions concerning the distribution of the predictor variables must be met. One model requires that the distribution of the X variables be continuous and that the joint distribution of Y and X variables be normal. This means that each variable has a normal distribution, with its own mean and variance, and that each pair of variables taken jointly has a bell-shaped distribution. For the social sciences, this is a very limited model, since it disallows the use of variables such as sex, attitude as measured on a Likert scale, treatment, and other dichotomous, discrete, and qualitative variables.

A second model for regression allows the inclusion of these kinds of variables as predictors. In this model, the predictors are considered to be fixed constants, known in advance. For example, consider the first subject in Table 45-1, who had a mental age of 9.2 and a reading test score of 61. Under this model, the two values are considered to be measured without error. We know that this is unlikely and that if we measured these scores again, they would likely change because of measurement error. Because of this fixed-predictor assumption, our generalizations are limited to populations consisting only of values equal to those in our sample. Therefore, it is imperative that our sample be representative of the population of interest. In the remaining sections on regression analysis, we operate under this model, and so these assumptions should be kept firmly in mind.

45-13. EXERCISES

45-1. For your sample of 40 students, find $r_{YX_1 \cdot X_2}$ and $r_{YX_2 \cdot X_1}$, where $Y =$ score on final, $X_1 =$ College Board score, and $X_2 =$ pretest.

45-2. Test the hypotheses $H_0: \rho_{YX_1 \cdot X_2} = 0$ and $H_0: \rho_{YX_2 \cdot X_1} = 0$.

45-3. Find the 95 percent confidence intervals for $\rho_{YX_1 \cdot X_2}$ and $\rho_{YX_2 \cdot X_1}$.

45-4. In Exercises 45-2 and 45-3, two tests and two confidence intervals were examined. What is the limit to the risk of a type I error in either problem for the critical values you used?

45-5. In a comparative study of the teaching of reading in which 50 students were assigned to a control group the following sample correlation coefficients were obtained:

	Y	X_1	X_2
Y	1.00	.61	.39
X_1		1.00	.24
X_2			1.00

For an experimental program, the corresponding correlations were

	Y	X_1	X_2
Y	1.00	.71	.29
X_1		1.00	.22
X_2			1.00

Is there any reason to believe that $\rho_{YX_1 \cdot X_2}^{(C)} = \rho_{YX_1 \cdot X_2}^{(E)}$?

45-6. For your sample of size 40, find $r_{Y(X_1 \cdot X_2)}$ and $r_{Y(X_2 \cdot X_1)}$, where the variables are defined in Exercise 45-1.

45-7. Is there any reason to believe that $\rho_{Y(X_1 \cdot X_2)} = 0$ and $\rho_{Y(X_2 \cdot X_1)} = 0$? (Refer to Exercise 45-6.)

45-8. Combine your data of 40 subjects with two other students to obtain a total sample size of 120. Obtain, on a computer, the multiple regression equation for $Y =$ final, predicted from $X_1 =$ sex, $X_2 =$ College Board score, $X_3 =$ high school biology, and $X_4 =$ pretest.

45-9. For your combined sample of $N = 120$ subjects, is there any reason to believe that $R_{Y \cdot X_1 X_2 X_3 X_4}^2 = 0$?

45-10. Find the 95 percent confidence interval for $\sigma_{Y \cdot X_1 X_2 X_3 X_4}^2$.

45-11. Obtain the multiple regression equation of Y on X_2 and X_3, and compare $\hat{R}_{Y \cdot X_2 X_3}^2$ to $\hat{R}_{Y \cdot X_1 X_2 X_3 X_4}^2$. Explain what $\Delta = \hat{R}_{Y \cdot X_1 X_2 X_3 X_4}^2 - \hat{R}_{Y \cdot X_2 X_3}^2$ measures.

45-12. Some statisticians argue that variables such as X_1 and X_3 cannot be used in regression analysis. Comment on this statement.

45-13. For your example, show that

a. $\hat{R}_{Y \cdot X_1 X_2 X_3 X_4}^2 =$
$$r_{YX_1} b_1 + r_{YX_2} b_2 + r_{YX_3} b_3 + r_{YX_4} b_4$$

b. $\hat{R}_{Y \cdot X_1 X_2 X_3 X_4}^2 =$
$$\sum_{p=1}^{4} b_p^2 + \sum_{p=1}^{4} \sum_{\substack{p'=1 \\ p < p'}}^{4} b_p b_{p'} r_{X_p X_{p'}}$$

Identification of Significant Predictors for a Multiple Regression Equation

46-1. TESTING THE REGRESSION WEIGHTS FOR STATISTICAL SIGNIFICANCE

It is possible to test each B_p separately, or all coefficients simultaneously, for statistical significance. In either case, standard statistical hypothesis testing procedures are used, wherein one simply compares each B_p to its standard error. In the planned case, the separate test statistics are referred to the critical values reported in the Dunn table with $C = P$ comparisons and with $v = N - P - 1$ degrees of freedom. In the post hoc Scheffé model, the test statistic is referred to $S = \sqrt{PF_{P,N-P-1:1-\alpha}}$.

The standard error of an unstandardized regression coefficient, such as B_1, is given by the following extension of the formulas in Chapter 44.

Standard error of an unstandardized regression coefficient

The squared standard error of B_1 is

$$SE_{B_1}^2 = \frac{MS_{R(Y \cdot X_1 X_2 \ldots X_P)}}{SS_{R(X_1 \cdot X_2 X_3 \ldots X_P)}}$$

where

$$MS_{R(Y \cdot X_1 X_2 \ldots X_P)} = \frac{SS_T(1 - R_{Y \cdot X_1 X_2 \ldots X_P}^2)}{N - P - 1}$$

and

$$SS_{R(X_1 \cdot X_2 X_3 \ldots X_P)} = SS_{T(X_1)}(1 - R_{X_1 \cdot X_2 X_3 \ldots X_P}^2)$$
$$= (N - P)MS_{R(X_1 \cdot X_2 X_3 \ldots X_P)}$$

The standard errors of $B_2, B_3, \ldots, B_P$ are defined in a similar fashion.

The statistical test of $H_0 : \beta_p = 0$ proceeds according to familiar test theory. The test is described in Box 46-1.

Box 46-1   Procedure for testing $H_0 : \beta_p = 0$ against $H_1 : \beta_p \neq 0$

Step 1. Compute

$$t = \frac{B_p - 0}{SE_{B_p}}$$

Step 2. The hypothesis is rejected with a risk of a type I error set at α according to the following decision rules:

a. For a single test

Decision Rule: Reject H_0 if $t < t_{v_2 : \alpha/2}$ or if $t > t_{v_2 : 1-\alpha/2}$

where $v_2 = N - P - 1$.

b. For a planned testing of all P regression coefficients

Decision Rule: Reject H_0 if $t < t_{\alpha : P, v_2}^{\text{Dunn}}$ or $t > t_{\alpha : P, v_2}^{\text{Dunn}}$

c. For a post hoc testing of the regression coefficients

Decision Rule: Reject H_0 if $t < -S$ or $t > +S$

where $S = \sqrt{PF_{P, N-P-1 : 1-\alpha}}$.

We now apply these procedures to the data of Table 45-4, for which $B_1 = 6.6485$. To determine whether this value differs significantly from zero, we must first determine the value of SE_{B_1}. From Table 45-5 we find

$$\text{MS}_{R(Y \cdot X_1 X_2)} = 341.19$$

and

$$\text{SS}_{R(X_1 \cdot X_2)} = (N - 2)\text{MS}_{R(X_1 \cdot X_2)} = 38(1.5015) = 57.0570$$

As a result,

$$\text{SE}_{B_1} = \sqrt{\frac{341.19}{57.0570}} = 2.4454$$

and

$$t = \frac{6.6485}{2.4454} = 2.72$$

1. If a single test were performed with $\alpha = .05$, the critical values would be $t = \pm 2.02$, with $v = 37$. We would reject H_0.

2. If each of the two regression weights were tested by Dunn's procedure with $C = 2$, $\alpha = .05$, and $v = 37$, the critical values would be $t = \pm 2.33$. We would reject H_0.

3. If a familywise Scheffé post hoc analysis were performed with $\alpha = .05$, the critical values would be defined by $S = \pm\sqrt{2F_{2,37:.95}} = \pm\sqrt{2(3.26)} = \pm 2.55$. We would reject H_0.

Thus, according to each of the above comparison procedures, we would conclude that β_1 differs significantly from zero. That is, mental age is statistically related to performance on the arithmetic test, even when the contribution of the reading test is considered. In addition, $H_0: \beta_2 = 0$ is also rejected, since the statistical test of B_2 gives

$$t = \frac{0.7648}{0.2203} = 3.47$$

This t value corresponds exactly to that obtained for testing $H_0: \rho_{YX_2 \cdot X_1} = 0$ in Chapter 45. This is analogous to the simple regression model where the test of $\rho_{YX} = 0$ was identical to the test of $\beta_1 = 0$.

Confidence intervals for the beta weights are determined according to familiar interval estimation procedures. In addition to testing β_p values for significance from zero, we can place the $1 - \alpha$ percent confidence intervals about the unknown values. The model is shown in Box 46-2.

Box 46-2   Confidence intervals for regression coefficients

The $100(1 - \alpha)$ percent confidence interval for β_p is

$$B_p - t(SE_{B_p}) < \beta_p < B_p + t(SE_{B_p})$$

where $v = N - P - 1$ and the value of t is chosen according to the procedures in Box 46-1, step 2.

The following respective confidence intervals for β_1 are:
For a per comparison control:

$$\beta_1 = 6.6485 \pm 2.02(2.4454) = 6.6485 \pm 4.9397$$

For a $C = 2$ planned analysis control:

$$\beta_1 = 6.6485 \pm 2.33(2.4454) = 6.6485 \pm 5.6978$$

For a post hoc analysis control:

$$\beta_1 = 6.6485 \pm 2.55(2.4454) = 6.6485 \pm 6.2358$$

Since zero is not included in any of the intervals, $\beta_1 \neq 0$. These results are, of course, consistent with the tests of hypothesis that were previously performed.

It cannot be emphasized too strongly that one must commit oneself to only one of these three models. For the per comparison control, the hypothesis test of $H_0: \beta_1 = 0$ should have been the only test of interest, since the entire $\alpha = .05$ is used for this *one* comparison. The Dunn procedure must be planned in advance, and the test of $H_0: R^2_{Y \cdot X_1 X_2} = 0$ should not be performed. The only case that permits a justified test of $H_0: R^2_{Y \cdot X_1 X_2} = 0$, $H_0: \beta_1 = 0$, and $H_0: \beta_2 = 0$ is the third case, referred to as post hoc analysis control. First testing $R^2_{Y \cdot X_1 X_2}$ for significance and then conducting a post hoc examination of the beta weights is permissible, because it is a direct application of Scheffé's method. In addition, under this model, a test of $H_0: \beta_1 = \beta_2$ could also be performed.

Comparing corresponding beta weights in two different samples involves a direct extension of the methods of Section 44-3. Thus, to test $H_0: \beta_p^{(1)} = \beta_p^{(2)}$, we use

$$t = \frac{B_p^{(1)} - B_p^{(2)}}{\sqrt{SE_{B_p}^{2(1)} + SE_{B_p}^{2(2)}}}$$

with $v = N_1 - P - 1 + N_2 - P - 1 = v_1 + v_2$ and with each standard error based on a pooled estimate of the common unknown variance. In this case,

$$MS_R = \frac{v_1 MS_{R(1)} + v_2 MS_{R(2)}}{v_1 + v_2}$$

This model extends directly to cover the K-sample problem, in terms of pairwise comparisons. The assumption required are:

1. Samples are independent.
2. Observations within samples are independent.
3. Residual variances within populations are equal.
4. Error deviations are normally distributed.

46-2. ASSESSMENT OF VARIATION EXPLAINED BY INDIVIDUAL PREDICTORS

In Section 9-2 we saw that r^2_{YX} could be used as an estimate of the proportion of the variability in Y that could be explained by the linear relationship between X and Y. In Section 45-7 we saw that $R^2_{Y \cdot X_1 X_2 \ldots X_P}$ could be used, similarly, as an estimate of the percentage of variation in Y that could be explained by the linear relationship of Y with $X_1, X_2, \ldots, X_P$ collectively. It certainly makes sense to ask how much of the total variation is explained by X_1 alone, by X_2 alone, etc. Unfortunately, as soon as $P > 1$, no simple method is recommended by statisticians to do this. The complication in this case arises because the components of explained variation associated with X_1, with X_2, etc., are themselves correlated.

Consider, for example, the two methods for computing $\hat{R}^2_{Y \cdot X_1 X_2 \ldots X_P}$ as described in Section 45-9. For $P = 2$, $\hat{R}^2$ reduces to

$$\hat{R}^2 = b_1^2 + 2b_1 b_2 r_{X_1 X_2} + b_2^2$$

For the data of Table 45-1,

$$.5840 = .1379 + .2214 + .2247$$

We see that X_1 appears to account for 14 percent of the explained variability in Y, that X_2 appears to account for 22 percent of the explained variability, and that X_1 and X_2 appear to share 22 percent of the explained variability. A difficulty becomes obvious if b_1, b_2, or $r_{X_1 X_2}$ is negative. Under this condition the middle term will have a negative algebraic value and sums of squares are always positive.

According to the second formula for computing $\hat{R}^2$ when $P=2$,

$$\begin{aligned}\hat{R}^2 &= r_{YX_1}b_1 + r_{YX_2}b_2\\ &= (.6700)(.3714) + (.7080)(.4746)\\ &= .2480 + .3360\\ &= .5840\end{aligned}$$

One is advised against saying that X_1 explains 25 percent of the total variation, since r_{YX_1} does not have X_2 partialed out. In like manner, 34 percent is not the amount of explained variation associated with X_2, since r_{YX_2} does not have X_1 partialed out.

As these two methods for computing $\hat{R}^2$ illustrate, it is easy to fall into the trap of thinking that we can determine the percentage of variability explained individually by $X_1, X_2, \ldots, X_P$. However, it must be emphasized that this must not be done. In addition, there is the substantive problem that the apparent contribution of any variable to the regression equation is intimately related to the nature and number of other predictor variables included by the researcher in the analysis. The amount of variability explained by a variable, whether it is large or small, is strictly a function of how many other predictor variables accompany it in the equation, as well as the intercorrelations among all variables.

46-3. METHOD OF ALL POSSIBLE REGRESSIONS

One way that researchers have tried to estimate the amount of explained variation associated with a particular variable is to examine the multiple correlation coefficients generated by using all possible combinations of predictors. The method is not very useful, since it was originally designed to solve a different problem. The different problem is the determination of the minimum number of variables required to give a satisfactory prediction equation. The method is best illustrated by an example.

Consider predicting Y from the set of variables X_1, X_2, and X_3. If the cost of measurement were high, such as in economic or industrial investigations, one may wish to use the fewest number of variables that give an adequate prediction for practical purposes. In this case, seven different possible regressions could be used: Y could be predicted from X_1, X_2, or X_3 alone; from the combinations X_1 and X_2, X_1 and X_3, and X_2 and X_3; or from X_1, X_2, and X_3 together. Suppose the multiple correlations for these seven different regressions are as reported in Table 46-1. As we see, the use of X_1, X_2, and X_3 provides the best prediction, with $\hat{R}^2_{Y \cdot X_1 X_2 X_3} = .62$. The next best prediction is offered with X_2 and X_3, for which $\hat{R}^2_{Y \cdot X_2 X_3} = .60$.

Since $\hat{R}^2_{Y \cdot X_2 X_3} = .60$ is almost equal to $\hat{R}^2_{Y \cdot X_1 X_2 X_3} = .62$, one might be advised to use X_2 and X_3 alone, because the expense involved in measuring X_1

Table 46-1. Measures of association for all possible regressions of three variables used to predict one variable

Predictors	$\hat{R}^2$
X_1	.18
X_2	.25
X_3	.55
X_1 and X_2	.29
X_1 and X_3	.38
X_2 and X_3	.60
X_1, X_2, and X_3	.62

increases the percentage of explained variation only minimally. In this example, even X_3 alone might be sufficient, since $r^2_{YX_3} = .55$. This is only .05 less than the best two-variable solution. In the final analysis, the economics of the situation determine the best strategy.

46-4. METHODS OF BACKWARD ELIMINATION AND FORWARD SELECTION

Alternate procedures have been proposed that alleviate the problem of examining all possible regressions. In many cases, these models are preferable since the number of possible regression equations for P variables can become very large. These methods are called *backward elimination* and *forward selection*.

Backward elimination begins with the full regression equation involving $X_1, X_2, \ldots, X_P$. For the full set of predictors, $\hat{R}^2_{Y \cdot X_1 X_2 \ldots X_P}$ is computed. Next, one computes the P regression equations that result from the removal of one predictor variable. Then the various P values of $\hat{R}^2$ are computed, and each is compared to $\hat{R}^2_{Y \cdot X_1 X_2 \ldots X_P}$. The equation, with one variable removed, that produces an $\hat{R}^2$ closest to the full squared correlation is retained. With this equation as a new starting point, the process of removing one variable is repeated, so that $P - 1$ regression equations and associated $\hat{R}^2$ values are computed. These $P - 1$ squared correlations are compared to the $\hat{R}^2$ from the previous step, and the equation with the largest one is retained. The process continues in this fashion. At any step along the way, however, whenever a noticeable decrease in $\hat{R}^2$ is observed, relative to $\hat{R}^2$ in the preceding step, a judgment is made to terminate the process.

Forward selection is the reverse of backward elimination. In this approach, one starts with the single predictor that has the largest correlation with Y. Then the variable that increases $\hat{R}^2$ the most is added. This process is repeated, and judgment is made to terminate the process when the addition to $\hat{R}^2$ is deemed negligible.

46-5. METHOD OF STEPWISE REGRESSION

The most popular method in use for selecting the fewest number of predictor variables necessary to guarantee adequate prediction is based on a model referred to as *stepwise regression*, which is actually a combination of the forward and backward methods. We now examine the stepwise procedure. According to this method, the X variable exhibiting the highest zero-order correlation, in absolute value, with Y enters into the regression equation first. Let the first variable selected be X_1. Thus, with X_1 in the model, $\hat{R}^2$ is $r^2_{YX_1}$. Second, the next variable selected, say X_2, will produce the greatest increment in $\hat{R}^2$. The X variable that will satisfy this condition is the one with the largest squared part correlation $r^2_{Y(X_2 \cdot X_1)}$. At this point a test is made to determine whether X_2 should be added to X_1. If the test of $H_0: \rho_{Y(X_2 \cdot X_1)} = 0$ is rejected, X_2 is added. Most computer programs use an alpha value of about .05 for this test. If the test is not significant, the process is terminated. Let us say that X_2 enters. With both X_1 and X_2 in the equation, the tests of $H_0: \rho_{YX_1 \cdot X_2} = 0$ and $H_0: \rho_{YX_2 \cdot X_1} = 0$ are performed. These tests are usually performed at an α value of about .10. If a variable does not surpass the criterion, it is eliminated.

The procedure extends in a straightforward fashion, described in Box

---

Box 46-3   Procedures for performing a stepwise regression

Step 1. Select the independent variable with the largest correlation with Y. Let it be X_1. The amount of variability in Y explained by this variable is

$$\hat{R}^2_{YX_1} = r^2_{YX_1}$$

Step 2. Compute, for the remaining $P - 1$ predictor variables, the squared part correlations with Y.

Step 3. Select the variable with the largest squared part correlation with Y, and enter it into a multiple regression along with X_1, if it exceeds the selected criterion. Let X_2 be the variable selected.

Step 4. Test each variable in the equation for retention.

Step 5. Repeat the process until all P independent variables have been included or until none of the variables meet the criterion for entry or removal.

46-3. After P successive steps,

$$\hat{R}^2_{Y \cdot X_1 X_2 ... X_P} = r^2_{YX_1} + r^2_{Y(X_2 \cdot X_1)} + r^2_{Y(X_3 \cdot X_1 X_2)} + \cdots + r^2_{Y(X_P \cdot X_1 X_2 ... X_{P-1})}$$

Stepwise regression requires a test of the part correlation coefficient. We derive the general form of the test in the chapter appendix. The model for testing the part correlation is given in Box 46-4.

Box 46-4   How to perform a partial F test

Step 1. Suppose p variables $X_1, X_2, \ldots, X_p$ have entered a regression equation. Let the sum of squares explained by $X_1, X_2, \ldots, X_p$ be denoted $SS_{X_1, X_2, ..., X_p}$. For this sum of squares, $v_p = p$.

Step 2. Add the variable $X_{(p+1)}$ to the regression, and let the sum of squares with this larger set of variables be denoted $SS_{X_1, X_2, ..., X_p, X_{(p+1)}}$. For this sum of squares $v_{(p+1)} = p + 1$.

Step 3. The additional contribution to the sum of squares explained by adding $X_{(p+1)}$ is given by

$$SS_{X_1, X_2, ... X_p, X_{(p+1)}} - SS_{X_1, X_2, ..., X_p} = SS_{add}$$

and its degrees of freedom are

$$v = v_{(p+1)} - v_p = p + 1 - p = 1$$

Step 4. With the first $p + 1$ variables in the equation, compute the sum of squares residual as

$$SS_R = (1 - \hat{R}^2_{Y \cdot X_1 X_2 ... X_p X_{(p+1)}}) SS_T$$

and the mean square residual as

$$MS_R = \frac{SS_R}{N - (p+1) - 1} = \frac{SS_R}{N - p - 2}$$

Step 5. Test the hypothesis

$$H_0: \rho^2_{Y(X_{(p+1)}) \cdot X_1 X_2 ... X_p} = 0$$

with

$$F = \frac{MS_{add}}{MS_R}$$

and reject H_0 if $F > F_{1, N-p-2:1-\alpha}$. Note that $MS_{add} = SS_{add}$.

As a simple example of the stepwise procedure, recall when mental age and reading scores were used to predict performance on the arithmetic test. In this example, X_2 = reading score would be selected first as a candidate for the regression equation, since $r_{YX_1} = .6700$ and $r_{YX_2} = .7080$. Since r_{YX_2} is statistically different from zero at $\alpha = .05$, it would be entered into the equation in step 1. In step 2, one would evaluate the part correlation $r_{Y(X_2 \cdot X_1)} = .3681$. With $\hat{R}^2_{Y \cdot X_1 X_2}$ given previously as .5840, we have, for the test of H_0: $\rho_{Y(X_2 \cdot X_1)} = 0$, that

$$F = \frac{40 - 1 - 2}{1} \left(\frac{0.3681^2}{1 - 0.5840} \right) = 12.05$$

is significant at $\alpha = .05$. Since the tests of both partial correlations were significant, neither would be removed, and the procedure is terminated.

In a variation of forward selection, researcher-defined sets of variables are added in groups, rather than individually, at each step of the forward selection process. In this case, SS_{added} represents the additional explained variation provided by the set of, for instance, q predictors beyond that explained by the previously entered p predictors. As shown in the chapter appendix, the only change would come in the appropriate degrees of freedom for the SS added (add) and SS residual (R), which would now be given by $v_1 = q$ and $v_2 = N - (p + q) - 1$. Then

$$F = \frac{SS_{add}/q}{SS_R/(N - p - q - 1)} = \frac{MS_{add}}{MS_R}$$

46-6. APPENDIX

To determine whether adding q predictors to an equation already containing p predictors increases $\hat{R}^2$ by a statistically significant amount, determine $\hat{R}^2_{Y \cdot x_1 \dots x_p x_{p+1} \dots x_{p+q}}$ and $\hat{R}^2_{Y \cdot x_1 \dots x_p}$. Then

$$\hat{R}^2_{Y \cdot x_1 \dots x_{p+q}} = \hat{R}^2_{Y \cdot x_1 \dots x_p} + \hat{R}^2_{add}$$

Since

$$1 = 1 - \hat{R}^2_{Y \cdot x_1 \dots x_{p+q}} + \hat{R}^2_{Y \cdot x_1 \dots x_{p+q}}$$

it follows that

$$1 = (1 - \hat{R}^2_{Y \cdot x_1 \dots x_{p+q}}) + \hat{R}^2_{Y \cdot x_1 \dots x_p} + \hat{R}^2_{add}$$

If we now multiply this equation by $(N - 1)S_Y^2 = SS_T$,

$$SS_T = (1 - \hat{R}^2_{Y \cdot x_1 \dots x_{p+q}})SS_T + \hat{R}^2_{Y \cdot x_1 \dots x_p}SS_T + \hat{R}^2_{add}SS_T$$

with associated degrees of freedom given by

$$N - 1 = (N - p - q - 1) + (p) + (q)$$

In this notation,

$$SS_R = (1 - \hat{R}^2_{Y \cdot X_1 \ldots X_{p+q}})SS_T$$

$$SS_{X_1 \ldots X_p} = \hat{R}^2_{Y \cdot X_1 \ldots X_p}SS_T$$

and

$$SS_{add} = \hat{R}^2_{add}SS_T$$

So

$$MS_{add} = \frac{\hat{R}^2_{add}SS_T}{q}$$

and

$$MS_R = \frac{(1 - \hat{R}^2_{Y \cdot X_1 \ldots X_{p+q}})SS_T}{N - p - q - 1}$$

Thus, we can construct an F ratio to test

$$H_0: R^2_{add} = 0$$

by computing

$$F = \frac{MS_{add}}{MS_R}$$

The resulting F ratio is often called a *partial F test*. The hypothesis of the partial F test is rejected if $F > F_{v_1, v_2 : 1 - \alpha}$, where $v_1 = q$ and $v_2 = N - p - q - 1$.

46-7. EXERCISES

46-1. Consider the data of Exercise 45-1. Test the hypothesis that each of the regression coefficients is equal to zero.
 a. Do the test as a planned analysis with $\alpha = .05$.
 b. Do the test as a post hoc analysis with $\alpha = .05$.

46-2. Find the confidence intervals for the beta weights under models a and b of Exercise 46-1.

46-3. Do a stepwise regression on the data of Exercise 45-1, letting the computer select the order.

46-4. Report the results of Exercise 46-1 in a short article suitable for a professional journal.

CHAPTER 47

Analysis of Variance as a Multiple Regression Model

47-1. CODING QUALITATIVE VARIABLES FOR THE TWO-GROUP t TEST

We have seen on several occasions that a relationship exists between the two-sample t test and the point biserial correlation coefficient. Because both models reflect mean differences, we can use either as a basis for testing H_0: $\mu_{Y_1} = \mu_{Y_2}$. In this chapter we show that a simple extension of the model that connects $\hat{\psi} = \overline{Y}_1 - \overline{Y}_2$ to r_{pb} can be made that permits the use of regression theory to test the ANOVA hypothesis $H_0: \mu_{Y_1} = \mu_{Y_2} = \cdots = \mu_{Y_K}$.

To facilitate understanding this procedure, we examine in some detail the two-sample case. In calculating the point biserial correlation coefficient in Chapter 10, we assigned values of 0 and 1 to designate to which of the two groups a subject or observation belonged. We then showed that if the regression equation were determined, the slope equaled the difference in group means. Because the correlation coefficient is scale-free and location-free, we know that any other choice of values to designate group membership will yield the same correlation. Let us examine why the choice of 0 and 1 is preferred in most situations.

Let us call the predictor variable X_1. To denote the value of this variable in each group, we let X_{11} be the value in the first group and X_{21} the value in the second group. Following the procedures first presented in Chapter 10, let us predict the Y scores, using these coded values of X_{11} and X_{21}. The layout of the data is shown in Table 47-1. As before, the regression equation connecting $\hat{Y}$ to X_1 is

$$\hat{Y} = B_0 + B_1 X_1$$

Because the values of X_1 are all equal to X_{11} and X_{21}, it can be shown that

$$B_1 = \frac{\bar{Y}_2 - \bar{Y}_1}{X_{21} - X_{11}}$$

From this we see that the slope is equal to the difference in the group means on Y divided by the difference in the coded values. If we select X_{11} and X_{21} so that $X_{21} - X_{11} = 1$, then B_1 reduces to

$$B_1 = \bar{Y}_2 - \bar{Y}_1$$

or just a contrast or simple difference in mean values. Let us say that we choose X_{21} and X_{11} so that the slope equals $\bar{Y}_2 - \bar{Y}_1$.

Table 47-1. Data for predicting dependent variable Y from coded values representing group membership

Group 1		Group 2	
Y	X_1	Y	X_2
Y_{11}	X_{11}	Y_{12}	X_{21}
Y_{21}	X_{11}	Y_{22}	X_{21}
.	.	.	.
.	.	.	.
.	.	.	.
$Y_{N_1 1}$	X_{11}	$Y_{N_2 2}$	X_{21}

If we now examine the intercept

$$B_0 = \bar{Y} - B_1 \bar{X}$$

we have

$$B_0 = \bar{Y} - (\bar{Y}_2 - \bar{Y}_1)\bar{X}_1$$

We can show that

$$B_0 = \frac{X_{21}\bar{Y}_1 - X_{11}\bar{Y}_2}{X_{21} - X_{11}}$$

We have already seen that B_1 reduces to $\hat{\psi} = \bar{Y}_2 - \bar{Y}_1$ if we choose X_{21} and X_{11} so that $X_{21} - X_{11} = 1$. In addition, we can simplify B_0 if we make a judicious choice for X_{11} and X_{21}. Note that if we let $X_{11} = 0$ and $X_{21} = 1$, then B_0 reduces to

$$B_0 = \frac{1(\bar{Y}_1) - 0(\bar{Y}_2)}{1 - 0} = \bar{Y}_1$$

of just the mean value of Y in group 1. Thus not only does B_1 have a simple interpretation, but so, also, does B_0, provided we let $X_{11} = 0$ and $X_{21} = 1$.
   In addition, the regression equation then becomes

$$\hat{Y} = \bar{Y}_1 + (\bar{Y}_2 - \bar{Y}_1)X_1$$

If we substitute $X_1 = 0$, we have $\hat{Y} = \bar{Y}_1$. Similarly, substituting $X_1 = 1$ gives us $\hat{Y} = \bar{Y}_2$. Thus, the predicted value for any observation in a particular group is that group's mean. If we would like to maintain, as in previous chapters, the notation of membership in the kth group in terms of $k = 1$ and $k = 2$, we can denote the regression equation as

$$\bar{Y}_k = \bar{Y}_1 + (\bar{Y}_2 - \bar{Y}_1)X_{k1}$$

where $X_{k1} = 0$ for $k = 1$ and $X_{k1} = 1$ for $k = 2$.

47-2. DUMMY CODING FOR MORE THAN TWO GROUPS

The results examined for two groups can be extended to more than two groups. Suppose there are $K = 3$ groups. Because the degrees of freedom between groups are given by $v = K - 1 = 3 - 1 = 2$, we need to use a regression equation based on two coding variables, X_1 and X_2. In this case, we have

$$\hat{Y} = B_0 + B_1 X_1 + B_2 X_2$$

Box 47-1   Procedure for dummy-coding a qualitative variable to produce contrasts to a given group

Step 1. Determine the number of levels of the qualitative variable of interest. Let the number be denoted K.

Step 2. Define $K - 1$ dummy variables $X_1, X_2, \ldots, X_{K-1}$, which are given as follows:

Group	X_1	X_2	$\ldots$	X_{K-1}
1	1	0	$\ldots$	0
2	0	1	$\ldots$	0
$\cdots$				
K	0	0	$\ldots$	0

For this choice of codes, group K serves as the reference group. As a consequence,

$$B_0 = \bar{Y}_K$$

$$B_1 = \bar{Y}_1 - \bar{Y}_K = \hat{\psi}_{1,K}$$

$$B_2 = \bar{Y}_2 - \bar{Y}_K = \hat{\psi}_{2,K}$$

$$\cdot$$

$$\cdot$$

$$\cdot$$

$$B_{K-1} = \bar{Y}_{K-1} - \bar{Y}_K = \hat{\psi}_{K-1,K}$$

The regression equation is defined as

$$\bar{Y}_k = \bar{Y}_K + (\bar{Y}_1 - \bar{Y}_K)X_1 + \cdots + (\bar{Y}_{K-1} - \bar{Y}_K)X_{K-1}$$

The problem is to define X_1 and X_2 so that B_0, B_1, and B_2 have simple interpretations. Following the model of Section 47-1, we define X_1 and X_2 so that

$$B_0 = \bar{Y}_1 \qquad B_1 = \bar{Y}_2 - \bar{Y}_1 \qquad B_2 = \bar{Y}_3 - \bar{Y}_1$$

As shown in the appendix, the coding that achieves these slope values can be summarized as follows:

Group (k)	X_{k1}	X_{k2}
1	0	0
2	1	0
3	0	1

Coded values chosen in this way, so that the intercept equals the mean of a given group (in this example, the first group) and the slopes equal the differences between the means of the other groups and the given group, are called *dummy codes*.

We can see from this three-group example that one of the groups is given zeros on all codes. This group becomes a reference group for all the other groups, and the intercept of the regression equation B_0 equals the mean of the reference group. The other groups are given a coded score of 1 on one of the coding variables and a coded score of 0 on all the others. In the regression equation, the slope of a particular coded variable compares the mean of the group scored 1 on that variable to the mean of the reference group.

In our example, the first group is the reference group, since it received a code score of 0 on both coded variables. Variable X_1 was coded 1 in the second group, so that $B_1 = \bar{Y}_2 - \bar{Y}_1$. Similarly, variable X_2 was coded 1 in the third group, so that $B_2 = \bar{Y}_3 - \bar{Y}_1$.

We can extend these results to the K-group case. We will need $K - 1$ coded variables $X_1, X_2, \ldots, X_{K-1}$. We assign 0s and 1s to the variables to produce slopes that represent simple contrasts in means with all groups contrasted to the group coded $(0, 0, \ldots, 0)$. For this model, dummy coding proceeds as described in Box 47-1.

47-3. ANALYSIS OF VARIANCE AS A MULTIPLE REGRESSION PROBLEM

Not only do coded values allow the estimation of contrasts of interest via the regression slopes, but also we show in the chapter appendix that the sums of squares in the regression (reg) model actually reduce to those in the analysis of variance. In particular,

$$SS_{reg} = SS_B \quad \text{and} \quad SS_R = SS_W$$

As an example, consider the data of Table 47-2, which represent the pretest scores of the 39 students of Table 2-2 classified by college major

Table 47-2. Quantification of qualitative data to convert an ANOVA to a regression model where $Y =$ score on pretest and where college major for humanities, natural sciences, social sciences, and others is represented by X_1, X_2, and X_3

	Group 1				Group 2				Group 3				Group 4		
Y	X_1	X_2	X_3	Y	X_1	X_2	X_3	Y	X_1	X_2	X_3	Y	X_1	X_2	X_3
28	1	0	0	13	0	1	0	10	0	0	1	24	0	0	0
17	1	0	0	18	0	1	0	28	0	0	1	23	0	0	0
25	1	0	0	13	0	1	0	25	0	0	1	16	0	0	0
13	1	0	0	20	0	1	0	10	0	0	1	26	0	0	0
30	1	0	0	28	0	1	0	13	0	0	1	29	0	0	0
16	1	0	0	28	0	1	0	30	0	0	1	5	0	0	0
13	1	0	0	9	0	1	0					8	0	0	0
3	1	0	0	30	0	1	0					10	0	0	0
16	1	0	0									22	0	0	0
17	1	0	0									17	0	0	0
15	1	0	0									14	0	0	0
17	1	0	0									15	0	0	0
												16	0	0	0

(humanities, natural science, and social science), with others and unknowns treated as a fourth group. The ANOVA table for these data is presented in Table 47-3. The mean values are $\bar{Y}_1 = 17.5000$, $\bar{Y}_2 = 19.8750$, $\bar{Y}_3 = 19.3333$, and $\bar{Y}_4 = 17.3077$.

To show that the individual group means are obtained when dummy cod-

Table 47-3. Analysis of variance table for data of Table 47-2

Source	df	SS	MS	F	$\hat{\eta}^2 = \dfrac{SS_B}{SS_T}$
Between groups	3	46.38	15.46	0.26	.0217
Within groups	35	2093.98	59.83		
Total	38	2140.36			

ing is used, we now code all students with dummy variables as follows:

Major	X_1	X_2	X_3
Humanities	1	0	0
Natural science	0	1	0
Social science	0	0	1
Others and unknown	0	0	0

With these dummy-coded variables, the regression coefficients are

$$B_0 = \bar{Y}_4 = 17.3077$$
$$B_1 = \bar{Y}_1 - \bar{Y}_4 = 17.5000 - 17.3077 = 0.1923$$
$$B_2 = \bar{Y}_2 - \bar{Y}_4 = 19.8750 - 17.3077 = 2.5673$$
$$B_3 = \bar{Y}_3 - \bar{Y}_4 = 19.3333 - 17.3077 = 2.0256$$

The regression equation is

$$\hat{Y} = 17.3077 + 0.1923X_1 + 2.5673X_2 + 2.0256X_3$$

From this equation,

$$\hat{Y}_{hum} = 17.3077 + 0.1923(1) + 2.5673(0) + 2.0256(0)$$
$$= 17.5000 = \bar{Y}_1$$

$$\hat{Y}_{nat\ sci} = 17.3077 + 0.1923(0) + 2.5673(1) + 2.0256(0)$$
$$= 19.8750 = \bar{Y}_2$$

$$\hat{Y}_{soc\ sci} = 17.3077 + 0.1923(0) + 2.5673(0) + 2.0256(1)$$
$$= 19.3333 = \bar{Y}_3$$

$$\hat{Y}_{other} = 17.3077 + 0.1923(0) + 2.5673(0) + 2.0256(0)$$
$$= 17.3077 = \bar{Y}_4$$

As expected, the regression equation reproduces the group means.

47-4. OTHER CODING CHOICES

We can use the concepts underlying the choice of dummy codes to specify other code possibilities. The dummy codes of the previous section generate slopes equal to pairwise contrasts in means, with $(0, 0, \ldots, 0)$ serving as a reference group. Different contrasts can also be represented by slopes when other coding schemes are used. For example, assume we are analyzing a four-group design that involves two independent variables. Such a design is shown in Figure 47-1. Standard two-way ANOVA would extract the sums of squares explained by the two main-effects contrasts and the interaction contrast. The analysis can also be performed with multiple regression, with the proper codes chosen to produce slopes equal to the desired contrasts.

To generate the codes, we again set up the regression equation so that the predicted values equal the group means. Since there are three between-group degrees of freedom, we need three coded variables. The regression equation is then

$$\bar{Y}_k = B_0 + B_1 X_{k1} + B_2 X_{k2} + B_3 X_{k3}$$

We define coded values so that

$$B_0 = \text{grand mean} = \frac{\bar{Y}_1 + \bar{Y}_2 + \bar{Y}_3 + \bar{Y}_4}{4}$$

$$B_1 = \text{sex difference} = \frac{\bar{Y}_1 + \bar{Y}_3}{2} - \frac{\bar{Y}_2 + \bar{Y}_4}{2} = \bar{Y}_M - \bar{Y}_F$$

$$B_2 = \text{treatment difference} = \frac{\bar{Y}_1 + \bar{Y}_2}{2} - \frac{\bar{Y}_3 + \bar{Y}_4}{2} = \bar{Y}_T - \bar{Y}_C$$

$$B_3 = \text{interaction} = \bar{Y}_1 - \bar{Y}_2 - \bar{Y}_3 + \bar{Y}_4$$

After substituting these values into the regression equation and combining terms involving each of the means, we have

$$\bar{Y}_k = \left(\frac{1}{4}\bar{Y}_1 + \frac{1}{4}\bar{Y}_2 + \frac{1}{4}\bar{Y}_3 + \frac{1}{4}\bar{Y}_4 \right) + \left(\frac{\bar{Y}_1 + \bar{Y}_3}{2} - \frac{\bar{Y}_2 + \bar{Y}_4}{2} \right) X_{k1}$$

$$+ \left(\frac{\bar{Y}_1 + \bar{Y}_2}{2} - \frac{\bar{Y}_3 + \bar{Y}_4}{2} \right) X_{k2} + (\bar{Y}_1 - \bar{Y}_2 - \bar{Y}_3 + \bar{Y}_4)X_{k3}$$

$$= \left(\frac{1}{4} + \frac{X_{k1}}{2} + \frac{X_{k2}}{2} + X_{k3} \right) \bar{Y}_1 + \left(\frac{1}{4} - \frac{X_{k1}}{2} + \frac{X_{k2}}{2} - X_{k3} \right) \bar{Y}_2$$

$$+ \left(\frac{1}{4} + \frac{X_{k1}}{2} - \frac{X_{k2}}{2} - X_{k3} \right) \bar{Y}_3 + \left(\frac{1}{4} - \frac{X_{k1}}{2} - \frac{X_{k2}}{2} + X_{k3} \right) \bar{Y}_4$$

Letting $k = 1, 2, 3, 4$, we can solve these equations for the codes. For example, for $k = 1$, the equation reduces to

$$\bar{Y}_1 = \left(\frac{1}{4} + \frac{X_{11}}{2} + \frac{X_{12}}{2} + X_{13} \right) \bar{Y}_1 + \left(\frac{1}{4} - \frac{X_{11}}{2} + \frac{X_{12}}{2} - X_{13} \right) \bar{Y}_2$$

$$+ \left(\frac{1}{4} + \frac{X_{11}}{2} - \frac{X_{12}}{2} - X_{13} \right) \bar{Y}_3 + \left(\frac{1}{4} - \frac{X_{11}}{2} - \frac{X_{12}}{2} + X_{13} \right) \bar{Y}_4$$

	Sex	
Treatment	Males	Females
One	$\overline{Y}_1$	$\overline{Y}_2$
Two	$\overline{Y}_3$	$\overline{Y}_4$

Figure 47-1.
Two-factor study of sex $\times$ treatment

To satisfy this equation, the coefficients of $\overline{Y}_2$, $\overline{Y}_3$, and $\overline{Y}_4$ must equal zero and the coefficient of $\overline{Y}_1$ on the right must equal 1. These conditions are satisfied if

$$X_{11} = \tfrac{1}{2} \qquad X_{12} = \tfrac{1}{2} \qquad X_{13} = \tfrac{1}{4}$$

Similar considerations for the other groups yield the following code scheme, called *contrast coding:*

	Contrast code		
Group	X_1	X_2	X_3
Treatment male	$\tfrac{1}{2}$	$\tfrac{1}{2}$	$\tfrac{1}{4}$
Treatment female	$-\tfrac{1}{2}$	$\tfrac{1}{2}$	$-\tfrac{1}{4}$
Control male	$\tfrac{1}{2}$	$-\tfrac{1}{2}$	$-\tfrac{1}{4}$
Control female	$-\tfrac{1}{2}$	$-\tfrac{1}{2}$	$\tfrac{1}{4}$

Note that X_1 defines the weights for the gender differences, X_2 defines the weights for treatment differences, and X_3 defines the weights of a tetrad interaction contrast. For any code choice, dummy or contrast, in most situations the slopes take on their specified values only when all the codes are entered into the equation. Therefore, we strongly recommend whenever a coding scheme is used that the slopes be interpreted only when all predictors are included in the regression equation.

47-5. NONORTHOGONAL TWO-FACTOR ANALYSIS OF VARIANCE USING REGRESSION

At this point, we have seen how analysis of variance can be performed with regression analysis. In addition, coded variables may be used to set the regression coefficients equal to contrasts among means. Of course, since we already know how to perform the analysis of variance and to test contrasts, this equality between the two analysis procedures may seem an aesthetically pleasing result, but no more. The use of regression to perform analysis of variance, however, is extremely important in analyzing two- or higher-factor designs with unequal cell sizes. Up to now, we have not even considered analyzing a two-factor design with unequal cell sizes in ANOVA terms. For these designs, the sums of squares for the various families of hypotheses are not orthogonal, so that adding the sums of squares explained by the separate families to the unexplained sums of squares does not yield the sum of squares total. In parallel with our discussion of Section 46-2, a certain amount of the sums of squares explained by the families cannot be uniquely attributed to any one of them. The unequal cell sizes make it impossible to determine the unique contribution of each family in a single analysis.

We saw in Section 45-4, however, that squared part correlation coefficients can be used to determine the contribution of a variable or a set of variables to the regression, with the variables already in the equation being partialed from the variables added last. We can use this notion here to attempt to measure the contribution of a particular family or contrast that is free of the contributions of other families. To do so, we define coded variables representing contrasts that examine effects within the various families. Then, by adding a set of coded variables for a particular family into the equation last, we can get a measure of the sum of squares due to that family not shared by the other families. We must do this for each family in a different regression equation. We illustrate these procedures for the data of Table 47-4.

Table 47-4. Final examination score by major and treatment group for data of Table 2-2

	Humanities (1)	Natural science (2)	Social science (3)	Other (4)
Laboratory group	69	50	59	47
	68	57	45	80
	59	54	67	45
	38	68		71
	59			46
	43			47
	21			42
				35
				37
Discussion group	43	19	30	52
	24	20	64	43
	48	39	19	35
	48	31		42
	31			47

Table 47-5. Planned contrasts for nonorthogonal data of Table 47-4

		Contrast coefficients				Contrast coefficients			
		L(1)	L(2)	L(3)	L(4)	D(1)	D(2)	D(3)	D(4)
Treatment	ψ_1	7/23	4/23	3/23	9/23	-5/17	-4/17	-3/17	-5/17
Major	ψ_2	7/12	-4/8	0	0	5/12	-4/8	0	0
	ψ_3	0	-4/8	3/6	0	0	-4/8	3/6	0
	ψ_4	0	-4/8	0	9/14	0	-4/8	0	5/14
$T \times M$	ψ_5	1	-1	0	0	-1	1	0	0
	ψ_6	0	-1	1	0	0	1	-1	0
	ψ_7	0	-1	0	1	0	1	0	-1
Grand mean		7/40	4/40	3/40	9/40	5/40	4/40	3/40	5/40

The data in this table are taken from Table 2-2. It is a two-factor design with unequal sample sizes. Because there are eight cells in the design, we can define seven coding variables to predict Y, the final test scores. To generate the coding variables, assume we wish to test the seven contrasts of Table 47-5. Then ψ_1 is the contrast of the laboratory condition compared to the discussion condition, ψ_2 contrasts the humanities majors to the natural science majors, ψ_3 is a similar contrast of social science majors to natural science majors, and ψ_4 contrasts others to natural science majors. The natural science majors constitute the reference group for the coding scheme. Finally, ψ_5, ψ_6, and ψ_7 are tetrad differences used to measure the interaction of treatment and major.

To determine the appropriate codes that set the regression coefficients equal to the desired contrasts among the means, we write the regression equation as

$$\bar{Y}_k = B_0 + B_1 X_{k1} + B_2 X_{k2} + \cdots + B_7 X_{k7}$$

We then specify that

$$B_1 = \frac{7}{23}\bar{Y}_1 + \frac{4}{23}\bar{Y}_2 + \cdots + (-\frac{5}{17})\bar{Y}_8$$
$$B_2 = \frac{7}{12}\bar{Y}_1 - \frac{4}{8}\bar{Y}_2 + \cdots + 0\bar{Y}_8$$

and so on. We set the intercept equal to the grand mean of all the observations:

$$B_0 = \frac{7}{40}\bar{Y}_1 + \frac{4}{40}\bar{Y}_2 + \cdots + \frac{5}{40}\bar{Y}_8$$

After these values are substituted into the regression equation, a computer

Table 47-6. Final examination scores Y and seven coded variables defined by contrasts of Table 47-5

Y	X_1	X_2	X_3	X_4	X_5	X_6	X_7
69	0.42	0.70	−0.13	−0.39	0.29	−0.06	−0.14
68	0.42	0.70	−0.13	−0.39	0.29	−0.06	−0.14
59	0.42	0.70	−0.13	−0.39	0.29	−0.06	−0.14
38	0.42	0.70	−0.13	−0.39	0.29	−0.06	−0.14
59	0.42	0.70	−0.13	−0.39	0.29	−0.06	−0.14
43	0.42	0.70	−0.13	−0.39	0.29	−0.06	−0.14
21	0.42	0.70	−0.13	−0.39	0.29	−0.06	−0.14
50	0.51	−0.31	−0.13	−0.40	−0.15	−0.08	−0.17
57	0.51	−0.31	−0.13	−0.40	−0.15	−0.08	−0.17
54	0.51	−0.31	−0.13	−0.40	−0.15	−0.08	−0.17
68	0.51	−0.31	−0.13	−0.40	−0.15	−0.08	−0.17
59	0.51	−0.31	0.87	−0.40	−0.15	0.42	−0.17
45	0.51	−0.31	0.87	−0.40	−0.15	0.42	−0.17
67	0.51	−0.31	0.87	−0.40	−0.15	0.42	−0.17
47	0.36	−0.30	−0.13	0.61	−0.11	−0.06	0.24
80	0.36	−0.30	−0.13	0.61	−0.11	−0.06	0.24
45	0.36	−0.30	−0.13	0.61	−0.11	−0.06	0.24
71	0.36	−0.30	−0.13	0.61	−0.11	−0.06	0.24
46	0.36	−0.30	−0.13	0.61	−0.11	−0.06	0.24
47	0.36	−0.30	−0.13	0.61	−0.11	−0.06	0.24
42	0.36	−0.30	−0.13	0.61	−0.11	−0.06	0.24
35	0.36	−0.30	−0.13	0.61	−0.11	−0.06	0.24
37	0.36	−0.30	−0.13	0.61	−0.11	−0.06	0.24
43	−0.59	0.71	−0.18	−0.29	−0.41	0.09	0.19
24	−0.59	0.71	−0.18	−0.29	−0.41	0.09	0.19
48	−0.59	0.71	−0.18	−0.29	−0.41	0.09	0.19
48	−0.59	0.71	−0.18	−0.29	−0.41	0.09	0.19
31	−0.59	0.71	−0.18	−0.29	−0.41	0.09	0.19
19	−0.51	−0.29	−0.17	−0.30	0.15	0.08	0.17
20	−0.51	−0.29	−0.17	−0.30	0.15	0.08	0.17
39	−0.51	−0.29	−0.17	−0.30	0.15	0.08	0.17
31	−0.51	−0.29	−0.17	−0.30	0.15	0.08	0.17
30	−0.51	−0.29	0.83	−0.30	0.15	−0.42	0.17
64	−0.51	−0.29	0.83	−0.30	0.15	−0.42	0.17
19	−0.51	−0.29	0.83	−0.30	0.15	−0.42	0.17
52	−0.65	−0.29	−0.18	0.71	0.19	0.10	−0.43
43	−0.65	−0.29	−0.18	0.71	0.19	0.10	−0.43
35	−0.65	−0.29	−0.18	0.71	0.19	0.10	−0.43
42	−0.65	−0.29	−0.18	0.71	0.19	0.10	−0.43
47	−0.65	−0.29	−0.18	0.71	0.19	0.10	−0.43

Table 47-7. ANOVA table for regression of Y on X_1, $X_2, \ldots, X_7$

Source	df	SS	MS	F ratio	$\hat{\eta}^2$
Regression	7	3086.1	440.9	2.29	.334
Residual	32	6157.8	192.4		
Total	39	9243.9			

program can be used to solve for the required codes. The results are summarized in Table 47-6.

When Y is predicted from all seven codes, the results correspond to a one-way ANOVA. The ANOVA table is shown in Table 47-7. The mean square residual is equal to the mean square within groups. Table 47-8 contains the regression coefficients, their standard errors, and the associated t statistics. The coefficients, as desired, are equal to the contrasts among means. For example, from Table 47-9, we see that the combined mean for the laboratory group equals 52.48 and that for the discussion group equals 37.35. The difference between them does, in fact, equal B_1. The equivalence of the other coefficients and the contrasts among the means can also be established. In addition, the standard error for $\hat{\psi}_1$ equals

$$SE_{\hat{\psi}_1} = \sqrt{MS_R(\tfrac{1}{23} + \tfrac{1}{17})} = 4.45$$

as reported. Since these contrasts have been planned, the decision rule for the

Table 47-8. Planned contrasts analysis of Table 47-7

Source	Value of $\hat{\psi}$	$SE_{\hat{\psi}}$	t	Sum of squares added last
ψ_1	15.13	4.45	3.42	2249.5
ψ_2	3.67	6.30	0.57	62.7
ψ_3	5.08	7.49	0.68	88.6
ψ_4	5.54	6.15	0.89	152.8
ψ_5	−17.80	12.59	−1.38	367.5
ψ_6	−10.67	14.98	−0.71	97.5
ψ_7	−23.80	12.37	−1.90	694.5

Table 47-9. Mean values for data of Table 47-4

	Humanities	Natural science	Social science	Other	Total
Laboratory	51.00	57.25	57.00	50.00	52.48
Discussion	38.80	27.25	37.67	43.80	37.35
Total	45.92	42.25	47.33	47.79	46.05

single contrast family is given with $C = 1$, $\alpha = .05$, and $v = 32$ as

Decision Rule: Reject H_0 $\psi_1 = 0$ if $t_\psi < -2.04$ or if $t_\psi > 2.04$

The decision rules for $\hat{\psi}_2$, $\hat{\psi}_3$, and $\hat{\psi}_4$ are given for $C = 3$, $\alpha = .05$, and $v = 32$ by

Decision Rule: Reject H_0 if $t_\psi < = -2.53$ or if $t_\psi > = 2.53$

Similarly, for $\hat{\psi}_5$, $\hat{\psi}_6$, and $\hat{\psi}_7$, the decision rules are

Decision Rule: Reject H_0 $\psi = 0$ if $t_\psi < -2.53$ or if $t_\psi > 2.53$

Hence, only the main effect due to treatment is significant. Students placed in the laboratory attained higher final examination scores.

If we attempted to find the sums of squares associated with these contrasts, we would find that they would not sum to $SS_B = SS_{reg} = 3086.1$, because they are not orthogonal. Similarly, if we found the sums of squares associated with the families by using our familiar ANOVA formulas, they would not sum to SS_{reg} either, and for the same reason. Therefore, in an attempt to find the sums of squares associated with the contrasts, we use the method developed for part correlations. We perform seven regression analyses, adding a different one of the coded variables last in each analysis. The sums of squares added at the last step of each equation measure the amount of variability associated with the code added last, and this variability will have had partialed from it the variability associated with the other coded variables. The results are shown in Table 47-8, under the column "Sum of Squares Added Last." Since each sum of squares added has 1 degree of freedom associated with it, we can test the significance of the amount added. For ψ_1, for example,

$$F_{\psi_1 \text{ added last}} = \frac{SS_{\psi_1} \text{ added last}/1}{MS_{Res}} = \frac{2249.5}{192.4} = 11.69$$

By comparing this to $F_{1,32:.95} = 4.16$, we again conclude ψ_1 is significantly different from zero. Of course, F_{ψ_1} added last is the square of the t statistic for $\hat{\psi}_1$. Notice, however, that

$$SS_{\hat{\psi}_1} = \frac{\hat{\psi}_1^2}{\sum\limits_{k=1}^{K} W_k^2/N_k} = \frac{15.13^2}{1/17 + 1/23} = 2237.7$$

is not equal to SS_{ψ_1} added last.

Suppose we did not wish to analyze the data in a planned fashion. We want to determine the significance of the hypotheses through three omnibus tests, one per family. We perform these tests by adding the codes associated with a family's contrasts into the regression last, and we use the partial F test of Section 46-5. For the treatment effect represented by X_1, we find $\hat{R}^2_{Y \cdot X_2 X_3 \dots X_7} = .0905$. Since $\hat{R}^2_{Y \cdot X_1 X_2 \dots X_7} = .3339$,

$$F_{treat} = \frac{(\hat{R}^2_{Y \cdot X_1 X_2 \dots X_7} - \hat{R}^2_{Y \cdot X_2 X_3 \dots X_7})/1}{(1 - \hat{R}^2_{Y \cdot X_1 X_2 \dots X_7})/32}$$

$$= \frac{(.3339 - .0905)/1}{(1 - .3339)/32} = 11.69$$

The sum of squares associated with treatment, with the other effects partialed out, is

$$SS_{\substack{treatment \\ added\ last}} = SS_T(\hat{R}^2_{Y \cdot X_1 X_2 \dots X_7} - \hat{R}^2_{Y \cdot X_2 X_3 \dots X_7})$$
$$= 9243.9(.3339 - .0905) = 2249.5$$

This is identical to the value reported in Table 47-8. In like manner, since $\hat{R}^2_{Y \cdot X_1 X_5 X_6 X_7} = .3159$,

$$SS_{\substack{major \\ added\ last}} = 9243.9(.3339 - .3159) = 166.39$$

Further,

$$F_{\substack{major \\ added\ last}} = \frac{(.3339 - .3159)/3}{(1 - .3339)/32} = 0.29$$

Finally, since $\hat{R}^2_{Y \cdot X_1 X_2 X_3 X_4} = .2529$,

$$SS_{\substack{interaction \\ added\ last}} = 9243.9(.3339 - .2529) = 748.76$$

and

$$F_{\substack{interaction \\ added\ last}} = \frac{(.3339 - .2529)/3}{(1 - .3339)/32} = 1.30$$

These results are summarized in Table 47-10.

Table 47-10. ANOVA table for post hoc analysis of data of Table 47-4

Source	df	SS[a]	MS	F	$\hat{\eta}^2$
Treatment	1	2249.5	2249.5	11.69	.24
Major	3	166.39	55.46	0.29	
$T \times M$	3	748.76	249.59	1.30	
Residual	32	6157.80	192.40		
Total	39				

[a] Sums of squares are not additive.

We have provided two strategies for analyzing nonorthogonal designs. Of the two, the added-last strategy is recommended. This is true for both the omnibus tests followed by a post hoc analysis and the individual contrast tests involving a preplanned partitioning of the risk of a type I error.

47-6. APPENDIX

We derive the coding scheme for $K = 3$ independent groups. If we let X_{k1} and X_{k2} represent the coded values for X_1 and X_2, respectively, in group k, then for the kth group the predicted value equals the kth group mean:

$$\bar{Y}_k = \bar{Y}_1 + (\bar{Y}_2 - \bar{Y}_1)X_{k1} + (\bar{Y}_3 - \bar{Y}_1)X_{k2}$$

Let us write out these equations in detail for each group. For group 1,

$$\bar{Y}_1 = \bar{Y}_1 + (\bar{Y}_2 - \bar{Y}_1)X_{11} + (\bar{Y}_3 - \bar{Y}_1)X_{12}$$

To make the right-hand side identical to $\bar{Y}_1$, we must choose $X_{11} = 0$ and $X_{12} = 0$, so that

$$\bar{Y}_1 = \bar{Y}_1 + (\bar{Y}_2 - \bar{Y}_1)0 + (\bar{Y}_3 - \bar{Y}_1)0 = \bar{Y}_1$$

In group 2,

$$\bar{Y}_2 = \bar{Y}_1 + (\bar{Y}_2 - \bar{Y}_1)X_{21} + (\bar{Y}_3 - \bar{Y}_1)X_{22}$$

If we choose $X_{21} = 1$ and $X_{22} = 0$, then

$$\bar{Y}_2 = \bar{Y}_1 + (\bar{Y}_2 - \bar{Y}_1)1 + (\bar{Y}_3 - \bar{Y}_1)0 = \bar{Y}_2$$

Finally, for group 3,

$$\bar{Y}_3 = \bar{Y}_1 + (\bar{Y}_2 - \bar{Y}_1)X_{31} + (\bar{Y}_3 - \bar{Y}_1)X_{32}$$

As with group 2, we see that the choice of $X_{31} = 0$ and $X_{32} = 1$ satisfies the equation since

$$\bar{Y}_3 = \bar{Y}_1 + (\bar{Y}_2 - \bar{Y}_1)0 + (\bar{Y}_3 - \bar{Y}_1)1 = \bar{Y}_3$$

If we choose to use coded variables, then we know that the predicted value for all scores in a given group equals the particular group mean. Recall from Chapter 9 that the total deviation d_T is

$$d_{T_{ik}} = Y_{ik} - \bar{Y}$$

the explained deviation d_E is

$$d_{E_{ik}} = \hat{Y}_{ik} - \bar{Y}$$

and the unexplained deviation d_U is

$$d_{U_{ik}} = Y_{ik} - \hat{Y}_{ik}$$

where $\bar{Y}$ is the grand mean of all observations and $\hat{Y}$ is the predicted value of Y computed from the regression equation. Because, with our coding, the predicted value for a particular group equals $\bar{Y}_k$, we have for the kth group

$$d_{E_{ik}} = \bar{Y}_k - \bar{Y} \quad \text{and} \quad d_{U_{ik}} = Y_{ik} - \bar{Y}_k$$

Squaring these deviations and adding across groups, we see that, because the predicted value in a particular group is the same for all that group's subjects,

$$SS_{reg} = \sum_{i=1}^{N} (\hat{Y}_i - \bar{Y})^2 = \sum_{k=1}^{K} N_k (\bar{Y}_{.k} - \bar{Y})^2 = SS_B$$

and

$$SS_R = \sum_{i=1}^{N} (Y_i - \hat{Y}_i) = \sum_{k=1}^{K} \sum_{i=1}^{N_k} (Y_{ik} - \bar{Y}_{.k}) = SS_W$$

where Y_{ik} implies that $\bar{Y}_k$ is subtracted from each subject only in group k.

47-7. EXERCISES

47-1. Use a computer to analyze the data of Table 36-1 as a multiple regression, using dummy coding.

47-2. What is measured by B_0, B_1, B_2, and B_3?

47-3. Show that

$$SS_{reg} = (N-1)(B_1^2 S_{X_1}^2 + B_2^2 S_{X_2}^2 + B_3^2 S_{X_3}^2) + 2(B_1 B_2 r_{X_1 X_2} S_{X_1} S_{X_2} + \cdots)$$

and

$$\hat{\eta}^2 = \hat{R}_{Y \cdot X_1 X_2 X_3}^2$$

47-4. Combine your data with that of two other students and divide your sample of 120 subjects into males and females and programs 1 and 2. Use a computer and the contrast coding of Section 47-4 to analyze your data.

47-5. Use a computer to analyze the data of Table 39-1 in terms of a multiple regression model using coding.

    a. Do this for an interaction model.

    b. Do this for a design with a simple effect nested in sex.

CHAPTER 48

Analysis of Covariance Viewed from a Multiple Regression Perspective

48-1. CODING IN ANCOVA

We examine in this chapter how analysis of covariance can be performed with regression analysis. As with analysis of variance, one major use of the regression approach to ANCOVA occurs when we have a two- or higher-order design with unequal cell sizes. In the case of ANCOVA, however, an additional important feature is that more than one covariate can be used.

Consider again the two-group case. We know from the previous chapter that we need only one coded variable to represent group membership. Let this variable be a dummy code, denoted X_1, and let the second group be the reference group, coded zero. We examine what effect the addition of a covariate C has on the regression results. With one code X_1 and one covariate

C, the regression equation connecting these variables to the dependent variable Y is

$$\hat{Y}_{ik} = B_0 + B_1 X_{k1} + B_C C_{ik}$$

where $k = 1, 2, \ldots , K$ and $i = 1, 2, \ldots , N_k$. If we sum the Y_{ik} values across the $i = 1, 2, \ldots , N_k$ observations in group k and then divide by N_k, we obtain the mean value of Y in group k. For this model,

$$\bar{Y}_{\cdot k} = B_0 + B_1 X_{k1} + B_C \bar{C}_{\cdot k}$$

Without a covariate, B_0 equaled $\bar{Y}_2$ and B_1 equaled $\bar{Y}_1 - \bar{Y}_2$. The addition of the covariate to the equation changes what B_0 and B_1 estimate. We show in the chapter appendix that, with the covariate included, B_1 estimates the difference between the covariate-adjusted group means. Therefore, B_1 estimates the variability between the groups after the covariate adjustment is completed. In addition, B_0 is the mean of the second group, less a constant term involving the covariate. Finally, B_C is the pooled within-group slope relating Y to C.

As an example, consider the analysis of covariance discussed in Section 43-4, in which six educational groups were compared on their mean composition scores, with verbal test score as a covariate. We need five dummy codes to account for the between-group degrees of freedom. Assume we choose these dummy codes:

Program	X_1	X_2	X_3	X_4	X_5
Business administration	1	0	0	0	0
Engineering	0	1	0	0	0
Chemistry	0	0	1	0	0
English	0	0	0	1	0
History	0	0	0	0	1
Mathematics	0	0	0	0	0

Using C to denote the verbal score covariate, we set up our regression equation as

$$\hat{Y} = B_0 + B_1 X_1 + \cdots + B_5 X_5 + B_{Y \cdot C(W)} C$$

When the analysis is performed via a computer program, the multiple regression equation is

$$\hat{Y} = 208 + 55X_1 + 46X_2 + 95X_3 + 124X_4 + 96X_5 + 0.5067C$$

For these data, $B_{Y \cdot C(W)} = .5067$ equals the value of the pooled within-group regression coefficient for predicting the composition score from the verbal score, while at the same time $B_1, B_2, \ldots, B_5$ represent covariate-adjusted composition mean differences between each of the groups and the mathematics group represented by $k = 6$. Although B_0 is not the covariate-adjusted mean for the mathematics group, B_0 is the constant amount $B_{Y \cdot C(W)} \overline{C}_{..}$ less than the mathematics group's adjusted mean. The adjusted mean for the mathematics group is given by

$$\overline{Y}^A_{\cdot 6} = B_0 + B_{Y \cdot C(W)} \overline{C}_{..}$$

The adjusted means for the other groups are

$$\overline{Y}^A_{\cdot k} = \overline{Y}^A_{\cdot 6} + B_{\cdot k}$$

Table 48-1 contains the original group mean for composition, as well as the $B_{\cdot k}$ values and the covariate-adjusted means, $\overline{Y}^A_{\cdot k}$.

In recapitulation, we see that $B_{Y \cdot C(W)} = .5067$ equals the pooled within-group regression coefficient reported originally in Section 43-4. Further, the intercept $B_0 = 208$ equals the covariate-adjusted mean for the mathematics group less the constant amount $.5067(541) = 274$, so that the adjusted mean for the mathematics group is

$$\overline{Y}^A_6 = 208 + .5067(541) = 482$$

In addition, $B_1 = 52 = \overline{Y}^A_{\cdot 1} - \overline{Y}^A_{\cdot 6}$, so that

$$\overline{Y}^A_{\cdot 1} = \overline{Y}^A_{\cdot 6} + B_1 = 482 + 55 = 537$$

Table 48-1. Means on composition, both original and adjusted for verbal score covariate

Program	$\overline{Y}_k$	$B_{\cdot k}$	$\overline{Y}^A_k$
Business administration	494	55	537[a]
Engineering	517	46	528
Chemistry	564	95	577
English	636	124	606
History	597	96	578
Mathematics	490		482

[a] The adjusted means in this column differ slightly from the values reported in Chapter 43, owing to the use of integers in their calculation.

The remaining values are given in Table 48-1. We see that the codes cause the intercept and coded variable coefficients to represent the same statistical quantities as they did without a covariate, but now they do so after adjustment for the covariate.

48-2. ANALYSIS OF COVARIANCE USING REGRESSION

Because we can interpret the regression coefficients when a covariate and codes are used as predictors, we can form a plan for performing an analysis of covariance using regression analysis. The hypothesis tested in ANCOVA is that there is no difference in group means, once the variation explained by the covariate is accounted for. Hence, we wish to test the additional amount of variation explained by group membership, above and beyond that explained by the covariate. The incremental F test examined in Chapter 46 does just that. Our plan, then, would involve entering the covariate into the regression as a first step and then testing the significance of the set of coded variables added collectively on a second step.

For our example, we would first predict composition scores from verbal scores only. The results of this analysis are given in Table 48-2. Because only the verbal scores have been entered, the F ratio reported in Table 48-2 would test the significance of the total regression coefficient B_T. We see that the squared multiple correlation coefficient equals .4095. From Table 48-3, we find that $\hat{R}^2$ for predicting composition scores from verbal scores and the five coded variables is .5631. Hence, the increment in $\hat{R}^2$ due to adding the coded variables is

$$\hat{R}^2_{Y(X_1 X_2 \cdots X_5 \cdot C)} = \hat{R}^2_{Y \cdot C X_1 X_2 \cdots X_5} - \hat{R}^2_{Y \cdot C} = .5631 - .4095 = .1536$$

We use the procedures of Chapter 46 to test the additional amount of explained variation for significance from zero. The results of the incremental F test should equal those for the analysis of covariance. Thus, we test

$$H_0 : R^2_{Y(X_1 X_2 \cdots X_{K-1} \cdot C)} = 0$$

Table 48-2. Results for regression of composition scores on verbal scores

Source	df	SS	MS	F	$\hat{R}^2$
Regression	1	302,360	302,360	45.77	4095
Residual	66	436,003	6,606		
Total	67	738,363			

Table 48-3. Summary results for regression analysis of composition scores on verbal scores and five coded variables

Source	df	SS	MS	F	$\hat{R}^2$
Regression	6	415,771	69,295	13.10	.5631
Residual	61	322,589	5,288		
Total	67	738,360			

In this case, we are adding $q = K - 1$ variables to the $p = 1$ variable already in the equation. Hence

$$F = \frac{(\hat{R}^2_{Y \cdot CX_1 X_2 \cdots X_{K-1}} - \hat{R}^2_{Y \cdot C})/(K - 1)}{(1 - \hat{R}^2_{Y \cdot CX_1 X_2 \cdots X_{K-1}})/[N - 1 - (K - 1) - 1]}$$

In this example, $N = 68$ and $K = 6$. Thus

$$F = \frac{(.5631 - .4095)/(6 - 1)}{(1 - .5631)/(68 - 1 - 5 - 1)} = 4.29$$

This is the same F ratio as reported in Table 43-6. In addition, the degrees of freedom for the incremental F test, $v_1 = 5$ and $v_2 = 61$, are the same as those for the analysis of covariance. The two procedures yield identical results.

These concepts extend to more than a single covariate and to any number of groups. For example, consider 216 subjects who are classified according to religion as stated by responses to a questionnaire given to entering students in a large university. Let the groups be denoted

G_1: Protestant G_3: Jewish
G_2: Catholic G_4: Other and unknown

Let the covariates be

C_1: High school grade point average (GPA)
C_2: Score on a 20-item test measuring liberal-conservative political philosophy
C_3: Score on a 20-item test of locus of control

Let the dependent variable be denoted Y: (total score on a questionnaire designed to measure attitudes toward women's role as breadwinner).

We perform the analysis using regression, entering the three covariates first and then examining the increment accounted for by the three coded variables representing group membership. The results of the regression analysis at step 1 are shown in Table 48-4. As we see, the three covariates account for $\hat{R}^2_{Y \cdot C_1 C_2 C_3} = .5624$ of the total variation.

At this point, the F ratio tests the regression of Y on C_1, C_2, and C_3 without regard to group membership. Suppose we now wish to determine how much impact religion has upon the attitude toward women's role scores, above that accounted for by the three covariates. When this ANCOVA hypothesis is viewed from a multiple regression perspective, this amounts to testing how much additional variation can be explained by the inclusion of the religion variable in an equation that already includes three covariates.

We can introduce the qualitative variable, religion, into the regression equation by using dummy coding. Thus, each group is represented in the regression equation as follows:

Religion	X_1	X_2	X_3
Protestant	1	0	0
Catholic	0	1	0
Jewish	0	0	1
Unknown and other	0	0	0

We now enter the set of three dummy variables into the regression equation. The results of this analysis are shown as step 2 in Table 48-4. The resulting standardized regression equation is

$$Y = .3270C_1 + .2577C_2 + .2806C_3 + .0181X_1 + .0757X_2 + .0413X_3$$

The partial F test for this set of three variables is given by

$$F = \frac{(\hat{R}^2_{Y \cdot C_1 C_2 C_3 X_1 X_2 X_3} - \hat{R}^2_{Y \cdot C_1 C_2 C_3})/(4-1)}{(1 - \hat{R}^2_{Y \cdot C_1 C_2 C_3 X_1 X_2 X_3})/[216 - 3 - (4-1) - 1]}$$

$$= \frac{(.5306 - .5264)/3}{(1 - .5306)/209} = 0.62$$

which is very small and not statistically significant when compared to $F_{3,209;.95} = 3.28$. Thus, it would be concluded that stated religion is not significantly related to the attitude questionnaire scores after the effects of high school GPA, liberal-conservative political leanings, and locus of control are removed.

Although we have illustrated the model for only a single group member-

Table 48-4. Analysis of covariance performed as a regression analysis

Source	df	SS	MS	F	$\hat{R}^2$	Increment $\hat{R}^2$
			Step 1			
Regression on C_1,C_2,C_3	3	89,686.81	29,855.60	78.54	.5264	.5264
Residual	212	80,691.83	380.62			
Total	215	170,378.64				
			Step 2			
Regression on C_1,C_2,C_3,X_1,X_2,X_3	6	90,399.83			.5306	.0042
C_1,C_2,C_3	3	89,686.81	29,895.60			
X_1,X_2,X_3	3	713.02	237.67	.62		
Residual	209	79,978.82	382.67			
Total	215	170,378.65				

ship variable or factor, clearly it can be used for multiple factors and more complex designs. In general, there should be little conceptual difficulty in performing a general analysis of covariance with many covariates and many ANOVA factors. A computer, of course, would be required for the calculations.

For completeness, we provide directions for performing an analysis of covariance as a regression in Box 48-1.

Even though our demonstration of the flexibility of the regression model was performed for the purpose of testing the ANCOVA hypothesis, another hypothesis can be tested with the covariates and coded variables as predictors. Entering the set of covariates *after* the set of dummy variables is in the equation permits a test of the pooled within-group relationship between the dependent variable and the covariates. In particular,

$$F = \frac{(\hat{R}^2_{Y \cdot C_1 C_2 \ldots C_P X_1 X_2 \ldots X_{K-1}} - \hat{R}^2_{Y \cdot X_1 X_2 \ldots X_{K-1}})/P}{(1 - \hat{R}^2_{Y \cdot C_1 C_2 \ldots C_P X_1 X_2 \ldots X_{K-1}})/(N - K - P)}$$

is referred to an F distribution with the P and $N - K - P$ degrees of freedom. This F tests the hypothesis that all the within-slope regression coefficients are equal to zero.

Box 48-1 **Procedure for performing an analysis of covariance using the partial F test**

Step 1. Perform a regression on the P covariates $C_1, C_2, \ldots, C_P$. Let the squared multiple correlation coefficient associated with these P variables be denoted $\hat{R}^2_{Y \cdot C_1 C_2 \ldots C_P}$.

Step 2. Consider a qualitative factor defined in terms of K unique levels. Introduce $v = K - 1$ dummy variables as

Group	X_1	X_2	$\ldots$	X_{K-1}
1	1	0	$\ldots$	0
2	0	1	$\ldots$	0
$\cdots$				
K	0	0	$\ldots$	0

Step 3. Enter these dummy variables into the regression equation as a set of $K - 1$ variables. Let the squared multiple correlation associated with both covariates and dummy variables in the equation be denoted

$$\hat{R}^2_{Y \cdot C_1 C_2 \ldots C_P X_1 X_2 \ldots X_{K-1}}$$

Step 4. Compute

$$F = \frac{(\hat{R}^2_{Y \cdot C_1 C_2 \ldots C_P X_1 X_2 \ldots X_{K-1}} - \hat{R}^2_{Y \cdot C_1 C_2 \ldots C_P})/(K - 1)}{(1 - \hat{R}^2_{Y \cdot C_1 C_2 \ldots C_P X_1 X_2 \ldots X_{K-1}})/(N - K - P)}$$

Step 5. With a chosen α level of significance, reject H_0 of no difference in adjusted averages if

$$F > F_{K-1, N-K-P : 1-\alpha}$$

48-3. TESTING K REGRESSION LINES FOR PARALLELISM BY USING MULTIPLE REGRESSION THEORY

Recall that one of the assumptions underlying ANCOVA is that the regression coefficients for predicting the dependent variable from the covariate are the same in all the groups. For a single covariate, this is the assumption of the parallelism of the regression lines. The regression model is so flexible that one can test a hypothesis of parallelism by using multiple regression theory. To do so, we define a set of codes that test contrasts among the group slopes themselves. Since there are K slopes, we will need $K-1$ dummy codes to account for the degrees of freedom among the slopes.

Consider again the simple two-group problem introduced in Chapter 47. Use of a dummy code allowed us to express group mean differences in terms of B_1, whereas the use of this code scheme in the presence of a covariate represented differences in adjusted means.

We now write a regression equation involving the covariate, the dummy code, and a parallelism code, and we then specify the code required so that the regression coefficient for this code represents the difference in the two groups' slopes. We denote this code P, for parallelism, and its regression coefficient B_P. Our equation then becomes

$$\hat{Y} = B_0 + B_1 X + B_C C + B_P P$$

Recall from Chapter 40 that contrast coefficients for interactions in ANOVA can be calculated by taking the product of the corresponding main-effect contrast coefficients. Analogously, we have examined in ANCOVA the "main effects" explained by the covariate and by group differences. To examine whether the effects of the covariate differ among the groups, that is, whether the group slopes differ, we must create a variable representing the group by covariate interaction. To do so, we set $P = CX$. If we arrange this coding and perform the resulting algebra, we can show that

$$B_C = B_{Y \cdot C(2)}$$

and

$$B_P = B_{Y \cdot C(1)} - B_{Y \cdot C(2)}$$

where

$$B_{Y \cdot C(1)} = \text{slope of group 1}$$

and

$$B_{Y \cdot C(2)} = \text{slope of group 2}$$

Thus, testing $H_0: \beta_P = 0$ is identical to testing $H_0: \beta_{Y \cdot C(1)} - \beta_{Y \cdot C(2)} = 0$.

As might be expected, this model can be extended to cover the testing of K regression lines for parallelism. Similar to the logic for means and adjusted means, the group coded $(0, 0, \ldots, 0)$ will serve as the comparison group. All other group slopes will be contrasted to this one single group slope. In addition, the model can be extended to cover multiple covariates.

As an example, consider again the analysis involving six educational programs. For the analysis of covariance, we entered the covariate and five group

Table 48-5. Regression of composition scores on verbal scores, five group codes, and five product codes

Source	df	SS	MS	F	$\hat{R}^2$
Regression	11	425,960	38,724	6.94	.5769
Residual	56	312,400	5,579		
Total	67	738,360			

codes into the equation. To test parallelism, we need to enter the covariate, the five group codes, and five product variables $CX_1, CX_2, \ldots, CX_5$. We enter them in an ordered fashion, first the covariate and the five group codes and then the product variables. Parallelism is tested by using the partial F test on the additional sums of squares explained by the product terms. Table 48-5 summarizes this 11-variable analysis. After the first six variables have been entered, we saw in Table 48-3 that $\hat{R}^2 = .5631$. According to Table 48-5, the 11-variable equation has $\hat{R}^2 = .5769$. From the partial F test

$$F = \frac{(.5769 - .5631)/5}{(1 - .5769)/56} = 0.37$$

Since $F_{5,56:.95} = 2.39$, we conclude that the slopes do not differ significantly from one another.

From the computer results for this analysis, the regression equation is

$$\hat{Y} = (278 - 2.6X_1 - 20.9X_2 + \cdots + 107.1X_5) + 0.3813C$$
$$+ (0.0998P_1 + 0.1208P_2 + \cdots - 0.0136P_5)$$

where $X_1, X_2, \ldots, X_5$ are dummy codes for groups, C is the covariate (verbal score), and $P_1, P_2, \ldots, P_5$ are the products of C and each X. The coefficient of C equals the slope in the sixth group; thus, $B_{Y \cdot C(6)} = .3813$, the value reported in Table 43-3. The difference

$$B_{Y \cdot C(1)} - B_{Y \cdot C(6)} = .4810 - .3813 = .0997 = B_{P_1}$$

is the coefficient of P_1. Thus, the coefficients of the products have the same interpretation as those of the original dummy codes used in ANOVA, except that they represent contrasts in group slopes. Unfortunately, in the 11-variable equation, no coefficients other than those for the covariate and the product variables have a statistically meaningful interpretation.

This analysis can be extended to testing parallelism with P covariates. In addition to the inclusion of P covariates and $K - 1$ dummy-coded variables in

---

Box 48-2 **Procedure for testing K regression lines for parallelism by using dummy codes**

Step 1. Continue the ANCOVA process of Section 48-2 by introducing dummy codes

$$P_1 = C_1 X_1, \qquad P_2 = C_1 X_2, \qquad \ldots, \qquad P_{P(K-1)} = C_P X_{K-1}$$

Step 2. Compute

$$F = \frac{(\hat{R}^2_{Y \cdot C_1 C_2 \ldots C_P X_1 X_2 \ldots X_{K-1} P_1 P_2 \ldots P_{P(K-1)}} - \hat{R}^2_{Y \cdot C_1 C_2 \ldots C_P X_1 X_2 \ldots X_{K-1}}) / [P(K-1)]}{(1 - \hat{R}^2_{Y \cdot C_1 C_2 \ldots C_P X_1 X_2 \ldots X_{K-1} P_1 P_2 \ldots P_{P(K-1)}}) / [N - K(P+1)]}$$

Step 3. Reject the hypothesis of parallelism if

$$F > F_{v_1, v_2 : 1 - \alpha}$$

where $v_1 = P(K - 1)$ and $v_2 = N - K(P + 1)$.

---

the model, one can define $P(K - 1)$ products in which each covariate is multiplied by each dummy variable. This will result in a total of $P + K - 1 + P(K - 1) = PK + K - 1$ variables. If one enters the $P(K - 1)$ products after the $P + K - 1$ original variables are already in the regression, then one can perform a partial F test for parallelism. The reference F distribution is based on $P(K - 1)$ and $N - K(P + 1)$ degrees of freedom. The procedure is summarized in Box 48-2.

48-4. APTITUDE-BY-TREATMENT INTERACTIONS

As an example of a further use of the equation involving a covariate, group codes, and product codes, consider designing two programs intended to improve reading ability. Assume that the students had taken a verbal ability test prior to being given one of the programs and that a reading test is given upon completion of the programs. It is desired to determine which program is better and whether the effectiveness of the programs depends on the ability of the student before the course work began. One possible outcome is shown in Figure 48-1, in which the regression lines for reading scores predicted from the verbal scores have been graphed separately for the students in each program. Since the lines cross, it seems that students possessing high verbal ability benefit more from program 2 than program 1, whereas the reverse is true for students with a lower verbal ability. Hence, there appears to be an interaction between treatment and ability.

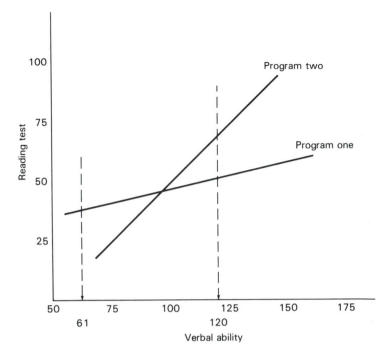

Figure 48-1.
The two regression lines predicting reading outcomes from initial verbal ability.

The question, then, naturally arises as to whether the two lines are significantly far apart for any values of verbal ability and, if so, for which values. This information allows us to pick the particular program that is better for a given student. If the two values of $\hat{Y}_1$ and $\hat{Y}_2$ for the programs do not differ significantly, then the choice of program can be made based on considerations of time, availability, or cost, since the reading ability outcomes for the two are statistically the same.

We have seen how coding schemes can be used to test the identity of the adjusted means (ANCOVA) or the identity of the slopes (parallelism). But if we test the identity of the adjusted means and slopes simultaneously, we are testing the *identity of the regression lines*. If the lines are not identical, then they must differ significantly at some values of the verbal score. To perform the test, we enter the covariate at the first step and then use the partial F test to determine whether the addition of the group codes and the product codes, all at once, significantly increases $\hat{R}^2$.

For example, in the analysis of the two programs, the data of Table 48-6 show that the verbal score by itself produced $\hat{R}^2 = .3931$, whereas the equation involving the covariate, one group code, and one product code yields $\hat{R}^2 = .6922$. Therefore,

$$F = \frac{(.6922 - .3931)/2}{(1 - .6922)/27} = 13.12$$

Table 48-6. Aptitude-treatment interaction data for $X =$ verbal ability test and $Y =$ score on a reading test for two different teaching methods

	Method 1		Method 2	
	X	Y	X	Y
	119	51	131	90
	113	36	116	65
	159	53	68	27
	104	52	109	58
	109	63	129	59
	104	41	95	45
	136	58	144	107
	115	58	100	36
	91	60	105	52
	111	56	114	70
	59	33	104	61
	99	38	123	79
	106	29	95	52
	121	59	95	35
	79	40	117	62
Mean	108.8	48.3	109.7	59.2
SD	22.3	10.8	18.57	21.11
r	.45		.89	
Slope	0.2193		1.0064	
Intercept	24.39		−51.16	

which is compared to $F_{2,27:.95} = 3.35$. We thus conclude that the two regression lines are not identical.

The Scheffé coefficient is given by

$$S = \sqrt{v_1 F_{v_1,v_2:.95}} = \sqrt{2F_{2,27:.95}} = 2.59$$

Thus, to be significant, our test statistic (TS) must exceed this value. Using

---

Box 48-3   **Procedure for testing K regression lines for identity**

Step 1. Enter the covariate C, the dummy codes for group means $X_1, X_2, \ldots, X_{K-1}$ and the dummy codes for parallelism $X_1C, X_2C, \ldots, X_{K-1}C$, all at once into the regression equation.

Step 2. Enter only the covariate into the regression equation.

Step 3. Compute the increment in $\hat{R}^2$, using the step 1 and step 2 measures of explained variation.

Step 4. Conclude that the increment is significant if the partial F test is significant. Use

$$v_1 = 2(K-1) \qquad \text{and} \qquad v_2 = N - 2K$$

Step 5. If H_0 is rejected, find the regions of difference following the example of this section.

---

the standard errors derived in Section 44-4, we have

$$(TS)_{\hat{\psi}} = \frac{\hat{Y}_1 - \hat{Y}_2}{\sqrt{SE_{\hat{Y}_1}^2 + SE_{\hat{Y}_2}^2}}$$

$$= \frac{75.56 - .7871X}{\sqrt{(101.7)[\frac{1}{16} + (X - 108.8)^2/7460.7 + \frac{1}{15} + (X - 109.7)^2/4827.3]}}$$

We must solve for the values of X, if any exist, for which $(TS)_{\hat{\psi}} > S$ or $(TS)_{\hat{\psi}} < -S$. We see that it is a complex task. Solving the equation, we find that the lines differ significantly for $X < 61$ and for $X > 120$. For students with verbal ability less than 61, we would recommend program 1; for students whose verbal ability exceeds 120, program 2 would be suggested; and for other students it would not matter which program were used. For completeness, in Box 48-3 we provide directions for testing identity through regression analysis.

48-5. APPENDIX

We now establish the coding schema for ANCOVA. Recall that regression coefficients are based on partial correlations. Each coefficient reflects an association between Y and a predictor that has associations with all other predictors partialed out. Variable X is used to measure the variability *between* groups. Once X is used to partial out the group differences, $B_{YC \cdot X}$ must reflect the association between Y and C that takes place *within* the groups. Therefore, $B_{YC \cdot X}$ must equal the pooled within-group regression coefficient $B_{Y \cdot C(W)}$.

Let us now determine the characteristics of B_0 and B_1. If we subtract $B_{Y \cdot C(W)}\overline{C}$ from both sides of the equation defining $\overline{Y}_{.k}$ in terms of B_0, B_1, and $B_{Y \cdot C(W)}$, we have

$$\overline{Y}_{.k} - B_{Y \cdot C(W)}\overline{C}_{.k} = B_0 + B_1 X_k$$

The expression on the left resembles the adjusted mean for the kth group. We now determine how it can be related to the covariate-adjusted mean. The covariate-adjusted mean is defined as

$$\begin{aligned} \overline{Y}_{.k}^A &= \overline{Y}_{.k} + B_{Y \cdot C(W)}(\overline{C} - \overline{C}_{.k}) \\ &= (\overline{Y}_{.k} - B_{Y \cdot C(W)}\overline{C}_{.k}) + B_{Y \cdot C(W)}\overline{C} \end{aligned}$$

where $\overline{C}$ is the grand mean on the covariate. Therefore,

$$\overline{Y}_{.k} - B_{Y \cdot C(W)}\overline{C}_{.k} = \overline{Y}_{.k}^A - B_{Y \cdot C(W)}\overline{C}$$

The term on the left side equals the covariate-adjusted mean less the constant $B_{Y \cdot C(W)}\overline{C}$.

Thus,

$$\overline{Y}_{.k} - B_{Y \cdot C(W)}\overline{C}_{.k} = B_0 + B_1 X_k$$

can be treated as the two-group coding problem of the ANOVA presented in Chapter 47, but here the results are interpreted in terms of $\overline{Y}_{.k} - B_{Y \cdot C(W)}\overline{C}_{.k}$. In Chapter 47, the intercept in the two-group case equaled the mean of the second group. Here,

$$B_0 = \overline{Y}_{.2} - B_{Y \cdot C(W)}\overline{C}_{.2}$$

Similarly, in Chapter 47, B_1 equaled the difference between the two group means. Here,

$$B_1 = (\overline{Y}_{.1} - B_{Y \cdot C(W)}\overline{C}_{.1}) - (\overline{Y}_{.2} - B_{Y \cdot C(W)}\overline{C}_{.2})$$

Thus, the coding problem here is interpreted in the same way as ANOVA coding, except that we deal with $\overline{Y}_{.k} - B_{Y \cdot C(W)}\overline{C}_{.k}$, instead of $\overline{Y}_{.k}$.

Although these contrasts may not seem to be comparing actual covariate-adjusted means, they are. We now demonstrate this result. By definition,

$$\begin{aligned} \hat{\psi} = \overline{Y}_{.1}^A - \overline{Y}_{.2}^A &= [\overline{Y}_{.1} + B_{Y \cdot C(W)}(\overline{C} - \overline{C}_{.1})] - [\overline{Y}_{.2} + B_{Y \cdot C(W)}(\overline{C} - \overline{C}_{.2})] \\ &= (\overline{Y}_{.1} - B_{Y \cdot C(W)}\overline{C}_{.1}) - (\overline{Y}_{.2} - B_{Y \cdot C(W)}\overline{C}_{.2}) \\ &= B_1 \end{aligned}$$

Therefore, the regression coefficient B_1 is the adjusted mean contrast of group 1 and group 2. In the K-group case, this result can be generalized. The slopes in ANOVA represent contrasts among means. With the covariate in the regression equation, the slopes represent contrasts among covariate-adjusted means.

48-6. EXERCISES

48-1. Combine your data deck of 40 subjects with that of two other students to obtain a total sample size of 120. Treat the four groups of students defined by sex and program as a one-way design, and assign dummy codes to identify group membership. Using a statistical computer package, perform an analysis of covariance on the four groups, using final examination scores as the dependent variable and College Board scores as the covariate. Use multiple regression theory as described in this chapter.

48-2. For Exercise 48-1, how much of the variability is associated with the College Board scores entered on the first step? How much is associated with group membership?

48-3. Test the four regression lines of Exercise 48-1 for parallelism, using multiple regression theory as described in this chapter. How much of the variation is absorbed by the deviations of the lines from parallelism?

48-4. Repeat Exercises 48-1 and 48-2 by using as covariates College Board scores and the dichotomous variable associated with having

had or not having had a previous course in high school biology.

48-5. Treat sex and program as fully crossed factors, and repeat Exercises 48-1 and 48-2.

48-6. Treat sex and program as fully crossed factors, and repeat Exercise 48-4, testing for sex differences, program differences, and interaction effects of sex and program.

48-7. Divide the 120 subjects according to program assignment, and test for an aptitude by treatment interaction. For the aptitude measure use College Board scores.

48-8. Repeat Exercise 48-7, using the pretest scores as the aptitude measure. Which of the two variables, College Board or pretest, is more indicative of a treatment by aptitude interaction?

48-9. Repeat Exercise 48-5, using contrast codings for sex, program, and the interaction of sex by program.

48-10. Summarize the results of Exercises 48-1 through 48-9 in a short "results" section for a professional journal.

CHAPTER 49

Log-Linear Analysis

49-1. QUALITATIVE INDEPENDENT VARIABLES

In the preceding chapters, we have seen how regression analysis can be used to great effect in solving difficult ANOVA and ANCOVA problems. In particular, we could avoid some of the problems of confounding in nonorthogonal designs by using the partial F test. In this chapter, we see how the concepts underlying the partial F test can be used in the analysis of second- and higher-order contingency tables for qualitative variables. The major difficulty in making this transition lies in defining the nature of the dependent variable, which is an unordered qualitative variable, in a regression context. This is done through the use of *odds ratios*, to which we now turn. In addition, odds ratios allow us to define meaningful contrasts for higher-order contingency tables.

49-2. ODDS RATIO FOR A 2 × 2 CONTINGENCY TABLE

Reconsider the data of Table 10-3. In particular, consider the 23 subjects in program 1. Nineteen passed and four failed the final examination. Thus, for each subject who failed, $19/4 = 4.75$ have passed. In program 2, the ratio of passed to failed is given by $8/9 = 0.89$. Clearly, the odds favor passing for a student in program 1, whereas the odds are fairly close to even for the passing or failing of students in program 2. As we saw earlier, we had reason to believe that for these data the hypotheses $H_0: p_1 = p_2$ and $H_0: \phi = 0$ were false. Our interpretation here agrees with this prior knowledge.

Note that we compared the odds, $\hat{r}_1 = f_{11}/f_{21}$, in program 1 to the odds, $\hat{r}_2 = f_{12}/f_{22}$, in program 2. In the population, the odds are defined in terms of the appropriate parameters underlying the model. For example, in the independence model, we have in the single sample

$$\hat{r}_1 = \frac{f_{11}}{f_{21}} = \frac{f_{11}/N}{f_{21}/N} = \frac{\hat{p}_{11}}{\hat{p}_{21}}$$

and

$$\hat{r}_2 = \frac{f_{12}}{f_{22}} = \frac{f_{12}/N}{f_{22}/N} = \frac{\hat{p}_{12}}{\hat{p}_{21}}$$

So in terms of population values, we define

$$r_1 = \frac{p_{11}}{p_{21}} \quad \text{and} \quad r_2 = \frac{p_{12}}{p_{22}}$$

Similarly, in the homogeneity model, we have in the samples

$$\hat{r}_1 = \frac{f_{11}}{f_{21}} = \frac{f_{11}/N_1}{f_{21}/N_1} = \frac{\hat{p}_1}{\hat{q}_1}$$

and

$$\hat{r}_2 = \frac{f_{12}}{f_{22}} = \frac{f_{12}/N_2}{f_{22}/N_2} = \frac{\hat{p}_2}{\hat{q}_2}$$

In terms of population values, we define

$$r_1 = \frac{p_1}{q_1} \quad \text{and} \quad r_2 = \frac{p_2}{q_2}$$

We now examine the null hypothesis of homogeneity and independence in terms of the population odds ratios. Under the null hypothesis in the homogeneity model, $p_1 = p_2$ and $q_1 = q_2$. Therefore, $r_1 = p_1/q_1 = p_2/q_2 = r_2$ under H_0. Thus, we can write $H_0: r_1 = r_2$ or $H_0: g = r_1/r_2 = 1$. In the latter form, g is called the *odds ratio*, it being the ratio of the odds of success to those of failure in the two populations.

When the hypothesis of independence is true, $p_{11} = p_{1.}p_{.1}$, $p_{12} = p_{1.}p_{.2}$, $p_{21} = p_{2.}p_{.1}$, and $p_{22} = p_{2.}p_{.2}$. If these are substituted into the equations defining r_1 and r_2, then $r_1 = r_2$. Hence, for the independence model, the null hypothesis can again be written as $H_0: r_1 = r_2$ or as $H_0: g = r_1/r_2 = 1$.

In both cases, g is estimated as

$$\hat{g} = \frac{f_{21}/f_{11}}{f_{12}/f_{22}}$$

This means that with the concept of odds ratio, questions of homogeneity and independence can be answered with a single statistical procedure.

For our example,

$$\hat{g} = \frac{19/4}{8/9} = \frac{19(9)}{4(8)} = 5.34375$$

We now want to know whether the sample g indicates that the sample could have come from a population where $g = 1$. This can be done directly, but a simpler method is achieved if we transform g and $\hat{g}$ by using natural logarithms. If we do this and we denote the transformed value as $\hat{\gamma}$ (gamma), we see that

$$\hat{\gamma} = \ln \hat{g} = (\ln f_{11} - \ln f_{21}) - (\ln f_{12} - \ln f_{22})$$

is a linear combination in the logarithms of the frequencies. $\hat{\gamma}$ is called the *log odds ratio*. If f_{11}, f_{21}, f_{12}, and f_{22} are sufficiently large, then $\hat{\gamma}$ has a sampling distribution that is normal with $E(\hat{\gamma}) = 0$ if H_0 is true and for which $\text{Var}(\hat{\gamma}) = 1/f_{11} + 1/f_{21} + 1/f_{12} + 1/f_{22}$. Thus

$$Z = \frac{\hat{\gamma} - 0}{\sigma_{\hat{\gamma}}}$$

can be used as a test statistic for testing

$$H_0: \gamma = 0 \quad \text{or} \quad H_0: g = 1$$

against

$$H_1: \gamma \neq 0 \quad \text{or} \quad H_1: g \neq 1$$

For our example,

$$\hat{\gamma} = \ln \frac{19/4}{8/9}$$

$$= (\ln 19 - \ln 4) - (\ln 8 - \ln 9)$$
$$= (2.9444 - 1.3863) - (2.0794 - 2.1972)$$
$$= 1.6758$$

and

$$\text{Var}(\hat{\gamma}) = 1/19 + 1/4 + 1/8 + 1/9 = 0.5387$$

so that

$$Z = \frac{1.6758 - 0}{\sqrt{0.5387}} = \frac{1.6758}{0.7340} = 2.28$$

With the $\alpha = .05$ decision rule to reject H_0 if $Z < -1.96$ or if $Z > 1.96$, we reject H_0 and conclude that $\gamma \neq 0$ and $g \neq 1$. This agrees with the analysis of Section 26-2.

The 95 percent confidence interval for γ is given by

$$1.6758 - 1.96(0.7340) < \gamma < 1.6758 + 1.96(0.7340)$$

$$0.2372 < \gamma < 3.1144$$

As expected, $\gamma = 0$ is not in the interval.

Another form of this test has greater utility, since it extends to contingency tables of size greater than 2×2. This form makes use of the observed frequencies and the expected frequencies computed in the same manner as for the Karl Pearson X^2 statistic. This statistic is defined as

$$G^2 = 2 \sum_{i=1}^{2} \sum_{j=1}^{2} f_{ij} \ln \frac{f_{ij}}{F_{ij}}$$

If the F_{ij} exceed 5, this statistic has a distribution that is approximately χ^2 with $\nu = 1$. Let us examine this form of the test, using the expected values of Table 26-2 and natural logarithms. For these data,

$$G^2 = 2 \left(19 \ln \frac{19}{15.525} + 4 \ln \frac{4}{7.475} + 8 \ln \frac{8}{11.475} + 9 \ln \frac{9}{5.525} \right)$$

$$= 2 \,(19 \ln 1.224 + 4 \ln 0.535 + 8 \ln 0.697 + 9 \ln 1.629)$$
$$= 5.68$$

Since $G^2 = 5.68$ is larger than $\chi^2_{1:.95} = 3.84$, H_0 is rejected at $\alpha = .05$. Again, this agrees with the earlier findings.

Box 49-1   Procedure for testing H_0: $\gamma = 0$ or H_0: $g = 1$ in a 2 $\times$ 2 table

Step 1. Compute

$$Z = \frac{\hat{\gamma} - 0}{\sigma_{\hat{\gamma}}}$$

Step 2. Reject H_0 if $Z < Z_{\alpha/2}$ or if $Z > Z_{1-\alpha/2}$.

Step 3. If H_0 is rejected, determine a $1 - \alpha$ percent confidence interval for γ as

$$\hat{\gamma} + Z_{\alpha/2}\sigma_{\hat{\gamma}} < \gamma < \hat{\gamma} + Z_{1-\alpha/2}\sigma_{\hat{\gamma}}$$

We have now produced four different procedures for analyzing 2×2 contingency tables. All procedures have produced the same conclusions, and all the test statistics are close to one another in numerical value. We provide directions for testing odds ratios for statistical significance in Box 49-1.

Sometimes a researcher finds that the frequency in one of the cells is zero. This creates a problem since the logarithm of zero is not defined. The solution to the problem is to add ½ to each cell of the table before beginning the arithmetic computations.

49-3. G^2 STATISTIC FOR AN $I \times J$ CONTINGENCY TABLE

As defined in Section 49-2, G^2 can be used for testing independence or homogeneity in any $I \times J$ contingency table. In these cases,

$$G^2 = 2 \sum_{i=1}^{I} \sum_{j=1}^{J} f_{ij} \ln \frac{f_{ij}}{F_{ij}}$$

When H_0 is true, G^2 has an approximate chi-square distribution with $v = (I - 1)(J - 1)$. We illustrate the method for the data of Tables 26-2 and 26-3. For these data,

$$G^2 = 2 \left(45 \ln \frac{45}{33.85} + 8 \ln \frac{8}{9.11} + \cdots + 5 \ln \frac{5}{13.59} \right)$$

$$= 2(42.2450) = 84.49$$

In this case, G^2 is slightly larger than $X^2 = 77.92$ found in Section 26-4 for these data. As before, H_0 is rejected since with $\alpha = .05$, $v = (I - 1)(J - 1) = (4 - 1)(5 - 1) = 12$, and $\chi^2_{12:.95} = 21.03$. We provide directions in Box 49-2 for testing for no association or for homogeneity of distribution in an $I \times J$ contingency table.

Box 49-2   **Procedure for testing independence or homogeneity in an $I \times J$ contingency table**

Step 1. Compute

$$G^2 = 2 \sum_{i=1}^{I} \sum_{j=1}^{J} f_{ij} \ln f_{ij}/F_{ij}$$

Step 2. Reject H_0 if $G^2 > \chi^2_{v:1-\alpha}$ where $v = (I-1)(J-1)$.

49-4. MULTIPLE COMPARISONS FOR TWO-FACTOR TESTS OF INDEPENDENCE

In a series of papers that appeared in the late 1960s and early 1970s. Goodman provided methods for examining contrasts with log odds ratios. He showed how contrasts should be defined and how they can be tested for both a priori and post hoc investigations. As we saw in Section 49-2, the odds ratio $g = p_{11}p_{22}/(p_{12}p_{21})$ could be analyzed in terms of

$$\gamma = \ln p_{11} - \ln p_{12} - \ln p_{21} + \ln p_{22}$$

In this form, γ resembles an interaction contrast, not in terms of $p_{11}, p_{12}, p_{21}, p_{22}$ but in terms of their logarithms. Goodman made an investigation of the hypothesis of independence, and he found that for an $I \times J$ contingency table, one could define contrasts as

$$\psi = \sum_{i=1}^{I} \sum_{j=1}^{J} W_{ij} \ln F_{ij}$$

where

$$\sum_{i=1}^{I} W_{ij} = 0 \quad \text{and} \quad \sum_{j=1}^{J} W_{ij} = 0$$

He also noted that in a sample of size N, contrasts could be estimated as

$$\hat{\psi} = \sum_{i=1}^{I} \sum_{j=1}^{J} W_{ij} \ln f_{ij}$$

In addition, the variance of these contrasts is

$$\mathrm{Var}(\hat{\psi}) = \sum_{i=1}^{I} \sum_{j=1}^{J} \frac{W_{ij}^2}{f_{ij}}$$

If the expected values are sufficiently large, the $\hat{\psi}$ values have sampling distributions that are normal. It was also shown that the critical value for testing

$$H_0: \psi = 0$$

against

$$H_1: \psi \neq 0$$

with

$$Z = \frac{\hat{\psi} - 0}{\sigma_{\hat{\psi}}}$$

was given by $S^* = \sqrt{\chi^2_{v:1-\alpha}}$ with $v = (I-1)(J-1)$ in the post hoc case and by $Z_{1-\alpha/2C}$ in the a priori case, for C a priori defined contrasts.

Let us apply the a priori procedure to the data of Table 26-2. As might be expected, an infinite number of contrasts exist that one could define on the 20 eye color $\times$ hair color cells of Table 26-2. Those that make the most sense are the ones defined for the tetrad odds ratios. Since one can choose 2 rows and 2 columns from Table 26-2 in $\binom{4}{2} = 6$ ways and $\binom{5}{2} = 10$ ways, respectively, the total number of tetrad odds ratios is $C = 6(10) = 60$. For rows i and i' and j and j', these contrasts can be examined for significance by comparing each $Z = \hat{\gamma}_{(ii')(jj')}/\sigma_{\hat{\gamma}_{(ii')(jj')}}$ to $Z = 3.33$, the Z value found by interpolation in Table A-11 for $v = \infty$, $C = 50$, $C = 100$, and $\alpha = .05$. Since the sample sizes are small, most will be nonsignificant. Rather than test all 60 contrasts for significance, let us illustrate this procedure for one which we think might be significant. A likely candidate is the one defined for black and blond hair color with brown and blue eyes. For this contrast,

$$\hat{\gamma}_{(13)(15)} = \ln 45 - \ln 3 - \ln 7 + \ln 18 = 3.6526$$

with

$$\text{Var}(\hat{\gamma}_{(13)(15)}) = \tfrac{1}{45} + \tfrac{1}{3} + \tfrac{1}{7} + \tfrac{1}{18} = 0.5540$$

For the test of $H_0: \gamma_{(13)(15)} = 0$ against $H_1: \gamma_{(13)(15)} \neq 0$, we have

$$Z = \frac{\hat{\gamma}_{(13)(15)}}{\sigma_{\hat{\gamma}_{(13)(15)}}} = \frac{3.6526}{\sqrt{0.5540}}$$
$$= \frac{3.6526}{0.7442} = 4.914$$

In this case H_0 is rejected, since Z is in the critical region defined by $Z < -3.33$ or $Z > 3.33$. This procedure could be used to examine the remaining 59 contrasts.

If a post hoc analysis is of interest, the critical value is given by $S^* = \sqrt{\chi^2_{12:.95}} = \sqrt{21.03} = 4.59$. This can be applied to the 60 tetrad odds ratios and other more complicated contrasts of interest to a researcher. For example, with this critical value, we could examine the contrast for individuals with black and dark brown hair treated as a group and red- and blond-haired individuals treated as a group and compared on brown and blue eye color. Essentially, this contrast serves as a test of a correlation of eye color, brown and blue, with hair color, dark and light. It serves as a test of the hypothesis that brown eyes go with dark hair and blue eyes go with light hair. For this contrast,

$$\hat{\gamma} = (\ln 45 + \ln 50) - (\ln 6 + \ln 3) - (\ln 7 + \ln 5) + (\ln 13 + \ln 18)$$
$$= 6.7283$$

with

$$\mathrm{Var}(\hat{\gamma}) = \tfrac{1}{45} + \tfrac{1}{50} + \tfrac{1}{6} + \tfrac{1}{3} + \tfrac{1}{7} + \tfrac{1}{5} + \tfrac{1}{13} + \tfrac{1}{18}$$
$$= 1.0176$$

For this contrast,

$$Z = \frac{\hat{\gamma}}{\sigma_{\hat{\gamma}}} = \frac{6.7283}{\sqrt{1.0176}} = \frac{6.7283}{1.0087} = 6.67$$

As we see, $H_0 : \gamma = 0$ is rejected.

Before we close this discussion, note that we did not *pool* the data before computing $\hat{\gamma}$ and $\sigma_{\hat{\gamma}}$. This is because the contrasts are defined on the separate p_{ij} parameter values and not on the pooled values. A researcher should define contrasts carefully and correctly and should use the above method to test research questions of interest, be they planned prior to data collection or suggested by relationships among the observed frequencies.

We are now in a position to define H_0 and H_1 in tests of independence for qualitative variables. For a two-dimensional contingency table, the general form of H_0 is given by

$$H_0 : \text{all } \psi = \sum_{i=1}^{I} \sum_{j=1}^{J} W_{ij} \ln p_{ij} = 0$$

where

$$\sum_{i=1}^{I} W_{ij} = 0 \qquad \text{and} \qquad \sum_{j=1}^{J} W_{ij} = 0$$

Box 49-3   Procedures for testing odds ratios in a two-dimensional contingency table

Step 1. Define and count the number C of contrasts of interest to be investigated. For an $I \times J$ table, the number of tetrads is $\binom{I}{2}\binom{J}{2}$. For an $I \times J$ table they are of the form, for rows, (ii'), and for columns, (jj'):

$$H_0: \psi = \gamma_{(ii')(jj')} = 0$$
$$= \ln p_{ij} - \ln p_{ij'} - \ln p_{i'j} + \ln p_{i'j'}$$

Step 2. Compute the variances for a two-dimensional table as

$$\text{Var}(\hat{\psi}) = \frac{1}{f_{ij}} + \frac{1}{f_{ij'}} + \frac{1}{f_{i'j}} + \frac{1}{f_{i'j'}}$$

Step 3. Make the test of $H_0: \psi = 0$, using

$$Z = \hat{\psi}/\sigma_{\hat{\psi}}$$

Step 4. If these contrasts are planned, reject H_0 if

$$Z < -Z_{1-\alpha/2C} \text{ or if } Z > Z_{1-\alpha/2C}$$

where the critical values are read from the last column of Table A-11. If they are post hoc, use $S = \sqrt{\chi^2_{(I-1)(J-1):1-\alpha}}$.

Step 5. For more complex contrasts involving more than four cells, follow the example in the text.

---

with H_1 defined as

$$H_1: \text{at least one } \psi \neq 0$$

For completeness, we provide the procedure for testing contrasts in a two-dimensional contingency table in Box 49-3.

49-5. CALCULATING EXPECTED VALUES FOR FREQUENCY TABLES BASED ON THREE OR MORE VARIABLES

In the preceding chapters, we examined the ANOVA model for one, two, and more independent variables and a quantitative dependent variable. We now turn to similar multifactor designs in which the variables are qualitative. Contingency tables based on three or more variables have been of interest to researchers in the social sciences for many years.

In an $I \times J$ table, the estimated expected frequencies would be given simply as $F_{ij} = N(F_{i.}/N)(F_{.j}/N)$. This simplicity does not hold in contingency tables with three or more variables. In a two-dimensional contingency table, the F_{ij} are such that the marginal totals in the expected table equal the corresponding marginal totals in the observed table. For the more complicated tables, if the expected values are calculated in the same fashion as in the $I \times J$ table, this is no longer true. In these cases a lengthy process of *iteration* is required to equalize the marginal totals in the observed and expected tables.

Although the usual procedure for estimating expected cell frequencies is to compute F_{ij} as $F_{ij} = F_i F_j / N$, other methods can be used. We wish to illustrate one used for contingency tables with three or more dimensions. Even though it can be used for two-dimensional tables, it rarely is, because it is time-consuming. We illustrate it for the data of Table 26-2.

In the iterative procedure, each step in the iteration is denoted by a superscript. First, one makes an initial estimate of each F_{ij}, labeled $F_{ij}^{(1)}$. The usual practice is to set each $F_{ij}^{(1)}$ equal to 1. With this estimate, we see that for the first row

$$F_{1.}^{(1)} = F_{11}^{(1)} + F_{12}^{(1)} + F_{13}^{(1)} + F_{14}^{(1)} + F_{15}^{(1)}$$
$$= 1 + 1 + 1 + 1 + 1 = 5$$

whereas in Table 26-2 the corresponding row value is

$$f_{1.} = f_{11} + f_{12} + f_{13} + f_{14} + f_{15} = 45 + 8 + 7 + 2 + 7 = 69$$

Thus, each estimate is too small. We now adjust the estimates so that

$$F_{1.}^{(2)} = F_{11}^{(2)} + F_{12}^{(2)} + F_{13}^{(2)} + F_{14}^{(2)} + F_{15}^{(2)} = 69$$

This second step is achieved by multiplying each $F_{ij}^{(1)}$ by the ratio of the

Table 49-1. Second estimated frequencies for data of Table 26-2

| Hair color | Eye color | | | | | |
	Brown	Hazel	Green	Gray	Blue	Total
Black	13.8	13.8	13.8	13.8	13.8	69
Red	7.8	7.8	7.8	7.8	7.8	39
Blond	7.4	7.4	7.4	7.4	7.4	37
Dark brown	13.4	13.4	13.4	13.4	13.4	67
Total	42.4	42.4	42.4	42.4	42.4	212

desired row total to the present row total. Thus, we have

$$F_{11}^{(2)} = F_{11}^{(1)}\left(\frac{f_{1.}}{F_{1.}^{(1)}}\right) = 1\left(\frac{69}{5}\right) = 13.8$$

In like manner,

$$F_{12}^{(2)} = F_{13}^{(2)} = F_{14}^{(2)} = F_{15}^{(2)} = 13.8$$

This process is repeated for each row. This gives the estimates reported in Table 49-1. Even though the marginal totals for the rows are correct, the marginal totals for the columns are in error. They need to be corrected. For this correction we use

$$F_{11}^{(3)} = F_{11}^{(2)}\left(\frac{f_{.1}}{F_{.1}^{(2)}}\right) = 13.8\left(\frac{104}{42.4}\right) = 33.85$$

$$F_{21}^{(3)} = F_{21}^{(2)}\left(\frac{f_{.1}}{F_{.1}^{(2)}}\right) = 7.8\left(\frac{104}{42.4}\right) = 19.13$$

$$F_{31}^{(3)} = F_{31}^{(2)}\left(\frac{f_{.1}}{F_{.1}^{(2)}}\right) = 7.4\left(\frac{104}{42.4}\right) = 18.15$$

$$F_{41}^{(3)} = F_{41}^{(2)}\left(\frac{f_{.1}}{F_{.1}^{(2)}}\right) = 13.4\left(\frac{104}{42.4}\right) = 32.87$$

These estimates are identical to those of Table 26-3. These computations are even more lengthy for higher-dimensional tables and are not illustrated. In practice, a computer would be used.

49-6. TESTING TWO VARIABLES IN A THREE-VARIABLE CONTINGENCY TABLE

Consider the data of Table 27-1, which involve two independent variables

$$X_1 = \text{sex: male, female}$$

$$X_2 = \text{college major: sociology, other}$$

and one dependent variable:

Y: The most important way to reduce crime in the streets is to:

1. increase penalties
2. increase police force
3. increase welfare payments and social services
4. none of these

These data were examined in Section 27-2 in terms of the Karl Pearson test of homogeneity, where the distinction between sex and college major was not maintained. The model that we examine here keeps the distinction. The data are reported in Table 49-2.

In this design, even though seven sources of variation could be accounted for, a researcher often will not be interested in testing all seven of the corresponding hypotheses. These seven effects, analogous to a three-factor ANOVA with all possible interactions, would be sex, major, response, $S \times M$, $S \times R$, $M \times R$, and $S \times M \times R$. These sources of variation would examine the following seven hypotheses:

1. For sex, the null hypothesis is
   $H_0: P(\text{male}) = P(\text{female}) = \frac{1}{2}$.
2. For major, the null hypothesis is
   $H_0: P(\text{sociology}) = P(\text{other}) = \frac{1}{2}$.
3. For response, the null hypothesis is
   $H_0: P(\text{response } 1) = P(\text{response } 2) = P(\text{response } 3) = P(\text{response } 4) = \frac{1}{4}$.
4. For $S \times M$, the null hypothesis is

$H_0: P(\text{male, sociology}) = P(\text{male})P(\text{sociology})$
$P(\text{female, sociology}) = P(\text{female})P(\text{sociology})$
$P(\text{male, other}) = P(\text{male})P(\text{other})$
$P(\text{female, other}) = P(\text{female})P(\text{other})$

This hypothesis could be more succinctly specified in terms of Cramer's V as $H_0: V_{S \times M} = 0$. We write the remaining hypotheses in terms of V:

5. For $S \times R$, the null hypothesis, in terms of Cramer's V, is
   $H_0: V_{S \times R} = 0$.

Table 49-2. Responses to an attitude question by sex and major

	Sociology		Other	
Response	Male	Female	Male	Female
1	1	0	5	10
2	6	2	16	12
3	16	19	8	7
4	20	15	10	13

6. For $M \times R$, the null hypothesis, in terms of Cramer's V, is
$H_0: V_{M \times R} = 0$.

7. For $S \times M \times R$, the null hypothesis, in terms of Cramer's V, is
$H_0: V_{S \times M \times R} = 0$.

Let us examine these hypotheses in terms of their usefulness and interpretability. The first two hypotheses are uninteresting since one would not expect, or even necessarily wish to discover, that a population contains equal proportions of males and females or of sociology and other majors. The third hypothesis, however, testing for equal proportions of the population supporting each attitude, would be of some interest. The fourth hypothesis could be of interest if one had a random sample from the population, since one could then determine whether the selection of a major is independent of sex. Because we started with an intact classroom, we do not have a random sample. Hypotheses 5 through 7 are of definite interest in this context.

Let us examine hypothesis 5, which states that response is independent of sex. Embodied in this hypothesis is a question concerning the effects of a single independent variable, sex, on a single dependent variable, response. We wish to know whether the dependent variable differs in some way for males and females. Hence, we see that testing the independence of sex and response can be conceptualized as a test of main effect. We also saw this kind of equivalence in Section 16-5, where the median test was used to examine a two-group main effect of median difference. Although the analysis was performed on a 2×2 contingency table, testing for independence, the hypothesis was in the form of a main effect.

Why, then, is the source of variation examining the independence of response and sex written as an interaction? Let us examine the log odds ratio γ that is used to test this hypothesis, to better understand why this is so. As we recall, the log odds ratio for rows i and i' and columns j and j' would be

$$\hat{\gamma}_{(ii')(jj')} = (\ln f_{ij} - \ln f_{ij'}) - (\ln f_{i'j} - \ln f_{i'j'})$$

The right-hand side, being a difference of differences, is a tetrad interaction contrast as defined in two-factor ANOVA. It is because of this identity that tests of independence appear as interactions in this model, even though they test hypotheses of main effects on a single dependent variable.

In a similar fashion, we can create an argument to show that the $S \times M \times R$ source of variation can be thought to test a hypothesis that is really a two-factor interaction. Again, we have only the single dependent variable of response, and we wish to determine whether the two independent variables of sex and major exert interactive effects on it. The log odds ratio testing this hypothesis is in a form resembling the difference of interactions and, thus, is similar to a three-way ANOVA interaction contrast. Despite the difference between the conceptualization of the hypothesis and the appearance of the contrasts, we label the hypothesis in log-linear terminology, which is consistent with the form of the contrasts.

One problem in testing the two-dimensional contingency tables $S \times R$, $M \times R$, and $S \times M$ provided we wish to test the associated hypotheses, is that none of them can be tested free of the interaction involving $S \times M \times R$. For a three-dimensional contingency table, all two-factor tests are confounded with the three-factor interaction.

As an example of this confounding, consider the situation illustrated by the data of Table 49-3. If one were merely to test the $A \times B$ interaction in the table of totals (T), one would conclude that A and B were independent, since $X^2_{AB \cdot T} = 0.84$. But this conclusion is somewhat questionable. If we examined the individual tables, we would find that $X^2_{AB \cdot C_1} = 10.00$ and that $X^2_{AB \cdot C_2} = 4.00$, individually suggesting a lack of independence between A and B. There is, however, a reversal of the association from table C_1 to table C_2, so a three-factor interaction must be involved. Simply adding $X^2_{AB \cdot C_1}$ and $X^2_{AB \cdot C_2}$ would seriously overestimate the strength of the $A \times B$ association. Thus, any test based on the sum of the separate chi-square values must be adjusted for the three-factor interaction.

As another way of delineating this confounding, consider the hypothesis of no $S \times R$ effect in Table 49-2. We can calculate a G^2 statistic *within* each of the majors. If we sum these *within* G^2 statistics, calling the resulting value $G^2_{S \times R \cdot W}$, then $G^2_{S \times R \cdot W}$ has a large sample chi-square distribution whose degrees of freedom are cumulative across the M contingency tables. In other words,

$$v_{S \times R \cdot W} = v_{S \times R(1)} + v_{S \times R(2)} + \cdots + v_{S \times R(M)}$$
$$= (S - 1)(R - 1) + (S - 1)(R - 1) + \cdots + (S - 1)(R - 1)$$
$$= M(S - 1)(R - 1)$$

But this is the wrong number of degrees of freedom for this test, since we know in the two-dimensional case that $v_{S \times R} = (S - 1)(R - 1)$. The problem is that $G^2_{S \times R \cdot W}$ is inflated by the value of $G^2_{S \times R \times M}$ for which $v_{S \times R \times M} =$

Table 49-3. Example of confounding of a two-factor interaction

	B_1	B_2		B_1	B_2		B_1	B_2
A_1	5	15	A_1	12	6	A_1	17	21
A_2	15	5	A_2	6	12	A_2	21	17

(C_1)	(C_2)	(T)
$X^2_{AB \cdot C_1} = 10.00$	$X^2_{AB \cdot C_2} = 4.00$	$X^2_{AB \cdot T} = 0.84$

$(S - 1)(R - 1)(M - 1)$. The test statistic for testing the two-factor interaction is given as

$$G^2_{S \times R \cdot P} = G^2_{S \times R \cdot W} - G^2_{S \times R \times M}$$

with degrees of freedom given by

$$\begin{aligned} v_{S \times R \cdot P} &= M(S - 1)(R - 1) - (S - 1)(M - 1)(R - 1) \\ &= (S - 1)(R - 1) \end{aligned}$$

This latter test of hypothesis is referred to as a *partial test of association*. It should be accompanied by a marginal test of association based on a table collapsed across major. For this marginal test, one sums the frequencies across the levels of M to produce a two-dimensional frequency table of size $S \times R$. The G^2 for this table is computed by using the methods of Section 49-3. We denote the marginal G^2 for this collapsed total table $G^2_{S \times R \cdot T}$: It is compared to the chi-square distribution with $v_{S \times R \cdot T} = (S - 1)(R - 1)$ to determine the rejection of H_0. Under this formulation one of four things can happen:

1. Both $G^2_{S \times R \cdot P}$ and $G^2_{S \times R \cdot T}$ are significantly large.
2. Neither $G^2_{S \times R \cdot P}$ nor $G^2_{S \times R \cdot T}$ is significantly large.
3. The $G^2_{S \times R \cdot P}$ is significantly large, and $G^2_{S \times R \cdot T}$ is not.
4. The $G^2_{S \times R \cdot P}$ is not significantly large, and $G^2_{S \times R \cdot T}$ is.

The first two situations provide no problem. For the latter two situations, a researcher must make decisions based on theory or practical considerations. In these cases, we suggest tentatively rejecting the null hypothesis, contingent on substantive interpretation.

Let us examine the hypotheses of interest. But as we do, remember that the value of $G^2_{S \times R \times M}$ must be available. We compute $G^2_{S \times R \times M}$ in Section 49-7, where we see that $G^2_{S \times R \times M} = 3.20$. We use this value in this section.

There are seven hypotheses that one could test with the data of Table 49-2. We examine three:

1. Responses to the question are independent of sex.
2. Responses are independent of major.
3. Responses are independent of major and sex when they are considered simultaneously.

As we have seen, the first two hypotheses are conceptualized as *main-effect* hypotheses, even though contrasts associated with them resemble two-factor interactions, while the third hypothesis would be recognized as an *interaction-effect* hypothesis, even though contrasts associated with it resemble three-fac-

Table 49-4. Observed and expected frequencies for main effect of sex on response

Sex	R_1	R_2	R_3	R_4	Total
			Sociology		
		Observed frequencies			
Male	1	6	16	20	43
Female	0	2	19	15	36
Total	1	8	35	35	79
		Expected frequencies			
Male	0.544	4.354	19.051	19.051	43
Female	0.456	3.646	15.949	15.949	36
Total	1	8	35	35	79

tor interactions. We describe in more detail what these hypotheses mean as we examine the three hypotheses under consideration.

We begin by testing the first hypothesis. In this case we see that the test of independence of response and sex can be written as

$$H_0: P(\text{response 1}|\text{male}) = P(\text{response 1}|\text{female})$$
$$P(\text{response 2}|\text{male}) = P(\text{response 2}|\text{female})$$
$$P(\text{response 3}|\text{male}) = P(\text{response 3}|\text{female})$$
$$P(\text{response 4}|\text{male}) = P(\text{response 4}|\text{female})$$

In what follows, we let f_{smr} represent the frequency in

1. The sth sex: $1 = $ male and $2 = $ female
2. The mth major: $1 = $ sociology and $2 = $ other
3. the rth response: $1 = $ penalties, $2 = $ police, $3 = $ welfare, and $4 = $ none.

We begin the estimation procedure by making a guess about the expected frequencies, and we apply the iteration procedure of Section 49-5.

The two variables of interest of this hypothesis are sex and response, so that within each level of the third variable, major, we require the expected values to sum to the marginal totals. Resulting expected values are reported in Table 49-4.

Table 49-4. *(Continued)*

Sex	R_1	R_2	Other R_3	R_4	Total
			Observed frequencies		
Male	5	16	8	10	39
Female	10	12	7	13	42
Total	15	28	15	23	81
			Expected frequencies		
Male	7.222	13.481	7.222	11.074	39
Female	7.778	14.519	7.778	11.926	42
Total	15	28	15	23	81

For these estimated expected frequencies, the conditional test of $S \times R$ can be calculated from

$$G^2_{S \times R \cdot W} = 2 \left(1 \ln \frac{1}{0.544} + 6 \ln \frac{6}{4.354} + \cdots + 13 \ln \frac{13}{11.926} \right)$$
$$= 6.45$$

Thus

$$G^2_{S \times R \cdot P} = G^2_{S \times R \cdot W} - G^2_{S \times R \times M} = 6.45 - 3.20 = 3.25$$

with

$$v_{S \times R \cdot P} = (S - 1)(R - 1) = (2 - 1)(4 - 1) = 3$$

With $\alpha = .05$, H_0 is not rejected since $\chi^2_{3;.95} = 7.81$.

For the marginal test, we sum the frequencies across the two majors to give the data reported in Table 49-5. The $G^2_{S \times R \cdot T}$ for these frequencies is found in the usual way for a two-dimensional table and is given by $G^2_{S \times R \cdot T} = 2.85$. Again H_0 is not rejected.

We now consider the hypothesis of homogeneity of response distribution

Table 49-5. Summed frequencies for the sex × response marginal test of hypothesis

| | Sex | | |
Response	Male	Female	Total
1	6	10	16
2	22	14	36
3	24	26	50
4	30	28	58
Total	82	78	160

for the two majors. The hypothesis of this test is

$$H_0: P(\text{response } 1|\text{sociology}) = P(\text{response } 1|\text{other})$$
$$P(\text{response } 2|\text{sociology}) = P(\text{response } 2|\text{other})$$
$$P(\text{response } 3|\text{sociology}) = P(\text{response } 3|\text{other})$$
$$P(\text{response } 4|\text{sociology}) = P(\text{response } 4|\text{other})$$

Table 49-6. Observed and expected frequencies for testing the main effect of major on response

| | Males | | | | |
Major	R_1	R_2	R_3	R_4	Total
	Observed frequencies				
Sociology	1	6	16	20	43
Other	5	16	8	10	39
Total	6	22	24	30	82
	Expected frequencies				
Sociology	3.146	11.537	12.585	15.732	43
Other	2.854	10.463	11.415	14.268	39
Total	6	22	24	30	82

We must now generate F_{smr} values for this test. We use the same procedure as for the test across the two sexes, but this time we start with the data shown in Table 49-6 and estimate the expected values within the levels of sex. The expected values are also shown in Table 49-6. For these data,

$$G^2_{M \times R \cdot W} = 2 \left(1 \ln \frac{1}{3.146} + 6 \ln \frac{6}{11.537} + \cdots + 13 \ln \frac{13}{15.077} \right)$$
$$= 40.77$$

Thus,

$$G^2_{M \times R \cdot P} = G^2_{M \times R \cdot W} - G^2_{S \times R \times M} = 40.77 - 3.20 = 37.57$$

with

$$v_{M \times R \cdot P} = (M - 1)(R - 1) = (2 - 1)(4 - 1) = 3$$

With $\alpha = .05$, H_0 is rejected since $\chi^2_{3:.95} = 7.81$.

For the marginal test we sum the frequencies across the two sexes to give the data reported in Table 49-7. The $G^2_{M \times R \cdot T}$ for these frequencies is $G^2_{M \times R \cdot T} = 37.17$. Again, H_0 is rejected.

Table 49-6. *(Continued)*

			Females		
Major	R_1	R_2	R_3	R_4	Total
			Observed frequencies		
Sociology	0	2	19	15	36
Other	10	12	7	13	42
Total	10	14	26	28	78
			Expected frequencies		
Sociology	4.615	6.462	12.000	12.923	36
Other	5.385	7.538	14.000	15.077	42
Total	10	14	26	28	78

Table 49-7. Summed frequencies for major × response marginal test of hypothesis

	Major		
Response	Sociology	Other	Total
1	1	15	16
2	8	28	36
3	35	15	50
4	35	23	58
Total	79	81	160

We provide directions for testing two variables for independence in a three-dimensional contingency table in Box 49-4.

49-7. TESTING THREE VARIABLES IN A THREE-DIMENSIONAL CONTINGENCY TABLE

Testing three variables in a three-dimensional contingency table, in which two of the variables are independent variables and one is a dependent variable, is equivalent to testing for *no interaction* between the two independent variables on the dependent variable. In the context of our example, the hypothesis of no two-way interaction between sex and response means that each of the response odds ratios for the males is equal to the corresponding response odds ratios for the females. The lack of a three-way interaction means that the $S \times R$ interaction for sociology majors is equal to the corresponding interaction for the nonmajors. If we let $g_{(ss')(rr')m}$ represent the odds

Table 49-8. Expected values for test of no interaction between sex and major on response

	Major: Sociology				
Sex	R_1	R_2	R_3	R_4	Total
Male	.458	5.416	17.756	19.371	43.001
Female	.543	2.589	17.240	15.629	36.001
Total	1.001	8.005	34.996	35.000	79.002

Box 49-4 **Procedure for testing two variables for independence in a three-dimensional table**

Step 1. Denote the variables A, B, and C, with categories

$$A: A_1, A_2, \ldots, A_I$$
$$B: B_1, B_2, \ldots, B_J$$
$$C: C_1, C_2, \ldots, C_K$$

Step 2. To test the hypothesis that A and B are independent, estimate the expected frequencies in the $A_i B_j C_k$ cell by using the iterative procedure, illustrated in Section 49-3, within each level of C. Let the estimates be denoted F_{ijk}.

Step 3. Compute

$$G^2_{A \times B \cdot W} = 2 \sum_{k=1}^{K} \sum_{i=1}^{I} \sum_{j=1}^{J} f_{ijk} \ln \frac{f_{ijk}}{F_{ijk}}$$

Step 4. Use the method of Section 49-7 to compute $G^2_{A \times B \times C}$ and then compute

$$G^2_{A \times B \cdot P} = G^2_{A \times B \cdot W} - G^2_{A \times B \times C}$$

Reject H_0 if $G^2_{A \times B \cdot P} > \chi^2_{\nu; 1-\alpha}$, where $\nu = (I-1)(J-1)$.

---

ratio in major category m for the (s, s') rows and (r, r') responses, and if we let $g_{(ss')(rr')m'}$ represent the corresponding ratio in the m' major category, then H_0 can be written

$$H_0: \text{all } g_{(ss')(rr')m} = g_{(ss')(rr')m'}$$

Truly, this is a complex hypothesis.

Table 49-8. *(Continued)*

			Other		
Sex	R_1	R_2	R_3	R_4	Total
Male	5.537	16.573	6.254	10.636	39,000
Female	9.465	11.418	8.751	12.367	42.001
Total	15.002	27.991	15.005	23.004	81.001

Box 49-5   Procedure for testing three variables for independence

Step 1. Follow the steps for testing two variables for independence, but in this case balance the margins for all three variables simultaneously.

Step 2. Reject H_0 if G^2 is greater than $\chi^2_{\nu;1-\alpha}$, where $\nu = (I-1)(J-1)(K-1)$.

The expected values for this test are required to sum to three marginal totals simultaneously. After an initial guess, the iteration procedure outlined in Section 49-3 is used on each pair of marginal totals, in sequence, until all three marginal totals are met. These values are reported in Table 49-8. For these values

$$G^2_{S \times M \times R} = 2 \left(1 \ln \frac{1}{0.458} + 5 \ln \frac{5}{5.416} + \cdots + 13 \ln \frac{13}{12.367} \right)$$

$$= 3.20$$

With $\nu = (S-1)(M-1)(R-1) = (2-1)(2-1)(4-1) = 3$, we see that H_0 is not rejected, since $\chi^2_{3;.95} = 7.81$. We provide directions for testing three variables for independence in Box 49-5.

49-8. HIGHER-ORDER CONTINGENCY TABLES

Clearly hand calculator operations are not advised for third- or higher-order contingency tables. Even though we do not provide an example, a researcher should be able to generalize conceptually from the presentation in this chapter to higher-dimensional tables. Finally, complex tables involve some complex statistical theory and complications. We have not discussed them. Again, one is advised to consult more complete references on the topic.

49-9. PLANNED AND POST HOC CONTRASTS IN MULTIDIMENSIONAL CONTINGENCY TABLES

As we saw in the context of ANOVA, the null hypotheses could be expressed in terms of contrasts among means. The same is true in multidimensional contingency tables, where the null hypotheses can be expressed in terms of contrasts among odds ratios or log frequencies.

For an example of a hypothesis concerning the independence of two factors in a three-dimensional table, consider the major $\times$ response effect. The null hypothesis tested for this effect was written in Section 49-2 in terms of probabilities. In terms of odds ratios, this hypothesis would be written

$$H_0: \text{all contrasts among } \gamma_{(mm')(rr')} = 0$$

From this formulation of H_0, one would think that $\gamma_{(12)(12)}$ would be estimated from the frequencies of Table 49-7 as

$$\hat{\gamma}_{(12)(12)} = \ln 1 - \ln 15 - \ln 8 + \ln 28$$

Unfortunately, this is not correct. Notice that when this hypothesis was tested, the G^2 test statistic contained contributions from each of the 16 separate cells. For this reason, contrasts among log frequencies must be defined in terms of the separate cell frequencies, without collapsing, to correspond correctly to the null hypothesis under examination. Thus, for this example,

$$\hat{\gamma}_{(12)(12)} = (\ln 1 + \ln 0) - (\ln 5 + \ln 10) - (\ln 6 + \ln 2) + (\ln 16 + \ln 12)$$

Before we compute this, we must realize that $\ln 0$ is undefined; the standard practice is to replace this value by $\ln \frac{1}{2}$. Then

$$\begin{aligned}
\hat{\gamma}_{(12)(12)} &= [0 + (-0.6931)] - (1.6094 + 2.3026) \\
&\quad - (1.7918 + 0.6931) + (2.7726 + 2.4829) \\
&= -1.8326
\end{aligned}$$

As we have seen previously, the variance of $\hat{\gamma}$ is given by the sum of the reciprocals of the cell frequencies. Thus for these data

$$\sigma^2_{\hat{\gamma}(12)(12)} = \frac{1}{1} + \frac{1}{\frac{1}{2}} + \cdots + \frac{1}{12} = 4.1125$$

and

$$Z = \frac{\hat{\gamma}_{(12)(12)}}{\sigma_{\hat{\gamma}(12)(12)}} = \frac{-1.8326}{2.0279} = -0.9037$$

Since H_0 was tested with 3 degrees of freedom, the critical value for testing H_0 in terms of $\gamma_{(12)(12)}$ is given by $= S^* = \sqrt{\chi^2_{3;.95}} = 2.79$. Thus, $H_0: \gamma_{(12)(12)} = 0$ is not rejected. The remaining tests of $\gamma_{(mm')(rr')}$ are given in Table 49-9.

Although the test of the three-factor interaction was not significant, we examine contrasts to test this hypothesis for illustrative purposes. Consider the sex $\times$ major $\times$ response categories of Table 49-4. Since we will again be examining $2 \times 2 \times 2$ frequency tables, we have six contrasts to examine. As an example, consider associating sex and responses 1 and 2. In the three-factor interaction, this is compared between sociology and nonsociology majors. As before, 0 is replaced by $\frac{1}{2}$. With this adjustment, we have

$$\begin{aligned}
\hat{\psi}_1 &= [(\ln 1 - \ln \tfrac{1}{2}) - (\ln 6 - \ln 2)] - [(\ln 5 - \ln 10) - (\ln 16 - \ln 12)] \\
&= 0.5754
\end{aligned}$$

Table 49-9. The $C = (\frac{M}{2})(\frac{R}{2}) = (\frac{2}{2})(\frac{4}{2}) = 6$ two-factor major $\times$ response contrasts for data of Table 49-4

| | | Sociology | | Other | | | | |
| | Response | Male | Female | Male | Female | $\hat{y}$ | Var($\hat{y}$) | Z |
Contrast	category							
1	1	1	0	5	10	−1.8326	4.1125	−0.90
	2	6	2	16	12			
2	1	1	0	5	10	−6.2968	3.6830	−3.28[a]
	3	16	19	8	7			
3	1	1	0	5	10	−5.4414	3.5936	−2.87[a]
	4	20	15	10	13			
4	2	6	2	16	12	−4.4643	1.1955	−4.08[a]
	3	16	19	8	7			
5	2	6	2	16	12	−3.6088	1.1061	−3.43[a]
	4	20	15	10	13			
6	3	16	19	8	7	0.8554	0.6766	1.04
	4	20	15	10	13			

[a] Significant at $\alpha = .05$

with

$$\text{Var}(\hat{\psi}_1) = \frac{1}{1} + \frac{1}{\frac{1}{2}} + \frac{1}{6} + \frac{1}{2} + \frac{1}{5} + \frac{1}{10} + \frac{1}{6} + \frac{1}{12}$$

$$= 4.1125$$

and

$$Z = \frac{\hat{\psi}_1}{\sigma_{\hat{\psi}_1}} = \frac{0.5754}{\sqrt{4.1125}} = \frac{0.5754}{2.0279} = 0.28$$

With $\alpha = .05$ and $C = 6$, the decision rule for testing each is

Decision Rule: Reject H_0 if $Z < -2.64$ or if $Z < 2.64$

Thus, this contrast is nonsignificant. We provide directions for testing contrasts in multidimensional contingency tables in Box 49-6.

Box 49-6   **Procedure for testing contrasts in multidimensional contingency tables**

Step 1. Define the contrasts of interest as

$$\psi = \sum_{i=1}^{I}\sum_{j=1}^{J}\sum_{k=1}^{K} W_{ijk} \ln p_{ijk}$$

with

$$\sum_{i=1}^{I} W_{ijk} = \sum_{j=1}^{J} W_{ijk} = \sum_{k=1}^{K} W_{ijk} = 0$$

Choose these W_{ijk} to reflect the hypothesis being tested.

Step 2. Estimate them as

$$\hat{\psi} = \sum_{i=1}^{I}\sum_{j=1}^{J}\sum_{k=1}^{K} W_{ijk} \ln f_{ijk}$$

Step 3. Determine the variances as

$$\mathrm{Var}(\hat{\psi}) = \sum_{i=1}^{I}\sum_{j=1}^{J}\sum_{k=1}^{K} W_{ijk}^{2}/f_{ijk}$$

Step 4. Compute

$$Z = \frac{\hat{\psi}}{\sigma_{\hat{\psi}}}$$

Step 5. For a post hoc analysis, reject H_0 if $Z < -S$ or if $Z > S$, where

$$S = \sqrt{\chi_{\nu:1-\alpha}^{2}}$$

and where ν = degrees of freedom for the test. For a planned analysis, replace S by critical values read from Table A-11 for C = number of contrasts of interest.

49-10. LOG-LINEAR MODEL

As mentioned in Section 49-1, the concepts of regression analysis are helpful in analyzing higher-order contingency tables. To see why this is so, we now present the log-linear model. For the two-factor example of eye color and hair color, let F_{ij} be the expected value in the ith row and jth column of the table. The model for this design is written as

$$\ln F_{ij} = \mu + \alpha_i + \beta_j + \gamma_{ij} \qquad i = 1, 2, \ldots, I; j = 1, 2, \ldots, J$$

In addition, there are side restrictions to be met by these parameters:

$$\sum_{i=1}^{I} \alpha_{i.} = 0 \qquad \sum_{j=1}^{J} \beta_{.j} = 0 \qquad \sum_{i=1}^{I} \gamma_{ij} = \sum_{j=1}^{J} \gamma_{ij} = 0$$

The model and the restrictions are similar to those in the model for two-factor ANOVA, except here the dependent variable is ln F_{ij}. Thus, we should be able to use coded variables and regression analysis in log-linear analysis.

This is, in fact, the case. Coded variables can be prepared that represent contrasts among the main-effect and interaction parameters in the model. With these coded variables entered into the model, the predicted values are actually the expected values F_{ij} required for performing the G^2 test. Thus, to test the sex main effect, the coded variable representing the sex contrast could be entered and the F_{ij} determined. Then, G_S^2 could be calculated. To determine whether the main effect for sex should be considered significant, the model containing only the grand mean μ would be examined, G_μ^2 would be calculated, and the sex main effect would be tested by examining $G_S^2 - G_\mu^2$.

When all the coded variables are entered into the equation and all the degrees of freedom are accounted for, the model is said to be *saturated* (sat). In this case, all the expected values equal the corresponding observed frequencies, and so $G_{sat}^2 = 0$. To test the highest-order interaction for its contribution to the model, we would compare the G^2 value when the interaction is included to that obtained when it is excluded. However, the inclusion of the highest-order interaction makes the model saturated, with a G^2 value of zero. Therefore, the G^2 value obtained when this interaction is excluded is equal to the G^2 statistic for testing the highest-order interaction. For our example, when the model includes all the main effects and all the $S \times R$, $S \times M$, and $M \times R$ interactions, the G^2 value equals 3.20, the value reported for $G_{S \times M \times R}^2$.

The importance of this result relates to the marginal tests described in Section 49-6. To understand these tests in regression terms, consider the marginal test of the $S \times R$ interaction. First, the table is summed across the levels of the missing variable, here major, yielding the values reported in Table 49-5. This table is then analyzed by using a model containing only the sex and response main effects. As explained above, the G^2 for this analysis is identical to the test of the highest-order interaction in this table, which is the $S \times R$ interaction. But since this table has been achieved by summing across major, the result is the test of the *marginal* $S \times R$ interaction, the value we called $G_{S \times R \cdot T}^2$.

Of course, any effects in our model could be confounded with other effects owing to the nonorthogonal nature of the design. For this reason, it makes sense to examine each particular effect after the others have been partialed out. For example, consider again the $S \times R$ interaction, but let us try to partial major from it. To do so, we enter all the main effects plus the $S \times R$, $S \times M$, and $R \times M$ interactions. As we have seen, the G^2 for this model (actually the test of the $S \times M \times R$ interaction) equals 3.20. If we now calculate G^2 for the model including the main effects, plus the $S \times M$ and $R \times M$ interactions only, we have an indication of how well the model fits without the $S \times R$ interaction. This G^2 value is equal to 6.45, identical to $G^2_{S \times R \cdot W}$ in Section 49-6. The difference between $G^2_{S \times R \cdot W}$ and $G^2_{S \times M \times R}$ is the partial test of the association between sex and response

$$G^2_{S \times R \cdot P} = G^2_{S \times R \cdot W} - G^2_{S \times M \times R} = 6.45 - 3.20 = 3.25$$

as before.

The concepts underlying regression analysis can be applied to the log-linear model. Indeed, many computer programs have stepwise procedures helpful in determining which of the effects seem to be relatively important factors in the design. As is true of stepwise regression, however, stepwise log-linear analysis does not ensure that the best set of independent variables will be found. The only way to do so is to examine all possible models. Unfortunately, the number of possible models increases quickly with an increase in the number of variables in the design. For our example, 18 models are possible — the grand mean only, three main effects separately, three pairs of main effects, all three main effects together, three two-factor interactions separately, each of these with the one other main effect, three pairs of two-factor interactions, and all first-order interactions together. For larger tables, the time required to examine all possible models mounts up rapidly, even for computers.

Because of the relationship between the tests of models and the marginal and partial tests examined in Section 49-6, a reasonable model-building procedure can be used. First, perform the marginal and partial tests. If both are significant, the effect should definitely be included in all models. If neither is significant, the effect is always excluded. The only models that then have to be compared are ones which contain the definitely significant effects, plus those effects that are significant on only the marginal or the partial test. Substantive interpretation and incremental tests would be used to determine whether the tentatively rejected factors should be included in the model.

49-11. EXERCISES

49-1. Analyze the data of Exercise 26-2, using the log-linear model. Do the analysis, using a statistical computer program. Add $\frac{1}{2}$ to all the cells before beginning the analysis. This correction will adjust for the zero cell frequencies.

49-2. Analyze the data of Exercise 26-4 as a log-linear model with G^2 statistics. Use a statistical

computer program. Add $\frac{1}{2}$ to each cell of the design before performing the analysis.

49-3. Make a post hoc analysis of the odds ratios for the data of Exercise 49-2.

49-4. Examine the data of Exercise 26-2 in terms of
a. The Fisher Irwin test for large samples
b. The G^2 statistic

c. The test of the hypothesis that the odds ratio is zero

d. The phi coefficient.

49-5. The study of Exercise 26-1 also involved men who were asked whether they thought women should abort unwanted babies. The results are as follows:

	Age		
Response	Under 30	Over 30	Total
Yes	42	10	52
No	6	48	54
Total	48	58	106

Analyze the data for the two tables in terms of three-factor log-linear model. Use statistical software. Compare the odds ratio for the males to that of females.

49-6. In a survey of student attitudes following a year of school integration, students were asked: How well do you get along with your classmates this year (as compared to last year) — better or worse? The results are as shown.

	School 1		School 2		School 3	
Attitude	White	Black	White	Black	White	Black
Better	76	107	91	73	96	59
Worse	37	25	39	49	43	36
Total	113	132	130	122	139	95

Analyze these data using the log-linear model. Determine the odds ratios for each school, and use contrasts to determine whether a three-factor interaction is significant. Are the three-factor interaction contrasts tests of three factors or two factors? Explain what you mean. Remember that attitude represents a response variable and not an independent variable. What are the independent variables?

49-7. Test the three odds ratios of Exercise 49-6 for significance.

49-8. Contrast school 1 against schools 2 and 3 taken collectively. In this study this contrast made sense because school 1 was essentially untouched by the integration program.

49-9. Write up the results of Exercises 49-6, 49-7, and 49-8 for a professional report.

49-10. The data of Exercise 49-6 can be examined in terms of three separate Fisher Irwin tests. How does this analysis relate to Exercise 49-7? Which model is superior — that of Exercise 49-7 or the one proposed here? Why?

PART IX

POWER AND SAMPLE SIZE

Research and statistical investigations cost money. Most researchers work with a minimal budget and therefore want to maximize the information they can collect for a fixed amount of money. One way to do this is to use statistically powerful procedures. In this last chapter we discuss the problem of power and show how one can determine appropriate sample sizes for most of the statistical models considered in previous chapters.

CHAPTER 50

Power and Sample Size

50-1. POWER OF A STATISTICAL TEST

We are all familiar with how a microbiologist rates a microscope in terms of quoting its power. A microscope with a power of 10 will take an object and expand it for viewing by a factor of 10. A 50-power microscope will increase the dimensions of an object by a factor of 50. A 50-power microscope is more powerful than a 10-power microscope. Statisticians use the same terms to define the power of a statistical test. A test based on 50 observations is more powerful than one based on 10 observations in its ability to reject H_0 if it is false.

Consider a researcher who has a choice among the sign test, the matched-pair Wilcoxon test, or the matched-pair t test for testing $H_0 : \mu_1 = \mu_2$. Naturally, she wants to use the test that has the highest probability of rejecting H_0 if it is false. The test that has this property is called the *most powerful test*. In this case, it is the t test, *provided that the underlying variable has a normal distribution*. Of the three tests, the least powerful for normal data is the sign test. However, it does not follow that the power of the Wilcoxon test is midway between the two for such data. Statisticians have shown that a t test based on 100 observations is as powerful as a Wilcoxon test based on 105 observations and a sign test based on 157 observations. This means that the relative power of the Wilcoxon test to the t test is given by $100/105 = 0.955$, the relative power of the sign test to the t test is $100/157 = 0.637$, and the relative power of the sign test to the Wilcoxon test is $105/157 = 0.667$. A researcher should always choose the t test over the Wilcoxon or sign test *if the assumptions for the t test are valid*. However, almost no loss accrues if the Wilcoxon test is adopted. Surprisingly, at times the Wilcoxon test is more powerful than the t test. This occurs when the distribution of the variable is platykurtic. On the other hand, the sign test is preferred when the distribution of the variable is leptokurtic. As this discussion implies, the power of a test determines its utility.

50-2. CONTROLLING THE POWER OF A STATISTICAL TEST

In Chapter 12, we saw that the ability to reject H_0 if it is false depends on three conditions:

1. The risk of a type I error
2. The value of the population parameters as defined under the alternative hypothesis
3. The number of trials or the sample size

Of these three conditions, the one under most direct control of the researcher is the sample size. The probability of a type I error is typically controlled in the social and behavioral sciences at 1 or 5 percent, although smaller values are sometimes used. Thus, since nature determines the values of the parameters, the only freedom that a researcher has to reduce the risks of making a type II error is control of the sample size.

Statisticians have formulated ways to determine the appropriate sample size in advance of data collection if the following characteristics can be specified:

1. The risk of a type I error
2. The risk of a type II error
3. An educated guess of the parameter values associated with H_1

Of these three characteristics, specification of H_1 is most difficult to satisfy. If it can be stated in approximate terms, then ballpark estimates of the sample size can be specified. We consider some special cases for which solutions exist. The tables we present have been adapted from *Statistical Power Analysis for the Behavioral Sciences* by Jacob Cohen, published by Academic Press in 1969.

50-3.   SAMPLE SIZES FOR TWO-SAMPLE t TEST

The sample sizes for the two-sample t test can be determined provided that a researcher can specify the values of the two unknown means and of the unknown population standard deviation. We illustrate the method by an example. The method is based on the determination of

$$\Delta = \left| \frac{\mu_1 - \mu_2}{\sigma} \right|$$

where

μ_1 = population mean for group 1

μ_2 = population mean for group 2

σ = standard deviation of each population

The vertical lines indicate that the algebraic sign of the standardized difference is ignored. Once the value of Δ is known, Table 50-1 can be used to determine the appropriate sample size. This table gives sample sizes for $N_1 = N_2$ with $\alpha = .05$ and $\beta = .30$, $\beta = .20$, $\beta = .10$, and $\beta = .05$.

Suppose a researcher wishes to compare a new reading program to an old program with $\alpha = .05$ and $\beta = .10$. And suppose it is known that, over a long period, students taught with the old method tend to have test scores with an average value of $\mu_1 = 35$ and a standard deviation of $\sigma = 12$. Since there is no way to know the value of μ_2 under the new program, it may be decided that there is no interest in the new program unless it increases the mean value by one-third of a standard deviation. This means that we are interested in alternatives that have $\mu_2 \geq \mu_1 + \frac{1}{3}\sigma = 35 + \frac{1}{3}(12) = 39$. With $\mu_1 = 35$ and $\mu_2 = 39$,

$$\Delta = \left| \frac{\mu_1 - \mu_2}{\sigma} \right| = \left| \frac{35 - 39}{12} \right| = 0.33$$

Notice that Δ measures the distance between the populations in standard deviation units. In practice, this means that a researcher does not need to know the values of μ_1, μ_2, and σ to determine the appropriate sample sizes. A simple statement of mean differences in terms of standard deviation units achieves the desired end. Since $\Delta = 0.33$ is not in the table, we must perform some interpolation. For $\beta = .10$ and $\Delta = 0.30$, each sample size should con-

Table 50-1. Sample sizes for two-sample t test for $\alpha = .05$, $\beta = .30$, $\beta = .20$, $\beta = .10$, $\beta = .05$, and $N_1 = N_2$

	Sample size for type II error probabilities			
Δ	$\beta = .30$	$\beta = .20$	$\beta = .10$	$\beta = .05$
.10	1235	1571	2102	2600
.20	310	393	526	651
.30	138	175	234	290
.40	78	99	132	163
.50	50	64	85	105
.60	35	45	59	73
.70	26	33	44	54
.80	20	26	34	42
1.00	13	17	22	27
1.20	10	12	16	19
1.40	7	9	12	14

Adapted with permission from Table 2.4.1, n to detect d-by-t test, in J. Cohen, *Statistical Power Analysis for the Behavioral Sciences*, New York: Academic Press, 1969.

sist of about 234 students, and for $\Delta = 0.40$, each sample size should consist of about 132 students. Interpolating between these values, we find $N_1 = N_2 = 234 - \frac{1}{3}(234 - 132) = 234 - 34 = 200$.

From an applied point of view, the considerations made in determining the sample sizes of the previous example are very exacting. Rarely do researchers place such tight requirements on the risk of a type II error, because it is expensive to keep it low. A more typical situation would be to let $\beta = .30$ and let $\mu_2 \geq \mu_1 + \frac{1}{2}\sigma$. If this were acceptable, it would be found that $\mu_2 \geq 35 + \frac{1}{2}(12) = 41$, so that

$$\Delta = \left| \frac{\mu_1 - \mu_2}{\sigma} \right| = \left| \frac{35 - 41}{12} \right| = 0.50$$

With $\beta = .30$ and $\Delta = 0.50$, the sample sizes are given approximately by $N_1 = N_2 = 50$. Such smaller sample sizes are easier to work with and easier to obtain.

50-4. SAMPLE SIZE FOR POINT BISERIAL CORRELATION COEFFICIENT

Since the two-sample t test and the point biserial correlation coefficient are based on the same model, Table 50-1 should be useful in determining the sample size for testing $H_0 : \rho_{pb} = 0$ against $H_1 : \rho_{pb} \neq 0$. For equal-size samples, the square of the point biserial correlation is associated with Δ according to the following equation:

$$\Delta^2 = \frac{4\rho_{pb}^2}{1 - \rho_{pb}^2}$$

We show how Table 50-1 can be used to determine the sample sizes for testing $\rho_{pb}^2 = 0$.

Suppose a researcher is interested in comparing a verbal reinforcement schedule with a candy reinforcement, but is interested in declaring that a significant difference exists between the two types of reinforcement only if $\rho_{pb}^2 > 0.10$. Substituting this value into the equation that relates ρ_{pb}^2 to Δ gives

$$\Delta = \frac{2}{3}$$

Since $\Delta = \frac{2}{3}$ is not in the table, it is necessary to interpolate. For $\Delta = 0.60$, the sample sizes for β values of .30, .20, .10, and .05 are 35, 45, 59, and 73, respectively. For $\Delta = 0.70$, the sample sizes are 26, 33, 44, and 54. By interpolating between these figures for $\Delta = \frac{2}{3}$, the four possible sample sizes are 29, 33, 49, and 60. If the researcher can afford to test $N_1 = N_2 = 60$ subjects, he can have a study with a low probability of a type II error. However, a study with $N_1 = N_2 = 29$ will provide a test with $\beta = .30$.

50-5. SAMPLE SIZE FOR A SINGLE-SAMPLE CORRELATION COEFFICIENT

Sample sizes needed to test whether a population correlation coefficient ρ is significantly different from zero are reported in Table 50-2. This table is entered with the value of ρ defined under the alternative hypothesis, along with the probability of a type II error that a researcher is willing to tolerate for $\alpha = .05$.

As an example, consider a researcher who wishes to study the relationship between an independent and a dependent quantitative variable. Suppose interest exists in the relationship only if $\rho \geq 0.50$. The sample sizes at this level of correlation for β values of .30, .20, .10, and .05 are, respectively, 66, 84, 112, and 139.

Table 50-2.   Sample sizes for testing H_0: $\rho = 0$ against the two-sided alternative H_1: $\rho \neq 0$ for $\alpha = .05$ and β values of .30, .20, .10, and .05

	Sample size			
ρ	$\beta = .30$	$\beta = .20$	$\beta = .10$	$\beta = .05$
.10	616	783	1046	1308
.20	152	193	258	322
.30	66	84	112	139
.40	37	46	61	75
.50	23	28	37	46
.60	15	18	24	30
.70	10	12	16	19
.80	7	9	11	13
.90	5	6	7	8

Adapted with permission from Table 3.4.1, n to detect r-by-t test, in J. Cohen, *Statistical Power Analysis for the Behavioral Sciences,* New York: Academic Press, 1969.

50-6. SAMPLE SIZES FOR TESTING EQUALITY OF TWO CORRELATION COEFFICIENTS

In Section 24-4, the test of $H_0 : \rho_1 - \rho_2 = 0$ against $H_1 : \rho_1 - \rho_2 \neq 0$ was performed in terms of the Fisher z transformation, which is summarized in Table A-9. The sample size determination is made in terms of this transformation. If we let Z_1 and Z_2 be the Fisher Z values for ρ_1 and ρ_2, respectively, and consider

$$d = |Z_2 - Z_1|$$

then the figures of Table 50-3 can be used to determine the values of $N_1 = N_2$ for $\alpha = .05$ and β values of .30, .20, .10, or .05.

As an example, consider a researcher who believes that the correlation coefficients between an independent and a dependent variable in a control and experimental group should be close in numerical value to $\rho_1 = 0.25$ and $\rho_2 = 0.50$, respectively. The Fisher z values for these correlation coefficients are $z_1 = 0.2554$ and $z_2 = 0.5493$, so that $|d| = 0.2939 \approx 0.30$. For $d = 0.30$, the sample sizes for β values of .30, .20, .10, and .05 are 140, 177, 236, and 292, respectively.

Table 50-3. Sample sizes for testing H_0: $p_1 - p_2 = 0$ against the two-sided alternative H_1: $p_1 - p_2 \neq 0$ for $\alpha = .05$, β values of .30, .20, .10, and .05, and $N_1 = N_2$

	Sample size			
$|Z_1 - Z_2|$	$\beta = .30$	$\beta = .20$	$\beta = .10$	$\beta = .05$
.10	1237	1573	2104	2602
.20	312	395	528	653
.30	140	177	236	292
.40	80	101	134	165
.50	52	66	87	107
.60	37	47	61	75
.70	28	35	46	56
.80	22	28	36	44
1.00	15	19	24	29
1.20	12	14	18	21
1.40	9	11	14	16

Adapted with permission from Table 4.4.1, n to detect $q = z_1 - z_2$ by Fisher z transformation of r, in J. Cohen, *Statistical Power Analysis for the Behavioral Sciences*, New York: Academic Press, 1969.

50-7. SAMPLE SIZES FOR CONTINGENCY TABLES

Of the sample size determination procedures, the most difficult to execute is the one associated with contingency tables, since the specification of the alternate hypothesis is virtually impossible. However, if a researcher can specify the value of Cramer's V of interest, it is possible to determine the appropriate sample size for $\alpha = .05$ by using the figures of Table 50-4. This table is entered by means of the index

$$e = MV^2$$

where

$$M = \text{minimum of } I - 1 \text{ and } J - 1$$

$$I = \text{number of rows}$$

$$J = \text{number of columns}$$

Table 50-4. Sample sizes for testing H_0: $V = 0$ against H_1: $V \neq 0$ for $\alpha = .05$; β values of .30, .20, .10, .05; and $v = 1, 2, 3, 4, 5, 6, 7, 8, 9, 10, 12, 16, 20,$ and 24

							Degrees of freedom								
β	e	1	2	3	4	5	6	7	8	9	10	12	16	20	24
.30	.10	62	77	88	97	105	111	118	123	129	134	144	160	175	188
	.20	31	39	44	48	52	56	59	62	63	67	72	80	87	94
	.30	21	26	29	32	35	37	39	41	43	45	48	53	58	63
	.40	15	19	22	24	26	28	29	31	32	34	36	40	44	47
	.50	12	15	18	19	21	22	24	25	26	27	29	32	35	38
	.60	10	13	15	16	17	19	20	21	21	22	24	27	29	31
	.70	9	11	13	14	15	16	17	18	18	19	21	23	25	27
	.80	8	10	11	12	13	14	15	15	16	17	18	20	22	24
.20	.10	78	96	109	119	128	136	144	150	156	162	173	193	210	225
	.20	39	48	55	60	64	68	72	75	78	81	87	96	105	112
	.30	26	32	36	40	43	45	48	50	52	54	58	64	70	75
	.40	20	24	27	30	32	34	36	38	39	42	43	48	52	56
	.50	16	19	22	24	26	27	29	30	31	32	35	39	42	45
	.60	13	16	18	20	21	23	24	25	26	27	29	32	35	37
	.70	11	14	16	17	18	19	21	21	22	23	25	28	30	32
	.80	10	12	14	15	16	17	18	19	20	21	22	24	26	28
.10	.10	105	127	142	154	165	174	183	191	198	205	218	241	261	279
	.20	53	63	71	77	82	87	91	95	99	103	109	121	131	140
	.30	35	42	47	51	55	58	61	64	66	68	73	80	87	93
	.40	26	32	35	39	41	44	46	48	50	51	55	60	65	70
	.50	21	25	28	31	33	35	37	38	40	41	44	48	52	56
	.60	18	21	24	26	27	29	30	32	33	34	36	40	44	47
	.70	15	18	20	22	24	25	26	27	28	29	31	34	37	40
	.80	13	16	18	19	21	22	23	24	25	26	27	30	33	35
.05	.10	130	154	172	186	198	209	218	227	236	244	259	285	307	328
	.20	65	77	86	93	99	104	109	114	118	122	129	142	154	164
	.30	43	51	57	62	66	70	73	76	79	81	86	95	102	109
	.40	32	39	43	46	49	52	55	57	59	61	65	71	77	82
	.50	26	31	34	37	40	42	44	45	47	49	52	57	61	66
	.60	22	26	29	31	33	35	36	38	39	41	43	47	51	55
	.70	19	22	25	27	28	30	31	33	34	35	37	41	44	47
	.80	16	19	21	23	25	26	27	28	29	30	32	36	38	41

Adapted with permission from Tables 7.3.15 to 7.3.28, Power of χ^2 at $a = 0.5$, $\mu = 1, 2, 3, 4, 5, 6, 7, 8, 9, 10, 12, 16, 20,$ and 24, in J. Cohen, *Statistical Power Analysis for the Behavioral Sciences*, New York: Academic Press, 1969.

As an example, consider a researcher who wishes to detect $V^2 = 0.10$ for $I = 4$ and $J = 3$ with $\alpha = .05$. In this case,

$$e = MV^2 = (J - 1)V^2 = 2(0.10) = 0.2$$

With $e = 0.2$ and $v = (I - 1)(J - 1) = (4 - 1)(3 - 1) = 6$, sample sizes for β values of .30, .20, .10, and .05 are 56, 68, 87, and 104, respectively.

Note that if $I = J = 2$, then e reduces to

$$e = \phi^2$$

This means that Table 50-4 can be used to obtain the sample sizes for a 2×2 contingency table. For example, the test of $H_0 : \phi^2 = 0$ against $H_1 : \phi^2 > 0.10$ requires a sample size of 62, 78, 105, or 130 for β values of .30, .20, .10, or .05, respectively.

This table can also be used to set up the sample size for testing $H_0 : \Delta = P_1 - P_2 = 0$. As shown in Section 16-4, the connection between $\hat{\phi}$ and $\hat{\Delta}$ is

$$\hat{\phi} = \sqrt{\frac{N_1 N_2}{f_{1.} f_{2.}}} \, \hat{\Delta}$$

With $N_1 = N_2 = N$ and $E(f_{1.}) = 2Np$ and $E(f_{2.}) = 2Nq$, we have

$$\phi = \sqrt{\frac{N^2}{(2N)p(2N)q}} \, \Delta = \frac{\Delta}{\sqrt{4pq}}$$

The largest sample size will be required when $p = q = \frac{1}{2}$. In this case

$$\phi = \Delta$$

so that

$$e = \Delta^2$$

For $\Delta = 0.32$, $e = (0.32)^2 = 0.1024 \approx 0.10$, we determine the total number of subjects to be 62, 78, 105, or 130 for β values of .30, .20, .10, or .05, respectively. Thus each group should be based on sample sizes of 31, 39, 53, or 65.

50-8. SAMPLE SIZES FOR ONE-WAY ANALYSIS OF VARIANCE

Just as the two-sample t test can be associated with a measure of explained variation, so can the multiple-sample F test. In particular, as shown in Section 36-3, the F test and the sample correlation ratio are associated by

$$F = \frac{N - K}{K - 1} \left(\frac{\hat{\eta}^2}{1 - \hat{\eta}^2} \right)$$

Thus, sample sizes can be determined as soon as α, β, K, and η^2 can be specified. Of these four conditions, η^2 is the most difficult to determine, but a researcher can always specify the minimum η^2 of interest. This is illustrated by an example based on the sample size tabulations of Table 50-5.

Table 50-5. Sample sizes for the K-sample F test for $\alpha = .05$; β values of .30, .20, .10, and .05; $\nu_1 = 1, 2, 3, 4, 5, 6, 8,$ and 10; and $N_1 = N_2 = \cdots = N_K$

		Degrees of freedom for numerator of F test							
β	f	1	2	3	4	5	6	8	10
.30	.10	310	258	221	195	175	160	138	123
	.20	78	65	56	49	44	41	35	31
	.30	35	29	25	22	20	18	16	14
	.40	20	17	15	13	12	11	9	8
	.50	13	11	10	9	8	7	6	6
	.60	10	8	7	6	6	5	5	4
	.70	7	6	6	5	5	4	4	3
	.80	6	5	5	4	4	4	3	3
.20	.10	393	322	274	240	215	195	168	148
	.20	99	81	69	61	54	50	42	38
	.30	45	36	31	27	25	22	19	17
	.40	26	21	18	16	14	13	11	10
	.50	17	14	12	10	9	9	8	7
	.60	12	10	9	8	7	6	6	5
	.70	9	8	7	6	5	5	4	4
	.80	7	6	5	5	4	4	4	3
.10	.10	526	421	354	309	275	250	213	187
	.20	132	106	89	78	69	63	54	48
	.30	59	48	40	35	31	29	24	22
	.40	34	27	23	20	18	16	14	13
	.50	22	18	15	13	12	11	9	8
	.60	16	13	11	10	9	8	7	6
	.70	12	10	8	7	7	6	5	5
	.80	9	8	7	6	5	5	4	4
.05	.10	651	515	430	372	331	299	254	223
	.20	163	130	108	94	83	75	64	56
	.30	73	58	49	42	38	34	29	26
	.40	42	33	28	24	22	20	17	15
	.50	27	22	18	16	14	13	11	10
	.60	19	15	13	11	10	9	8	7
	.70	14	12	10	9	8	7	6	5
	.80	11	9	8	7	6	6	5	4

Adapted with permission from Tables 8.4.4 to 8.4.5, n to detect f-by-F test at $a = .05, \mu = 1, 2, 3, 4, 5, 6, 7, 8,$ and 10, in J. Cohen, *Statistical Power Analysis for the Behavioral Sciences,* New York: Academic Press, 1969.

Table 50-5 gives the sample sizes needed for each sample, provided that $N_1 = N_2 = \cdots = N_K$ and that $\alpha = .05$. The table is entered not with η^2, but with a related number defined as

$$f = \sqrt{\frac{\eta^2}{1 - \eta^2}}$$

Suppose a researcher is planning a study with $K = 4$ groups, and suppose interest exists in rejecting $H_0 : \mu_1 = \mu_2 = \mu_3 = \mu_4$ only if the independent variable accounts for at least 10 percent of the variation. For $\eta^2 = 0.10$,

$$f = \sqrt{\frac{0.10}{1 - 0.10}} = \frac{1}{3}$$

Since $f = \frac{1}{3}$ is not in the table, we must interpolate. With $v_1 = K - 1 = 4 - 1 = 3$ and $f = 0.30$, the sample sizes for β values of .30, .20, .10, and .05 are 25, 31, 40, and 49, respectively. For $f = 0.40$, the corresponding sample sizes are 15, 18, 23, and 28. By interpolating for these values, possible sample sizes are 22, 27, 35, and 42 per group.

50-9. SAMPLE SIZES FOR THE SIGN TEST

Sample size determination for the sign test is not easy because researchers find it difficult to specify the value of $P(+)$ if H_0 is false and H_1 is true. However, if $P(+)$ can be approximated, then Table 50-6 can be used to determine sample size, provided $\alpha = .05$.

Suppose a researcher wishes to perform the sign test and has reason to believe that under H_1 the value of $P(+)$ will be close to 0.70. According to Table 50-6, possible sample sizes for β values of .30, .20, .10, and .05 are 37, 49, 61, and 75, respectively.

Table 50-6. Sample sizes for the sign test with $\alpha = .05$

	Sample size			
$P(+)$	$\beta = .30$	$\beta = .20$	$\beta = .10$	$\beta = .05$
.45 or .55	616	783	1047	1294
.40 or .60	153	194	259	319
.35 or .65	67	85	113	138
.30 or .70	37	49	61	75
.25 or .75	25	30	40	49
.20 or .80	17	20	28	32
.15 or .85	12	15	17	23

Adapted with permission from Table 5.4.1, Power of sign test ($P = .50$), in J. Cohen, *Statistical Power Analysis for the Behavioral Sciences*, New York: Academic Press, 1969.

50-10. SAMPLE SIZES FOR MULTIPLE REGRESSION

Suppose a researcher wishes to determine the sample size required to detect an R^2 equal to .3 in a regression analysis involving five predictors. The appropriate F test of the null hypothesis

$$H_0: R^2 = 0$$

has, as degrees of freedom, $v_1 = 5$ and $v_2 = N - 6$. Substituting $R^2 = .3$ in place of η^2 in the equation for f in Section 50-8,

$$f = \sqrt{\frac{R^2}{1 - R^2}} = \sqrt{\frac{.3}{1 - .3}} = 0.65$$

We can use Table 50-5 to determine the required sample size to provide the appropriate power. To use the table, we must relate regression parameters to ANOVA values. Since the table has been designed for analysis of variance, degrees of freedom in the numerator equal $K - 1$, whereas they equal P in regression analysis. Hence, we can set

$$P = K - 1$$

so that

$$K = P + 1$$

Further, $v_2 = N - P - 1$ in regression analysis, whereas $v_2 = K(n - 1)$ in ANOVA, where n will be read from the table. Therefore

$$N - P - 1 = K(n - 1)$$

and since $K = P + 1$, we have

$$N = (P + 1) + (P + 1)(n - 1) = n(P + 1)$$

For a power of 0.7 and $v_1 = 5$, we would need $n = 5.5$ subjects per cell. Therefore, for our regression we need $N = 5.5(5 + 1) = 33$ subjects.

50-11. DETERMINATION OF EXPLAINED VARIATION

The problem that a researcher must face when determining the sample size is that knowledge about the alternative hypothesis must be available. Rarely does this knowledge exist, and so many researchers do not use the methods illustrated in this chapter. This is unfortunate, since ballpark values can be determined that are adequate for most studies. Inspection of the literature shows that very few relations between independent and dependent variables explain more than 10 percent of the total variation. Thus, if a researcher plans a study to explain at least 10 percent of the variation, it will be relatively sure to detect any measure of explained variation that exceeds 10 percent. This high probability of detection is guaranteed, since smaller sample sizes suffice for larger measures of explained variation.

50-12. EXERCISES

50-1. How many observations are needed for a t test in which $\mu_1 = 80$, $\mu_2 = 90$, and $\sigma = 30$, where $\alpha = .05$, $N_1 = N_2$, and $\beta = .20$?

50-2. How many observations are needed for a t test where $\rho_{pb} = 0.40$, $\alpha = .05$, $N_1 = N_2$, and $\beta = .20$?

50-3. How many observations are needed to reject $\rho_1 = \rho_2$ if $\alpha = .05$, $\beta = .20$, $N_1 = N_2$ and if $\rho_1 = 0.40$ and $\rho_2 = 0.50$?

50-4. How many observations are needed to reject $\rho_1 = \rho_2$ if $\alpha = .05$, $\beta = .20$, $N_1 = N_2$ while $\rho_2 = \rho_1 + 0.10$?

50-5. How many observations are needed for the Fisher-Irwin test if $p_1 = .3$, $p_2 = .6$, $\alpha = .05$, and $\beta = .20$?

50-6. How many observations are needed for a one-way ANOVA where $K = 4$, $\eta^2 = .10$, $\alpha = .05$, $\beta = .10$, and $N_1 = N_2 = N_3 = N_4$?

50-7. How many observations are needed to test $H_0: p = .5$ against $H_1: p = .6$, where $\alpha = .05$ and $\beta = .20$?

50-8. How many observations are needed to test these three hypotheses:
a. $H_A: \alpha_{1..} = \alpha_{2..} = \alpha_{3..}$
b. $H_B: \beta_{.1.} = \beta_{.2.} = \beta_{.3.} = \beta_{.4.}$
c. $H_{A \times B}: \gamma_{11} = \gamma_{12} = \cdots = \gamma_{34}.$

if $\eta_A^2 = .10$, $\eta_B^2 = .05$, $\eta_{A \times B}^2 = .15$, $\alpha_A = \alpha_B = \alpha_{AB} = .05$, and $\beta_A = \beta_B = \beta_{AB} = .20$?

50-9. How many observations are needed to test Cramer's V if $V^2 = 0.20$, $I = 3$, $J = 6$, and $\alpha = .05$?

50-10. How many observations are needed for a multiple regression analysis based on five predictors with $\alpha = .05$, $\beta = .10$, and $R^2_{Y \cdot X_1 X_2 X_3 X_4 X_5} = .40$?

STATISTICAL TABLES

Table A-1. Table of random numbers.

10	09	73	25	33	76	52	01	35	86	34	67	35	48	76	80	95	90	91	17	39	29	27	49	45
37	54	20	48	05	64	89	47	42	96	24	80	52	40	37	20	63	61	04	02	00	82	29	16	65
08	42	26	89	53	19	64	50	93	03	23	20	90	25	60	15	95	33	47	64	35	08	03	36	06
99	01	90	25	29	09	37	67	07	15	38	31	13	11	65	88	67	67	43	97	04	43	62	76	59
12	80	79	99	70	80	15	73	61	47	64	03	23	66	53	98	95	11	68	77	12	17	17	68	33
66	06	57	47	17	34	07	27	68	50	36	69	73	61	70	65	81	33	98	85	11	19	92	91	70
31	06	01	08	05	45	57	18	24	06	35	30	34	26	14	86	79	90	74	39	23	40	30	97	32
85	26	97	76	02	02	05	16	56	92	68	66	57	48	18	73	05	38	52	47	18	62	38	85	79
63	57	33	21	35	05	32	54	70	48	90	55	35	75	48	28	46	82	87	09	83	49	12	56	24
73	79	64	57	53	03	52	96	47	78	35	80	83	42	82	60	93	52	03	44	35	27	38	84	35
98	52	01	77	67	14	90	56	86	07	22	10	94	05	58	60	97	09	34	33	50	50	07	39	98
11	80	50	54	31	39	80	82	77	32	50	72	56	82	48	29	40	52	42	01	52	77	56	78	51
83	45	29	96	34	06	28	89	80	83	13	74	67	00	78	18	47	54	06	10	68	71	17	78	17
88	68	54	02	00	86	50	75	84	01	36	76	66	79	51	90	36	47	64	93	29	60	91	10	62
99	59	46	73	48	87	51	76	49	69	91	82	60	89	28	93	78	56	13	68	23	47	83	41	13
65	48	11	76	74	17	46	85	09	50	58	04	77	69	74	73	03	95	71	86	40	21	81	65	44
80	12	43	56	35	17	72	70	80	15	45	31	82	23	74	21	11	57	82	53	14	38	55	37	63
74	35	09	98	17	77	40	27	72	14	43	23	60	02	10	45	52	16	42	37	96	28	60	26	55
69	91	62	68	03	66	25	22	91	48	36	93	68	72	03	76	62	11	39	90	94	40	05	64	18
09	89	32	05	05	14	22	56	85	14	46	42	75	67	88	96	29	77	88	22	54	38	21	45	98
91	49	91	45	23	68	47	92	76	86	46	16	28	35	54	94	75	08	99	23	37	08	92	00	48
80	33	69	45	98	26	94	03	68	58	70	29	73	41	35	53	14	03	33	40	42	05	08	23	41
44	10	48	19	49	85	15	74	79	54	32	97	92	65	75	57	60	04	08	81	22	22	20	64	13
12	55	07	37	42	11	10	00	20	40	12	86	07	46	97	96	64	48	94	39	28	70	72	58	15
63	60	64	93	29	16	50	53	44	84	40	21	95	25	63	43	65	17	70	82	07	20	73	17	90

```
61 19 69 04 46   26 45 74 77 74   51 92 43 37 29   65 39 45 95 93   42 58 26 05 27
15 47 44 52 66   95 27 07 99 53   59 36 78 38 48   82 39 61 01 18   33 21 15 94 66
94 55 72 85 73   67 89 75 43 87   54 62 24 44 31   91 19 04 25 92   92 92 74 59 73
42 48 11 62 13   97 34 40 87 21   16 86 84 87 67   03 07 11 20 59   25 70 14 66 70
23 52 37 83 17   73 20 88 98 37   68 93 59 14 16   26 25 22 96 63   05 52 28 25 62

04 49 35 24 94   75 24 63 38 24   45 86 25 10 25   61 96 27 93 35   65 33 71 24 72
00 54 99 76 54   64 05 18 81 59   96 11 96 38 96   54 69 28 23 91   23 28 72 95 29
35 96 31 53 07   26 89 80 93 54   33 35 13 54 62   77 97 45 00 24   90 10 33 93 33
59 80 80 83 91   45 42 72 68 42   83 60 94 97 00   13 02 12 48 92   78 56 52 01 06
46 05 88 52 36   01 39 09 22 86   77 28 14 40 77   93 91 08 36 47   70 61 74 29 41

32 17 90 05 97   87 37 92 52 41   05 56 70 70 07   86 74 31 71 57   85 39 41 18 38
69 23 46 14 06   20 11 74 52 04   15 95 66 00 00   18 74 39 24 23   97 11 89 63 38
19 56 54 14 30   01 75 87 53 79   40 41 92 15 85   66 67 43 68 06   84 96 28 52 07
45 15 51 49 38   19 47 60 72 46   43 66 79 45 43   59 04 79 00 33   20 82 66 95 41
94 86 43 19 94   36 16 81 08 51   34 88 88 15 53   01 54 03 54 56   05 01 45 11 76

98 08 62 48 26   45 24 02 84 04   44 99 90 88 96   39 09 47 34 07   35 44 13 18 80
33 18 51 62 32   41 94 15 09 49   89 43 54 85 81   88 69 54 19 94   37 54 87 30 43
80 95 10 04 06   96 38 27 07 74   20 15 12 33 87   25 01 62 52 98   94 62 46 11 71
79 75 24 91 40   71 96 12 82 96   69 86 10 25 91   74 85 22 05 39   00 38 75 95 79
18 63 33 25 37   98 14 50 65 71   31 01 02 46 74   05 45 56 14 27   77 93 89 19 36

74 02 94 39 02   77 55 73 22 70   97 79 01 71 19   52 52 75 80 21   80 81 45 17 48
54 17 84 56 11   80 99 33 71 43   05 33 51 29 69   56 12 71 92 55   36 04 09 03 24
11 66 44 98 83   52 07 98 48 27   59 38 17 15 39   09 97 33 34 40   88 46 12 33 56
48 32 47 79 28   31 24 96 47 10   02 29 53 68 70   32 30 75 75 46   15 02 00 99 94
69 07 49 41 38   87 63 79 19 76   35 58 40 44 01   10 51 82 16 15   01 84 87 69 38
```

Reprinted from A Million Random Digits with 100,000 Normal Deviates by The Rand Corporation. New York: The Fress Press, 1955, page 1. Copyright 1955 and 1983 by The Rand Corporation. Used by permission.

Table A-2. Critical values for the sign test.

N	.005	.025	.050	.950	.975	.995
			Percentile value for X, the number of + signs			
5			0	5		
6		0	0	6	6	
7		0	0	7	7	
8	0	0	1	7	8	8
9	0	1	1	8	8	9
10	0	1	1	9	9	10
11	0	1	2	9	10	11
12	1	2	2	10	10	11
13	1	2	3	10	11	12
14	1	2	3	11	12	13
15	2	3	3	12	12	13
16	2	3	4	12	13	14
17	2	4	4	13	13	15
18	3	4	5	13	14	15
19	3	4	5	14	15	16
20	3	5	5	15	15	17
21	4	5	6	15	16	17
22	4	5	6	16	17	18
23	4	6	7	16	17	19
24	5	6	7	17	18	19
25	5	7	7	18	18	20

For $N \geq 26$, use the integer below:

$$P_{.005} = \left(\frac{N}{2} - \frac{1}{2}\right) - 2.58\sqrt{\frac{N}{4}}$$

$$P_{.025} = \left(\frac{N}{2} - \frac{1}{2}\right) - 1.96\sqrt{\frac{N}{4}}$$

$$P_{.050} = \left(\frac{N}{2} - \frac{1}{2}\right) - 1.645\sqrt{\frac{N}{4}}$$

For $N \geq 26$, use the integer above:

$$P_{.995} = \left(\frac{N}{2} + \frac{1}{2}\right) + 2.58\sqrt{\frac{N}{4}}$$

$$P_{.975} = \left(\frac{N}{2} + \frac{1}{2}\right) + 1.96\sqrt{\frac{N}{4}}$$

$$P_{.950} = \left(\frac{N}{2} + \frac{1}{2}\right) + 1.645\sqrt{\frac{N}{4}}$$

Table A-3. Binomial coefficients $\binom{N}{X}$.

N	$\binom{N}{0}$	$\binom{N}{1}$	$\binom{N}{2}$	$\binom{N}{3}$	$\binom{N}{4}$	$\binom{N}{5}$	$\binom{N}{6}$	$\binom{N}{7}$	$\binom{N}{8}$	$\binom{N}{9}$	$\binom{N}{10}$
0	1										
1	1	1									
2	1	2	1								
3	1	3	3	1							
4	1	4	6	4	1						
5	1	5	10	10	5	1					
6	1	6	15	20	15	6	1				
7	1	7	21	35	35	21	7	1			
8	1	8	28	56	70	56	28	8	1		
9	1	9	36	84	126	126	84	36	9	1	
10	1	10	45	120	210	252	210	120	45	10	1
11	1	11	55	165	330	462	462	330	165	55	11
12	1	12	66	220	495	792	924	792	495	220	66
13	1	13	78	286	715	1287	1716	1716	1287	715	286
14	1	14	91	364	1001	2002	3003	3432	3003	2002	1001
15	1	15	105	455	1365	3003	5005	6435	6435	5005	3003
16	1	16	120	560	1820	4368	8008	11440	12870	11440	8008
17	1	17	136	680	2380	6188	12376	19448	24310	24310	19448
18	1	18	153	816	3060	8568	18564	31824	43758	48620	43758
19	1	19	171	969	3876	11628	27132	50388	75582	92378	92378
20	1	20	190	1140	4845	15504	38760	77520	125970	167960	184756

Table A-4. Critical values for the matched-pair Wilcoxon test.

N	.005	.025	.050	.950	.975	.995
			Percentile value for T, the sum of the positive ranks			
5			0	15		
6		0	2	19	21	
7		2	3	25	26	
8	0	3	5	31	33	36
9	1	5	8	37	40	44
10	3	8	10	45	47	52
11	5	10	13	53	56	61
12	7	13	17	61	65	71
13	9	17	21	70	74	82
14	12	21	25	80	84	93
15	15	25	30	90	95	105
16	19	29	35	101	107	117
17	23	34	41	112	119	130
18	27	40	47	124	131	144
19	32	46	53	137	144	158
20	37	52	60	150	158	173

For $N \geq 21$, use the integer below:

$$P_{.005} = \frac{N(N+1)}{4} - \frac{1}{2} - 2.58 \sqrt{\frac{N(N+1)(2N+1)}{24}}$$

$$P_{.025} = \frac{N(N+1)}{4} - \frac{1}{2} - 1.96 \sqrt{\frac{N(N+1)(2N+1)}{24}}$$

$$P_{.050} = \frac{N(N+1)}{4} - \frac{1}{2} - 1.645 \sqrt{\frac{N(N+1)(2N+1)}{24}}$$

For $N \geq 21$, use the integer above:

$$P_{.995} = \frac{N(N+1)}{4} + \frac{1}{2} + 2.58 \sqrt{\frac{N(N+1)(2N+1)}{24}}$$

$$P_{.975} = \frac{N(N+1)}{4} + \frac{1}{2} + 1.96 \sqrt{\frac{N(N+1)(2N+1)}{24}}$$

$$P_{.950} = \frac{N(N+1)}{4} + \frac{1}{2} + 1.645 \sqrt{\frac{N(N+1)(2N+1)}{24}}$$

Adapted from the table of critical values of the signed-rank statistic T originally published in W. J. Dixon and F. J. Massey, Jr. *Introduction to Statistical Analysis*, 4th ed., New York: McGraw-Hill, 1983. Used by permission.

Table A-5. Critical values for the two-sample Wilcoxon test.

N_1	N_2	.005	.025	.050	.950	.975	.995
2	5			3	13		
2	6			3	15		
2	7			3	17		
2	8		3	4	18	19	
2	9		3	4	20	21	
2	10		3	4	22	23	
3	3			6	15		
3	4			6	18		
3	5		6	7	20	21	
3	6		7	8	22	23	
3	7		7	8	25	26	
3	8		8	9	27	28	
3	9	6	8	10	29	31	33
3	10	6	9	10	32	33	36
4	4		10	11	25	26	
4	5		11	12	28	29	
4	6	10	12	13	31	32	34
4	7	10	13	14	34	35	38
4	8	11	14	15	37	38	41
4	9	11	14	16	40	42	45
4	10	12	15	17	43	45	48
5	5	15	17	19	36	38	40
5	6	16	18	20	40	42	44
5	7	16	20	21	44	45	49
5	8	17	21	23	47	49	53
5	9	18	22	24	51	53	57
5	10	19	23	26	54	57	61
6	6	23	26	28	50	52	55
6	7	24	27	29	55	57	60
6	8	25	29	31	59	61	65
6	9	26	31	33	63	65	70
6	10	27	32	35	67	70	75
7	7	32	36	39	66	69	73
7	8	34	38	41	71	74	78
7	9	35	40	43	76	79	84
7	10	37	42	45	81	84	89
8	8	43	49	51	85	87	93
8	9	45	51	54	90	93	99
8	10	47	53	56	96	99	105
9	9	56	62	66	105	109	115
9	10	58	65	69	111	115	122
10	10	71	78	82	128	132	139

For $N_1 > 10$ or $N_2 > 10$, use the integer below:

$$P_{.005} = N_1 \left(\frac{N_1 + N_2 + 1}{2} \right) - \frac{1}{2} - 2.58 \sqrt{\frac{N_1 N_2}{12} (N_1 + N_2 + 1)}$$

$$P_{.025} = N_1 \left(\frac{N_1 + N_2 + 1}{2} \right) - \frac{1}{2} - 1.96 \sqrt{\frac{N_1 N_2}{12} (N_1 + N_2 + 1)}$$

$$P_{.050} = N_1 \left(\frac{N_1 + N_2 + 1}{2} \right) - \frac{1}{2} - 1.645 \sqrt{\frac{N_1 N_2}{12} (N_1 + N_2 + 1)}$$

For $N_1 > 10$ or $N_2 > 10$, use the integer above:

$$P_{.995} = N_1 \left(\frac{N_1 + N_2 + 1}{2} \right) + \frac{1}{2} + 2.58 \sqrt{\frac{N_1 N_2}{12} (N_1 + N_2 + 1)}$$

$$P_{.975} = N_1 \left(\frac{N_1 + N_2 + 1}{2} \right) + \frac{1}{2} + 1.96 \sqrt{\frac{N_1 N_2}{12} (N_1 + N_2 + 1)}$$

$$P_{.950} = N_1 \left(\frac{N_1 + N_2 + 1}{2} \right) + \frac{1}{2} + 1.645 \sqrt{\frac{N_1 N_2}{12} (N_1 + N_2 + 1)}$$

Table A-6. Critical values for the Mann-Whitney U test.

N_1	N_2	.005	.025	.050	.950	.975	.995
2	5			0	10		
2	6			0	12		
2	7			0	14		
2	8		0	1	15	16	
2	9		0	1	17	18	
2	10		0	1	19	20	
3	3			0	9		
3	4			0	12		
3	5		0	1	14	15	
3	6		1	2	16	17	
3	7		1	2	19	20	
3	8		2	3	21	22	
3	9	0	2	4	23	25	27
3	10	0	3	4	26	27	30
4	4		0	1	15	16	
4	5		1	2	18	19	
4	6	0	2	3	21	22	24
4	7	0	3	4	24	25	28
4	8	1	4	5	27	28	31
4	9	1	4	6	30	32	35
4	10	2	5	7	33	35	38
5	5	0	2	4	21	23	25
5	6	1	3	5	25	27	29
5	7	1	5	6	29	30	34
5	8	2	6	8	32	34	38
5	9	3	7	9	36	38	42
5	10	4	8	11	39	42	46
6	6	2	5	7	29	31	34
6	7	3	6	8	34	36	39
6	8	4	8	10	38	40	44
6	9	5	10	12	42	44	49
6	10	6	11	14	46	49	54
7	7	4	8	11	38	41	45
7	8	6	10	13	43	46	50
7	9	7	12	15	48	51	56
7	10	9	14	17	53	56	61
8	8	7	13	15	49	51	57
8	9	9	15	18	54	57	63
8	10	11	17	20	60	63	69
9	9	11	17	21	60	64	70
9	10	13	20	24	66	70	77
10	10	16	23	27	73	77	84

For $N_1 > 10$ or $N_2 > 10$, use the integer below:

$$P_{.005} = \frac{N_1 N_2}{2} - \frac{1}{2} - 2.58 \sqrt{\frac{N_1 N_2}{12}(N_1 + N_2 + 1)}$$

$$P_{.025} = \frac{N_1 N_2}{2} - \frac{1}{2} - 1.96 \sqrt{\frac{N_1 N_2}{12}(N_1 + N_2 + 1)}$$

$$P_{.050} = \frac{N_1 N_2}{2} - \frac{1}{2} - 1.645 \sqrt{\frac{N_1 N_2}{12}(N_1 + N_2 + 1)}$$

For $N_1 > 10$ or $N_2 > 10$, use the integer above:

$$P_{.995} = \frac{N_1 N_2}{2} + \frac{1}{2} + 2.58 \sqrt{\frac{N_1 N_2}{12}(N_1 + N_2 + 1)}$$

$$P_{.975} = \frac{N_1 N_2}{2} + \frac{1}{2} + 1.96 \sqrt{\frac{N_1 N_2}{12}(N_1 + N_2 + 1)}$$

$$P_{.950} = \frac{N_1 N_2}{2} + \frac{1}{2} + 1.645 \sqrt{\frac{N_1 N_2}{12}(N_1 + N_2 + 1)}$$

Table A-7. Critical values of the standard normal distribution.

Z	Y	Cumulative probability
−3.25	$\mu - 3.25\sigma$	.0006
−3.20	$\mu - 3.20\sigma$	.0007
−3.15	$\mu - 3.15\sigma$	.0008
−3.10	$\mu - 3.10\sigma$	.0010
−3.05	$\mu - 3.05\sigma$	.0011
−3.00	$\mu - 3.00\sigma$	.0013
−2.95	$\mu - 2.95\sigma$	.0016
−2.90	$\mu - 2.90\sigma$	.0019
−2.85	$\mu - 2.85\sigma$	.0022
−2.80	$\mu - 2.80\sigma$	.0026
−2.75	$\mu - 2.75\sigma$	.0030
−2.70	$\mu - 2.70\sigma$	.0035
−2.65	$\mu - 2.65\sigma$	.0040
−2.60	$\mu - 2.60\sigma$	.0047
−2.55	$\mu - 2.55\sigma$	.0054
−2.50	$\mu - 2.50\sigma$	.0062
−2.45	$\mu - 2.45\sigma$	.0071
−2.40	$\mu - 2.40\sigma$	.0082
−2.35	$\mu - 2.35\sigma$	.0094
−2.30	$\mu - 2.30\sigma$	.0107
−2.25	$\mu - 2.25\sigma$	.0122
−2.20	$\mu - 2.20\sigma$	.0139
−2.15	$\mu - 2.15\sigma$	.0158
−2.10	$\mu - 2.10\sigma$	.0179
−2.05	$\mu - 2.05\sigma$	.0202
−2.00	$\mu - 2.00\sigma$	.0228
−1.95	$\mu - 1.95\sigma$	.0256
−1.90	$\mu - 1.90\sigma$	.0287
−1.85	$\mu - 1.85\sigma$	.0322
−1.80	$\mu - 1.80\sigma$	.0359
−1.75	$\mu - 1.75\sigma$	.0401
−1.70	$\mu - 1.70\sigma$	.0446
−1.65	$\mu - 1.65\sigma$	.0495
−1.60	$\mu - 1.60\sigma$	.0548
−1.55	$\mu - 1.55\sigma$	.0606
−1.50	$\mu - 1.50\sigma$	.0668
−1.45	$\mu - 1.45\sigma$	.0735
−1.40	$\mu - 1.40\sigma$	.0808
−1.35	$\mu - 1.35\sigma$	.0885
−1.30	$\mu - 1.30\sigma$	.0968
−1.25	$\mu - 1.25\sigma$	.1056
−1.20	$\mu - 1.20\sigma$	.1151
−1.15	$\mu - 1.15\sigma$	.1251
−1.10	$\mu - 1.10\sigma$	.1357
−1.05	$\mu - 1.05\sigma$	.1469
−1.00	$\mu - 1.00\sigma$	.1587
−0.95	$\mu - 0.95\sigma$	.1711
−0.90	$\mu - 0.90\sigma$	.1841
−0.85	$\mu - 0.85\sigma$	.1977
−0.80	$\mu - 0.80\sigma$	.2119
−0.75	$\mu - 0.75\sigma$	.2266
−0.70	$\mu - 0.70\sigma$	.2420

Table A-7. *(continued)*

Z	Y	Cumulative probability
−0.65	$\mu - 0.65\sigma$	.2578
−0.60	$\mu - 0.60\sigma$	.2743
−0.55	$\mu - 0.55\sigma$	.2912
−0.50	$\mu - 0.50\sigma$	.3085
−0.45	$\mu - 0.45\sigma$	.3264
−0.40	$\mu - 0.40\sigma$	.3446
−0.35	$\mu - 0.35\sigma$	.3632
−0.30	$\mu - 0.30\sigma$	.3821
−0.25	$\mu - 0.25\sigma$	.4013
−0.20	$\mu - 0.20\sigma$	.4207
−0.15	$\mu - 0.15\sigma$	.4404
−0.10	$\mu - 0.10\sigma$	.4602
−0.05	$\mu - 0.05\sigma$	.4801
0.00	μ	.5000
0.05	$\mu + 0.05\sigma$	.5199
0.10	$\mu + 0.10\sigma$	.5398
0.15	$\mu + 0.15\sigma$	.5596
0.20	$\mu + 0.20\sigma$	.5793
0.25	$\mu + 0.25\sigma$	.5987
0.30	$\mu + 0.30\sigma$	.6179
0.35	$\mu + 0.35\sigma$	.6368
0.40	$\mu + 0.40\sigma$	.6554
0.45	$\mu + 0.45\sigma$	.6736
0.50	$\mu + 0.50\sigma$	.6915
0.55	$\mu + 0.55\sigma$	.7088
0.60	$\mu + 0.60\sigma$	.7257
0.65	$\mu + 0.65\sigma$	.7422
0.70	$\mu + 0.70\sigma$	.7580
0.75	$\mu + 0.75\sigma$	.7734
0.80	$\mu + 0.80\sigma$	.7881
0.85	$\mu + 0.85\sigma$	.8023
0.90	$\mu + 0.90\sigma$	.8159
0.95	$\mu + 0.95\sigma$	.8289
1.00	$\mu + 1.00\sigma$	.8413
1.05	$\mu + 1.05\sigma$	.8531
1.10	$\mu + 1.10\sigma$	.8643
1.15	$\mu + 1.15\sigma$	.8749
1.20	$\mu + 1.20\sigma$	.8849
1.25	$\mu + 1.25\sigma$	.8944
1.30	$\mu + 1.30\sigma$	.9032

Table A-7. *(continued)*

Z	Y	Cumulative probability
1.35	$\mu + 1.35\sigma$	.9115
1.40	$\mu + 1.40\sigma$	.9192
1.45	$\mu + 1.45\sigma$	.9265
1.50	$\mu + 1.50\sigma$	.9332
1.55	$\mu + 1.55\sigma$	.9394
1.60	$\mu + 1.60\sigma$	.9452
1.65	$\mu + 1.65\sigma$	.9505
1.70	$\mu + 1.70\sigma$	.9554
1.75	$\mu + 1.75\sigma$	.9599
1.80	$\mu + 1.80\sigma$	.9641
1.85	$\mu + 1.85\sigma$	.9678
1.90	$\mu + 1.90\sigma$	.9713
1.95	$\mu + 1.95\sigma$	.9744
2.00	$\mu + 2.00\sigma$	.9772
2.05	$\mu + 2.05\sigma$	.9798
2.10	$\mu + 2.10\sigma$	.9821
2.15	$\mu + 2.15\sigma$	.9842
2.20	$\mu + 2.20\sigma$	.9861
2.25	$\mu + 2.25\sigma$	.9878
2.30	$\mu + 2.30\sigma$	.9893
2.35	$\mu + 2.35\sigma$	.9906
2.40	$\mu + 2.40\sigma$	.9918
2.45	$\mu + 2.45\sigma$	.9929
2.50	$\mu + 2.50\sigma$	.9938
2.55	$\mu + 2.55\sigma$	.9946
2.60	$\mu + 2.60\sigma$	.9953
2.65	$\mu + 2.65\sigma$	.9960
2.70	$\mu + 2.70\sigma$	.9965
2.75	$\mu + 2.75\sigma$	.9970
2.80	$\mu + 2.80\sigma$	.9974
2.85	$\mu + 2.85\sigma$	.9978
2.90	$\mu + 2.90\sigma$	.9981
2.95	$\mu + 2.95\sigma$	.9984
3.00	$\mu + 3.00\sigma$	.9987
3.05	$\mu + 3.05\sigma$	.9989
3.10	$\mu + 3.10\sigma$	.9990
3.15	$\mu + 3.15\sigma$	.9992
3.20	$\mu + 3.20\sigma$	.9993
3.25	$\mu + 3.25\sigma$	.9994

Table A-7. *(continued)*

Z	Y	Cumulative probability
−3.09	$\mu - 3.09\sigma$	.0010
−2.58	$\mu - 2.58\sigma$	.0050
−2.33	$\mu - 2.33\sigma$	.0100
−1.96	$\mu - 1.96\sigma$	.0250
−1.645	$\mu - 1.645\sigma$	.0500
−1.28	$\mu - 1.28\sigma$	.1000
−0.67	$\mu - 0.67\sigma$	.2500
0.67	$\mu + 0.67\sigma$	.7500
1.28	$\mu + 1.28\sigma$	.9000
1.645	$\mu + 1.645\sigma$	.9500
1.96	$\mu + 1.96\sigma$	.9750
2.33	$\mu + 2.33\sigma$	.9900
2.58	$\mu + 2.58\sigma$	.9950
3.09	$\mu + 3.09\sigma$	.9990

Table A-8. Critical values of the Spearman rank correlation
coefficient.

N	.005	.025	.05	.95	.975	.995
5						
6		−.89	−.83	.83	.89	
7		−.79	−.71	.71	.79	
8	−.88	−.74	−.64	.64	.74	.88
9	−.83	−.70	−.60	.60	.70	.83
10	−.79	−.65	−.56	.56	.65	.79
11	−.75	−.62	−.54	.54	.62	.75
12	−.73	−.59	−.50	.50	.59	.73
13	−.70	−.56	−.48	.48	.56	.70
14	−.68	−.54	−.46	.46	.54	.68
15	−.66	−.52	−.45	.45	.52	.66
16	−.64	−.50	−.43	.43	.50	.64
17	−.62	−.49	−.41	.41	.49	.62
18	−.60	−.47	−.40	.40	.47	.60
19	−.58	−.46	−.39	.39	.46	.58
20	−.57	−.45	−.38	.38	.45	.57
21	−.56	−.44	−.37	.37	.44	.56
22	−.54	−.43	−.36	.36	.43	.54
23	−.53	−.42	−.35	.35	.42	.53
24	−.52	−.41	−.34	.34	.41	.52
25	−.51	−.40	−.34	.34	.40	.51
26	−.50	−.39	−.33	.33	.39	.50
27	−.49	−.38	−.32	.32	.38	.49
28	−.48	−.38	−.32	.32	.38	.48
29	−.47	−.37	−.31	.31	.37	.47
30	−.47	−.36	−.31	.31	.36	.47

Permission granted by The Institute of Mathematical Statistics for reprinting the
table of critical values of the Spearman rank correlation coefficient, originally in
E. G. Olds. Distribution of sums of squares of rank differences for small numbers
of individuals, *Annals of Mathematical Statistics, 9* (1938).

Table A-9. Table of the Fisher's z transformation for correlation coefficients

r	Z	r	Z
.01	0.010	.50	0.549
.02	0.020	.51	0.563
.03	0.030	.52	0.577
.04	0.040	.53	0.590
.05	0.050	.54	0.604
.06	0.060	.55	0.618
.07	0.070	.56	0.633
.08	0.080	.57	0.648
.09	0.090	.58	0.663
.10	0.100	.59	0.678
.11	0.110	.60	0.693
.12	0.121	.61	0.709
.13	0.131	.62	0.725
.14	0.141	.63	0.741
.15	0.151	.64	0.758
.16	0.161	.65	0.775
.17	0.172	.66	0.793
.18	0.182	.67	0.811
.19	0.192	.68	0.829
.20	0.203	.69	0.848
.21	0.213	.70	0.867
.22	0.224	.71	0.887
.23	0.234	.72	0.908
.24	0.245	.73	0.929
.25	0.255	.74	0.950
.26	0.266	.75	0.973
.27	0.277	.76	0.996
.28	0.288	.77	1.020
.29	0.299	.78	1.045
.30	0.310	.79	1.071
.31	0.321	.80	1.099
.32	0.332	.81	1.127
.33	0.343	.82	1.157
.34	0.354	.83	1.188
.35	0.365	.84	1.221
.36	0.377	.85	1.256
.37	0.389	.86	1.293
.38	0.400	.87	1.333
.39	0.412	.88	1.376
.40	0.424	.89	1.422
.41	0.436	.90	1.472
.42	0.448	.91	1.528
.43	0.460	.92	1.589
.44	0.472	.93	1.658
.45	0.485	.94	1.738
.46	0.497	.95	1.832
.47	0.510	.96	1.946
.48	0.523	.97	2.092
.49	0.536	.98	2.298
		.99	2.647

Table A-10. Critical values of the chi-square distribution.

df	$P_{0.5}$	P_{01}	$P_{02.5}$	P_{05}	P_{10}	P_{90}	P_{95}	$P_{97.5}$	P_{99}	$P_{99.5}$
1	0.000039	0.00016	0.00098	0.0039	0.0158	2.71	3.84	5.02	6.63	7.88
2	0.0100	0.0201	0.0506	0.1026	0.2107	4.61	5.99	7.38	9.21	10.60
3	0.0717	0.115	0.216	0.352	0.584	6.25	7.81	9.35	11.34	12.84
4	0.207	0.297	0.484	0.711	1.064	7.78	9.49	11.14	13.28	14.86
5	0.412	0.554	0.831	1.15	1.61	9.24	11.07	12.83	15.09	16.75
6	0.676	0.872	1.24	1.64	2.20	10.64	12.59	14.45	16.81	18.55
7	0.989	1.24	1.69	2.17	2.83	12.02	14.07	16.01	18.48	20.28
8	1.34	1.65	2.18	2.73	3.49	13.36	15.51	17.53	20.09	21.95
9	1.73	2.09	2.70	3.33	4.17	14.68	16.92	19.02	21.67	23.59
10	2.16	2.56	3.25	3.94	4.87	15.99	18.31	20.48	23.21	25.19
11	2.60	3.05	3.82	4.57	5.58	17.28	19.68	21.92	24.72	26.76
12	3.07	3.57	4.40	5.23	6.30	18.55	21.03	23.34	26.22	28.30
13	3.57	4.11	5.01	5.89	7.04	19.81	22.36	24.74	27.69	29.82
14	4.07	4.66	5.63	6.57	7.79	21.06	23.68	26.12	29.14	31.32
15	4.60	5.23	6.26	7.26	8.55	22.31	25.00	27.49	30.58	32.80
16	5.14	5.81	6.91	7.96	9.31	23.54	26.30	28.85	32.00	34.27
18	6.26	7.01	8.23	9.39	10.86	25.99	28.87	31.53	34.81	37.16
20	7.43	8.26	9.59	10.85	12.44	28.41	31.41	34.17	37.57	40.00
24	9.89	10.86	12.40	13.85	15.66	33.20	36.42	39.36	42.98	45.56
30	13.79	14.95	16.79	18.49	20.60	40.26	43.77	46.98	50.89	53.67
40	20.71	22.16	24.43	26.51	29.05	51.81	55.76	59.34	63.69	66.77
60	35.53	37.48	40.48	43.19	46.46	74.40	79.08	83.30	88.38	91.95
120	83.85	86.92	91.57	95.70	100.62	140.23	146.57	152.21	158.95	163.65

From W. J. Dixon and F. J. Massey, Jr., *Introduction to Statistical Analysis*, 3d ed. Copyright 1969 by McGraw-Hill, Inc., New York. Used with permission of McGraw-Hill Book Company.

Table A-11. Percentage points of the Dunn multiple-comparison test.

Number of comparisons C	α	Error df 5	7	10	12	15	20	24	30	40	60	120	∞
2	.05	3.17	2.84	2.64	2.56	2.49	2.42	2.39	2.36	2.33	2.30	2.27	2.24
	.01	4.78	4.03	3.58	3.43	3.29	3.16	3.09	3.03	2.97	2.92	2.86	2.81
3	.05	3.54	3.13	2.87	2.78	2.69	2.61	2.58	2.54	2.50	2.47	2.43	2.39
	.01	5.25	4.36	3.83	3.65	3.48	3.33	3.26	3.19	3.12	3.06	2.99	2.94
4	.05	3.81	3.34	3.04	2.94	2.84	2.75	2.70	2.66	2.62	2.58	2.54	2.50
	.01	5.60	4.59	4.01	3.80	3.62	3.46	3.38	3.30	3.23	3.16	3.09	3.02
5	.05	4.04	3.50	3.17	3.06	2.95	2.85	2.80	2.75	2.71	2.66	2.62	2.58
	.01	5.89	4.78	4.15	3.93	3.74	3.55	3.47	3.39	3.31	3.24	3.16	3.09
6	.05	4.22	3.64	3.28	3.15	3.04	2.93	2.88	2.83	2.78	2.73	2.68	2.64
	.01	6.15	4.95	4.27	4.04	3.82	3.63	3.54	3.46	3.38	3.30	3.22	3.15
7	.05	4.38	3.76	3.37	3.24	3.11	3.00	2.94	2.89	2.84	2.79	2.74	2.69
	.01	6.36	5.09	4.37	4.13	3.90	3.70	3.61	3.52	3.43	3.34	3.27	3.19
8	.05	4.53	3.86	3.45	3.31	3.18	3.06	3.00	2.94	2.89	2.84	2.79	2.74
	.01	6.56	5.21	4.45	4.20	3.97	3.76	3.66	3.57	3.48	3.39	3.31	3.23
9	.05	4.66	3.95	3.52	3.37	3.24	3.11	3.05	2.99	2.93	2.88	2.83	2.77
	.01	6.70	5.31	4.53	4.26	4.02	3.80	3.70	3.61	3.51	3.42	3.34	3.26
10	.05	4.78	4.03	3.58	3.43	3.29	3.16	3.09	3.03	2.97	2.92	2.86	2.81
	.01	6.86	5.40	4.59	4.32	4.07	3.85	3.74	3.65	3.55	3.46	3.37	3.29
15	.05	5.25	4.36	3.83	3.65	3.48	3.33	3.26	3.19	3.12	3.06	2.99	2.94
	.01	7.51	5.79	4.86	4.56	4.29	4.03	3.91	3.80	3.70	3.59	3.50	3.40
20	.05	5.60	4.59	4.01	3.80	3.62	3.46	3.38	3.30	3.23	3.16	3.09	3.02
	.01	8.00	6.08	5.06	4.73	4.42	4.15	4.04	3.90	3.79	3.69	3.58	3.48
25	.05	5.89	4.78	4.15	3.93	3.74	3.55	3.47	3.39	3.31	3.24	3.16	3.09
	.01	8.37	6.30	5.20	4.86	4.53	4.25	4.1*	3.98	3.88	3.76	3.64	3.54
30	.05	6.15	4.95	4.27	4.04	3.82	3.63	3.54	3.46	3.38	3.30	3.22	3.15
	.01	8.68	6.49	5.33	4.95	4.61	4.33	4.2*	4.13	3.93	3.81	3.69	3.59
35	.05	6.36	5.09	4.37	4.13	3.90	3.70	3.61	3.52	3.43	3.34	3.27	3.19
	.01	8.95	6.67	5.44	5.04	4.71	4.39	4.3*	4.26	3.97	3.84	3.73	3.63
40	.05	6.56	5.21	4.45	4.20	3.97	3.76	3.66	3.57	3.48	3.39	3.31	3.23
	.01	9.19	6.83	5.52	5.12	4.78	4.46	4.3*	4.1*	4.01	3.89	3.77	3.66
45	.05	6.70	5.31	4.53	4.26	4.02	3.80	3.70	3.61	3.51	3.42	3.34	3.26
	.01	9.41	6.93	5.60	5.20	4.84	4.52	4.3*	4.2*	4.1*	3.93	3.80	3.69
50	.05	6.86	5.40	4.59	4.32	4.07	3.85	3.74	3.65	3.55	3.46	3.37	3.29
	.01	9.68	7.06	5.70	5.27	4.90	4.56	4.4*	4.2*	4.1*	3.97	3.83	3.72
100	.05	8.00	6.08	5.06	4.73	4.42	4.15	4.04	3.90	3.79	3.69	3.58	3.48
	.01	11.04	7.80	6.20	5.70	5.20	4.80	4.7*	4.4*	4.5*		4.00	3.89
250	.05	9.68	7.06	5.70	5.27	4.90	4.56	4.4*	4.2*	4.1*	3.97	3.83	3.72
	.01	13.26	8.83	6.9*	6.3*	5.8*	5.2*	5.0*	4.9*	4.8*			4.11

* Obtained by graphical interpolation. Permission granted by the American Statistical Association to reproduce the table of percentage points of the Dunn multiple comparison test from O.J. Dunn. Multiple comparisons among means, *Journal of the American Statistical Association*, **56** (1961), 52–64.

Table A-12. Critical values of Student's t distribution.

df	.005	.01	.025	.05	.10	.90	.95	.975	.99	.995
1	−63.657	−31.821	−12.706	−6.314	−3.078	3.078	6.314	12.706	31.821	63.657
2	−9.925	−6.965	−4.303	−2.920	−1.886	1.886	2.920	4.303	6.965	9.925
3	−5.841	−4.541	−3.182	−2.353	−1.638	1.638	2.353	3.182	4.541	5.841
4	−4.604	−3.747	−2.776	−2.132	−1.533	1.533	2.132	2.776	3.747	4.604
5	−4.032	−3.365	−2.571	−2.015	−1.476	1.476	2.015	2.571	3.365	4.032
6	−3.707	−3.143	−2.447	−1.943	−1.440	1.440	1.943	2.447	3.143	3.707
7	−3.499	−2.998	−2.365	−1.895	−1.415	1.415	1.895	2.365	2.998	3.499
8	−3.355	−2.896	−2.306	−1.860	−1.397	1.397	1.860	2.306	2.896	3.355
9	−3.250	−2.821	−2.262	−1.833	−1.383	1.383	1.833	2.262	2.821	3.250
10	−3.169	−2.764	−2.228	−1.812	−1.372	1.372	1.812	2.228	2.764	3.169
11	−3.106	−2.718	−2.201	−1.796	−1.363	1.363	1.796	2.201	2.718	3.106
12	−3.055	−2.681	−2.179	−1.782	−1.356	1.356	1.782	2.179	2.681	3.055
13	−3.012	−2.650	−2.160	−1.771	−1.350	1.350	1.771	2.160	2.650	3.012
14	−2.977	−2.624	−2.145	−1.761	−1.345	1.345	1.761	2.145	2.624	2.977
15	−2.947	−2.602	−2.131	−1.753	−1.341	1.341	1.753	2.131	2.602	2.947
16	−2.921	−2.583	−2.120	−1.746	−1.337	1.337	1.746	2.120	2.583	2.921
17	−2.898	−2.567	−2.110	−1.740	−1.333	1.333	1.740	2.110	2.567	2.898
18	−2.878	−2.552	−2.101	−1.734	−1.330	1.330	1.734	2.101	2.552	2.878
19	−2.861	−2.539	−2.093	−1.729	−1.328	1.328	1.729	2.093	2.539	2.861
20	−2.845	−2.528	−2.086	−1.725	−1.325	1.325	1.725	2.086	2.528	2.845
21	−2.831	−2.518	−2.080	−1.721	−1.323	1.323	1.721	2.080	2.518	2.831
22	−2.819	−2.508	−2.074	−1.717	−1.321	1.321	1.717	2.074	2.508	2.819
23	−2.807	−2.500	−2.069	−1.714	−1.319	1.319	1.714	2.069	2.500	2.807
24	−2.797	−2.492	−2.064	−1.711	−1.318	1.318	1.711	2.064	2.492	2.797
25	−2.787	−2.485	−2.060	−1.708	−1.316	1.316	1.708	2.060	2.485	2.787
26	−2.779	−2.479	−2.056	−1.706	−1.315	1.315	1.706	2.056	2.479	2.779
27	−2.771	−2.473	−2.052	−1.703	−1.314	1.314	1.703	2.052	2.473	2.771
28	−2.763	−2.467	−2.048	−1.701	−1.313	1.313	1.701	2.048	2.467	2.763
29	−2.756	−2.462	−2.045	−1.699	−1.311	1.311	1.699	2.045	2.462	2.756
30	−2.750	−2.457	−2.042	−1.697	−1.310	1.310	1.697	2.042	2.457	2.750
40	−2.704	−2.423	−2.021	−1.684	−1.303	1.303	1.684	2.021	2.423	2.704
60	−2.660	−2.390	−2.000	−1.671	−1.296	1.296	1.671	2.000	2.390	2.660
120	−2.617	−2.358	−1.980	−1.658	−1.289	1.289	1.658	1.980	2.358	2.617
∞	−2.576	−2.326	−1.960	−1.645	−1.282	1.282	1.645	1.960	2.326	2.576

Table A-13. Critical values of the Tukey test

Error df	α	\multicolumn{10}{c}{r = number of means or number of steps between ordered means}
		2	3	4	5	6	7	8	9	10	11
5	.05	3.64	4.60	5.22	5.67	6.03	6.33	6.58	6.80	6.99	7.17
	.01	5.70	6.98	7.80	8.42	8.91	9.32	9.67	9.97	10.24	10.48
6	.05	3.46	4.34	4.90	5.30	5.63	5.90	6.12	6.32	6.49	6.65
	.01	5.24	6.33	7.03	7.56	7.97	8.32	8.61	8.87	9.10	9.30
7	.05	3.34	4.16	4.68	5.06	5.36	5.61	5.82	6.00	6.16	6.30
	.01	4.95	5.92	6.54	7.01	7.37	7.68	7.94	8.17	8.37	8.55
8	.05	3.26	4.04	4.53	4.89	5.17	5.40	5.60	5.77	5.92	6.05
	.01	4.75	5.64	6.20	6.62	6.96	7.24	7.47	7.68	7.86	8.03
9	.05	3.20	3.95	4.41	4.76	5.02	5.24	5.43	5.59	5.74	5.87
	.01	4.60	5.43	5.96	6.35	6.66	6.91	7.13	7.33	7.49	7.65
10	.05	3.15	3.88	4.33	4.65	4.91	5.12	5.30	5.46	5.60	5.72
	.01	4.48	5.27	5.77	6.14	6.43	6.67	6.87	7.05	7.21	7.36
11	.05	3.11	3.82	4.26	4.57	4.82	5.03	5.20	5.35	5.49	5.61
	.01	4.39	5.15	5.62	5.97	6.25	6.48	6.67	6.84	6.99	7.13
12	.05	3.08	3.77	4.20	4.51	4.75	4.95	5.12	5.27	5.39	5.51
	.01	4.32	5.05	5.50	5.84	6.10	6.32	6.51	6.67	6.81	6.94
13	.05	3.06	3.73	4.15	4.45	4.69	4.88	5.05	5.19	5.32	5.43
	.01	4.26	4.96	5.40	5.73	5.98	6.19	6.37	6.53	6.67	6.79
14	.05	3.03	3.70	4.11	4.41	4.64	4.83	4.99	5.13	5.25	5.36
	.01	4.21	4.89	5.32	5.63	5.88	6.08	6.26	6.41	6.54	6.66
15	.05	3.01	3.67	4.08	4.37	4.59	4.78	4.94	5.08	5.20	5.31
	.01	4.17	4.84	5.25	5.56	5.80	5.99	6.16	6.31	6.44	6.55
16	.05	3.00	3.65	4.05	4.33	4.56	4.74	4.90	5.03	5.15	5.26
	.01	4.13	4.79	5.19	5.49	5.72	5.92	6.08	6.22	6.35	6.46
17	.05	2.98	3.63	4.02	4.30	4.52	4.70	4.86	4.99	5.11	5.21
	.01	4.10	4.74	5.14	5.43	5.66	5.85	6.01	6.15	6.27	6.38
18	.05	2.97	3.61	4.00	4.28	4.49	4.67	4.82	4.96	5.07	5.17
	.01	4.07	4.70	5.09	5.38	5.60	5.79	5.94	6.08	6.20	6.31
19	.05	2.96	3.59	3.98	4.25	4.47	4.65	4.79	4.92	5.04	5.14
	.01	4.05	4.67	5.05	5.33	5.55	5.73	5.89	6.02	6.14	6.25
20	.05	2.95	3.58	3.96	4.23	4.45	4.62	4.77	4.90	5.01	5.11
	.01	4.02	4.64	5.02	5.29	5.51	5.69	5.84	5.97	6.09	6.19
24	.05	2.92	3.53	3.90	4.17	4.37	4.54	4.68	4.81	4.92	5.01
	.01	3.96	4.55	4.91	5.17	5.37	5.54	5.69	5.81	5.92	6.02
30	.05	2.89	3.49	3.85	4.10	4.30	4.46	4.60	4.72	4.82	4.92
	.01	3.89	4.45	4.80	5.05	5.24	5.40	5.54	5.65	5.76	5.85
40	.05	2.86	3.44	3.79	4.04	4.23	4.39	4.52	4.63	4.73	4.82
	.01	3.82	4.37	4.70	4.93	5.11	5.26	5.39	5.50	5.60	5.69
60	.05	2.83	3.40	3.74	3.98	4.16	4.31	4.44	4.55	4.65	4.73
	.01	3.76	4.28	4.59	4.82	4.99	5.13	5.25	5.36	5.45	5.53
120	.05	2.80	3.36	3.68	3.92	4.10	4.24	4.36	4.47	4.56	4.64
	.01	3.70	4.20	4.50	4.71	4.87	5.01	5.12	5.21	5.30	5.37
∞	.05	2.77	3.31	3.63	3.86	4.03	4.17	4.29	4.39	4.47	4.55
	.01	3.64	4.12	4.40	4.60	4.76	4.88	4.99	5.08	5.16	5.23

Table A-13. *(continued)*

r = number of means or number of steps between ordered means

12	13	14	15	16	17	18	19	20	α	Error df
7.32	7.47	7.60	7.72	7.83	7.93	8.03	8.12	8.21	.05	5
10.70	10.89	11.08	11.24	11.40	11.55	11.68	11.81	11.93	.01	
6.79	6.92	7.03	7.14	7.24	7.34	7.43	7.51	7.59	.05	6
9.48	9.65	9.81	9.95	10.08	10.21	10.32	10.43	10.54	.01	
6.43	6.55	6.66	6.76	6.85	6.94	7.02	7.10	7.17	.05	7
8.71	8.86	9.00	9.12	9.24	9.35	9.46	9.55	9.65	.01	
6.18	6.29	6.39	6.48	6.57	6.65	6.73	6.80	6.87	.05	8
8.18	8.31	8.44	8.55	8.66	8.76	8.85	8.94	9.03	.01	
5.98	6.09	6.19	6.28	6.36	6.44	6.51	6.58	6.64	.05	9
7.78	7.91	8.03	8.13	8.23	8.33	8.41	8.49	8.57	.01	
5.83	5.93	6.03	6.11	6.19	6.27	6.34	6.40	6.47	.05	10
7.49	7.60	7.71	7.81	7.91	7.99	8.08	8.15	8.23	.01	
5.71	5.81	5.90	5.98	6.06	6.13	6.20	6.27	6.33	.05	11
7.25	7.36	7.46	7.56	7.65	7.73	7.81	7.88	7.95	.01	
5.61	5.71	5.80	5.88	5.95	6.02	6.09	6.15	6.21	.05	12
7.06	7.17	7.26	7.36	7.44	7.52	7.59	7.66	7.73	.01	
5.53	5.63	5.71	5.79	5.86	5.93	5.99	6.05	6.11	.05	13
6.90	7.01	7.10	7.19	7.27	7.35	7.42	7.48	7.55	.01	
5.46	5.55	5.64	5.71	5.79	5.85	5.91	5.97	6.03	.05	14
6.77	6.87	6.96	7.05	7.13	7.20	7.27	7.33	7.39	.01	
5.40	5.49	5.57	5.65	5.72	5.78	5.85	5.90	5.96	.05	15
6.66	6.76	6.84	6.93	7.00	7.07	7.14	7.20	7.26	.01	
5.35	5.44	5.52	5.59	5.66	5.73	5.79	5.84	5.90	.05	16
6.56	6.66	6.74	6.82	6.90	6.97	7.03	7.09	7.15	.01	
5.31	5.39	5.47	5.54	5.61	5.67	5.73	5.79	5.85	.05	17
6.48	6.57	6.66	6.73	6.81	6.87	6.94	7.00	7.05	.01	
5.27	5.35	5.43	5.50	5.57	5.63	5.69	5.74	5.79	.05	18
6.41	6.50	6.58	6.65	6.73	6.79	6.85	6.91	6.97	.01	
5.23	5.31	5.39	5.46	5.53	5.59	5.65	5.70	5.75	.05	19
6.34	6.43	6.51	6.58	6.65	6.72	6.78	6.84	6.89	.01	
5.20	5.28	5.36	5.43	5.49	5.55	5.61	5.66	5.71	.05	20
6.28	6.37	6.45	6.52	6.59	6.65	6.71	6.77	6.82	.01	
5.10	5.18	5.25	5.32	5.38	5.44	5.49	5.55	5.59	.05	24
6.11	6.19	6.26	6.33	6.39	6.45	6.51	6.56	6.61	.01	
5.00	5.08	5.15	5.21	5.27	5.33	5.38	5.43	5.47	.05	30
5.93	6.01	6.08	6.14	6.20	6.26	6.31	6.36	6.41	.01	
4.90	4.98	5.04	5.11	5.16	5.22	5.27	5.31	5.36	.05	40
5.76	5.83	5.90	5.96	6.02	6.07	6.12	6.16	6.21	.01	
4.81	4.88	4.94	5.00	5.06	5.11	5.15	5.20	5.24	.05	60
5.60	5.67	5.73	5.78	5.84	5.89	5.93	5.97	6.01	.01	
4.71	4.78	4.84	4.90	4.95	5.00	5.04	5.09	5.13	.05	120
5.44	5.50	5.56	5.61	5.66	5.71	5.75	5.79	5.83	.01	
4.62	4.68	4.74	4.80	4.85	4.89	4.93	4.97	5.01	.05	∞
5.29	5.35	5.40	5.45	5.49	5.54	5.57	5.61	5.65	.01	

Table A-14. Contrast weights for trend analysis.

k	Polynomial				Coefficients							Σc_{ij}^2
3	Linear	−1	0	1								2
	Quadratic	1	−2	1								6
	Linear	−3	−1	1	3							20
4	Quadratic	1	−1	−1	1							4
	Cubic	−1	3	−3	1							20
	Linear	−2	−1	0	1	2						10
5	Quadratic	2	−1	−2	−1	2						14
	Cubic	−1	2	0	−2	1						10
	Quartic	1	−4	6	−4	1						70
	Linear	−5	−3	−1	1	3	5					70
6	Quadratic	5	−1	−4	−4	−1	5					84
	Cubic	−5	7	4	−4	−7	5					180
	Quartic	1	−3	2	2	−3	1					28
	Linear	−3	−2	−1	0	1	2	3				28
7	Quadratic	5	0	−3	−4	−3	0	5				84
	Cubic	−1	1	1	0	−1	−1	1				6
	Quartic	3	−7	1	6	1	−7	3				154
	Linear	−7	−5	−3	−1	1	3	5	7			168
	Quadratic	7	1	−3	−5	−5	−3	1	7			168
8	Cubic	−7	5	7	3	−3	−7	−5	7			264
	Quartic	7	−13	−3	9	9	−3	−13	7			616
	Quintic	−7	23	−17	−15	15	17	−23	7			2184
	Linear	−4	−3	−2	−1	0	1	2	3	4		60
	Quadratic	28	7	−8	−17	−20	−17	−8	7	28		2772
9	Cubic	−14	7	13	9	0	−9	−13	−7	14		990
	Quartic	14	−21	−11	9	18	9	−11	−21	14		2002
	Quintic	−4	11	−4	−9	0	9	4	−11	4		468
	Linear	−9	−7	−5	−3	−1	1	3	5	7	9	330
	Quadratic	6	2	−1	−3	−4	−4	−3	−1	2	6	132
10	Cubic	−42	14	35	31	12	−12	−31	−35	−14	42	8580
	Quartic	18	−22	−17	3	18	18	3	−17	−22	18	2860
	Quintic	−6	14	−1	−11	−6	6	11	1	−14	6	780

Extract from Table xxxiii from R.A. Fisher and F. Yates. *Statistical Tables for Biological, Agricultural and Medical Research*, 6th ed., 1974. Reprinted with the permission of Longman Group Ltd.

Table A-15. Critical values of the F distribution.

v_1, Degrees of freedom for numerator

v_2	Cum. prop.	1	2	3	4	5	6	7	8	9	10	11	12	15	20	24	30	40	60	120	∞	Cum. prop.
1	.005	$.0^462$	$.0^251$	.018	.032	.044	.054	.062	.068	.073	.078	.082	.085	.093	.101	.105	.109	.113	.118	.122	.127	.005
	.01	$.0^325$	.010	.029	.047	.062	.073	.082	.089	.095	.100	.104	.107	.115	.124	.128	.132	.137	.141	.146	.151	.01
	.025	$.0^215$	.026	.057	.082	.100	.113	.124	.132	.139	.144	.149	.153	.161	.170	.175	.180	.184	.189	.194	.199	.025
	.05	$.0^262$	.054	.099	.130	.151	.167	.179	.188	.195	.201	.207	.211	.220	.230	.235	.240	.245	.250	.255	.261	.05
	.95	161	200	216	225	230	234	237	239	241	242	243	244	246	248	249	250	251	252	253	254	.95
	.975	648	800	864	900	922	937	948	957	963	969	973	977	985	993	997	100^1	101^1	101^1	101^1	102^1	.975
	.99	405^1	500^1	540^1	562^1	576^1	586^1	593^1	598^1	602^1	606^1	608^1	611^1	616^1	621^1	623^1	626^1	629^1	631^1	634^1	637^1	.99
	.995	162^2	200^2	216^2	225^2	231^2	234^2	237^2	239^2	241^2	242^2	243^2	244^2	246^2	248^2	249^2	250^2	251^2	253^2	254^2	255^2	.995
2	.005	$.0^450$	$.0^250$	.020	.038	.055	.069	.081	.091	.099	.106	.112	.118	.130	.143	.150	.157	.165	.173	.181	.189	.005
	.01	$.0^320$	.010	.032	.056	.075	.092	.105	.116	.125	.132	.139	.144	.157	.171	.178	.186	.193	.201	.209	.217	.01
	.025	$.0^213$	.026	.062	.094	.119	.138	.153	.165	.175	.183	.190	.196	.210	.224	.232	.239	.247	.255	.263	.271	.025
	.05	$.0^250$	.053	.105	.144	.173	.194	.211	.224	.235	.244	.251	.257	.272	.286	.294	.302	.309	.317	.326	.334	.05
	.95	18.5	19.0	19.2	19.2	19.3	19.3	19.4	19.4	19.4	19.4	19.4	19.4	19.4	19.4	19.5	19.5	19.5	19.5	19.5	19.5	.95
	.975	38.5	39.0	39.2	39.2	39.3	39.3	39.4	39.4	39.4	39.4	39.4	39.4	39.4	39.4	39.5	39.5	39.5	39.5	39.5	39.5	.975
	.99	98.5	99.0	99.2	99.2	99.3	99.3	99.4	99.4	99.4	99.4	99.4	99.4	99.4	99.4	99.5	99.5	99.5	99.5	99.5	99.5	.99
	.995	198	199	199	199	199	199	199	199	199	199	199	199	199	199	199	199	199	199	199	200	.995
3	.005	$.0^446$	$.0^250$	.021	.041	.060	.077	.092	.104	.115	.124	.132	.138	.154	.172	.181	.191	.201	.211	.222	.234	.005
	.01	$.0^319$	.010	.034	.060	.083	.102	.118	.132	.143	.153	.161	.168	.185	.203	.212	.222	.232	.242	.253	.264	.01
	.025	$.0^212$	.026	.065	.100	.129	.152	.170	.185	.197	.207	.216	.224	.241	.259	.269	.279	.289	.299	.310	.321	.025
	.05	$.0^246$	.052	.108	.152	.185	.210	.230	.246	.259	.270	.279	.287	.304	.323	.332	.342	.352	.363	.373	.384	.05
	.95	10.1	9.55	9.28	9.12	9.01	8.94	8.89	8.85	8.81	8.79	8.76	8.74	8.70	8.66	8.63	8.62	8.59	8.57	8.55	8.53	.95
	.975	17.4	16.0	15.4	15.1	14.9	14.7	14.6	14.5	14.5	14.4	14.4	14.3	14.3	14.2	14.1	14.1	14.0	14.0	13.9	13.9	.975
	.99	34.1	30.8	29.5	28.7	28.2	27.9	27.7	27.5	27.3	27.2	27.1	27.1	26.9	26.7	26.6	26.5	26.4	26.3	26.2	26.1	.99
	.995	55.6	49.8	47.5	46.2	45.4	44.8	44.4	44.1	43.9	43.7	43.5	43.4	43.1	42.8	42.6	42.5	42.3	42.0	42.0	41.8	.995
4	.005	$.0^444$	$.0^250$	.022	.043	.064	.083	.100	.114	.126	.137	.145	.153	.172	.193	.204	.216	.229	.242	.255	.269	.005
	.01	$.0^318$	.010	.035	.063	.088	.109	.127	.143	.156	.167	.176	.185	.204	.226	.237	.249	.261	.274	.287	.301	.01
	.025	$.0^211$	.026	.066	.104	.135	.161	.181	.198	.212	.224	.234	.243	.263	.284	.296	.308	.320	.332	.346	.359	.025
	.05	$.0^244$	.052	.110	.157	.193	.221	.243	.261	.275	.288	.298	.307	.327	.349	.360	.372	.384	.396	.409	.422	.05
	.95	7.71	6.94	6.59	6.39	6.26	6.16	6.09	6.04	6.00	5.96	5.94	5.91	5.86	5.80	5.77	5.75	5.72	5.69	5.66	5.63	.95
	.975	12.2	10.6	9.98	9.60	9.36	9.20	9.07	8.98	8.90	8.84	8.79	8.75	8.66	8.56	8.51	8.46	8.41	8.36	8.31	8.26	.975
	.99	21.2	18.0	16.7	16.0	15.5	15.2	15.0	14.8	14.7	14.5	14.4	14.4	14.2	14.0	13.9	13.8	13.7	13.7	13.6	13.5	.99
	.995	31.3	26.3	24.3	23.2	22.5	22.0	21.6	21.4	21.1	21.0	20.8	20.7	20.4	20.2	20.0	19.9	19.8	19.6	19.5	19.3	.995
5	.005	$.0^443$	$.0^250$	.022	.045	.067	.087	.105	.120	.134	.146	.156	.165	.186	.210	.223	.237	.251	.266	.282	.299	.005
	.01	$.0^317$	.010	.035	.064	.091	.114	.134	.151	.165	.177	.188	.197	.219	.244	.257	.270	.285	.299	.315	.332	.01
	.025	$.0^211$	.025	.067	.107	.140	.167	.189	.208	.223	.236	.248	.257	.280	.304	.317	.330	.344	.359	.374	.390	.025
	.05	$.0^243$	.052	.111	.160	.198	.228	.252	.271	.287	.301	.313	.322	.345	.369	.382	.395	.408	.422	.437	.452	.05
	.95	6.61	5.79	5.41	5.19	5.05	4.95	4.88	4.82	4.77	4.74	4.71	4.68	4.62	4.56	4.53	4.50	4.46	4.43	4.40	4.36	.95
	.975	10.0	8.43	7.76	7.39	7.15	6.98	6.85	6.76	6.68	6.62	6.57	6.52	6.43	6.33	6.28	6.23	6.18	6.12	6.07	6.02	.975
	.99	16.3	13.3	12.1	11.4	11.0	10.7	10.5	10.3	10.2	10.1	9.96	9.89	9.72	9.55	9.47	9.38	9.29	9.20	9.11	9.02	.99
	.995	22.8	18.3	16.5	15.6	14.9	14.5	14.2	14.0	13.8	13.6	13.5	13.4	13.1	12.9	12.8	12.7	12.5	12.4	12.3	12.1	.995

Denominator degrees of freedom

Read $.0^562$ as .00056, 200^1 as 2,000, 162^4 as 1,620,000, and so on.

Table A-15. (continued)

v_1, Degrees of freedom for numerator

Denominator degrees of freedom

Denominator df = 6

Cum. prop.	1	2	3	4	5	6	7	8	9	10	11	12	15	20	24	30	40	60	120	∞	Cum. prop.
.005	$.0^4 43$	$.0^2 50$	.022	.045	.069	.090	.109	.126	.140	.153	.164	.174	.197	.224	.238	.253	.269	.286	.304	.324	.005
.01	$.0^3 17$	.010	.036	.066	.094	.118	.139	.157	.172	.186	.197	.207	.232	.258	.273	.288	.304	.321	.338	.357	.01
.025	$.0^2 11$	.025	.068	.109	.143	.172	.195	.215	.231	.246	.258	.268	.293	.320	.334	.349	.364	.381	.398	.415	.025
.05	$.0^2 43$	.052	.112	.162	.202	.233	.259	.279	.296	.311	.324	.334	.358	.385	.399	.413	.428	.444	.460	.476	.05
.95	5.99	5.14	4.76	4.53	4.39	4.28	4.21	4.15	4.10	4.06	4.03	4.00	3.94	3.87	3.84	3.81	3.77	3.74	3.70	3.67	.95
.975	8.81	7.26	6.60	6.23	5.99	5.82	5.70	5.60	5.52	5.46	5.41	5.37	5.27	5.17	5.12	5.07	5.01	4.96	4.90	4.85	.975
.99	13.7	10.9	9.78	9.15	8.75	8.47	8.26	8.10	7.98	7.87	7.79	7.72	7.56	7.40	7.31	7.23	7.14	7.06	6.97	6.88	.99
.995	18.6	14.5	12.9	12.0	11.5	11.1	10.8	10.6	10.4	10.2	10.1	10.0	9.81	9.59	9.47	9.36	9.24	9.12	9.00	8.88	.995

Denominator df = 7

Cum. prop.	1	2	3	4	5	6	7	8	9	10	11	12	15	20	24	30	40	60	120	∞	Cum. prop.
.005	$.0^4 42$	$.0^2 50$	.023	.046	.070	.093	.113	.130	.145	.159	.171	.181	.206	.235	.251	.267	.285	.304	.324	.345	.005
.01	$.0^3 17$	.010	.036	.067	.096	.121	.143	.162	.178	.192	.205	.216	.241	.270	.286	.303	.320	.339	.358	.379	.01
.025	$.0^2 10$	.025	.068	.110	.146	.176	.200	.221	.238	.253	.266	.277	.304	.333	.348	.364	.381	.399	.418	.437	.025
.05	$.0^2 42$	.052	.113	.164	.205	.238	.264	.286	.304	.319	.332	.343	.369	.398	.413	.428	.445	.461	.479	.498	.05
.95	5.59	4.74	4.35	4.12	3.97	3.87	3.79	3.73	3.68	3.64	3.60	3.57	3.51	3.44	3.41	3.38	3.34	3.30	3.27	3.23	.95
.975	8.07	6.54	5.89	5.52	5.29	5.12	4.99	4.90	4.82	4.76	4.71	4.67	4.57	4.47	4.42	4.36	4.31	4.25	4.20	4.14	.975
.99	12.2	9.55	8.45	7.85	7.46	7.19	6.99	6.84	6.72	6.62	6.54	6.47	6.31	6.16	6.07	5.99	5.91	5.82	5.74	5.65	.99
.995	16.2	12.4	10.9	10.0	9.52	9.16	8.89	8.68	8.51	8.38	8.27	8.18	7.97	7.75	7.65	7.53	7.42	7.31	7.19	7.08	.995

Denominator df = 8

Cum. prop.	1	2	3	4	5	6	7	8	9	10	11	12	15	20	24	30	40	60	120	∞	Cum. prop.
.005	$.0^4 42$	$.0^2 50$	.023	.047	.072	.095	.115	.133	.149	.164	.176	.187	.214	.244	.261	.279	.299	.319	.341	.364	.005
.01	$.0^3 17$	.010	.036	.068	.097	.123	.146	.166	.183	.198	.211	.222	.250	.281	.297	.315	.334	.354	.376	.398	.01
.025	$.0^2 10$	.025	.069	.111	.148	.179	.204	.226	.244	.259	.273	.285	.313	.343	.360	.377	.395	.415	.435	.456	.025
.05	$.0^2 42$	.052	.113	.166	.208	.241	.268	.291	.310	.326	.339	.351	.379	.409	.425	.441	.459	.477	.496	.516	.05
.95	5.32	4.46	4.07	3.84	3.69	3.58	3.50	3.44	3.39	3.35	3.31	3.28	3.22	3.15	3.12	3.08	3.04	3.01	2.97	2.93	.95
.975	7.57	6.06	5.42	5.05	4.82	4.65	4.53	4.43	4.36	4.30	4.24	4.20	4.10	4.00	3.95	3.89	3.84	3.78	3.73	3.67	.975
.99	11.3	8.65	7.59	7.01	6.63	6.37	6.18	6.03	5.91	5.81	5.73	5.67	5.52	5.36	5.28	5.20	5.12	5.03	4.95	4.86	.99
.995	14.7	11.0	9.60	8.81	8.30	7.95	7.69	7.50	7.34	7.21	7.10	7.01	6.81	6.61	6.50	6.40	6.29	6.18	6.06	5.95	.995

Denominator df = 9

Cum. prop.	1	2	3	4	5	6	7	8	9	10	11	12	15	20	24	30	40	60	120	∞	Cum. prop.
.005	$.0^4 42$	$.0^2 50$	.023	.047	.073	.096	.117	.136	.153	.168	.181	.192	.220	.253	.271	.290	.310	.332	.356	.382	.005
.01	$.0^3 17$	.010	.037	.068	.098	.125	.149	.169	.187	.202	.216	.228	.257	.289	.307	.326	.346	.368	.391	.415	.01
.025	$.0^2 10$	.025	.069	.112	.150	.181	.207	.230	.248	.265	.279	.291	.320	.352	.370	.388	.408	.428	.450	.473	.025
.05	$.0^2 42$	.052	.113	.167	.210	.244	.272	.296	.315	.331	.345	.358	.386	.418	.435	.452	.471	.490	.510	.532	.05
.95	5.12	4.26	3.86	3.63	3.48	3.37	3.29	3.23	3.18	3.14	3.10	3.07	3.01	2.94	2.90	2.86	2.83	2.79	2.75	2.71	.95
.975	7.21	5.71	5.08	4.72	4.48	4.32	4.20	4.10	4.03	3.96	3.91	3.87	3.77	3.67	3.61	3.56	3.51	3.45	3.39	3.33	.975
.99	10.6	8.02	6.99	6.42	6.06	5.80	5.61	5.47	5.35	5.26	5.18	5.11	4.96	4.81	4.73	4.65	4.57	4.48	4.40	4.31	.99
.995	13.6	10.1	8.72	7.96	7.47	7.13	6.88	6.69	6.54	6.42	6.31	6.23	6.03	5.83	5.73	5.62	5.52	5.41	5.30	5.19	.995

F-distribution critical values. Numerator degrees of freedom across the top; denominator degrees of freedom (df2) down the left side; tail probability (p) in the second column.

df2	p	∞	120	60	40	30	24	20	15	12	11	10	9	8	7	6	5	4	3	2	1
10	.005	.397	.370	.344	.321	.299	.279	.260	.226	.197	.185	.171	.156	.139	.119	.098	.073	.048	.023	$.0^250$	$.0^441$
	.01	.431	.405	.380	.357	.336	.316	.297	.263	.233	.220	.206	.190	.172	.151	.127	.100	.069	.037	.010	$.0^317$
	.025	.488	.464	.441	.419	.398	.379	.360	.327	.296	.283	.269	.252	.233	.210	.183	.151	.113	.069	.025	$.0^210$
	.05	.546	.523	.502	.481	.462	.444	.426	.393	.363	.351	.336	.319	.299	.275	.246	.211	.168	.114	.052	$.0^241$
	.95	2.54	2.58	2.62	2.66	2.70	2.74	2.77	2.85	2.91	2.94	2.98	3.02	3.07	3.14	3.22	3.33	3.48	3.71	4.10	4.96
	.975	3.08	3.14	3.20	3.26	3.31	3.37	3.42	3.52	3.62	3.66	3.72	3.78	3.85	3.95	4.07	4.24	4.47	4.83	5.46	6.94
	.99	3.91	4.00	4.08	4.17	4.25	4.33	4.41	4.56	4.71	4.77	4.85	4.94	5.06	5.20	5.39	5.64	5.99	6.55	7.56	10.0
	.995	4.64	4.75	4.86	4.97	5.07	5.17	5.27	5.47	5.66	5.75	5.85	5.97	6.12	6.30	6.54	6.87	7.34	8.08	9.43	12.8
11	.005	.412	.382	.355	.330	.308	.286	.266	.231	.200	.188	.174	.158	.141	.121	.099	.074	.048	.023	$.0^240$	$.0^440$
	.01	.444	.417	.391	.366	.344	.324	.304	.268	.237	.224	.210	.193	.175	.153	.128	.100	.069	.037	.010	$.0^316$
	.025	.503	.476	.450	.429	.407	.386	.368	.332	.301	.288	.273	.256	.236	.212	.185	.152	.114	.069	.025	$.0^210$
	.05	.559	.535	.513	.490	.469	.452	.433	.398	.368	.355	.340	.323	.302	.278	.248	.212	.168	.114	.052	$.0^241$
	.95	2.40	2.45	2.49	2.53	2.57	2.61	2.65	2.72	2.79	2.82	2.85	2.90	2.95	3.01	3.09	3.20	3.36	3.59	3.98	4.84
	.975	2.88	2.94	3.00	3.06	3.12	3.17	3.23	3.33	3.43	3.47	3.53	3.59	3.66	3.76	3.88	4.04	4.28	4.63	5.26	6.72
	.99	3.60	3.69	3.78	3.86	3.94	4.02	4.10	4.25	4.40	4.46	4.54	4.63	4.74	4.89	5.07	5.32	5.67	6.22	7.21	9.65
	.995	4.23	4.34	4.45	4.55	4.65	4.76	4.86	5.05	5.24	5.32	5.42	5.54	5.68	5.86	6.10	6.42	6.88	7.60	8.91	12.2
12	.005	.424	.393	.365	.339	.315	.292	.272	.235	.204	.191	.177	.161	.143	.122	.100	.075	.048	.023	$.0^250$	$.0^441$
	.01	.458	.428	.401	.375	.352	.330	.310	.273	.241	.227	.212	.196	.176	.155	.130	.101	.070	.037	.010	$.0^316$
	.025	.514	.487	.461	.437	.416	.394	.374	.337	.305	.292	.276	.259	.238	.214	.186	.153	.114	.070	.025	$.0^210$
	.05	.571	.545	.522	.499	.478	.458	.439	.404	.372	.358	.343	.325	.305	.280	.250	.214	.169	.114	.052	$.0^241$
	.95	2.30	2.34	2.38	2.43	2.47	2.51	2.54	2.62	2.69	2.72	2.75	2.80	2.85	2.91	3.00	3.11	3.26	3.49	3.89	4.75
	.975	2.72	2.79	2.85	2.91	2.96	3.02	3.07	3.18	3.28	3.32	3.37	3.44	3.51	3.61	3.73	3.89	4.12	4.47	5.10	6.55
	.99	3.36	3.45	3.54	3.62	3.70	3.78	3.86	4.01	4.16	4.22	4.30	4.39	4.50	4.64	4.82	5.06	5.41	5.95	6.93	9.33
	.995	3.90	4.01	4.12	4.23	4.33	4.43	4.53	4.72	4.91	4.99	5.09	5.20	5.35	5.52	5.76	6.07	6.52	7.23	8.51	11.8
15	.005	.457	.422	.389	.360	.333	.308	.286	.246	.212	.198	.183	.166	.147	.125	.102	.076	.049	.023	$.0^241$	$.0^441$
	.01	.490	.456	.425	.397	.370	.346	.324	.284	.249	.235	.219	.202	.181	.158	.132	.103	.070	.037	.010	$.0^316$
	.025	.546	.514	.485	.458	.433	.410	.389	.349	.315	.300	.284	.265	.244	.219	.190	.156	.117	.070	.025	$.0^210$
	.05	.600	.571	.545	.519	.496	.474	.454	.416	.382	.368	.351	.333	.311	.285	.254	.216	.170	.115	.052	$.0^240$
	.95	2.07	2.11	2.16	2.20	2.25	2.29	2.33	2.40	2.48	2.51	2.54	2.59	2.64	2.71	2.79	2.90	3.06	3.29	3.68	4.54
	.975	2.40	2.46	2.52	2.59	2.64	2.70	2.76	2.86	2.96	3.01	3.06	3.12	3.20	3.29	3.41	3.58	3.80	4.15	4.76	6.20
	.99	2.87	2.96	3.05	3.13	3.21	3.29	3.37	3.52	3.67	3.73	3.80	3.89	4.00	4.14	4.32	4.56	4.89	5.42	6.36	8.68
	.995	3.26	3.37	3.48	3.59	3.69	3.79	3.88	4.07	4.25	4.33	4.42	4.54	4.67	4.85	5.07	5.37	5.80	6.48	7.70	10.8
20	.005	.500	.457	.419	.385	.354	.327	.308	.258	.220	.206	.190	.171	.151	.129	.104	.077	.050	.023	$.0^239$	$.0^439$
	.01	.532	.491	.455	.422	.392	.365	.340	.297	.259	.244	.227	.208	.187	.162	.135	.105	.071	.037	.010	$.0^316$
	.025	.585	.548	.514	.484	.456	.430	.406	.363	.325	.310	.292	.273	.250	.224	.193	.158	.117	.071	.025	$.0^210$
	.05	.637	.603	.572	.544	.518	.493	.471	.430	.393	.377	.360	.340	.318	.290	.258	.219	.172	.117	.052	$.0^240$
	.95	1.84	1.90	1.95	1.99	2.04	2.08	2.12	2.20	2.28	2.31	2.35	2.39	2.45	2.51	2.60	2.71	2.87	3.10	3.49	4.35
	.975	2.09	2.16	2.22	2.29	2.35	2.41	2.46	2.57	2.68	2.72	2.77	2.84	2.91	3.01	3.13	3.29	3.51	3.86	4.46	5.87
	.99	2.42	2.52	2.61	2.69	2.78	2.86	2.94	3.09	3.23	3.29	3.37	3.46	3.56	3.70	3.87	4.10	4.43	4.94	5.85	8.10
	.995	2.69	2.81	2.92	3.02	3.12	3.22	3.32	3.50	3.68	3.76	3.85	3.96	4.09	4.26	4.47	4.76	5.17	5.82	6.99	9.94
24	.005	.527	.479	.437	.400	.367	.337	.310	.264	.226	.210	.193	.175	.154	.131	.106	.078	.050	.023	$.0^240$	$.0^439$
	.01	.558	.513	.473	.437	.405	.376	.350	.304	.264	.249	.231	.211	.189	.165	.137	.106	.072	.038	.010	$.0^316$
	.025	.610	.568	.531	.498	.468	.441	.415	.370	.331	.315	.297	.277	.253	.227	.195	.159	.117	.071	.025	$.0^210$
	.05	.659	.622	.588	.558	.530	.504	.480	.437	.399	.383	.365	.345	.321	.293	.260	.221	.173	.116	.051	$.0^240$
	.95	1.73	1.79	1.84	1.89	1.94	1.98	2.03	2.11	2.18	2.21	2.25	2.30	2.36	2.42	2.51	2.62	2.78	3.01	3.40	4.26
	.975	1.94	2.01	2.08	2.15	2.21	2.27	2.33	2.44	2.54	2.59	2.64	2.70	2.78	2.87	2.99	3.15	3.38	3.72	4.32	5.72
	.99	2.21	2.31	2.40	2.49	2.58	2.66	2.74	2.89	3.03	3.09	3.17	3.26	3.36	3.50	3.67	3.90	4.22	4.72	5.61	7.82
	.995	2.43	2.55	2.66	2.77	2.87	2.97	3.06	3.25	3.42	3.50	3.59	3.69	3.83	3.99	4.20	4.49	4.89	5.52	6.66	9.55

Denominator degrees of freedom

Read $.0^456$ as .00056, 200^1 as 2,000, 162^4 as 1,620,000, and so on.

Table A-15. (continued)

v_1, Degrees of freedom for numerator

Denominator degrees of freedom

df	Cum. prop.	1	2	3	4	5	6	7	8	9	10	11	12	15	20	24	30	40	60	120	∞	Cum. prop.
30	.005	$.0^4 40$	$.0^2 50$	.024	.050	.079	.107	.133	.156	.178	.197	.215	.231	.271	.320	.349	.381	.416	.457	.504	.559	.005
	.01	$.0^3 16$	.010	.038	.072	.107	.138	.167	.192	.215	.235	.254	.270	.311	.360	.388	.419	.454	.493	.538	.590	.01
	.025	$.0^2 10$	.025	.071	.118	.161	.197	.229	.257	.281	.302	.321	.337	.378	.426	.453	.482	.515	.551	.592	.639	.025
	.05	$.0^2 40$	.051	.116	.174	.222	.263	.296	.325	.349	.370	.389	.406	.445	.490	.516	.543	.573	.606	.644	.685	.05
	.95	4.17	3.32	2.92	2.69	2.53	2.42	2.33	2.27	2.21	2.16	2.13	2.09	2.01	1.93	1.89	1.84	1.79	1.74	1.68	1.62	.95
	.975	5.57	4.18	3.59	3.25	3.03	2.87	2.75	2.65	2.57	2.51	2.46	2.41	2.31	2.20	2.14	2.07	2.01	1.94	1.87	1.79	.975
	.99	7.56	5.39	4.51	4.02	3.70	3.47	3.30	3.17	3.07	2.98	2.91	2.84	2.70	2.55	2.47	2.39	2.30	2.21	2.11	2.01	.99
	.995	9.18	6.35	5.24	4.62	4.23	3.95	3.74	3.58	3.45	3.34	3.25	3.18	3.01	2.82	2.73	2.63	2.52	2.42	2.30	2.18	.995
40	.005	$.0^4 40$	$.0^2 50$	.024	.051	.080	.108	.135	.159	.181	.201	.220	.237	.279	.331	.362	.396	.436	.481	.534	.599	.005
	.01	$.0^3 16$	.010	.038	.073	.108	.140	.169	.195	.219	.240	.259	.276	.319	.371	.401	.435	.473	.516	.567	.628	.01
	.025	$.0^2 99$	.025	.071	.119	.162	.199	.232	.260	.285	.307	.327	.344	.387	.437	.466	.498	.533	.573	.620	.674	.025
	.05	$.0^2 40$	.051	.116	.175	.224	.265	.299	.329	.354	.376	.395	.412	.454	.502	.529	.558	.591	.627	.669	.717	.05
	.95	4.08	3.23	2.84	2.61	2.45	2.34	2.25	2.18	2.12	2.08	2.04	2.00	1.92	1.84	1.79	1.74	1.69	1.64	1.58	1.51	.95
	.975	5.42	4.05	3.46	3.13	2.90	2.74	2.62	2.53	2.45	2.39	2.33	2.29	2.18	2.07	2.01	1.94	1.88	1.80	1.72	1.64	.975
	.99	7.31	5.18	4.31	3.83	3.51	3.29	3.12	2.99	2.89	2.80	2.73	2.66	2.52	2.37	2.29	2.20	2.11	2.02	1.92	1.80	.99
	.995	8.83	6.07	4.98	4.37	3.99	3.71	3.51	3.35	3.22	3.12	3.03	2.95	2.78	2.60	2.50	2.40	2.30	2.18	2.06	1.93	.995
60	.005	$.0^4 40$	$.0^2 50$	.024	.051	.081	.110	.137	.162	.185	.206	.225	.243	.287	.343	.376	.414	.458	.510	.572	.652	.005
	.01	$.0^3 16$	.010	.038	.073	.109	.142	.172	.199	.223	.245	.265	.283	.328	.383	.416	.453	.495	.545	.604	.679	.01
	.025	$.0^2 99$	.025	.071	.120	.163	.202	.235	.264	.290	.313	.333	.351	.396	.450	.481	.515	.555	.600	.654	.720	.025
	.05	$.0^2 40$	.051	.116	.176	.226	.267	.303	.333	.359	.382	.402	.419	.463	.514	.543	.575	.611	.652	.700	.759	.05
	.95	4.00	3.15	2.76	2.53	2.37	2.25	2.17	2.10	2.04	1.99	1.95	1.92	1.84	1.75	1.70	1.65	1.59	1.53	1.47	1.39	.95
	.975	5.29	3.93	3.34	3.01	2.79	2.63	2.51	2.41	2.33	2.27	2.22	2.17	2.06	1.94	1.88	1.82	1.74	1.67	1.58	1.48	.975
	.99	7.08	4.98	4.13	3.65	3.34	3.12	2.95	2.82	2.72	2.63	2.56	2.50	2.35	2.20	2.12	2.03	1.94	1.84	1.73	1.60	.99
	.995	8.49	5.80	4.73	4.14	3.76	3.49	3.29	3.13	3.01	2.90	2.82	2.74	2.57	2.39	2.29	2.19	2.08	1.96	1.83	1.69	.995
120	.005	$.0^3 39$	$.0^2 50$	.024	.051	.081	.111	.139	.165	.189	.211	.230	.249	.297	.356	.393	.434	.484	.545	.623	.733	.005
	.01	$.0^3 16$	.010	.038	.074	.110	.143	.174	.202	.227	.250	.271	.290	.338	.397	.433	.474	.522	.579	.652	.755	.01
	.025	$.0^2 99$	.025	.072	.120	.165	.204	.238	.268	.295	.318	.340	.359	.406	.464	.498	.536	.580	.633	.698	.789	.025
	.05	$.0^2 39$	.051	.117	.177	.227	.270	.306	.337	.364	.388	.408	.427	.473	.527	.559	.594	.634	.682	.740	.819	.05
	.95	3.92	3.07	2.68	2.45	2.29	2.18	2.09	2.02	1.96	1.91	1.87	1.83	1.75	1.66	1.61	1.55	1.50	1.43	1.35	1.25	.95
	.975	5.15	3.80	3.23	2.89	2.67	2.52	2.39	2.30	2.22	2.16	2.10	2.05	1.95	1.82	1.76	1.69	1.61	1.53	1.43	1.31	.975
	.99	6.85	4.79	3.95	3.48	3.17	2.96	2.79	2.66	2.56	2.47	2.40	2.34	2.19	2.03	1.95	1.86	1.76	1.66	1.53	1.38	.99
	.995	8.18	5.54	4.50	3.92	3.55	3.28	3.09	2.93	2.81	2.71	2.62	2.54	2.37	2.19	2.09	1.98	1.87	1.75	1.61	1.43	.995
∞	.005	$.0^3 39$	$.0^2 50$	.024	.052	.082	.113	.141	.168	.193	.216	.236	.256	.307	.372	.412	.460	.518	.592	.699	1.00	.005
	.01	$.0^3 16$	.010	.038	.074	.111	.145	.177	.206	.232	.256	.278	.298	.349	.413	.452	.499	.554	.625	.724	1.00	.01
	.025	$.0^2 98$	.025	.072	.121	.166	.206	.241	.272	.300	.325	.347	.367	.418	.480	.517	.560	.611	.675	.763	1.00	.025
	.05	$.0^2 39$	.051	.117	.178	.229	.273	.310	.342	.369	.394	.417	.436	.484	.543	.577	.617	.663	.720	.797	1.00	.05
	.95	3.84	3.00	2.60	2.37	2.21	2.10	2.01	1.94	1.88	1.83	1.79	1.75	1.67	1.57	1.52	1.46	1.39	1.32	1.22	1.00	.95
	.975	5.02	3.69	3.12	2.79	2.57	2.41	2.29	2.19	2.11	2.05	1.99	1.94	1.83	1.71	1.64	1.57	1.48	1.39	1.27	1.00	.975
	.99	6.63	4.61	3.78	3.32	3.02	2.80	2.64	2.51	2.41	2.32	2.25	2.18	2.04	1.88	1.79	1.70	1.59	1.47	1.32	1.00	.99
	.995	7.88	5.30	4.28	3.72	3.35	3.09	2.90	2.74	2.62	2.52	2.43	2.36	2.19	2.00	1.90	1.79	1.67	1.53	1.36	1.00	.995

Table A-16. Hypothetical population of numerical values used to illustrate statistical theory.

Code number	Sex	College Board score	High school biology	Major	Pretest score	Final	Experimental program
001	1	560	0	4	10	42	2
002	0	390	0	4	20	57	1
003	1	650	1	5	29	78	1
004	1	520	1	—	06	38	2
005	0	450	1	4	16	39	2
006	1	500	1	3	18	78	1
007	0	590	0	3	10	53	1
008	0	710	1	2	30	82	1
009	1	650	1	5	30	68	2
010	0	580	0	5	14	56	2
011	1	510	0	4	22	47	1
012	0	400	0	5	21	52	1
013	1	700	0	2	14	47	2
014	1	480	1	2	07	49	1
015	1	800	1	1	26	88	1
016	1	430	1	1	17	43	1
017	1	470	1	—	05	45	1
018	1	420	0	5	21	51	1
019	0	620	0	2	23	57	1
020	1	470	—	4	18	27	1
021	0	610	0	4	14	42	1
022	1	410	0	1	17	43	2
023	1	600	0	2	19	45	2
024	0	490	0	2	18	20	2
025	0	560	0	1	15	40	2
026	1	690	0	2	30	49	1
027	0	450	1	1	15	41	2
028	0	630	1	1	16	68	1
029	1	550	1	5	28	50	2
030	1	610	1	5	20	50	1
031	1	470	1	2	06	50	1
032	1	520	0	4	22	30	2
033	0	430	1	5	30	63	1
034	—	500	1	1	15	21	1
035	1	530	0	2	21	40	2
036	1	820	0	1	30	73	2
037	1	630	1	—	08	71	1
038	1	410	0	—	04	40	2
039	1	610	1	1	16	59	1
040	1	610	0	3	13	45	1
041	0	560	1	4	16	48	2
042	1	460	1	1	16	45	2
043	1	470	1	5	27	70	2
044	1	510	1	3	02	70	2
045	1	420	1	2	17	45	2

Table A-16. *(continued)*

Code number	Sex	College Board score	High school biology	Major	Pretest score	Final	Experi- mental program
046	0	490	0	2	19	36	2
047	0	600	0	1	03	38	1
048	1	550	1	2	16	48	2
049	0	410	0	1	28	41	1
050	0	390	—	5	12	40	1
051	0	640	1	5	27	72	1
052	1	370	1	1	14	55	2
053	1	700	1	1	28	69	1
054	1	470	1	2	08	38	1
055	1	410	0	4	24	52	2
056	0	430	1	1	10	43	1
057	0	410	0	2	10	50	2
058	1	620	0	2	16	61	1
059	1	610	1	2	08	50	1
060	0	570	1	5	24	60	1
061	0	460	0	5	16	37	1
062	—	500	—	—	12	22	1
063	—	480	0	—	—	40	2
064	1	690	1	1	19	65	2
065	1	500	0	2	10	51	1
066	0	580	1	1	28	64	1
067	0	550	1	5	27	65	2
068	1	510	1	1	17	37	2
069	—	460	0	4	18	23	2
070	0	590	1	3	28	59	1
071	1	490	0	4	17	47	2
072	1	610	1	1	18	51	1
073	1	440	1	1	13	35	2
074	1	210	1	5	26	35	2
075	1	510	0	2	13	47	1
076	0	390	0	2	27	49	1
077	0	600	0	3	15	44	2
078	0	400	0	—	—	46	1
079	—	410	0	4	14	18	2
080	1	460	1	2	04	50	1
081	1	410	0	1	—	52	1
082	0	580	0	2	20	50	2
083	0	580	0	5	30	55	2
084	0	510	0	3	01	16	2
085	0	560	0	2	25	39	1
086	0	490	1	5	24	59	1
087	1	510	0	1	30	56	2
088	1	540	0	1	17	31	2
089	1	580	0	3	15	27	1
090	0	500	0	1	17	45	2

Table A-16. *(continued)*

Code number	Sex	College Board score	High school biology	Major	Pretest score	Final	Experi-mental program
091	0	470	1	3	26	61	2
092	1	470	1	3	—	61	1
093	1	420	0	5	12	40	2
094	0	610	0	1	16	59	1
095	1	410	1	5	05	41	2
096	1	470	1	1	09	40	2
097	—	470	1	—	12	43	2
098	1	550	1	1	08	47	1
099	1	480	0	2	17	51	2
100	0	790	1	1	29	73	2
101	1	460	1	—	08	49	1
102	1	400	0	3	10	19	2
103	1	410	1	1	16	52	1
104	1	610	0	2	28	57	1
105	0	430	1	2	16	22	2
106	0	460	0	5	16	37	1
107	1	540	0	2	16	50	1
108	1	410	—	2	29	55	1
109	0	710	1	3	15	74	1
110	1	420	0	2	13	43	2
111	0	500	0	—	—	13	2
112	—	470	0	5	28	57	1
113	1	500	1	4	28	70	1
114	1	600	0	1	21	22	2
115	1	490	0	2	09	31	2
116	1	560	1	2	22	48	1
117	1	580	0	4	—	50	1
118	0	490	0	4	19	47	2
119	0	470	0	2	02	43	2
120	1	610	0	5	30	54	2
121	1	410	1	4	08	39	1
122	1	410	0	1	09	28	1
123	0	510	1	1	25	68	1
124	1	680	1	3	17	60	1
125	0	550	0	1	15	51	1
126	0	590	0	5	17	57	2
127	—	470	1	5	15	35	1
128	1	610	1	5	15	43	1
129	1	390	—	3	25	55	2
130	1	400	1	4	19	55	2
131	1	410	0	2	13	19	2
132	0	410	0	1	14	44	1
133	0	460	0	5	—	47	1
134	—	400	1	1	04	27	1
135	1	790	1	4	29	80	1

Table A-16. *(continued)*

Code number	Sex	College Board score	High school biology	Major	Pretest score	Final	Experi- mental program
136	0	610	1	3	30	67	1
137	0	710	0	1	18	40	2
138	1	400	1	5	21	40	2
139	1	510	0	3	16	44	2
140	1	610	1	1	13	48	2
141	1	510	0	1	09	50	2
142	1	470	1	4	10	40	2
143	1	660	1	3	26	67	1
144	1	610	0	3	25	64	2
145	0	490	—	5	16	25	2
146	1	430	1	1	15	40	1
147	0	600	0	1	15	34	2
148	1	430	0	1	13	24	2
149	1	720	0	3	03	49	2
150	1	590	1	3	08	66	2
151	0	390	0	1	16	49	1
152	1	600	1	2	09	52	1
153	1	640	1	5	27	56	2
154	0	410	0	1	16	41	2
155	0	550	—	5	16	61	1
156	0	720	1	3	08	56	2
157	1	490	0	1	14	59	2
158	0	390	0	1	30	47	2
159	0	590	1	3	28	59	1
160	1	600	1	1	21	58	1
161	1	410	1	2	13	45	1
162	1	800	1	2	28	54	1
163	1	820	1	3	18	63	1
164	1	470	1	3	20	50	2
165	0	610	1	1	10	50	2
166	1	490	1	1	20	18	2
167	1	530	0	2	17	44	2
168	—	580	0	3	10	30	2
169	1	500	0	3	12	54	1
170	1	560	0	5	30	49	1
171	0	470	0	2	13	39	2
172	1	470	1	4	10	46	2
173	0	500	—	1	13	26	2
174	0	650	1	2	14	54	1
175	0	550	0	2	13	50	1
176	0	670	1	5	26	59	2
177	1	720	1	3	27	59	2
178	1	500	0	1	15	25	1
179	1	480	0	1	18	59	1

Table A-16. *(continued)*

Code number	Sex	College Board score	High school biology	Major	Pretest score	Final	Experimental program
180	1	620	1	5	27	50	1
181	1	410	0	4	15	50	1
182	0	510	0	1	28	49	2
183	1	390	0	1	10	50	1
184	1	560	0	4	30	50	2
185	0	510	0	1	21	47	1
186	1	510	0	5	13	33	2
187	1	390	0	2	20	50	1
188	0	710	1	2	27	51	2
189	0	760	1	1	27	60	1
190	1	500	1	2	30	68	1
191	0	390	0	2	12	50	1
192	1	390	0	5	01	42	1
193	1	790	1	4	29	80	1
194	1	700	1	4	29	75	1
195	0	460	1	1	30	48	2
196	1	500	1	5	27	56	2
197	0	560	0	2	02	37	2
198	—	510	0	5	28	31	2
199	0	600	1	3	07	45	1
200	1	470	0	2	03	46	2
201	1	390	0	4	23	43	2
202	1	670	1	1	13	61	2
203	1	460	0	1	10	38	2
204	0	420	0	2	18	31	2
205	1	610	1	5	—	59	1
206	0	410	0	2	05	51	1
207	1	430	1	1	17	42	1
208	1	440	1	1	18	39	2
209	1	600	0	2	10	47	1
210	1	410	0	2	18	38	1
211	0	490	0	2	18	20	2
212	0	600	0	2	27	60	1
213	0	800	1	5	20	77	1
214	1	510	0	—	12	36	2
215	1	510	0	1	15	66	1
216	1	510	0	1	06	46	1
217	1	580	0	2	12	49	1
218	1	430	0	2	15	39	1
219	1	420	0	1	—	53	1
220	0	570	0	2	20	50	2
221	1	450	0	2	03	44	2
222	1	460	1	1	13	40	2
223	1	680	1	1	15	63	2

Table A-16. *(continued)*

Code number	Sex	College Board score	High school biology	Major	Pretest score	Final	Experi- mental program
224	1	440	0	1	08	35	2
225	0	430	0	2	20	35	2
226	1	600	1	5	20	60	1
227	0	400	0	2	05	48	1
228	1	480	0	5	22	53	1
229	1	720	0	3	30	65	1
230	1	590	0	2	18	42	2
231	1	450	—	4	16	25	1
232	0	570	0	1	17	42	2
233	1	650	0	2	30	45	1
234	0	420	1	1	14	38	2
235	0	640	1	1	19	70	1
236	1	600	0	—	16	47	1
237	1	550	1	5	27	52	2
238	1	600	1	5	19	49	1

Selected Additional Readings

PARTS I AND II

Ferguson, G. A. *Statistical analysis in psychology and education,* 5th ed. New York: McGraw-Hill, 1981.

Loftus, G. R., and E. F. Loftus. *Essence of statistics.* Belmont, Calif.: Brooks/Cole, 1982.

PARTS III, IV, V, AND VI

Conover, W. J. *Practical nonparametric statistics.* New York: John Wiley, 1980.

Dixon, W. J., and F. J. Massey. *Introduction to statistical analysis,* 4th ed. New York: McGraw-Hill, 1983.

Fleiss, J. L. *Statistical methods for rates and proportions,* 2d ed. New York: John Wiley and Sons, 1981.

Marascuilo, L. A., and M. McSweeney. *Nonparametric and distribution-free methods for the social sciences.* Belmont, Calif.: Brooks/Cole, 1977.

PART VII

Cook, T. D., and D. T. Campbell. *Quasi-experimentation.* Chicago: Rand McNally, 1979.

Dixon, W. J., and F. J. Massey. *Introduction to statistical analysis,* 4th ed. New York: McGraw-Hill, 1983.

Dunn, O. J., and V. A. Clark. *Analysis of variance and regression.* New York: John Wiley, 1974.

Keppel, G. *Design and analysis,* 2d ed. Englewood Cliffs, N.J.: Prentice-Hall, 1982.

Kirk, R. E. *Experimental design,* 2d ed. Belmont, Calif.: Brooks/Cole, 1982.

Kirk, R. E. *Introductory statistics.* Belmont, Calif.: Brooks/Cole, 1978.

Loftus, G. R., and E. F. Loftus. *Essence of statistics.* Belmont, Calif.: Brooks/Cole, 1982.

Winer, B. J. *Statistical principles in experimental design,* 2d ed. New York: McGraw-Hill, 1971.

PART VIII

Cohen, J., and P. Cohen. *Applied regression/correlation analysis for the behavioral sciences,* 2d ed. New York: John Wiley, 1982.

Draper, N., and H. Smith. *Applied regression analysis,* 2d ed. New York: John Wiley, 1981.

Everitt, B. S., and G. Dunn. *Advanced methods of data exploration and modelling.* London: Heinemann Educational Books, 1983.

Fienberg, S. E. *The analysis of cross-classified categorical data,* 2d ed. Cambridge, Mass.: MIT Press, 1980.

Marascuilo, L. A., and J. R. Levin. *Multivariate statistics in the social sciences: A researcher's guide.* Belmont, Calif.: Brooks/Cole, 1983.

Pedhazur, E. J. *Multiple regression in behavioral research,* 2d ed. New York: Holt, Rinehart and Winston, 1982.

PART IX

Cohen, J. *Statistical power analysis for the behavioral sciences.* New York: Academic Press, 1969.

Dixon, W. J., and F. J. Massey. *Introduction to statistical analysis,* 4th ed. New York: McGraw-Hill, 1983.

Answers to Selected Exercises

CHAPTER 1

1-5. a. $68\%_{16} \leq$ true height $\leq 68^{11}\!/_{16}$
 b. $68\%_8 \leq$ true height $\leq 68\%_8$
 c. $68\%_8 \leq$ true height $\leq 68\%_8$

CHAPTER 3

3-2. Bar graph, since the variable is ordered qualitative

CHAPTER 4

4-8. Mean $= 9.48$

4-9. $\alpha = 6.12,$ $\alpha_2 = -3.18,$ $\alpha_3 = -1.08,$
 $27(6.12) + 36(-3.18) + 47(-1.08) = 0$

CHAPTER 6

6-3. a. 36 f. 402
 b. 48 g. 654

c. 24   h. 222
d. 108   i. 3618
e. 12   j. 44.67

6-4. a. 50 in
b. 77 in
c. 74 in
d. 187.96 cm

6-5. a. 4 in
b. 103.2256

6-6. $A = -{}^{80}/_{36}, B = {}^{1}/_{36}$

6-10. Positively skewed

CHAPTER 7

7-4. Same

CHAPTER 10

10-1. Spearman correlation = .846
Pearson correlation = .855

10-3. $\phi = .339$

CHAPTER 11

11-1. Multiplication

11-2. Addition
$P(X = 0) = .0123$
$P(X = 1) = .0988$
$P(X = 2) = .2963$
$P(X = 3) = .3951$
$P(X = 4) = .1975$

11-4. a. .0769
b. .0769
c. .1538
d. .2500
e. .3077
f. .0192

11-5. P(king and queen) = .0059

11-6. a. .0148
b. .0887

c. .0011
d. .0310
e. .0118

11-8. $2^{10} = 1024$

11-12. a. .0000
b. .3000
c. .6000
d. .1000

11-13. a. .1200
b. .4200
c. .2800

11-14. a. .2244
b. .4986
c. .2770

11-15. a. .4737
b. 47.37

CHAPTER 12

12-1. .2617

12.2. .6488

12-3. a. .00137
b. .01646

12-4. .1780
.3560

12-5. c. .4661

CHAPTER 13

13-1. .3995

13-2. .3955

13-3. .0508

13-5. .1094

13-6. a. 1140
b. 720
c. 120
d. 120

13-11. Yes, P(no black) = .0016

13-14. 175,760,000

CHAPTER 14

14-2.   a. $N = 12$, $X = 9$; do not reject H_0
      b. $N = 16$, $X = 9$; do not reject H_0

14-3. $N = 13$, $X = 10$; reject H_0 one-tailed

14-6.   Reject H_0 if X is 15 or more

14-7. $13.8 \leq M \leq 30.8$

14-8.   No

14-12. Old program: $X = 3$, do not reject directional hypothesis
New program: $X = 12$, do not reject directional hypothesis

14-14. $\phi = -.46$

CHAPTER 15

15-1.   a. 15,504
      b. 184,756
      c. 15,504

15-2.   a. 792
      b. 3960
      c. 6160
      d. 3696
      e. 840
      f. 56

15-3.   a. .0512
      b. .2554
      c. .3973
      d. .2384
      e. .0542
      f. .0036

15-4.   a. .0000
      b. .1250
      c. .2500
      d. .3750
      e. .5000
      f. .6250

15-5.   a. .0196
      b. .1413
      c. .3391
      d. .3391
      e. .1413
      f. .0196

15-6.   a. .2222
      b. .0494
      c. .2324, with replacement

15-7.   .0598, without replacement

15-8.   30

15-9.   .3077

15-10. a. .0588
      b. .0196
      c. .2353
      d. .2941

15-11. 3750

15-12. 52,360

15-14. a. .5714
      b. .5714
      c. .4286
      d. .7142

15-15. a. .000004
      b. .0002
      c. .0024
      d. .0183
      e. .0815
      f. .2148
      g. .3281
      h. .2664
      i. .0883

15-17. a. 5040
      b. 35

15-20. $\frac{1}{5} = .2000$

CHAPTER 16

16-2. a. $\phi = .7035$
      b. Reject H_0

16-3. No

16-4. No

16-5. a. Male vs. female: Reject H_0
        Male vs. neither: Do not reject
        Female vs. neither: Reject H_0
     b. Male vs. female: Do not reject
        Male vs. neither: Do not reject
        Female vs. neither: Do not reject

CHAPTER 17

17-1. a. $T = 31$, reject H_0
b. $-1.55 \le M_d \le -.05$

17-5. a. $T = 49$, reject H_0
b. $M_d \ge 6$, one-tailed

17-6.
a.

	Sign test	Wilcoxon test
Old program	$T_+ = 15.5$, reject H_0	$T = 135.5$, reject H_0
New program	$T_+ = 16$, reject H_0	$T = 136$, reject H_0

17-6.
b. Old program: $8 \le M_d \le 12$, $7.5 \le M_d \le 11.5$
New program: $12 \le M_d \le 18$, $12 \le M_d \le 17.5$

CHAPTER 18

18-4. No, $T_W = 90$, do not reject H_0

18-5. $-.32 \le M_d \le .91$

18-7. $S_F^2 = .6922$, $S_M^2 = .1560$

CHAPTER 19

19-1. a. 75.5–78.5 in
b. 74–80 in
c. 72.5–81.5 in
d. 75.99 in
e. 76.62 in
f. 78.55 in
g. .7477
h. .6566

19-2. a. .2500
b. .0637
c. .2523
d. .4409

19-3. a. .3655
b. .0238

CHAPTER 20

20-1. a. $\mu = 36$, $\sigma^2 = 60$
b. $\mu = 12$, $\sigma^2 = 6.6667$
c. $\mu = 82$, $\sigma^2 = 1690$
d. $\mu = -14$, $\sigma^2 = 970$

20-2. a. .6972
b. .7807
c. .1919
d. .9998

20-3. $E(Y) = 3.5$, $\text{Var}(Y) = 2.9167$

20-4. $E(T) = 7.0$, $\text{Var}(T) = 5.8333$

20-5. $E(T) = 35$, $\text{Var}(T) = 29.1667$, $P(T \ge 40) = .1773$

CHAPTER 21

21-2. Yes, we should be surprised

21-4. No, we should not be surprised

21-6. Mean = 80, variance = 8, $z = 1.4142$, no surprise

21-7. a. $73.7998 \le \mu \le 76.2002$
b. $95.5467 \le \mu \le 116.4533$

21-8. a. 390,625
b. 12,650

21-9. $\mu = 22,000$, $\sigma^2 = 492,187.5$ (without replacement)

CHAPTER 22

22-1. a. $E(X) = 37.5$, $\text{Var}(X) = 18.75$
b. $E(E) = 50.0$, $\text{Var}(X) = 16.6667$
c. $E(X) = 56.25$, $\text{Var}(X) = 14.0625$

22-2. $z = 2.6969$

22-3. a. $E(p) = .5$, $\text{Var}(p) = .0033$
b. $E(p) = .6667$, $\text{Var}(p) = .0030$
c. $E(p) = .75$, $\text{Var}(p) = .0025$

CHAPTER 23

23-1. Exact critical value = 45; approximate critical value is the integer above $44.1386 = 45$

23-2. Exact critical value = 93; approximate critical value is the integer above $92.8689 = 93$

23-7. Heterosexual vs. others: $z = 4.3881$
Bisexual vs. others: $z = -2.4254$
Homosexual vs. others: $z = -2.3612$

23-8. Heterosexual: $.4132 \leq p \leq .6812$
Bisexual: $.0304 \leq p \leq .2821$
Homosexual: $.0717 \leq p \leq .3092$

23-10. Exact critical value = 6,18; approximate critical values are the integer below $6.7 = 6$ and the integer above $17.3 = 18$

CHAPTER 24

24-8. a. 1 vs. 2: $z = -.7843$
1 vs. 3: $z = -.5656$
1 vs. 4: $z = .6443$
2 vs. 3: $z = .2187$
2 vs. 4: $z = 1.4286$
3 vs. 4: $z = 1.2099$
b. Do not reject any of the six H_0
c. Do not reject any of the six H_0

24-9. $.24 \leq \text{rho} \leq .62$

CHAPTER 25

25-1. .9545

25-2. $\mu = 3$, $\sigma^2 = 6$; $\mu = 11$, $\sigma^2 = 22$; $\mu = 100$, $\sigma^2 = 200$

25-3. 25

25-4. 232.9

25-5. 233.9960

CHAPTER 26

26-1. $\phi = .64$, $X^2 = 39.2078$

26-2. $V = .24$, $X^2 = 19.1528$

26.3. $r_s = .2647$, $z = 2.7381$

26.4. $V = .2896$, $X^2 = 68.4533$

26-6. $\phi = .3777$, $X^2 = 12.1251$

26-7. $V = .4743$, $X^2 = 45.00$

26-8. $V = .5987$, $X^2 = 25.4525$

CHAPTER 27

27-2. $\phi = .1464$, $X^2 = 93.7427$

27-3. $V = .2898$, $X^2 = 25.7876$

27-4. $V = .3466$, $X^2 = 72.07$

27-5. $r_s = -.4238$, $z = 5.9483$

CHAPTER 28

28-1. $\psi_1 = .3909$, $z = 3.7116$, reject H_0
$\psi_2 = .3567$, $z = 3.6700$, reject H_0
$\psi_3 = -.0342$, $z = -.3100$, do not reject

28-2. $\psi_1 = .3909$, $z = 4.1684$, reject H_0
$\psi_2 = .3567$, $z = 3.9043$, reject H_0
$\psi_3 = -.0342$, $z = -.3878$, do not reject

28-3. 24 pairwise contrasts, planned critical value = 3.08, $S* = 4.11$, need 250 contrasts

28-4.

Contrast	z(planned)	z(post hoc)
a vs. b	3.23	3.45
a vs. c	5.65	6.40
a vs. d	4.44	4.39
b vs. c	2.42	2.53
b vs. d	1.21	1.13
c vs. d	-1.21	-1.13

CHAPTER 29

29-1. a. $X_B^2 = 0$, $X_W^2 = 28.8$, $X_O^2 = .2927$

29-2. $.02 \leq \psi_{AB} \leq .26$ (95% confidence interval)

29-3. $-.02 \le \psi_{AB} \le .30$
$.12 \le \psi_{AW} \le .36$
$-.04 \le \psi_{AO} \le .28$
$-.03 \le \psi_{BW} \le .23$
$-.16 \le \psi_{BO} \le .12$
$-.21 \le \psi_{WO} \le -.03$

29-4. $X^2_{\text{Bowker}} = 207.44$

29-5. $-.02 \le \psi_{12} \le .10$
$-.12 \le \psi_{13} \le .05$
$.11 \le \psi_{23} \le .23$

29-6. $Z_1 = 10.62$
$Z_2 = -8.47$
$Z_3 = -1.93$

29-7. $-.11 \le \psi_1 \le .12$
$.04 \le \psi_2 \le .22$
$-.25 \le \psi_3 \le -.02$

CHAPTER 30

30-1. $\chi^2 = 8.64$
Two-tailed critical values = 12.40, 39.36

30-2. One-tailed critical value = 13.85

30-3. $9.37 \le \sigma \le 16.69$

30-4. $\sigma \le 15.80$

CHAPTER 31

31-1. a. $t_{10:.95} = 1.812$
b. $t_{15:.95} = 1.753$
c. $t_{25:.95} = 1.708$

31-2. a. $t_{10:.025} = -2.228, t_{10:.05} = -1.812$
b. $t_{30:.025} = -2.042, t_{30:.05} = -1.697$

31-3. 17

CHAPTER 32

32-1. $t = -4.2647, t_{24:.025} = -2.064,$
$t_{24:.975} = 2.064$

32-2. $t_{24:.05} = -1.711$

32-3. $57.0894 \le \mu \le 65.5106$

32-4. $\mu \le 64.7904$

32-9. $t = -1.1255, t_{13:.025} = -2.160,$
$t_{13:.975} = 2.160$

32-10. $-3.1276 \le \mu \le .9848$

CHAPTER 33

33-1. a.

Contrast	t
1 vs. 2	-2.0728
1 vs. 2	-13.4731
1 vs. 4	-17.6187
2 vs. 3	-11.4003
2 vs. 4	-15.5459
3 vs. 4	-4.1456

Dunn critical value = 2.71

b. Tukey critical value = 2.64

c.

Contrast	t	df
1 vs. 2	-2.7472	37
1 vs. 3	-15.6275	34
1 vs. 4	-16.0349	28
2 vs. 3	-12.8046	36
2 vs. 4	-13.8675	30
3 vs. 4	-3.4658	34

33-3.

Contrast	t	Tails
1 vs. 2	4.7828	1
3 vs. 4	1.4113	1
5 vs. 6	4.8612	1
7 vs. 8	2.2738	1
1 vs. 3	-0.7841	2
2 vs. 4	-4.1555	2
5 vs. 7	-1.0193	2
6 vs. 8	-3.6067	2
1 vs. 5	1.4897	2

Contrast	t	Tails
2 vs. 6	1.5681	2
3 vs. 7	1.2545	2
4 vs. 8	2.1170	2

Two-tailed critical value = 2.92
One-tailed critical value = 2.69

33-4.

Contrast	t	Tails	df	C.V.
1 vs. 2	6.4039	1	23	2.89
3 vs. 4	2.0602	1	24	2.88
5 vs. 6	3.2039	1	17	3.00
7 vs. 8	2.7760	1	27	2.86
1 vs. 3	−1.4090	2	27	3.13
2 vs. 4	−4.9139	2	27	3.13
5 vs. 7	−1.4229	2	27	3.13
6 vs. 8	−2.2996	2	19	3.26
1 vs. 5	2.3555	2	27	3.13
2 vs. 6	0.9998	2	19	3.26
3 vs. 7	1.9243	2	25	3.15
4 vs. 8	2.5033	2	27	3.13

CHAPTER 34

34-1.
 a. $t = -3.4928$
 b. $t = -3.2711$
 c. $t = -0.1568$
 d. $t = 4.3799$
 e. $t = 5.0452$
 f. $t = -0.4704$

34-2. $t_{Mono} = 2.9052$

34-3. Old vs. (phonics, linguistic) $t = -5.5496$
Phonics vs. linguistic $t = 0.6812$
(Male vs. female)$_{old}$ $t = 0.3853$
(Male vs. female)$_{phonics}$ $t = -0.8135$
(Male vs. female)$_{linguistic}$ $t = -2.1193$
Dunn $t_{.05;5,54} = 2.67$

34-4. Dunn $t_{.05;6,54} = 2.74$
$t_{54;.975} = 2.01$

CHAPTER 36

36.2

Source	df	SS	MS	F
Between	4	8136	2034	6.85
Within	45	13354	297	
Total	49	21490		

36-4. $\eta^2 = .3786$, $F = 6.85$

CHAPTER 38

38-1. $S = 3.26$; $C = 20$

38-2. $df_1 = 5$, $df_2 = 24$, $S^* = 3.81$

38-3. $t_{Lin} = 5.1316$
$t_{Quad} = 0.7654$
$t_{Cub} = -0.6269$
$t_{Quart} = 0.3247$

38-6.

Source	df	SS	MS	F
Between	5	162433	32487	
Prof vs. acad	1	35363	35363	4.44
Bus vs. engin	1	2420	2420	0.30
Hum vs. sci	1	106090	106090	13.32
English vs. hist	1	2880	2880	0.36
Chem vs. math	1	15680	15680	1.97
Within	54	430099	7965	
Total	59	592532		

Planned critical value = $(2.67)^2 = 7.13$

38-7.

Source	df	SS	MS	F
Between	5	3989.2	797.8	
Old vs. (P,L)	1	3360.2	3360.2	30.80
Phon vs. ling	1	50.6	50.6	0.46
Sex in old	1	16.2	16.2	0.15
Sex in phon	1	72.2	72.2	0.66
Sex in ling	1	490.0	490.0	4.49
Within	54	5891.7	109.1	
Total	59	9880.9		

CHAPTER 39

39-2.

Source	df	SS	MS	F
Type	1	148.84	148.84	23.7
Amount	1	234.04	234.04	27.3
$T \times A$	1	69.34	69.34	11.1
Within	56	350.84	6.27	
Total	59	803.06		

39-3.

Source	df	SS	MS	F
Amount	1	234.04	234.04	27.3
Type in Amt	2	218.18		
Type in 0	1	7.50	7.50	1.20
Type in 3	1	210.68	210.68	23.60
Within	56	350.84	6.27	
Total	59	803.06		

39-4.

Source	df	SS	MS	F
Type	1	130.54	130.54	7.20
Amount	1	310.54	310.54	17.1
$T \times A$	1	40.84	40.84	2.3
Within	56	1015.56	18.14	
Total	59	1497.48		

39-5.

Source	df	SS	MS	F
Amount	1	310.54	310.54	17.1
Type in Amt	2	171.38		
Type in 0	1	12.68	12.68	0.70
Type in 3	1	158.70	158.70	8.75
Within	56	1015.56	18.14	
Total	59	1497.48		

39-6.

Source	df	SS	MS	F
Gender	1	236	236	2.16
Method	2	3411	1705.5	15.63
$G \times M$	2	342	171	1.57
Within	54	5892	109	
Total	59	9881		

39-7.

a.

Source	df	SS	MS	F
Method	2	3411	1705.5	15.63
Gender in M	3	578		
Gender in O	1	16	16	0.15
Gender in P	1	72	72	0.66
Gender in L	1	490	490	4.50
Within	54	5892	10	
Total	59	9881		

b.

Source	df	SS	MS	F
Gender	1	236	236	2.16
Method in G	4	3753		
Method in M	2	1030	515	4.72
Method in F	2	2723	1361.5	12.49
Within	54	5892	109	
Total	59	9881		

39-8.

Source	df	SS	MS	F
Education	3	389.35	129.78	23.09
Religion	4	986.55	246.64	43.85
$E \times R$	12	240.15	20.01	3.55
Within	60	337.50	5.63	
Total	79	1953.55		

CHAPTER 40

40-1. a. Old vs. (P,L) $t = -5.55$
Phon vs. ling $t = 0.68$

Dunn critical value $t_{.05:2,54} = 2.31$
Gender in O $t = 0.39$
Gender in P $t = -0.81$
Gender in L $t = -2.12$
Dunn critical value $t_{.10:3,54} = 2.16$
b. Gender $t = 1.47$
Critical value $t_{54,.975} = 2.01$
In Male:
    Old vs. (P,L) $t = -2.86$
    P vs. L $t = 1.14$
Dunn critical value $t_{.05:2,54} = 2.31$
In Female:
    Old vs. (P,L) $t = -5.00$
    P vs. L $t = -0.17$
Dunn critical value $t_{.05:2,54} = 2.31$

40-2. a. Assume all 10 contrasts were planned; Dunn critical value $t_{.15:10,54} = 2.51$
b. $S^2 = 5F_{5,54}(.85) = 8.50$

CHAPTER 41

41-1.

Source	df	α
Sex	1	.05
Ability	2	.05
Method	2	.05
$S \times A$	2	.05
$S \times M$	2	.05
$A \times M$	4	.05
$S \times A \times M$	4	.05
Residual	162	
Total	179	

41-2. See table for Exercise 41-1

41-3.

Source	df	α
Ability	2	.05
Within Low	5	.10
Sex	1	.033

Source	df	α
Method	2	.033
$S \times M$	2	.033
Within Ave (See Low)	5	.10
Within High (See Low)	5	.10
Residual	162	
Total	179	

41-4. See table for Exercise 41-3

41-6.

Source	df	SS	α
Religion	4	11564.2	.05
Education	3	9830.2	.05
Gender	1	1.0	.05
$R \times E$	12	2822.6	.05
$R \times G$	4	88.0	.05
$E \times G$	3	80.0	.05
$R \times E \times G$	12	164.3	.05
Residual	120	6196.5	
Total	159	30746.8	

41-7.

Source	df	SS	α
Education	3	9830.2	.05
R in E_1	4	2505.9	.025
G in E_1	1	18.2	.025
$R \times G$ in E_1	4	113.2	.025
R in E_2	4	4851.5	.025
G in E_2	1	12.1	.025
$R \times G$ in E_2	4	84.4	.025
R in E_3	4	4123.6	.025
G in E_3	1	16.9	.025
$R \times G$ in E_3	4	11.1	.025
R in E_4	4	2905.9	.025

Source	df	SS	α
G in E_4	1	34.2	.025
$R \times G$ in E_4	4	43.2	.025
Residual	120	6196.5	
Total	159	30746.8	

CHAPTER 42

42-1.

Source	df	SS
Subjects	4	300.27
Time	2	89.73
Residual	8	64.93
Total	14	454.93

42-2.

Source	df	SS
Subjects	4	686.8
Within Subj	40	3378.0
Time	2	382.5
Method	2	2222.5
$T \times M$	4	74.9
Residual	32	698.1
Total	44	4064.8

42-3.

Source	df	SS
Subjects	9	1823.5
Gender	1	256.7
Residual	8	1566.8
Within Subj	80	5407.1
Time	2	537.2
Method	2	3227.3
$T \times M$	4	107.5
$G \times T$	2	69.6
$G \times M$	2	112.1

Source	df	SS
$G \times T \times M$	4	31.8
Residual	64	1321.6
Total	89	7230.6

42-7. Friedman chi-square $= 6.0556$, $df = 2$

42-8. $Q = 3.5$, $df = 2$

42-10.

Source	df	SS
Subjects	31	216.43
Group	3	153.77
Residual	28	62.66
Within Subj	96	499.75
Trial	3	426.46
$G \times T$	9	47.32
Residual	84	25.97
Total	127	716.18

CHAPTER 43

43-1. Means: 51.01, 45.18, 49.94, 54.94, 55.23

43-2. Adjusted means: 50.39, 50.36, 51.42, 54.03, 54.35

43-3. Standard errors: 0.7869, 1.0116, 0.6082, 0.6566, 0.6332

43-4. Control vs. Expt: $z = 3.67$, $\alpha = .05$
1 vs. 2 in Cont: $z = 0.02$, $\alpha = .05$
3 vs. 4 in Expt: $z = -2.76$, $\alpha = .0167$
3 vs. 5 in Expt: $z = -3.34$, $\alpha = .0167$
4 vs. 5 in Expt: $z = -0.35$, $\alpha = .0167$

43-7. 36.62, 48.12, 59.62

43-10. a.

Source	df	SS
Subjects	33	77.70
Group	1	12.71
Residual	32	64.99
Within Subj	34	71.25

Source	df	SS
Trial	1	46.78
$G \times T$	1	10.72
Residual	32	13.75
Total	67	148.95

b.

Source	df	SS
Between (Adj)	1	20.635
Within (Adj)	31	24.554
Total (Adj)	32	45.189

c. $t = 4.99$, $df = 32$

CHAPTER 44

44-9. a. For the most disparate slopes, β_{13} vs. β_{15}, $t = 1.07$

b. For the most disparate slopes, β_{13} vs. β_{15}, $t = 0.98$

CHAPTER 45

45-5. $Z = 0.9261$

CHAPTER 47

47-1.

Source	df	SS
Regression	3	208.87
Residual	36	1932.90
Total	39	2141.77

47-2. $B_0 = 15.6 = $ Group 4 mean
$B_1 = 5.8 = $ Group 1 mean $-$ Group 4 mean
$B_2 = 0.9 = $ Group 2 mean $-$ Group 4 mean
$B_3 = 3.6 = $ Group 3 mean $-$ Group 4 mean

47-3. $S^2 = 0.1923$, $r = -0.3333$;
$$SS_{\text{Reg}} = 39[5.8^2(0.1923) + \cdots$$
$$+ 3.6^2(0.1923) +$$
$$2\{5.8(0.9)(-0.3333)$$
$$\times (0.1923) + \cdots +$$
$$0.9(3.6)$$
$$\times (-0.3333)(0.1923)\}] = 208.87$$

47-5. a. For $B_0 = $ Grand mean
$B_1 = $ Male listener vs. female listener
$B_2 = $ Lead singer vs. no lead singer
$B_3 = $ Male lead vs. female lead
$B_4 = $ (Lead vs. no lead)$_{\text{male listener}}$ vs. (Lead vs. no lead)$_{\text{female listener}}$
$B_5 = $ (Male lead vs. female lead)$_{\text{male listener}}$ vs. (Male lead vs. female lead)$_{\text{female listener}}$

Use as codes:

Listener	Lead	X_1	X_2	X_3	X_4	X_5
Male	Male	$\frac{1}{3}$	$\frac{1}{4}$	$\frac{1}{2}$	$\frac{1}{2}$	1
	Female	$\frac{1}{3}$	$\frac{1}{4}$	$-\frac{1}{2}$	$\frac{1}{2}$	-1
	None	$\frac{1}{3}$	$-\frac{1}{2}$	0	-1	-1
Female	Male	$-\frac{1}{3}$	$\frac{1}{4}$	$\frac{1}{2}$	$-\frac{1}{2}$	1
	Female	$-\frac{1}{3}$	$\frac{1}{4}$	$-\frac{1}{2}$	$-\frac{1}{2}$	0
	None	$-\frac{1}{3}$	$-\frac{1}{2}$	0	1	0

b. For $B_0 = $ Grand mean
$B_2 = $ Male listener vs. female listener
$B_2 = $ (Lead vs. no lead)$_{\text{male listener}}$
$B_3 = $ (Male lead vs. female lead)$_{\text{male listener}}$
$B_4 = $ (Lead vs. no lead)$_{\text{female listener}}$
$B_5 = $ (Male lead vs. female lead)$_{\text{female listener}}$

Use as codes:

Listener	Lead	X_1	X_2	X_3	X_4	X_5
Male	Male	$\frac{1}{2}$	$\frac{1}{3}$	$\frac{1}{2}$	0	0
	Female	$\frac{1}{2}$	$\frac{1}{3}$	$-\frac{1}{2}$	0	0
	None	$\frac{1}{2}$	$-\frac{2}{3}$	0	0	0
Female	Male	$-\frac{1}{2}$	0	0	$\frac{1}{3}$	$\frac{1}{2}$
	Female	$-\frac{1}{2}$	0	0	$\frac{1}{3}$	$-\frac{1}{2}$
	None	$-\frac{1}{2}$	0	0	$-\frac{2}{3}$	0

CHAPTER 49

49-1. $G^2 = 17.819$ (Pearson $X^2 = 16.886$)

49.2. $G^2 = 63.812$, $df = 15$

49-4. a. $z = 6.2289$
b. $G^2 = 42.020$
c. $z = 5.5893$
d. $X^2 = 39.208$

49-5. $G^2_{AR.T} = 98.08$, $G^2_{AR.P} = 99.18$
For male vs. female gamma, $z = 0.5059$

49-6. School$_1$ vs. School$_2$: $z = -2.9549$
School$_1$ vs. School$_3$: $z = -2.5457$
School$_2$ vs. School$_3$: $z = 0.3615$

49-7. School$_1$: $z = -2.4538$
School$_2$: $z = 1.6875$
School$_3$: $z = 1.1039$

49-8. $z = -3.1259$

50-3. $N_1 = N_2 = 1271$

50-4. $N_1 = N_2 = 1573$, to ensure $\beta = .20$

50-5. $N_1 = N_2 = 24$

50-6. 35 per cell

50-7. $N = 194$

50-8. For A: 31 per level
For B: 58 per level
For AB: 13 per cell
To ensure β's as specified, use 15 per cell

50-9. For $\beta = .3, .2, .1, .05$, use $N = 34, 42, 51, 61$

50-10. Need 30 observations, by extrapolation

CHAPTER 50

50-1. $N_1 = N_2 = 150$

50-2. $N_1 = N_2 = 23$

Index

Pages on which procedures appear are indicated by an italic number. Pages on which definitions appear are indicated by a bold number.